ALSO BY MEGAN KATE NELSON

*The Three-Cornered War: The Union, the Confederacy,
and Native Peoples in the Fight for the West*

*Saving Yellowstone: Exploration and Preservation
in Reconstruction America*

Ruin Nation: Destruction and the American Civil War

Trembling Earth: A Cultural History of the Okefenokee Swamp

THE WESTERNERS

Mythmaking and Belonging
on the American Frontier

———◆◆———

MEGAN KATE NELSON

SCRIBNER
New York   Amsterdam/Antwerp   London
Toronto   Sydney/Melbourne   New Delhi

Scribner
An Imprint of Simon & Schuster, LLC
1230 Avenue of the Americas
New York, NY 10020

For more than 100 years, Simon & Schuster has championed authors and the stories they create. By respecting the copyright of an author's intellectual property, you enable Simon & Schuster and the author to continue publishing exceptional books for years to come. We thank you for supporting the author's copyright by purchasing an authorized edition of this book.

No amount of this book may be reproduced or stored in any format, nor may it be uploaded to any website, database, language-learning model, or other repository, retrieval, or artificial intelligence system without express permission. All rights reserved. Inquiries may be directed to Simon & Schuster, 1230 Avenue of the Americas, New York, NY 10020 or permissions@simonandschuster.com.

Copyright © 2026 by Megan Kate Nelson

All rights reserved, including the right to reproduce this book or portions thereof in any form whatsoever. For information, address Scribner Subsidiary Rights Department, 1230 Avenue of the Americas, New York, NY 10020.

First Scribner hardcover edition March 2026

SCRIBNER and design are registered trademarks of Simon & Schuster, LLC

Simon & Schuster strongly believes in freedom of expression and stands against censorship in all its forms. For more information, visit BooksBelong.com.

For information about special discounts for bulk purchases, please contact Simon & Schuster Special Sales at 1-866-506-1949 or business@simonandschuster.com.

The Simon & Schuster Speakers Bureau can bring authors to your live event. For more information or to book an event, contact the Simon & Schuster Speakers Bureau at 1-866-248-3049 or visit our website at www.simonspeakers.com.

Interior design by Kyle Kabel

Manufactured in the United States of America

1   3   5   7   9   10   8   6   4   2

The Library of Congress Cataloging-in-Publication Data has been applied for.

ISBN 978-1-6680-0434-0
ISBN 978-1-6680-0436-4 (ebook)

Let's stay in touch! Scan here to get book recommendations, exclusive offers, and more delivered to your inbox.

To my fellow Westerners,
especially those who never thought these histories belonged to them

CONTENTS

Prologue XIII

PART I
CURIOSITY IN MOTION 1

PART II
THE BRINGERS OF CHANGE 49

PART III
A GOOD TIME TO BE IN THE PICK AND SHOVEL BUSINESS . . 103

PART IV
VIOLENCE PUSHED TO ITS LIMITS 149

PART V
IT WILL BIND THEM TOGETHER AND TEAR US APART 199

PART VI
SURVIVAL IS A PRESENCE AND AN ABSENCE 271

Epilogue 329

Acknowledgments 337
Notes 341
Bibliography 389
Index 421

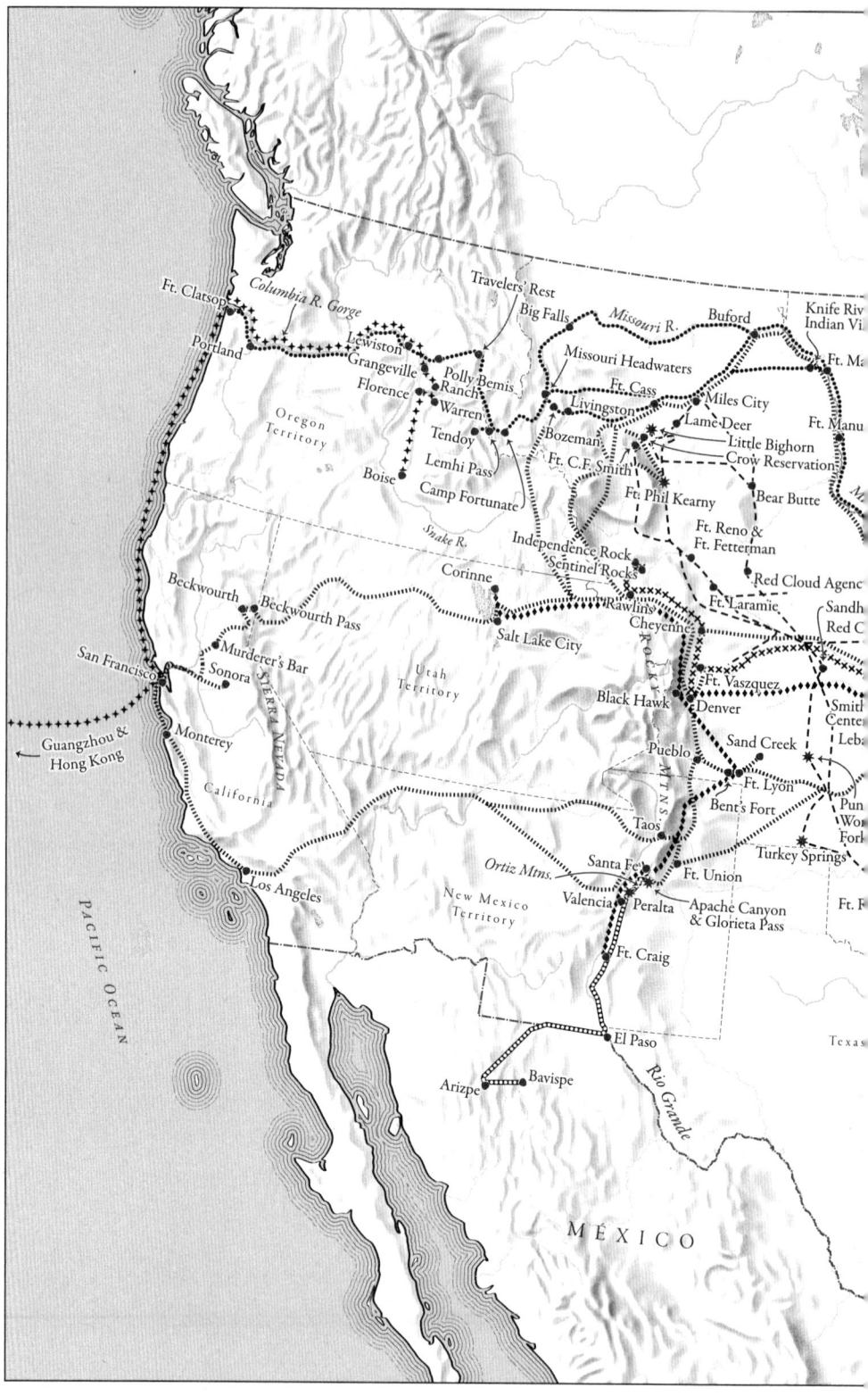

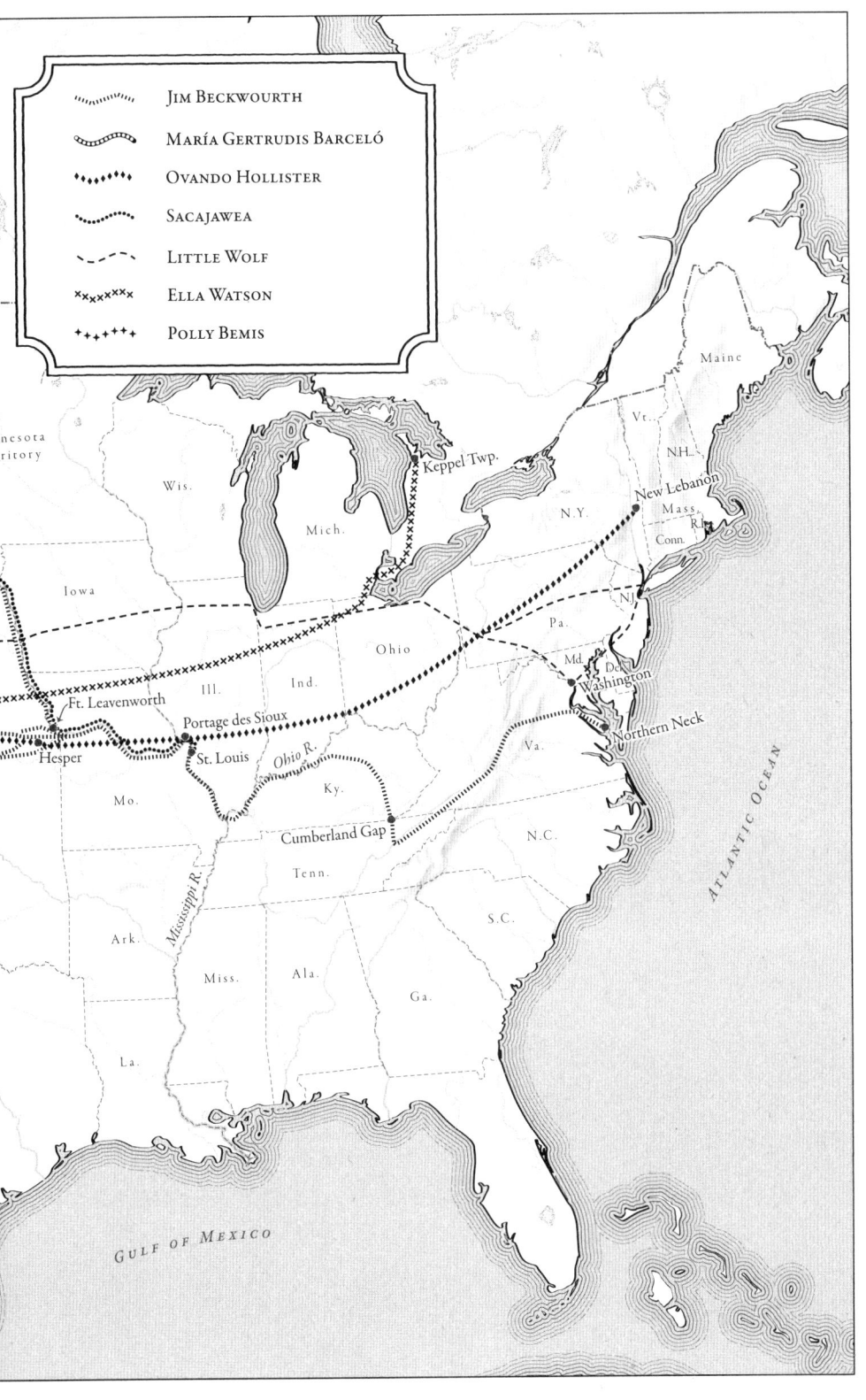

PROLOGUE

Chicago. July 1893.

It was already warm when Mae Turner left the University of Chicago campus and joined some friends to spend the day at the Columbian Exposition (known more popularly as the World's Fair). She and her husband, Frederick Jackson Turner, had left their two toddlers back home in Wisconsin, so this trip to Chicago was a vacation for Mae—but not for Turner. He was in the "final agonies" of finishing a paper he was giving to an audience of his fellow history professors at the American Historical Association meeting in two days' time. So, his wife went to the fair without him.

When Mae and her friends arrived at the exposition, there were already tens of thousands of people roaming the grounds: 630 acres of bright white Beaux Arts buildings, stuffed with the evidence of American achievement in mining, electricity, manufacturing, and agriculture; and a system of lagoons designed by the famous landscape architect Frederick Law Olmsted. Hawkers offered hot food and souvenirs along the Midway Plaisance, a carnival promenade on the west side of the grounds displaying "living villages" of African and American Indigenous peoples. A 264-foot-high Ferris wheel towered above it all, a feat of engineering that provided visitors with a spectacular view of Lake Michigan.[1]

All the states and territories in the Union were represented at the fair. Colorado's pavilion boasted a re-creation of Mesa Verde, a collection of Ancestral Puebloan cliff ruins in the southwestern part of the state, and a larger-than-life sculpture of an Indigenous hunter, standing upon the body of a buffalo he had just slain. The sculpture was titled "The Closing Era," but most journalists called it "The Last of His Race."[2]

Turner would have liked to see this sculpture, along with Buffalo Bill's Wild West Show, which was set up outside the fairgrounds. The ten-year-old show was immensely popular across the United States, depicting a West in which white pioneers conquered both Indigenous peoples and the "wilderness."[3] Turner had been studying American expansion and conquest across the continent; it was the subject of the talk he had to finish.

The American Historical Association was less than a decade old and had been incorporated in 1889. Historians founded it amid the professionalization of academic disciplines in the United States, envisioning a society of trained scholars who engaged in rigorous historical research and educated future historians at the nation's growing number of colleges and universities. Every year, members convened in Washington, D.C., to present new research and exchange ideas.[4]

The meeting in 1893 was special, however. Association officers had decided to hold it in Chicago, in conjunction with the World's Fair. Presenting a paper at the conference was a big moment for the thirty-one-year-old Turner. Although he had earned his PhD at Johns Hopkins University, acknowledged as one of the leading history programs in the nation, he was relatively unknown in the profession. He was hoping to make his mark with a talk that was more manifesto than research paper.

Two days after Mae left him in a university dorm to go to the fair, Turner took a horse-drawn streetcar eight miles north for the association's second session, which began at 8:00 p.m. The Art Institute, a building that had opened to the public just a few months before, was hosting a series of lectures and meetings to highlight the world's intellectual progress since 1492.[5] It was an imposing two-story building clad in limestone, with symmetrical wings extending out from its central hall.

Walking up a 120-foot-wide flight of steps, Turner stepped through the doorway and found himself in a broad, high-ceilinged lobby. Huge columns made of light pink and dove gray Tennessee marble shone in the evening light filtering in from the glass roof. Most of the Art Institute's antiquities, silver objects, and musical instrument collections were still in storage, but the trustees had placed statuary, paintings, and other items in the halls. Hundreds of people milled around, looking at the work of Dutch and French masters mounted on walls painted in shades of crimson, to set off the artworks' gilded frames.[6]

Hall Three, where Turner was scheduled to give his paper, was a long room on the north side of the building, with five windows that had been opened to let in the breeze after a hot summer day. The hall was already filling up with more than two hundred historians, who sat in chairs in front of an elevated platform for the speakers. Electric lights gave the room a warm glow. A portion of the Art Institute's historical cast collection was mounted on the walls: sculptural fragments, bas-reliefs, pilasters, and doors from some of Europe's most famous architectural sites.[7]

As the sun set, the session began. Turner sat through four talks before he rose to give his own. In college, Turner had won several awards for his oratorical skills, and he had abundant experience talking to large audiences. It was late, however—probably after 10:00 p.m.—and even the lakeshore breezes could not dispel the heat from the day in Hall Three. Turner figured he would outline the major points of his paper and skip some of the details. At this point in the program, no one would complain about a paper that was shorter than expected.[8]

Turner began his talk by explaining the significance of the "frontier" in American history. Most of his audience members understood this term in different ways. Geographically, it was the border between nations, or the raw, unrefined edge of human civilization where countries sent armies to guard against their enemies. Metaphorically, frontiers could exist everywhere, as the furthermost limit of human understanding. To Turner, however, the frontier was a historical process of nation-making.

"Up to our own day American history has been in a large degree the history of the colonization of the Great West," Turner argued. "The existence of an area of free land, its continuous recession, and the advance of American settlement westward, explain American development."[9]

This argument about the frontier was new, and it was controversial. In the last decade of the nineteenth century, most historians of the United States were convinced that America's unique social and political institutions had come directly from Europe. But Turner was suggesting that the heart of the nation's history was not in England or in the American colonies along the eastern seaboard, but on the western frontier.[10]

Turner read on, declaring that the American frontier itself was not a single place, but a line between "savagery" and "civilization" that shifted westward over time. During the colonial period, the frontier lay in the original thirteen colonies. As the forces of American politics, economics, and culture triumphed over Indigenous lifeways, the frontier moved on to the Ohio River Valley, then Kentucky and Tennessee, and Kansas and Nebraska. By the mid-nineteenth century, the frontier crossed the Great Plains and leapt over the Rocky Mountains to California.

For the previous fifty years, Turner argued, the frontier had become synonymous with the large region now known as "the American West." There, the pioneers—practical, inventive, restless, exuberant white men—clashed with Indigenous peoples, subduing them and a wilderness filled with wild animals and abundant natural resources. They paved the way for those to come: American farmers and ranchers and, ultimately, industrialists and city dwellers. These white settlers came in successive waves. They wiped out the towns, networks, and communities that Indigenous peoples had built and established their own uniquely American institutions.[11]

This historical process was a series of "perennial rebirths," Turner contended, as pioneers tamed the frontier over and over and over again, for two centuries. It was these actions, he emphasized, that "furnish the forces dominating American character."[12]

Sensing, perhaps, that the patience of his audience was nearing its end, Turner brought his talk to a close. The federal census of 1890, he pointed out, had determined that there were no longer any sparsely populated portions of the United States that remained in a frontier condition. This, Turner believed, was alarming news.

"Now, four centuries from the discovery of America, at the end of a hundred years of life under the Constitution," he asked, what would happen to the "vital force" animating the country if the frontier no longer existed?[13]

Turner gathered his papers, stepped off the platform, and walked back to his seat to a smattering of applause. There were no questions. The historians filed out of the hall and into the outer galleries, happy to stretch their legs. Turner must have been disappointed. He had put forward a brazen theory of the origins of national institutions, one that rooted

American exceptionalism in the frontier experience rather than European precedents. His theory flew in the face of everything the members of the American history profession had been arguing for years. At that moment, however, it seemed that nobody cared. Turner could not have known that his manifesto would define scholarly and popular understandings of American and western history for the next one hundred years.

After he and Mae returned to Wisconsin, Frederick Jackson Turner revised his paper slightly and read it to the members of the Wisconsin Historical Society, who proved a much more receptive audience than the historians in Chicago. In 1894, they published his paper in their journal, as did the American Historical Association. Almost immediately, Turner received a note from a fellow historian of the American West.

"I have been greatly interested in your pamphlet on the frontier," Theodore Roosevelt wrote. The future president was putting together the third volume of his own history, *Winning of the West*, and he found that many of Turner's ideas about westward expansion and its pioneer heroes dovetailed with his own. "You have put definite shape to a good deal of thought," Roosevelt added, "that has been floating around rather loosely."[14]

Roosevelt was right. The ideas about the frontier that Turner had articulated in his paper might have been radical in the historical field in the 1890s. But as was abundantly clear at many of the World's Fair exhibits and at Buffalo Bill's Wild West Show, they were already commonplace in American culture.

For almost a century, a popular image of the vast lands between the Pacific coast and the Missouri River had been taking shape. As the U.S. government acquired territory by purchase, diplomacy, and warfare, American explorers, mapmakers, and Army officers wrote vivid reports of the region. They highlighted its harsh and challenging landscapes and its possibilities for farming and ranching.

Fiction writers published cheap paperbacks called "dime novels" and ghostwritten autobiographies of men like Kit Carson, creating heroes out of Indian fighters who rescued white families from "savage" dangers.

Landscape painters, lithographers, and photographers introduced Easterners to the Romantic West of sublime landscapes filled with towering peaks and deep canyons and Indians who seemed to exist only in small numbers, fated to disappear as American pioneers swept westward.

At the same time, more and more Americans embraced Manifest Destiny, the idea that continental conquest was inevitable and that the lands stretching from the Atlantic Ocean to the Pacific (and possibly beyond) were American by divine right. Rugged, determined white men with wives and children in tow made their way west, staking their claims and living independent lives without any help from the federal government. With grit and determination, they built houses and tilled farms and built their fortunes alongside other pioneers, who were, like them, white Americans. This preordained process became the core of the American Dream, as white families envisioned themselves pursuing life, liberty, and happiness in the American West.[15]

By the time Turner gave his paper in Chicago in 1893, the myth of the frontier already had an irresistible pull in American culture, a simple rhetorical trajectory that made white men and women feel proud of themselves and their past. Even Turner admitted that these ideas were already dominant in the zeitgeist.

"The ideas underlying my 'Significance of the Frontier' would have been expressed in some form or another in any case," he reflected later. "They were part of the growing American consciousness of itself."[16]

In the decade after the publication of Turner's "The Significance of the Frontier in American History," more and more historians integrated his arguments into their own work and taught "the frontier thesis" to their students. They bestowed upon the popular vision of the frontier and its pioneer heroes the imprimatur of historical truth. By the early 1900s, the field of U.S. western history became a viable and respected area of study in the historical profession. The pioneers and their frontier adventures dominated histories of the U.S. West and the United States for more than a century. Their appeal rarely waned, even as scholars in the 1980s began to publish books and articles that challenged this vision of regional and national history. Despite their work, the frontier myth continues to influence popular histories and portrayals of the West in media, ranging from books to movies to video games.[17]

The frontier myth is a fantasy that white Americans have repeated over time to create a national community.[18] It has, from the beginning, marginalized, ignored, or entirely erased the actual people who explored, fought over, excavated, and built the American West in the nineteenth century. They were Indigenous peoples who had claimed this region as their homelands for thousands of years; women and men who were at first Spanish, then Mexican, then American citizens as national borders moved around them; Black Americans, who migrated with their enslavers and then claimed for themselves the freedoms the West offered; white women who rejected cultural expectations and forged paths of their own; and Asian immigrants, who arrived at Pacific ports and spread out from there to build lives in a foreign land.

The frontier myth's erasure of their lives was no accident. Politicians, newspaper editors, surveyors, artists, writers, and historians did it deliberately.[19] Removing people from a central national narrative effectively eliminates them from the body politic, making it easier to take their property and their civil rights away.[20]

While the West offered opportunities and freedoms to all comers in the early nineteenth century, it became a more restrictive place in the years after the Civil War. The federal government, controlled mostly by the Republican Party, increasingly exerted its power in the West and provided incentives for white settlers to migrate to the region. The frontier myth undergirded their policies.

Proponents of the frontier myth tried to obscure the fact that the real people who built the West had much in common with white pioneers. They had a high tolerance for risk. They traveled thousands of miles as they chased their own dreams, crossing paths in unexpected ways.

They faced challenges on their journeys throughout the region and often persevered.

Unlike the pioneers of the frontier myth, however, these real people journeyed through the West not only from the East, but in many different directions.[21] Sacajawea, for example, was born in Shoshone lands in the northern Rocky Mountains. Her first movement through what became the American West was eastward, when she was stolen from her people and taken to the Knife River Villages in the Upper Missouri River Valley, where she met Meriwether Lewis and William Clark. Her subsequent journey to the Pacific and back again traversed a vast and diverse landscape filled with Indigenous polities.

The West in the early nineteenth century was also a Spanish domain of movement and far-flung networks of exchange. Those who succeeded there, like María Gertrudis Barceló, were adept at navigating these spaces. Barceló was born in Sonora, one of the northernmost provinces of New Spain, the same year that Sacajawea was stolen from her people. She moved north with her family in 1815, ultimately making her home in Santa Fe and establishing herself as one of the most powerful businesswomen in Nuevo México.

The fur trader, scout, and entrepreneur Jim Beckwourth also made a name for himself in the West in the 1820s and '30s, after migrating with his enslaver father from Virginia to lands northwest of St. Louis. As a biracial man moving through the West in the first half of the nineteenth century, Beckwourth found freedom in nascent towns and mining camps from the Rocky Mountains to the Pacific coast. Like Sacajawea and Gertrudis Barceló, he became a cultural broker, expertly traversing multiple racial worlds in the West.

The region's transformations attracted migrants from all over the nation and the world. Ovando Hollister, a white man who appeared to be a typical pioneer, left a Shaker community in New York to make his way to the Rocky Mountains to take part in the Colorado gold rush. He arrived in 1860, just a year before the event that would change the nature of the West for the rest of the century: the American Civil War.

Hollister and his fellow U.S. soldiers helped defend Colorado and New Mexico Territory from a Confederate invasion during the Civil War, securing the larger West for the Union. The war brought thousands of soldiers into the region, who helped clear the way for hundreds of thousands of additional migrants. The federal government increasingly took an interest in controlling the West, and Hollister was happy to support this effort. After his discharge from the Army, he started a local newspaper and promoted the Republican Party's visions for the white settlement of the West.

Like Frederick Jackson Turner, Hollister imagined the future West as a land without Indians. But Indigenous peoples who had lived in these lands for thousands of years were determined to assert their sovereignty and retain their homelands. The Northern Cheyenne chief Little Wolf exemplified this resolve in the 1860s and '70s, leading his people in many different battles to defend the North Country of his ancestors. Until the end of the century, Little Wolf resisted removal to reservations and fought and negotiated with U.S. federal forces to ensure his people's survival.

The Canadian immigrant Ella Watson, who entered the American West from the north, was one of the white settlers who coveted Northern Cheyenne and other Plains tribal lands. In the late 1870s and early 1880s, she worked in hotel kitchens in Kansas and Nebraska, ultimately saving enough money to travel to the windswept prairies of Wyoming and establish herself as a cattle rancher. But Watson, too, struggled to survive in a landscape increasingly dominated by white men.

The frontier myth—and its core belief that the West belonged only to white Americans—had become a national ideology by the 1880s and '90s, ushering in an age of oppression and migration restriction. Chinese immigrants who arrived during the California gold rush and built the Central Pacific railroad were attacked and expelled from towns and mining camps across the American West. Polly Bemis, who had been trafficked from Hong Kong to San Francisco and then taken to the gold fields of Idaho in the early 1870s, did not initially experience these pressures in her remote, Chinese-majority town. The federal government ultimately found her, however, and defined Bemis as an "other" in a place she had helped create.

All seven of these women and men, and the communities to which they belonged, shaped the American West by the time Frederick Jackson

Turner published his frontier thesis. Their stories prove that Turner was right about one thing: that a distinctive American culture emerged on the frontier. But it was Indigenous peoples, Hispanos, Asian immigrants, Black Americans, and women (along with men), working alongside the white pioneers, who created it. They were and are the central protagonists in U.S. western history.

These seven people moved within and across sprawling landscapes, extending from the high deserts of New Mexico to the mountains of Idaho to the ever-changing riverbanks of the Upper Missouri River.

On topographical maps, the West is obvious to the eye. Light and dark brown crests rise suddenly along a narrow strip near the Pacific coast and mark its western border. Wrinkles and ridges cover more than one thousand miles and then ease down into the Great Plains. The West's eastern border shades into green, marking the point where rainfall amounts no longer necessitate irrigation in its extensive farmlands.

Its towering mountain ranges—the Cascades, the Sierra Nevadas, and the Rockies—are interspersed with lush valleys, vast deserts, and rolling prairies of deeply rooted grasses. They are all high-elevation landscapes, with dry air and abundant sunshine. The headwaters of the continent's major river systems emerge in the West, but much of its lands nurture only scrub brush and bunchgrass at lower elevations. This is big sky country. The land of little rain. A landscape of migration.

The American West was and is expansive. As is its true history.[22]

Centering diverse communities in a history of the nineteenth-century American West challenges popular notions of what the region was and is, who created it, and who is allowed to claim it as home.[23] It helps us understand how the erasure of many and diverse peoples from our national history leads to racist and oppressive policies that impact all American lives, across the country. The national embrace of the frontier myth obscured, recast, or erased the lives of the real people who shaped national events. It was one of the most egregious acts of revisionist history in American life.

The truth of western history remains in family and community stories, archives, museums, historic sites, and the landscape itself. These sources show us that Sacajawea, Jim Beckwourth, María Gertrudis Barceló, Ovando Hollister, Little Wolf, Ella Watson, and Polly Bemis lived remarkable lives that crossed and doubled back, wove together and broke apart, revealing contradictions and surprising connections. Their stories allow us to see the full shape of the American West and its history.

PART I
CURIOSITY IN MOTION

CHAPTER 1

The water in the narrow river was rushing with spring snowmelt when a Northern Shoshone woman knelt on the bank with her infant daughter in her arms. She bathed her in the river water, just as the god Coyote had washed the Shoshone people after he created them. Wrapping her in deerskins, the woman introduced the baby to her father, a chief of the Agai-dika band (Salmon-eaters), and her two brothers and older sister. They named her Sacajawea (boat launcher).[1]

The Agai-dika were relatively new arrivals in the Bitterroot Mountains. An Indigenous fight for control over the Black Hills earlier in the eighteenth century had pushed many tribal nations into the Great Plains and the Rocky Mountains. In 1782, a smallpox epidemic had weakened the Agai-dika; their Indigenous enemies took advantage and forced them into these mountains. Here they found a varied ecosystem suited to their lifeways, which had long been based in hunting, fishing, and foraging. The Agai-dika found plentiful fish in what became known as the Lemhi River, salmon and trout that had swum more than eight hundred miles from the Pacific to spawn here. They built brush lodges along its banks, the waters a blue ribbon unfurling through a light brown valley.[2]

Sacajawea's brothers and father went out with bows and arrows made of cedar and pine to hunt deer, elk, and small game while her mother dug in the soil with a curved stick, prying out yampa and camas roots, which they dried or baked like potatoes. She also gathered red and purple berries and pine nuts, dropping them into bags made of silk grass.[3]

Every autumn, the family rode east over high mountain passes and down into a wide, green valley. There, three rivers twisted up from the south and joined together, forming a large channel that disappeared into the shadow of tall limestone cliffs, heading toward an unknown end.

These were the Three Forks, the headwaters of what French traders thousands of miles downstream called "Le Missouri"; but in the 1780s and '90s, neither American nor European explorers had set foot in the Three Forks. Two thousand miles to the east, the Americans had been free of British control for only a generation. Most of their population was still confined to the eastern seaboard, although some farmers and slaveholders were climbing up and over the Appalachian Mountains to see what lands lay beyond.

Spanish colonists, with their capital in Mexico City, had been moving north into the southern Rocky Mountains for more than two hundred years. They had enslaved Indigenous peoples to build Catholic missions and defensive presidios along New Spain's most important interior river: the Rio Grande. They had acquired a massive tract of land ("Louisiana") from the French in the 1760s but had not yet established towns or cities in its vast expanse.

The French still controlled the great Gulf port of New Orleans and many of the trading towns along the Mississippi River up to the Great Lakes. Napoleon Bonaparte, who was embroiled in a war to suppress an uprising among enslaved peoples on the Caribbean island of Saint-Domingue, wanted to take back Louisiana so its traders could supply his armies with food.

These far-flung events had little impact on the Agai-dika. They knew of Europeans, of course, having traded for their goods with Indigenous neighbors. British and French muskets and Spanish horses had been a vital part of their economy and culture for more than fifty years. But they were still quite secluded in the Rocky Mountains and knew little of the dramas unfurling at the distant edges of their homelands. The Bitterroots and the Three Forks were the heart of an Indigenous world, a place of overlapping territories and relationships largely independent of European or American influence.[4]

THE WESTERNERS

In 1800, Sacajawea's family made their autumn journey to the Three Forks. Riding down into the valley was an annual homecoming, and as usual, the landscape was slightly different than the year before. The waters were always choosing new courses, rising and falling with a particularly rainy season or a drought. But the immense rock shaped like an arrowhead, looming eighty feet above the waterways, was constant. If you climbed to the top and walked out toward its vertiginous, northernmost edge, you could see for miles around.

Twelve-year-old Sacajawea's parents identified their campsite, and she helped her mother build a wickiup, propping willow tree limbs against one another and covering them with brush. The men took their guns, bows and arrows, and bags filled with dried salmon and currants and loaded them onto their horses. They said goodbye to Sacajawea and her mother and rode out to meet kin from other Shoshone bands and Salish (Flathead) and Apsáalooke (Crow) allies. The buffalo herds were on the move from the Great Plains to the mountains, and these animals would feed and clothe the family for the winter.[5]

The men were not expected back for another week or two, but the women had to be ready when they returned. The hunters would bring giant, shaggy buffalo carcasses, secured behind their horses on travois. It was the women's job to strip the hides and cure them, then break down the animals' bodies into piles of muscle, organs, and bones. In their capable hands, the bison would be converted into food, paints, medicines, and tools.[6] The Agai-dika would trade excess meat and hides to Bannock, Apsáalooke, and other Shoshone bands for items they could not produce on their own: tobacco, iron kettles, Spanish saddles, obsidian carved from tall cliffs near the Yellowstone Basin, and guns or ammunition if they were lucky.[7]

A few days after the men left, Sacajawea stopped along a slough to investigate seedpods that she might pluck and store for winter. Nature in all its forms—fish, water, animals, plants—was not just a resource to mine for the Agai-dika. These seedpods connected Sacajawea to her own past travels to the Three Forks and those of her ancestors. They were evidence of the Northern Shoshone's kinship with nature and would both sustain Sacajawea and her family and connect them to the earth and its waters.[8]

Suddenly, the sound of pounding hooves reverberated across the waterways. The riders came closer, and the women emerged from their wickiups, wondering why the hunters were back already. They soon realized, however, that these riders were not the Agai-dika but enemies from the eastern prairies. The Hidatsa had ridden hundreds of miles from their villages at the confluence of the Knife and Missouri Rivers to raid the Agai-dika camps while the men were away and take as many women, children, and horses as they could.[9]

While the Hidatsa attack was unexpected, its purpose was well understood. After the smallpox epidemic, many tribal nations sent raiders out in search of captives to increase their populations—especially women and children. Some of these captives married into their new communities, while others were traded away in exchange for goods that circulated widely through the region.[10]

As the Hidatsa raiding party swept into the Three Forks camp, the Agai-dika women raised the alarm and then scattered into the woods, running southwest along a riverbank. Sacajawea plunged into the shallow water, half running and half swimming. She had almost reached an island in the middle of the channel when a Hidatsa raider named Red Arrow grabbed the back of her buckskin dress and hauled her up onto his horse. As her captor galloped away, the screams of the pursued and the injured grew fainter. They followed the course of the Missouri River downstream, and soon other horsemen pulled alongside. After a few hundred miles, the Hidatsa turned from the river and rode hard to the east. Sacajawea was not their only captive. There were four boys and two more girls—Otter Woman and Leaping Fish Woman—along with a handful of others.[11]

It took them three weeks to ride six hundred miles to the Knife River, an area that the French and Spanish claimed on paper but the Hidatsa and their southern neighbors, the Mandan, controlled on the ground.[12]

Like the Agai-dika, the Hidatsa were relative newcomers to these lands. Twenty years before, their enemies the Lakota had pushed them westward, and they built three villages on a high bluff above the river. The largest was Metaharta, with almost two thousand residents; they walked or rode to the other two villages on hard-packed trails that wound through the prairie grass.[13]

Red Arrow brought Sacajawea and the other Agai-dika captives to Metaharta just as the Hidatsa women were caching their corn in deep pits and preparing for their annual winter move. They were not going far, just from the bluffs to the bottomlands along the river. There, among the cottonwood trees, they would be protected from the winter's howling winds and driving snow but still have access to their earthen lodges on the bluff.[14]

Although some Agai-dika and other Shoshone bands frequented the trading fairs that the Hidatsa and the Mandan held every autumn, Sacajawea had never been to the Knife River Villages. Over the next few months, as she and her fellow captives lived with Red Arrow's family, they encountered a landscape that was, to them, discombobulating. Although Europeans often called all Indigenous peoples "Indians," each tribal nation had its own way of living.

In the valleys of Sacajawea's homeland in the Rockies, she could look out at the mountain peaks in the distance, up at the highest branches of a pine forest, or sit by a narrow river tumbling down over a series of boulders. Here in Metaharta, there was little visual relief. The rolling plains of the Missouri Plateau stretched out to the horizon in all directions, broken up only by the bluffs lining the river and sporadic clusters of cottonwood trees. The sky was huge. The Knife and the Missouri were muddy and wide, churning up the soil with currents that seemed sluggish but could pull you under in a matter of seconds.

The Hidatsa villages, too, were large and imposing. The village that Sacajawea had grown up in was small and far away from neighboring bands. This distance between villages helped prevent overfishing in the region's mountain rivers. The three Hidatsa towns and the two Mandan villages to the south, however, were densely settled. Their compact organization helped them defend themselves from Indigenous attackers and sheltered their residents during harsh weather.

The tall, domed lodges, each thirty to forty feet in diameter, were framed in cottonwood limbs and covered with grass and wildflowers. They housed multiple families and sometimes, their horses. Tall racks leaned against the walls, strips of orange squash and red-brown buffalo meat hanging from the rungs. The lodges were impressive feats of domestic architecture, longer-lasting and more spacious than the tipis covered with deerskins or the brush wickiups that Sacajawea had lived in as a child.[15]

Metaharta was often teeming with people. Apsáalooke, Assiniboine, Cheyenne, and Kiowa women and men were there to trade, offering up leather clothing, iron kettles, strings of beads and shells, pouches filled with rifle ammunition, and hardy western horses.[16] Hidatsa women walked among them, making good deals in exchange for their corn, pumpkins, sunflowers, beans, and tobacco.[17]

Instead of a diet of predominantly salmon, nuts, and berries, Sacajawea now ate more buffalo meat and abundant vegetables. The Hidatsa did fish in the waters of the Knife, and the rainbow, brown, and brook trout they prepared were a familiar taste, a reminder of home. When spring came, the women of Red Arrow's lodge planted and tended corn in the bottomland gardens. This crop was at the center of the Hidatsa trading economy, and the control women had over this vital resource gave them power. They also introduced Sacajawea to the local flora, which differed from those in her homeland. She learned which plants were edible and which were poisonous and how to clean, store, and cook the root vegetables she dug out of the ground.[18]

As women tended to the earth, men went off to hunt or to trade beaver pelts and buffalo robes with English and French fur traders. More than one hundred years before, these Europeans had followed Canadian rivers south and west to the Indigenous communities of the Upper Missouri region. Most of them worked for trading companies, but some moved permanently into the Knife River Villages; these men became known as "residenters." The Hidatsa welcomed them, recognizing the value of having Europeans in their communities to promote diplomacy and commerce.[19]

In 1800, the Indigenous polities of the Upper Missouri Valley, the Great Plains, and the Rocky Mountains far outnumbered the Europeans in their midst. Some prophets, however, were having disturbing visions.

Hundreds of miles southwest of Metaharta in the Black Hills, a Cheyenne prophet named Sweet Medicine lay dying. As a young man, he had given the Cheyenne their political structure and unified them as a people. Now, at the dawn of a new century, he worried for their future. A new people were on the rise.

"They will be people who do not get tired but who will keep pushing forward, going, going all the time," Sweet Medicine warned. "They will keep coming, coming. . . . They are coming all the time."[20]

Sacajawea and Otter Woman remained in Red Arrow's lodge for two years after their capture. Leaping Fish Woman was no longer there; she had escaped from the Villages and disappeared into the prairies, and they did not know what became of her. One day, Red Arrow sent Sacajawea and Otter Woman to meet Toussaint Charbonneau, a French Canadian fur trader and hunter who had been living in Metaharta for several years, and who was a generation older than they were. Charbonneau had worked his way from Quebec to the Upper Missouri Valley, representing the European fur companies. By the time he arrived in the Knife River Villages, Charbonneau spoke several Indigenous languages and was regularly hired on to French and British trading expeditions as a guide, hunter, and interpreter.[21]

Charbonneau took an interest in the two Shoshone women and came to the lodge to negotiate with Red Arrow. The two men smoked and talked, and Charbonneau likely presented Red Arrow with buffalo robes or trade items of great value. When they were done, Sacajawea and Otter Woman packed up their belongings and moved to Charbonneau's lodge as his wives. Intermarriage between traders and Indigenous women was not unusual in the Knife River Villages; such alliances strengthened ties between communities and gave some families more control over trade in the region. As captive women, Sacajawea and Otter Woman had no say in the matter.[22]

After they married Charbonneau, the women processed the buffalo, deer, and antelope hides he brought back to the village. Sacajawea and Otter Woman also grew and harvested corn and other vegetables to feed him and themselves and to trade in the Metaharta market. They learned to speak Hidatsa and probably a smattering of French as well. One of their duties as Charbonneau's wives was to have sex with him, and by the spring of 1804, sixteen-year-old Sacajawea was pregnant with her first child.[23]

That autumn, the Hidatsa heard that a large group of American men were coming up the Missouri in a flat-bottomed fifty-five-foot keelboat, with two pirogues (long, narrow canoes) trailing behind. This was surprising news. The traditional trading season was over, and the winds that carried a chill into Metaharta signaled a shift to the winter season. But the Hidatsa were always looking to make good deals. They would welcome the visitors when they arrived and hold a calumet ceremony, passing a pipe with a dark brown bowl and abundance of eagle feathers to acknowledge the white men as kin. Then they would trade.[24]

In the third week of October, as the temperatures fell below freezing at night, Sacajawea and Otter Woman gathered corn and cured buffalo meat and packed them into a saddlebag for Charbonneau. The Americans had arrived in the Mandan villages, and he was going south to meet them. Perhaps these traders—Meriwether Lewis and William Clark—needed a hunter or guide; if so, he would offer them his services.[25]

As Sacajawea worked, the green and pink lights of the aurora borealis danced in the night sky above Metaharta.[26] The northern lights were a relatively common sight, but there had been many celestial displays in 1804. Indigenous communities of the North Country told conflicting stories about these illuminations, which appeared throughout the late fall and winter. Some believed they were the work of benevolent spirits, reminding the people of their presence. Others were wary, seeing in them the spirits of the dead who sought to take the people with them into the heavens.[27]

The appearance of the aurora borealis just as the Americans arrived might have seemed like a mere coincidence. After all, even though these traders arrived late in the season, they were part of a much longer history of commercial exchange in the Knife River Villages. At that moment, the Americans did not seem to be particularly noteworthy visitors.

"They were few," the Kiowa poet N. Scott Momaday later put it, "and they seemed very small against the great land and the great sky."[28]

CHAPTER 2

Although the Hidatsa and Mandan controlled the lands and waters of the Upper Missouri River Valley, European powers considered it their own. For more than a century, France claimed the Villages as well as more than 800,000 square miles of the North American interior, from the eastern slopes of the Rocky Mountains to the Mississippi River, and from north of the Great Lakes to the Gulf of Mexico. This massive Territory of Louisiana changed hands several times and in 1800, Spain returned control of the territory to France.[1]

This shift concerned American president Thomas Jefferson and the U.S. Congress. Spain was a relatively weak power in the region and had not established many cities or forts in the almost forty years they claimed Louisiana. But France was much more powerful, and Jefferson was wary of their presence on the Mississippi River. The population of Tennessee, Kentucky, and the Upper Midwest had exploded in the years since the American Revolution, and these new residents relied on unrestricted access to the Mississippi River for transporting their goods. If France denied entry into New Orleans or closed the river to American boats, the economic effects would be disastrous for the nascent United States.[2]

Jefferson, who had been elected president the same year that Sacajawea arrived in Metaharta, had big dreams for the United States. He envisioned "a rising nation, spread over a wide and fruitful land," he wrote in his first inaugural, "advancing rapidly to destinies beyond the reach of mortal eye."[3] This was one of the first iterations of the frontier myth, a narrative that imagined a bountiful future for Americans in western lands. To make this dream a reality, the federal government needed to take control of the interior from France and initiate a productive relationship with the Hidatsa, Mandan, and other Indigenous peoples of the region.

In January 1803, the president asked Congress for money to fund an expedition to the Upper Missouri River Valley. "An intelligent officer, with ten or twelve chosen men, fit for the enterprise," he suggested, would explore that country as far as the Western Ocean. They might find a river route across the continent (a long-held dream for many), and they would "have conferences with the natives on the subject of commercial intercourse, get admission among them for our traders."[4]

When Jefferson sent diplomats to Paris a few weeks later to negotiate with Napoleon Bonaparte, however, his goals were more modest. He wanted to purchase the port of New Orleans, which was clearly the most valuable asset that France held in North America, and maybe Florida. On a warm July day, he received a communiqué from the diplomats with an update. When the president opened the letter and read its contents, he was shocked. Napoleon had not only sold them New Orleans and its upriver neighbor Baton Rouge; he had offered up the entirety of Louisiana Territory as well for $15 million. It seemed auspicious to Jefferson that he received this offer on July 3, the day before the nation celebrated its founding and the Declaration of Independence.[5]

As the U.S. Congress discussed ratification of the purchase treaty and hammered out the details of integrating hundreds of thousands of French, British, Spanish, and Indigenous people into the American body politic, Jefferson turned once again to the expedition he had envisioned. Congress appropriated $2,500 to outfit a corps led by two military men, Meriwether Lewis and William Clark, and the hunters and explorers they saw fit to hire.

By March 1804, Lewis and Clark were in St. Louis and witnessed the ceremony that U.S. officials held to mark the transfer of Louisiana from European to American control.[6] Two months later, along with more than thirty men—including Clark's enslaved man named York—they pushed off from the docks and into the Mississippi River. Battling the strong current upstream, they turned west into the Missouri River. For the next five months, as they moved more than one thousand miles north and west of St. Louis, Lewis and Clark met with the Osage, Arikara, and Dakota/Lakota. During the councils they held with tribal chiefs, the captains announced that their homelands were now American territory. Lewis and Clark imagined themselves the vanguards of American conquest, the harbingers of civilization. In reality, the expedition had already moved beyond the reach of federal power and into an Indigenous world.

That fall, several days after Lewis and Clark's expedition landed in the Mandan Villages, Toussaint Charbonneau met with them. When he returned to Metaharta, Charbonneau told Sacajawea and Otter Woman what he had seen. The Americans had large parcels of goods packed in their keelboat, but they were not traders. Instead, they were there to pave the way for future commercial relationships with the United States. The parcels—stuffed with glass beads, camp kettles, brass buttons, ivory combs, fishhooks, rings with glass stones affixed to them, and ruffled shirts, among other things—were meant for the tribal chiefs as gifts.[7]

Lewis and Clark were also there to explore. They told the Mandan and Hidatsa leaders that they would spend the winter nearby in a fort of their own construction. When the river ice thawed in the spring of 1805, they would row up the Missouri as it arced west toward its headwaters at the Three Forks. From there, the expedition members hoped to traverse the Rocky Mountains (about which the Americans knew almost nothing), buy horses and other supplies from the Northern Shoshone (about whom they knew little), and then find a route to the Pacific Ocean. They were in search of scientific information and an understanding of the nature of the country.

To the Hidatsa, the idea that men would travel so far solely for the purpose of exploration was probably surprising. Like other Indigenous peoples across the continent, the Hidatsa had a multifaceted relationship with the landscape. The earth and the water, and its animals and plants, were kin to the Hidatsa, part of their tribal history and their sense of themselves as a people. They marked distances and the territorial boundaries of their own and other tribal nations with natural features, and they moved across the lands between their villages on the Upper Missouri and the Three Forks to hunt and trade, and to raid or make war on their enemies. Both men and women were keen observers of new landscapes and the waters, their bounty and their dangers. They returned home to share this knowledge with their kin and sometimes, with allies, trading in both material goods and information that improved their lives and asserted their control in the region. The Hidatsa understood the point of exploration to determine resources, but to move across these lands *only* to gain knowledge, as the Americans said they were doing, must have seemed odd.[8]

The Hidatsa and other Indigenous peoples along the Missouri were right to be wary, for the Americans did have other motives. The Lewis and Clark Expedition—also known as the Corps of Discovery—was intended to legitimize the Louisiana Purchase and secure the nation's new borders. The thirty-three men of the Corps, who were soldiers but also skilled at river navigation, hunting, and trading, would then move beyond Louisiana. They were agents of empire.[9]

During Charbonneau's discussion with Lewis and Clark, he had told them that both Sacajawea and Otter Woman were Northern Shoshone and had grown up in the Bitterroot Mountains in the northern Rockies. Later that evening at the half-built Fort Mandan, Clark pulled out his diary. "A French man by Name Chabonah . . . visit[ed] us," he wrote. "We engaged him to go on with us and take one of his wives to interpret the Snake [Shoshone] language."[10]

A few days later, Sacajawea and Otter Woman went with Charbonneau to the Americans' fort, ten miles south and on a big bend in the Missouri River. As they neared, they heard the sharp thunk of axes cutting into cottonwood logs, the slap and smear of daub applied to seal the gaps in the walls. The women dismounted, pulled their bundles off the horses, and the Americans stopped working and gathered around. Sacajawea and Otter Woman presented Lewis and Clark with buffalo robes, then turned to offer more robes to the rest of the Corps.[11] For the Shoshone women these gifts indicated the women's goodwill and their new relationship with the Americans.

The next week, Sacajawea, Otter Woman, and Charbonneau returned to Fort Mandan, with all their belongings packed on a travois. Instead of moving to the Knife River bottomlands with the Hidatsa, they would spend the winter at the fort.

The fort was shaped like an arrowhead, with gates at the base, lodgings for the Corps members built from the gates to the point, and an open space in the middle. Once inside, Sacajawea and Otter Woman assembled their tent: cottonwood logs arranged in a circle, raised on their ends and fitted together in the middle. They covered the structure with tanned buffalo hides sewn with sinew and tied their four horses to posts they drove into the dirt. There was not much room in the fort's courtyard; it was barely larger than the interior of their Metaharta lodge. The tent would provide them with only a modicum of privacy.[12]

As the ice grew thick on the river, Sacajawea and Otter Woman welcomed Hidatsa kin and friends to their new home. Some of them came to trade with the Americans or with Charbonneau. Others came to socialize and keep the women company while Charbonneau departed for long stretches, hiring on for winter hunts and trading expeditions up and down the river. Digging into their sacks of green corn and dried squash, Sacajawea and Otter Woman lifted out palmfuls to cook over the tent's hearth fire. They prepared and repaired deerskins to sew into dresses and leggings for themselves and tiny versions for Sacajawea's baby.

Sometimes the American captains summoned Sacajawea and Otter Woman to their headquarters, asking for information about Shoshone country and where they might expect to find Agai-dika bands with large horse herds in the mountains. The two women explained to Charbonneau in Hidatsa, then he translated into French for one of the traders at the fort, who told Lewis and Clark what they wanted to know in English. The Americans used the knowledge these women gave them to start sketching a map of a country they had never seen themselves. Lewis and Clark hoped that this map would not only help them navigate their way through the mountains and whatever lay beyond but also render this massive region intelligible to President Jefferson and the other government officials who waited for their return in the East.[13]

As winter settled in, temperatures often fell well below zero, and snow piled up in drifts against the edges of the Charbonneaus' tent.[14] One morning Sacajawea and Otter Woman were awakened by the boom of the Corps's swivel gun. They emerged to find that the Americans had raised their flag above the fort. It was Christmas Day, the Americans said, and they celebrated the holiday by drinking and eating and dancing into the night. Sacajawea and Otter Woman attended the festivities but "took no other part," one of the Corps members observed, beyond "the amusement of looking on."[15]

In January, Sacajawea fell sick several times. Whether her illnesses were due to the frigid temperatures or her advanced pregnancy was unclear.[16] Her large belly pushed up against her rib cage and made most tasks uncomfortable; she could no longer bend over to pick up baskets or buffalo robes.[17] In the second week of February, her water broke, pooling on the dirt floor of the tent.

If she had been in Metaharta or along the riverbank of her birth in her homeland, this would have been the signal for her female kin to gather in the lodge to prepare for the birth. The Hidatsa would have gathered grass and covered it with deerskins and buffalo robes, speaking in hushed tones to keep the expectant mother calm. They would have raised two posts on either side of the bed for Sacajawea to grip as she squatted, bearing down through the shattering pain of contractions. She would have relied upon the prayers of the women's societies or the visions of owners of the sacred bundles for a safe birth and a healthy baby. They would not have called for a medicine man unless the birth was incredibly difficult, and Sacajawea's life was in danger.[18]

But Sacajawea was in a military camp full of men with only Otter Woman (who was newly pregnant herself) to help her. Lewis and Clark had some medical training but had never aided in a childbirth before and so had little knowledge to offer her. Sacajawea pushed and panted and strained throughout the day. Outside, the frozen currents of the river shrieked as ice-cold water roiled beneath, echoing her pain.[19] A French trader, who was married to a Mandan woman, suggested a treatment of a rattlesnake's rattle, broken into pieces and taken with water. Ten minutes after swallowing the rattles and taking small sips of water, Sacajawea bore down one final time, and a wailing Jean-Baptiste Charbonneau emerged into the world. Otter Woman took him up in a buffalo calfskin and bathed him in warm water.[20]

Two weeks later, the ice began to crack and boom in the river. As Sacajawea recovered from childbirth in the tent at Fort Mandan, the Hidatsa rode out into the prairie west of their villages and set it on fire. The scorched earth would make it easier to see migrating antelope and elk and to track them in the spring hunts. Smoke drifted through the air as the men of the Corps began to prepare for the next phase of their expedition. They cut their boats out of the melting river ice and pulled them up onto the banks, then began to organize their supplies.

They also bickered with Toussaint Charbonneau, accusing him of colluding with the British to prevent the Corps and future American traders from establishing a foothold in the beaver pelt trade. The captains also argued with him about the work he would and would not do on the expedition. Ultimately, they dismissed him, and Charbonneau stormed back to the tent and made Sacajawea and Otter Woman dismantle it and move out of the fort.[21]

Charbonneau soon thought better of his obstinate behavior and apologized, and Lewis and Clark rehired him. On March 18, 1805, the trader took up a pen and scratched an X beside his name on an employment contract. Sacajawea and Otter Woman did not make their marks on the paper, for their names were not included in the list of Corps employees. But William Clark considered them part of the expedition. "Our party will consist of . . . one French man as an interpreter with his two wives," Clark wrote in his diary on April 1. "[T]his man Speaks Minetary [Hidatsa] to his wives who are . . . Snake Indians [Shoshone] of the nation through which we Shall pass, and to act as interpretress thro him."[22]

On April 3, the Corps loaded a large trunk, four boxes, and three cages of live animals onto a barge. The boxes contained specimens: the skins and bones of pronghorns, coyotes, jackrabbits, badgers, and squirrels; Mandan bows and arrows, Arikara tobacco, and several samples of pottery. About a dozen of the boatmen who accompanied the Corps to the Mandan villages were returning to St. Louis, and they would transport the specimens there and then send them on to Thomas Jefferson's library at his home in Virginia and the Academy of Natural Sciences in Philadelphia.[23]

When the Corps put eight boats in the water, Charbonneau, Sacajawea, and Jean-Baptiste were on board a white pirogue. Otter Woman was not coming after all. Although Indigenous women were used to delivering babies while on the move, Sacajawea's hard labor had likely convinced Lewis and Clark that overseeing a childbirth in river rapids or mountain passes would be more than *they* could handle. So Sacajawea and Otter Woman parted ways for the first time in more than four years. They had shared so much: the trauma of their kidnapping and captivity, their forced integration into Hidatsa society, marriage to a man not of their choosing, the birth of Jean-Baptiste. These were experiences that many Indigenous women shared across the Great Plains. But Sacajawea and Otter Woman would not take this journey back to the Three Forks together.[24]

"We were now about to penetrate a country at least two thousand miles in width, on which the foot of civilized man had never trodden," Lewis mused in his diary. "The good or evil it had in store for us was for experiment yet to determine."[25]

Of all the members of the Corps of Discovery, Sacajawea knew best what lay ahead. For her, it was not the Territory of Louisiana but a land of turbulent rivers and jagged mountains and countless Indigenous polities. As the boats moved north, a flock of cedar waxwings alighted on the riverbanks, their tail feathers fringed bright yellow. Like them, Sacajawea was taking flight and going home.[26]

CHAPTER 3

It was the middle of summer before Americans across the seventeen states of the Union received word that Lewis and Clark had set out up the Missouri River to the Knife River Villages. The specimens, journals, and map of the country the captains packed in a keelboat arrived in St. Louis, while letters to government officials in Washington, D.C., and to their friends in Virginia and Kentucky were sent on by express.

"By reference to the muster rolls forwarded to the war department," Meriwether Lewis wrote to President Jefferson, "you will see the state of the party; in addition to which we have two interpreters, one negro man servant to captain Clarke and one Indian woman, wife to one of the interpreters." Sacajawea would serve as a diplomat as well as a translator "to restore peace between the Snake [Shoshone] Indians and those in this neighborhood."[1] This was the first that Americans east of the Mississippi River heard of the "wife to one of the interpreters" and the roles she would play in the expedition.

That William Clark took his enslaved man, York, with him on the expedition was not surprising. Clark was born in Virginia, and his parents were planters who owned several estates where they enslaved Black men and women as laborers. When the Clarks migrated to Kentucky after the American Revolution, they brought their enslaved people to clear, plant, and harvest the Indigenous lands they claimed. Clark was accustomed to having York with him as a manservant; York was also a good shot with a rifle, which would come in handy on the journey.[2]

Clark did not need to worry that York would become free by virtue of his travel through the Louisiana Purchase lands. Although the U.S. Congress had outlawed slavery in the newly acquired Northwest Territories fifteen years before, the international slave trade and enslavement were still legal in every state in the country. In colonial Louisiana, France had a long-established system of African slavery, and New Orleans was one of the most vigorous slave-trading markets on the continent. In 1726, the French Louisiana census counted 1,385 enslaved Black people as residents. The shift to Spanish control in the 1760s did not stem the tide of slavery's expansion. By 1800, the Black population in Louisiana had grown to almost twenty thousand.[3]

When the U.S. Congress created the Louisiana Territory in March 1805, they debated whether to outlaw slavery in one or both of its districts: Orleans (New Orleans and its environs) and the enormous district of Louisiana, which extended from the Canadian border south to the Red River bottomlands, an area that Caddo and Quapaw peoples claimed and would later become southern Arkansas. But slavery was already central to the lives of white settlers in these lands, as well as the Ohio Valley farther north and east.

Congressmen therefore reasoned that outlawing slavery in Louisiana would cause more problems than it solved. Within a year, enslaved men and women accounted for 25 percent of what would become Missouri Territory and nearly one-third of the population living around the French trading town of St. Louis.[4]

For the slave-owning planters of Virginia, this was welcome news. International demand for tobacco was growing, and slavers clamored for the right to import and purchase more enslaved men and women.[5] Their lands, however, would not sustain increased production. Planting only tobacco for decades had leeched the formerly rich soil of its nutrients. By 1800, they wanted more slaves, but they needed new lands.

In the spring of 1805, just as Sacajawea was moving north on the Missouri River with the Corps of Discovery, the enslaved people on Jennings Beckwith's plantation between the Rappahannock and the Potomac Rivers in Virginia (known as the Northern Neck) did not sow tobacco seeds into the dry, crumbly soil, as they usually did that time of year. Instead, Jennings gathered them together and told them they were moving to the western bank of the Mississippi River, in Louisiana Territory.

The Beckwiths had been in Virginia for almost one hundred years, ever since Jennings's grandfather had migrated there from England. At first Marmaduke worked as a clerk. He saved enough money to buy a few acres of prime tobacco land, and after several years he could afford to buy more acreage and enslave several African men and women. They built his house, slave quarters, and a tobacco-curing shed. The Beckwith estate was nowhere near as large or impressive as other slave plantations in the Northern Neck, like Landon Carter's Sabine Hall, a towering, red, Georgian-style brick mansion with a massive, four-columned white portico. Or Stratford Hall, home to the Lee family, already storied in American history due to the heroics of Light-Horse Harry Lee in the American Revolution. But the property was substantial enough to allow Marmaduke's son Jonathan to build upon the family's fortunes. In 1796, Jonathan Beckwith died and left the house, hundreds of acres of tobacco land, and thirty-four enslaved people to his eldest son, Jennings.[6]

This inheritance should have set up Jennings Beckwith for life. But by then, the soil of the Northern Neck was producing fewer tobacco plants and leaves of lesser quality than ten years before. In 1800, Jennings sold more than three hundred acres to pay his debts. That cash infusion did not last. So, he sold more than ten of his enslaved men and women away from their families and the only home they had ever known. The money this traffic in human beings brought in sustained the Beckwiths for a while, but then it, too, ran out. When the news began to spread about the Louisiana Purchase, it seemed to Jennings that it was the perfect opportunity to start anew.[7]

Although the Territory of Orleans had proven lucrative for sugar planters, the northern part of Louisiana was more appealing to Jennings Beckwith. From the reports of traders and travelers, the area—referred to as Upper Louisiana—seemed to have a climate suitable for tobacco production, as well as corn and wheat. These lands, especially those near the confluence of the Missouri and the Mississippi Rivers just north of St. Louis, were cheaper than acreage near Baton Rouge or New Orleans.

In 1805, territorial officials were in the process of clearing all previous land titles around St. Louis and pushing the Osage, Missouria, and Illini peoples to the west. Soon, huge tracts of rich, dark brown soil would enter the market at $1.25 an acre, almost half of the going rate for American public lands.[8]

Jennings Beckwith could be assured that the new territory would support his claims to the twenty-two enslaved people he was bringing with him, including his young son Jim. After their decision to permit slavery and the slave trade in Upper Louisiana, the U.S. Congress adopted a slave code based on France's Code Noir and Virginia's slave laws, confirming the right of white men to buy, sell, and treat enslaved people however they wished, throughout the new American territory.

For seven-year-old Jim Beckwith, the move from the Northern Neck to Louisiana Territory would be sad in some ways. He was one of his father's favorite children, so he lived in the Big House with his father rather than in the slave quarters with his mother. Jim would miss the nights when his father's fellow Revolutionary War veterans came over to the house to drink brandy and tell war stories. "My youthful mind was vividly impressed," he said later, "with the stirring scenes depicted by those old soldiers."[9]

But Jim was an adventurous boy, and the idea of a long journey to an unknown place did not bother him at all. He could not have known at the time how important this moment was for him, and for what he would become. And of course, he had no say in the matter. His father made the decisions in the family and for the people he enslaved.

But how would the Beckwiths get to St. Louis from southeastern Virginia? In 1805, there were two options. Both routes would require the Beckwiths to travel from the Northern Neck across the state of Virginia and over the Shenandoah Mountains. Then they would strike southwest until they crossed the Cumberland Gap into Kentucky. From there, they could take the Wilderness Road, a game trail long used by Shawnee, Cherokee, and many other Indigenous peoples in the region. They would cross Kentucky, Indiana, and Illinois on a series of unimproved roads and paths until they arrived at the eastern bank of the Mississippi River, across from St. Louis.

The other option was to board flatboats at a navigable point on the Cumberland River and float downstream. The river ultimately joined the Ohio, which flowed on to the Mississippi. From there, they would propel the boats upstream, working against strong currents to make the landing at St. Louis.

It is likely that Jennings Beckwith chose the river route. It was faster and cheaper, which were primary concerns for a man with a large group of people and belongings to move. When they left the Northern Neck and set out for Louisiana Territory, the Beckwiths were one of many migrant groups who followed rivers and roads to St. Louis in the first years after the "Great Bargain" that brought Louisiana into the United States. Like them, most of these travelers were white Southerners. Some of them, like Jennings Beckwith, were planters with enslaved people in tow.[10] The majority were small farmers who hoped to do well enough on their Louisiana landholdings to purchase enslaved men and women of their own.[11]

A few months after their departure, the Beckwiths docked north of St. Louis, at the small town of Portage des Sioux. The town's name reflected the significance of the area as a trading thoroughfare for bands of Lakota, Dakota, and Yankton/Yanktonai peoples (whom the Americans knew as the Sioux) who routinely crossed through this strip as a shortcut between the Missouri and the Mississippi. Here, in a two-mile-wide stretch between waterways, there were rich soils that could grow a variety of crops. The area may have reminded Jennings Beckwith of the Northern Neck. Whatever the reason, he decided that this would be the site of his new plantation.

At first, Beckwith did not bother to file a land claim. He had arrived in advance of the land surveyors, as well as any law enforcement officials who might evict them. And like most white migrants, Beckwith believed Indigenous homelands in Louisiana Territory to be American public lands, free for the taking. He squatted on a tract and marked its boundaries, then ordered his enslaved people to build a house and slave quarters and clear the land. They cut down trees, plowed the soil, then planted and harvested tobacco, corn, and hemp. Ultimately, Jennings

Beckwith claimed more than 1,200 acres outside Portage des Sioux through this process of preemption. When the Land Office opened, he bought the parcel for a minimum price of $1.25 per acre. After harvests, he took most of his crops a short distance to the wharves at St. Charles to be transported by boat down the Mississippi River and sold in St. Louis and New Orleans.[12]

Within four years of the ratification of the Louisiana Purchase, the Beckwiths and other families from the eastern states were serving the purpose that Thomas Jefferson imagined for them. They were taking up land and cultivating it, establishing American habits and practices as the vanguard of democracy in the American West.

"Is it not better that the opposite bank of the Mississippi should be settled by our own brethren and children," Jefferson asked in his second inaugural address in 1805, "than by strangers of another family?"[13]

"Beckwith's Settlement" and those around it in Portage des Sioux were making another of the Louisiana Purchase's unstated goals manifest. The purchase not only secured land from France, but it also signaled that the United States would continue to acquire Indigenous territory, through diplomacy or forced removal.[14] President Jefferson had always admired the long histories of Indigenous communities across the continent. But he also believed that they were vanishing as a people. He first elaborated his ideas about this process in his *Notes on the State of Virginia* in 1785, and by 1805, he embraced a view that would come to dominate U.S. Indian policy in the nineteenth century.

"Occupying a country which left them no desire but to be undisturbed," the president wrote that year, "the stream of overflowing population from other regions directed itself on these shores; without power to divert, or habits to contend against, they have been overwhelmed by the current or driven before it."[15]

In reality, the Indigenous peoples who lived in Upper Louisiana were not disappearing. They remained in large numbers and were prepared to defend their homelands. As Americans like the Beckwiths began to arrive in St. Louis and its surrounding counties, the Osage and the Sauk and Fox were wary. "We had always heard bad accounts of the Americans," the Sauk leader Black Hawk said later, "from Indians who had lived near them."[16]

The year before the Beckwiths arrived, Sauk warriors had killed three American settlers on the plains northwest of St. Louis. In the wake of this attack, Indiana's territorial governor William Henry Harrison requested a parlay with Sauk leaders in Portage des Sioux. At the end of the talks, Harrison persuaded a few chiefs to sign what they thought was a peace agreement. It was a treaty that ceded over fifteen million acres of Sauk land to the U.S. government.[17]

Given Harrison's trickery, the Sauk and Fox did not consider the treaty binding. And they were angry. The number and severity of their attacks on American settlements increased.[18] By the time the Beckwiths began planting their new lands with corn in 1806, the American settlers in St. Charles and Portage des Sioux were building forts for defense as well as farms and houses.

"Inhabitants of four adjoining sections would unite," Jim Beckwith remembered, "and build a block-house in the centre of their possessions, so that in case of alarm they could all repair to it as a place of refuge from the savages." While enslaved people labored, overseers and others stood guard with muskets in their arms. They alternately watched the men and women in the fields and scanned the horizon for signs of Indigenous war bands on the move. There were constant alarms. "Hardly a day passed without the inhabitants being compelled to seek [the block-houses] for protection," Jim noted.[19]

One day, when Jim was only nine years old, Jennings sent him to deliver a large sack of corn to the mill. It was the first time his father had entrusted such a task to Jim, and he was thrilled to be thought man enough to shoulder the responsibility. He was also looking forward to the excitement of town and to calling on a few of his friends along the way.

As he trotted up to the fence that separated their house from the road, all was unusually still and quiet. It was not until he drew closer that Jim could see his playmates' bodies lying strewn about the yard and those of their parents farther back, in the doorway. "Their throats [were] cut," he remembered later, "their scalps torn off, and the warm life-blood still oozing from their wounds!"[20]

Jim wheeled his horse around and galloped back to his family's plantation. Breathless, he told his father what he had seen, and Jennings Beckwith headed out with a posse of white migrants to seek revenge. Two days later, his father returned with scalps hanging from his saddle.[21] He had cut them from the heads of Sauk and Fox men and women, mostly likely, or perhaps Osage raiders. Jim was pleased that his friends' murders had been avenged and did not seem shocked at the violence.

"The backwoodsman fought the savage in Indian style," he reasoned, "and it was scalp for scalp between them."[22]

After some raids, settlers sent translators to try to negotiate with Indigenous leaders.[23] This more diplomatic strategy thwarted some attacks but not others. It seemed to many Americans in Louisiana Territory that a larger conflict might be brewing. More than twenty years after the end of the American Revolution, British traders and settlers still moved up and down the Mississippi and Missouri Rivers, and they had amicable relationships with the Indigenous peoples living along their banks. An official alliance between the British and the Indians was a worrisome prospect, as it would prevent American settlement in Upper Louisiana.

When there were no alarms and Jennings had business in town, Jim liked to ride with his father and walk through St. Charles. It was a bit larger than Portage des Sioux, and its buildings sat atop a range of little hills. The streets ran right down to the bank of the Mississippi River, and Jim could see the keelboats and pirogues churning through the brown water, steered by voyageurs (boatmen) and carrying trappers, hunters, interpreters, guides, cooks, and stewards.[24]

One of the boats passing by at that time likely belonged to Manuel Lisa, a Spanish entrepreneur intent on establishing trade relationships with the Indigenous peoples of Upper Louisiana. He was setting out to build a fort more than one thousand miles north of St. Louis, near the Knife River Villages. One of the men who worked for Lisa was Edward Rose, an expert hunter already legendary in the region, the son of a white man and a woman with both Black American and Cherokee parentage.[25]

If Jim Beckwith had met Rose, he would have found much to admire in the hunter, who was living the kind of life the boy already wanted for himself. Like Rose, Jim wanted to be out on the road instead of stuck at home. And like Rose, he was a child born into multiple racial worlds.

In St. Louis and the rest of Louisiana Territory, Jim's status was not all that unusual. A network of multiracial families had been shaping the political and economic development of the region for years. French, Spanish, and English traders married Indigenous women from tribal nations that controlled the Missouri River trade in furs and other commercial items. Their children were multilingual cultural brokers who expanded the family's trade connections and diplomatic power along the region's riverways.[26]

The long history of enslavement in St. Louis meant that children like Jim were not alone in the city and its hinterlands. It also meant, however, that Jim and other biracial children with Black enslaved mothers were considered slaves. Laws in both Virginia and Louisiana Territory determined that "all children born into this country shall be held bond or free only according to the condition of the mother."[27] The Code Noir applied to Jim and the growing numbers of enslaved and free Black people in Upper Louisiana. But in the first decade of the nineteenth century, race relations in St. Louis and towns like Portage des Sioux and St. Charles were relatively fluid. The area was a borderland of Indigenous, European, and American territories. Racial codes in the region were not yet hardened by the national fights over the expansion of slavery. It was common to see free Black business owners and men like Edward Rose and other multiracial guides and hunters in St. Louis and on the boats moving up and down the Missouri and Mississippi.

Jennings Beckwith had realized early on that Jim was smart and a fast learner. Virginia had not outlawed Black literacy before they left, and there was no such provision in Louisiana's Code Noir. Jennings wanted to send Jim to school to learn to read and write and do simple math; after he was done with his education, Jennings would set him up in a business in Portage des Sioux or St. Charles. Jim Beckwith, however, had other ideas. Even as a young boy he knew he would not stay in one place very long. And the dynamic world of Upper Louisiana would provide him with many opportunities to embark on a life of adventure.

CHAPTER 4

As white Americans began moving into Upper Louisiana, the Corps of Discovery made steady progress up the Missouri River, traveling six hundred miles in two months. Then they encountered the Great Falls. There were five waterfalls in all, descending more than six hundred feet in ten miles, their spray drifting up over the plains like smoke. They were beautiful, but they posed a problem for the Corps; it would take them four weeks to portage all their supplies and the boats up the riverbank to get past them.

Sacajawea was sick for the first week they were encamped along the falls, sweating with fever and breathless from a searing pain in her abdomen. Both Meriwether Lewis and William Clark treated her, applying Peruvian bark poultices and dosing her with salts and sulfur tonics. These treatments did not work, and Sacajawea refused additional medicines they offered her. On a particularly bad morning, Clark scraped at the skin below her belly button, then placed a dome-shaped glass over it. Her blood seeped into it, a slowly rising tide.

The captains had learned about bloodletting from Dr. Benjamin Rush, Philadelphia's most prominent surgeon, who taught them that restrictions in the blood vessels were the root of all disease. Whatever was ailing Sacajawea, the captains believed, would leave her body with her blood.[1] The men of the Corps waited for her to recover from her illness, and worried. The next phase of their exploration depended on her expertise.

"What a great loss she would be, if she died," one of them wrote in his journal, "she being our only Interpreter, for the Snake [Shoshone] Indians."[2] The Corps members did not know much about the Rocky Mountains, but they knew they needed to secure horses from the Shoshone to cross over and through them. Their survival depended on Sacajawea's.

Whether it was due to the Americans' ministrations or despite them, Sacajawea began to feel better after about ten days in camp. She left her tent and set out on her own along the Great Falls, rigging up a fishing line to see what she could catch. She stopped when she saw a clutch of blue-purple pea-shaped flowers tucked in among the riverbank grasses. Reaching down to grasp the stalks, she pulled them out and brushed the dirt from their bulbs. Tsoaika: Indian breadroot (prairie turnip). The Hidatsa and other Great Plains peoples picked and then cached these vegetables, pulling them out of storage to eat year-round. They dried them over a hot fire or out in the sun and then ate them boiled or roasted, mixed with buffalo grease and berries, or pounded into a powder to thicken soups.[3]

Sacajawea had been foraging from the first days of the expedition. She often joined Clark when he left the boats to walk along the shore, placing Jean-Baptiste in a cradle on her back. On these walks, she gathered several items, in addition to the prairie turnip: wild licorice, their bristled pods filled with aromatic seeds; artichokes growing in clumps with their purple crowns not yet in bloom; and golden currant bushes, growing tall with their star-shaped yellow flowers smelling like cloves.[4]

At first, she gathered these plants to supplement her family's diet. She soon realized, however, that Clark and Lewis were always interested in what she found. They were especially pleased if she gave them something they had never seen before, a plant that American scientists had not yet recorded. For this, too, was part of their charge as a Corps of Discovery. They were to collect and record "objects worthy of notice," Thomas Jefferson had written to Lewis in his instructions. These might include "the soil & face of the country, its growth & vegetable productions, especially those not of the U.S."[5]

Jefferson was eager to analyze these botanical specimens because as a natural scientist, he was invested in the expedition as a pursuit of knowledge. He was the president of the American Philosophical Society, an organization founded by Benjamin Franklin in 1743 to pursue "all philosophical Experiments that let Light into the Nature of Things."[6] As the president of the United States, however, he had other motives. In recent years, French scientists had cast aspersions on the North American continent as inferior in every way to Europe. If Lewis and Clark could collect a wide variety of animal and botanical samples that proved America's uniqueness, Jefferson could use these to construct a sense of American identity. Scientific understanding was a tool of nation building.[7]

These botanical collections were also a way to determine if the lands of the Louisiana Purchase could sustain American farmers. If the soil was rich enough to grow a variety of vegetables in the wild, then perhaps it could nurture millions of acres of corn and wheat. American farmers could grow enough to sustain themselves and their families and then ship the rest down the Missouri and the Mississippi to sell in St. Louis or New Orleans. They would create the "empire of liberty" that Jefferson envisioned, its roots digging deep into the prairie soil. That these lands were Indigenous did not concern Jefferson in the least. To him and to most Americans, Louisiana Territory was public land the moment the United States purchased it. The federal government was free to survey it and sell it, converting it to private property that would sustain the nation.[8]

Sacajawea's knowledge was central to the creation of this continental community of farmers. While the captains had initially believed that she would be most valuable as an asset when they reached her people in the Rocky Mountains, she was the only expedition member who was familiar with the flora and fauna between the Knife River Villages and the headwaters of the Missouri. Within a few months, she was already a central player in the pursuit of scientific knowledge on the expedition—and through it, the conquest of the West.[9]

After the portage around the Great Falls, the next section of the Missouri River seemed placid. Soon, limestone cliffs rose up on either side of the expedition boats, dark gray at the base fading into a creamy yellow at the top. The Corps members paddled slowly through the canyon, staring up at vivid red and orange drawings of people and animals, images that the Shoshone's ancient ancestors had painted to track their histories. These Indigenous peoples no doubt had a name for this canyon, but Meriwether Lewis decided to call it "The Gates of the Rocky Mountains." By giving it a name, he believed he was claiming it for the United States of America. But it was an act of usurpation rather than a discovery.[10]

Sacajawea recognized the pictographs and additional evidence of Shoshone inhabitation along the water's edge: scattered wickiups on small landings, the pine trees around them peeled of their bark. These were defensive structures, used for hunting and warfare.[11] Two days later, the boats left the shadows of the limestone cliffs, and the country opened before them, the river widening into an extensive green plain. Flocks of geese and cranes flew low over the water, alighting on numerous islands that crowded the valley.

"This is the river on which my relations live," Sacajawea told Lewis. "The three forks are at no great distance."[12] Lewis asked her if they should expect more rough water or cataracts. She shook her head. "The river continues much as we see it." But the captain was skeptical. "I can scarcely form an idea of a river running to great extent through such a rough mountainous country," Lewis wrote in his notes, "without having its stream intercepted by some difficult and dangerous rapids or falls."[13]

Lewis should have trusted her memory and experience; the expedition found nothing but calm currents ahead. Their arrival at the Three Forks, the headwaters of the Missouri River, marked the end of the first phase of the expedition. Soon they would enter the Rocky Mountains and trade their boats for horses, acquired from Sacajawea's relatives.[14]

The captains decided to stay at the Three Forks for a few days. They sensed that the headwaters of the Missouri were an essential point in western geography and wanted to accurately convey its location and features.[15] The day after their arrival, Sacajawea placed Jean-Baptiste into a cradleboard and walked with Lewis and Charbonneau through the bottomlands of the waterway that Lewis renamed the Jefferson River, in honor of "that illustrious personage" who was the "author of their enterprise."[16]

"Here I was taken prisoner," Sacajawea told Lewis. On that walk and then again back in camp, she told the story of how she ran and tried to hide from the Hidatsa raiders five years before. How the enemy pursued and killed several men and women and boys and took her, Otter Woman, and Leaping Fish Woman away with them.[17] The memories of that traumatic day had clearly remained with Sacajawea, in all their vivid detail.[18] Her fellow Corps members recognized the emotional power of her story; almost all those who were keeping journals of the expedition wrote it down.

When they left the Three Forks a few days later, the captains were feeling a sense of urgency. It was already August, and they knew that within weeks, snowstorms would bury the high mountain passes in the Bitterroots, the forbidding mountain range to the West. Lewis took several men with him to travel overland ahead of the main group, and Sacajawea stayed in the boat party with Jean-Baptiste, Charbonneau, and Clark. For the next ten days, they struggled upriver. Often forced to disembark and walk along the riverbank, they tugged the canoes with elk skin ropes.[19] Long grasses and hardy serviceberry shrubs crowded the banks.

Sacajawea fetched a pail from a canoe and filled it with clusters of dark purple fruit to share with her fellow expedition members. The men delighted in the bounty, which tasted like mild blueberries with almond-flavored seeds inside. Clark was so pleased he renamed the landscape they were moving through Service Valley, in honor of the abundant fruit.[20]

The next morning, after they had moved just a few miles upriver, an unusual sound reached them: singing. Sacajawea recognized the tune, and soon a group of men came through the trees, riding fine horses. They stopped when they saw her. "Captain Lewis is up the river waiting for you," they said to her, in Shoshone. The captain had found their encampment at the confluence of the Beaverhead River and Horse Prairie Creek.[21] The messengers offered the Corps two of their horses, and Sacajawea and Charbonneau, along with Jean-Baptiste, mounted one while Clark took the other. As they rode off toward the camp, the boat party shoved back into the river and followed behind.[22]

Lewis's bivouac—which the Corps would come to call Camp Fortunate—was set up close to a cluster of wickiups. When Sacajawea, Charbonneau, and Clark appeared at the edge of the camp, Shoshone men, women, and children gathered around the horses. Sacajawea dismounted and sucked her fingers, a sign of Shoshone kinship. Suddenly, a young woman separated herself from the group and approached. She was Leaping Fish Woman, who had been taken captive with Sacajawea and escaped from Red Arrow's lodge.[23] How had she survived the journey back to their homeland, alone and without resources? As much freedom and possibility as there were in these lands, there was also always danger. Her presence here seemed miraculous. Clearly, she—like Sacajawea—had a geographical memory of her homeland and the expertise to guide herself home.[24]

Later that afternoon, when Lewis and Clark drew Sacajawea and Charbonneau into a tent to translate, Sacajawea was presented to the Agai-dika chief and felt another shock. His face was thinner, and his hair was cut short to indicate he was in mourning, but she knew her brother Cameahwait almost instantly.[25] The two had only a few moments to talk before the council began; a more extensive private conversation would be delayed.

Lewis started to speak. The Corps of Discovery was in Shoshone country, Sacajawea explained to her brother and his fellow chiefs, to explore the country and to follow the rivers across the mountains to the Pacific. They wished to go that far, she said, to "find out a more direct way to bring merchandise to the Shoshone." The Americans would build forts, where Shoshone and American traders would meet and forge an extensive commercial network.

The captains did not divulge to Cameahwait that President Jefferson had yet another motive to explore and build trading forts in the region. A vigorous frontier trade would not only boost the U.S. economy, but it would also push Indigenous communities into debt and force them to cede their lands as payment.

"In this way our settlements will gradually circumscribe and approach the Indians," Jefferson believed, "and they will in time either incorporate with us as citizens of the United States, or remove."[26]

Cameahwait was receptive to their overtures, because he knew the Americans could provide the Agai-dika with guns and ammunition. They needed to defend themselves against their Indigenous enemies, most of whom had already established direct relationships with English and French traders and acquired many muskets. The conversation soon turned to the purchase of Shoshone horses and the possibility that Cameahwait would supply the Corps with a guide to lead them over the Bitterroot Mountains. When the negotiations were over, the gifting began. The captains gave Cameahwait the largest of the American peace medals they had in their bags, along with a uniform coat and other clothing items, a twist of tobacco, and an assortment of knives, beads, and magnifying glasses.[27]

As the members of the council began to disperse, Sacajawea finally had a chance to talk with her brother. She asked about the rest of their family and discovered that in her absence her parents had died, along with the rest of their family, except one brother and the son of her eldest sister. There had been such joy when she found Leaping Fish Woman and Cameahwait, but now she sorrowed to know the fates of her kin.[28]

For the next week, Sacajawea traveled with the captains as they scouted for routes through the mountains and translated as Cameahwait and other Shoshone described their tribal culture and explained the local geography. At one point, a man more than twice Sacajawea's age approached her. When she was a young girl, her father had promised her in marriage to this man once she came of age. This was a Shoshone tradition, and the man had the right to claim her as his third wife. The man looked at Sacajawea, at Jean-Baptiste, and at Charbonneau. "As you have a child by another man," he said to her, "I do not want you."[29]

Sacajawea may have felt some relief when she heard this. Charbonneau could be violent—he had struck her just the week before during a dinner they shared together—and he was probably not the man she would have chosen for herself.[30] Their marriage had given her a link to the larger Hidatsa community, however, and now to the Corps of Discovery as well. This Shoshone man, on the other hand, was a stranger.[31] His rejection of her also meant that Sacajawea and Jean-Baptiste could continue westward with the expedition. She could contribute more botanical knowledge to the expedition report. And she could map the region beyond the mountains for herself, information that might be useful to her, the Shoshone, or the Hidatsa one day. At this point in the journey, Sacajawea was becoming an explorer too.

In early September, Sacajawea rode up and over a high mountain pass on horseback, Jean-Baptiste strapped to her back. Cameahwait had helped them obtain horses and provided a guide, and then the Agai-dika left for the Three Forks; it was time for their annual buffalo hunt. The Corps paused at the summit and looked at the jagged peaks of the Bitterroot Range extending all the way to the western horizon. They had just crossed the continental divide, that great backbone of North America. All the rivers west of here ran to the Pacific.[32]

It took the Corps three weeks to get through the Bitterroots. Even with their guide, they stumbled along trails that suddenly ended or backtracked on themselves, late-summer snowstorms pelting them as they rode. Game was scarce, and they were often hungry. The Bitterroots were "the most terrible mountains I ever beheld," wrote one of the Corps members.[33]

Finally, they emerged from the pine forests and into a fertile valley. This was the Nez Perce homeland, and soon they met with men and women of that tribal nation. After agreeing to sit with the Americans in several councils, the Nez Perce gave them salmon and berries for their packs and pointed them toward the northwest, sending a few men with them as additional translators. With this help, the Corps made their way to the Clearwater River and then the Snake. After stopping to construct canoes, they traveled downriver until they steered into the Columbia, the confluence surrounded by low plains crowded with sagebrush. There the Corps found the villages of Yakama and Wanapum peoples.[34]

Sacajawea did not know their language, nor did they have Shoshone captives among them. Once she appeared, however, women and men came out of their lodges and seemed at ease. In Indigenous communities, the presence of women in a group was a form of gendered diplomacy; their inclusion suggested peace rather than war, alliance rather than antagonism.[35]

"The wife of Shabono [Charbonneau] our interpreter we find reconciles all the Indians as to our peaceful intentions," Clark wrote in his diary.[36] Reassured by Sacajawea's presence, great numbers of Yakama and Wanapum arrived at the Corps's camp, and a vigorous trading session began. They spent several days in this area and then moved on. It was late October, and they needed to reach the Pacific before stopping to build winter quarters.[37]

As the Corps floated down the Columbia River, they passed through a region of fault zones and volcanic peaks before entering the coastal lowlands, an area Russian traders called "the rain coast." Nearly constant fog and damp began to rot Sacajawea's clothing, Jean-Baptiste's blankets, and the tent they shared with Charbonneau.[38] The riverbanks were dense with plank houses, their steep roofs and gables covered with white cedar bark. The Clatsop and Chinook who lived there wore sailor's jackets and cotton shirts and carried muskets and pistols along with war axes and bows and arrows.

Some of these items they had scavenged from shipwrecks along the Pacific coast; others they had acquired through trade with English, French, and Russian mariners who entered their lands from the West. They were experienced negotiators and refused most of the meager and cheap goods Lewis and Clark offered them.[39] During one trading session, a Chinook man declined to exchange a sumptuous robe of sea otter skins that the captains coveted for a few of the Corps's ratty blankets. He surveyed the Americans' camp and decided he would accept only a belt that Sacajawea wore, which she had decorated with blue beads. The captains forced her to give it up so they could obtain the robe. A few days later, they gave her a blue cotton coat from their bundles to make up for her loss. It was not an equal trade for her.[40]

The captains did, at least, ask for Sacajawea's input when they were deciding where to establish their winter camp. Sacajawea pointed out that the south bank of the Columbia had plentiful game, as well as an abundant supply of wapato, a small, cream-colored, potato-like vegetable that grew among the reeds. The Chinook dug them out of the mud with their toes, and Sacajawea could do the same and cook them up like she would other roots. She could also use them to trade for other items.[41] Lewis and Clark found her arguments convincing but decided that all Corps members should weigh in on the decision. Sacajawea and York participated in the subsequent vote, and the majority chose the south bank.[42]

Over the next few weeks, Charbonneau built their hut a short walk from the wapato fields near the water. After the first of the year, Sacajawea went to see Clark. "I have traveled a long way with you to see the great waters," she told him. And yet Charbonneau and the captains had left her behind when they followed the Columbia to its outlet and looked upon the mighty Pacific, its waves pounding on a wide sand beach with a huge whale carcass decomposing upon it. "And now that the monstrous fish is also to be seen," she said, "I think it very hard that I should not be permitted to see either." She was adamant, so Lewis agreed to take her.[43]

On January 8, 1806, Sacajawea climbed up a high promontory that the captains called Tillamook Head. From the top, she and Jean-Baptiste finally saw the Pacific. After taking in the view, Sacajawea made the steep descent to a visit a Tillamook village with Clark and Charbonneau and to walk on the beach. The whale carcass, unfortunately, was no longer there. The Tillamook had long since stripped it of its organ meat, blubber, and skin. This must have been disappointing, but at least Sacajawea was able to stand and watch the ocean waves crash upon the sand—an experience that none of her Shoshone and Hidatsa kin would have had. A few days later, Sacajawea returned to the fort, satisfied.[44]

The weather warmed a bit over the next three months, but the rain never slackened. The days in camp were long and uneventful, and Sacajawea likely spent most of the time trying to keep herself and Jean-Baptiste dry and comfortable. Lewis and Clark managed to accumulate enough supplies from the hard-bargaining Clatsop and Chinook to prepare for the return journey. On March 23, 1806, Sacajawea turned to the east with the rest of the Corps and left the dampness of the western coast and the roaring waves of the Pacific Ocean behind.

The Corps retraced its steps, and three weeks later, they were once again climbing up into the Bitterroots. Along the way, Sacajawea noticed the delicate white petals of a wildflower pushing up from a melting ridge of snow. Recognizing it from her childhood, she pulled up a bunch and brought it to the captains. Lewis tasted the roots and found them pleasing; he and Clark then described them in detail in their journals. The western spring beauty, as it came to be called, was unknown to American or European scientists, and the captains gave Sacajawea credit for discovering it.[45]

Eager to get back to the Upper Missouri, the Corps did not tarry at the Three Forks, and Sacajawea did not see her brother again. From this point on, they split into two groups. Sacajawea, Jean-Baptiste, and Charbonneau went with Clark, following buffalo roads overland toward another set of mountains to the east. Sacajawea recognized this place as well.

"A few years ago, buffalo was very plentiful in these plains and valleys," she told Clark. "But [the Shoshone] don't come into these valleys of late," fearing a clash with Apsáalooke (Crow) or Lakota bands who claimed these lands."[46] Sacajawea pointed out a gap in the mountains and suggested the party head there instead of a route that Clark had mapped out farther north and then follow the Yellowstone River eastward. Clark took her advice.[47]

"The Indian woman has been of great service to me," the captain noted in his diary, "as a pilot through this Country."[48]

They made good time, and by late July, Sacajawea could no longer see the Rocky Mountains if she turned back to look toward the west. Large streams joined the Yellowstone from the south, one after the other, and the country flattened out and trees became sparse. Soon the Yellowstone poured its silt and mud (some of it still carrying the sulfur and calcium carbonate from the geothermal basins at its source) into the Missouri River. Here the Clark party slowed down to wait for Captain Lewis and his group. Reunited little more than a week later, the Corps of Discovery turned their boats downstream and soon landed at the Knife River Villages.[49]

The Corps had been gone for more than a year and a half. It was mid-August 1806, and the Villages were full of Indigenous and European traders. The Corps fired a salute, and several Hidatsa chiefs gathered to welcome them. Sacajawea carried Jean-Baptiste and what was left of her belongings off the boat. As she walked through the village, the bustle of the trading plaza eased into the quiet of the lodges. There had been a whooping cough epidemic while the Corps had been gone, and more than one hundred Hidatsa children had died.[50] Sacajawea likely went looking for Otter Woman and her baby; whether she found them or not is unknown.

While Lewis and Clark were preparing for their final councils with the Hidatsa and Mandan chiefs, Clark came to see Sacajawea and Charbonneau. He told them that he wanted to take Jean-Baptiste with him to St. Louis. He had grown fond of the boy on the journey (and had even named a geological feature after him, using the pet name he gave him, Pompey), and he wanted to adopt him into his own family.

Sacajawea refused. Jean-Baptiste was not yet weaned; he could not be separated from her. Charbonneau did not question her decision. The French trader also declined Clark's invitation to journey with them to St. Louis and then on to Washington, D.C., to report directly to Thomas Jefferson. Clark was disappointed but paid Charbonneau his wages for the expedition, a little more than $500. Although Sacajawea had contributed to the Corps's success in unanticipated and valuable ways—collecting specimens, cooking, translating, mapping, and guiding—she was an uncontracted member of the Corps and therefore received no pay.[51]

"Your woman who accompanied you [on] that long dangerous and fatiguing route to the Pacific Ocean and back," Clark later wrote to Charbonneau, "deserved a greater reward for her attention and services on that route than we had in our power to give her at the Mandans."[52] He offered to procure the family some land to farm around St. Louis, should they visit and then decide to settle there.

As the American boats disappeared downriver, Sacajawea turned her attention to her lodge and to the trading season. Soon the temperatures would drop, and Jean-Baptiste would need warmer clothes. The baby was now nineteenth months old, walking unsteadily and showing a few tiny teeth when he smiled.

Sacajawea had traveled over more of the continent than most other people of that era, men or women, Indigenous, European, or American. She may have told the stories of her explorations to Otter Woman, or to the Hidatsa in Metaharta. But for the most part, residents of the Knife River Villages soon forgot about the Corps's passage through their homelands. The Americans were a curiosity and a trade opportunity in 1805 and 1806, but nothing more.[53] Sacajawea could not have known how eagerly Americans perused the newspapers for updates on the expedition's progress, how much they wanted to know about what the Corps of Discovery had found in the western interior of the continent.[54] And she could not have predicted how powerful the publication of Lewis and Clark's journals would become in shaping the frontier myth and the American desire to claim the lands between the Pacific Ocean and the Mississippi River.

CHAPTER 5

When Meriwether Lewis and William Clark left the Knife River Villages, they took a Mandan chief named Sheheke and his family with them. They stopped for several weeks in St. Louis, and by December 1806 they were in Washington, D.C. After a series of receptions and public engagements, the Mandan couple attended a dinner with Thomas Jefferson. The president may have been disappointed that Sheheke did not stop at Monticello on the way. He had suggested to Lewis that they all go to see the "tokens of friendship" the captains had sent back in their specimen boxes, which Jefferson had arranged in "a kind of Indian hall" in his stately manor house in the Virginia countryside.[1]

Jefferson stood up to make a speech at the dinner, aware that he needed to walk a fine line between offering friendship to Indigenous chiefs like Sheheke and asserting power.

"My friends and children," he began in his speech at dinner, "we are descended from the old nations which live beyond the great water, but we and our forefathers have been so long here that we seem like you to have grown out of this land." The United States was no longer a part of Europe, he told the Mandan, "but as united in one family with our red brethren here."

Jefferson advised Sheheke to be at peace with his Indigenous neighbors and with the Americans in their midst. He invited the chief to visit all the great cities of the eastern seaboard and tell everyone at the

Knife River and Mandan Villages what he had seen. He wanted all Indigenous peoples of the Louisiana Purchase lands to understand the kind of economic and military strength that the United States—now a nation of five million people—could wield. Jefferson was sure that the more these tribal nations knew of Americans, "the more they will be our hearty friends" and choose peace over war.[2]

The president also told the Mandan that "the French, the English, the Spaniards, have now agreed . . . to retire from all the country which you and we hold between Canada and Mexico, and never more to return to it."[3] This was disingenuous. European traders remained at forts along the Mississippi and the Missouri Rivers after Louisiana Territory changed hands. Even as President Jefferson hosted Sheheke and his family in Washington, D.C., he awaited news of a treaty with Great Britain, one that would confirm America's neutral trading rights and prevent British naval captains from boarding American ships to search for deserters and force ("impress") U.S. sailors into service.

Three months later, just as his Mandan visitors returned to St. Louis, Jefferson rejected the treaty because the British had not agreed to discontinue impressment. In December 1807, the president signed the Embargo Act, which closed American ports to all exports and disallowed British imports. The act made only a small dent in the British economy, but it drove the United States into a depression. It also cut off the flow of European goods into the Knife River Villages markets.

Although the Spanish trader Manuel Lisa arrived and established a fur trading post on the Bighorn River in the winter of 1807, by the spring of 1808 the Mandan and Hidatsa were feeling the pinch of the embargo. They began to fight one another to control the fur trade with Lisa and to secure British and American traders as allies. Discontent spread.[4]

More than one thousand miles to the southeast, a Shawnee prophet and his brother, a chief named Tecumseh, founded a town along the Wabash River in Indiana Territory. The prophet had had a vision of a giant crab that crawled from the sea, promising to overturn the land so white people would be covered with it. The brothers planned to build a pan-tribal confederacy to protect Indigenous land, based in what they called Prophetstown. Another vision promised an earth-shattering end to all white settlement in the region and any Indigenous communities that did not join them.⁵

Amid this chaos in the heart of the continent, Sacajawea and other women who went out into the prairies surrounding Metaharta in the spring of 1809 had to be vigilant. The Arikara had been raiding from the south, and there was always the danger of an attack from the Lakota to the east. One day, as dusk gathered itself in the sky, the Hidatsa climbed onto the roofs of their lodges to chat. From there, someone spied a fleet of boats arriving from the south. It was Manuel Lisa, who was returning from St. Louis for another trapping and trading season. He intended to build a new trading fort just north of Metaharta.⁶

On their way, Lisa's boats had stopped at the Mandan Villages to drop off Sheheke and his family, who had been waiting for two years to return home after their journey to Washington, D.C. The stories that President Jefferson wanted Sheheke to tell—about the Americans' large cities and vast farmlands—had the effect that the president desired. The Mandan and Hidatsa heard these stories, and they seemed an ill omen.

A few weeks later, when Lisa's boats pushed off to head downriver, Sacajawea, Jean-Baptiste, and Toussaint Charbonneau were on board. They had finally decided to take up William Clark's earlier offer and visit St. Louis. Perhaps it was the growing violence of the Knife River Villages that convinced them to go. Or maybe Charbonneau was looking for a wider variety of employment. Or perhaps Sacajawea was yearning, once again, to explore. Jean-Baptiste was almost five years old, dashing about the boat and talking to his parents in multiple languages. It was the third long voyage of Sacajawea's young life, but the first time she would be moving southward rather than to the west or east.⁷

A few weeks later, the boats navigated a big turn as the Missouri River's roiling waters joined the wide, slow Mississippi, and soon after, they drew up at the docks on the west bank below a high bluff. Sacajawea, Jean-Baptiste, and Charbonneau disembarked, then walked up the path that led them onto La Rue Royale, a narrow street that stretched the length of St. Louis.

The city was about the same size as Metaharta, with 1,500 residents, although thousands more lived in the surrounding farmlands. Unlike Metaharta's densely packed domed lodges, however, the square buildings of St. Louis were evenly spaced on generous lots that lined the city's gridded streets, the spaces between them planted with fragrant gardens and shade trees. Most structures were made of cedar or mulberry logs set vertically into the ground, although some Americans had rejected this French style and stacked their logs horizontally. Several larger houses were made of stone or brick, and some of them bore dark scars of fires set during an Osage raid on the city the previous year.[8]

The streets were busy, packed with both city residents and those who lived on the outskirts, running their errands and going to and from their workplaces or the docks.[9] "Here to be seen about the river banks," the American writer Washington Irving observed, "were the hectoring, extravagant, bragging boatmen of the Mississippi, with the gay, grimacing, sighing, good-humored Canadian voyageurs."[10] Osage, Otoe-Missouria, and Ioway men and women joined them, along with white American migrants just arriving from Louisiana, Kentucky, and Tennessee.

There were enslaved Black women and men in the city, more than Sacajawea or Charbonneau had ever seen in one place. York was not among them. William Clark, angry that York had refused to relocate to another of Clark's plantations because it would mean leaving his family, hired him "out to Some Severe Master" in Kentucky.[11]

Across the river and north of the city, several large, grassy mounds rose up in the landscape. They were the remnants of Cahokia, a trading center of ten thousand people that connected the Great Lakes to the Gulf of Mexico, built by the Mississippian peoples in the eleventh century. At one time there had been at least 120 mounds towering over the floodplains of the river. By 1350, the city's residents had abandoned Cahokia, migrating northward along the midcontinent's rivers. Their descendants were the Arikara, the Mandan, and the Hidatsa.[12]

Sacajawea, Jean-Baptiste, and Charbonneau set off to find William Clark. When Clark had returned from Washington, D.C., with Sheheke in 1807, President Jefferson had appointed him the U.S. agent for Indian affairs in the region. Two years later, his office was busy with men buying licenses to trade with the Missouri River tribal nations and fur traders returning from trips upriver. Hanging above his desk was a copy of the map that Sacajawea and Otter Woman had helped him draw at Fort Mandan. Clark also owned a large house outside town on Beaver Pond, where he lived with his seventeen-year-old wife, Julia, whom he called Judith. Clark had named a river after her during the Corps's trip to the Pacific, and they had been married on her father's Virginia plantation in 1808. They had a new baby, a boy whom Clark had named after Meriwether Lewis.[13]

Clark was happy to see the Charbonneaus, especially Jean-Baptiste, for whom he still had great affection. They talked about their lives since the expedition, and Clark told them the sad news that Meriwether Lewis had died. He had left the city a few weeks before to travel to Washington, D.C., and at an inn on the Natchez Trace, he had apparently taken his own life. Lewis left no word as to why, but Clark had long been worried about his bouts of depressive melancholy.[14] Lewis had taken the only copies of the Corps of Discovery's journals with him, but they were secure.

They also discussed the family's plans. Charbonneau, in addition to receiving extra pay for the expedition, had been awarded a land grant of 320 acres outside the city. The rolling hills west of St. Louis, like the Beckwith plantation farther north in Portage des Sioux, had rich, deep soils. Sacajawea would clear and plant the fields with corn and Charbonneau would continue his work as a hunter and guide on the river. If it did not work out, Charbonneau could always sell the land. White migrants were arriving in St. Louis every day, looking to wrest farms out of the bottomlands and make them pay.[15]

Clark took the family around St. Louis and introduced them to sixty-year-old Auguste Chouteau, who had helped found St. Louis in 1764, building a fort on the western bank of the Mississippi across from Cahokia on behalf of a New Orleans trader. He was part of a multiracial family who had long-established trade and diplomatic relationships with the Osage and a large network of kin and business connections throughout the region. Over the next few months, the Charbonneaus and Chouteau came to know each other well enough that when Jean-Baptiste was baptized after Christmas, Chouteau agreed to be the boy's godfather.[16]

This relationship with Chouteau strengthened the Charbonneau family's ties to the geography of empire in the Missouri River world and enlarged their network of friends and relations to call upon in a crisis.[17] Ultimately, Sacajawea and Charbonneau stayed in St. Louis more than a year. They bought additional acreage from Clark, paying for it with yet another bonus that Congress awarded them. Charbonneau met with Clark to answer some queries sent by Nicholas Biddle, the editor of the journals of the Lewis and Clark expedition, to clarify some of the Corps's activities.[18]

By the spring of 1811, however, they had grown restive. Sacajawea was tiring of life in St. Louis, and Charbonneau itched to get back to his work in the fur trade. Manuel Lisa was taking another fleet of Missouri Fur Company boats up the Missouri to the Knife River Villages in April, and Charbonneau signed on to work as an interpreter for him. William Clark, as he had in 1806, begged the Charbonneaus to leave Jean-Baptiste with him. The boy was now six years old, and Clark wanted to take him under his wing and send him to school.[19]

This time, Sacajawea agreed. A child in the family who could speak English—the increasingly dominant language of trade along the Missouri River—would be helpful in the future. And establishing a kin tie to the powerful Clark family would create another productive connection between the Knife River and St. Louis, the Hidatsa and the Americans.[20] Given that diplomatic relations between Great Britain and the United States had deteriorated further, this could help Sacajawea and Charbonneau navigate the conflict to come. And so, Jean-Baptiste remained in St. Louis. In late June 1811, Sacajawea and Toussaint Charbonneau stepped off Manuel Lisa's fur company boats and returned to their lodge in Metaharta. Sacajawea never saw her son again.[21]

In late fall that year, after the trading season was over in the Knife River Villages, word came that there had been a major battle between U.S. forces and Indigenous warriors at Prophetstown in Indiana. The territorial governor, William Henry Harrison, had gathered more than one thousand volunteer militia and Army regulars (men already mustered into the U.S. Army) to crush the growing insurgency led by Tecumseh and his brother.

"If some decisive measures are not speedily adopted," he wrote to the secretary of war, "we shall have a general combination of all the tribes against us."[22]

The Americans marched against the town in late November, and while they were encamped along the Tippecanoe River, five hundred Kickapoo, Winnebago, and Potawatomi warriors attacked them. Harrison's troops held their positions and then pushed the warriors back. The next day, Harrison marched to Prophetstown and burned it to the ground. The governor believed this to be a great victory for the United States, but it did nothing to quell Indigenous resistance in the region. The number of raids on American towns and forts increased the next year, and many white settlers abandoned their farms and fled to safety. Tribal chiefs sent runners to British traders, offering an alliance if a war with the Americans came to pass.[23]

A little more than a month after the Battle of Tippecanoe, residents of the Louisiana Purchase lands felt the earth begin to rumble and roll beneath their feet. Near New Madrid, a Mississippi River town 160 miles south of St. Louis, sand boiled up from the earth and overflowed. Compressed quartz crystals emitted flashes of light from large fissures in the ground. It was the first of over 1,800 shocks and aftershocks that unsettled the Upper Missouri region for three months. During one intense quake in February 1812, one section of the Mississippi riverbank heaved up, turning the waterway back on itself. For several hours, Old Man River ran backward.[24]

People felt the New Madrid earthquake and its reverberations more than one thousand miles away. Many Indigenous peoples believed them to be the fulfillment of the Shawnee prophet's vision of the giant crab overturning the earth. According to the prophecy, the quakes were not a disaster but a correction. They would turn back the tide of white settlement, and the Shawnee and many other tribal nations would heal their relationships with the land.[25]

It is possible that the residents of the Knife River Villages felt the New Madrid tremors that winter. Still living in Metaharta, Sacajawea was pregnant with her second child, and Charbonneau was scouting and hunting for Manuel Lisa's Missouri Fur Company. But after the United States officially declared war on Great Britain in June 1812, Lisa began to build a fort farther south on the Missouri River, closer to American territories. He shut down his Knife River fort and sent word to Charbonneau to join him at a new site he was calling Fort Manuel.

British forces allied with several Indigenous nations, including the Shawnee, and won several major battles near the small town of Detroit. Sacajawea was in the last weeks of her pregnancy and may have preferred to stay put, but she and Charbonneau packed their belongings and headed south. When they arrived in August, Lisa and his men were constructing the fort. The rudimentary stockade sat on a bluff along the river's edge, the logs used to build it cut from the river bottoms.

Sacajawea gave birth there a few weeks later. Just as she had in 1805, she labored in an American military installation, without a physician or any of her kin around her. Luckily, there were no complications, and soon Sacajawea was gathering up her daughter Lizette and putting her in a cradleboard for walks along the riverbank.[26] The fall of 1812, however, was tumultuous. The Indigenous polities of the Upper Missouri Valley attacked one another, stealing horses and food and children. Charbonneau left Fort Manuel several times on reprisal raids or to translate during peace negotiations with the Hidatsa, Arikara, and Lakota.[27]

In early December, Sacajawea felt a sudden headache, and then her body was racked with chills and fever. She developed a rash and soon became delirious. On the clear, cold night of December 20, 1812, Sacajawea died within the walls of Fort Manuel, eight hundred miles east of the Bitterroots and the river valley in which she was born.

"She was a good and best Woman in the fort, aged about 25 years," the trader John Luttig wrote in his diary. "She left a fine infant girl."[28]

Luttig did not note a burial ceremony at the fort, or if Charbonneau had sent Sacajawea's body back to the Knife River Villages. Two months later, Charbonneau went out on a scout and did not return; everyone at Fort Manuel assumed he was dead, a victim of a Lakota attack or a casualty in the War of 1812. That winter, the conflict between Great Britain, the United States, and the Upper Missouri tribal nations escalated once again, and Manuel Lisa abandoned Fort Manuel. In March 1813, when he and Luttig departed for St. Louis, they took Lizette Charbonneau with them. That summer, William Clark became Lizette's guardian, and she went to live with him and his wife and their children and with her brother Jean-Baptiste.[29]

Two years later, as the American soldiers still battled with British and Indigenous troops in Mississippi, northern New York, and Canada, a Philadelphia publisher printed two thousand copies of *History of the Expedition under the Command of Captains Lewis and Clark*. The editor based the account on expedition diaries but often embellished them to create a dramatic narrative of an adventure into the wilderness, with Lewis and Clark as the frontier heroes. He omitted many of the Corps's encounters with Indigenous peoples and much of its scientific work.[30] A more complete edition of the journals themselves would not be published until 1893, the same year that Frederick Jackson Turner gave his talk at the Art Institute in Chicago.

Sacajawea did not appear often in these volumes, and for the rest of the nineteenth century, most Americans did not even know her name. In their original journals, Meriwether Lewis and William Clark had referred to her in several ways: Interpreter's Wife. Our Indian Woman. Squaw. Clark sometimes called her Janey, a name commonly given to enslaved Black women on southern plantations. He used her Shoshone name only a few times.[31]

But Sacajawea is present in the records that the men of the Corps kept in 1805 and 1806. They mention her and her work hundreds of times. They listened to her stories and her advice, and they accepted her as a member of the Corps. Sacajawea was so much more than just the interpreter's wife. She was an interpreter in her own right. A cultural broker. A botanist. A mother. And an explorer. She was an Indigenous woman traveling through an Indigenous world, taking its measure. It would take more than one hundred years for Americans to recognize the vital role she played in the federal government's first survey of the lands between the Pacific and the Knife River Villages.[32]

PART II
THE BRINGERS OF CHANGE

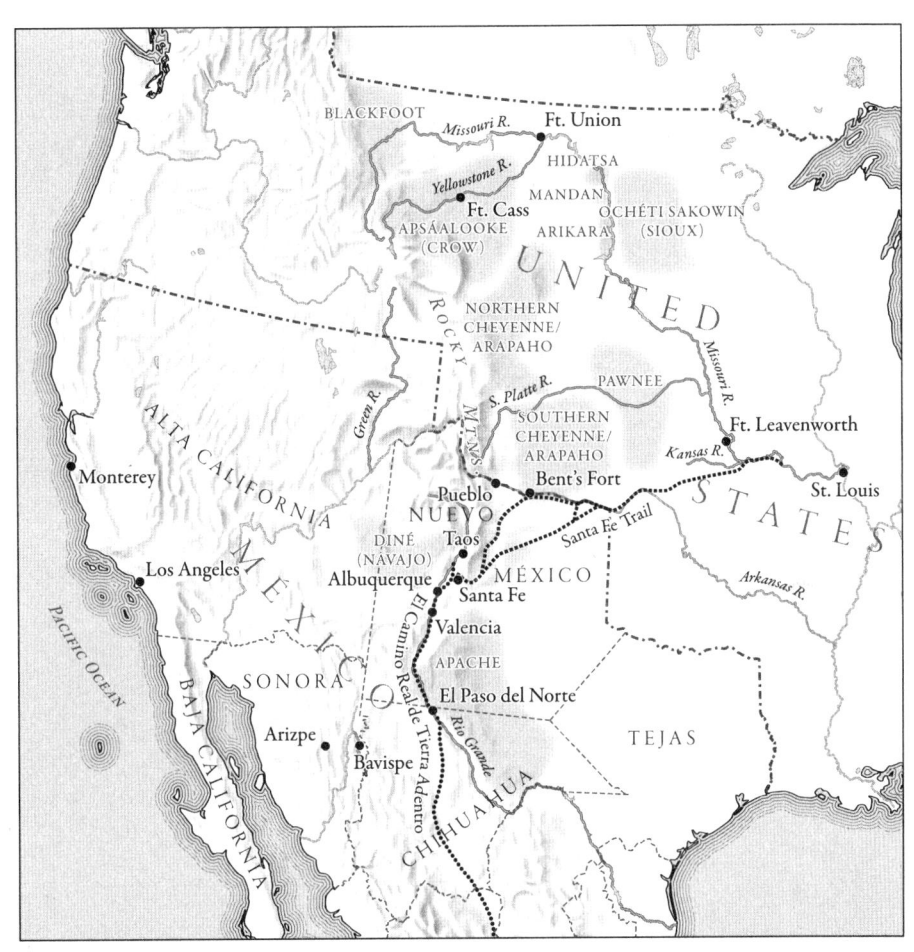

CHAPTER 6

Many decades after Sacajawea's death, rumors about her circulated in Hidatsa and Shoshone villages. Perhaps she had not died. Maybe she had lived for many more years in the Knife River Villages. Or perhaps she had escaped Charbonneau and the Hidatsa amid the chaos of the War of 1812 and traveled southward to live with the Comanche.[1] If she had gone south, Sacajawea would have left one region of warfare and entered another. In the lands that Spain claimed in North and Central America, a colonial rebellion had begun in 1810.

Colonists living in New Spain—provinces as far north as San Francisco and as far south as the Yucatán—had been inspired by the uprisings against colonial powers that defined the "Age of Revolution" in the Atlantic World. The United States. France. The French colony of Saint-Domingue (now known as Haiti). If agitators could take control of New Spain's government in Mexico City and the other provinces, perhaps they could make strides toward racial equality and land redistribution. On a fall day in 1810, a rebellious Catholic priest who had been spreading such ideas received word of his imminent arrest. The priest, whose parish lay 250 miles northwest of the colonial capital of Mexico City, did not run. Instead, he rang his church bell and called his parishioners to the nave. He armed them, then gave an impassioned speech advocating for a revolt against Spain and freedom for its colonists in North America.[2]

This speech sparked the first of a series of passionate but uncoordinated insurgencies that broke out across New Spain over the next five years. Spanish authorities, calling troops from presidios (military forts) across the colony and mobilizing local militias, defeated most of the rebels. But in 1815, the rebellion was still a strong undercurrent, pulling at New Spain's communities. The constant violence wreaked havoc on commercial networks, cutting ties between Mexico City and its northern provinces of Sonora, Tejas, Nuevo México, and Alta California.

Spain had founded towns and built presidios and missions in these lands long before the English established Jamestown, Virginia, in 1607. The Spanish farmers and ranchers who settled in the northern provinces often clashed with the region's Indigenous peoples, who still claimed these lands and defended them from incursions. Apache, Navajo, Tohono O'odham, and Yaqui raiders took sheep, mules, crops, and women and children from Spanish settlers, and settlers raided in return, creating a cycle of violence that fed the trading markets of northern New Spain.[3]

In the narrow, green valleys of the rugged Sierra Madre Occidental range in northern Sonora, farmers planted maize (corn), beans, pumpkins, and other crops to feed the province's gold and copper miners.[4] María Gertrudis Barceló's grandfather had come to this valley from Spain in the 1750s, to take up lands along the banks of the Bavispe River. There was a Spanish mission in the town and a presidio housing soldiers who protected the valley farmers from Apache raids. Hundreds of feet above the Barceló farm, a rock ledge perched atop the foothills of the Sierra Madre Oriental, a crown of jagged teeth.[5]

Gertrudis's father, Juan Ignacio, did well enough for himself and his wife, Dolores Herrero, that they earned the titles of Don and Doña Barceló. They were able to educate their children; Gertrudis, her older brother Trinidad, and her younger sister María de la Luz could read, and they could write their own names.[6]

As a man of some standing, Juan Ignacio had reason to worry that revolutionaries—or perhaps even Opata rebels—would come for his land and his family. He had heard from one of his relatives who owned a hacienda near the small town of Valencia, south of Albuquerque in Nuevo México, offering refuge. The hacienda edged the Rio Grande, one of the great waterways of northern New Spain, and was planted with corn, wheat, and grapevines. Although the threats of Indigenous raids were ever present in Nuevo México, the province had a reputation for openness and opportunity. There were rumors, too, of gold strikes in the mountains north and east of Albuquerque. Valencia was five hundred miles away from their homestead on the Bavispe, but Juan Ignacio believed that the move would be worth it.[7]

The Barcelós loaded a cart, hitched up their mules, and set out from their farm, heading out of the valley to the west, toward the main road to Arizpe, the capital of Sonora. The road climbed into a mountain range and then down into a valley before turning north along the Rio Sonora. It was a roundabout way to get to Arizpe, but roads in this part of New Spain were few and narrow. They followed the rivers that had carved a path through the earth and the trails that animals and then men had pounded out alongside them. Such roads often meandered and doubled back on themselves.

Along the way, fifteen-year-old Gertrudis and her younger sister took turns walking and riding in the cart, gathering up their long skirts to keep them from dragging in the dirt. Gertrudis pulled up her blue-and-white rebozo (shawl) over her auburn hair and down over her brown eyes, to protect her face from the sun.[8] It is hard to know how she felt at this moment, leaving her home for an uncertain future. But it was already clear to her family that Gertrudis Barceló had inherited her father's business sense, along with a prodigious memory and a mathematical mind. The towns along the Rio Grande would offer her the chance to do something more than be a farmer's wife, an idea that likely had some appeal.

When they arrived in Arizpe, the Barcelós visited the market in the city's central plaza, where they could buy fresh milk and eggs and other supplies for the journey ahead. It was imperative that they stock up now, for there were only a handful of towns in the desert between Arizpe and the Rio Grande, 350 miles to the northeast. The Barcelós packed up and joined a caravan of travelers who would provide both company and protection on the road.[9]

As the migrants moved north, the land and the sky expanded. The desert was dotted with thorny shrubs and saguaro cacti. Puffy clouds moved rapidly overhead, boiling into dark gray towers of rain with little or no warning. In the distance, the ground shimmered with the rising heat of the day.[10] The caravan turned eastward onto a trail that the Spanish military had blazed to connect the presidios of Alta California to the missions of Tucson and Tubac, and then to El Paso del Norte. The Barcelós and the other families scanned the landscape in all directions, alert to oncoming danger. They knew that when they entered these deserts, they entered the heartland of Apachería.

Like the Knife River country and St. Louis, northern Mexico was a borderland in the early nineteenth century. The Chiricahua and Western Apache peoples who claimed these lands rode Spanish horses and carried French and British muskets, secured in the many trading rendezvous that took place throughout the region. Warfare between the Apache and Spanish soldiers had raged for more than a century, in a seemingly unending cycle of raids and counterraids across Apachería.[11]

Stories circulated through the Barcelós' caravan that there was a young Chiricahua Apache war leader rising to the fore, intent on accumulating horses and taking captives in raids on Spanish migrants heading to and from the Rio Grande. Some in Sonora called him Fuérte. The residents of Nuevo México called him Mangas Coloradas. He had already gained a reputation as a fierce fighter with a bitter hatred for Mexicans, especially those living in Sonora.[12]

After a tense two weeks, the caravan made it to El Paso del Norte, a town of reddish-pink adobe structures built along a big curve in the Rio Grande as it moved through two mountain ranges rising out of the desert. Mangas Coloradas had not ridden down upon them after all, and their supplies had sustained them on the journey. Green farmlands rolled out from the banks of the river, and people thronged the plaza to buy and sell wheat, fruit, and wine made from the region's vineyards.

El Paso del Norte had long been a crucial outpost for New Spain, a trading center for the northern provinces. Royal officials had already forced many of the military and civic leaders there to declare their loyalty to the mother country and disavow the War of Independence from Spain. It did not cost them much to do so; the rebellion was centered much farther south.[13]

From El Paso, the Barcelós turned north along the legendary El Camino Real de Tierra Adentro (the Royal Road of the Interior), the first Euro-American trade route in North America. Spanish conquistadors had created this road during their explorations of the region in the 1550s, as they searched for golden cities to capture and Indigenous peoples to convert to Catholicism. The camino connected Mexico City to Santa Fe, and smaller towns like El Paso, Valencia, and Albuquerque sat along it, links in a 1,600-mile-long chain.[14]

During their migration north, the Barcelós passed hundreds of carts moving south, carrying loads of yellow corn and sacks of squash and onions. Gertrudis could smell just-picked peaches, apricots, plums, and apples that filled wagons bound for the city of Chihuahua, two hundred miles due south.[15] Spanish ricos (wealthy men) in fancy jackets rode horses while pobres (the poor) on foot drove small herds of sheep. Spanish slave traders urged on groups of Apache and Navajo women and children, on their way to the regional slave markets.[16] Two weeks later, the Barcelós arrived in Valencia, eager to get settled at the hacienda. It was a quiet town not far from the road.

El Camino was a dynamic place, a force of change in Nuevo México. Gertrudis Barceló did not know where it would take her in the future. South? North? East, even? She was young but already considered a woman. In New Spain, that meant she had rights that many Indigenous and American women did not have. According to Spanish law, Gertrudis could run a business. She could keep her property and her given name when she married. She could smoke and drink and gamble if she chose.[17] She had come with her family to a new land, in the middle of a revolution. She would find her place, and she would stake a claim to it.

In 1821, colonial rebels and the government of Spain negotiated the Treaty of Córdoba and created the Mexican Empire in North America. Although Spain did not recognize this treaty for another fifteen years, it was a pivotal moment. The Barcelós and millions of other residents of New Spain were no longer Spanish subjects. They were Mexicans.[18]

Trade restrictions that protected Spanish merchants were one of the rebels' central complaints during the war, so one of the first official acts of the Mexican government was to establish free trade with many foreign countries, especially the United States.[19] Within weeks, American merchants from Missouri steered their wagons into the plaza at Santa

Fe, and the number of Anglos in Nuevo México proliferated. They had followed a trading route long used by many Indigenous communities in the high deserts and the Great Plains, and the Spanish traders who met them along the Arkansas River. The ruts the Americans' wagon wheels pushed into the ground along this road from Independence, Missouri, became known as the Santa Fe Trail.[20]

Two years later, Gertrudis Barceló met Manuel Antonio Sisneros. His family came from Bernalillo, a small town farther north along the Rio Grande. When they married, twenty-two-year-old Gertrudis was already four months pregnant with a son, José Pedro. Soon after the wedding celebrations, however, Gertrudis's father died. Later that year, after just a month of life, José Pedro also died. She lost a second son, Miguel Antonio, in 1825; he lived only four months.

Unsure if she could become pregnant again, Barceló found another way to bring children into her life. In 1826, she and Manuel Antonio attended the baptism of a baby girl named Refugio. As the priest poured the water over the infant's head, Gertrudis and Manuel Antonio promised to care for her as her godparents. This was an act of support for Refugio's parents, part of a growing kinship network that brought the community together. Godparenting was also a ritual that moved Mexican children from one household to another, often as laborers but sometimes as kin. Gertrudis and Manuel Antonio must have taken to Refugio, because soon after the baptism, they brought her home to live with them. Within the year, they formally adopted her as their own.[21]

The next year, in the Ortiz Mountains near Santa Fe, a herder looking for a lost sheep spied a chunk of gold-bearing quartz in a dry arroyo. Like the Barcelós, he was from Sonora, and he had seen such rock before there, at a mine that had produced thousands of dollars a day. The word got out, and soon there were thousands of Mexican miners digging out dirt and sifting it in pans. Gertrudis Barceló, her husband, and her daughter soon followed. They were not there to mine, but to mine the miners. Early in their marriage Manuel Antonio had taught Barceló to play monte, a game of chance based on a Spanish deck of forty cards. She found that her quick mind and ability to read people were skills perfectly suited to such a game. Barceló soon won enough money in Valencia to buy her own table and become a dealer.[22]

Nuevo México was no stranger to gambling, or to gold rushes. The obsessive desire to find the mythical, gleaming cities of Cibola had driven Spanish exploration and settlement in this region in the late sixteenth century. By the nineteenth century, both North and South America, along with Australia and Africa, were entering an Age of Gold. Strikes of varying sizes instigated migrations that connected far-flung places across the globe.[23]

By the 1820s, there were Mexican miners but also Anglos and some Europeans roaming through Nuevo México, ready to jump on the next strike. They heard about the Ortiz Mountains discoveries, and soon there were flush times in the diggings and the nearby boomtown, both now known as Real de Dolores. The miners sifted thousands of dollars' worth of dust and nuggets from the gullies and then carried their lodes more than two miles to the closest stream to wash the minerals from the dirt. At the end of the day, the miners left the gullies, ate their dinners out of dented pans over campfires, and made their way to the makeshift saloons and shops along the main street.

In a nearby alley, Gertrudis Barceló set up her monte table, sitting so that her back was to the slanting wall of a building. That way, she could see potential gamblers (or thieves) coming and prevent anyone from seeing the cards she dealt. Gambling was widespread in Nuevo México but technically illegal, so she had to assemble and pull apart the table quickly if the alcalde (mayor) or his men wandered past. Barceló was fined several times for card dealing in her first few months in Real de Dolores. Then the alcalde of Santa Fe quietly sold her a license to operate—and pocketed the money, a crime for which he was later indicted.[24]

Each night, miners gathered around Gertrudis Barceló's monte table, eager to wager on the cards.[25] The games probably went like this.[26]

Barceló shuffled her deck. Four suits, ten cards each. She signaled to the players that the game was about to begin. The men leaned forward, palms gripping the wooden edges of the table, staring intently at the cards Barceló laid down.

Five of swords. Queen of clubs. The top layout, dealt from the bottom of the deck.

Barceló paused. Several players reached out over the table, placing Mexican coins next to the cards. When the flurry of betting abated, she took two cards from the top of the deck.

Four of swords. The players murmured to themselves and to one another. Six of suns. More coins appeared on the table, along with small bags of gold dust.

Barceló memorized the bets and calculated the gold's value. She glanced up at the remaining players, waiting for them to decide which risks they would take. After the last of the players made their final bets and stood back from the table, she turned the deck up, exposing the bottom card.

King of cups. The players groaned and cursed. Barceló swept the dealt cards to one side and the coins and gold dust into a purse tied around her waist. If the bottom card had been a sword, club, or sun, she would have paid equal money to those who bet on that suit, in either deal. After several more hours of bets, wins, and losses, the miners wandered off, heading back to their lean-tos or to the saloons for a consoling shot of whiskey. Barceló packed up her table and returned to the small cabin she shared with Manuel Antonio and Refugio.

Barceló was making a decent living, but she knew that Real de Dolores was too small a place to put down roots. The town would fade away as quickly as it had sprung up once the gold ran out. If she wanted to make real money, she needed to be in Santa Fe. The capital of Nuevo México had always been a thriving center of commerce in New Spain, but its population and power had grown since the opening of the Santa Fe Trail.[27] The city's economy boomed, bringing in gold, American and Mexican currency, and material goods from all directions. It was as essential to the commercial life of the Southwest as the Knife River Villages were to the Upper Missouri Valley.[28] Santa Fe was where the action was in Nuevo México. Gertrudis Barceló wanted to be there too.

CHAPTER 7

Santa Fe was not the only city to welcome a rush of American traders and merchants in the wake of Mexican Independence. Migrants moving along the Santa Fe trail from Nuevo México to the eastern terminus at Independence, Missouri, usually continued their travels eastward, to the growing city of St. Louis. By the early 1820s, more than 4,500 people lived in St. Louis (a 200 percent increase since Sacajawea and Charbonneau had lived there), and ten thousand others made their homes in the surrounding county. The city was a gateway to the Upper Missouri River Valley to the north and the rolling plains of the western interior.[1]

Although St. Louis still attracted a heterogenous mix of travelers and prospective settlers and only 14 percent of the city's households included enslaved men and women, the city was in an era of transition. The diplomatic and economic power of multiracial families like the Chouteaus had waned, and a population of white slaveholders was on the rise.[2]

Little more than fifteen years after the return of the Corps of Discovery, St. Louis was fully ensnared in the slave trade, sending boats full of Black men and women down the river to the teeming slave markets of New Orleans. White leaders like the Missourian Thomas Hart Benton argued that enslavement was good for everyone: it controlled and "civilized" Black men and women, and denied them citizenship and belonging in American society. This meant that the wealthiest planters and the poorest white farmers were assured of their racial supremacy in Missouri.

In 1820, Missouri came into the Union as part of a compromise that kept the balance of powers in Congress. The Mason-Dixon Line running from the southern border of Pennsylvania to the Mississippi River was established, and an agreement made that slavery would exist only south of that line. The free state of Maine was admitted alongside Missouri, whose constitution legalized slavery and included a provision "to prevent free negroes and mulattoes from coming to and settling in this State, under any pretext whatsoever." Slave hunters had appeared on the streets of St. Louis. Soon, the state would require free Black women and men to carry their papers or risk being jailed as runaways and sent south to the slave markets.[3]

It is unclear if Jim Beckwith had free papers or if he traveled without them. He had left school after just a few years in the classroom, and Jennings sent him to a blacksmith shop to work as an apprentice. Jim liked the work fine but hated laboring for someone else. A disagreement with the blacksmith had led to a fistfight, and Jim fled from the shop. He stowed away on a keelboat that was heading north, but his boss found him and sent him home to his father. They argued. Jennings wanted him to behave and to learn a trade.

"I expressed a growing wish to travel," Beckwith remembered.

Jennings was exasperated, but Jim was adamant. Jennings, seeing his determination, finally consented. He gave his son $500 in cash and took him out to the stable to pick a horse, saddle, and bridle.[4] These were valuable gifts. It would have taken Jim almost a year to make that much money as a blacksmith, and a good horse cost $150.[5] With this kit and cash on hand, Jim could take up any profession that would have him. Jennings helped him onto his horse, and bade him godspeed upon his journey. Jim Beckwith rode out toward St. Louis and his future.

In 1823, St. Louis became the headquarters of a new outfit intent on making millions of dollars in the lands to the west: the Rocky Mountain Fur Company.[6] The skins and fur of beaver, deer, elk, mountain sheep, and bears had been the center of an extensive trade network of Indigenous peoples for hundreds of years. Europeans and then Americans were relative newcomers to this trade and were eager to make their fortunes.[7] The fur trader William Ashley, one of the company's founders, had (like the Beckwiths) come to Missouri from Virginia. He and his business partner saw an opportunity to participate directly in the western fur trade, cutting out the Indigenous hunters who had been supplying Missouri River traders with beaver and racoon skins.

The company hired white trappers and provided them with guns, powder, lead, traps, and transportation to the Rocky Mountains. After several months, the men returned to a base camp with beaver furs, and deer and raccoon skins to pack and ship to St. Louis or Santa Fe. Each trapper gave half his haul to the company in exchange for their initial investment in his supplies. The rest he could sell for profit or trade with other Indigenous, European, and American trappers.[8]

The fur trade was the first major extractive industry that Americans established in the lands between the Pacific Ocean and the Missouri River, and after only a few years the federal government ceased to regulate it. The market for beaver pelts was booming, and the Rocky Mountain Fur Company could sell them for $3–$10 per pound—the equivalent of a week's wages for a farm laborer. By replacing the Indigenous supply chain with a set of commercial linkages that they controlled themselves, William Ashley and his partner stood to make hundreds of thousands of dollars in just one season.[9]

Jim Beckwith saw the appeal of joining this fledgling company. He would be an employee of sorts, but he would have the freedom to move around as he saw fit in a western landscape that was in a state of transformation.

The work, however, would be dangerous. Arikara and Lakota warriors defending their homelands had attacked white trappers and traders moving up the Missouri River in previous years. But Jim was willing to face any number of dangers to live an independent life. In September 1823, William Clark, whom President James Monroe had appointed Missouri's superintendent of Indian affairs, issued Ashley a license to trap and trade furs. Ashley wanted to avoid the Arikara and the Lakota, so he planned to take a different route on this expedition. A few days later, Beckwith set out with twenty-nine other men for the Kansas River, hoping to follow it westward across the Great Plains to the Rockies.[10]

The Fur Company may have benefited from the map Sacajawea had helped Lewis and Clark produce, which had been published as an engraving in the first edition of the journals. They may have also had access to published accounts and maps from the explorers who followed in the Corps of Discovery's wake, Zebulon Pike and Stephen Long among them.[11]

Even with this knowledge of the country at their disposal, Jim Beckwith's first foray with the Fur Company was a disaster. The trappers' horses gave out long before they reached the headwaters of the Kansas, and an effort to find the Pawnee to trade for more animals failed. Beckwith went out on a scout with a fellow trapper and got lost. Only days away from starving to death, they found their way to an Osage camp and then to a trading post on the Missouri River.[12] When he finally made it back to St. Louis, Beckwith ran into William Ashley on the street. Ashley was shocked; he thought that Beckwith had died on the prairie.

Impressed with the young man's resilience, Ashley offered him a job as a trapper for the company's 1824–25 expedition. Beckwith initially demurred. The memory of his near-death experience lingered, and he planned to join his father on the plantation at Portage des Sioux. And he had started courting several women in the city, which was an impetus to stay. He had made *all* of these ladies certain promises, however, so perhaps leaving was a better option. Ashley's offer was tempting and lucrative, so ultimately Jim said yes.[13]

At some point during his first few years in the fur trade, Jim Beckwith changed the spelling of his last name to Beckwourth. It is unclear why he did so. He may have wanted to establish some distance between himself and his father, lest Missouri slave catchers find him west of the river. Or Ashley may have misheard his accent and spelled his last name wrong on his contract, and Jim figured it was not worth the trouble to correct him.

In May 1824, Beckwith—now Beckwourth—left St. Louis once again, moving upriver to Council Bluffs by boat, where the Rocky Mountain Fur Company purchased horses and set out westward along the Platte. The men ran out of rations and had to eat some of their horses; Arapaho and then Apsáalooke (Crow) raiders stole many of the rest. It took the trappers twelve months to make it to the Green River, a narrow channel that rose from the ground in the Wind River Mountains and cut southwest for more than seven hundred miles through the Wyoming Basin.

This area, which was east of where Sacajawea had grown up with her Shoshone family in the northern Rockies, was a continental borderland in the mid-1820s. It was a homeland or hunting ground to Apsáalooke, Lakota, Cheyenne, Arapaho, Eastern Shoshone, Shoshone-Bannock, Salish (Flathead), Blackfoot, and Nez Perce peoples. Their territorial borders overlapped with Oregon Country (occupied jointly by the United States and Great Britain), the Louisiana Purchase lands north of the new state of Missouri, and northern Mexico.

Ashley told his trappers to head to the mountains, catch and kill as many beavers as possible, and meet back at the river in July 1825. Beckwourth joined a small group of more experienced men, and they followed small creeks upstream from their confluences with the Green. The older men showed Jim how to look for dams and other signs that beavers were active. When they found a dam, the trappers waded into the cold water, carrying several traps with care so they would not cut themselves on the sharpened edges. They lowered the traps into the water with lengths of chain, set the springs that held the metal jaws apart, and attached the chains to stakes they drove into the creek bed. After rubbing castoreum oil (which beavers used to attract one another during mating season) on the stakes, the trappers clambered out of the water. Hopefully, several curious beavers would swim up to the traps, searching for the sources of the castoreum, and step on the triggers.

For two months, Beckwourth worked hard as his team set hundreds of traps. When they returned a few weeks later, Jim learned how to remove the trapped beavers and cut off their heads, feet, and tails. He sliced the beavers' pelts away from their connective tissues, muscle, and fat, making sure that the soft underfur (known as felt) was intact. This was the most valuable part of the animal; milliners used it to make hats that had become wildly popular in America and Europe. The ground in their processing camp was saturated with bright red blood and strewn with organs. Jim hung the pelts he claimed from tree branches and, after they dried, packed them together and strapped them to his horse.[14]

In July, Beckwourth and his group came down from the mountains to the banks of the Green River and found the Rocky Mountain Fur

Company's rendezvous. It was the first such American gathering in the region, a sign of the changes to come. More than two hundred French, English, and some Indigenous trappers had arrived with their families, and they were talking, eating, and making deals with one another.[15]

Beckwourth traded some of his pelts with other trappers and gave half his haul to Ashley. By the end of the summer, the Rocky Mountain Fur Company had accumulated pelts worth almost $200,000 in the St. Louis markets.

From the rendezvous, Beckwourth and most of the company trappers made their way northeast to the Wind River country and then even farther north to the Yellowstone River. They constructed boats to carry them and their heavy packs of pelts downriver, boating the same waters Sacajawea had twenty years before.

At that river's confluence with the Missouri, they disembarked at Fort Clarke, one of the U.S. Army's new installations in the Upper Missouri Valley. Before 1825, it had been rare to see U.S. soldiers along the northern reaches of the river. But the Department of War had determined that the U.S. Army was a necessary symbol of federal power in this part of the continent. Military leaders therefore created the Department of the West, based in St. Louis, and housed and trained both infantry and cavalry at Jefferson Barracks. The Missouri River was now a staging ground for military campaigns whose goal was to protect white settlers of the Louisiana Purchase lands from Indigenous raids.[16]

Jim Beckwourth was not thinking of any of this as he sat in the boat on its way south to St. Louis. Instead, he was thinking of home. "Those who reside in maritime places and have witnessed the hardy tars step ashore in their native land," Beckwourth mused, "can form an adequate idea of the happy return of the mountaineers from their wanderings on the Plains to St. Louis, which is their great sea-port."[17]

The couriers had ridden ahead to bring news of their arrival, and Beckwourth disembarked to find his father waiting for him at the landing. Jim was delighted to see Jennings after more than a year away from home but noticed that his father seemed haggard and worried. He soon found out why. Eager to promote the future of Portage des Sioux, Jennings had loaned money to several other planters. These debtors had either been ruined or had run off, so Jennings had been forced to sell his own plantation and move into the city. When William Ashley paid Jim $300 for his services in the Rockies, he was able to give his father some of the money to pay his debts.[18]

After visiting with Jennings, Beckwourth went to see a woman named Eliza. Although he had been wooing several women before he left for the West, he had thought mostly of her during his time away. Despite his long absence, Eliza agreed to marry him. But before Jim could start making plans to establish a business in St. Louis to support his fiancée, William Ashley came to see him. He needed a man to carry dispatches to William Sublette, one of his captains in the field, and he believed that Beckwourth was just the man to get the job done. Ashley offered him $1,000 to make the trip, which was too large of a sum for Jim to turn down.

Beckwourth called on Eliza and told her he was leaving again. She wept and protested that she cared nothing for money, only for him. Beckwourth promised to come back to St. Louis as quickly as he could. Then he went to see his father. The two men talked a bit and then bid each other farewell.[19]

It took Jim Beckwourth several months to find William Sublette and deliver William Ashley's message to him at the fur company's camp in the Rockies. By that time, snow blanketed the mountains and Beckwourth resigned himself to staying over the winter. Eliza would wait for him, he was sure of it.[20]

When the snowpack began to melt, Beckwourth figured he might as well hire onto the Rocky Mountain Fur Company's spring 1826 expedition. He would earn $500 as a base salary and then make thousands more selling his extra pelts. Beckwourth spent the next year in Blackfoot country, trapping and building a trading fort for the company.

The Blackfoot, whose three bands ranged the high plains east of the Rocky Mountains from southern Canada to the Yellowstone Basin, had established ties with Canadian and British traders in the 1780s. When Beckwourth arrived in their homelands, the Blackfoot sought him out. They took him to the lodge of a chief named Heavy Shield. The two men smoked, and then the chief offered Jim one daughter in marriage, then another. Women (like Sacajawea and Otter Woman) had long been essential to cementing ties with other Indigenous communities and later, Europeans. Through his daughters, Heavy Shield hoped to benefit from this alliance with an American trader.[21]

Beckwourth thought it over and agreed. A connection with Heavy Shield's family would benefit him as well, guaranteeing his own survival and securing part of the Blackfoot fur trade for the Rocky Mountain Fur Company. He was following in the footsteps of the Chouteaus, Toussaint Charbonneau, and many other European and American trappers and traders, who married Indigenous women and exploited their kinship networks, as well as their bodies and their labor.[22]

When Beckwourth returned to the fur company camp two weeks later, however, he did so without his Blackfoot wives. His marriages had been short-lived and diplomatic. He did not consider them lasting commitments. He also returned with more confidence in his abilities to trap beaver and broker agreements with Indigenous peoples on his own. Jim quit the Rocky Mountain Fur Company and became a free trapper, selling his furs to any buyer at whatever price he could negotiate.[23]

It was a lonely life, however, and Beckwourth was a man who liked company. He soon joined up with a group of free trappers, including Jim Bridger, who was (like Beckwourth), a Virginia-born adventurer. Such arrangements were common during this period, as people moving through the West found safety and conviviality in alliances and communities.[24]

One day, when he was out trapping with Bridger, the two men were separated, and Beckwourth suddenly found himself surrounded by Apsáalooke warriors. The men pointed their weapons at him, and he slowly laid down his own. He mounted his horse and returned with them to their camp, resigned to the fact that he was now their prisoner. When they arrived at the village, the warriors indicated that they wanted to take him to the chief's lodge.[25]

On the way, several Apsáalooke women approached him. They were women who had lost sons, nephews, and brothers in Cheyenne attacks. They walked around him, inspecting his body and his face. One woman, overcome with grief, thought she saw her son in Beckwourth and claimed him as hers.

"The dead was alive again," he marveled, "and the lost one was found."[26] The band embraced him, inviting them into their lodges. A chief offered him his daughter in marriage. As he had among the Blackfoot, Beckwourth accepted. He might have felt a pang about Eliza, but his survival was paramount. At this point, Beckwourth said, "I began my Indian life."[27]

The Apsáalooke community that Beckwourth joined traced their ancestry back to a band of Hidatsa kin. They had separated from them around the same time that Spanish explorers founded Mexico City, in the early sixteenth century. The band had walked westward and soon found the Yellowstone River and the large tributaries that rushed in to meet it from the south (the Tongue, Powder, Bighorn, Clark's Fork, and Stillwater). Along its banks, there were lush grasses, bounding deer, and antelope. The large mountains to the west harbored more animals, elk and mountain sheep that would provide meat and skins that could keep the Apsáalooke alive during the harsh winters that characterized the region.[28]

The Apsáalooke knew they had come home, so they stayed.[29] Their communities flourished, but Indigenous enemies soon arrived at their borders, hoping to take their lands from them: Blackfoot from the northwest, Cheyenne and Arapaho peoples from the southeast, and Shoshone from the southwest. The Apsáalooke were not worried. The First Maker (Lone Man), who had made them, "told us that we should always have to fight to hold our country, but said that He would always be with us, because we would be outnumbered."[30]

They lived on these lands for several generations before Comanche traders brought horses—bought or stolen from Spanish colonists far to the south—to their trading rendezvous. The Apsáalooke, like the other Indigenous peoples of the mountains and plains, quickly saw the utility of horses; they could use them to travel, hunt, and fight. They could raid their enemies' growing herds, divide the horses among their allies, and build wealth and power. The Apsáalooke soon accumulated thousands of these animals and called them "ichilay" (to search with).[31]

French and English Canadian trappers first appeared in their territory in the 1740s, canoeing up the Yellowstone and Missouri Rivers looking for furs to buy.[32] The first American the Apsáalooke met was William Clark, moving through their lands with Sacajawea, in July 1806. After that, they began to encounter American fur traders on a regular basis.[33] Like their Blackfoot enemies, the Apsáalooke saw the potential in cultivating relationships with the Americans. They hoped these newcomers would help them control the region's ebb and flow in beaver pelts and, later, buffalo robes.

Jim Beckwourth found that he enjoyed living in an Indigenous world. The Apsáalooke moved several times a year to provide their horses with fresh grass, hunt bison on the plains, and meet up in large gatherings with their relatives in other bands. The constant motion suited Jim and gratified the sense of adventure that had propelled him from his father's plantation to St. Louis and then from St. Louis to the Rocky Mountains.

Beckwourth soon discovered that the Apsáalooke valued feats in warfare that proved a man's ability to lead other men.[34] He did not hesitate, therefore, to join war and horse-raiding parties when he had the opportunity. At the time, he noted, "the Crows were incessantly at war with all the tribes within their reach" and fought large-scale battles with the Blackfoot and the Cheyenne.[35]

He established his reputation in several battles, and soon Beckwourth was leading his own war parties. After each major victory, Beckwourth took a new Apsáalooke name. The Antelope. Big Bull. Enemy of Horses. Bobtail Horse. Red Wing. Bloody Arm. Good War Road. These new names marked his achievements in warfare and his continuous acts of reinvention within the world of the American West.[36]

In the wake of these battles, Beckwourth sometimes thought of his friends and family in St. Louis. They must be wondering, he mused, "how a man who had been reared in civilized life could ever participate in such scenes of carnage and rapine." Beckwourth justified his violence by arguing that he might be fighting alongside the Apsáalooke, but he killed only Indigenous enemies, never white men. He often called up the memory of that day in 1809, riding along the road from his father's plantation to town. "I hardly ever struck down an Indian," he mused, "but my mind reverted to the mangled bodies of my childish play-fellows, which I discovered on my way to the mill."[37]

Beckwourth began to refer to his adoption into the Apsáalooke tribe as his "translation." It was a transformation, a shifting of one sense of himself to another. Like Sacajawea and Gertrudis Barceló, he was able to take on new identities because he was moving from place to place. Geographic mobility required adaptability. To Beckwourth and many like him, the West in the 1830s was the ideal place for such transitions. The vastness of the region and the lack of federal oversight meant that you could lose and then find yourself again, and again, and again.[38]

Five years passed. Beckwourth married several more Apsáalooke women and relentlessly pursued a young woman named Pine Leaf, who often joined him in battle and was known as a fierce warrior. His kin and relatives rode out with him to fight, and to trap beaver along the Yellowstone River and its tributaries. By 1831, Beckwourth had accumulated beaver pelts worth $3,000 in St. Louis. Cash was worthless within Indigenous communities, but Beckwourth could stash this money or use it to buy other items. So he took a few men with him (who had their own packs of pelts) and rode more than 250 miles to Fort Union, a trading installation built on the banks of the Upper Missouri River a few years earlier.[39]

Beckwourth walked into the trading fort and spoke with the trader in Apsáalooke. He was dressed in a deerskin shirt and leggings, and his hair was long. His dark skin likely registered with the trader as Indigenous, given his outfit and the language he was speaking.

"No one at the post doubted my being a Crow," Beckwourth bragged.

He was feeling mischievous, however, so when one of the Apsáalooke asked the trader a question, Beckwourth translated the query into English. The trader and his clerks were astonished. It was "as if a bomb-shell had exploded in the fort," Beckwourth reported with glee. He enjoyed both passing as Apsáalooke *and* orchestrating a sudden reveal of his identity. Jim was somewhat chagrined, however, to hear that his fellow American traders believed that he had perished in the Rocky Mountains.[40]

While he was at Fort Union, he contracted with an American Fur Company trader to build a fort at the confluence of the Bighorn and the Yellowstone. In exchange, the trader appointed Beckwourth the representative for his Apsáalooke band. It was another year until the fort, a large square of vertically planted logs with block houses at opposite corners, sat atop white limestone cliffs. The American Fur Company called it Fort Cass.[41]

Jim Beckwourth likely did not know anything about the man for whom it was named. New Hampshire–born Lewis Cass had come to Ohio with his family and then fought against British troops and their Indigenous allies in the War of 1812. As a reward for his service, President James Madison appointed him the territorial governor of Michigan. Ultimately, Cass created the plan for a new federal U.S. Indian policy: the forced migration of Indigenous peoples from their homelands to reservations often hundreds or thousands of miles away—in the West.

In his political speeches and a series of articles he wrote for the *North American Review* in the late 1820s, Cass championed a turn away from cultural assimilation (bringing Indigenous peoples into the body politic) and toward expulsion (segregating and controlling them far away from white settlements). Americans had the right to take Indigenous lands for themselves, Cass argued, and force Native peoples to live beyond the nation's borders. Articulating a core tenet of the evolving frontier myth, Cass wrote that the lands between the Appalachians and the Mississippi River were the inheritance of America's Revolutionary patriots. According to him, it was absurd to think that Indigenous peoples should be given title to lands that Providence had designed to be "civilized" by Americans.[42]

By December 1829, when President Andrew Jackson suggested in his first address to Congress that they set aside "an ample district west of the Mississippi . . . to be guaranteed to the Indian tribes as long as they shall occupy it," Lewis Cass was one of the leading voices advocating this policy. Congress passed the Indian Removal Act in 1830, giving the president of the United States the power to create an Indian Territory in part of the Louisiana Purchase lands and forcibly deport Indigenous peoples from their homelands for resettlement there.[43] In the summer of 1831, Jackson appointed Cass as his new secretary of war.[44]

Just as the first boatloads of trade goods began to arrive at the fort named after him in Apsáalooke territory, Secretary Cass was waging a war against Indigenous peoples on another front. Under the leadership of Black Hawk, the Sauk and Fox had attempted to recross the Mississippi River in 1832 to return to their homelands. Cass was determined to send them back to Indian Territory. He marshaled a combined force of U.S. Army regulars and volunteers (including twenty-three-year-old Abraham Lincoln) and sent them to fight a group of Sauk and Fox men, women, and children. Black Hawk and his men attacked U.S. forts, and the Army pursued them. Ultimately, Black Hawk surrendered to the government, and army officials sent him and other leaders as prisoners of war to St. Louis, and then Washington, D.C.

"An example must be made of the Sauks," Cass declared, "the effect of which will be everlasting."[45]

Indian removal campaigns had not yet reached the Yellowstone River, but the naming of a trading fort after Lewis Cass was an ominous sign. Beckwourth did not seem to notice, however, and he oversaw a vigorous trade at the fort, between Americans and the Apsáalooke. He sent thousands of furs to St. Louis and built five Mackinaw boats (light boats with three sails that traders had long used to carry cargo on the West's many rivers) to transport them.[46]

Initially the Apsáalooke, camped outside Fort Cass's walls, were happy to trade for guns, ammunition, and other valuable goods. Access to the fort enabled them to exert more direct control over the fur trade. But when they convened at the fort and left their horses to graze in the surrounding lands, they became vulnerable. Their Blackfoot and Cheyenne enemies knew where they were and launched several surprise attacks on their camps over the next few years, killing many Apsáalooke warriors and siphoning off large numbers of horses.[47]

Beckwourth worked happily at Fort Cass for four years but then began to tire of his Indian life. "What had I done?" he mused. "What had been my career?" He had gone west to "gratify a youthful thirst for adventure; I had narrowly escaped starvation in a service in which I had no interest; I had traversed the fastnesses of the far Rocky Mountains in summer heats and winter frosts." That he had survived the battles he fought thus far was something of a miracle. While he still lived, he thought, there was time to "take more heed unto my ways." So Beckwourth decided to go home to St. Louis.[48]

When Beckwourth departed from Fort Cass in the fall of 1836, the women and men of his Apsáalooke band came to see him off. He made a speech, thanking them for their kindness to him and promising to return in the future. And then he boarded a boat to Fort Union, leaving his wives behind. Farther south on the Mississippi, there were boats churning northward, carrying Creek men, women, and children away from their homelands in Alabama toward a newly created reservation in Indian Territory.[49]

During his time with the Apsáalooke, Jim Beckwourth had been a witness to and a participant in a changing Indigenous world. Many forces that the United States had brought to bear in the early decades of the nineteenth century—exploration, white settlement, fur trapping and trading, warfare, and Indian removal—were changing the geopolitics of the American West. They put pressure on Indigenous peoples, who, in turn, put pressure on one another. A new era in American-Indigenous relations had begun. As for Beckwourth, his "Indian life" was over. Whether his family and friends in St. Louis would welcome him back to "civilization" remained to be seen.[50]

CHAPTER 8

Jim Beckwourth was not the only Westerner on the move in the 1830s. After five years in the gold camps of Real de Dolores, Gertrudis Barceló finally earned enough money dealing Spanish monte to buy a house in Santa Fe. She, Manuel Antonio, Refugio, her mother, and her mother's new husband packed up their belongings and established themselves in a comfortable adobe residence at the base of a high cliff north of the city.[1] Barceló walked to the plaza along small lanes that wound through cornfields, irrigated by the Santa Fe River and its acequia madre (mother ditch), then past the city barracks and the Palace of the Governors.[2]

At first, Barceló set up her monte table in back alleys between adobe buildings just off the plaza. From there, she could see the steady stream of traffic coming into the city on the Santa Fe Trail. American drovers, wagon masters, and trappers arrived with red dust on their boots and money in their pockets. They found their way to her monte table, and she gladly took whatever coins or gold nuggets they had on them.[3] One trader from Kentucky named Lucius Thruston was a frequent player, and they became friends. Barceló's somewhat unusual profession, as well as her success at it, soon drew attention in the city of Santa Fe.

One of Barceló's neighbors, Doña Rendón, seeing that Thruston was often at the Barceló house—and noticing that her husband Manuel Antonio was frequently away—made an official complaint that Barceló and the Kentuckian were having an extramarital affair, and perhaps even illegally cohabitating. Married women were accorded more freedom in Mexico than they were in the United States. They could keep their names when they married, maintain separate finances from their husbands, and leave marriages without much trouble. But personal reputations were still important—especially women's reputations—in the changing social and business worlds of Santa Fe. So Barceló sued her accuser for slander.[4]

At the trial, both women appeared as witnesses, and within minutes Barceló argued her neighbor into a corner. Rendón backed down and withdrew her statement. The clerk, sure that an agreement had been reached, produced a document of conciliation. Doña Rendón marked an X by her name, and then Gertrudis took up the pen. She signed her full name and added several loops below the o in Barceló. This was her rubric, a flourish that was both decorative and a protection against forgery.[5]

A few months later, Barceló was back in court. "I have been done harm by Doña Josefa Tenorio," she declared. The nature of this second dispute went unrecorded, but the outcome was the same. "I cannot recall that I have done anything to harm you," Tenorio swore. "But if I did do so, I repent and retract whatever I did." Barceló acceded and the two women signed the conciliation. Such legal quarrels were common in Santa Fe, and Mexican women often used the courts to assert their rights and defend themselves. Barceló's civil suits had the effect that she desired; they defended her reputation as one of the most successful businesswomen in Santa Fe.[6]

The city's busy streets were a sign of the Mexican government's continued interest in cultivating international trade relationships with the United States. There were now three thousand people living in the city and another three thousand in the surrounding mesas and valleys, where dark green piñon pines and junipers dotted the landscape. The plaza was busiest in the spring, when American merchants arrived from Independence, Missouri, with wagons stuffed with goods. They would stay until the fall and then return to the United States, hauling Mexican goods more than eight hundred miles to the east. Mexican farmers made daily or weekly trips to the city, offering fruit, vegetables, firewood, and chickens for sale from their carts.[7]

Many of the other goals that Mexican revolutionaries had hoped to achieve through independence from Spain, particularly racial equality and land redistribution, had gone by the wayside. Nuevo México's wealthiest residents (ricos) benefited most from international trade and dominated local politics. The gap between the privileged and the poor in the province widened. The ricos looked after Nuevo Méxican affairs without much interference from the central government in Mexico City, and residents were able to elect their own governors, until the mid-1830s. One of the nation's other northern territories, Texas, rebelled after the presidential administration of Antonio López de Santa Anna tried to exert control of the growing Anglo population there by restricting immigration, establishing taxes, and outlawing enslavement.[8]

Nuevo México's ricos and Anglos showed no signs of a similar revolt, but Santa Anna was not taking any chances. He sent a new governor to the territory in May 1835, a fellow soldier named Albino Pérez.[9] Immediately, rumors about restrictive measures to come began to circulate. The residents whispered that Pérez, acting on orders from México City, would be levying exorbitant taxes on Santa Fe residents to pay for the war against the Texans. He would force men into town militias to fight Navajos and Apaches. Nuevo Méxicans, particularly peons (laborers) and Indigenous and mestizo (biracial) residents of Taos Pueblo, increasingly believed that Pérez's policies would grind the people of Nuevo México down into further poverty and take away the freedoms they had gained with Mexican independence.

Resentments simmered. In the summer of 1836, news came of the Texans' victory over Santa Anna's troops at San Jacinto and the Mexican retreat south across the provincial border. Mexico City officials blamed the United States for these developments; 40 percent of the Texan troops had been Americans. They changed their policies and began to clamp down on trade with the United States, to the chagrin of most of the citizens of Santa Fe. The next summer, Governor Pérez jailed the alcalde of a small town between Santa Fe and Taos for refusing to pay a fine. A mob broke him out, and the Taos Rebellion of 1837 began.[10]

In early August, the gamblers of Santa Fe were just beginning to gather around Barceló's monte table when a large group of men rode into town, yelling and whooping. They dismounted and planted a spike in the dirt in the middle of the plaza. One of their number took an object out of a rucksack and shoved it down on the top of the spike. As the townspeople began to gather around, they recognized the object as the head of Albino Pérez.[11]

Gertrudis Barceló and her family retreated to her house during the mêlée. She and Manuel Antonio had a lot to protect: their home and all their belongings, along with Refugio and their niece Petra, who was living with them and was newly pregnant.[12] While they hunkered down, the American merchants of Santa Fe assembled in front of their stores on the plaza. "We had at the minimum 500 to 600 loaded guns and prepared for a hot battle," a wine merchant wrote to his sister. "Saddled horses and mules stood prepared in the courtyards and stables so that we could escape if necessary."[13] They waited anxiously for the Taos rebels to appear and attack them and their businesses. The revolutionaries did arrive and occupied the city, but they were not interested in fighting Anglo businessmen; they were focused on their fight against the Mexican government. The rebels named one of their own the governor of Nuevo México and organized a Junta Popular (People's Assembly) to establish a new government.[14]

More conservative Nuevo Méxicanos were initially supportive of the rebellion, figuring that they would benefit from the greater freedoms it might bring. But the mounting violence and the Junta Popular threatened their livelihoods, and they turned against the rebels. Pulling together a militia of almost a thousand men, a former governor and rico named Manuel Armijo marched into Santa Fe and occupied it. Then he moved north, pursuing the rebels to Taos. More than four months of skirmishes, negotiations, and flare-ups followed, but Armijo ultimately defeated the rebels in a battle in a narrow valley north of Santa Fe. As a reward, government leaders in Mexico City declared Armijo the governor of Nuevo México.[15]

Although the Taos Rebellion of 1837 created chaos in Santa Fe, the rebels' defeat turned out to be a boon for Gertrudis Barceló's business. Just a few months after taking up his office, Manuel Armijo decided to legalize gambling in Santa Fe. Dealers and players would pay fees instead of fines, with no threats of arrest.[16] With this new measure in place, Barceló was able to buy a building just off the plaza, between Palace and San Francisco Streets. She placed the front door in Burro Alley—a nod to her first days as a side-street dealer—and whitewashed its walls, inside and out. A barroom just inside the entrance offered gamblers whiskey and wine. In the back room Barceló arranged her monte tables. The dealers, as was tradition, sat with their backs to the walls while gamblers milled about in the middle of the room, choosing the table where they would try their luck.[17]

It was a lucrative enterprise. Within the year, Barceló—now often referred to by a nickname, La Tules (the reed)—owned a fancy carriage, a wardrobe full of silk dresses, and a box stuffed with fine jewelry. Mexican peons and Navajo and Apache women and children almost certainly labored in her house and at the sala (hall). Although Mexico had outlawed slavery after independence, coercive servitude was still common in Nuevo México. Gertrudis Barceló was a rico now, and Indigenous and Mexican "servants" were a sign of her status. She and her husband also became the godparents of more than ten children during this period; this process was one of the ways in which ricos brought laborers into their households.[18]

Barceló also invested in currency and mules and sent both along the Santa Fe and Chihuahua Trails in wagon trains, bound for trading houses. When she held dinner parties and receptions, guests ate off silver plates and lounged on expensive carpets. Barceló's gambling sala was not so unusual as a business in Mexico, but it and Barceló herself became tourist attractions for Americans arriving in Santa Fe.

Many of America's thousands of newspapers had been reporting the traffic between Missouri and Nuevo México for more than ten years. They also published travelers' accounts of the Santa Fe Trail, with detailed descriptions of the Mexican towns and their residents. In the wake of the Taos Rebellion, a former actor named Matt Field joined a wagon train to Nuevo México. When the train encamped each evening, Field leaned back against a wagon, opened his journal, and recorded everything that he had done and seen that day, much of it in poetic verse.[19]

He and his companions reached Santa Fe in the fall of 1839 and applied to the alcalde for a tour of the town. While they sauntered down one of the streets off the plaza, Gertrudis Barceló's carriage dashed by them, drawn by three mules. Barceló bowed her head at the alcalde, and her dark-haired niece Petra gave them a smile. Later that evening, Field joined the alcalde at Barceló's house, where they met Governor Armijo, several of his officers, and the sons of the city's wealthiest residents.

Field found the company convivial, and although he did not think the thirty-nine-year-old, auburn-haired Barceló was particularly handsome, he did admire her eyes, which were full of shrewd intelligence. When the alcalde translated Field's questions for her, Barceló's dark eyes brightened with a mischievousness that "can make any countenance agreeable." She was beautifully dressed and had a graceful ease about her that, Field argued, would have made her a popular attraction at parties held anywhere in the United States.

Field had never heard of or played Spanish monte, but he was impressed by the sheer variety of gamblers the game drew to Barceló's sala. "By this business has Señora Toulous amassed a fortune," Field wrote, "and made herself a person of no small distinction."[20]

When he was not chatting with Barceló or her guests, Field was looking around her house. The beds were folded up against the walls in the Mexican style, serving as couches and covered with Mexican and Navajo blankets. Field admired an elaborate clock hanging on the wall. It was of American manufacture, and it did not keep the time; its hands were stuck at twelve and six.

"I am economical with my clock, it being too handsome to work," Barceló told him with a wink. "Not wishing to grow old too fast, I only let it go on holidays." This "supreme queen of refinement and fashion" charmed Field, and he was not surprised to find that in Santa Fe, "the highest court her favor, and the lowest look at her with wonder."[21]

He and other American visitors were fascinated to find a woman of such prominence in Santa Fe, and they were similarly curious about her sala. When Field visited, he found her sitting at a dealer's table, abandoning her silks for a plain white dress, her blue rebozo loose on her shoulders. She calmly eyed the gamblers as she shuffled and dealt and took bets, losing some hands but winning more. Monte was a game of chance, and the house almost always won in the end—especially when the gamblers were knee-walking drunk on whiskey. Players could lose an entire year's wages in just a few hours.

One night, an Irish American "scalp hunter" named James Kirker, whom the Mexican government paid to attack Apache and Comanche villages and kill both men and women, was sitting at Barceló's table. He was "betting largely, and losing," Field observed, "and the other gamesters had ceased their own play to be spectators of the exciting contention." As Barceló dealt the cards and swept the coins off the table after each hand, she watched Kirker intently. She did not trust him. Earlier that summer, she had to sue him to recover four hundred pesos he had borrowed from her and then lost playing at her tables.[22] During this game, Kirker alternately cursed and gulped from a tumbler of whiskey, and at one point he sent a friend to fetch another bag of gold coins from his rooms. Kirker was determined to win and would stay at the sala as long as it took to double his money.

La Tules won a few hands, but Kirker won more. The game went on for hours and everyone stayed, sitting with their elbows on the other tables and their chins resting in their hands, watching. "The slip, slip of the cards, and now and then the jingling of coin, as the stakes were removed and replaced," Field recorded, "alone broke the midnight stillness of the apartment." Kirker began to lose big on every hand. At one point, Barceló paused and gestured to one of her attendants.

"Tráeme una nueva baraja de cartas," she said. *Bring me a new deck of cards.*

"No, Señora," Kirker interjected. "We have played so far with this pack, and they are good enough for the rest of the game."

La Tules shrugged and waved her man away, dealing another hand with the old deck. The monte tables were often jovial but could turn easily to violence. Kirker killed people for a living, and she did not want to rile him. The game continued, and it was not until the sun rose that Kirker laid down his last bet. "Señora Toulous once more swept the table," Field wrote, "and the reckless trader was left without a dollar."

There was a tense moment as everyone waited to see how Kirker would react to his loss. He jumped up from the table and started shouting. "Wake snakes! Hail Columbia! I'm off for California tomorrow!" he yelled. He turned to La Tules. "And I say, old lady, I'll see you again in the fall!" La Tules arose, curtsied to Kirker, and disappeared through the side door. Her attendants followed, carrying several heavy sacks of gold and Mexican dollars.[23]

Journalists and travelers were captivated by such scenes and wrote about them in detail for American audiences. Matt Field published more than eighty articles on his western journey for the *New Orleans*

Times-Picayune in 1839–40. Most of them reinforced a growing narrative of American dominion in the West and the confidence white migrants had that they would settle the Southwest once they had spread across the lands of the Louisiana Purchase.

Two of Field's articles featured Gertrudis Barceló, who displayed many ideal American traits—perseverance, savvy, strength—but who did not fit the image of a pioneer because she was a Mexican woman. Americans continued to be fascinated. Josiah Gregg's 1842 guidebook, *Commerce of the Prairies*, included several accounts of Barceló and her gambling empire. She was one of the wealthiest women in Nuevo México. She had powerful friends, although her sala was open to all.[24]

"The grave magistrate and the priestly dignity, the gay caballero and the titled señora may all be seen staking their doubloons upon the turn of a card," Gregg observed, "while the humbler ranchero, the hired domestic and ragged pauper, all press with equal avidity to test their fortune at the same shrine."[25]

Barceló relished the attention and the power that her standing gave her in Santa Fe. Her sala was a convening site, a place where all Santa Fe's residents and traders and travelers passing through mixed with relative ease. Like Sacajawea and Jim Beckwourth, Gertrudis Barceló was a cultural broker who expertly navigated the multiple communities that came together in the West. The Americans who came off the Santa Fe Trail in the early 1840s were of all types: merchants, trappers, scouts, traders, adventurers, journalists. Gertrudis Barceló sat at her monte table and watched them come and go from her sala, taking some of her money with them but leaving more. It was hard to know if their business would bring her great profits or ultimately cause her immense sorrow.[26]

CHAPTER 9

One of the travelers joining the crowds of traders and journalists on the Santa Fe Trail in the summer after the Taos Rebellion was Jim Beckwourth. He had not stayed long in St. Louis after his return from Apsáalooke country. Most of his family members had left, including his father, who had returned to Virginia and died there. Beckwourth went to see Eliza but found that she was married to someone else. She believed he was dead and, understandably, had moved on with her life.[1]

St. Louis, the town that had welcomed him home so many times, had a darker edge to it in the mid-1830s. While he was gone, the city had been the site of several infamous racial murders. A U.S. Army officer stationed at Jefferson Barracks south of the city and already known for his cruelty in campaigns against Indigenous peoples, had beaten one of the women he enslaved to death. And just a few months before Beckwourth's return, a free Black steamboat steward disembarked in St. Louis and moments later was accosted by several white men. In the fight that followed, the sailor killed two of his attackers. Later that afternoon, an enraged white mob took him from his jail cell and burned him to death on one of the city's main thoroughfares.[2]

"Though slavery is thought, by some, to be mild in Missouri, when compared with the cotton, sugar, and rice growing states," the fugitive slave William Wells Brown would later write, "no part of our slaveholding country is more noted for the barbarity of its inhabitants than St. Louis."[3]

So, Jim Beckwourth left Missouri once again. Initially he went east, to scout for troops fighting Seminoles in the Florida swamps. Although the federal government had succeeded in forcing thousands of these men and women from their homelands to the newly created Indian Territory (reorganized later as Oklahoma) as part of their Indian removal campaign, many Seminoles remained and were resisting their deportation with force.[4] The Florida swamps seemed more likely to give Beckwourth yellow fever than the notoriety he craved, so he left the Gulf South and returned to St. Louis.

He was there only a few days before signing on to work as a fur trader for the new firm of Sublette & Vasquez, led by two men he knew from his trapping days. With Andrew Sublette and a group of hunters, trappers, and wagon masters, Jim set out on the Santa Fe Trail. A day's ride out of Bent's Fort, a trading installation on the Arkansas River, Beckwourth started to feel ill. When he tried to speak, he slurred his words, and he seemed confused about where he was and why he was there. His compatriots quickly diagnosed his symptoms: sunstroke.

That night, the team rolled up to the fort's gate and carried Beckwourth into a large, sandy square lined with trading rooms and sleeping quarters on every side. Thick cottonwood trunks held up the crossbeams in the Spanish style; the exterior adobe walls were more than fourteen feet high, with watchtowers at each corner.

The fort, built in 1833 by the brothers Charles and William Bent and their friend Ceran St. Vrain, perched at a curve of the Arkansas, in territory claimed by Kiowa, Osage, Southern Cheyenne, Arapaho, Ute, Lipan Apache, and Jicarilla Apache peoples. The river marked the international boundary between the United States and Mexico. To the Bents and St. Vrain, this geopolitical borderland was the perfect place to build a permanent trading fort. They could take advantage of traffic moving both east- and westbound on the Santa Fe Trail and become central brokers in the growing trade in buffalo robes.[5]

Trappers like Beckwourth had decimated beaver populations by the late 1820s, and then the rage for felt hats had waned. Ten years later, buffalo robes were retaining their value—and they brought two to three times the money of any other pelt. Indigenous and Anglo buffalo hunters killing animals not for consumption of their meat but for trade in robes stood to make a fortune out of the giant, shaggy hides.[6]

Beckwourth spent several days at the fort recovering from his bout with sunstroke while his compatriots haggled with Indigenous, Mexican, and American traders. They kept quiet about their reason for traveling the Santa Fe Trail. The Bents and St. Vrain would not appreciate competition in the region. Within a few days, Beckwourth was able to ride his horse again, so he took up scouting duties on the rest of their journey.

Instead of taking the Cimarron cutoff toward Santa Fe, they turned north along a Ute trail that followed the foothills of the Rocky Mountains until the landscape shifted slightly, becoming higher, drier, and flatter. There, the South Platte rushed out of the mountains onto the flats and then turned north, its shallow waters full of rolling sand and gravel scraped from the high country. The men of Sublette & Vasquez followed it until they reached a place where the water had carved through the soft sandstone for hundreds of thousands of years, creating a cliff about thirty to forty feet high.[7]

Beckwourth and the men reined their horses and dismounted, then began to unload the wagons. Over the next several weeks, they constructed a square building in the style of Bent's Fort and a barn for storing hay to feed their horses and mules. They called it Fort Vasquez, after Pierre "Louis" Vasquez, a partner in their enterprise.[8]

Soon afterward, Sublette announced that he was returning to St. Louis. He was leaving the installation in the capable hands of Jim Beckwourth, in whom "I have implicit confidence," Sublette said, "and whose long experience and intimate acquaintance with the Indian character preeminently entitle him to the trust."[9]

Beckwourth was delighted to be given such responsibility, and his first act was to send men out to establish satellite posts closer to the summer villages of the Southern Cheyenne and Arapaho. After several of his men returned having failed to locate the Southern Cheyenne encampments, Beckwourth decided to deal with them himself. He took one man with him and set out to find them.[10]

It was a huge risk. While he was living with the Apsáalooke, Beckwourth had attacked and killed many Cheyenne warriors. It was quite likely they would seek revenge upon him when they discovered who he was. A few days later, they followed a herd of buffalo to a Southern Cheyenne camp, where they also found William Bent. The trader offered to translate for him, but Beckwourth asked to speak through an Apsáalooke captive instead. He opted for audaciousness in his message to the chiefs—and a lie.

"Tell the Cheyennes that I have fought them many winters," he told the Apsáalooke translator. "I have killed a great Crow chief, and am obliged to run away." He explained that he had come to the Cheyenne, "the bravest people in the mountains, as I do not wish to be killed by any of the inferior tribes."

When William Bent heard this message, he could not believe it. "You are certainly bereft of your senses," he told Beckwourth. "The Indians will make sausage-meat of you."[11]

The Southern Cheyenne were curious and gathered around Beckwourth as their chiefs arrived to speak with him. In council, Jim told them who he was and offered them his life. Old Bark was impressed with the trader's boldness.

"We know you," he said. "You say you have killed many of our warriors; we know you do not lie. We like a great brave," he added, "and we will not kill you."

In exchange for his life, Beckwourth promised to trade with them fairly.[12]

Jim Beckwourth gave himself a lot of credit for this exchange in the moment and afterward. But for the Southern Cheyenne, sparing an American trader's life was not a surprising choice. Over the previous twenty years, they had become the dominant brokers of buffalo robes as well as guns and horses in the region. Establishing a relationship with Beckwourth and the men of Fort Vasquez would only increase the Southern Cheyenne's power in the Great Plains.[13]

And apparently, they did believe that Beckwourth would treat them fairly. Perhaps because he had fought fiercely against them in battle. Or because he knew their history and their ways. The Southern Cheyenne may have trusted him more than the other American traders in their midst, however, because he was not white. Beckwourth was once again living between worlds, an ideal situation for a trader in the West.

Although Beckwourth did not know it at the time, this initial negotiation with the Southern Cheyenne was the beginning of a long and varied relationship with that tribal nation, which would last for more than twenty years.[14]

For the next two years, Beckwourth commanded Fort Vasquez on the South Platte. He managed the traders who worked for Sublette & Vasquez and the free hunters who came in, looking to off-load buffalo robes or purchase goods. Riding out to Southern Cheyenne camps, he traded with them directly and invited them to camp near the fort. He went to the women first, for they were the ones who processed the buffalo hides.

Beckwourth did not, however, make good on his promise to treat the Southern Cheyenne fairly. He felt no compunction about trading buffalo robes for whiskey and making thousands of dollars from this lopsided exchange. At one point he gave Southern Cheyenne hunters sixty gallons of whiskey (which likely cost around $15) as payment for $6,000 worth of bison robes and eighteen hardy prairie horses.

"The sale of liquor is one of the most profitable branches of a trader's business," he shrugged, "and since the appetite for the vile potion had already been created, my personal influence in the matter was slight."[15] Beckwourth was becoming an expert at abdicating responsibility for such transactions and focusing instead on how he could profit from them.

In 1840, Beckwourth received a note from Sublette that he and Vasquez were closing the fort, even though it had been flourishing. Disappointed, he offered his services to the Bent brothers and St. Vrain. Working on their behalf, he traded with the Southern Cheyenne along the South Platte for another year. At that point, Beckwourth decided to make a change. He had heard tell of a thriving trading center in the mountains of northern Mexico and thought he might make a go of it there.

"I had now accumulated a considerable sum of money," Beckwourth remembered later, "and thought I might as well put it to some use for my own profit, as risk my life in the service of others, while they derived the lion's share from my industry."[16]

In the summer of 1841, Jim Beckwourth arrived in Taos, New Mexico. The town had recovered from the 1837 rebellion and its suppression, although the ties between the Mexican population and the Pueblo peoples living at Taos Pueblo remained a strong one. Taos had a printing press and a newspaper, and its plaza was crowded with farmers and ranchers and laborers bringing goods in and out.[17]

Beckwourth also found several American traders in town, supplying Apache, Navajo, Ute, Southern Cheyenne, and Arapaho communities, as well as a growing number of American residents working in the area. The Kentuckian Kit Carson (who, like Beckwourth, had absconded from an apprenticeship as a young man and then gone west) lived in Taos but traveled much of the year, working for Bent's Fort as a hunter.[18]

Just a few weeks after his arrival, Beckwourth sensed that the Nuevo Méxicanos in Taos were looking upon him and the other American traders with suspicion. That summer, an army of Anglo Texans (who had successfully declared their independence from Mexico in 1836), announced their intention to expand the borders of their new republic. They believed that Santa Fe belonged to Texas and had organized a campaign to march into Nuevo México to claim its capital city for themselves.[19] Disorganized and inadequately equipped, the "Santa Fe Pioneers" struggled through the high deserts of eastern Nuevo México until mid-September 1841, when they surrendered to a company of Mexican soldiers. The territory's governor—and one of Gertrudis Barceló's patrons—Manuel Armijo sent the Texans to Mexico City, where they languished in jail for six months.[20] It was the first time that Anglos attempted to invade and occupy Nuevo México. It would not be the last.

In the spring of 1842, Beckwourth and his new wife, Luisa Sandoval, left Taos and traveled through the Sangre de Cristo foothills and down onto the eastern prairies to trade. They established a supply depot along the Arkansas River, a camp that would later become the town of Pueblo, Colorado. They moved between there and the South Platte, where Fort Vasquez had once stood. The place was still a thriving trading center; since 1840 it had been under the control of another biracial man who had decided that his future lay west of St. Louis: Jean-Baptiste Charbonneau.[21]

Sacajawea's son had grown up in St. Louis with William Clark's family. They sent him to St. Louis Academy for his education, and then he traveled through Europe with an acquaintance before heading to the

Rocky Mountains. American traders and travelers were rather astonished to meet such an educated man out on the sandy plains in what became known later as the Front Range of Colorado.

"He had acquired a classical education and could converse quite fluently in German, Spanish, French, and English, as well as several Indian languages," one writer reported. Charbonneau had a keen sense of humor, and he was shrewd. He commanded the respect of everyone who visited his camp. Those visitors included Beckwourth and Luisa, as well as the explorer John C. Frémont, who stopped by in 1842, on his way to Alta California with Kit Carson as his guide.[22]

Beckwourth was making money trading with Charbonneau and the Southern Cheyenne, but his marriage to Luisa was not going well. In the fall of 1843, he did what he usually did when he felt bored or frustrated or under threat. Jim Beckwourth hit the road.

In January 1844 Beckwourth and a group of fifteen men, including three Hispanos, arrived with a train of goods and forty horses in Los Angeles, in Mexican California. The town consisted of one-story adobe houses, stores, Spanish mission buildings, and Catholic churches, surrounded by farms, vineyards, and ranchlands. Enslaved Indigenous peoples worked in the fields and as vaqueros (cowboys), fetching their water from a series of acequias, ditches cut into the earth to connect the Los Angeles River to the town's fields and meadows.[23]

As Beckwourth looked for a store in which to trade his goods, he faced some resistance. Los Angeles residents did not welcome Americans, whom they saw as rabble-rousers at best and imperialists at worst. Too many Americans in the town would bring the attention of Mexico City, which Los Angelenos did not want. For the previous five years, Alta California's officials had been expelling Americans who refused to learn Spanish or engage in business with Mexican residents.[24]

Beckwourth avoided this fate, using the diplomatic skills he had honed during his fur-trapping days and at the trading forts of Nuevo México. He was comfortable in Los Angeles, which was about half the size of Santa Fe with its 2,500 Californios (Hispano Californians) and their enslaved Indigenous people. It was just the kind of nascent multicultural community in which Beckwourth thrived. He found business partners and customers easily.

"I indulged my new passion for trade," he reported, "and did a very profitable business for several months."[25]

Just nine months after his arrival, however, the conflict between Californios and Mexico City officials that Los Angelenos had feared derailed Beckwourth's business. President Antonio López de Santa Anna sent troops to occupy Los Angeles, claiming they would protect the town and its ports from potential American incursions.[26] Instead, the soldiers pillaged Californio homes and businesses and assaulted women. By November 1844, the Californios in Los Angeles had had enough. Under the leadership of a local militia leader, they formed companies throughout the region and attacked federal positions. Most of the Americans in Alta California, "according to their interests and predilections," chose sides. Beckwourth was sympathetic to the Californios. The Mexican federals were "worthless vagabonds," he believed, and their armies constituted an invading force.

Beckwourth joined a militia with several other Americans to support the Californio cause, but in the end, there wasn't much of a fight at all. After an early morning cannonade, the Californios managed to pin down the federal troops and force them to surrender.[27] Beckwourth and his men rode back to Los Angeles, and the celebrations of their bloodless victory lasted for a week. Once his hangover had dissipated, Beckwourth returned to his business. But less than a year later, to his chagrin, "fresh political commotions supervened."[28]

While Beckwourth was in Los Angeles, white men gathered at polling stations across the United States and elected Democrat James K. Polk, a wealthy slaveholder and land speculator from Tennessee who came into office on the strength of his expansionist promises.

In the years since the Louisiana Purchase, the War of 1812, and the 1830 Indian Removal Act, federal politicians were taking a more aggressive stance toward land acquisition across the continent, so Polk's election was not a surprise. He pledged to settle the Oregon boundary dispute with Great Britain and began negotiations to purchase California and Nuevo México from Mexico. When the Republic of Texas applied for annexation to the United States, threatening to disturb the balance of free and slave state representation in Congress, President Polk rallied to their cause. While many northern politicians resisted annexation because this would bring another slave state into the Union, many Americans favored the addition of Texas to the body politic.

"It is time now for the opposition to the Annexation of Texas to cease," the popular newspaper editor John O'Sullivan wrote in the summer of 1845. Given the number of Americans already settled there, drawn by the incentives that the Mexican government had offered up after they achieved independence from Spain, "the sweep of our eagle's wing already includes within its circuit the wide extent of her fair and fertile land."

Any American politician who tried to prevent the Republic's entrance into the Union, O'Sullivan argued, was no better than England, France, or Mexico, all countries that had tried to hamper American power, "limiting our greatness and checking the fulfillment of our manifest destiny to overspread the continent allotted by Providence for the free development of our yearly multiplying millions."[29]

The ideology of Manifest Destiny that O'Sullivan articulated so well—a central set of beliefs in the frontier myth—had been pervading American politics and social life for years. Polk embraced it. When Mexico declined his offer to purchase its remaining northern provinces, he turned to military force. Hoping to provoke Mexican soldiers into firing first, he sent troops to the Nueces River, the disputed boundary between Texas and Mexico. Polk also dispatched a note to John C. Frémont, an explorer who had embarked on his third journey to the Pacific coast that year. The president suggested that Frémont ready his men to occupy vital ports in Alta California, should war be declared.

In the spring of 1846, just after Texas was officially admitted as America's twenty-eighth state, Frémont and his men—including the scout and Indian fighter Kit Carson—arrived in Monterey Bay, in northern Alta California. Mexican officials stationed there demanded that they leave immediately. Frémont pretended to agree but took command of an army of American trappers, fur traders, and scouts in the foothills of the Sierra Nevada mountains.[30]

By June 1846, Frémont's army was making its way down the coast, stealing horses, pillaging houses, assaulting women, and threatening the lives of Californios who did not agree to help them. They ultimately joined a force of U.S. marines who docked in Monterey. Everywhere they went, Frémont's men raised a flag with a grizzly bear on it, proclaiming that northern California was now the "Bear Flag Republic."[31]

Jim Beckwourth was somewhat astonished by these events. The Americans who had stood with the Californios against Mexico just a year earlier were now clamoring for battle against their former allies. "Matters seemed to be growing too warm to be pleasant," he determined.[32]

In early July 1846, news reached the residents of Los Angeles that the United States and Mexico were officially at war. Mexico had had enough of Polk's threats and demands and declared war on the United States. The two nation's troops clashed along the Nueces River, and a little more than two weeks later, President Polk asked Congress to declare war and Congress agreed.[33]

The standing U.S. Army was not large (little more than seven thousand cavalry and infantry garrisoned posts across the country), but Polk had confidence in them and the volunteers who he felt sure would enlist in state and territorial militias.[34] And he was, like many Americans, even more convinced that Mexico could not possibly win a war against the United States. An untrained army of planters and farmers had defeated Santa Anna in Texas just ten years before. Most politicians believed, as John O'Sullivan did, that Mexico was "imbecile and distracted" and unable to exert any real authority in the far-flung northern provinces.[35] Their soldiers, scattered among just a handful of presidios, had been unable to prevent regular attacks by Apache, Navajo, and Comanche raiders. Mexico's War of Independence had given them freedom from Spain, the Americans believed, but had not yet made them into a great nation able to win international wars.

Beckwourth would have liked to join Frémont's forces but thought it would be impossible to get to them. It was likely he would be captured and imprisoned. "If I looked south, the same difficulties menaced me," he thought, "and the west conducts me to the Pacific Ocean." His only route of escape, he believed, was eastward.

A few days later, Beckwourth left Los Angeles with five other Americans and a large herd of horses that they stole from Californio ranches in the area. Clearly, he did not consider them his allies any longer. By the time Beckwourth arrived back at his trading fort at Pueblo, almost half of the horses had died or faltered due to the rapid pace. He and his friends divided the remaining animals among them, and Beckwourth drove his herd to Taos.

His flight from California had been exhilarating, but his arrival at home left much to be desired.[36] In his absence, Luisa had remarried. She believed that Beckwourth had abandoned her, and therefore they were legally divorced. Beckwourth could not blame her and did not protest. "I preferred to enjoy once more the sweets of single blessedness," he admitted.[37]

In Taos, Beckwourth discovered that a large army under the command of General Stephen Watts Kearny was on the move from the United States, to invade and occupy Nuevo México and then California. He saddled and mounted his horse and rode eastward, toward Bent's Fort. Beckwourth was not going there to muster into the U.S. Army. He was in his late forties and had no interest in soldiering. He was going to meet the army because he knew that a military force on the move always needed fresh mounts, and Jim Beckwourth had a herd of horses to sell them.

CHAPTER 10

As Beckwourth rode out to meet the American army, Nuevo México's governor Manuel Armijo gathered Mexican federal troops and the city's militia in Santa Fe. He told them that "the giant, our Neighbor," had taken Texas, and now they were on the way to take Nuevo México in another act of usurpation. He needed their help to protect the province on behalf of their comrades and their federal government.[1] The men cheered, but the outlook for Santa Fe was not encouraging.

The city had no fortifications, and the military force under Armijo's command was small. Federal soldiers usually worked as a city police force, breaking up fights and dragging drunks to the local jail. The city's civilian militia, which rode out against Indigenous raiders, was independent of local government and funded their own campaigns. Armijo needed money to raise more troops and seasoned soldiers from the southern territories to help Nuevo México win a potential battle with an American army.

Over the summer of 1846, Governor Armijo visited Gertrudis Barceló and other prominent Nuevomexicanos, urging them to do all they could to defend the nation against an American invasion. He made impassioned speeches to the provincial legislature, proposing a new tax on residents to provide for their own protection. He wrote a series of letters to Mexico City, pleading for military aid. And he issued a proclamation to the Mexican citizens of Santa Fe.

"At this very moment, forces of the United States are now advancing on the department," he wrote. "Let us be ready for war since we are provoked to it. Let us not look to the strength of our enemies, nor at the size of the obstacles to overcome." Instead, the city's citizens needed to defend themselves and their nation with decisiveness and conviction.[2]

Armijo also met with Santa Fe's Anglo business and landowners, who now numbered in the hundreds. They had established themselves in the city after the opening of the Santa Fe Trail more than twenty years before, and their population had grown steadily in the years since. Armijo told them that he sympathized with their plight, for he also wanted to sustain a commercial relationship with the United States. He traded in sheep the way Gertrudis Barceló traded in mules, and like her, Armijo regularly sent Mexican and American goods to Missouri along the Santa Fe Trail. "I wish for the peace and welfare of our two countries," he told the Americans in Santa Fe.[3]

Gertrudis Barceló, whose livelihood depended on the free flow of people and goods in and out of the city and across national borders, was similarly conflicted. If the war came to Santa Fe, would she choose Mexico or the United States? Barceló had become the wealthiest woman in the province by being patient and playing the odds. She would wait to see how the suits fell in this latest skirmish before deciding what to do.

In early August 1846, Mexican army scouts returned with reports that a large army of two thousand Americans had arrived in the town of Las Vegas, seventy miles east of Santa Fe. On the evening of August 12, a small group of Anglo soldiers and civilians arrived, sent in advance of the main body of American soldiers. The city's residents may have recognized James Magoffin, one of the civilians. An American trader who had married into a Mexican family, Magoffin had been sending trade caravans between Chihuahua, Santa Fe, and Missouri for fifteen years.

The group dismounted and ducked into the Palace of the Governors, the historic government building constructed in 1610. When they entered Armijo's office, the governor rose to meet them. "I am sent to you by the general commanding the American Army," a U.S. cavalry officer, Philip St. George Cooke, informed Armijo. "I have a letter, which I can present at your convenience." Armijo took the letter, broke the seal, and unfolded it.[4]

"I come as a friend," General Stephen Watts Kearny had written, "and with the disposition, and intention, to consider all Mexicans and others as friends who will remain peaceably at their homes and attend to their own affairs." He then demanded Armijo's capitulation and the surrender of the city of Santa Fe to the United States Army.[5]

Magoffin sat with Armijo that night, trying to convince him that submission was the best course of action. The governor's ragtag army of poorly trained soldiers was no match for Kearny's troops with their gleaming carbines, pistols, and sabers and their artillery regiment with sixteen cannons. But Armijo would hear none of it.[6] The next morning, the Americans rode out of town, bearing a letter from the governor to the general.

"You have notified me that you intend to take possession of the country I govern," Armijo wrote. "The people of the country have risen, en masse, in my defense. If you take the country, it will be because you prove the strongest in battle." Armijo promised that his troops would march the next day toward Las Vegas. "We will meet and negotiate on the plains."[7]

The next morning, Gertrudis Barceló and the other residents of Santa Fe watched as the governor rode out of the city to the east, leading a few hundred soldiers and militia. The next several days were full of worry. Both Kearny's and Armijo's armies had blocked all traffic on the Santa Fe Trail, so there was no news from that quarter. Men and women still came to drink whiskey and play monte at Barceló's sala, but the atmosphere was subdued.

On August 17, word reached the city that before a battle with the Americans could even begin, Governor Armijo had skedaddled. Instead of marching to Santa Fe to defend it, he had abandoned his position and ridden hard for Albuquerque, via a cutoff that allowed him to avoid returning to the capital city. Armijo would later defend himself by saying that his officers had disputed his authority and urged surrender. That he had too few men to win the oncoming battle, and he decided he would not send them into a slaughter. Most of Santa Fe's Mexican residents scoffed at his excuses.[8]

Gertrudis Barceló was in a difficult situation. Manuel Armijo had been a friend and an ally, but now he was a traitor. A coward. He had left the people of Santa Fe at the mercy of the American military. The final card had turned, and Barceló knew what she had to do.

The next afternoon, the U.S. Army arrived in Santa Fe Plaza. Kearny rode at the head of the column, leading hundreds of cavalrymen dressed in blue uniforms covered with dust from the road.[9] Jim Beckwourth, wearing his usual outfit of buckskins, was with them. He had sold as many horses as he could to the soldiers and sent the rest back to his ranch in Pueblo. When the sale was completed, Kearny had asked him to come with the Army of New Mexico on their march to Santa Fe.

"You like war," the general told Beckwourth. "I have good use for you now."[10]

It took three hours for the entire American force to arrive, a mix of horsemen and soldiers on foot and horses dragging artillery caissons. The officer in command of the artillery was Meriwether Lewis Clark, the son of William Clark. Santa Fe's residents came out of their houses and businesses and watched the American soldiers pass by. The Anglos cheered. The Hispanos did not. "Women could be seen in various parts of town," one soldier observed, "with their hands covering their faces or sobbing aloud."[11]

Armijo's lieutenant governor, now in command of the city, came out of the Palace of the Governors and welcomed Kearny and his officers. The American general did not mince words.

"I have come amongst you by order of my government, to take possession of your country, and extend over it the laws of the United States," he said. "We come amongst you as friends, not as enemies; as protectors—not as conquerors." Kearny promised that the U.S. government would help defend New Mexicans against Navajo, Apache, and Comanche raiders and that his soldiers would respect their private property and that of the Catholic Church.

Kearny and the officers then went inside the palace, and the lieutenant governor offered them wine and brandy, the best that the vineyards of El Paso had to offer. "We were too thirsty to judge of its merits," one of the Americans noted, "anything liquid and cool was palatable."[12] While they drank, the sun began to set. Suddenly, the boom of a cannon echoed over the town. Then twelve more. Kearny looked pleased. "There," he said, "my guns proclaim that the flag of the United States floats over this capital."[13]

The party rose and walked into the plaza. Snapping in the breeze from the top of a newly cut pole, was the American flag. Twenty-seven white stars on a blue field and alternating stripes in red and white. This banner was already out of date; on July 4 the federal government had added a star for the state of Texas, but Kearny's army had not received the new flags before setting out from Bent's Fort.

Under the shadow of the Stars and Stripes, Nuevo México's provincial officials took an oath of loyalty to the United States. Then the group went to the house of one of Santa Fe's leading Hispano citizens, where they ate fresh bread and multiple courses of vegetables and meat, washed down with more El Paso wine.[14] When the American officers returned to the palace after the meal, they found the American trader Lucius Thruston waiting for them. After the customary introductions, Thruston passed on a message for the officers: Gertrudis Barceló hoped to see them at her home for another supper that night, in honor of their arrival. The Americans were impressed.

"This is a lady who has amassed a large fortune here and at Chihuahua," one of them noted, "by gambling and other accomplishments."[15]

This was the first night Barceló entertained U.S. Army soldiers at her home and at her sala on Burro Alley, and it was the first of many. At the sala, she sold them Santa Fe's finest whiskey and taught them how to play Spanish monte. The soldiers grew to love the game and her sala. One evening, a handful of officers lost hundreds of dollars to her in just a few hands. Barceló chatted with them while she dealt and between games. The Americans were excellent sources of information on the U.S. Army's plans for Nuevo México and for Santa Fe's Mexican residents.

A few days after his arrival, Kearny established martial law and issued a proclamation of annexation, claiming Santa Fe and Nuevo México "as part of the United States, and under the name of the Territory of New Mexico." He promised protection, a new government, and citizenship. He asked for peace and tranquility in return. "Those who are encountered with arms, or instigating others against the United States," his proclamation read, "shall both be looked upon as traitors and treated as such."[16]

Over the objections of the Mexican residents, who were used to choosing one of their own to lead them, Kearny appointed an American territorial governor. Charles Bent, the former soldier and fur trapper who had built Bent's Fort with his brother on the Arkansas River, had also managed a store in Taos for more than fifteen years. He was married to Maria Jaramillo and was Kit Carson's brother-in-law. Carson had become famous when John Frémont wrote admiring descriptions of him and his talents in his 1840s exploration reports. Kearny believed that Bent had enough local connections and knowledge to govern New Mexico and enough patriotism to keep it in American hands.[17]

The American soldiers, with the help of Mexican adobe artisans and builders, constructed a fort on a cliff on the north edge of town, while Kearny prepared for the Army's march to California. He wrote a series of dispatches and handed them off to Jim Beckwourth, who rode more than nine hundred miles to deliver them to the officers in command of Fort Leavenworth, on the Missouri River.

"This was my service," Beckwourth said. "The occupation was a tolerably good one, and I never failed in getting my dispatches through."[18] While Beckwourth was gone, the plaza in Santa Fe resumed its bustle as merchants and country farmers led their burros into the large square, "laden with kegs of Taos whiskey or immense packs of fodder, melons, wood, or grapes." Pueblo women arrived with large baskets of peaches, and soldiers and civilians mingled as they bought chilis, onions, toasted pine nuts, or tobacco that they rolled into long, thin cigarritos.[19]

The soldiers and the American merchants and traders who followed in the U.S. Army's wake already knew about Gertrudis Barceló from the accounts that journalists and travelers had published in the early 1840s. Like them, these new arrivals found Barceló mesmerizing, even as they became alarmed at the ease with which she separated men from their money. "Señora Barcelo dealt monte with a firm hand and a winning smile that enticed gold from the pockets of the jeunesse d'orée of the regiment," wrote William Clark Kennerly, a nephew of William Clark and a trader from St. Louis. "The charming Señora was quite a character, possessing great wealth which she had earned through her own efforts by turning the right card."[20]

Susan Magoffin, the young, dark-haired wife of American trader Samuel Magoffin (James's brother), was similarly impressed but also scandalized. Barceló was "a stately dame of a certain age," Magoffin wrote in her journal after meeting the monte dealer at a fandango, "the possessor of a portion of that shrewd sense and fascinating manner necessary to allure the wayward, inexperienced youth to the hall of final ruin."[21]

The soldiers who left Barceló's sala in the early hours of the morning staggered through the city streets. Some shouted and sang and shot their pistols in the air, while others started fights and were thrown into the city jail as a result. "What an everlasting noise these soldiers keep," Magoffin complained, "from early dawn till late at night."[22]

Santa Fe quieted down a bit in late September, when Kearny left with three hundred soldiers to march through the heart of Apachería, toward California. Two weeks later, another army arrived from the east, a battalion of five hundred Mormon soldiers with their families, with a seventy-wagon train rolling along behind them. They stayed for only nine days, and for the most part they refrained from visiting Gertrudis Barceló's sala. When they marched out of town under the command of Philip St. George Cooke to follow Kearny's route to the west, they were led by a scout they had hired at Bent's Fort: the "French Pilot," Jean-Baptiste Charbonneau.[23]

Although Gertrudis Barceló was developing cordial and mostly profitable relationships with U.S. Army personnel, there was never a unanimous embrace of the American occupation among Santa Fe's Hispano families. Many local farmers began to lose their land to American speculators mere months after Kearny's arrival, and the appointment of Anglo territorial officials instead of Hispano political leaders angered many residents. In the Catholic churches of Santa Fe and Taos, priests railed against the annexation of Nuevo México to the United States in their sermons.

In early December 1846, word spread that an uprising would begin on Christmas night in Santa Fe. The Mexican rebels would reassert their sovereignty and take back Nuevo México for their nation.[24] Barceló heard about the specifics of this plan from women she knew. At her sala, she passed along the information to Donaciano Vigil, one of Armijo's former soldiers who had impressed Stephen Kearny so much that he appointed him to be Charles Bent's lieutenant governor. Vigil told Bent about the plot and informed the U.S. commander in charge of Santa Fe, Colonel Sterling Price.[25] As snow fell in thick flakes on the streets of Santa Fe and Taos, Bent's and Price's men made arrests. On Christmas night, some soldiers dragged prisoners to the city jail while others patrolled the streets. The artillery commander moved several cannons into the plaza, and Price declared martial law in the city.[26]

On January 5, 1847, Governor Bent tried to appease the restive residents by issuing an official proclamation assuring them of his commitment to their future and urging them to believe in the power of the United States rather than local rebel leaders. He believed that his words had had some effect and that the situation was mostly resolved. Two weeks later, against the advice of his friends and fellow officials, Bent left Santa Fe for his home in Taos.[27] After he arrived home on the evening of January 18, one of his good friends came to see him.

"For God's sake, Don Carlos," he urged the governor, "saddle your horse and get away from here, as sure as there is a God in heaven, they are going to kill you." Despite this warning and several others, Bent stayed with his family in their house. "He [just] could not believe that they wanted to kill him," his daughter remembered later.[28]

The next morning, a large group of rebels surrounded Bent's house. While someone pounded on the front door, several went up on the roof to rip off the grasses and cattails and the cedar planks beneath. Bent told his wife and children to hide and opened the door, stepping onto the porch. While he argued with the men outside, Ignacia Bent uncovered a passageway they had excavated to her sister's house next door. The children got down on their bellies and crawled through it.[29]

Bent was not able to convince the rebels of his good intentions. The crowd surged toward him, and he staggered back into the house with several arrows already imbedded in his body. He managed to drag himself through the tunnel to Josefa Carson's house, but the rebels burst in there as well. They shot him with several more arrows and pistol balls, and as he lay dying on the floor, they attacked him with hatchets. Ignacia and Josefa got onto their knees and begged the rebels to spare their lives and the lives of their children. The leaders of the rebellion conferred and left them alive, then went off in search of the other Americans living in Taos.[30]

Throughout the day and into the next, the attack on the Bents turned into a general uprising. The rebels killed seventeen Americans in Taos and nearby towns. When Colonel Price received word of Bent's brutal murder and the continued insurrection, he became convinced that the rebels aimed to kill every American and every Mexican whom Kearny had appointed to a territorial office. He issued a call for all the Americans in the city to join his soldiers.

"The ox-drivers, mule-drivers, merchants, clerks, and commissariat-men were formed into rank and file," Jim Beckwourth (who joined the militia) reported, "and placed in a condition for holding the city."[31] Price gathered them all and marched north to Taos. For the next three weeks, they pursued the insurgents through the Taos Valley and into the mountain town of Mora.[32] After fighting a series of battles in frigid temperatures and taking hundreds of prisoners, including two leaders of the revolt, the U.S. Army returned to Santa Fe.[33]

"I hope soon the insurrection is completely quieted," one U.S. soldier named Alexander Dyer confessed to a friend. "I fear the annexation of this country was both a moral and a political error." Dyer was worried that the United States could never hold New Mexico firmly in its grasp. It was too far from Washington, D.C., and its Mexican and Indigenous residents could never be integrated into American society. To distract himself from these gloomy thoughts, Dyer left the barracks and went out to Gertrudis Barceló's sala, which had not shut down during the chaos of the Taos Revolt.

"It was the first time I had ever seen a woman gamble," Dyer wrote in his journal. "The room was crowded" with bettors willing to risk all their cash on hand for a chance of winning.[34] He continued to go to the sala whenever he had a chance, placing his bets with Barceló herself or with another dealer in a room crowded with traders, soldiers, merchants, and travelers. In August, a new U.S. Army officer in command of the city issued a proclamation closing all gambling saloons and public fandangos. Barceló's sala was, of course, exempt.[35]

As a reward for her loyalty during the occupation and the revolt, the U.S. Army provided Gertrudis with an escort of Missouri Volunteers whenever she made long trips out of town to visit family or trade some of the mules in her large herd. They guarded her against Navajo or Apache attacks, Taos rebels who had not been apprehended, and bandits who might be operating along the Santa Fe or Chihuahua Trails.[36] It was on such a trip that Barceló met the Prussian soldier August de Marle, and after that, it was rumored that he took the place of Lucius Thruston in La Tules's affections, and in her bed.[37]

By the spring of 1847, Gertrudis Barceló had successfully brokered a future for herself and her family and a new role in Santa Fe society. This was entirely due to her ability to assess the rapidly changing geopolitics of Nuevo México. The American occupiers became her friends, lovers, and customers. She passed on information to them, and they, in turn, gambled at her monte tables and protected her interests. The only event to mar what was a triumphant period for Gertrudis Barceló was the death of her granddaughter, who was only five years old.[38] But there was reason to celebrate life amid that sorrow: soon after the funeral, Barceló's daughter Refugio gave birth to another daughter, Delfinea.[39]

The U.S. Army established a tenuous hold on Nuevo México, and the other campaigns that President Polk had set in motion were similarly successful. General Kearny had arrived in southern California and met some resistance from Mexican troops but ultimately took control of the region. Frémont's "Bear Flags" were still flapping in the breeze in the northern part of the province. The soldiers Polk had sent with Zachary Taylor into Texas crossed into Mexico and won a series of battles south of the Rio Grande. And in March 1847, General Winfield Scott brought soldiers by sea to the port of Veracruz and took that city after a three-week siege. Six months later, Scott's army marched on to Mexico City and occupied it.

In February 1848, more than 1,400 miles southeast of Santa Fe, four men—three Mexicans and one American—took up their pens and ink in the sanctuary of a sixteenth-century basilica. On this spot, Our Lady of Guadalupe had appeared to an Indigenous man and instructed him to build a church there. The structure was imposing, with two high towers on either side of the entry and a golden dome that soared above the center of the nave. As the men signed the document laid out for them, one of the Mexicans turned to the American.

"This must be a proud moment for you," the man said. He was one of three commissioners negotiating the end of the Mexican-American War. "We are making peace," replied Nicholas Trist, the American diplomatic envoy. "Let that be our only thought."[40]

After they had all signed, a clerk took the document and gave it to a messenger, who began a seventeen-day journey to present it to President Polk in Washington, D.C. The signing of the Treaty of Guadalupe Hidalgo was a watershed moment for both Mexico and the United States. Mexico lost Texas, Nuevo México, and California—more than 500,000 square miles of land—to its northern neighbor. In return, they received $15 million and several unfulfilled promises regarding protection against Indigenous enemies, recognition of Mexican land grant rights, and citizenship for Mexican residents of the new American territories.[41]

When the U.S. Congress ratified the treaty a month later, on March 10, 1848, the borders of the United States now extended from the Pacific to the Atlantic. All the continent's major mountain ranges and river systems were in American hands. And Gertrudis Barceló, who had already built a life on the choices that she and her family had made, was no longer a Mexican Northerner. She was now, by treaty, an American Westerner.

PART III
A GOOD TIME TO BE IN THE PICK AND SHOVEL BUSINESS

CHAPTER 11

A week before the signing of the Treaty of Guadalupe Hidalgo, a carpenter named James Marshall walked along the banks of the American River in northern California. He had temporarily dammed the river, hoping to use the force of its water to wash the dirt from the sawmill he was building for John Sutter. Marshall looked down at the exposed riverbank and saw flecks of gold glinting in the sun. He immediately sent samples to the governor of California in Monterey to stake the claim. After that, the news began to spread. There was gold in the Sierra Nevada Mountains, and any man with a pan or a pickax could strike it rich there.[1]

That summer, Jim Beckwourth was continuing his work for the U.S. Army, carrying dispatches between Fort Leavenworth and New Mexico. Some of the messages Beckwourth carried were bound for California and when the gold strike rumors reached Santa Fe, he decided that he would take them all the way himself.

Within days, Beckwourth left Santa Fe with a group of fifteen men. He was acting as both a courier and an escort for a lawyer bound for Oregon, appointed by President Polk to be a judge in that territory's supreme court. Presidential appointments were one way for federal politicians to control the political future of the American West. With friendly governors, judges, and other civil officials installed across the region, the party that held the White House could exert power and court future voters thousands of miles from Washington, D.C.

Beckwourth's group set out on the Spanish Trail to Los Angeles, a road used by Indigenous, Spanish, and Mexican traders and raiders to transport mules, horses, and enslaved Navajo, Apache, and Paiute women and children back and forth between Santa Fe and Los Angeles.[2] They made good time, covering more than eight hundred miles in a little more than a month. As they moved west, the news of Marshall's discovery moved east.

After Marshall filed his claim, California's territorial governor sent a letter to President Polk and enclosed a few samples of gold from Sutter's Mill. It took several months to arrive in the nation's capital, stuffed into a mailbag placed on board a ship that traveled down the Pacific coast, then on mules to cross the Isthmus of Panama, then on another ship sailing from the Gulf of Mexico to the Chesapeake Bay. By that time, many Californio and Anglo residents had already left for the Sierra Nevada Mountains.[3]

Most newspaper editors scoffed at the reports on Sutter's Mill and published only brief notices. It was President Polk himself who confirmed the rumors in his fourth and final annual address to Congress, in December 1848. First, he detailed the astonishing changes in American geography during his first (and only) administration. "Within less than four years the annexation of Texas to the Union has been consummated," Polk bragged, "all conflicting title to the Oregon Territory south of the forty-ninth degree of north latitude, being all that was insisted on by any of my predecessors, has been adjusted, and New Mexico and Upper California have been acquired by treaty." The United States had obtained more than one million square miles of land, a larger territory than the Louisiana Purchase, "a country more than half as large as all that which was held by the United States before their acquisition."[4] Then Polk dropped the bombshell.

"It was known that mines of the precious metals existed to a considerable extent in California," he wrote. "Recent discoveries render it probable that these mines are more extensive and valuable than was anticipated." The gold strike at Sutter's Mill had been confirmed as legitimate, and miners were already in the diggings. "The explorations [have shown] that the supply is very large and that gold is found at various places in an extensive district of country."[5]

When the president's address was reprinted in newspapers across the nation, it caused a sensation. It also prompted a massive migration that changed the population demographics, transformed the economy, and altered natural environments across the West. Hundreds of thousands of Americans, as well as prospectors from Mexico, Hawai'i, Chile, Peru, France, and Australia, packed their bags. Most Americans coming from the east traveled to California overland on a trail that extended more than two thousand miles from the Missouri River to Sutter's Mill. Most did not arrive until the late summer or fall of 1849. By that time, Jim Beckwourth had been in the diggings for six months.

Beckwourth had not gone there directly. After delivering his dispatches to the U.S. Army headquarters in the coastal town of Monterey, he spent the next few months (and most of his money) rambling through the area. When he needed cash, he found work riding between Monterey and a ranch more than 150 miles south. There, he handed off packets of mail and U.S. Army dispatches to a rider from Los Angeles and collected others to carry back.[6] In the spring of 1849, Beckwourth and a group of fifteen others stepped on board the steamship *California*, which was heading north to San Francisco.[7]

From that port, they made their way to Stockton, a town along the San Joaquin River in the Central Valley, eighty miles east of San Francisco. It was the gateway to the mining camps of the southern Sierras, a place to spend the night, buy supplies, and throw back a few shots of whiskey at any number of saloons. Beckwourth bought clothing and other goods there, and then he and a business partner continued eastward. They went to Sonora, a mining town founded by experienced Mexican prospectors that was already one of the largest and most productive gold camps in the region. In a matter of hours, Beckwourth sold all his goods at exorbitant prices and sent his partner back to Stockton to buy more.[8]

Business boomed, and soon Beckwourth replaced his tent with a house built of wooden boards, and a corral. He also hired Miwok men to go out into the hills and prospect, stake claims, dig, and pan for gold. In exchange for housing and tools, the Miwok men gave him half of their earnings.[9]

By the fall of 1849, there were more than ten thousand Mexican and Californio miners in the Sonora diggings, laboring alongside four thousand Americans and Europeans.[10] All of them were hoping to make their fortune. In reality, it was hard work to make even a few dollars a day by digging gold out of the ground in the Sierras. Miners stood in frigid mountain waters, panning thousands of pounds of dirt, sand, and gravel for months on end, sifting out the gold dust and small nuggets. If granite outcroppings in gullies and narrow canyons showed "signs of color," the men built wooden structures to funnel river water down the banks. The force of the water would scour the banks and bring the gold to the miners.

This was the first phase of prospecting, known as placer mining. It did not require much capital, just a pickax and shovel and some construction tools. At a certain point, however, gold mining would become impossible for individual prospectors. Mining companies with the money and technologies to dig deep shafts in the earth and pound the rock into dust would replace them.[11]

Within a few months of his arrival in Sonora, Beckwourth was, as usual, feeling restless. After selling his part of the business to his partner for $6,000, he threw a poncho over his shoulder, donned a slouchy hat, and mounted a gray horse. He rode to Murderer's Bar, a camp on the American River upstream from Sutter's Mill.[12]

Murderer's Bar came by its name honestly. The previous spring, seven men from Oregon had arrived at Sutter's Mill, stopped for provisions, then rode up the north fork of the American River. Soon they came upon an Indigenous rancheria, with good pasturage and a small house. The men found several Nisenan women there, whom they backed into a corner and attempted to rape. The women's screams brought their men to the house; the Oregon miners drew their revolvers and shot down three of them.

The Oregonians fled north. After setting up a temporary camp, two of them went out prospecting into the hills. When they returned, they found the dead bodies of the men they had left behind. Outraged, they headed to the small town of Coloma and raised a posse to seek their revenge. They were persuaded by other posse members to go to Sutter's Mill and attack the Miwok men who were working for James Marshall instead of the Nisenan men who had murdered their friends. "There was not the shadow of justification for the atrocious deed," Marshall's biographer later wrote, "for the whole of the slaughtered men were constantly employed as mill-hands by Marshall and his partners, and therefore could not have had anything to do with the killing of the white men at Murderer's Bar."[13]

Beckwourth was likely not surprised to hear this story. Alta California in 1849 was a place of chaotic violence. Since the end of the Mexican-American War, six different military leaders had overseen the territory, and the provisional government had not held any sanctioned elections. Miners and town residents created their own laws and tried and executed thieves and murderers on the spot. It was usually only the fear of this "lynch law" that kept criminals in check.[14] Many crimes went unpunished, however, particularly if the victim was an Indigenous person or one of the enslaved Black men and women whom some migrants from the South brought with them to the gold mines.

California was still in political limbo because the U.S. Congress was fractured by debates over the expansion of slavery into the Mexican cession lands. Southern and northern Democrats argued that slave owners should be able to move to California and New Mexico with all their property, including the men and women they enslaved. Antislavery Whigs and Democrats, who joined together to create the Free-Soil Party after the signing of the Treaty of Guadalupe Hidalgo, argued that slavery should be excluded from all federal territories, which would include the Mexican cession. The congressional fight that ensued delayed the passage of legislation providing for the new territories' governance and prevented appointments of federal officials to oversee government transitions.[15]

"At this time society in California," Beckwourth judged, "was in the worst condition to be found, probably, in any part of the world."[16]

For Beckwourth, the chaos was double-edged. It made life dangerous for anyone like him who lived a life out on the road. But it also provided him with opportunities. California did not yet have a legislature to pass Black codes. The gold camps were, for the moment, open to anyone who could get there. The lack of social order in such places often allowed Black men and women to establish themselves and succeed, at least in the short term.[17] Beckwourth was a man who thrived in these kinds of conditions. A life of calm did not appeal to him at all.

When Beckwourth arrived in Murderer's Bar, the camp was a mass of white tents clustered along the edges of the American River, housing more than two hundred men. Some of the miners were waist-deep in holes on the hillsides, throwing dirt out like they were digging their own graves. Others crouched on the riverbanks, washing gravel in tin pans. Small groups were partially submerged in the river itself, building a dam that would turn the water's course to the side, exposing the gravel bed below and drying it out to make placer mining easier.[18]

The miners in California did not hesitate to overhaul nature to meet their own needs. They believed that the natural resources of the mountains were theirs for the taking. They did not consider the potential costs of diverting the river's water or how their use of quicksilver (mercury) to process the gold they found might slip through their sluices and poison the river's fish or their fellow residents at Murderer's Bar. They thought only of gold and of the changes that striking a rich vein would bring to their lives.[19]

Beckwourth walked into the village of tents, looking for the business district. There he found—much to his surprise—Jean-Baptiste Charbonneau, whom he had first met at Vasquez Fort and who had arrived in California with the Mormon Battalion two years before.[20] As a reward for his work for the U.S. Army, Charbonneau had been appointed the alcalde (mayor) of Mission San Luis Rey, between San Diego and Los Angeles. That appointment was short-lived, however, because Sacajawea's son had proven too kind and flexible in his treatment of the Kumeyaay and Luiseño peoples who lived and labored there. When he heard about the gold strikes in northern California, Charbonneau was one of the first to arrive on the north fork of the American River. He had been prospecting and working as a mail carrier ever since.[21]

Charbonneau had a small house on the main road, and Beckwourth found this convenient for his own purposes. "[I] staid with him," he noted, "until the rainy season set in."[22]

While Beckwourth and Charbonneau set up housekeeping in the gold fields, a group of thirty-eight men met in the second story of a schoolhouse in Monterey. Ten of them were Californios, and the rest were Anglos, and most hailed from districts in northern California. They were seated at long tables in one half of the room while spectators observed from the other half. Someone distributed copies of the constitution of the state of Iowa, which had been admitted to the Union in 1846. They would use it as a model as they hammered out the details of the California constitution.[23]

The delegates agreed on most matters and passed a measure outlawing slavery. But they hotly debated two topics: the eastern boundary of the proposed state of California and the civil rights of Black and Indigenous Californians. On the first issue, they reached a compromise: the border would lie between the Sierras and the Rocky Mountains so it would not encroach upon the land claims of the Mormons, who had arrived around the Great Salt Lake in 1847 and established the giant territory of "Deseret" across much of the Great Basin. They also wanted to keep the size of the state reasonable for governing purposes.[24]

On the second issue, the delegates argued about whether they should restrict the immigration of Black Americans into the state. There were already almost one thousand Black men and women in residence, including Jim Beckwourth. Most of them, unlike Beckwourth, were enslaved. They came to the state with their enslavers, who hoped to buy up huge tracts of land in the fertile valleys of California and extend the South's empire of slavery to the Pacific.[25]

The delegates who originally hailed from the South argued against restrictions, hoping to bring more of their fellow enslavers to California. The delegates who considered themselves antislavery but could not endorse racial equality thought migration restriction seemed a good compromise.[26] In the end, the measure did not pass. But another article did, despite vociferous objections from a handful of Californio and Anglo delegates: a law that disfranchised Black and Indigenous men. That the first constitution of California denied the vote to non-whites was indicative of the power of racism and of the frontier myth in American culture by 1849. The beliefs it disseminated resulted in the separation of Black and Indigenous people from the body politic.[27]

By mid-October 1849, the constitution was finalized and signed. The Army fired salutes from their cannons in Monterey, and there were impromptu celebrations. On November 13, 1849, more than twelve thousand men voted to approve the constitution and forward it to Washington, D.C., as part of California's application to join the Union as the nation's thirty-first state. It is unclear if the copies of the constitution and the ballots reached the miners at Murderer's Bar. If residents had voted in that mining town, Jim Beckwourth and Jean-Baptiste Charbonneau would not have been allowed to cast their ballots.[28]

California was officially a free territory and would soon be a free state. There had been an opportunity in this moment to write racial equality and full citizenship for all comers into the constitution and set a precedent for the other territories that would ask to join the Union in the 1850s. But the white Americans who migrated to California had already bought into the frontier myth and the power it promised them in society. They would not let Indigenous peoples or free Black men like Jim Beckwourth stand in their way. From this point on, people of color found it more and more difficult to claim the freedoms that the American frontier had seemed to promise.

CHAPTER 12

The California gold rush had not yet brought a stream of Anglo migrants into Santa Fe, but the demographic shift that resulted from it was powerful, changing the nature of cities and towns across the region. Anglo-American men were buying up lands in northern New Mexico and starting businesses to exploit the rising tide of American migration through the territory in the wake of the Mexican-American War. To the Anglo-Americans, the Hispanos who had helped them establish their foothold in New Mexico Territory ceased to be allies by 1849. They were now competitors.[1]

Gertrudis Barceló's influence in the city began to wane, but she did what she could to retain her status. She ran her sala. She invested in land and mules. And she loaned people money. Most of her debtors were Anglos like George Coulter, owner of the U.S. Hotel off the plaza, who had come to her in 1848 asking to borrow a substantial sum. When she gave him $500, he signed a promissory note agreeing to pay the amount back in full plus 2 percent interest within a month. When he did not make his payment, Barceló filed suit against him. His lawyers requested a continuance; Coulter, like Jim Beckwourth, had gone to California chasing dreams of gold.

When court finally convened to consider the matter, the Santa Fe jury, now made up mostly of Anglos rather than Hispano citizens, could not decide how much Coulter owed. Barceló believed that Coulter's allies had an undue influence on the jurors. So she made a request of the court. "I wish to change the venue [of this suit]," she declared, "because the public mind in this county is so prejudiced against me that I cannot have a fair trial in the county of Santa Fe." Two days later, the court granted Barceló's request.[2]

While she waited for the trial to begin, Barceló returned to her family and her sala. Over the winter, a merchant who was looking after Coulter's business concerns at the U.S. Hotel while he was in California came to see Barceló with a proposition. Barceló and her lover, Auguste de Marle, would set up tables and deal monte at the hotel. He would pay them $200 up front, and they would deal at the hotel rent-free until Coulter's debt was paid. At first Barceló refused.

"I will not deal monte in that house," she retorted, "while Coulter continues to owe me the debt."[3] After some discussion with de Marle, however, she agreed. The hotel would become a second location of her gambling enterprise. The guests staying there would not be able to resist making a bet if she was right there in the lobby, turning cards. In January 1850, Barceló and de Marle set up their tables and dealt hundreds of games at the U.S. Hotel, taking money from Anglo and Hispano gamblers alike.

One night, Gertrudis and Auguste walked over to the hotel from the sala, as usual. They set up their tables, and a few guests began to wander by. They laid down their bets and some of them won. But most of them lost. It was nearing the end of the night, and Gertrudis was satisfied. They had done well, and this arrangement with Coulter seemed to be working out for them. At his table, de Marle dealt the fifth card of a final game and began to sweep Mexican and American coins on the table into his dealer's bag. One of the gamblers who had lost grew agitated, demanding a loan from de Marle to continue playing. When de Marle refused, the man pulled out a gun and began shooting. Barceló flipped her table on its side and dove behind it, taking shelter until several citizens subdued the shooter. While U.S. Army officers dragged him to the city jail, Barceló and de Marle packed up their tables and went back to her sala. The deal with the merchant—and through him, Coulter—was off.[4]

In the spring of 1850, when the court convened in a different location to decide the case of *Barceló v. Coulter*, the Hispano-dominated jury found in favor of Gertrudis Barceló. They awarded her $257, the balance of the debt that Coulter owed her.[5] She was not in the courtroom to savor her victory, however. She was not feeling well, and consultations with a physician had not determined what ailed her.

Two months later, Gertrudis Barceló walked into the office of James Giddings, a trader from Kentucky who was the clerk of Santa Fe's probate court. He was also her son-in-law; he had married her niece Petra (whom Gertrudis had adopted as her daughter) in 1842.[6] Barceló began to speak in Spanish while Giddings translated, and the lawyer who had represented her in her suit against Coulter transcribed her words into English.

"First, I declare and state I am entirely free from debt," Barceló said, "and that the property of every kind that I am about to dispose of has been accumulated by my own labor and exertions."

Barceló had single-handedly built her gambling empire since those first days at the rickety tables in Real de Dolores in the 1820s, and she had always managed her own finances. She wanted to make sure that her family members—particularly the women—benefited from her achievements. To her sister Maria de la Luz, she left most of her estate: the house in which she and de Marle resided (where she was also boarding several U.S. Army officers) and the land it sat on, as well as her carriage, jewelry, household furniture, and half of her herd of mules. The other half went to Barceló's brother Trinidad.

Maria de la Luz and Trinidad, as well as Barceló's daughter Refugio, would receive equal shares of the money in her accounts and any debts still owed to her. To Petra's thirteen-year-old daughter Rallitos (whom Giddings had adopted), Barceló left her gambling sala. Refugio's daughter Delfinea would receive another house Barceló had acquired west of Santa Fe and its lands.[7]

While Barceló waited for Giddings to prepare her will, Congress argued about whether New Mexico should enter the Union as a free state, along with California. The admission of these two states would disrupt the balance of power in Congress and tip it away from proslavery Southerners. Southern Democrats were desperate for control of the Senate so that they could continue to pass proslavery legislation or at least prevent Free Soilers in the House of Representatives from passing abolitionist laws. The initial efforts at compromise failed, and ultimately Congress had to pass three separate acts to make Northerners and Southerners happy, or at least equally disgruntled.

These acts, collectively known as the Compromise of 1850, brought New Mexico and Utah in as territories. Federal politicians saw both places as problematic, given the number of Hispano residents in New Mexico and the common practice of polygamy in Mormon Utah. Nevertheless, these residents would have "popular sovereignty," the right to determine whether their territories would allow slavery or abolish it, by a vote of the people. Congress also admitted California as a free state under the constitution negotiated in Monterey and outlawed the slave trade (though not slavery itself) in Washington, D.C. They also passed a newer and stronger Fugitive Slave Act, which meant that any enslaved person escaping to California (or any other free state or territory) had to be returned to her or his enslaver.

New Mexico's new territorial status did not make much of a difference in Gertrudis Barceló's life. She continued to deal monte, gather with her family and Santa Fe officials, and initiate more legal tussles with debtors. In late October 1850, when her will was ready, Barceló went back to Giddings's office. Seven men joined her there. After Barceló signed the will, a group that included her physician, the governor of New Mexico Territory, and a prominent Hispano merchant added their signatures. When they were done, Giddings stamped and sealed the will, and it was published and declared according to the law.[8]

That Barceló took such measures was not unusual in New Mexico. Most wealthy Hispanas drew up wills to distribute their property after death—although they usually signed their wills and had them witnessed by female friends and relatives. By inviting some of New Mexico's most powerful men to be the witnesses to her last will and testament, Gertrudis Barceló once again made her own way and diverged from tradition. She also established that she still had power and status in Santa Fe.

By Christmas 1851, Barceló's health had deteriorated to the point that she and her family knew the end was near. The specifics of her will suggested everything that she had valued in life: her family, her business, and her wealth. The Mexican War for Independence that had prompted her family's migration to Nuevo México had given her rights and freedoms that American women could only imagine in the mid-nineteenth century. It changed the trajectory of her life and gave her the opportunity to gain an unusual amount of cultural and social power.

An independent Mexico had also become alluring to expansionist Americans, and Barceló exploited this change for her own gain. As the war came to Santa Fe and Nuevo México, Gertrudis had tried to control the game. She used her talents to manipulate the men around her and protect her family. And her actions helped pave the way for American occupation and settlement of New Mexico Territory.[9] She had a canny ability to recognize when and where power was shifting, and this skill helped her succeed in a complicated geopolitical world.

When she realized that her days were near an end, Barceló initially refused to confess her sins, believing that God would welcome her into heaven regardless. After the New Year, she relented, and a priest arrived to bestow the final rites: confession, an anointment with oil, and a final Communion. On January 17, 1852, María Gertrudis Barceló, the "notorious gambler" and "supreme queen of refinement and fashion," died in her home in Santa Fe.[10]

True to her character, Barceló planned every detail of her own funeral. Her coffin was "richly bound and lined, and draped with costly silk," one American resident of Santa Fe reported. A group of priests dressed in gold and lace accompanied the coffin in a procession from her house to the Parroquia church on the other side of the plaza. Chanters followed, swinging their censers. A huge crowd walked behind, all of them holding lit wax candles. "The whole form[ed] a galaxy," an observer noted, "which at night would have made a very imposing illumination." When they reached the church, Archbishop Jean-Baptiste Lamy led the funeral service in a nave draped with white and black silk and illuminated with yet more candles. At her request, Barceló's body was interred in a side chapel next to her granddaughter, Maria Rosa.[11]

To many Anglo-Americans, Barceló's funeral was scandalous, because of "all that pomp and ceremony with which ill-gotten wealth delights to gild its obsequies." Barceló reportedly paid more than $2,000 for the event, more than a farm laborer in California earned in four years of work.[12] To the Hispano residents of Santa Fe, who pressed into the streets and the church to witness the funeral, it was an appropriate celebration of a woman whose keen business sense made her the wealthiest woman in New Mexico Territory and one of the most well-known residents of the Mexican North and the American West.

For all New Mexicans, the year of Barceló's death was a transformative moment. In the wake of the Mexican-American War and the California gold rush, Americans became increasingly dominant in civil, political, and economic life in the territory. The cross-cultural alliances that characterized early encounters between Hispanos and Anglos were less common. Hispanas lost much of the power they had and were relegated to domestic and agricultural work. They lost the property rights they had under Spanish and then Mexican laws and had fewer legal options if they needed to leave a bad marriage. Local power shifted from brokers who could navigate multiple worlds toward Anglo merchants and civil officials, whose power rested in their whiteness.[13]

One month after Barceló died, her granddaughter Rallitos married Lorenzo Labadie, a Hispano farmer and future federal Indian agent whose French grandfather had come to New Mexico to work as a physician.[14] Rallitos was young—a teenager, still—and the couple needed money to begin their life together. So they sold Barceló's sala.

"The office of the *Santa Fe Weekly Gazette* has been removed," the city's year-old newspaper announced to its readers in November 1852, "to the house formerly occupied by the late Gertrude Barceló."[15] And so the sound of the printing press and the smell of hot metal and fresh ink replaced the slap of the cards and the cheers and moans of gambling patrons off Burro Alley. Barceló would have been chagrined to see her family members abandon the business that had made her so wealthy and famous. But she may have appreciated the motto of the paper that replaced her sala in Santa Fe: "Independent in all things, neutral in nothing."[16]

CHAPTER 13

Three months after Gertrudis Barceló's funeral in Santa Fe, the *New York Times* reported on her death, noting that she was "known to all Americans who have known any-thing of New Mexico for the last quarter of a century."[1] She was one of the few women in a growing group of famous Westerners; most of them were frontier scouts and "mountain men" like Kit Carson and Jim Bridger. This group would soon include Jim Beckwourth.

Jim had left Jean-Baptiste Charbonneau's house in the Murderer's Bar mining camp after only a year and prospected his way northeast until he happened upon a valley in northern California, "already robed in freshest verdure, contrasting most delightfully with the huge snow-clad masses of rock we had just left." A series of streams ran through it, all of them tributaries of the Feather River. The vast, bright green plain was an extensive stretch of freshwater marsh that attracted flocks of large sandhill cranes, their foreheads a vivid red against their white heads and necks. Herds of deer and antelope grazed on the valley floor.[2]

Beckwourth built a cabin for himself in the northeast end of the valley, and during his explorations of the area, he saw there was a gap in the mountains to the east, where the "rain shadow" of the Sierras marked a transitional zone between the lush valley and the high deserts of the Great Basin and Salt Lake City far beyond.[3] He knew that, despite the dangers, white emigrants would continue crossing those deserts to reach

California. Without any experience as an engineer, Beckwourth began building a wagon road over the pass. It was little more than a mile long and the grade was not severe, but it took him several months to complete the trail, and then several weeks to recover his health.

He took the first few wagon trains over the pass from the east, and it did not take long for word of this new trail to spread. Soon, Beckwourth watched wagon trains wind their way down to the bright green marshlands from his cabin's porch. The emigrants arrived exhausted and half-starved. They asked Beckwourth to let their oxen and horses loose in lands around his house, to feast on the red and white clovers waving in the breeze. They offered some of their meager domestic goods in exchange for the cabbages, turnips, and radishes growing in his kitchen garden. Although Beckwourth did not have much to spare—he had spent more than $1,500 of his own money on the migrant road's construction—he did not deny them.

"They were never refused what they asked for at my house," he declared.[4]

By this time, Beckwourth was starting to feel every one of his fifty-six years, although his body was still strong and muscular. He had traded in his trapper deerskins, poncho, and slouchy hat for the "civilized" clothes of a respectable gentleman. Under his shirt, however, Beckwourth still wore a thread of sinew. A perforated bullet hung from it, with two oblong beads on either side. He had salvaged the bullet from a Blackfoot battlefield during his "Indian life" with the Apsáalooke in the 1830s; it hit a dagger he was wearing instead of puncturing his skin, but the impact of the shot knocked him out. When he revived with no visible wound, the Apsáalooke believed that his "medicine" was infallible. Beckwourth had worn the bullet as an amulet ever since.[5]

Life was relatively quiet in what was sometimes known as Beckwourth Valley, despite the stream of travelers moving both west and east along his road. The racially restrictive laws that the California legislature had passed did not seem to touch Beckwourth here. He hunted for deer, rabbits, sage hens, and grouse and fetched his water from the marshes. His closest neighbors were four miles away. This was a relief, as it meant that "social broils" in the mountains of northern California did not often disturb him.[6]

Some of these fights originated in local feuds. Others were sparked by intense disagreements that continued to tear America apart in the early 1850s. Several of Beckwourth's neighbors argued on behalf of the southern states, advocating for the continued legalization of slavery and the congressional balance of power among all the states. Others pointed out that many white migrants had come to California looking for land they could buy and work as free laborers. They did not want to compete with slave owners or their enslaved workers.

In 1853, emigrants brought news to Beckwourth Valley of the congressional fight over the route for a transcontinental railroad, which would span the Louisiana Purchase and the Mexican cession lands. Sectional rancor defined the debates about where to lay the track: northern politicians argued for a line from Chicago to San Francisco, while southern politicians pushed for a southern route from Missouri to Los Angeles. To determine the feasibility of the possible routes, Congress dispatched four exploration teams made up of soldiers, surveyors, scientists, and artists. These railroad surveys and their thirteen volumes of descriptions, data, and visual images of the American West introduced many Americans to these lands. They also exacerbated tensions between Northerners and Southerners over who would control the West.[7]

If the transcontinental railroad followed the central route, the state of Illinois would benefit economically and politically as the eastern terminus. Illinois's Democratic senator Stephen Douglas needed his southern colleagues to help him push through a vote for the central route. But he had to give them something in return. In December 1853, when a bill was introduced in the Senate to create a new territory of Nebraska out of Louisiana Purchase lands, Douglas recognized his opportunity.

In January 1854, Douglas proposed a new bill to create two territories instead of one. In their constitutional conventions, the American men who settled in Kansas and Nebraska would exercise popular sovereignty, voting whether to allow slavery within their borders. Southerners were satisfied with this plan, but Northerners were outraged because this legislation meant that if the voters of Nebraska so chose, they could legalize slavery north of the Mason-Dixon Line.

To convince his fellow legislators to pass the bill, Douglas argued that it was incumbent upon Congress to organize the lands of the Louisiana

Purchase and the Mexican cession. If they did not, the entire West would become as lawless as California had been before its admittance into the Union.

"How long could you have postponed action with safety?" he asked his colleagues. "Do you suppose that you could keep that vast country a howling wilderness in all time to come, roamed over by hostile savages, cutting off all safe communication between our Atlantic and Pacific possessions?" By this time, Douglas and most white Americans believed in the ideology of Manifest Destiny and the important role that the West would play in the nation's future. "You cannot fix the bounds to the onward march of this great and growing country," Douglas argued. "You cannot fetter the limbs of the young giant. He will burst all your chains."[8]

Five months later, a majority in the Senate supported Douglas's plan and passed the Kansas-Nebraska Act.[9] The matter of the transcontinental route, however, would have to wait. Even with southern Senators on his side, Douglas could not bring a transcontinental railroad act to the floor. There was too much division and rancor in both houses of Congress. And while the Kansas-Nebraska Act may have appealed to many Americans who embraced the federal conquest of the West, the provision regarding popular sovereignty rang national alarm bells.

"The proposition to repeal the Missouri Compromise," the Black abolitionist Frederick Douglass told a crowd in Chicago a few months later, "was a stunning one. It fell upon the nation like a bolt from a cloudless sky."[10] Kansas and Nebraska, the eastern edge of the American West, would now be the crucible that determined whether the Mason-Dixon Line would hold.[11] If it did not, this meant that California—where Jim Beckwourth had just built himself a house in a valley he loved—could conceivably become a slave state.

The next winter, as snowstorms began to roll into the valley from the west, Jim Beckwourth had a visit from Thomas D. Bonner, an itinerant justice of the peace. Bonner hailed from western Massachusetts and had spent most of his life as a newspaper editor, publishing tracts advocating for temperance and giving lectures on the New England lyceum circuit.

He came to California at the same time Beckwourth did and in 1852 was elected in Butte County to hear civil cases and hand down sentences for petty crimes and misdemeanors. What qualified him for this job, no one knew.[12]

Beckwourth first met Bonner at a mining camp on the Feather River. The two men got along well, and Beckwourth often invited Bonner up to his cabin for evenings of drinking and conversation.[13] The justice of the peace had clearly given up his temperate ways. He was also curious about Beckwourth's past and astonished to learn that he had been involved in so many of the century's momentous events: the fur trade of the 1820s and '30s, the Mexican-American War, the California gold rush. Beckwourth had known some of the most famous men in the West like William Ashley, Kit Carson, and Jim Bridger. Most amazing to Bonner, however, were Beckwourth's stories about the ten years he spent with the Apsáalooke. The idea of a man leaving the crowded settlements of the East for so long and "domiciliated among the wild beasts and wilder savages" captivated Bonner.[14]

The "white man gone Native" had been a central figure in a growing American fictional literature for almost seventy years. Daniel Boone became famous after dictating his own life story to the writer John Filson, who published the Kentucky explorer's autobiography in 1784. And Natty Bumppo, the hero frontiersman of James Fenimore Cooper's five Leatherstocking Tales (1823–1841), inhabited an interstitial space on the frontier: not quite settler, not quite Indigenous, but somehow embodying the best of both worlds.[15]

Bonner believed that he and Beckwourth could make some money from a book about the old trader's life, especially one that emphasized his time living with the Apsáalooke. Americans had been clamoring for stories of the American West since the newspaper accounts of the Lewis and Clark expedition and John C. Frémont's reports, and the nationwide dissemination of an interview with Kit Carson in the early 1850s. Carson became the star of several cheap "dime novels," including Charles E. Averill's *Kit Carson, the Prince of the Gold Hunters*. These and other narratives had white male protagonists like Carson, intrepid pioneers and frontiersmen, battling Indigenous people for supremacy in the vast expanses of the West, which was a landscape made for storytelling.[16]

Even with these tales in circulation, there was a relative dearth of literature about the Indigenous peoples in America. Most journalists and writers lived east of the Mississippi and rarely ventured from their homes. "No one who could wield the pen had banished himself for years among our savage tribes," a writer for *Harper's Monthly* complained, "and thus been enabled to learn the truth regarding the habits and customs of these children of the forest."[17] Beckwourth's story, then, could shade from autobiography to ethnography, from a daring adventure story ranging across the American West to a detailed and instructive study of Indigenous life.[18]

Bonner wrote up a contract, and in it Beckwourth agreed "to relate in person to T.D. Bonner, a history of my life and adventures as a 'Mountaineer'" in addition to his experiences in the Mexican-American War and as a forty-niner in California. He would also relate his life "among all the tribes of Indians in North America according to the best of my recollections." For his part, Bonner would "faithfully and truly record in writing all the incidents which the said Beckwith [*sic*] may relate in plain hand" and prepare the text "for the press according to the best of my abilities." In addition, a man from west of the valley named Joseph Davis would give them $200 to buy paper and ink (and perhaps some rum and whiskey) and then would help with getting the book ready for market. The three men would share the copyright and the profits.[19] Beckwourth signed the contract, and Bonner rode off to the county courthouse to file it with the clerk.[20]

Over the next few months, Beckwourth dictated what would become a published autobiography of more than five hundred pages. He briefly described his early life in Virginia and St Louis. Prompted by Bonner's questions—or perhaps because this time in his life loomed large in his memory—Beckwourth talked mostly about his time with the Apsáalooke. Anticipating that this section of the autobiography might be too much to be believed, Bonner promised readers in his preface that every story that appeared in the ensuing pages was the truth.

"The author has in no instance departed from the story of the narrator," the former journalist insisted, "but it was taken down literally as it was from day to day related."[21] Readers might find the dates a little fuzzy, Bonner admitted, but that was only because Beckwourth, like so many other fur trappers and traders in his day, did not keep a journal that he could reference. And of course, an account of more than fifty years of one's life was bound to contain a few misremembered or even invented moments. Autobiography, after all, was both a historical and a literary act. Then there was the fact that many Americans believed trappers and mountain men to be inveterate liars. They often relayed tales about grizzly bear fights and perilous river crossings around the campfire, and exaggeration was one of their storytelling tools.

Bonner was adamant that both the larger narrative and details in the autobiography were true. Any readers who were excessively concerned with accuracy could ask Beckwourth's many friends across the West for corroboration.[22] When Beckwourth was done talking and Bonner finished writing, Bonner bundled up the papers and gave them to Davis, who shopped them around to publishers.

A few months after Beckwourth and Bonner finished the book, emigrants arriving in Beckwourth Valley relayed the news that hundreds of armed Missourians had poured over the border into Kansas Territory, intent on establishing residency and voting to legalize slavery in the first territorial election. The New England Emigrant Aid Society sent abolitionist settlers there to counter their votes.

"Civil feud, strife, and continual agitation have been the result in all communities," the Massachusetts emigrant Sara Robinson wrote. She was optimistic, however. Kansas, "with its mountains, prairies, and valleys, lying midway between the north and south, east and west, in the very heart of the United States, was never to be cursed with the blackest of all [villainies], the bitterest of all evils—human slavery."[23]

The next year, in the congressional debates over admitting the clearly riven state of Kansas to the Union, Massachusetts senator Charles Sumner gave a speech on the floor of the Senate. He castigated several of his fellow senators, including Stephen Douglas and South Carolina's Andrew Butler, for bringing "that harlot, slavery" into Kansas. Three days later, Butler's cousin Preston Brooks beat Sumner almost to death while he sat at his Senate desk, signing copies of his speech. This attack in the halls of Congress came on the heels of a proslavery attack on the free-state town of Lawrence in Kansas. Missouri men set fire to the Free State Hotel and threw the *Herald of Freedom* printing press into the Kansas River, then looted the town.[24]

During these violent attempts to determine the future of the West and of the United States, Harper & Brothers in New York City published the first edition of *The Life and Adventures of James P. Beckwourth, Mountaineer, Scout, and Pioneer, and Chief of the Crow Nation of Indians*, with twelve original illustrations, including a portrait of Beckwourth himself. Through the summer and fall of 1856, booksellers advertised the autobiography in newspapers across the nation, offering it for sale for $1.25 a copy.[25]

The response was largely positive. "A personal witness of most of the events which extended our conquests in those regions and of a restless, daring spirit himself," wrote the reviewer for the *New York Daily Herald*, "there are few careers which present so many features of interest as that of Beckwourth." The *Christian Advocate and Journal* found it "one of the best illustrations of frontier and ultra-frontier life in our literature."[26] Others were more skeptical. "Parts of the tale smack of the 'fish story,'" the Washington, D.C., *National Era* declared. "Mr. Beckwourth, or his narrator, has it all his own way, and we can fancy a lurking smile at the thought of how glibly he puts together such a discordant mass of material brought out from the storehouse of memory."[27]

Stories about Beckwourth and his book began to circulate in local and national newspapers. The most famous one involved a group of miners sending a comrade to a neighboring camp to borrow a copy of Beckwourth's autobiography. The man, who could not read, obtained a copy of the Bible by mistake. When one of the miners opened the book and began to read about Samson catching three hundred foxes, his audience listened with rapt attention. When he finished, one of the men jumped up. "One of Jim Beckwourth's lies!" he exclaimed. "It sounds adzactly [*sic*] like him!"[28]

The autobiography's fictive qualities were not its biggest problem, however, according to the *National Era*'s reviewer. He found Beckwourth's vices and violent crimes—especially those enacted while he lived with the Apsáalooke—appalling and his apologies for them insufficient. "We suspect that many of the Missouri outlaws, whose barbarities in Kansas are so well known, might find their counterpart here."[29] Despite the crudeness of these elements of the book, the reviewer at *Harper's Monthly* was elated to find in Beckwourth's book a rich and detailed account of Indigenous life in the American West.

"We have at last something really genuine about the privations of the mountaineer; something to be relied upon relating to the inner life of the savage," the reviewer wrote.[30] He recommended that the reader buy the book "to be introduced into the very arcana of the wild life of the great prairies and towering mountains of our Western world."[31] Only a man like Beckwourth could have written it, the reviewer judged. "He combines the superior intelligence of the white man (and that of a high order)," he wrote, "with the cunning of the aborigines."[32]

That the *Harper's Monthly* reviewer believed Beckwourth to be white was not an unusual response for readers of his autobiography, who did not know him personally. Because while Bonner wrote many pages describing how Beckwourth "passed" as Apsáalooke in the company of both Indigenous and white people at rendezvous and trading posts, nowhere in the book did Bonner reveal that Beckwourth's father was white and his mother was Black. This may have been because Jim did not tell him. Or it could have been that the frontier myth had already taken hold in American culture and readers thought of Kit Carson and Jim Bridger as the only "true" frontiersmen. Bonner may have thought that Americans would not believe that a biracial man could have a similar career in the West.

The twelve illustrations that Harper & Brothers commissioned to accompany the text deliberately blurred Beckwourth's racial identity. Ten of the twelve depicted his time with the Apsáalooke, where he is shown as having slightly darker skin than the white men in his midst and lighter skin than his Apsáalooke kin. The final image in the book is a portrait of Beckwourth "in Citizen's Dress"—a fitted coat, vest, and cravat. His hair is dark and curly, and he sports a goatee. His eyes are black, and his skin is pale. Most readers who looked at this image would likely assume, as the *Harper's Monthly* reviewer had, that Beckwourth was white.[33]

Because both the text and the illustrations manipulated his racial identity, Beckwourth could claim the title of "pioneer," and white readers could admire him as an agent of American conquest in the West. The publication of *The Life and Adventures of James P. Beckwourth* in 1856 was another successful moment of "translation" in Beckwourth's life. As he became a protagonist in the pages of a "Western," Beckwourth shifted from a phenotypically Black frontiersman into a white gentleman. It was a transformation that he and Bonner found useful for the purposes of selling a frontier memoir, especially in an increasingly racialized United States of America.[34]

There was one newspaper, however, whose editors called out Beckwourth for passing as white on the page. The first Black newspaper in California made a short statement in an issue published a few months after the book's release. The *Mirror of the Times*, printed in San Francisco "by an association of colored individuals," pronounced "James Beckwourth, whose life and adventures has recently appeared in print, a person of their own color."[35] Neither Bonner nor Beckwourth responded to this statement, and Beckwourth continued to obscure his racial identity on the page and in life.

Although the autobiography did well enough to be published in London and Paris, Jim Beckwourth did not receive any money from the publication, despite his contract with Bonner. For a time, he remained at his home in Beckwourth Valley, farming and guiding and greeting passers-by. In the spring of 1857, a cousin of Kit Carson's named George Jackson arrived and sat down for a chat with Beckwourth. Jackson was done with the California diggings, he told Jim, and he was going home to Missouri. He might make a stop along the way in the Rocky Mountains, however. Jackson had heard that prospectors found gold along the South Platte. Beckwourth mulled this over and told Jackson he might see him there in a year's time.[36]

It may have been the allure of gold. Or the restlessness that usually came upon Jim after living in one place for too long. There were also whispers along the Feather River that he had done something—it was not clear exactly what—to anger local vigilantes, who let it be known that they were coming for him. Whatever it was, something prompted Jim Beckwourth to think about moving on. In the early spring of 1859, Beckwourth left the little cabin in the valley that bore his name. He saddled his horse and rode east toward home.[37]

CHAPTER 14

Beckwourth's route took him over the pass he had carved out of the mountains, across the Great Basin to Salt Lake City, and through the Rockies. He passed but did not take the trail that would have led him south to the rumored gold discoveries on the South Platte. If he had taken the turnoff, Beckwourth may have been present when two miners emerged from a canyon twenty miles west of the new boomtown of Denver, covered in a layer of sleet from an April storm, bearing a bag of gold dust and nuggets.

Subsequent prospecting in what became known as Gregory Gulch revealed that the steep hillsides near the headwaters of Clear Creek were full of gold-bearing quartz. By the end of May 1859, the month-old Denver newspaper the *Rocky Mountain News* reported that "there are extensive gold washings all along the foot of the mountains which will pay from one to three dollars a day to the man, with occasional larger strikes." William Byers, the editor, mused that the news "will induce thousands of persons in the crowded East to migrate to this country with a view of making it their home."[1]

That summer, the *New York Tribune* editor Horace Greeley arrived in Denver with an entourage, interviewed miners in the gold diggings, and gave a "fine speech" in front of a crowd of two thousand men and a few women. The mineral belt was within the borders of Kansas, and Greeley urged the miners to create their own territory. Based on the gold strikes he was already seeing in Gregory Gulch, the editor believed that the miners' success was assured.²

"This district yet prospected," Greeley later wrote, must be "a mere corner of the Rocky Mountain Gold Region."³ The area was soon "crowded with canvas tents, log shanties, and bough houses, as thick as they could stand," and in Gregory Gulch alone, miners built more than one hundred sluices to funnel creek water for pan washing. The Colorado gold rush was underway.⁴

Jim Beckwourth missed the chance to go to Denver that spring, but by the fall of 1859 he was there, working once again for Louis Vasquez. The trader had bought land in Auraria, a small settlement across Cherry Creek from Denver, and Beckwourth helped Vasquez's nephew A.P. set up shop there. They unloaded supplies that would appeal to the area's migrants as winter set in: nails, window glass and dishes, candles, wool clothing, and deerskins, in addition to dried and preserved fruits, pickles, sugar and fresh flour, and—perhaps of most interest to idle miners—"Champaign & Catawba Wines."⁵

It took several days for them to unpack. Once his work was done, Beckwourth walked around the town. The most imposing building along Auraria's main road was a one-and-a-half-story storehouse with a clapboard roof and the town's only glass window. Wooten's Store was home to a New Mexico trader and his family and had quickly become a hub of the district. There was a mercantile on the ground floor and the *Rocky Mountain News* press office on the second.⁶

Beckwourth climbed the stairs, and there he found William Byers, several junior editors, and a group of local citizens. Everyone knew who he was. They invited the "celebrated mountaineer" to stay, and Beckwourth entertained them for several hours retelling the stories that some of them had read in his autobiography. It was "quite a conversation," one of the editors recorded in his diary later that night.⁷

The editors found that the sixty-two-year-old "looks scarce fifty, hale, hearty, and straight as an arrow." They were also impressed by his eloquence. "We had formed the opinion, as has, we presume, almost everyone," Byers wrote in a feature published the next week, "that Capt. Beckwourth was a rough, illiterate backwoodsman." But they were "most agreeably surprised to find him a polished gentleman, possessing a fund of general information which few can boast."[8]

Beckwourth had planned to stay for only a short time. But he liked what he saw in this "Queen City of the Plains." It was chaotic and rough enough to welcome a man like him. There were not yet restrictive racial laws (or many laws at all), and the population was still heterogenous. It was in places like this that Jim Beckwourth flourished. He bought land from Vasquez in Auraria and began to build a house.[9]

Denver and Auraria were like many of the western towns and cities Beckwourth had visited and lived in over the years: growing with unimaginable speed and full of contradictions. Most of the miners had come to the Rockies to escape from federal reach, for example, and yet they were already campaigning to separate from Kansas Territory and create the "Territory of Jefferson," named after the president who brought most of the Rocky Mountain mineral belt into the United States with the Louisiana Purchase. They elected local officials and planned to send a delegate to Congress.[10]

Depending on the time of year, Denver's streets—eighty feet wide with large, deep lots—were either jammed with miners, migrants, and businessmen or they were empty, abandoned for the diggings in the mountains. When the *Tribune* editor Horace Greeley visited, he found this constant movement in western towns to be disconcerting.

"The first circumstance that strikes a stranger traversing this wild country," he wrote, "is the vagrant instincts and habits of the great majority of its denizens." Everyone he talked to in Denver and the Rocky Mountain diggings had come there from California, Texas, Kansas, or Nebraska. Most of these people—many of them white Americans but Hispanos as well as Chinese and European immigrants—had arrived in the West in the previous thirty years, part of a migration of more than 300,000 fortune hunters to and through these high, dry lands.[11]

After only a year in existence, both Auraria and Denver were established sites of supply for the diggings in the mountains. They already had bakeries, jewelers, Masonic groups, saloons, and a Ladies Aid Society. One migrant had opened a bookstore and lending library under a cottonwood tree on the banks of Cherry Creek. "The collection of volumes was not large," a city chronicler wrote, "but it served to assist much in giving food for the mind to a community, which, then as now, contained more than an ordinary amount of literary taste."[12]

Although there were no church buildings constructed yet, there were Sunday services. "The City now seems more like a civilized community than of yore for they have meetings here now upon the Sabbath," one gold miner noted. But there was also "swearing and pistol shooting, and the hoots and yells of the meanest, and those with delirium [tremors] caused by the strychnine"—a wheat-based whiskey that Gertrudis Barceló had often served in her gambling sala, called "Taos Lightning."[13]

The drunken carousing often turned violent. Men fought one another in Auraria's gridded streets for many reasons, or sometimes for no reason at all. A few weeks before Beckwourth arrived, two Black migrants punched one another until one of them, a man named William Payne, pulled out a pistol and shot his antagonist. He was arrested, claimed self-defense, and was acquitted. At a public dinner, two elected officials argued over the language one of them used in a toast. One of them was injured in their duel the next day; he lingered for five months before dying. When a farmer arrived in Denver with a wagonload of turkeys to sell, a gang of "desperados" intercepted him and stole all his birds. A vigilance committee traded shots with them before running them out of town.[14]

"These white men are as far behind the wild Indians as the Indians are behind the white men that are supposed to be the most civilized people in the United States," one miner complained.[15]

Whether they were violent or peaceful, these newly arrived white settlers were living on Indigenous lands. The 1851 Treaty of Fort Laramie had designated the plains near Wichita, Kansas, westward to the Rocky Mountains and from the North Platte south to the Arkansas River as Cheyenne territory. The federal government had not recognized the division of this tribal nation into Northern and Southern bands in the 1830s, and Americans' general lack of knowledge complicated this and every treaty with Cheyenne peoples to come. The flood of white gold seekers into their lands disrupted the migration of buffalo herds in this region of the Great Plains and aggravated tensions with neighboring tribal nations.[16]

"I feel like prosecuting the settlers," Beckwourth told his friends at the *Rocky Mountain News*, "who are encroaching, and building cities on [the Cheyenne's] old hunting grounds."

Given that Beckwourth himself was a settler encroaching on Cheyenne lands, this statement was a bit rich. The editors, however, dismissed his concerns not because of their irony but because to them, it did not matter whether the government recognized the Northern and Southern Cheyenne as separate entities with their own territories. Their land claims did not matter at all. Like many white Americans in the 1850s, they believed that the American West belonged to whoever could develop its lands. And they knew that the U.S. government supported their right to take Indigenous lands for their own, despite treaty agreements.

"We hope [Beckwourth] may live to see a great city," the editors wrote, "where, no doubt forty years ago, he did not dream of seeing a white man, except his fellow trappers and traders."[17]

On a Friday evening in late March 1860, nine Southern Cheyenne men walked down the streets of Auraria. The residents in the town stared at them but did not bid them welcome. Nor did they invite the men into their homes for a meal. The Southern Cheyenne, offended at this lack of hospitality, returned to their camp outside the town. The next day, they found Jim Beckwourth at the Vasquez store.[18]

"We are glad to see you," one of the chiefs told Beckwourth. They recognized him from his time trading for buffalo robes at the first Fort Vasquez in the 1840s. "Although we do not like to see you among the pale faces," they added. The Southern Cheyenne saw Jim as one of them, perhaps, and not a settler who wanted to take their lands. So they described the hostility of Denver and Auraria residents, behavior that was especially galling because the Southern Cheyenne had welcomed many American travelers as they passed through their homelands on their way to the gold diggings in California and in the Rockies. "Many a pale face has been lost," one chief said, "but never has one come to a Cheyenne lodge without getting plenty to eat, and being set on the right road to his people."[19]

Beckwourth invited the men to his house, and after they ate dinner, the Southern Cheyenne chiefs asked Beckwourth if he could be their federal Indian agent, negotiating with the U.S. government on their behalf. Most Indian agents in the West were political appointees, men from the eastern states with no experience and little to no knowledge of Indigenous communities. In the Southern Cheyenne's view, Beckwourth knew them better than any randomly assigned Bureau of Indian Affairs agent could. President James Buchanan's administration was trying to get them to move to a much smaller reservation than they had agreed to in 1851, and they believed that Beckwourth could represent their interests during councils with federal officials.

The old trader thought it over.

"Return to your tribe," he responded, "and consult with them." If all the Southern Cheyenne chiefs agreed that they wanted him as their agent, "I will do all in my power to consummate your wishes," he reassured them.[20] Two weeks later, a large group of Southern Cheyenne arrived south of town, dragging their belongings on travois attached to their horses. Sixty-three lodges soon sat among the blue grama and buffalo grass. A smaller contingent visited Auraria, which had, a few weeks before, officially merged with Denver as one city. They brought their buffalo robes to trade at A. P. Vasquez & Co. and other stores.

The next night, cries and shouts went up all over the Southern Cheyenne camp. A gang of white settlers ran through and into the lodges, dragging women out and sexually assaulting them. Then they stole several mules and rode out into the prairie east of the river. A group of warriors mounted their horses and pursued. They did not catch the gang, but they did find the mules they abandoned and brought them back to camp. Once the sun rose, several Southern Cheyenne chiefs rode into Denver and met with Beckwourth.[21] They reported the attack on their camp and demanded action. They told him that they were going back to meet in a council and decide whether to launch a reprisal raid on the people of Denver.

"Make no definite conclusion," Beckwourth replied, "until I [have] a talk with the whites." He would try to convince them to convene a meeting, and he would let the Southern Cheyenne know whether "the white men of Denver [would] tolerate such inhuman and ungrateful conduct."²² The Southern Cheyenne left, and Beckwourth composed a letter, handing it off to his friends at the *Rocky Mountain News*. They published it three days later.

"Justice to the Indian and security to my fellow citizens," Beckwourth began, "compel me to seek your columns to redress one of the grossest outrages ever perpetrated in this, or any other country." Beckwourth was sure that his fellow citizens would agree to find and punish the men responsible for the assaults and thefts. If they did not, he believed, the Southern Cheyenne would retaliate.

"The Indians are as keenly sensible to acts of injustice, as they are tenacious of revenge," he wrote in his letter, "and it is more humiliating to them to be the recipients of such treatment upon *their own lands*, which they have been deprived of, their game driven off and they made to suffer by hunger, and when they pay us a visit, abused more than dogs." To avoid a war with the Southern Cheyenne (and perhaps their Northern kin and Arapaho allies as well), Beckwourth wrote, Denver's residents should chastise the white men who attacked the camp and take measures to prevent future settler misbehavior. Most of the traders and scouts with as much experience as Beckwourth had agreed that Indigenous attacks on American wagon trains and towns were never unprovoked.

"All our Indian troubles are produced by the imprudent acts of unprincipled white men," he argued.²³

Thirty years after his first journey through the American West, Beckwourth was still acting as a cultural broker, using his unique position as a trader who knew both white and Indigenous Westerners well, to negotiate a peace between them. Nine days later, Denver's white residents gathered at Apollo Hall to hear Beckwourth give a report of his investigation of the attack on the Cheyenne. Beckwourth told them that the assault survivors named one of the men but refused to identify the rest, out of fear of reprisal. Given this lack of definitive evidence regarding the perpetrators, it seemed clear that trials and convictions would be impossible. Instead, Beckwourth asked the people of Denver to adopt two resolutions, which the audience members immediately passed.

"*Resolved*, That we condemn the outrages lately perpetrated upon our Indian brethren, and pledge ourselves to bring to punishment the guilty parties, in any further insults offered them of this character. *Resolved*,

That the citizens of Denver entertain the Indians hospitably, upon their visits to our city for purposes of trade."[24]

The town meeting participants also voted to appoint Jim Beckwourth a local Indian agent for the Cheyenne until the federal appointee, Colonel A. G. Boone (Kentuckian Daniel Boone's grandson) arrived in Denver. It was a rare moment in the city's history and showed the kind of policies that white Westerners could put into place if they acted with empathy. This would not be their approach to relations with Great Plains communities for long, however.[25]

Although the editors of the *Rocky Mountain News* begrudgingly acknowledged that "degraded as the Indian is, he has rights," they were steadfast in their belief that the Cheyenne, Arapaho, and other Plains peoples were not their equals. "Since our residence in the West," they wrote after the attack on the Southern Cheyenne camp, "we have learned to appreciate and share the general aversion felt for the red man." They agreed the attack was brutal but also suggested it might be useful for Denver's white residents.

"Will the Eastern press notice this affair as fit commentary upon our disorganized condition?" they wondered.

If so, Congress might accept the proposal for territorial organization that Denver residents had sent to Washington, D.C. The territorial creation process would extinguish all Indigenous land titles, including the Cheyenne and Arapaho claims to the proposed Jefferson Territory. The U.S. Army could then expel them from their homelands, force them onto reservations, and keep settlers and Indigenous peoples separate. This, they believed, was the only effective way to protect both communities.[26]

When the Southern Cheyenne returned to their summer camp along the Arkansas River, Jim Beckwourth stayed in Denver. He was managing A. P. Vasquez & Co., and he had planted "corn, potatoes, pumpkins, melons, and a variety of vegetables" in the rich bottomland soil along a bend in the South Platte.[27] He did not labor on the Vasquez farm alone. In June 1860, Jim Beckwourth and a Black woman named Elizabeth Lettbetter walked together to the offices of a Denver lawyer and got married. The *Rocky Mountain News* published a notice, as did the *Western Mountaineer*, a newspaper published in the new mining town of Golden.

"Capt. 'Jim Beckwourth,' the celebrated ex-chief of the Crow Indians, whose name is familiar as a household word throughout the West," the *Mountaineer* declared, "has lately again put his neck into the noose matrimonial." The editors noted that Beckwourth had been married eight times before, mostly to Indigenous women. Regardless, the *Mountaineer* editors believed, "the better half the Captain has lately taken to his bosom, surpasses all the others in worth and beauty."[28]

That summer, hopeful prospectors flooded into Denver from Nebraska and Missouri, northern Mexico and New Mexico, and California. "At the rate emigrants are now pouring into that region," one Topeka, Kansas, newspaper noted, "the Territory of Jefferson will by fall contain not less than 100,000 souls."[29] Gold rushes had the power to transform societies, and the Front Range of the Rocky Mountains had already become a contested landscape. Such a large influx of white miners would push the region toward large-scale violence.

CHAPTER 15

One of the new arrivals joining Jim Beckwourth and more than thirty thousand others along the Front Range was twenty-six-year-old farmer Ovando Hollister. He had most recently lived in eastern Kansas, but he grew up in New Lebanon, New York, a Shaker community that his parents had joined when he was four years old. Shakerism had been flourishing then, part of a Protestant revival that spawned many new religions and utopian societies—including Mormonism—in New England and New York. Ovando grew up believing that each person carried the divine light of God within them, making all human beings equal. The Hollisters were therefore abolitionists and proponents of women's rights.

Shakers also thought that the millennium was imminent and that practicing celibacy would bring them closer to Christ in preparation for that fateful day. They separated boys and girls and men and women and did not allow residents to marry. Ovando grew up and was educated only with other boys, including his three brothers and several cousins. He was comfortable in this kind of world, which boded well for him in the heavily male mining camps of the Rocky Mountains.[1]

Ovando's teachers instructed him in reading, writing, and math, as well as the art and science of herbalism.[2] He had a talent for writing, but the Shakers did not have a newspaper or a printer. When his schooling ended at age fourteen, the elders sent the brown-haired, gray-eyed teenager to the fields to work as a farmer. All children who grew up in

New Lebanon had the choice to leave or remain once they turned twenty-one. In the 1850s, 87 percent of young men left the Shakers when they reached adulthood. Ovando was one of them.[3]

After he left New York, Ovando Hollister cast about for a while, because jobs for young men were few and far between in the eastern states in the wake of the 1857 panic and depression.[4] Economic instability provoked geographic mobility, and Hollister, among hundreds of thousands of others, found his way to the Great Plains. In eastern Kansas, he bought land for less than a dollar an acre near the small town of Hesper, whose residents were mostly German immigrants. For a little more than a year, he cut down trees in the oak-hickory groves on his land and tilled up the prairie soil, seeding it with corn and wheat.[5]

His acreage had once been Kansas, Osage, and Otoe-Missouri land, but in the 1830s, the Shawnee arrived from Ohio, forced out of their homelands by the press of white American settlement and the Indian Removal Act. Twenty years later, the Shawnee had ceded this reservation to the federal government after the passage of the Kansas-Nebraska Act. Congress gave the Shawnee back two hundred acres per person in exchange, in the hope that this allotment would "civilize" them by turning them into private landowners. After they distributed the Shawnee land, the General Land Office sold the remaining acres to migrants like Ovando Hollister and, in 1859, one of his cousins.[6]

That summer, however, disaster struck. "The prairie grass, which other years often produces two tons of good hay to the acre," an observer noted, "was scarcely two inches high, and it was dried to a crisp." This was a sign of a serious drought; no one knew how long it would last.[7]

And so, in the spring 1860, Ovando Hollister decided that he was done with Kansas. The stories of all the gold to be found in Gregory Gulch were alluring. After growing up in the structured, rigid society of New Lebanon, Hollister was drawn to uncertainty and adventure. He packed up his belongings and said goodbye to his cousin, who decided to stay in Kansas.[8] Then he headed west, part of a massive migrant stream that would ultimately bring thousands of young men into the Rocky Mountains on the eve of the Civil War.

A few months later, when Ovando Hollister saw the Rocky Mountains rise from the rolling prairies, he was stunned. The mighty peaks impressed him, giving him a calming sense of "eternal and infinite solitude and solemnity, strength and repose." Hollister had seen mountains before, of course: the Berkshires of his youth near New Lebanon and the Appalachians on his way to Kansas. But the Rockies, a much younger and more jagged range, appealed to him immediately, with their "huge folds" and "great lateral spurs" and their summits "cutting boldly the evening sky."[9]

Soon Hollister was in Denver. He may have visited Vasquez & Co. and other stores to resupply, but he did not stay long. Just a few days later, Hollister rode west to the town of Golden and the road that would take him up Clear Creek Canyon to Gregory Gulch.[10] The route was thronged with wagons and carts, thousands of miners coming and going. For the first few miles it ascended a gentle slope. Then it pitched up an incline so severe that Horace Greeley had deemed it "Hill Difficulty."[11]

One miner's four mules balked at an especially steep section, and the wagon they pulled began to roll back. A man tried to stop it by putting a stone under a wheel but was crushed between the wagon and a tree.[12] After cresting this first pass, the road plummeted down to the banks of Clear Creek, leveled out, and then climbed again. The prospectors trudged up it as it wound through groves of aspen and pine for twenty more miles. Hollister estimated that ultimately, he crossed the creek fifty-eight times.[13]

As he moved up past seven thousand and then eight thousand feet above sea level, Hollister felt how much he did not yet belong to the mountains. He was "'filled plumb full of short wind,' as the Hoosiers say." His chest heaved as his body tried to deal with the lack of oxygen reaching his tissues. His lips chapped in the dry air, and he did not sleep well.[14] For Hollister and other migrants who came from lowlands and coastal areas across the continent, it would take more than a month to acclimate. Only then would they feel at home in the Rockies.[15]

When he finally arrived at Gregory Gulch, Hollister found the mining camp buzzing with activity. Prospectors had already torn up much of the ground in the placer mining phase, looking for the easily accessible gold veins within ten feet of the surface. Combing through the banks of Clear Creek, they had washed out the dirt and gravel in its waters to sort out the gold that sat close to the surface.[16] Now, it would take heavy machinery to get to the veins buried deep underground and quartz mills to crush the rock they pulled out.

Hollister decided to branch out and ultimately found his way to the nearby town of Missouri City. There were already more than five hundred people living there, and 90 percent of them were men. Some prospected while others worked for the Consolidated Ditch Company, which was diverting water from mountain creeks and constructing channels to transport it to the camps around Gregory Gulch. In an area with less than eight inches of rainfall a year, irrigation was necessary for both agriculture and mining.[17]

Four months after Hollister's arrival in Denver, a federal census taker found him living in a shanty in Missouri City with two other men. One of them, twenty-two-year-old Samuel S. Curtis, had been in the area since the summer of 1858, when he helped survey and plat 320 acres in Denver and, in the process, named one of its streets after himself.[18] Curtis reported to the census taker that he had a personal estate valued at $4,000.[19] That Ovando Hollister was living with him was either a stroke of incredible luck or an indication that he was able to make prominent friends in the most hardscrabble of places.

In the rest of the country, the fall and winter were tumultuous. On November 6, 1860, Republican Abraham Lincoln won the American presidency with less than 40 percent of the popular vote but a majority in the Electoral College. Six weeks later, more than 150 delegates convened at Institute Hall in Charleston, South Carolina. They voted unanimously to secede from the United States, citing "an increasing hostility on the part of the non-slaveholding States to the institution of slavery" and their conviction that Lincoln would prohibit its expansion into the western states and territories. The fight that had been tearing the country apart for more than forty years had finally come to a head.[20]

In January 1861, Mississippi, Florida, Alabama, Georgia, and Louisiana followed South Carolina's lead. The next month, Texas seceded as well, arguing not only that the federal government was hostile to the expansion of slavery but also that the U.S. Army had been unwilling or unable to protect white Texans and their enslaved people against Comanche and Apache raids on their farms and ranches.[21] As Democratic senators and congressmen from seceded states left the U.S. Congress en masse, Republicans (now in the clear majority) saw an opportunity to consolidate their power.[22]

Three days after Texas seceded, the U.S. Senate passed legislation carving out parts of western Kansas, western Nebraska, northern New Mexico, and eastern Utah to create Colorado Territory, and on the last day of February 1861, President James Buchanan signed the Colorado Organic Act. One week later, Congress also created Nevada and Dakota Territories and admitted Kansas as a free state. As the incoming president, Abraham Lincoln would appoint Republican officials to take political control of all the new territories, bringing them in on the side of the Union.[23]

"This is a consummation long desired," the *Rocky Mountain News* celebrated on March 5, "and there is now an assurance of established law and order, which will send a thrill of joy to every city, village, and hamlet throughout the Rocky Mountains."[24]

This issue of the *News* also noted the signing of the second Treaty of Fort Wise, a development necessary to the legal establishment of Colorado. In mid-February 1861, A. G. Boone, who had arrived and replaced Jim Beckwourth as the Southern Cheyenne and Arapaho Indian agent, called together chiefs including Black Kettle (Southern Cheyenne) and Left Hand (Arapaho) and U.S. Army officers at the fort, which sat on the banks of the Arkansas River. Representatives of the Northern Cheyenne were not present. After several days of gift-giving and negotiations, a small group of ten chiefs signed the treaty, ceding most of their land, including much of the eastern part of Colorado Territory. The Southern Cheyenne and Arapaho chiefs agreed to move to a small reservation along the Arkansas, in exchange for $30,000 a year for fifteen years and federal protection from white settlers who trespassed on their reservation.[25]

It remained to be seen, of course, whether Congress would ratify this treaty and whether the U.S. government, the Northern and Southern Cheyenne, or the Arapaho would abide by it. Most Denver residents likely shrugged at this news, given how little respect white settlers usually had for Indigenous land rights. But the treaty brought peace and quiet to the area, at least for the time being.[26]

There was no peace in the East, however. On April 18, Denver's newspapers reported that southern troops had fired on federal forces garrisoning Fort Sumter, in Charleston Harbor, South Carolina. The news was six days old but sensational all the same.

"The blow has come at last," the *News* lamented, "and civil war is upon our unhappy land."[27]

Although many Denver residents believed that Colorado Territory was for the Union, most towns and mining camps in the West had equal numbers of northern and southern prospectors.[28] On April 24, a small disunion flag appeared over a store in Denver. Although the staunchly Unionist editors of the *News* brushed this off—"aside from the bad taste displayed by the parties who allow such a rag to disgrace their premises, the event is of no importance"—the question of loyalty simmered in Colorado throughout the spring.[29]

In late May, the territory's first governor (and Lincoln appointee), William Gilpin, arrived in Denver. A Missouri lawyer who had traveled to the Pacific with John C. Frémont and fought in the Mexican-American War, Gilpin knew firsthand the mineral and strategic importance of the West. He was alarmed to hear about the raising of rebel flags in Denver and in the gold diggings. There were also rumors that Confederate sympathizers were gathering men and guns to attack and rob shops and wagon trains on the Santa Fe Trail, before leaving for Richmond to offer their services to the secessionists. Gilpin wrote to Washington, D.C., to ask for troops to defend Denver from this internal threat. Even though Colorado Territory occupied a pivotal place at the center of the American West, a region that the Republican administration coveted, Gilpin was rebuffed.[30]

Over the summer, Gilpin paid out of his own pocket for a series of advertisements in Denver's major newspapers, which were published in late July: "U.S. SOLDIERS WANTED," they said, under an illustration of an eagle, the symbol of the nation. Issuing more than $350,000 in paper money that he claimed was drawn on the U.S. Treasury, the governor paid merchants and farmers for supplies and began to secure housing and build barracks for several companies of soldiers who would become the 1st Regiment, Colorado Volunteers.[31]

As these ads appeared in the papers, Ovando Hollister sat around a fire with two of his friends in Missouri City. They were not having much luck with their claims. Most of the time they pulled just enough gold dust out of the dirt to pay for food and not much else. They agreed that mining had become quite disagreeable and discussed the future. Perhaps the fight for the country would become their new lode, a rich vein of patriotism they could work. They could raise a company and secure commissions in the U.S. Army, which would mean food and clothing and a decent monthly wage.[32]

Sam Cook, a fellow Kansan whom Hollister judged the most decisive and self-reliant of the three friends, sent off advertisements to the mining town and Denver papers. They proposed to gather the men into a company, convene in Denver, and then set out for Kansas to join troops deployed to the eastern theater. They had heard the news about the U.S. troops' disastrous loss to the Confederates at Bull Run in Virginia in late July. Clearly, the U.S. Army needed the help of some hardy mountaineers.[33]

Although these young men treated their decision to fight for the United States in a lighthearted way, they were all stalwart defenders of the federal government. Hollister's Shaker upbringing had taught him that slavery was a moral wrong; he had been drawn to Kansas and then to the Rockies in part because they were free-state communities. He and his compatriots believed in the cause of both the Union and abolition. They were certain that the Confederacy must be defeated and slavery outlawed across the nation. Or, at the very least, in the American West.[34]

In just a few weeks, they had recruited more than eighty volunteers. The miners packed their belongings and rode down to the valley, moving into furnished quarters on Ferry Street in West Denver. They expected to stay only a few days before procuring transportation to Fort Leavenworth, Kansas.[35] Then Governor Gilpin, who had already succeeded in filling two companies of 1st Colorado soldiers, came to see Sam Cook.

Word had just arrived that three hundred Texans had invaded southern New Mexico Territory, occupied the town of Mesilla, and forced the surrender of the entire federal garrison at Fort Fillmore. Their commander, a rancher and former state legislator named John R. Baylor, came from San Antonio to secure garrisons on the six-hundred-mile-long military road from that city to Fort Bliss, in El Paso. Baylor did not have orders to cross the border from Texas into New Mexico. He decided on his own to take this step to protect El Paso from any U.S. soldiers who might march down the Rio Grande to confront him.

Hollister and the others did not know it yet, but Baylor was also the vanguard of a campaign to take the entire American West for the Confederacy. The campaign was the brainchild of Henry Hopkins Sibley, a career military officer from Louisiana who had served for many years at U.S. Army forts in the Southwest. If he could march an army of Texans through New Mexico to California, Sibley told Confederate president Jefferson Davis, he could take control of the gold mines in the Sierra Nevadas and the Rockies. This would be a much-needed boost to the Confederate economy.

Securing California would give them access to Pacific ports from San Diego to San Francisco, where they could ship cotton out and bring supplies in while the U.S. Navy was blockading southern port cities in the Gulf and the Atlantic. A successful invasion of the Southwest might also bring Mexico in on the Confederate side and convince other foreign nations that the Confederacy could establish a coast-to-coast empire of slavery.[36]

On August 1, 1861, John Baylor declared the existence of new Confederate territory extending from the Rio Grande to the California border and named it Arizona. He did not have orders to do this either, but Baylor's superiors cheered the news when they heard. The Confederates were blocking the mail north of their position on the Rio Grande, so it had taken three weeks for the residents of Denver to hear this news.[37]

The threat of a Confederate invasion of the American West was now a reality. Governor Gilpin convinced Cook's company of miners to stay in Colorado, and on September 2, Ovando Hollister went with Sam Cook to a Denver recruiting office and mustered into Company F of the 1st Colorado Volunteers for a period of three years. The company would be a cavalry unit, attached to the infantry.[38] Hollister and Company F moved to a boardinghouse in the center of Denver and used a building nearby as a kitchen.[39]

For the next four months, Company F did not do much of anything. They escorted wagon trains bringing weapons and supplies into Denver and drilled at nearby Camp Weld. They were bored and disgruntled. Because Governor Gilpin had organized the 1st Colorado without authorization, the soldiers had not been paid since they enlisted.

Hollister began to regret his choice. There were plenty of hardships to be had in the 1st Colorado, with no chances at distinction. He thought about leaving, going east to reenlist with a Kansas company. There had not been any major fights in the East since Bull Run in July, but Confederates had won a battle at Wilson's Creek in Missouri and would likely take control of that border state in the coming weeks. If that happened, the people of Kansas would need more men to defend the nation's newest state.[40]

Hollister ultimately decided not to leave. In the first days of January 1862, an express arrived from the south. The three thousand Texas cavalry that Henry Sibley had recruited left San Antonio and marched northwest to El Paso, crossing into New Mexico Territory. The commander of the U.S. Army of New Mexico, E. R. S. Canby, had written to Colorado's Governor Gilpin, asking him to send troops to reinforce his own.[41]

A few weeks later, Hollister and the 1st Colorado were encamped near Fort Wise, on the Arkansas River in southern Colorado Territory. In late February, a rider galloped into the fort with a message: General Sibley's Confederates had marched north and fought an engagement with the U.S. Army at a ford in the Rio Grande called Valverde. The Texans had won the day, continued their march up the Rio Grande, and were currently approaching Albuquerque.[42] The report might not be reliable, Hollister thought. But it was exciting.

"Marching orders were immediately published," he wrote, "and gave universal joy."[43]

Two days later, Company F was on the road, heading west on the Santa Fe Trail toward Fort Union in New Mexico. Hollister and his compatriots were giddy with anticipation. Most of them had never fought in any kind of war or faced another man over the barrel of a gun, even in mining camps that were notorious for their violence. But the Civil War seemed to them another event in the exciting life that they were pursuing in the West.

"Whether it be in the battle, in the brawl, in the jayhawking or the mutiny—what matters how, so the blood is stirred," Hollister exclaimed.

Really, though, the Pikes Peakers (as they came to be called) had no idea what it meant to be soldiers. Or that the battles that the 1st Colorado would wage in the next month would be some of the most momentous of the American Civil War.

PART IV
VIOLENCE PUSHED TO ITS LIMITS

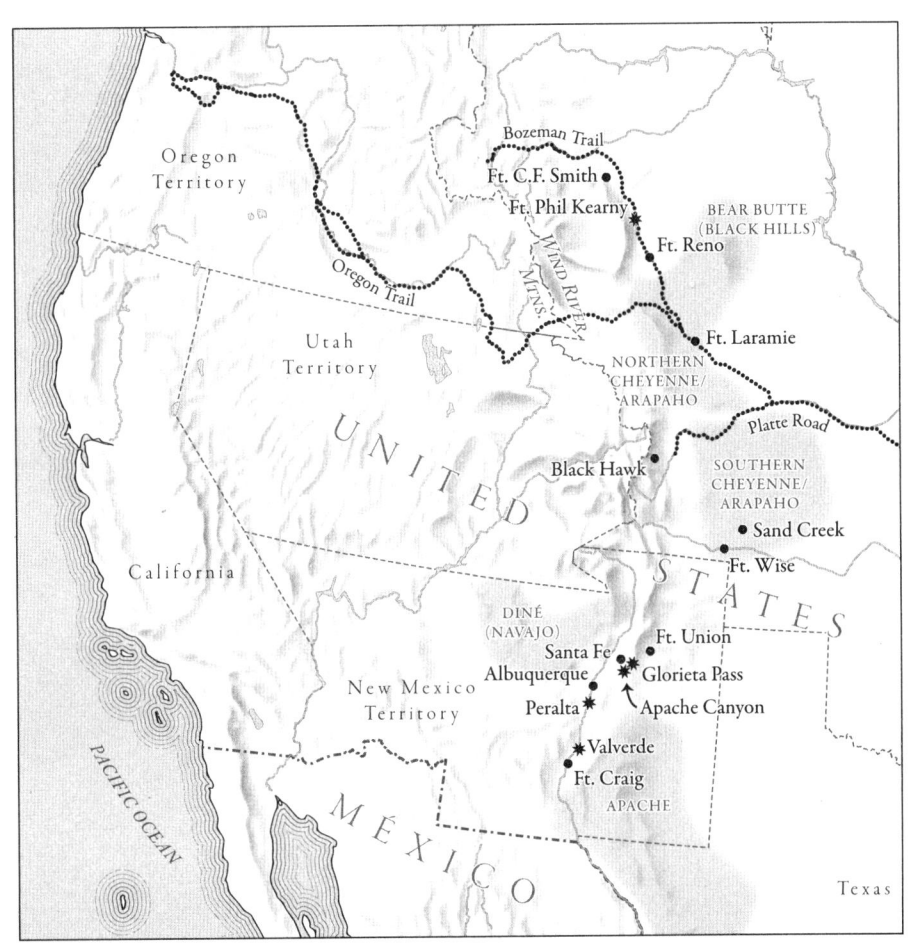

CHAPTER 16

After they left Fort Wise, the 1st Colorado marched more than two hundred miles to Fort Union in New Mexico. A few weeks later, they moved southwest toward Santa Fe. They followed the Santa Fe Trail, the route that General Stephen Kearny had taken fifteen years earlier during the Mexican-American War.

The morning of March 26, Ovando Hollister was up at dawn, filling his canteen at a spring bubbling up in the valley between the Sangre de Cristo mountains and Glorieta Mesa. The air was crisp and cold. Spring in the high desert was a changeable season; it could be a hot day, or a snow squall might descend upon them. The soldiers had to be ready for anything.

A few hours later, a report filtered through the ranks that the Texans had been spotted ahead on the road, just over the top of Glorieta Pass. They were heading to Fort Union, where Colonel Canby had a large supply cache, which the Confederates needed to continue their campaign of invasion. The men of the 1st Colorado stood between them and this goal.[1]

In the early afternoon, Hollister and his company, now under the command of Major John Chivington, reached the top of Glorieta Pass. One of their advance scouts appeared, riding at full speed toward them.

"Give them hell, boys!" he yelled as he passed. "Hurrah for the Pikes Peakers!"[2]

The Coloradans threw down their knapsacks, overcoats, canteens, and extra clothing by the side of the road.[3] Urging their horses onward, they entered Apache Canyon, a rift in the mountains with steep, rocky hillsides. Suddenly, they saw two cannons in the middle of the road, aimed right at them. Then they spotted several Confederate cavalrymen, one of whom held aloft a red flag with a white star: the banner of Texas.[4]

Chivington shouted out the order to charge, and the Coloradans were off, "like a parcel of wild Indians, cheering at the top of their lungs," Hollister wrote later.[5] The two small armies (about three to four hundred soldiers each) surged back and forth along the road until the sun began to sink behind mountain peaks beyond the canyon. As darkness fell, the firing ceased, and both sides withdrew. The 1st Colorado retreated along the Santa Fe Trail to a ranch east of Glorieta Pass.[6]

Hollister was elated for his company. "The action, though small, was conducted with great spirit and judgment," he believed. "Officers and men came to the scratch with enthusiasm."

That night, Colonel John Slough arrived with the rest of the 1st Colorado, boosting the U.S. troop strength to 1,300 men. He and his officers—Chivington and Lieutenant Samuel F. Tappan, an abolitionist and miner like Hollister—gathered at his field headquarters and discussed battle plans.[7]

Slough, a lawyer from Denver, had no practical military experience but had read tactical manuals in preparation for his command. He scouted the area and saw that he could use the Santa Fe Trail to his advantage. The Texans were stretched out along it and were therefore vulnerable to a flanking maneuver. Slough was somewhat worried that dividing his army would weaken the main body of soldiers who would face the Texans on the road, but if this gambit worked, it could win the battle for them. Tappan and Chivington agreed.[8]

On the morning of March 28, the Coloradans once again marched toward Santa Fe and the oncoming Texan army. Then Chivington and a group of almost five hundred men split off from the main column and turned onto a narrow road that wound southwestward through the forest. An offshoot of the trail led up and over Glorieta Mesa; Chivington's men would take this trail until they were behind the Texan lines. They were one of the most diverse commands to serve in all theaters of the Civil War in 1862: professional soldiers who had been in the U.S. Army before the war broke out, Rocky Mountain prospectors, and several companies of Hispano volunteers and officers from the 1st New Mexico. The Hispano soldiers knew the trail well and were the company's guides.[9]

As Chivington's group disappeared into the pines and oaks, Hollister and the others continued along the Santa Fe Trail. Early in the afternoon, Slough called a halt while the men rested their horses, gathered supplies, and visited their wounded friends at the field hospital. Suddenly, the bugles blared. Hollister and the others seized their weapons. Reinforcements had joined the Confederate company the Coloradans had faced in Apache Canyon. This combined force came over the pass and rushed upon them.[10]

The battle that followed was a messy one. It took place on the road, within the forests on either side, and among piles of rocks and boulders, shifting into hand-to-hand combat between scattered groups of soldiers.[11] The Texans' pressure was relentless, and the Coloradans fought well but were forced to moved back, and then back again. They were outnumbered, and Slough wanted to be cautious. Late in the afternoon, his order filtered through the lines: retreat.

As the skies darkened, a Texan arrived with a flag of truce from the Confederate officer in command. He suggested an eighteen-hour armistice while each army buried their dead and took their wounded from the battlefield to the hospitals. Slough agreed.[12]

Although the Texans held the field at the end of the day, Ovando Hollister and his comrades were satisfied with the battle. "The Coloradans are willing to fight them, man for man, every day in the year," he wrote.[13]

That night, Chivington and his men returned. The exciting news spread through the camp: they had found the lightly guarded wagon train the Confederates had left behind in Apache Canyon. Skidding down the slope of Glorieta Mesa and into the camp, they set fire to more than eighty wagons loaded with ammunition, clothing, subsistence, and forage. It was a devastating blow to the Confederates. Without their supplies, the Texans could not sustain themselves on the march to Fort Union or withstand another battle with federal forces in the high desert.[14]

The Coloradans celebrated into the night but were somber the next day as they buried thirty-five men on the field of battle.[15] Once the armistice ended, Colonel Slough planned to pursue the rebels—who he assumed were retreating to Santa Fe after the destruction of their wagon train—and force their surrender. Around midday, however, he received orders from Colonel Canby to retreat to Fort Union and defend it against a possible siege.[16]

Slough was incensed. He and his men had the advantage of the chase. They wanted to move forward. But orders were orders. The 1st Colorado withdrew to Fort Union, and soon after they arrived, Slough resigned his commission in protest.[17] Under a new commander, Hollister and Company F bedded down below the fort near a curving line of low foothills. Hollister was happy to be back.

"We had been gone eleven days—traveled 75 miles, fought two battles," he wrote in his diary, "and were glad of a chance to rest."[18]

Less than a week later, Hollister and Company F received orders to pack up and be ready to march. The Texans had left Santa Fe and were retreating down the Rio Grande. The 1st Colorado was to meet the rest of Canby's troops near Albuquerque.[19] Along the way, they picked up more than one hundred Texan prisoners from the battle at Glorieta Pass, who had been released on parole and were heading back to Santa Fe. Hollister rode among them for a while, and they argued about why the nation had torn itself apart in 1861.

Several of the Texans admitted that the U.S. government did have the constitutional right to restrict Southerners' ability to enslave men and women. Nevertheless, the prisoners argued, once Texas seceded and joined the Confederacy, they were duty-bound to join her in her cause: to establish an empire of slavery separate from the United States.

Hollister was exasperated by this argument. He could not understand why the Texans would cling to the Confederacy, even when they knew its cause was wrong and likely to fail. He debated them point by point, but the Confederates were obstinate.

"You have the argument," one of them said to Hollister, "but by God I know I am right." This attitude illustrated the spirit of the Confederacy for Hollister. "Pride of will is substituted for reason, and the chivalric courage . . . is desperately expended to make a bad matter worse."[20]

The prisoners went on to Santa Fe, and two days later the 1st Colorado joined Colonel Canby's soldiers south of Albuquerque. On April 14, they paused briefly at the small town of Peralta to hurl cannon shots at the Texans, and then the Confederates crossed over the Rio Grande. For the next two weeks, each army marched within sight of one another, the Texans on the west bank and the U.S. troops on the east.

The Coloradans passed through Valencia, where María Gertrudis Barceló and her family had first lived and farmed when they came to Nuevo México in 1815. Almost half a century later, the town was still small, with a few adobe houses, raised acequias bringing water from the Rio Grande to the fields, and herds of goats, burros, cattle, and sheep chewing on the grasses that grew along the riverbank.[21]

Hollister and the boys were disgruntled by the lack of action. They wanted to finish the fight they had started in Apache Canyon and force the Texans to submit. Winning a definitive battle in the Southwestern theater would bring them glory in a civil war that up to that point, the U.S. was losing.

But it was not to be.

Colonel Canby was content to keep track of the Confederates' progress and then wave goodbye as they crossed the border and returned to Texas. That way, he would not have to feed and house them as prisoners of war.[22] To Hollister, this was an infuriating waste of the 1st Colorado's effort. "Sixty miles per day to catch the traitors," he wrote with bitterness, "and ten to let them go."[23] But what could the Pikes Peakers do? They had committed to the U.S. Army and to their comrades for three years out of patriotism, excitement, and ambition.[24] They had to follow orders. At least they could feel pride about what they had achieved: they had turned back a Confederate invasion of a U.S. territory. No other fighting force in any of theater of the Civil War could claim that distinction by the spring of 1862.

The Coloradans did not know how their battle experiences compared to those of their fellow soldiers in the trans-Mississippi West or the eastern theater. With only around 3,800 fighting men, the U.S. Army in New Mexico was dwarfed by the Army of the Tennessee (with twenty-seven thousand soldiers) and the Army of the Potomac (ninety thousand).

But this small group could be proud of another achievement: they had secured the nation's largest region for the Union. The Sierra Nevada and Rocky Mountain gold mines would remain in the federal government's hands, as would California's Pacific ports. After their failed invasion of New Mexico, the Confederates would not be able to claim a continental empire of slavery.

By the end of April, the Coloradans were encamped along the riverbank at Valverde, where Canby's troops had lost a major battle to the Confederates back in late February. They built shelters of willow brush among the graves of Texan soldiers and read books looted from their camps. They played poker and Spanish monte for tobacco and other prized goods and strummed guitars and fiddles.

Bathing and washing their clothes in the Rio Grande, most of them stayed near the bank. There had been heavy snow in the Rockies over the winter, and the spring runoff had turned what was usually a placid stream into a raging torrent. The men who tried to swim across were trapped in eddies and whirlpools; their bodies were found weeks later, caught in sandbars downstream.[25]

Hollister and his comrades also read whatever newspapers they could get their hands on. In their pages, the Coloradans discovered that while they had been embroiled in the fight for New Mexico, federal forces had finally won several battles against the Confederates in other theaters of the war.

The U.S. Navy had forced the surrender of the city of New Orleans and was successfully blockading several other southern cities on the Gulf and the Atlantic. General Ulysses S. Grant had taken Forts Henry and Donelson and then defeated Confederate troops at Shiloh in Tennessee. The two-day battle at Shiloh had been a bloody one; each army experienced 25 percent casualties, and the Confederates lost their commander, Albert Sidney Johnston. Although the Pikes Peakers had sustained similar or higher casualty rates in their three fights with the Texans, battlefields strewn with thousands of wounded and dead soldiers were hard for them to imagine.

The Coloradans would have to wait several weeks to hear about the outcome of the spring campaigns in Virginia. And they did not know if anyone in Boston and New York City knew what had happened at Apache Canyon or Glorieta Pass.

"The eyes and hearts of the East were on greater battle-fields nearer home," one Colorado soldier wrote to his family, and "few realize how much was meant by that 'little fight' which . . . saved New Mexico, Colorado, Utah, Arizona, & California to the Union."[26]

For Hollister, the two months that the 1st Colorado spent encamped at Valverde in the wake of the Texans' retreat were "our golden age." The campsite, although it was messy and chaotic, felt like an oasis in the New Mexico desert. With "fine weather, light duty, discipline neither too lax nor too binding," Hollister wrote in his diary, the Valverde camp was "the acme of attainable bliss by unmitigated, unalloyed laziness."[27]

On several occasions, however, the soldiers did wake up in the night to find that Navajo raiders had galloped into their camp and siphoned off horses, cattle, and sheep. They could do nothing to defend themselves or deter these attacks. "Every expedition yet undertaken against them," Hollister observed, "has proven more disastrous to us than to them."[28] It was a harbinger of the battles to come in the West as the U.S. Army turned its attention toward the Indigenous peoples in its midst.

With no Confederates to fight and no organized campaign against the Navajo or Apache to engage in, it was unclear what the 1st Colorado would do for the rest of their service. The week of July 4, the U.S. Army paymaster from Colorado arrived at the Valverde camp. The men were ecstatic to receive their first pay as U.S. soldiers, eight months in arrears. They hardly knew what to do with so much money, after having none for so long. First on everyone's purchase list was tobacco.[29]

Hollister celebrated the nation's eighty-sixth birthday with his fellow soldiers, but he was distracted. For the previous few weeks, he had been suffering from an intense pain in his left hip, back, and leg. When he lay down, a bulge protruded from his groin. Hollister went to Fort Craig, and the post surgeon told him that it was likely an inguinal hernia: his intestines were pushing through a weak spot in his abdominal muscles. The surgeon could not do much for him except to wrap his hip and leg to keep the hernia in place until it resolved itself. And he could give him some opium or morphine for the pain.[30]

After resting at the fort hospital for more than a month, Hollister felt well enough to rejoin Company F when they accompanied the U.S. Army paymaster back to Fort Union.[31] They passed through Albuquerque and then Santa Fe and continued eastward along the Santa Fe Trail. When they entered Apache Canyon in late August, the men of Company F started talking at once, recalling every incident of the battle.[32] Their chatter died away when they passed the trailside ranch where several of their comrades were buried.

Company F stayed at Fort Union through September 1862, garrisoning the fort and riding out now and again, unsuccessfully, after Kiowa and Comanche raiders. Hollister had ample time to write in his diary and to talk with his fellow volunteers and the U.S. Army regulars posted at Fort Union about the Civil War and its purpose.

"Some thought that if a few of the leading Secessionists and Abolitionists could be hung together, the country would get on better," he wrote. Hollister thought this was a ridiculous notion, as it overlooked the great moral principles that underlay the struggle. He did not consider himself a blind, fanatical devotee of abolitionism, but he did see slavery as a national sin. The Civil War was meant to wipe it away, in Hollister's view, and all U.S. soldiers loyal to the Union were fighting for that noble cause.

In late September 1862, Abraham Lincoln issued a preliminary emancipation proclamation in the wake of the brutal carnage of the Battle of Antietam, in Maryland. The measure, which would take effect on January 1, 1863, freed all the enslaved people in parts of the Confederacy where the U.S. Army did not hold sway.

Hollister approved of this measure. The violence and destruction of the war would be worth it, he believed, if emancipation were the result. Every true patriot, Hollister argued, would rejoice in the destruction of slavery.[33]

In November 1862, Company F marched north to Denver, but Ovando Hollister was not with them. His hernia once again plagued him, and he remained at Fort Union through December, confined to a bed at the fort hospital.³⁴ He finally made it to Denver two months later, riding with several other 1st Colorado companies through the streets. The citizens cheered them for their part in defending New Mexico Territory—and thus the entire American West—against the Confederate invasion. Hollister wanted nothing more than to join them on their next campaign.³⁵

But Ovando Hollister would not take up arms for the Union again. In January 1863, he was honorably discharged from the U.S. Army, due to disability. John Chivington signed his papers at Camp Weld, and Hollister was left to find a new vocation.³⁶

He knew he did not want to return to the gold mines. He did not have enough money to buy land to farm. Ultimately Ovando Hollister decided that if he could no longer pick up a rifle to defend the Union, he would pick up a pen. Perhaps there was a place for him in one of the West's most storied institutions: the newspaper office.

CHAPTER 17

Americans across the nation heard about the fights on the battlefields of New Mexico a few weeks after the fact, given the hundreds of miles that lay between the high deserts and mountains of the West and the closest telegraph offices. Republicans were relieved that U.S. soldiers had forced the Confederates to retreat. The Department of War would not have to divert funds or soldiers from the other theaters of the war to defend the American West. The Lincoln administration could continue to squeeze the Confederates financially, preventing their use of Pacific ports and denying them access to western gold mines.

The U.S. Army's success in the far West also meant that Republicans in Congress could finally pass legislation that would enable and promote white settlement in the region. They had been trying to do so for the past twenty years, but the growing rancor between southern and northern politicians over the expansion of slavery had prevented it. Now, with a huge Republican majority after the flight of southern Democrats to the Confederacy and the U.S. Army in control of the lands between the Pacific and the Missouri River, the U.S. Congress and the Lincoln administration could act.

On May 20, 1862, President Lincoln signed the Homestead Act, allowing adult citizens loyal to the United States to claim 160 acres of public lands, improve this acreage by cultivating it, and secure ownership by paying a minimal registration fee.[1] And as the last of the Confederates crossed the New Mexico border and returned to Texas in early July, the president signed the Pacific Railway Act. Congress authorized the Union Pacific and the Central Pacific companies to begin construction on the track that would bind the West and the East together "in its iron clasp" and partially financed the project with government bonds and land cessions.[2]

At the same time, the Arizona Organic Act was under consideration in the Senate and the House, taking the western half of New Mexico and creating a new U.S. territory out of it. In the 1850s, Republicans had rejected calls for Arizona's territorial status because they were convinced it would become a slave state, given the number of Southerners who then lived in Tucson. The Confederate Territory of Arizona, which John Baylor had created in August 1861, had not lasted long.

When President Lincoln signed the legislation in early 1863, Congress admitted the first territory to the Union since the firing on Fort Sumter. The Organic Act created a provisional government for Arizona, whose civil officials would be Republicans. And one month after the enactment of the Emancipation Proclamation, it outlawed slavery and involuntary servitude in Arizona and in "all Territories now organized."[3] This provision suggested that Republicans in Washington, D.C., envisioned the American West as a region that would be free from slavery in the future.

This was good news for Jim Beckwourth, although he knew very well that the American West was not free of racism or discrimination, even if its states and territories had outlawed slavery. In the first months of 1863, Jim was still living in Denver, but he was not thriving. He had tried to secure a commission in the 2nd Colorado regiment, which had been raised in Denver while Ovando Hollister and his comrades were fighting the Confederate Texans in New Mexico.[4] But Beckwourth was sixty-four, much too old to shoulder a rifle to fight for the Union cause.

Mustering into the Army would have provided a steady income, which Beckwourth would have appreciated. In February 1863, he was charged with theft, accused of stealing saddles, bridles, and blankets from the Army's Camp Weld and receiving other stolen goods at his home. Beckwourth pleaded not guilty, and during the trial, which took place only a few days later, the jury could find no evidence of his wrongdoing and so returned no verdict.[5] While he was in the courtroom, the city of Denver fined him for failure to pay his $2 in city taxes, publishing his name among other delinquents in the newspapers.[6]

Beckwourth clearly had some money; his wife Elizabeth had been able to pay $30 for a cow and calf that same week. But a drought that had been plaguing the Great Plains for a year was killing the crops on his land, and the Beckwourths had a new mouth to feed: their daughter Julia was nine months old.[7]

Denver residents were hoping that spring rains would help ease the drought. Then in mid-April, a fire ripped through the city in the wee hours of the morning, consuming seventy buildings. Many of the city's residents camped along the banks of Cherry Creek, with their most precious belongings piled around them.[8]

Ensconced at Camp Weld just south of Denver, the soldiers of the 1st Colorado escaped the fire but were restless during the summer and fall of 1863. The mail had been delayed due to Northern Cheyenne, Arapaho, and Lakota raids along the Platte River Road from Kansas to Fort Laramie. Their barracks were deteriorating. They had little to entertain them, besides reading the *Rocky Mountain News* and the *Weekly Commonwealth* and discussing the battles taking place in Virginia, Pennsylvania, Mississippi, and Tennessee. Most of these fights were victories for the U.S. Army, now commanded by General Ulysses S. Grant. The federals were making inroads against the Confederates, it seemed. But still, the Civil War dragged on.

They may have also handed around copies of Ovando Hollister's *History of the First Regiment of Colorado Volunteers*, which he had written and published after his discharge from the Army. The book described the regiment's long marches to the battlefields of New Mexico, as well as the battles of Apache Canyon, Glorieta Pass, and Peralta. The *Rocky Mountain News* praised Hollister's account.

"Here is a pleasant, diversified, readable book," the reviewer said, "written in a good style by a man of ability."[9] The book was available for purchase at every retailer in Colorado, and the paper recommended that their readers procure copies for themselves.[10]

In the fall of 1863, Hollister was not in Denver. With several partners, he had purchased the presses, type, and printing materials of a defunct paper, the *Colorado Miner*, and moved to Black Hawk to run it. The office was on the central thoroughfare of the mining town, and Hollister lived above it and published the newly christened *Daily Mining Journal* while also running the commercial Pioneer Printing Press.[11]

"It will be our aim to elucidate all improvements in the art of mining," Hollister wrote in the paper's first column, and "to chronicle new discoveries in all parts of the world." They would not pay much attention to politics, they promised. But when they did speak about it, the *Mining Journal* would articulate the Republican position. "Believing that Mr. Lincoln's Administration has conducted the affairs of the nation in a very difficult crisis with the most signal wisdom, steadiness, and success," Hollister announced, "it will yield that Administration an undivided support."[12]

Through the *Daily Mining Journal*, Hollister also commented upon the growth and prospects of Colorado Territory, writing articles and opinion pieces on business development and Indian Affairs. Like many other frontier newspapermen, he became a local booster, arguing on behalf of the territory and its white residents.

In the spring of 1864, Hollister and every other newspaper editor in Colorado had a lot to say about the increase in Southern Cheyenne and Arapaho raids on ranches between the Arkansas and the Platte Rivers. These peoples were starving after a hard winter, and when they found no annuities waiting for them at Fort Wise, they stole horses and cattle and then disappeared into the prairies. Raiding had always been part of their culture, a way for them to build up valuable herds and survive throughout the year. They continued to consider these lands their own and saw American civilians and soldiers as trespassers.

Colorado's governor, John Evans, and Hollister's former officer John Chivington (now in command of the Colorado Military District) saw the Southern Cheyenne and Arapaho as dangerous enemies, people who would prevent the territory of Colorado from flourishing as a white settlement. They began to formulate plans for a response. Emboldened by recent U.S. Army campaigns against Navajos and Apaches in New Mexico, which had effectively forced thousands of Indigenous peoples to surrender and move to a reservation called Bosque Redondo, Evans and Chivington advocated for a merciless approach. They would send U.S. troops after Indigenous raiders and kill them if they found them.[13]

In May and June of 1864, Chivington authorized multiple campaigns against Indigenous communities throughout Colorado. One of these campaigns led to the death of the Southern Cheyenne chief Lean Bear, who had been advocating for peace with the Americans. Lean Bear's kin and allies were shocked at his death, and some of the more militant warrior societies swore that there would never be peace with the Americans after that. A few days later, Chivington wrote to Ned Wynkoop, the officer in charge at Fort Lyon (the former Fort Wise) in southern Colorado, relaying his orders.

"The Cheyennes will have to be soundly whipped before they will be quiet," he told Wynkoop. "If any of them are caught in your vicinity, kill them, as that is the only way."[14]

Ovando Hollister cheered Chivington and the troops on from his office in Black Hawk. "The Major has some reputation for energy and thoroughness," he wrote. Eradicating the Southern Cheyenne and Arapaho would be good for the territory. It would also improve the soldiers' morale. "It would be well to have the boys stirred up some," Hollister argued, "as they are losing both health and spirits in their long and isolated activity."[15]

The eastern plains were not the only violent place in Colorado that spring. On May 14, a blacksmith named Bill Payne had shown up at Jim Beckwourth's door, demanding to see his wife, Maria, who was a friend of Elizabeth's. The Beckwourths were sheltering her after the Paynes had a violent domestic dispute. Despite their concerns, they let Bill Payne into the saloon that was attached to their house and brought Maria to see him. When Payne tried to force the wedding ring off Maria's finger, Beckwourth intervened, ordering Payne out. The two men fought, scrambling to grab Beckwourth's shotgun, and several other patrons helped throw Payne outside.

"Bill immediately started to break in again to go for Beckwourth," the *Rocky Mountain News* reported, and Beckwourth "took up the gun and defended himself by firing at Bill as he was just approaching him, at the door." Payne was slowed by the bullets hitting his shoulder and neck but still made it a few steps into the saloon before collapsing near the fireplace. Within minutes, he was dead.[16]

After the inquest, Beckwourth was arrested for manslaughter. The Denver community's sympathies were with him, as Bill Payne was well-known in the city and had a history of violence, including the murder of another Black resident in 1859. The editors of the *Rocky Mountain News* believed that Jim Beckwourth had done the city a great service by killing him. "This Payne came out here as a slave with some persons connected with the old Express Company," they wrote. "He was considered a savage and dangerous character always and by almost all of our citizens. . . . He was large and strong of muscle and a rough case."[17]

Although fistfights and murders were somewhat common in Denver in the 1860s, it was another act of violence three weeks later that sent the city's residents over the edge into hysteria. A man rode into town with his horse in a lather with the news that Cheyenne raiders had attacked the Hungate family thirty miles southeast of the city. They had killed the father and mother, a four-year-old girl, and a baby and mangled them horribly. The residents of Denver did not know whether to believe him, as there had been several false alarms that spring and summer. But then a group of men brought the bodies into Denver. They placed all four into a box together, then propped the box up against a shed in the business district. Word of the spectacle grew, and hundreds of people lined up to gawk. Murmurs grew into agitated shouts.[18]

A U.S. Army officer proposed that the territorial government try to keep white Coloradans from roaming through the country. They "do not know one tribe from another," he protested, and "will kill anything in the shape of an Indian."[19]

The next week, Governor Evans issued a proclamation promising punishment for the raiders who had stolen cattle and destroyed property and for the band that had killed the Hungate family. Those Arapaho and Cheyenne peoples who wanted peace should go to Fort Lyon on the Arkansas River, Evans directed, where their Indian agent would distribute provisions and "show them a place of safety." Any Indigenous peoples who did not take this offer would be considered enemies. Evans sent the proclamation to Ned Wynkoop at Fort Lyon and told him to send a translator to the Southern Cheyenne peace camp under chief Black Kettle and read it aloud to them.[20]

Six weeks later, Evans was infuriated to find that only a few bands had taken up his offer of protection. On August 11, he issued another proclamation, abandoning any gesture toward peace and empowering private citizens to "go in pursuit of all hostile Indians on the plains," to kill and destroy as many of them as possible, and to take whatever property they found in Indigenous camps.[21] On the same day, he received authorization from the Department of War to raise a regiment of soldiers who would serve for one hundred days, pursuing the Southern Cheyenne and Arapaho.

Ovando Hollister scoffed at this plan. If Evans wanted troops to pursue Indigenous enemies, he should use the seasoned soldiers of the 1st and 2nd Colorado. "Calling out militia is a humbug," he wrote. "Bring back the troops or we are ruined."[22]

Ultimately, the Colorado 3rd Volunteer Regiment would count among its number many of Colorado's leading citizens. The campaign they launched, rooted in fear and anxiety about what was to become of white settlements in Colorado Territory, would become notorious. And it would provoke a new phase in the battle for control of the American West.[23]

CHAPTER 18

Four hundred miles northeast of Denver, more than one hundred Northern Cheyenne lodges were clustered together for the annual summer gathering of the tribal nation. The Northern Cheyenne knew about the escalating violence farther south between their Southern Cheyenne kin and the Americans. They, too, had raided along the Platte Road through Nebraska earlier in the spring. The summer, however, was about community, and preparation for the fall's buffalo hunts.

Across the camp, the high-pitched chirps of grassland sparrows swelled into a chorus and awakened many of the families. The breeze carried with it the smell of sagebrush, and a large herd of horses meandered through waving clumps of wheatgrass. There were games of chance and running races, stories and jokes told over cook fires, and trade in goods acquired or handcrafted.

One afternoon, forty-four men convened in a lodge large enough to seat them all. Four chiefs represented each of the ten bands of the Northern Cheyenne, and four council chiefs presided over them all. Every four years, they met to decide when to go to war, when to make treaties, where to establish summer and winter camps, and how to punish or reward tribal members for their actions.[1] Every ten years, they met at the summer encampment to choose a new round of leaders to protect the people and ensure their future.

Among the men who gathered in the Council of 1864 was a chief of his band and the headman of the Elk Horn Scrapers, one of the oldest and most respected of the military societies. Ó'kôhómôxháahketa (Little Wolf) had been born just as the Northern and Southern Cheyenne had separated in the 1820s, and his parents took him and his brothers to join the Northerners. He spent the first years of his life moving between the Yellowstone River and the Sand Hills of Nebraska. He hunted elk with his father in the Bighorn Mountains of Wyoming and chased buffalo across their range in South Dakota.

In the 1830s and '40s, this was a world that people like Jim Beckwourth thrived in, dominated by cross-cultural trade relationships. The Northern Cheyenne cultivated connections with other Indigenous bands and with a handful of European and American traders. But in the early 1840s, that world shifted. American troops entered the region more frequently as gold rushes, the Mexican-American War, and the Civil War reordered the West. White Americans poured into the Great Plains, and Little Wolf came of age during a time of violent conflicts between the Great Plains peoples and the U.S. government.[2]

Little Wolf was part of a Northern Cheyenne generation that saw both the commercial possibilities and the threat of colonization in their confrontations with Americans. Ultimately, they would defend their tribal sovereignty and their homeland until the end. Foremost in Little Wolf's mind, therefore, was the survival of his people.

Even as a young man, Little Wolf thought of others, not just himself. During a buffalo hunt one fall, for example, Little Wolf and his party were caught in a blizzard. They hunkered down in the snowdrifts for two days, and when they dug themselves out to return to the village, temperatures had fallen below zero. When Little Wolf saw that an older man had only a thin blanket, he gave the elder his own buffalo robe. He was younger and stronger, Little Wolf said, and could make do with the blanket.[3]

Later, when he joined war parties to fight against the Apsáalooke, Little Wolf fought well, drawing close enough to enemy warriors to tap them with a stick, demonstrating his bravery, and wounding or killing others with his bow and arrows. He also became a master strategist, planning campaigns that involved feints and surprise attacks, exploiting the terrain to gain advantages over the Apsáalooke and other Indigenous enemies in battle.

"He thought not merely of his individual deeds," the anthropologist George Bird Grinnell observed, "but of the battle as a whole."[4]

Generosity and bravery were two of the characteristics the Northern Cheyenne looked for in a leader. By the 1850s, Little Wolf joined the Elk Horn Scrapers and in 1854 became their headman. Military societies fought in battles and were also essential to the tribal governance system. They spent most of their time enforcing the council's decisions and helping tribal members settle domestic disputes.[5] The work that Little Wolf did as leader of the Elk Horn Scrapers and a chief in his band was a service to the Northern Cheyenne as a people, as well as a demonstration of his manhood.[6]

As they gathered in the Council of 1864, Little Wolf and the other chiefs had much to discuss. Like their Southern Cheyenne relatives, the Northern Cheyenne had been encountering more and more ve'ho'e (Americans) for the past fifteen years. The first were trappers and traders, who were followed by California gold seekers and Latter-day Saints.[7] Most of these white migrants did not stay in Northern Cheyenne territory very long, but their mules and oxen ate the grasses that the Great Plains bison and the tribal nation's horses needed to survive.[8]

In the past few years, the migration streams had changed. Americans arrived, and they stayed. Gold miners and U.S. soldiers flooded into Colorado in 1859 and then the mountain gulches in western Apsáalooke territory (what the Americans called Montana) in 1863.

It was the transformation in the Montana mountains that concerned the Northern Cheyenne chiefs most. By the time of the summer council, there were already ten thousand people living in the boomtowns of Bannock and Virginia City, far outnumbering the Northern Cheyenne's 150 lodges (1,300 people). Some of the miners had traveled north from New Mexico and Colorado along the western slopes of the Rockies. Most came from the east along the Oregon Trail and then cut northwest on a new road blazed by a miner named John Bozeman, who named the route after himself. More than one thousand migrants had come over the Bozeman Trail so far in 1864. For the Northern Cheyenne, the situation was untenable. They needed to elect council chiefs who could lead them wisely at this important moment in their history.[9]

After eating a feast that the women had prepared, the council discussed the matter at hand: Which of them would agree to serve another ten-year term to represent their band's interests and make decisions for the tribal nation, and who would step down and appoint another in his stead?[10]

The Seating Ceremony was a Cheyenne tradition that had been in place for hundreds of years, since the prophet Sweet Medicine had returned from Nóvávóse (Where Teachings Occur; Bear Butte) in the Black Hills and taught them to govern themselves. This was the eighth seating in Cheyenne history and the fourth since the Northern Cheyenne had separated from their southern kin in the 1820s.[11]

The business of the 1864 seating took most of the day that August, as some men chose to continue as members of the council and others stepped down and nominated others. Little Wolf, now in his forties, chose to remain the Elk Horn Scrapers headman, which was expected. After a long discussion about replacing two of the four council chiefs, they chose Little Wolf for one seat. They also named him the Sweet Medicine Chief, a great honor that recognized him as a singular leader among the rest.

This was a surprise. One man had never been a military society headman, a council chief, and Sweet Medicine Chief simultaneously. Little Wolf's fellow Northern Cheyenne chiefs clearly believed that he could lead his people into the future. They also thought it would be useful to have one man to put forward in future negotiations with the Americans, who could never understand that tribal leadership was shared among many. An elder presented Little Wolf with the Medicine Bundle, thought to have been handed down by Sweet Medicine himself. It was an item that bound both Little Wolf and the Northern Cheyenne to their history as a tribal nation.[12]

Little Wolf accepted the bundle and stood. In a short speech, he promised to make good on this great honor by sacrificing everything for the Northern Cheyenne. He would ignore all other annoyances and personal aggravations. "If a dog lifts its leg to my lodge, I will not see it," he announced, with some humor in his large, close-set eyes. Then he became serious. "Only danger that threatens my people will anger me now."[13] That danger would soon arrive on the borders of their homeland, changing the trajectory of their future.

The Northern Cheyenne were returning to their homelands from the annual buffalo hunt in the fall of 1864 when their Southern Cheyenne kin encamped fifty miles northeast of Fort Lyon, on the banks of Sand Creek. They had met with Colorado's governor John Evans and John Chivington the month before to negotiate a peace treaty. The peace chief Black Kettle wanted a reservation within the buffalo range of southern Colorado. Evans, however, met Black Kettle's conciliatory tone with hostility. He and Chivington agreed that there would be no peace without war.[14]

Soon afterward, Ned Wynkoop—who had been advocating for Black Kettle and for peace in southern Colorado—received word that he had been relieved of command of Fort Lyon. There had been complaints that "the Indians were running things" at the installation, and he was to report to Kansas to be reassigned.[15]

In Denver, John Chivington issued orders to the newly formed 3rd Colorado and several companies of the 1st Colorado—to march south toward Fort Lyon. Almost seven hundred soldiers prepared their kits and rations and readied their horses to ride more than one hundred miles south to the Arkansas River.[16] One of the officers, George Shoup, appeared at Jim Beckwourth's door, demanding that he join the 3rd Colorado as a guide and interpreter.[17]

Beckwourth agreed.

As the soldiers left the city, the residents of Denver watched them go and heaved a sigh of relief. Tensions were running high. Residents were paranoid and anxious and wanted Colorado's territorial government to protect them and their families.

"The soldiers have gone out at last," nineteen-year-old Anna Ronk wrote to her cousin. She hoped that they would find the Southern Cheyenne and "give them fits." If they did, it would be something the Indians would not soon forget.[18]

Within the week, an advance group of more than four hundred soldiers reached the pass that divided the South Platte and Arkansas River watersheds. The road descended from that high point of 7,300 feet toward

Colorado City, a small mining town at the base of Pikes Peak. The wind began to howl and dark clouds streamed over the mountains, dumping clumps of snow onto the soldiers. Colonel Shoup ordered the men to make camp, and Jim Beckwourth pitched his tent alongside the others. It snowed for the next two days, and he had to shovel himself out of drifts four feet deep.[19]

Beckwourth and the others struggled through the snow all the way to Fontaine qui Bouille (boiling fountain), a river named for its springtime runoff that tore down the mountain canyons and clawed at its banks until meeting the Arkansas at the town of Pueblo, where Beckwourth spent a year or two as a trader in the 1840s. The soldiers did not linger. They swung onto the Santa Fe Trail and moved east, heading for Fort Lyon.[20]

John Chivington and his three hundred soldiers caught up with Shoup and his four hundred troops a week later and took command. When they arrived at Fort Lyon, Chivington dismounted and went to find Major Scott Anthony, who had replaced Ned Wynkoop as commander. Anthony told him that the Cheyenne and a few Arapaho lodges were still encamped on Sand Creek. The soldiers had lost track of the larger Arapaho camp that had been on the Arkansas. Although Silas Soule and several others assured Chivington that these bands were not dangerous, both Chivington and Anthony dismissed their assessments.

"Some of those Indians ought to be killed," Anthony told Soule. "I have been waiting for a good chance to pitch into them."[21]

The orders filtered through the camp; they would leave Fort Lyon that night and march to the Sand Creek camp, using the darkness to preserve their advantage of surprise. Beckwourth went to the quartermaster's office to receive his ration of bacon and hardtack and packed it into his saddlebags. He fed his horse hay and corn and made sure he had his wool coat and bedroll. While the late November days were often in the fifties, the nighttime temperatures were already falling into the twenties.[22]

At 8:00 p.m. on November 28, the 3rd and the 1st Colorado, on horseback and accompanied by four pieces of artillery, rode out of Fort Lyon heading northeast. Watching them go was Samuel F. Tappan, who had been second-in-command at the battle of Glorieta Pass. Tappan had just arrived at the fort after visiting General Ulysses S. Grant and the

U.S. Army's winter camp at City Point, Virginia. He injured his foot on the journey and did not join the march to Sand Creek.[23]

Jim Beckwourth rode at the front of the column, alongside Robert Bent—the oldest son of William Bent, one of the region's most famous traders and the former owner of Bent's Fort—who had also been pressed into service as a guide and interpreter.[24] The regiment rode through the night, their exhalations crystallizing in the cold air. At dawn, they rode up over a small rise to see Sand Creek, just a trickle of water covered with a skim of ice, bending toward them and then away in the early morning light. The Southern Cheyenne and Arapaho camp sat on the northern bank, tucked into the inside arc of the creek bed for protection from the wind. Beyond the lodges was a large horse herd, grazing on dry scrub brush. Another smaller group of horses appeared beyond the bluffs to the west.

Although the Coloradans kept their talking to a minimum, their own horses had kicked up huge clouds of dust as they moved toward the camp over the plains. A woman out gathering water at dawn mistook them for a buffalo herd and ran into the camp to report their good luck.[25]

Chivington ordered two officers to take a few men and ride across the creek to cut off the northern horse herd from the camp and to gather the animals. He did not want the Cheyenne and Arapaho to be able to escape on horseback. As these small groups galloped off, they began to fire their revolvers and pistols into the camp, which they surrounded. The Sand Creek Massacre had begun.[26]

Jim Beckwourth followed closely as John Chivington brought the bulk of the army down the bluff, through the icy water, and onto the northern bank of Sand Creek. Chivington called at them to halt.

"Men, strip for action!" he yelled, taking off his own coat for quicker access to his guns. "I don't tell you to kill all ages and sex," Chivington added, "but look back on the plains of the Platte, where your mothers, fathers, brothers, sisters have been slain, and their blood saturating the sands on the Platte!" Then he turned toward the Cheyenne and Arapaho village and charged.[27]

Beckwourth had been both enemy to the Northern Cheyenne during his time with the Apsáalooke in the 1830s and friend to the Southern Cheyenne during his time as a trader and negotiator in the 1840s and early 1860s. He could have turned aside at this moment and joined the soldiers under the command of Silas Soule, who did not participate in the assault. Instead, in response to Chivington's rousing speech, he shed his coat and followed the colonel.

"I charged with the foremost," he admitted. "I was by the side of Colonel Chivington himself for a little ways" but soon lost ground. His slower pace was not due to a lack of enthusiasm: "His horse was fleeter than mine."[28]

This initial charge created chaos in the Southern Cheyenne camp. Women, children, men, and elders emerged from their lodges in confusion, then terror. The interpreter John Smith, who had arrived two days earlier to visit the Cheyenne with some traders, quickly assessed the situation. He found a stick, attached a white handkerchief to it, and walked toward the advancing soldiers, waving it in the air. Smith was wearing "citizen's dress" and figured there was no way that the men of the 3rd and 1st would mistake him for a Cheyenne warrior. The soldiers did recognize him but fired at him anyway.

"Shoot that old son of a bitch!" one of them shouted. "He is no better than an Indian!"[29] Another white flag went up in the middle of the camp, attached to a lodgepole along with an American flag waving above it. Before the makeshift flagpole stood Black Kettle, his wife, and another chief named White Antelope. "Don't be frightened!" Black Kettle yelled to his people during the charge. "The camp is under protection!"[30]

But the soldiers kept coming, and the gunfire intensified. Jim Beckwourth saw White Antelope leave Black Kettle's lodge and run out to meet the command. He recognized him because he had traded and held councils with the Southern Cheyenne chief.

"'Stop! Stop!'" White Antelope shouted, holding up his hands.

"He spoke it in as plain English as I can," Beckwourth said later. He was not sure if Chivington or Shoup had heard White Antelope, however. "There was such a whooping and hallooing that it was hard to hear what was said." The officers would have seen him, however, as White Antelope stopped shouting and folded his arms across his chest. It was a widely used gesture on the Great Plains, to show that he did not wish to fight.

"No attention was paid to White Antelope," Beckwourth noted, "only to shoot him, as I saw."[31] As White Antelope fell dead, women, men, and children continued to flee, heading northwest along the riverbank. A small group of warriors formed in a line to defend their families as they retreated, but then the artillerists of the 3rd began to fire from the southern bluffs. Cannons were a weapon that Indigenous communities had no answer for. The use of artillery in an Indian campaign usually ensured victory for the U.S. Army. Beckwourth watched as the shells plowed through the sand and exploded, breaking the warriors' line and driving them back. The Southern Cheyenne turned and followed the rest of their people, pursued by two companies of Coloradans.[32]

Beckwourth rode through the camp, firing his gun at moving bodies. He killed at least one man and watched as a U.S. soldier scalped the man he had killed. The officers of the 3rd did nothing to prevent the mutilation of Cheyenne and Arapaho men and women at Sand Creek. They also stood by as soldiers cut the ears, nose, and testicles from White Antelope's corpse. Soldiers rode through the camp, regardless of rank, and pursued and shot down men, women, and children alike.[33]

Two miles up Sand Creek, a group of old women and men were digging into a high sandbank, desperately trying to put the ground between them and the gunfire as protection. By the time George Bent, another of William Bent's sons, got there, "the soldiers were all around them shooting." Some survived, but many did not. "We past [sic] good many men women and children," Bent remembered later. "Killed."[34]

The massacre lasted most of the day. Colonel Shoup found Beckwourth and ordered him to take a group of prisoners to a lodge in the abandoned camp. Jack Smith, the son of John Smith and a Southern Cheyenne woman, had at first fled with his mother's kin. But then he decided to return and was taken prisoner with his father. They joined Beckwourth, along with another of William Bent's sons, Charles, and his Cheyenne wife, and a woman on her own with two children.[35]

The firing diminished and then ceased altogether as the sun set behind the distant mountains. The Southern Cheyenne and Arapaho who had survived the massacre continued to move to the west, gathering as many of their dead and wounded as they could as they fled from Sand Creek. The Colorado soldiers had succeeded in corralling their entire herd of six hundred horses, so they were mostly on foot. After the sun set, Charles Bent and his wife snuck out of the lodge Beckwourth was guarding and joined Charles's brother George, riding off with him and a string of ponies.

That night, Coloradans slept among and in the camp lodges, scavenging them for souvenirs. They built fires to cook their dinners and boasted to one another about how many scalps they had taken.[36] Several of them made threats against Jack Smith, vowing that he would not leave Sand Creek alive. It is unclear why they resented him so much. One of the soldiers was clearly worried enough that he informed John Chivington that the men were likely to kill Jack.

"I gave orders to take no prisoners," Chivington said with a shrug. "I have no new instructions now."[37] Later that night, Chivington sat in a lodge and wrote a dispatch to General Samuel Curtis, commander of the Department of Missouri (and the father of Sam Curtis, who lived with Ovando Hollister in Missouri City in 1860). He relayed the details of the massacre, delighted that he had fulfilled the general's desire to have "no peace till the Indians suffer more. . . . It is better to chastise before giving anything but a little tobacco to talk over."[38]

He also wrote a letter to William Byers at the *Rocky Mountain News*, bragging that his attack on the peaceful Southern Cheyenne and Arapaho camp was "one of the most bloody Indian battles ever fought on these plains." Chivington believed that the unprovoked assault was a necessary and noble act and should be listed among the achievements of Colorado's Civil War soldiers, alongside Apache Canyon and Glorieta Pass.[39]

The next day, the 3rd and 1st Colorado remained encamped at Sand Creek. In the early afternoon, a group of ten to fifteen men walked into the lodge where Jim Beckwourth was sitting with John and Jack Smith. Someone called for John Smith to come outside, and he left. Inside the lodge, a private approached Jack.

"You are a son of a bitch," he hissed, "and ought to have been shot long ago."

"I don't give a damn!" Jack replied. "If you want to kill me, shoot me."[40]

It was hard for Jim Beckwourth to see what exactly happened after that. It was possible that the soldier who had threatened Jack Smith shot him. Jim thought maybe someone fired a gun through a hole in the lodge from the outside. But one thing was certain. "The bullet entered below Jack's right breast," Beckwourth said. "He sprung forward and fell dead, and the lodge scattered, soldiers, squaws, and everything." Beckwourth moved with the surge outside and saw another soldier standing there with a pistol drawn. "I will finish him," he said to Beckwourth.

"Let him go to rest," Jim replied. "He is dead." The old trader went back into the lodge, picked up Jack's body, and carried him outside. "I do not know what they did with him afterwards," he confessed.[41]

That night, Chivington issued orders to his men to ready themselves for the march to the Arkansas River. They were going to track and then attack an Arapaho band encamped on the riverbank. He also told one of his lieutenants to burn the Southern Cheyenne village. On December 1, 1864, the Coloradans rode south. Behind them, the ashes of more than one hundred lodges were still smoking in the cold morning air.[42]

A little more than a week later, the Colorado soldiers returned to Fort Lyon, unsuccessful in their search for the Arapaho. John Chivington was pleased about his regiments' achievements, however. He left Colonel Shoup in command of all the soldiers, with directions to return to Denver as soon as the men were ready. He rode out ahead of them, eager to get back to the city that he was sure would welcome him with cheers and veneration.[43]

A few days later, Jim Beckwourth left Fort Lyon with Shoup and the rest of the regiment. A few days before Christmas, they arrived in Denver, parading through the business district with a live eagle tied to a pole. Some of the soldiers had attached the scalps of Southern Cheyenne men, women, and children to their saddles.

"As the 'bold sojer boys' passed along," the *Rocky Mountain News* reported, "the sidewalks and corner stands were thronged with citizens saluting their friends."[44]

The city continued to fete the soldiers through the holidays. In early January 1865, the Diana Theater in Denver exhibited the trophies of the Sand Creek Massacre to an admiring populace: "arrows, buffalo spoons, calumets of war, scalps and so forth."[45]

CHAPTER 19

It may have seemed to some Colorado residents that the Sand Creek Massacre was on par with U.S. General William Tecumseh Sherman's March through Georgia. Just two weeks before the 3rd Colorado left Denver, U.S. troops had set fire to the city of Atlanta and set out for Savannah and the Atlantic Ocean, burning some homes and foraging at plantations along the way. Both campaigns were meant as acts of destructive and psychological warfare. And both seemed to secure the U.S. Army's hold on enemy territory.

Outside Colorado, however, there was growing consternation about the nature and extent of the massacre at Sand Creek. The U.S. Congress had enough questions that the Committee on the Conduct of the War was considering an investigation.[1] After the 3rd Colorado was mustered out of the army, John Chivington and George Shoup resigned their commissions. From this point on, they would fight to defend their version of events at Sand Creek as civilians.

The U.S. Department of War wanted to gather all the information they could, and they sent Samuel Tappan to interview participants in the massacre. Tappan had impressed his superiors with his military record in Colorado and New Mexico and his humanitarian ideals. He seemed the obvious choice to lead the investigation of Sand Creek.[2]

In January 1865, Tappan came to see Jim Beckwourth in Denver. He asked him about how many Southern Cheyenne and Arapaho the soldiers had killed. While some newspaper accounts were putting the number at over five hundred, Beckwourth thought that "the Indian loss at Sand Creek [was] not over 160." He confirmed that it was likely that two-thirds of them were women, children, and old men.

Such a number was minuscule compared to the killing fields of the eastern theater, where thousands of men fell dead in a single day. But the deaths of more than one hundred civilians in an unprovoked assault was unheard of in any theater during the Civil War. The rules of warfare, established for the U.S. Army by the 1863 Lieber Code, prohibited deliberate attacks on unarmed civilians, especially women and children. Any soldiers found to have violated this rule of law would be rigorously punished.[3]

The Southern Cheyenne and Arapaho saw the deaths at Sand Creek for what they were: cold-blooded murders, acts of violence that must be avenged. Denver residents woke up in the first days of January to news that the massacre had galvanized war chiefs across the Great Plains. Joining forces in a military alliance that white settlers had always feared, they launched a series of reprisal raids along a one-hundred-mile front on the Platte Road in Colorado and Kansas. Southern Cheyenne warriors who had come directly from Sand Creek (including George Bent) joined their Northern Cheyenne kin and Arapaho and Lakota allies to attack American wagon trains, stage and telegraph stations, forts, and settlements along the Platte.[4]

On January 7, 1865, an Indigenous force of more than one thousand warriors launched a coordinated strike on Julesburg, a town 180 miles northeast of Denver. Leading the charge was a Lakota chief named Sitting Bull, who had already started to make a name for himself asserting his people's sovereignty in their homelands between the Missouri River and the Yellowstone Basin.[5]

Two days after the attack on Julesburg, Jim Beckwourth set out on his own to find the Southern Cheyenne camp, which he suspected was in the vicinity of Box Elder, a trapping site near the Smoky Hill River. It took him three days to find the camp, its lodges erected alongside those of Arapaho, Kiowa, and Comanche allies. The Kiowa and Comanche warriors had come from northern Texas, where they had fought U.S. troops led by Kit Carson four days before the massacre at Sand Creek.

The Kiowa and Comanche had been victorious in the Battle of Adobe Walls, driving Carson and his Hispano troops in the 1st New Mexico back to Santa Fe. Then they heard about the massacre at Sand Creek and rode to the Smoky Hill to join their allies.[6]

The camp was on the move, heading north toward the Platte Road. Beckwourth asked to speak to the Southern Cheyenne chiefs and eventually sat down with Leg in the Water and Little Robe. The Coloradans had killed the latter's father at Sand Creek.

"What have you come here for?" Leg in the Water asked Beckworth. "Have you fetched the white man to finish killing our families again?"

"I have come to talk to you," Beckwourth replied, "to persuade you to make peace with the whites." Their raids along the Platte Road might have been successful so far, he argued, but they did not have enough warriors to fight the Americans. "They are numerous as the leaves of the trees."

"We know it," the chiefs replied. "But what do we want to live for? The white man has taken our country, killed all of our game; was not satisfied with that but killed our wives and children." They had tried to broker an accord at the council with John Evans in Denver. But now, they told Beckwourth, there would be no peace. Then the chiefs called their former trading partner to count.

"Why did you come to Sand Creek with the soldiers," they asked, "to show them the country?"

"If I had not come," Beckwourth told them, "the white chief would have hung me." The Cheyenne chiefs were unimpressed. "Go stay with your white brothers," they retorted. Beckwourth knew when to stop pushing. He left the camp, saddled his horse, and rode three days back to Denver.[7]

Meanwhile, Samuel Tappan was at Fort Lyon with two other members of the investigative commission, interviewing Sand Creek witnesses. He talked with Ned Wynkoop, who had returned to the fort to retake command when Scott Anthony resigned. Wynkoop was livid when he found out about what had happened at the Southern Cheyenne camp. Chivington, he wrote to his superiors, was an "inhumane monster."[8]

On January 30, 1865, Ovando Hollister traveled down the Clear Creek Road from Black Hawk to Denver. The town was busier than when he was there last, but also more agitated. "People are divided into feuds and factions," he reported to the readers of his newspaper, "and everything goes as popular passion and prejudice sway for the moment." One of the things they were arguing about was Tappan's investigation. The Army officer was coming back to Denver to interview additional Sand Creek Massacre participants and witnesses.[9]

Although Hollister was a staunch abolitionist who had celebrated Lincoln's Emancipation Proclamation, he had never been sympathetic to Indigenous peoples' assertions of sovereignty. In this he was not alone. Most white settlers disagreed on many political issues in the 1860s, but they shared a conviction that the lands of the American West were theirs to occupy. Hollister was therefore initially hostile to the idea of an inquiry into the massacre. "We propose that the Colorado legislature fix a bounty of ten dollars on every Indian scalp taken between the Platte and Arkansas Rivers, the Missouri and the Mountains," he wrote in early January 1865, "as a counterpart to this threatened investigation."[10]

By late January, however, Hollister had changed his mind. He liked the idea that the military commission would determine the facts of the case and that this would help create an Indian policy that might bring real and long-lasting peace to Colorado. More importantly, settling the matter with the Southern Cheyenne and Arapaho would allow the traffic to flow once again on the Platte Road. The miners in Black Hawk were suffering for lack of food and supplies. He hoped, therefore, that Tappan and the others would be successful in their quest for the truth. "To do it they must be fearless and searching," he noted, and the people should encourage and support the commission, for it "was wholly for their interests that it was instituted."[11]

On February 9, 1865, Tappan and two fellow military commission members arrived in Denver.[12] They interviewed John Chivington (who protested that Tappan should not be a part of this investigation, given the well-known enmity between the two men) and Silas Soule.[13]

One month later, Samuel Tappan called Jim Beckwourth to appear before the commission and tell his story. Although the constitution of Colorado Territory did not allow Black men and women to serve on juries, testify against white people, or vote, this was a military investigation, not a court of law. Beckwourth's presence was unusual, but it was not illegal.[14]

When Beckwourth walked into the room, he saw that John Chivington was there. Although he was a civilian now and a minister rather than a lawyer, Chivington was calling witnesses and cross-examining them as part of the military inquiry. He turned to the commission members and asked them to administer his chosen oath, and they assented.

"Do you believe in the existence of a Supreme Being, of a God, by whom truth is enjoined and falsehood punished," a member of the commission asked Beckwourth, "and do you consider the form of administering an oath as binding upon your conscience?"

"I do," he answered.[15]

Tappan questioned Beckwourth for most of the day. He asked him why he joined the campaign as a guide, when the attack began, how many Southern Cheyenne and Arapaho lodges there were at the bend in Sand Creek, and how many men, women, and children the Colorado soldiers killed. Tappan was particularly interested to know whom the soldiers had targeted.

"There were all sexes, warriors, women, and children, and all ages, from one week old up to eighty years," Beckwourth testified.[16]

Tappan also asked for the details of White Antelope's murder and the number of soldiers Beckwourth saw scalping or otherwise mutilating the bodies of the dead. He also wanted to know what John Chivington had said to his troops as they charged the camp and if he or the other officers had tried to restrain the men at all. Beckwourth then spent the bulk of the afternoon explaining what had led to the murder of Jack Smith.

The next day, it was Chivington's turn to cross-examine Beckwourth. His questions forced the scout to admit that he rode at the front of the column and took part in the massacre. Beckwourth also acknowledged that he could not identify any of the soldiers he saw scalping Cheyenne and Arapaho bodies or the man who shot Jack Smith. Chivington also did not believe that Beckwourth ever got close enough to White Antelope to hear him shout at the soldiers to stop, but Beckwourth insisted that he did. The commission took a break for lunch, and then Beckwourth returned to several additional questions from Chivington.

"Is there any enmity existing between you and John Chivington?" the former colonel asked, referring to himself in the third person.

"None, so help me God," Beckwourth replied.

"Have you not used expressions of hostility towards Colonel Chivington within the six months last past?"

"Not to my knowledge."[17]

Unable to prove that Beckwourth was biased against him, Chivington decided to try another strategy: "To what race do you belong—the white, black, or Indian?"

Tappan objected to the question before Beckwourth could answer. He argued that if Beckwourth's racial identity was an issue, Chivington should have raised it before Beckwourth took the oath and gave his testimony. Even then, his attempt to bar Beckwourth's testimony because of his race would have been overruled. The other two commission members sustained Tappan's objection. Chivington rephrased.

"Were you a Crow chief?"

"Yes," Beckwourth replied.

Chivington hoped that Beckwourth's admission that he had a history with the Apsáalooke would discredit him.[18] To Beckwourth, this whole line of questioning was ridiculous. Anyone "could have found out my color by looking at me," he wrote later, willfully ignoring his own history with passing as both white and Indigenous. With this, the examination ended, Beckwourth was dismissed, and the commission adjourned until the next day.[19]

Beckwourth returned to his farm and saloon outside Denver and tried to resume his life. But the effort to undermine his Sand Creek testimony continued for several weeks. The commission's sessions had been closed to the public, and newspaper editors had only unsubstantiated rumors to cite in their articles about the investigation. David C. Collier, the editor of the Central City *Register*, who had known Beckwourth since he arrived in Colorado in 1860, attacked him on multiple fronts.

Tappan and the commission "could find no white witness mean enough," Collier wrote, "so adopted their last resort and introduced that negro renegade, Jim Beckwourth to testify." Collier clearly agreed with John Chivington that Beckwourth's race should have disqualified him as a witness. What was more, Collier argued, Beckwourth was a typical mountain man, regarded "by all who know him as the biggest liar and thief in the Territory." If that weren't bad enough, the editor argued, "for blood-thirsty cruelty he has no equal." Collier noted that Beckwourth had killed Bill Payne in cold blood, then went on to claim that during the Sand Creek Massacre, Beckwourth had murdered old women and babies.[20]

Ovando Hollister read Collier's editorial and was outraged. "In a strenuous effort to blacken Beckworth's character," he wrote in his own editorial in the *Daily Mining Journal*, Collier laid "the foulest crime . . . to his charge." And even if Beckwourth had taken part in the massacre, Hollister saw Collier's criticism of him for what it was. "At some future time, it may be pertinent to inquire," Hollister pointed out, "why an action denounced as barbarous in a poor devil of a negro should be entitled to commendation and support when performed by white men."[21]

A few days after his defense of Beckwourth appeared in the *Mining Journal*, Hollister received a letter at his office on Gregory Street in Black Hawk. It was from Jim Beckwourth, who had read Collier's editorial and Hollister's response. Beckwourth asked that Hollister print his own reply, in which he took on Collier's criticisms point by point. He was no liar, Beckwourth argued.

"I did not kill any woman or pappose [*sic*] at Sand Creek," he wrote, "neither did I shoot at any, nor did I imitate white men in scalping. Whoever states that I did either of these things, lies."

He noted that Collier had also identified him as a "full-blooded negro" who was accustomed to shooting Black men like Bill Payne for no reason. These were also falsehoods, Beckwourth wrote. He had shot Payne in a fair fight, defending a woman's honor. Beckwourth defied Collier and the Central City paper to "prove a single one of the charges they bring against me." In the meantime, he demanded that anyone who had anything to say about him bring proof and sign his name to the accusations.

"I have lived seventy years," Beckwourth wrote, "and if I live seventy more, I will always defend my character."[22]

Hollister published the letter in the March 17, 1865, issue of the *Daily Mining Journal*.

Three weeks later, residents of Denver and U.S. patriots across the continent were celebrating Robert E. Lee's surrender at Appomattox, Virginia.

"The End, of which prophetic souls saw the beginning in Vicksburg and Gettysburg, has at last come," Hollister wrote in his paper on April 10, "thank God!"[23] The next day, the U.S. Army fired a two-hundred-gun salute in Denver "to commemorate the surrender of the head and body of that bogus Confederacy under Lee."[24]

Samuel Tappan and the commission turned from the celebrations back to their investigation, but the proceedings were interrupted by two shocking events.

"President Lincoln Assassinated," the *Mining Journal* announced on April 15. Crowds in Black Hawk besieged the newspaper office, hoping for updates. The news "threw the community into the deepest consternation—the worse for the general elation caused by the late successes of our arms," Hollister wrote. The miners were horrified and seemed to want both vengeance and assurance that God would bring down no further terrible events upon them.

In Denver, little more than a week later, after returning from a dinner party, the former 1st Colorado officer Silas Soule bid his new wife goodbye and left their house. He was the commander of the city's provost guard, and he had been called to investigate a shoot-out in the street. As Soule turned into the business district, a man stepped out of the shadows with a pistol in his hand. Soule drew his own weapon but was not fast enough.

"The news of the cold-blooded assassination of Capt. Soule in Denver sent a thrill of horror to the heart of this community," Ovando Hollister wrote in his paper, "notwithstanding its recent violent excitement through an event of the same character."[25] Most Denver residents suspected that John Chivington was behind Soule's murder; his testimony against the former colonel in the Tappan investigation had been damning. Soule's assassin fled to New Mexico Territory, was arrested and brought back to Denver, but then escaped from jail.[26]

To Jim Beckwourth, Soule's murder must have felt like a warning. He began to spend more time away from Denver on hunting and trapping trips. Elizabeth left him. It was unclear why, although the death of their daughter Julia may have driven them apart. He met a Southern Cheyenne woman named Sue, and they married.[27] He also took a young hunter and painter under his wing, a white man named Charles S. Stobie. On one trip in the fall of 1865, the two men talked about Sand Creek. Beckwourth told Stobie that he had no idea that the 3rd Colorado would take things so far. He was still unsettled by his final meeting with the Southern Cheyenne and their brutal assessment of his character. He told Stobie what they yelled at him along the creek bank during the massacre: "You're a Ghost! You're a Liar! Why do you bring these white soldiers down on our village?"[28]

After Sand Creek, it was impossible for the Southern Cheyenne and Arapaho to trust any Americans, even men like Jim Beckwourth, who had been friends to them at one time. When their Northern Cheyenne kin and allies in the Plains heard about the massacre, they were incensed. During the Civil War, Americans had turned to an Indian policy rooted in the frontier myth, which embraced pitiless war and removal to reservations. But Indigenous peoples across the West also decided on a new approach to their relationship with the United States. From this point on, they would not submit. They would work together to fight the U.S. Army and to push white migrants from their lands.

"We have raised the battle-axe," the Southern Cheyenne told Beckwourth in January 1865. "We are going to fight until death."[29]

CHAPTER 20

On the morning of Abraham Lincoln's assassination, Indiana legislator and Speaker of the House of Representatives Schuyler Colfax had visited the president at the Executive Mansion. A stalwart Republican, Colfax was both a political ally and a friend of the president. They also shared a vision of the role of the American West in shaping the future of the nation.

"You are going to California, I hear," the president said to him. "How I would rejoice to make that trip! But public duties chain me down here, and I can only envy you its pleasures." Lincoln told Colfax that he and Mary were thinking of moving to the Pacific coast after his presidency was over, hoping that his sons would find employment opportunities there. He also recommended going west to the U.S. soldiers and veterans he had the pleasure of meeting and to recent immigrants who needed jobs.[1]

Lincoln, like Colfax, believed that the mineral wealth buried in the Rockies and the Sierra Nevada mountains was inexhaustible. The Pikes Peakers, Ovando Hollister among them, had helped to keep that wealth out of Confederate hands in 1862. "Now that the rebellion is overthrown," the president told his friend, "the more gold and silver we mine makes the payment of the [war] debt so much easier."[2]

The wealth of the West, unearthed and processed and sent eastward, would ensure the economic and political health of the entire United States. "Tell the miners from me," Lincoln said to Colfax, "that I shall promote their interests to the utmost of my ability; because their prosperity is the prosperity of the nation, and we shall prove in a very few years that we are indeed the treasury of the world."[3]

These were Lincoln's final words to Colfax—and possibly to any member of Congress—before the assassin's bullet ended his life. During his presidency, Lincoln had ensured that the federal government kept hold of the West and provided for its development. He sent Republican appointees to govern the new territories and states in the region. And he signed the Homestead Act and Pacific Railway Act, which would enable Americans loyal to the Union to settle the lands between the Pacific and the Missouri River. On the last day of his life, Lincoln was making plans for the West and its role in the future of the nation.

Colfax delayed his trip to California to stand vigil at the dying president's bedside, and then to attend funeral services. He was devastated by the loss. "How much I loved him personally," Colfax confessed.[4] When he finally embarked on his western tour in early summer, Colfax was determined to pass along Abraham Lincoln's message to American settlers in the West and to reassure them that they still had the support and protection of the federal government.

The Speaker also wanted to see the country, study its resources, and talk to Westerners. He believed he would return from the trip a more informed public servant who could bring a new perspective to legislation promoting the region's development. Colfax was confident that bringing this region into the nation, as part of the post–Civil War era of Reconstruction, would not only help all Americans to recover from the violence and destruction of the war. It would also further solidify loyalty to the Republican Party across the West.[5]

The Union Pacific railroad had laid only a few miles of track by the time Colfax embarked on his trip, so he and his party traveled by stage from Atchison, Kansas, to Denver.[6] This was a bold choice; the Smoky Hill route was a site of frequent Cheyenne and Arapaho attacks in the wake of Sand Creek. They made it through without incident and stayed for a few days in Denver with Colfax's sister Clara, who had come to Colorado with her husband during the gold rush. Then they piled into a carriage and followed the same road that Ovando Hollister had taken five years before to Gregory Gulch.

The coach jostled up the mountain road from Denver, its wooden wheels bumping over rocks and into deep ruts. Turning away from the banks of Clear Creek, it moved through the town of Black Hawk, turning onto Gregory Street and passing Ovando Hollister's printing and newspaper office and other clapboard and brick buildings advertising hardware, stoves, drugs, and meat. The coach did not stop, and the horses strained up another steep climb until the road curved to the south and narrowed, moving through a canyon of two- and three-story buildings.[7]

The men in the coach were "seemingly oblivious of the notice they attracted," Ovando Hollister wrote in the *Daily Mining Journal*, "and only intent on the new scenes presented to their gaze."[8]

At Central City's coach station, Colfax and his party disembarked, shook hands with local dignitaries, and then scattered into local hotels and residences. A few hours later, as the sun began to set, a crowd formed in front of the town bank on Main Street and on the rooftops in the vicinity. The mayor stepped out onto the bank's front step and quieted the throng. Then he introduced Colfax, a short man with dark hair, a heavy brow, and a chinstrap beard.

"It is with great pleasure that I meet and address the citizens of this Territory," Colfax intoned, "after my delightful journey across the plains."[9] This was his first trip to the American West, the Speaker said, and the journey had been "a succession of wonders."[10] God had created the precious metals in the molten rocks of the mountains and kept them hidden until Americans needed them. "Colorado will be the next scene in the development of this country which God had so peculiarly blessed." He could see the momentous changes already underway in the diggings that surrounded them, from the first days of the 1859 gold rush. "As you have gone on from pan to rocker, from rocker to tom and sluice, and thence to mills, so would the country advance in regular and rapid gradation," Colfax said.

The Speaker of the House had high hopes for Colorado. "She has only seen the dim twilight of the glorious sun which will dawn upon her," he told the residents of Central City. "Immigration will pour upon you as a flood, where there had been hundreds there would be thousands."[11]

When he finished his speech, the audience rewarded him with "long and hearty applause." Colfax retired to a house in town, whose doors were thrown open to welcome visitors who wished the Speaker well.[12] As the crowd milled around and then wandered off, Ovando Hollister returned to his printing office to write up an account of Colfax's speech for the next day's *Daily Mining Journal*. He was pleased with the Speaker's relaxed manner, the way he spoke with good humor, "sensitive to the feelings of his auditors." Colfax was also clearly interested in the territory's future.

"As he says he has been a friend to Colorado," Hollister noted. "He is a rising man, and under our circumstances, it is well to have such friends at court."

The Speaker's fellow travelers, all of whom were editors of the most prominent newspapers across America, were also, hopefully, impressed with the Rocky Mountains and all they had to offer. "Their observations in this country and all through the West will doubtless be read by millions. It is fitting that our people treat them with every consideration."[13]

For the next two days, the Colfax party toured the mines around Central City, Black Hawk, and the town of Empire, which lay farther south. Hollister joined them, reporting on the short speech that Colfax gave to the miners in Empire, and talking with the Speaker and the newspaper editors about the status of gold mining in Colorado in 1865. Production had fallen in the past two years, from a high of almost $3 million pulled out of the ground in 1863.[14]

In Hollister's view, this was not because there was no more gold in the mountains. Instead, he argued, it was because the mountain towns had no easy way to access resources like machinery, food supplies, or hardware. Colfax assured Hollister and the other prominent citizens of Black Hawk and Central City that the transcontinental railroad's completion would benefit Colorado. Spur lines connecting these communities to the main track would connect them to San Francisco and Chicago. Colfax also pledged to Coloradans that the federal government would do everything it could, including exterminating or removing Indigenous peoples from the West, to help white Americans establish themselves and flourish.

"If I ever had any romantic ideas of [Indians], derived from books of story and travel," Colfax said in his speeches, "what I have seen on this trip of their ravages has quite cured me of them." He did not believe that treaty-making would bring peace. Instead, he embraced U.S. Indian policy in the West that prioritized warfare and removal to reservations.

"I would say to them as we did to the South when they arose and left us," Colfax declared, that there was "no other course but to subjugate or annihilate them."[15]

Although Ovando Hollister welcomed the wave of white immigrants that the end of the Civil War brought to Denver, to Jim Beckwourth the city was starting to feel a bit too crowded. His habitual restlessness propelled him, once again, out on the road. In January 1866, Beckwourth left Denver—and his wife, Sue—and rode north to the banks of the Green River in Wyoming, where he had first learned to trap beaver more than forty years before.[16]

When he arrived at his old trapping grounds, however, Beckwourth discovered that even this region was not as remote as it once was. Across the Wind River Mountains to the east, the seven-hundred-mile-long Bozeman Trail provided a route from the Platte Road to the gold regions of the newly created Montana Territory. A stream of miners and migrants rode along it, and the mining camps in the northern Rockies were bustling. It looked to Beckwourth like this part of the West would soon resemble California, with its growing towns and road networks, and its legal system meant to concentrate power in white hands.[17]

From his homelands to the northeast of Beckwourth's trapping camp, the Northern Cheyenne chief Little Wolf watched these developments with anger. After many of the survivors of Sand Creek straggled into Northern Cheyenne villages, he and the council chiefs decided to ally with the Southern Cheyenne Dog Soldiers, along with Arapaho and several Lakota bands. This allied community of tribal nations congregated in the Powder River country, where buffalo, antelope, elk, and deer were plentiful despite the ongoing drought in the region.[18]

From there, they launched campaigns against U.S. Army posts and migration routes. Little Wolf led a force of three thousand Indigenous warriors in an attack on the North Platte Bridge, which spanned the river at a key point in the Platte Road, which fed into the Oregon and Bozeman Trails. The Northern Cheyenne and their allies killed dozens of U.S. soldiers. They also destroyed one thousand feet of telegraph wire and halted traffic on the Platte Road.[19] Farther north, the Hunkpapa Lakota chief Sitting Bull was marshaling his own warriors to sack U.S. forts built on the Upper Missouri River, on the eastern edge of their territory.

The U.S. federal government, eager to extend federal power into the West as the Civil War ended, sent officers and soldiers who chose to stay in the Army to the Platte Road and the Bozeman Trail. Two thousand soldiers converged on the Powder River country from the west, south, and east, but the battles they fought with allied Indigenous forces came to nothing. The Americans had meant to intimidate the Northern Cheyenne, Arapaho, and Lakota peoples with their numbers and their weapons. Instead, they enraged them further.

While Jim Beckwourth was skinning beavers along the Green River in the summer of 1866, an army of two thousand men led by Colonel Henry Carrington rode into Fort Laramie. Hundreds of mule teams followed, hauling huge quantities of supplies. Carrington had been sent to build several U.S. Army forts along the Bozeman Trail. He was also authorized to conduct treaty talks with the Northern Cheyenne and other tribal nations along the route if they were amenable. After the U.S. soldiers marched north from Laramie to Crazy Woman Fork and built Fort Reno, Carrington received a message from the Northern Cheyenne.

"Do you come for peace or war?" they asked.

"I shall be happy to have you come and tell me what you wish," Carrington wrote in a note that he handed to the courier. "The Great Father at Washington wishes to be your friend, and so do I and all of my soldiers."[20]

In mid-July, a Northern Cheyenne delegation (Little Wolf was not among them) arrived at Fort Reno. As they rode into the camp, the infantry band played a tune while the U.S. flag fluttered in the air overhead. After Carrington distributed tobacco and other gifts, the soldiers and the Northern Cheyenne sat down to talk. The chiefs made their demands: Carrington must not push farther into their homelands. They must not build more forts. The soldiers must keep white migrants on the roads farther south and prevent them from bringing their long wagon trains through the North Country.[21]

Carrington promised to pass along these words to President Andrew Johnson, in Washington, D.C. While he did make good on this promise, he did not wait for a response from the Department of War or the Bureau of Indian Affairs. He had his orders, so he marched on. Carrington moved northwest and encamped along Big Piney Creek, in the shadow of the Bighorn Mountains. There, he put his men to work building soldiers' quarters, a corral for cattle, stables for horses and mules, and blacksmith and woodshops. Carrington named the installation Fort Phil Kearny, after a beloved U.S. Civil War general (who was not related to General Stephen Kearny, who took New Mexico Territory for the Union in 1846).[22]

The fort sat on contested ground. The Lakota had taken it from the Apsáalooke in recent years, pushing their traditional enemies farther west beyond the Bighorn Mountains. Carrington had orders to establish contact with the Apsáalooke and convince them to ally with U.S. troops against the Lakota, to retake this part of their homelands. Luckily for Carrington, there were two men in the area who had abundant experience trading and treating with this tribal nation: Jim Bridger and Jim Beckwourth.[23]

After selling his pelts to traders in August, Beckwourth was happy to sign on as an emissary for Carrington in the fall of 1866. He also agreed to work as a scout and messenger, taking reports and letters more than two hundred miles between Fort Phil Kearny and Fort Laramie. After one round-trip, Beckwourth found that Jim Bridger and more than two hundred soldiers were marching ninety miles up the Bozeman Trail to build another fort in Montana Territory. Carrington wanted Beckwourth to head there as well, leading a party that included an Army officer on an inspection tour. Beckwourth would then take the party north to the Yellowstone River and return to establish contact with the Apsáalooke.[24]

Two weeks later, a soldier named George Templeton was sitting among the freshly hewn logs of the new fort (christened Fort C. F. Smith) as the sun began to set. "In the evening were somewhat surprised to see a mulatto ride into camp," Templeton wrote in his diary. "He proved to be the redoubtable 'Jim Beckwith' formerly chief of the Crows."[25]

Beckwourth did not stay long, but he returned on September 9 and helped the soldiers construct additional segments of the fort. A few days later, he and Templeton saw about twenty warriors come down to the banks of the Bighorn River. From a distance, Beckwourth thought they were Apsáalooke and convinced Templeton to take a canoe across the water to talk with them. When they reached the opposite bank, however, Beckwourth saw that they were Lakota.

"Come over to camp," Templeton said to them. The Lakota men shook their heads. "The whites don't love the Sioux," they replied. The Lakota invited them to come see a buffalo calf they had killed, which was in the brush behind the riverbank, but Templeton was suspicious. He pulled Beckwourth away, and they recrossed the water and went back to the fort. Templeton was relieved to have escaped. "They certainly played a treacherous, cunning game," he noted in his diary.[26]

A few days later, Beckwourth sought out Templeton and told him that he had a premonition that something bad was about to happen. Beckwourth had not lived among the Apsáalooke for thirty years, but he believed he carried "medicine" within him, in the form of the bullet necklace he still wore around his neck. It gave him a power and protection bestowed by the natural world. Beckwourth's medicine had not felt quite right, he told Templeton, and he was worried.[27]

In late September, Jim Bridger returned from a trip to the Gallatin Valley of Montana, north of the Yellowstone Basin. He had seen a party of Apsáalooke hunters and talked to them about coming in to meet with Army officers at the fort that winter and receive gifts and rations. "They are not intending to come in," he told Templeton and Beckwourth, "but may."[28]

That night, Beckwourth left Fort C. F. Smith to go to the Apsáalooke village that Bridger had told him about. The officer in charge of the fort offered him a detachment of soldiers for protection, but Beckwourth refused. Such a large group of armed soldiers might be seen as a sign of aggression, even if he was with them. And Beckwourth likely trusted in his ability to negotiate with the Apsáalooke on his own. He brought only one man with him, a soldier named Jim Thompson.[29]

The next morning, Beckwourth began bleeding from his nose. This was not so unusual during the onset of the winter season. The air was cold and dry, and even people who had lived in these arid lands for years had such reactions when the weather turned. By the time Beckwourth rode into the Apsáalooke camp, however, he felt terrible. He spoke with the chief, Iron Bull, for a few minutes and then asked to rest. Seeing his condition, Iron Bull and his wife offered Beckwourth their lodge.

Over the next few days, the old scout slept most of the time but had a few moments of clarity, during which he discussed plans with Iron Bull. "I want 100 young men to go with me next spring to fight the Sioux," he told the chief. Iron Bull and his fellow war leaders seemed willing to consider it.

That night, Beckwourth retreated to Iron Bull's lodge. It is unclear what happened over the next few hours, as no one was with him. Clearly, the nosebleed and the fatigue were symptoms of something else, perhaps internal bleeding or warning signs of a heart attack. Beckwourth was strong, but he had lived longer than most white Americans did in the 1860s, and twice as long as most Black men in the United States.[30]

The next morning, when Beckwourth did not appear around the cookfire, Iron Bull and Thompson entered the lodge and found his body. They took him outside and buried him among the prairie grasses near the Clark Fork River, its waters always moving and ever changing. Jim Beckwourth probably would have found it fitting that he died in an Apsáalooke lodge while doing what he did best: negotiating the boundaries of Indigenous and white worlds in the American West.[31]

On October 30, 1866, Jim Thompson returned to Fort C. F. Smith with a group of fifty or sixty Apsáalooke but without Jim Beckwourth. "I was very sorry to hear of his death," George Templeton remarked. He had liked Beckwourth and found him "a very pleasant man" even "with all his faults." Templeton never had any doubts that Beckwourth's loyalty lay with the United States. He was "one who would interpret for the best interests of the government and would fight besides."[32]

Two months later, Little Wolf sent a group of Lakota, Arapaho, and Northern Cheyenne horsemen to attract the notice of the soldiers at Fort Phil Kearny, while he and a large group of warriors waited in the grasslands along the southern edge of the Bozeman Trail. In front of them, the road descended a small hill and then crossed a shallow stream, its banks edged with frost. Around eleven in the morning, Little Wolf could hear the *pop-pop-pop* of rifles firing. The Northern Cheyenne warriors readied themselves. They checked their weapons and calmed their horses, pinching their noses so they would not whinny and give away their location.

U.S. troops began to come over the ridge in large numbers, chasing the group Little Wolf had sent. The horsemen split into two groups, rode in opposite directions for a moment, and turned and crossed one another's paths. This was the signal, one that Little Wolf and his fellow Lakota and Arapaho chiefs had decided upon in the council the night before. Although Fort Phil Kearny was the weakest of the American installations on the Bozeman Trail and they had the advantage of numbers, Little Wolf and the others knew they did not have the firepower to assault the fort directly. Drawing a contingent of the fort's soldiers into an ambush, therefore, was the best strategy.[33]

With shouts of encouragement and excitement, the Northern Cheyenne jumped onto their horses. They converged with Arapaho and Oglala Lakota warriors and galloped straight at the American soldiers while Minneconjou Lakota riders burst out of the grass and came up on their rear. The federals were stunned. They thought they had been pursuing a small band of raiders who had set upon a group of Fort Phil Kearny's woodcutters. Now they were surrounded by more than 1,500 Indigenous warriors. The soldiers retreated and took cover behind rocks along the slope of the ridge, and the warriors made fast approaches, hanging from the sides of their horses and shooting arrows at any American who showed himself.[34]

"The ground was so covered with arrows," the Minneconjou chief White Bull remembered, "that a warrior did not have to use his own, he could pick one up almost anywhere."[35] Little Wolf fought alongside his brothers, Big Nose and Swift Hawk, first on horseback and then on foot as the warriors dismounted and began to make their way up the ridge, "stabbing and scuffling there in the smoke."[36] This charge ended the battle; the Northern Cheyenne and their allies were victorious.

The warriors stripped the soldiers and rifled through their clothing, pocketing silver coins and ammunition. They cut some men to pieces and then scalped them. Others they shot with more than one hundred arrows. They left these bodies where they fell, along the road or the ridge, as a warning to the U.S. Army and the American federal government: anyone who came to steal their land would meet a similar fate.[37]

Little Wolf had much to celebrate in the wake of what the Lakota called the Hundred Men Killed Fight. The plan he had crafted with his fellow chiefs had worked just as they had envisioned it. The battle was as complete a victory as Indigenous warriors had ever achieved in their long war with American armies. His men had proven their bravery, and the alliance with the Lakota and Arapaho proved a strong one. But it was not a victory without sacrifice.

Little Wolf's little brother Swift Hawk was one of the two Northern Cheyenne killed that day, and his older brother Big Nose was injured.[38] As he gathered his men to return to their winter lodges along the Powder River, Little Wolf mourned his loss. He also knew that while the alliance had triumphed in this battle, there would be more to come.

The Hundred Men Killed Fight interrupted the mail, so the residents of Denver did not find out about that battle or Jim Beckwourth's death until late January 1867. Some greeted the news of Beckwourth's passing with a shrug.

"No loss to the country," one man said. "It was time," remarked another.

William Byers was immediately suspicious. He started a rumor that the Apsáalooke had poisoned Beckwourth, in revenge for a long-remembered slight or for representing the U.S. Army at such a destructive time for that tribal nation. Byers was also dismayed at the dismissive assessments of the man and his career.

"We know that many looked upon him as a bad man," the editor wrote in the *Rocky Mountain News*. "He doubtless had his faults, and who has not? Certainly, he was not worse than any of us would likely have been with such a beginning, and such surroundings through a long and eventful life."[39]

Jim Beckwourth was a complicated man, the editors of the *Denver Gazette* agreed. But "he was ever more sinned against than sinning."[40] Most Coloradans did admit that Jim Beckwourth's life was a remarkable one. He had taken part in so many of nineteenth-century America's most important events: fur trading, Indigenous land dispossession and warfare, the Mexican-American War, the California and Colorado gold rushes, and the Sand Creek Massacre. When he died in 1866, the Civil War was over, but the battles between Americans and Indigenous peoples in the American West, which had begun in the 1840s, continued.

"What a history there was in that life!" Byers exclaimed. "Almost from the Declaration of Independence by the thirteen feeble colonies, to the present day."[41]

Soon after learning of Beckwourth's death, the Denver photographer William Chamberlain placed an advertisement in the *Rocky Mountain News*. The scout had come to his studio with Sue, and each of them sat for a portrait. "He was one of the most famous men in his way that ever lived," the notice read, "and in a few years photographs of his face will be highly prized."[42]

William Byers purchased one and sent it to the editors of the *American Phrenological Journal* so they could read Jim Beckwourth's facial features for signs of his character. They saw in his bone structure a man who was perceptive, intuitive, remorseless, and generous. "Cautiousness was not large," they wrote in their assessment, "and he would venture where most others would not; would try experiments absolutely dangerous in themselves. The wonder is that he lived so long."[43]

Jim Beckwourth had been a trapper, a scout, a messenger, a miner, a merchant, and a farmer. Born into slavery, he lived to see it abolished when the Thirteenth Amendment was ratified in December 1865. Despite this, Jim did not have the right to vote in the state of California or the Territory of Colorado. He never overtly denied his biraciality, but he often chose to pass as Indigenous or white as the circumstances demanded in the dynamic communities of the American West. Sometimes the actions he took were violent or provoked violence. He was an unreliable husband, a man who thought nothing of abandoning both family and community. Beckwourth was also a successful cultural broker and made productive connections between communities. He embodied the complexities that defined the region he traveled through with such frenetic energy.

"Jim was a strong character," Beckwourth's former trapping associate Charles Stobie observed. "His reputation was as wide as the West itself."[44]

PART V
IT WILL BIND THEM TOGETHER AND TEAR US APART

CHAPTER 21

A few months before Jim Beckwourth died, Congress had passed the Fourteenth Amendment, declaring that all persons born or naturalized in the United States, excluding "Indians non-taxed" (Indigenous peoples not living on reservations), were American citizens.[1] This meant that Jim was now a fully recognized member of the body politic, along with four million formerly enslaved men and women who were transitioning to a life of freedom across the South. This was just one of the momentous changes in the post–Civil War world that shaped communities across the nation.

To secure the civil rights of Black Southerners, the U.S. Army posted tens of thousands of soldiers at forts across the former Confederacy. And to secure the rights of white Americans to fulfill their manifest destiny in the wake of a traumatic national conflict, they deployed thousands of soldiers across the American West, with new orders. Chase down Indigenous raiders who stole cattle and goods from white farmers and ranchers. Protect American migrants as they moved across the West. And defend Union Pacific railroad crews from potential attacks.

Although the Union Pacific corporation had formed after the passage of the Pacific Railway Act in 1862, the Civil War's chaos and destruction had delayed construction. The crews began laying down track in Omaha, Nebraska Territory, in 1865 and by the summer of 1867 had reached the high plains of southwestern Nebraska Territory. Railroad workers were a kind of army of their own: thousands of Irish, Italian, and German immigrants, U.S. and Confederate veterans, and formerly enslaved Black men who dug into the prairie soil, heaving it up and shaping it into a linear bed. In their wake came the tracklayers. One group laid out wooden crossties at regular intervals perpendicular to the line, while another lifted thirty-foot iron rails into position on the ties and clamped them together. Using mauls, the next crew pounded ten spikes into each rail.[2]

If the ground was flat enough and the weather cooperative, Union Pacific workers could lay eight miles of track in a day. Hundreds of men, followed by a massive cattle herd and supply trains carrying food and water, worked their way west that summer, crossing Pawnee and Lakota territory before reaching the Northern Cheyenne homelands.[3] To Little Wolf and his fellow chiefs, the appearance of the iron rails seemed to be Sweet Medicine's dying proclamation made manifest: the Americans "were coming, and they would keep on coming."

In late July 1867, a Northern Cheyenne war party crossed a completed section of the Union Pacific track in the Platte River lowlands, just as the waterway made a big bend southward. The track was built on a floodplain that attracted thousands of slate-gray sandhill cranes and provided nesting spots for piping plovers, identifiable by a band of black feathers around their necks.[4] The war party was on their way to find a Pawnee camp to attack. The two nations were traditional enemies, and they had been fighting one another since before Europeans and Americans ever set foot in the Great Plains.

A mile or so to the east, the Northern Cheyenne could see a handcar moving slowly toward them. There were several men aboard, working the pump that propelled them forward; they were mechanics who had been sent to fix the telegraph lines laid along the railroad right-of-way. After a short discussion, the war party rode a few miles to the west, then dismounted. They found some cottonwood logs the Union Pacific crews had left behind and piled them on the track. Then they hid themselves and their horses in a nearby gully.

When the handcar approached, the warriors jumped out and whooped at the mechanics, shaking their guns and lances over their heads. Distracted, the men grabbed for their guns and did not see the pile of wood on the track. Three of them were killed instantly in the wreck, and the Northern Cheyenne chased down the other two, scalping them and leaving them for dead. It was an unforeseen victory against a new enemy.[5]

While they were celebrating, the war party saw a light approaching from the east: a freight train pulling out from Plum Creek station. They had succeeded with the handcar, so they decided to try again. The men somehow managed to pry up a small section of iron and then hid in the tallgrass prairie. The conductor did not see the bent rail, and the seventeen-car train hit it at full speed. "The cars were literally jammed into a mass," a correspondent for the *Chicago Tribune* reported, "while their contents were crushed and scattered about in great confusion."[6]

The fireman and engineer were killed on impact, and the conductor and another man escaped. They ran back east along the track, waving down a passenger train that had been close behind. As the passenger engine reversed course and began pushing the cars back toward Plum Creek, the Northern Cheyenne came out of the grass and began to search the wreck for bounty. The first three cars were full of brick and coal; the rest carried food, textiles, and domestic goods bound for U.S. Army posts and the shops that lined Denver's business district.[7]

Several chiefs had brought their young sons along, hoping to give them an opportunity to count coup on a Pawnee (get close enough to him to tap him with a coup stick) and begin their journey into manhood. This was a different kind of lesson, one that taught the boys to take advantage of opportunities as they found them and to defend their homelands against any kind of incursion.

As their fathers piled up sacks of sugar, coffee, and tobacco to take back to their summer encampment, the boys got ahold of several bolts of fabric. They tied the cloth to their horses' tails and then leapt onto their backs. The warriors looked up to see the ponies flying across the prairie, the boys astride them yelling with glee. Long streamers of light yellow material printed with tiny red and blue flowers flowed behind them, snapping in the wind.[8]

The Union Pacific Railroad's response to the Plum Creek raid was immediate. They sent train cars full of workers to clean up the wreck, and they received help from the U.S. Army, whose officers ordered a contingent of soldiers and Pawnee scouts to find the band responsible for the attack. In the battles that ensued, the Northern Cheyenne lost several women and children to the Pawnee as captives.[9] Little Wolf and the other chiefs decided that the costs of another raid on the railroad were too high. They would focus instead on emigrant wagons on the Platte Road and the Bozeman Trail, striking them alongside the Southern Cheyenne Dog Soldiers and their Arapaho allies.[10]

Three weeks after the Plum Creek raid, Ovando Hollister took the Union Pacific from Omaha to Julesburg, Colorado Territory, and then boarded a horse-drawn coach to Denver.[11] He was returning from an eight-month sojourn on the East Coast, after selling the Black Hawk *Mining Journal* to the Times Publishing Company for $5,000. Hollister spent much of his trip in Springfield, Massachusetts, working with the editor and publisher Samuel Bowles, who had been part of Schuyler Colfax's entourage on his tour of the West in 1865. Hollister had pitched Bowles a book about Colorado's mining industry and a history of its white settlement. *The Mines of Colorado* would introduce eastern readers to the Rocky Mountains, he told Bowles, and it would be a useful guide for American migrants and investors.[12]

"The annexation of the Rocky Mountains to the Union by railways," Hollister argued, "will open a new world to [tourism and] science, a new field of adventure to money and muscle, a new and pleasant place of Summer resort to people of leisure."[13]

Hollister had hoped that the Union Pacific line would run through Denver. But the railroad's engineers had chosen a route to the north and would soon build a station in the town of Cheyenne, named by its white founders for the Indigenous peoples they displaced. The one-hundred-mile stretch between Cheyenne and Denver was relatively flat, with only a few creeks and rivers to cross. Hollister felt sure that Colorado residents could convince the Union Pacific to build a trunk line. Congress had passed an act in 1866 to fund construction of a track from Kansas City to Denver, but engineers had not started building it yet.[14] Hollister lobbied for both roads in *The Mines of Colorado*, which was 450 pages long and included a "new and intelligent map" of the territory.

The editors of the *Omaha Republican* were delighted with the book and suggested that Hollister send many copies to their city, for Union Pacific passengers to buy before climbing aboard. While a few miners in the Rockies criticized Hollister for emphasizing some gulches over others and suggested that the author was paid for coverage, most others came to Hollister's defense. He was not the kind of man, they argued, to degrade historical work for private gain. In early September 1867, when the editors of the *Rocky Mountain News* heard that Hollister had arrived back in town, they were pleased that one of the territory's most prominent boosters had returned.

"During his long absence," they wrote, he "has allowed no occasion to pass of defending the reputation of Colorado, or promoting her interests. He will receive the thanks of our people and their welcome home again."[15]

Hollister's boosterism had not been all that effective, however. Denver was still a sleepy town during the spring and summer, when the men left for the diggings in the mountains. Lakota and Northern Cheyenne raids on the Union Pacific and the Platte Road had slowed migration from the east to a trickle. Miners and migrants continued to arrive from the south and west, however, and the city now boasted a population of more than four thousand people. There was an array of activities to keep them busy: lyceums, charity events, lectures, concerts, fairs, theatricals, dinner and card parties, billiards, and horse races. If Denver residents wanted brisk exercise, it was a relatively short ride to the foothills, where they could ramble, ride, hunt, fish, camp out, or bathe in the frigid mountain creeks.

In Hollister's view, Colorado Territory was already developing a distinctive culture after only six years in existence. "There is a nameless, indefinable charm in the constitution of Rocky Mountain society," he believed, that was attributable to several factors, including "the incongruity of its original materials, drawn from every part of the Union." Building lives in Denver, the Rockies, and along the Front Range (a north–south corridor stretching more than two hundred miles along the foothills of mountains) forced the rich and poor to commingle. Hollister believed that this freed them from the usual restraints and customs of eastern society.

The American West also had the potential to change a person's inner life. "Beneath that sky of Heaven with its far horizons," he wrote in

The Mines of Colorado, "in presence of these colossal hills, . . . the soul expands."[16]

Hollister could not resist the allure of those colossal hills. Within two weeks of his arrival in Colorado, he was up in the mineral region. The gold diggings he had written about in his book were mostly played out, but miners had found silver veins embedded in lead deposits in nearby gullies. Hollister spent a month touring these lodes and meeting the miners who were working them. In one prospector's cabin, he was delighted to find a few books on a crooked, handmade wooden shelf.

"Plutarch, Macauley, . . . Thackeray, Dickens—and—no!—yes?— Hollister. See what it is to be the author of a book—what good company one gets into!"[17]

Hollister wrote letters to his former Black Hawk paper about the promise of silver extraction and compiled them into a short promotional pamphlet. "Very little can yet be certainly [predicted]" of the silver mines of Colorado, he wrote, "from the fact that exploration has only just commenced." To discover the true worth of these silver veins, the mines required an infusion of capital. Could there be a better or fresher field for investment? Hollister doubted it.[18]

The nation certainly needed an economic boost from successful mining in Colorado. The Civil War had ended only two years before, and it had taken both a human and a financial toll on the entire nation. Northern capitalists were funding the reconstruction of the South, and they wanted to develop the American West through national projects like the transcontinental railroad. Silver, a cheaper metal that could be exchanged widely as currency, could help stabilize the postwar economy. To exploit Colorado's silver veins, however, required an end to the hostilities between Colorado's white population and the Indigenous peoples whose lands they trespassed upon—particularly the Northern and Southern Cheyenne, and the Arapaho.

"Is the government to stand idly by and see the wild savages of the buffalo plains drive out the settlers of the west," Hollister asked in a letter to the *New York Times* in 1867, "the men who, through every conceivable hardship and privation, are extending our empire in the wilderness?"[19]

Hollister believed that he and other white Coloradans continued to be the vanguard of American conquest. They were the men and women whom Emanuel Leutze had depicted in the massive mural he painted in the U.S. Capitol during the Civil War, *Westward the Course of Empire Takes Its Way*. In the painting—a visual evocation of the frontier myth—hardy pioneers move up and over the mountains, pointing the way toward a glowing, sunlit future while holding an American flag.[20] The mural found the perfect home in the Capitol, where politicians had been supporting its ideals for years. And now Hollister felt that the federal government was duty-bound to step in and help the living pioneers of Colorado.

"It is war, and only war," Hollister wrote, "until the plains indians are wiped out."[21]

In 1867, many members of the U.S. Congress did not fully agree with Ovando Hollister's extreme take on federal Indian policy—at least not yet. The postwar government was mostly focused on bringing the former Confederate states back into the Union and protecting four million Black Americans' freedom and hard-won rights. It was a chaotic time, with congressional Republicans still reeling from Abraham Lincoln's assassination and embroiled in a nearly constant struggle with the conservative Democrat Andrew Johnson, who had succeeded Lincoln as president.[22]

Although most white Coloradans likely agreed with Hollister and with the violent actions that the U.S. Army had taken in Colorado, the 1864 Sand Creek Massacre had alarmed many Republican leaders in Washington, D.C. They wanted to prevent violence between American migrants and the West's tribal nations. The question was, how? The conflict over land in the region was long-standing and seemed inevitable. Congress created a commission to investigate clashes in the American West to find a resolution. When the Government Printing Office published its report *The Condition of the Indian Tribes* in 1867, the members of the commission embraced an Indian policy that had been part of the federal government's approach since the eighteenth century. They recommended that for the safety of both Indigenous peoples and white settlers in the American West, the two communities must be separated. If they were allowed to mingle freely, as they had in the past, the cycle of violence in the Great Plains would continue.[23]

To put this plan into motion, Congress created a Peace Commission, made up of four civilians and three military men, all of whom had experience in Indian affairs and represented a range of approaches. One of the civilian commission members was Samuel F. Tappan, who interviewed Jim Beckwourth as part of the U.S. Army's investigation of Sand Creek. One of the military commanders was William Tecumseh Sherman, who was Ulysses S. Grant's second-in-command in the post–Civil War Army, and who believed that the use of hard-war tactics against tribal nations was the only way to end the conflicts on the Plains.[24]

The commission's charge was to meet with as many Indigenous leaders as possible in the next year and to negotiate treaties that would achieve three goals: prevent warfare, provide for the safety of white residents, and "civilize the Indians."[25] The commissioners were also determined to ensure the construction of the transcontinental railroad. Every treaty they signed would require tribal nations to grant rights-of-way to the Union Pacific and all future railroads and to cease attacks on crews and surveyors.[26]

Late in the summer of 1867, the commission set out from St. Louis, taking a boat up the Missouri River and then the Union Pacific railroad to its westernmost stop, sixty-five miles east of Cheyenne. From there they rode to Fort Laramie on the North Platte, at its confluence with the Laramie River. They sent messengers out to the federal Indian agents in the region, asking them to bring chiefs to the fort for talks. They waited in vain for several weeks, wandering among the fort's scattered buildings tucked into a curve of the North Platte and surrounded by low hills. They watched the soldiers drill on the parade ground. In mid-October, part of the commission left to meet with the Comanche, Kiowa, Arapaho, Kiowa-Apache, and a few Southern Cheyenne leaders—including Black Kettle—at Medicine Lodge Creek in Kansas.[27]

When the commission members reconvened at Fort Laramie in November, only the Apsáalooke had arrived. The Lakota refused to come in, as did the Northern Cheyenne. The Americans returned to Washington, D.C. In their report to Congress, the peace commissioners noted that most existing Indian treaties were drawn up in total disregard of Indigenous desires and demands. It was no wonder, then, that tribal nations did not abide by them. Additionally, they observed, many of the federal

Indian agents tasked with forging connections between tribal nations and the federal government were corrupt. They stole money and goods from their own agencies and took kickbacks from suppliers who wanted contracts to provide reservations with meat, grain, tents, blankets, and other items the government promised as annuities.[28]

The commissioners also reported that the Great Plains peoples were most incensed by the construction of U.S. Army forts in their homelands.

"Our war against the whites is to save the valley of the Powder river," the Oglala Lakota chief Red Cloud told them in a message he sent by courier, "the only hunting ground left to our nation." If the United States withdrew the soldiers at Fort Phil Kearny and Fort C. F. Smith, the Lakota would come in for talks, and "the war on our part will cease."[29]

The General of the Armies, Ulysses S. Grant, read the Peace Commission's report and suggested that the Department of War might be willing to give up the forts along the Bozeman Trail to secure peace. In exchange, the Lakota and the Northern Cheyenne would have to move hundreds of miles away to a reservation in the Upper Missouri Valley. Armed with this offer, the commission members returned to Fort Laramie in early April 1868. Tappan and Sherman traveled together, and with them was the photographer Alexander Gardner, who had become famous during the Civil War for capturing that conflict's human and environmental carnage.[30]

Soon after they arrived, Sherman received word that he had been recalled to Washington to testify in the impeachment trial of Andrew Johnson. The president had tried to derail the Republicans' Reconstruction plans in the South one time too many, and they wanted to be rid of him. Before Sherman left Fort Laramie, he admonished Samuel Tappan and the other commission members to stay on task and convince the Plains chiefs to accept forced removal to a reservation in exchange for the abandonment of the Army's forts. If they did not agree, Sherman would "prosecute the war with vindictive earnestness against all hostile Indians, till they are obliterated or beg for mercy."[31]

When the Northern Cheyenne learned of the Peace Commission's offer to withdraw from the Bozeman Trail, they were intrigued. The

Americans never offered to abandon their fortifications in Indigenous territory. The Council of Forty-Four, the Northern Cheyenne's central governing body, discussed the matter and decided to send Little Wolf and several other emissaries to negotiate with the Americans. Little Wolf was more of a military leader than a diplomat, but he was his people's Sweet Medicine Chief and one of the Northern Cheyenne's most respected leaders. He would represent Northern Cheyenne interests with firmness and determination. As they traveled to Fort Laramie, the Northern Cheyenne crossed the dark scar of the Bozeman Trail as it cut its way through their homelands.

By the time they arrived at the fort, General Sherman had returned from Washington, D.C., having taken the Union Pacific line as far as it had been constructed, a few miles east of Laramie.[32] The commissioners had already met with several Lakota bands. The Northern Cheyenne erected their tipis on the plains outside the fort, along the banks of the Laramie River. On May 10, they put two tipis together to form a council lodge. Little Wolf and his fellow chiefs sat next to one another on overlapping blankets, flanked by three interpreters. When Tappan, Sherman, and two other commissioners entered the tent, the Americans settled themselves on stools and boxes.

"The government of the United States desires peace," the commissioners told Little Wolf and the others, "and its honor is hereby pledged to keep it."

The Department of War was willing to abandon their forts on the Bozeman Trail. In exchange, they wanted the Northern Cheyenne and their Northern Arapaho allies to relinquish their homelands. They would have to move five hundred miles south to the Arkansas River in Colorado with their Southern Cheyenne kin, or more than three hundred miles east to live near the Upper Missouri River with their Lakota allies. They would retain the right, however, to hunt in their ancestral lands if they ceased their attacks on white migrants and settlements, as well as railroad crews and passengers on the Union Pacific line.[33]

When the discussion was over, Little Wolf rose to place his mark beside his name on the treaty. The Northern Cheyenne would be giving up a lot. But continued access to their hunting lands was vital to their survival as a people. As was peace with the Americans.

Once all the other chiefs added their marks, the commissioners signed their names, and the clerk sealed the document. It was unclear whether Tappan and Sherman had explained all the treaty details, like the demand that the Northern Cheyenne cultivate wheat and corn on privately held tracts of land and send their children to American schools constructed by the Bureau of Indian Affairs.

Little Wolf left the council tent, wrapped in a dark blanket. He was talking with two of his fellow chiefs when the photographer Alexander Gardner approached him. For several months, Gardner had been taking photographs of the fort, its assembled Indigenous peoples, and the treaty negotiations. His stereographic camera produced doubled images, which appeared in three dimensions when seen through a stereograph viewer. Earlier that day, Gardner had captured the treaty negotiation in progress; the chiefs mostly had their backs to him while the commissioners sat in a row, some of them looking directly at the camera.[34]

Through gestures, Gardner indicated that he wanted Little Wolf and the others to pose for him. They agreed and stood in a row. Little Wolf leaned casually against a cottonwood stump, crossing his left leg over his right at the ankle. His long hair was parted in the middle and woven into two braids and wrapped in cloth. As Gardner exposed the camera's plate, Little Wolf held his blanket tightly around him and stared at the lens, his mouth pressed together in a grim line.[35]

That week, the *Rocky Mountain News* reported on the treaty negotiations at Fort Laramie. Although several of the commissioners had still not met with Sitting Bull or other Lakota bands, there was some hope that the commission had secured a peaceful future for the region. The chiefs of the Southern and Northern Cheyenne, the Apsáalooke, and the Arapaho had all agreed to terms. If the federal government did not ratify the treaties and begin providing food, clothing, agricultural tools, and money, however, the tribal nations "will not much longer remain quiet." If this happened, the *News* noted, "there will be no recourse but war."[36]

The article was not signed, but it is likely the author was Ovando Hollister, who had taken a job as associate editor of the *Rocky Mountain News* the week before Little Wolf sat down with the Peace Commission. Hollister had already begun writing the local columns of the paper, emphasizing Colorado's mineral and agricultural interests and giving readers "the freshest and fullest intelligence possible" of events in the territory and the West. And he argued for the importance of the transcontinental railroad as a national and regional project.[37]

Through his columns, Hollister continued his work as a Colorado booster. He wanted the territory to flourish and to become a state. As a devoted Republican, Hollister believed that Colorado would send Republican representatives and senators to Congress and increase the power of the party nationwide. Ten days after Little Wolf sat with the Peace Commission, Republican delegates met in Chicago and unanimously nominated Ulysses S. Grant to be their presidential candidate. In the first presidential election since the end of the Civil War, Grant would run against Democrat Horatio Seymour, a former New York governor who opposed Reconstruction policies that required the former Confederate states to protect Black civil rights before they could return to the Union.[38]

Two months later, Grant stepped out of a coach and onto Denver's streets. In the previous weeks, he had inspected U.S. Army garrisons across the Great Plains accompanied by two of his favorite Civil War officers (and fellow generals in the postwar U.S. Army), William Tecumseh Sherman and Major General Phil Sheridan.[39]

Grant made it clear to Denver's officials that this was not a campaign stop and he would not be making any political speeches. Instead, he and Sheridan strolled around the town and talked to residents. Ovando Hollister met Grant in the street and offered him a light for his cigar. The general gratefully accepted, and they chatted. Hollister was curious about the candidate's reasons for coming to the West. "We came because we had a chance," Grant told Hollister. "We don't know when we might have another, and we think it is every public man's duty to at least *see* the country."

"It gives one a broader outlook," Sheridan added, "and one's mind is apt to expand with his horizon."[40]

As they walked through Denver, a crowd started to gather around them. Grant made his excuses and quietly meandered away. "He seems to be the most unassuming man that ever lived," Hollister observed.[41] Over the next two days, Grant and his delegation rode up into the mountains, visiting the silver mines of Georgetown and the gold diggings at Black Hawk. When they returned to Denver, Grant, Sheridan, and Sherman attended a reception at the Masonic hall, then departed for Cheyenne the following morning.

Coloradans were delighted with the visit. If Grant won the presidency, he "will at least know there is such a place as Colorado." And perhaps Sherman and Sheridan would send soldiers to their aid more swiftly in the future. Accounts of the generals' trip might also encourage other tourists to brave the long journey to see the Queen City of the Plains and the astonishing peaks of the Rockies. All these developments would benefit Colorado and its white residents.[42]

Only a week or so after Grant's departure, his running mate Schuyler Colfax also arrived in Denver. He and his travel companions—including members of his family—took the Union Pacific to the end of the track, which was more than 730 miles west of Omaha. There, they took part in a ceremony driving a spike into the section of the track that crossed the Continental Divide. Then they returned to Cheyenne and boarded a coach to Denver.[43]

Colfax and his half sister Carrie Matthews stayed with their other sister Clara, who lived with her husband in Denver. Colfax gave several speeches in the city, expressing his delight at returning to Colorado after an absence of three years. He was impressed with their bountiful fields of wheat and corn and other vegetables. And he continued to have high hopes for the Rocky Mountains' rich veins of gold and, now, silver.[44]

"I believe that He who rules in Heaven and controls the destinies of men, has specially given them to you as a heritage," Colfax intoned, "had intended to indicate by this His own favored people."

At this, the crowd applauded wildly. They believed in Manifest Destiny and the idea that the federal government's conquest was inextricably linked with the nation's democratic institutions. They embraced the notion that as white American migrants to the West, they played a central role in this process, displacing Indigenous peoples and building settlements.[45] It was pleasing to hear Schuyler Colfax articulate what they believed to be the sacred nature of that mission.

"The people of Colorado love him," Hollister reported in the *Rocky Mountain News*.[46]

The next day, Colfax and a large party of about twenty rode up into the mountains, and Hollister went with them. Once again, they passed through Golden and followed Clear Creek up the canyon toward Black Hawk and Central City. As they rode, Hollister pulled alongside Carrie Matthews, who was riding sidesaddle and had tied up her long skirt so that the horse would not tread upon it. She had dark hair twisted into a braid and serious brown eyes. The group camped that night, staking their white tents into the rocky dirt, spreading their blankets, and kindling fires to cook their dinner. The conversation was varied and convivial.[47]

Ovando and Carrie hit it off. Before he left the next day to run the *Rocky Mountain News* while his fellow associate editor continued with the party, Ovando asked for Carrie's hand in marriage, and she said yes. Such a rapid engagement was unusual for the time, but Hollister and Carrie must have been able to envision a future together from the start.[48]

Back in Denver, Hollister rummaged through his belongings until he found a vial of gold dust that a friend had given him earlier in the summer. The gold came from the headwaters of the South Platte near the base of Mount Lincoln, named for the president Hollister had so admired and Schuyler Colfax had so loved. He visited a jeweler in town and asked him to convert the dust into to an engagement ring for Carrie. It would symbolize not only their betrothal but also the landscape of the American West and the Republican political convictions that brought the two of them together.[49]

That fall, Little Wolf rode through the gates of Fort Phil Kearny, 250 miles northwest of Fort Laramie. The fort and its environs had been the scene of the Hundred Men Killed Fight two years before, the Northern Cheyenne's greatest military victory over the Americans in the war to control the Great Plains. In a rare instance in which the federal government honored its treaty obligations, the cavalry and infantry garrisoning the Bozeman Trail's three installations had abandoned the forts.[50]

Now Little Wolf and his warriors galloped through the grounds and set fire to Fort Phil Kearny's buildings before withdrawing a short distance to watch the blaze. Little Wolf waited until every structure had burned, and all evidence of the federal government's presence was in ashes. The U.S. Army had abided by their promises. But the commissioners had not given Little Wolf and the other chiefs a timeline for their forced removal. So he turned his horse toward the grasslands of the North Country, determined to stay there as long as his people could defend their homelands.[51]

CHAPTER 22

As Americans picked up the pieces of the country in the late 1860s, they imagined the West as a landscape of reunion, to be settled by both Northerners and Southerners. It was also a landscape of opportunity. Commercial images of the West and all it had to offer proliferated, and almost all of them were visual representations of the frontier myth. Among the most popular was *Across the Continent: Westward the Course of Empire Takes its Way*, printed and distributed by Currier & Ives in New York City. First published in 1868 with a title taken from Emanuel Leutze's already famous mural, the print was the work of the firm's most productive lithographer, Frances Flora "Fanny" Palmer.

The components of *Across the Continent* were already familiar by 1868. A train steams out of a frontier town (its residents still chopping down trees to build homes and businesses clustered around the depot), heading into a vast, empty plain. They are the pioneers, the men and women transforming the West into usable space. The billowing smoke from the engine—"Through Line, New York to San Francisco"—threatens to engulf two Indigenous warriors who observe the scene from the margins and appear doomed to fade from the scene. The winding river and mountains that extend into the distance promise a prosperous and happy future for the train's passengers.[1]

Fanny Palmer had been born in England and migrated to the United States with her husband in the early 1840s. Since then, the Palmers had lived in Brooklyn and had never been west of New Jersey. She based her vision of the ideal western town on narratives already circulating in nineteenth-century culture. *Across the Continent* was both based on and further disseminated the central beliefs of the frontier myth.[2]

The ideas that *Across the Continent* embodied obviously appealed to Ovando Hollister, whose belief in the railroads to bring power and progress to the American West had never wavered. In January 1869, he was in Utah, having left his editorial job at the *Rocky Mountain News* (the publishers, apparently, could not afford to keep him). He had agreed, however, to remain on staff as a correspondent "from Mormondom." In the more than twenty years since the Latter-day Saints had made their way to the Great Salt Lake from Illinois, their "Deseret" settlements had flourished. One of the few new faiths to emerge from the Second Great Awakening and survive into mid-century, Mormonism involved several practices that fascinated Americans, none more so than polygamy.

As a man who had grown up in the world of Shakerism—itself a "burnt-over district" religion with a unique stance on relations between men and women—Hollister doubtless felt qualified to assess the impact of plural marriage on Latter-day Saint communities and on the future of Utah more generally. He had retained from his Shaker upbringing a firm belief in the equal rights of women and personally found polygamy to be "against human nature, so far as women are concerned." He believed that many of his fellow non-Mormon miners, newspapermen, and business owners agreed with him.

"Polygamy is what raises the gorge of all these noble-hearted Western boys, of the civilized world," Hollister wrote. "They don't care whether Joseph was a true prophet or not, whether the Mormons return to Missouri or not, but they will never give them peace in the enslaving and brutalizing of women in the United States."[3]

Hollister did not consult Mormon women to inquire if they felt brutalized by the practice of polygamy. If he had, he would have found that many of them were strong advocates of plural marriage as a foundational element of their religion. They did not want the federal government, or Gentile men (non-Mormons) like Hollister, to be their "saviors."[4] Nonetheless, it was Hollister's view that the Saints could not cling to polygamy for much longer, for the transcontinental railroad would bring the world to them. With a larger and more diverse population in Utah, American government officials and business leaders could not and would not ignore the Mormons' violation of human nature on such a grand scale.[5]

When Hollister arrived in Utah, the Latter-day Saints showed no signs of teetering on the edge of ruin. Salt Lake City had been perfectly placed as a supply depot for gold seekers heading to and from California. The Mormons, under the leadership of Brigham Young, had survived a war with U.S. forces in 1857–58 and proclaimed neutrality in the American Civil War soon afterward. They established a string of thriving towns and cities on the western side of the Rockies, from St. George to Provo to Salt Lake City to Ogden. By 1869, the Saints "occupied and possessed, (nearly) all the arable land and all the water that is available for irrigation," Hollister reported to Denver readers. There were more than eighty-five thousand people living in Utah when Hollister arrived, and 98 percent of them were Latter-day Saints.[6]

The imminent arrival of the transcontinental railroad did not, in fact, threaten Mormon existence in Utah. Instead, it strengthened the economic power of the church, through labor contracts Brigham Young had negotiated with the Union Pacific. The railroad's land bounties would also bring in bags of cash. "A Land Office is about to be opened, and they are going to pre-empt the land," Hollister complained, "there is thus no room for Gentile settlers." This is what concerned him more than the practice of polygamy. The American West was supposed to be open to all white settlers who chose to live there; the Mormons' monopoly in Utah was, according to him, a violation of American land rights.[7]

One month later, Hollister was living in a wooden shanty in the nascent town of Corinne, only steps away from the bridge that Union Pacific engineers were constructing across the Bear River. The crossing was sixty miles north of Salt Lake City and twenty-five miles east of Promontory Summit. Corinne "is fast becoming civilized," a caustic reporter for Salt Lake City's Mormon-supported *Deseret News* reported, "several men having been killed there already."[8]

Hollister admitted that the town was a little rough, as most settlements across the West were in their first months of existence. But "people are coming in pretty fast," he assured the readers of the *Rocky Mountain News*. The railroad brought them, and they were men with energy and money. Hollister hoped that Corinne would become a "Gentile colony," a business center filled with non-Mormons to rival Salt Lake City and Ogden. Corinne's residents would also welcome "apostate Mormons" and Mormon women who wanted to escape from the tyranny of polygamy.[9] He wrote about these ambitions for the Denver papers and for the Salt Lake City *Daily Reporter*. In March 1869, knowing that the junction of the Union Pacific and the Central Pacific was imminent, Hollister purchased land lots in Corinne and began to sell them, pitching settlement to merchants and suppliers in Denver and on the East Coast.

For his investment in Corinne to pay off, it was vital that Gentiles control the merchant and military business in the region, especially the trade routes from the Union Pacific track northward to mining towns and forts in Idaho and Montana. Ultimately, perhaps Gentiles would outnumber the Latter-day Saints in Utah and force the church to abandon plural marriage and submit to the federal government. "Experience goes to show that before and from a well-organized Christian society," Hollister wrote, "Mormonism shrinks away as reptiles from the light of the sun."[10]

As a Corinne booster, Hollister welcomed every non-Mormon who wanted to invest in the town. "Ping Chong has come and yesterday bought a lot," he told his Salt Lake City readers in early April, "although he protested against the price."[11]

Like Mormons, Chinese men had been traveling through and living in Utah Territory for two decades. Most of them, like Ping Chong, came from the rural lands near the city of Guangzhou (Canton), a major port city along the Pearl River in southeastern China. The region had been riven by social turmoil and economic instability since the 1830s, so when word came of the gold strikes on the American River near Sutter's Mill, southern Chinese men—like other men all over the world—jumped at the chance to make their fortunes in a new place. They traveled to Hong

Kong, where they secured passage to San Francisco on a steamship. They paid with their own money or, more often, funds negotiated through a broker.[12]

In 1850, while Jim Beckwourth and Jean-Baptiste Charbonneau were living together in Murderer's Bar, an initial group of 450 Chinese migrants arrived on the Pacific coast, bound for nearby gold fields. One year later, their numbers increased fivefold. By 1852, there were more than twenty thousand Chinese men and a few hundred Chinese women in California. In Cantonese, they called the state "Gam Saam": Gold Mountain.[13]

In the gold camps, Chinese, Mexican, European, and American miners lived in a nearly constant state of tension. Sometimes they worked together, pooling resources and trading with or buying goods from one another. Other times they beat each other bloody in the streets.[14]

Although Chinese miners had much in common with white migrants to the Sierras, white officials did not welcome them or see them as equals. First in 1850 and then two years later, California passed a foreign miners' tax that made it almost impossible for Chinese miners to make a profit in the Sierras. This tax was, like the constitutional provision that denied the vote to Black and Indigenous men, one of the first laws to reflect the power and persuasiveness of the frontier myth in the West. It separated Chinese miners from their compatriots in the diggings, punished them because of their racial identity, and took away any sense of belonging they may have felt in the mountains.[15]

Some Chinese miners stayed and worked their claims until the quartz veins were exhausted, while others went back to San Francisco or traveled through the West, taking on other work as laborers, cooks, or laundrymen. Others followed migrant trails eastward to Salt Lake City, stopping to resupply in Mormon stores before heading to the gold fields of Colorado or Montana.

Men like Ping Chong built businesses by hiring other Chinese miners to work for them and arranging for their room and board. If they died, he sent their remains back to China. During the 1860s, Ping moved back and forth between Montana's mining towns, Salt Lake City, and San Francisco. The Corinne lot he bought from Ovando Hollister was likely just one of his investments in American land and businesses.[16]

When Congress passed the Pacific Railway Act in the summer of 1862, there were thousands of Chinese men looking for work in California. The next January, the Central Pacific Railroad Company broke ground in Sacramento. When the company began construction ten months later, they hired mostly American and Irish workers. But by the spring of 1864 this labor force had abandoned the track, opting to head out to the newly discovered silver mines of Nevada and the gold diggings near Virginia City, Montana.

The railroad placed employment advertisements in San Francisco newspapers, but few white workers answered the call. Instead, Chinese men came to Sacramento from towns across the West. The Central Pacific's construction engineers hired a couple of dozen men on a provisional basis. Impressed by their work ethic and range of skills, they hired more. By the fall of 1865, thousands of Chinese men were working for the Central Pacific, drawn from a migrant population in California that had grown to more than fifty thousand.[17]

"Without them," the railroad's president and California Governor Leland Stanford wrote to President Andrew Johnson in October 1865, "it would be impossible to complete the western portion of this great national enterprise."[18]

Many of the Chinese railroad workers, like the miners who came before them, were from Guangzhou. In the years since the gold rush, a trans-Pacific network of labor migration emerged and professionalized, controlled by contractors and logistics firms based in Hong Kong and San Francisco. Central Pacific recruiters visited farms and towns across the Pearl River region, talking about the money to be made laying down track in California. It did not matter that these rural laborers had no experience with railroad construction, the recruiters assured them. They would learn on the job. After they signed their contracts and arrived in San Francisco, these men traveled by boat to Sacramento, then climbed aboard train cars that took them to the end of the line.

They were free workers, contracted and earning a weekly wage. When they arrived at the railroad's work camps, they organized themselves into "messes": small groups of workers who shared tents and ate together. Their work gangs were much larger, and they labored six days a week, eleven hours a day, in all weather conditions.

By the time the Central Pacific's tracks were nearing Promontory Summit in Utah in the spring of 1869, nearly twenty thousand Chinese workers had built the road from Sacramento. They were the single-largest workforce laboring for a private enterprise in American history.[19] Most moved ahead of the tracks, wielding axes to clear trees and stumps and shovels to remove rocks and other obstructions from the planned route. They graded and leveled the earth and built masonry walls and culverts, preparing the ground for the smaller groups of track layers coming up behind them (most of them Irish) who laid down the rails and hammered them together.[20]

Along the way, Chinese workers spent more than a year—including two brutal winters—scrambling up and down the steep slopes of the Sierra Nevadas, digging out and reinforcing fifteen tunnels through the mountains. They handled explosives and cut through solid granite to create passages for locomotives and train cars sixteen feet wide and eleven feet high.[21] It was "hard work, steady pounding on the rock," Charles Crocker, one of the Central Pacific's owners observed. "Bone-labor."[22]

By the time they made it through the Sierras, descended into the arid Great Basin of Nevada, and approached Promontory Summit in Utah, Chinese workers had prepared the way for more than 600 of the Central Pacific's 690 miles of railroad. They were initially paid $26 a month for a six-day workweek. They had to pay for their food and worked longer hours than their white coworkers, who earned a higher wage. As the Chinese moved into the Sierras, the Central Pacific raised their wages to $31 and then $35 a week.[23] Sensing their leverage, thousands of Chinese workers laid down their tools and stayed in their tents one morning in July 1867. Launching the most significant collective labor action up to that point in American history, the workers demanded a pay raise, shorter shifts, and safer working conditions.

"The truth is, they are getting smart," Crocker admitted condescendingly. "Who has stirred up the strike we don't know, but it was evidently planned and concerted."[24] Crocker responded by cutting off the workers' supplies, and the strikers were forced to return to work, lest they starve in the mountains. Crocker finally gave them a raise more than a year later as they made their way across the hot, dry sands of the Great Basin.

As the Central Pacific rails approached Promontory Summit from the west in the spring of 1869, Charles Crocker sent word to the Chinese camps that he had made a bet with Thomas Durant of the Union Pacific. Beginning at 5:00 a.m. on April 28, they would lay as much track as possible in fourteen hours. The construction crew that made it the farthest would win Crocker or Durant $10,000. That morning, more than five thousand Chinese workers moved up the sagebrush hillside, which shone blue-green in the rising sun. A squad of eight Irish rail-handlers followed behind. At 7:00 p.m., engineers determined that the Central Pacific workers had laid ten miles and fifty-six feet of track—and they had won the bet. When they returned to Sacramento, the Irish tracklayers were feted for their achievement. The names of the thousands of Chinese workers who had made it possible were not recorded. It is unclear whether Crocker ever claimed his winnings from Durant; what is clear is that the Chinese workers did not see a penny.[25]

Looking west from Corinne after this competition, Ovando Hollister could see a vast expanse of white tents, hundreds of wagons on the move, and thousands of men moving up the slope to Promontory Summit. Hollister visited the camps and probably felt like he was back in the Black Hawk diggings in 1860. The men working for Union and Central Pacific had the same look as gold miners: scruffy, lean, strong, and battered by the elements. Interspersed among the white tents pitched all over the ground were bales of blankets and teetering stacks of boxes and cooking pots piled on top of one another.[26] Two railroad cars sat on the tracks beside the Central Pacific camps, dispensing rice and vegetables for the Chinese workers.

The scene "presents the appearance of a mighty army," a correspondent for the *Deseret News* reported. And the noise was deafening. "The engine bell sending forth its cheering sound every hour," Hollister wrote to the *Rocky Mountain News*, "the rumble of the car wheels making bass for the lighter music of civilization, which always accompanies them, and the screech of the locomotive weakening echoes never so startled before."[27]

Even though Ovando Hollister had avidly followed and written about the progress of the transcontinental railroad in the spring of 1869, he left Corinne two days before the Union Pacific and Central Pacific lines officially joined at Promontory Summit. That Hollister should give up the chance to be present at one of the era's most significant moments (everyone who was involved knew it to be so) is unaccountable. Whatever his reasons for going, Hollister's week in Denver was convivial. His friends greeted him warmly, and he made his social rounds before heading back to Utah.[28]

The ceremony he missed was full of pomp and bloviation. One thousand people had gathered at Promontory Summit, including officials from both railroads, politicians from multiple states and territories, five companies of U.S. Army soldiers, Mormon dignitaries, members of the public, and Central Pacific and Union Pacific workers. After the speeches, and after Leland Stanford and Thomas Durant tried (and failed) to drive the commemorative Golden Spike into a rail, a Union Pacific worker drove it home. The crowd cheered.

The engineers brought the Union Pacific's engine number 119 up to meet the Central Pacific's Jupiter, nose to nose, and the photographer Andrew Russell set up his camera. Each of the locomotives' engineers climbed up on top of his engine's "cowcatcher" and leaned out toward one another, champagne bottles in hand. A crowd gathered around and then turned their heads toward Russell's camera. The photographer exposed the glass plate and captured the scene.[29]

After the crowd dispersed, eight Chinese men removed the ceremonial spikes and pounded the rails into place that joined the eastern and western lines. Russell took another photograph. This was the only image taken that day that depicted the Chinese workers whose labor made the construction of the Central Pacific line and the completion of the transcontinental railroad possible.[30]

The transcontinental was, to Ovando Hollister, the magnificent symbol of the "indomitable spirit of the intensely western men" who built it. To him, however, these western men were not Chinese. They were not Latter-day Saints. They were white Americans drawn from the towns and cities east of the Missouri River, working both sides of the line. Hollister's friend and editor Samuel Bowles agreed. In *Our New West* (1869), Bowles argued that in the wake of the Civil War, the railroad was an act of regional reunion, the work of white Northerners and Southerners in the West. Their achievement was uniquely American.

"No people other than ours—daring in conception, rapid in acquirement, bold in execution, beyond any other nation," Bowles boasted, "could have done it."[31]

The transcontinental, and the federal conquest of the continent that it both represented and promised, soon became an essential component of the ideologies of Manifest Destiny and American exceptionalism. The railroad did just as John O'Sullivan had promised in his 1845 essay "Annexation": it bound together "in its iron clasp our fast-settling Pacific region with that of the Mississippi Valley."[32]

Westerners could now board the transcontinental and ride all the way to California to dip their toes into the Pacific Ocean. Or they could go to the Missouri River and then take any number of train lines east to the Atlantic coast. Six months after its completion, Ovando Hollister did the latter, boarding the train at Corinne, heading east to its terminus in Omaha, and then traveling on to Washington, D.C. On December 1, 1869, he and Carrie Matthews were married in Vice President Schuyler Colfax's house. The president and Mrs. Grant witnessed the ceremony, as did a few of Grant's cabinet members and their wives.[33]

The newlyweds returned to the "aspiring town" of Corinne in the winter of 1870, where they moved into a plain board house in the middle of town. They would soon make improvements, for Hollister's new brother-in-law had secured him the position as the collector of internal revenue for Utah Territory, and President Grant had signed his appointment paperwork. He would now be making $2,500 a year in that role, along with whatever money his land sales and newspaper columns brought in.[34] In a neighborhood a few blocks away from the Hollisters, so many Chinese railroad workers and other laborers had moved in that the white residents now referred to it as Corinne's Chinatown.

While Utah's Chinese residents established themselves in the early 1870s, the families they left more than seven thousand miles away in southeastern China continued to endure political and economic chaos. Massive floods destroyed rice crops and silkworm harvests, and a regional famine sent bandits fanning out across the countryside in Guangzhou to take animals, foodstuffs, and women and children from their neighbors by force.

In a village in the Pearl River region, the parents of a teenage girl called her to them. They told her that they had sold her to a trader. She would be leaving soon, maybe for Guangzhou or perhaps even all the way to the mouth of the river at Hong Kong. With the money her parents would receive for her, they would be able to buy more rice seed and feed the rest of the family for a little longer. The girl, whose birth name we do not know, could not agree or object. She had no choice in the matter.

Trafficking in women and girls was a common practice in her village and across the region. Although this trade was technically illegal, local and national authorities allowed it to continue, because it was a necessary tool of survival in rural China. And the Three Obediences of Confucianism demanded that the girl obey her father at home. If the trader married her off, she would obey her husband after marriage, and then her eldest son when she became a widow. There was nothing to say, so the girl prepared herself for the journey to come.[35]

She parted her long, black hair in the middle and pulled it back into a bun at the nape of her neck. Although the robe she wore with its roomy sleeves and long pants were made of a coarse cloth, they were neat and clean. She was adept at sewing, and it mattered to her that her clothes were presentable.[36] When the trader came to fetch her, the girl took her meager belongings, said goodbye to her family, and traveled with him from her village to a riverboat. The two sails were unfurled, and the girl found a place to sit among stacked boxes, underneath arched wooden coverings that extended from port to stern.[37]

After more than a day of travel, the boat entered the main channel of the Pearl River and moved at a faster clip. When they finally stopped moving, the trader took her from the boat's hold, and they stepped out onto the docks of the port city of Hong Kong. Large trading ships were anchored in the harbor between the city and the rural lands of Kowloon to the north. The towering summit of Tai Ping Shan (Victoria Peak) loomed over the city, and hundreds of warehouses, stores, and customs offices clustered along the waterfront. Here and there across the city, British flags fluttered in the wind; Great Britain had occupied and controlled the island for thirty years, since the 1842 Treaty of Nanking ended the first Opium War.

As the girl entered the city, however, she could see that while Great Britain might oversee Hong Kong, Chinese people still ran it. Hundreds of thousands of men and women, almost all speaking various dialects of Cantonese, walked and rode through the streets that pitched upward toward the mountain's summit, going to and from work. Many were hawkers and shopkeepers, selling food and wares from shops and stands. She understood them, but they were all strangers to her. Although the trade in rural girls was common in China, she was likely not prepared at all for this experience, which was disorienting and terrifying.[38]

The trader took the girl to a shop, and the owner consulted his ledger and looked her over. At a little over four feet tall, she appeared younger than her eighteen years. She had high cheekbones and full lips. Money changed hands, and the trader left. The girl had been in the city for only a short time when the merchant took her down to the docks with two other girls.[39] All three of them boarded a ship, and within a few hours it steamed out of the harbor and moved north along the coast. Then it turned east to cross the Pacific Ocean on a journey that would take sixty days to complete. The girls were going to San Francisco, the other great hub of the trans-Pacific network that had brought Chinese gold miners and railroad workers to North America.[40]

San Francisco, like Hong Kong, was built on a series of hills along a deep harbor. Two- and three-story brick and plank houses huddled close together on its steep streets, and a few parks were scattered about.[41] The city had a large and thriving Chinatown, home to more than eleven thousand men and one thousand women in an overall urban population of around 150,000 people in 1872. The girl and her two companions were three of more than nine thousand arrivals from China that year alone.[42]

The steamship officers ushered the girls out onto the pier, which was packed with sailors, customs officials, merchants, and dockworkers unloading ships of every size and shape hailing from all over the world. Labor brokers fetched the Chinese men who had been with them on the ship, leading them from the pier and into the city streets. An old woman approached, handed money to the officers, and told the three girls to follow her. They stayed in the waterfront district, crossing over to another pier and boarding yet another steamship. They were going to the city of Portland in Oregon, she informed them. And then on to mining towns, where they would be able to pick up gold coins off the street. They were likely relieved, as many Chinese girls trafficked from Hong Kong were taken immediately to San Francisco's brothels and put to work.[43]

The girls did not stay in Portland long, either. The woman put them on another boat, which moved up the Columbia River to the town of Lewiston, Idaho, where a Chinese man named Ah Kan, who ran a mule pack train between Lewiston and Idaho's gold mines, picked them up. From this point on, they traveled on horseback, more than one hundred miles to the southeast. It is unclear if they had ever ridden horses before. If not, the journey must have been unimaginably painful. The girls crossed through the fertile prairies of Nez Perce territory (following some of the route that Sacajawea had ridden along almost seventy years before) and then up into the mountains on a trail muddy with spring runoff. Tall, green-needled firs and pines crowded each side of the narrow path, and a wrong step from the horses would have sent the girls tumbling down a steep slope.[44]

At the mining town of Florence, the girl was separated from her traveling companions. From this point on, she had no one to commiserate or laugh with, no one to talk with about the differences between these wet, stony American mountains and the gentler peaks around the farmlands of the Pearl River region.[45] The pack train moved directly south, across the Salmon River and through thick woods along an even narrower and more precipitous path.

For many miles, the girl could not see much beyond the next turn, but suddenly the trail widened, and a few wooden shanties appeared. She followed the pack driver onto a main street, riding past shops and saloons, a bank, and an assay office, which tested the gold that miners pulled from the mountains to determine its purity. They passed a bathhouse and a restaurant, and men came and went from a barber shop and two "hurdy" houses, where white women danced for money. Some of the signs that hung outside the buildings bore English words, but most displayed Cantonese characters.[46]

The town had been founded ten years before, after prospectors found gold veins worth working in the hills above Warren Creek, a tributary of the Salmon River. Its founders originally named it Washington, as an alternative to the nearby town of Richmond. The country was embroiled in the worst year of the American Civil War, and even in the gold diggings of the northern Rockies, miners picked sides.[47] Soon there were 1,500 prospectors in Washington, but the placer gold—nuggets and dust found easily by sifting—was gone within two years.[48]

The first Chinese miners arrived during the spring thaw of 1870, after leaving Central Pacific work camps or migrating from other diggings in Montana and Colorado. The white miners there, holding claims they believed were played out, were happy to sell them to the new arrivals for inflated prices. By this point, residents of Idaho Territory (created in 1863 after being cleaved from Washington) referred to the town as "Warren's Diggings" or just, "Warren." Within a few months, Chinese men outnumbered white families and had built homes and businesses on Main Street and in the meadows along Warren Creek. They built ditches to bring water to the neighborhood, and terraced gardens on the hillsides.[49]

The pack train halted in the meadows, and the girl looked around her. Chinese men, dressed in denim coveralls and rubber boots whose soles were studded with nails, walked and rode and worked all around her. That was a relief, at least. She had found people who looked like her and spoke her language in an alien landscape. No one seemed to pay her any mind, at first. Just a few weeks before, the summer snowmelt had pushed the creek over its banks and flooded much of the town of Warren, and its residents were still cleaning up.[50] They were happy to see the pack train. The road to Florence was newly opened, and the packer who had brought the girl to town was also bringing much needed supplies.

"Many articles had become extinct," a Boise newspaper reported, "even whisky, that necessity of a miner, was scarce, and only by diluting to the most extreme limit had the fountain been kept up."[51]

A Chinese man approached the girl and motioned for her to swing her leg over the saddle and dismount. He put his hands on her waist and helped her to the ground. As he did, he turned to some of the other men and said, "Here's Polly!"[52] The girl—Polly now, for she must have seen no reason to object to this new name—was an unfree woman in a country that had fought a war to free Black men and women from enslavement, in a region that was already mythologized in American literature and artworks as a land of freedom and self-determination.

She saw no gold coins in the streets, and she still did not know who had purchased her or why. Was she to be a prostitute hired out to the miners or a dancer at the hurdy houses? Or a concubine, a second wife to a miner or merchant who had left his first wife and children in China when he came to seek his fortune? Or a mui tsai, a domestic servant working in a white or Chinese family's household? These were all possible futures for a girl who had been sold and transported across the Pacific to the American West.[53]

CHAPTER 23

Around the time that the girl's parents informed her of her fate in rural China, the grassland prairies of eastern Wyoming had transformed from a rolling sea of green to a vast ocean of yellow. A small group of Northern Cheyenne couriers galloped through them on their approach to Fort Fetterman, a U.S. Army installation at the eastern terminus of the Bozeman Trail. The fort was still standing because they allowed it; the Northern Cheyenne found it a convenient house of call. They could receive annuities at the fort and acquire all manner of goods from the Army's traders.

The couriers splashed through the North Platte—the water was low but still running—and rode around the fort's eastern wall. At the gate, they passed along a message to Fetterman's commander, Colonel George Woodward. "Chief Little Wolf is on his way," they told him. And two other Northern Cheyenne bands were not far behind.[1]

The next day, the Sweet Medicine Chief arrived at the fort with more than two hundred people. The women dismounted, unpacked the horses, and put up the band's tipis along the south bank of the river. Little Wolf posted sentinels at the borders of the camp, then left the women to their labors and took several of his best warriors with him to a log cabin that sat just outside the fort. There he secured the services of Jose Merivale, a Mexican man who had long lived in the Great Plains and spoke Algonquian (the region's most common language) along with Spanish and English. The group rode into the fort and dismounted at Woodward's headquarters.[2]

Little Wolf walked up to the commander, shook his hand, and sat in a chair that Woodward offered to him. Merivale settled in beside him to translate while the other warriors sat on the floor and leaned back against the walls. The chief took out a pipe, packed it with kinnikinnik (a smokable shrub), lit it, and inhaled while gesturing down to Mother Earth and then up to the Great Spirit before passing the pipe to Woodward.

"I am glad to see you," Little Wolf said, "and my heart is good toward you." The Northern Cheyenne had had a prosperous hunt in the Powder River country the month before, and the women had dressed the buffalo robes and deer and antelope skins. The winter months were coming on, and the Northern Cheyenne were anxious to stockpile supplies. Little Wolf wanted permission from Woodward to visit traders inside and outside the fort's walls.

"Make the best bargains you can," Woodward replied, "and with whomever you choose."[3]

That day and the next, Northern Cheyenne children pressed around the traders' counters and flattened their noses against the windowpanes installed in the soldiers' quarters. Women brought buffalo tongues to the storehouses to trade for colorful calicos and bright beads. By then, the remaining Northern Cheyenne bands—one of them led by Little Wolf's fellow chief Dull Knife—had arrived.[4]

After they established their camp, a group of Dull Knife's men waded into a narrow spot in the North Platte and unfurled a seine (net) while a group of women and children on ponies splashed in upstream. At a signal, the riders formed a line and began shouting, walking their horses downriver toward the seine.

"The *net* result being a take of nine hundred fish," Woodward observed wryly, which "filled a hand-cart to overflowing."[5]

Such scenes had become more common in the Great Plains in the three years since the Treaty of Fort Laramie. There had been sporadic attacks on migrant trains that veered off the Oregon Trail and into Northern Cheyenne or Lakota territory, but for the most part, Little

Wolf and Dull Knife and their people were more interested in trade than in warfare. However, they had also consistently refused to abide by the Laramie Treaty's provision that they move southward to join their kin on their reservation along the Arkansas River. They wanted to remain in their homelands, which had been theirs for hundreds of years. And they needed to be able to defend them against the growing number of white Americans entering their territories.

Woodward could not initiate treaty talks with the Northern Cheyenne chiefs to negotiate their removal. Six months before, a debate between the Senate and the House of Representatives over which body was responsible for treaty-making led to the insertion of a rider in the 1871 Indian Appropriations Act. It designated tribal nations as "dependent domestic communities" with whom the U.S. government would no longer make treaties. This was the first step in a new postwar U.S. Indian policy, in which the federal government took a more aggressive stance toward Indigenous peoples who refused to make peace. The U.S. Army would declare war upon tribal nations, force them to surrender, and remove them from their homelands and onto reservations.[6]

The measure passed easily, but there were some politicians who saw the rider for what it was. "The adoption of this provision," one California senator believed, "is the beginning of the end in respect to Indian lands. It is the first step in a great scheme of spoliation, in which the Indians will be plundered, corporations and individuals enriched, and the American name dishonored in history."[7]

When Congress abandoned treaties as the primary tool of negotiation with tribal nations, they did not propose a new system to replace it. Commanders like Woodward, who represented federal power across the West, did not follow any unified Indian policy. They reacted to circumstances as they evolved. During their talk, Little Wolf and Dull Knife asked Woodward about a schedule for future annuity distribution. Because he could not negotiate such matters himself, the officer advised them to travel to Washington, D.C., to meet with President Ulysses S. Grant.[8]

In November 1872, Grant was reelected in a landslide over fellow Republican Horace Greeley, the *New York Tribune* editor who had visited Colorado's Gregory Gulch in 1859 and was known for exhorting aimless young men to "Go West!" It was the first presidential election in which Black men were able to vote, after the passage of the Fifteenth Amendment guaranteed them that right. White southern men attempted to keep them from the polls, however, as part of a violent campaign to take back their power and reaffirm white supremacy across the states of the former Confederacy. In 1871, Grant had given the U.S. Army and the Justice Department the job of pursuing, arresting, and prosecuting members of the Ku Klux Klan, and the ensuing trials captured American attention in 1872.[9]

Although defending the civil rights of four million freed people and bringing the Confederate states back into the Union took up most of Grant's time at the beginning of his second presidential term, he had other pressing concerns. The economy was still chaotic seven years after the end of the Civil War, and the transcontinental railroad was not yet the generator of wealth that promoters had imagined it to be. He knew that the West's transformation required the removal and "civilization" of its Indigenous peoples, but he was loath to turn to violence.

Wars of extermination, as Grant noted in his 1873 inaugural address, were demoralizing and wicked. They were also—and probably most importantly—expensive. As U.S. Army officials were fond of saying, "it was cheaper to feed Indians than fight them." Americans were superior in numbers and military strength, the president knew. These forms of power should result not in excessive force but in leniency toward the tribal nations. "The wrong inflicted upon [them] should be taken into account, and the balance placed to [their] credit," Grant believed. The resultant Indian policy should be humane and made in good faith. "We will stand better before the civilized nations of the earth," he intoned, "and in our own consciences for having made it."[10]

Receiving Indian delegations in the nation's capital city was an essential part of Grant's Peace Policy, which he had embraced in his first term. The meetings he held at the Executive Mansion were opportunities to persuade tribal nations to give up their homelands and move to reservations, where they would be subsisted and surveilled by the federal government. On reservations, they would send their children to school, become civilized through education and Christianization, and join the American body politic as useful and productive members of society.[11]

Grant, like many American presidents before him, believed that Indian delegations' travels from their homelands to Washington, D.C., would impress them with the size of America's population and its technological wonders and advances. There would be no more treaties, but that did not mean that President Grant could not engage in his own brand of coercive diplomacy.[12]

When Little Wolf, Dull Knife, and fourteen other Northern Cheyenne and Northern Arapaho chiefs set out on their journey to Washington, D.C., in late October 1873, they were accompanied by four translators and a Fort Laramie Army officer.[13] They rode their ponies from Laramie to a train station in western Nebraska near the site of the Plum Creek raid, where they boarded a Union Pacific car to take them east to Omaha. A few days later, they arrived at a redbrick railroad station built in the Victorian Gothic style and boasting three towers that overlooked the center of the National Mall in America's capital city.[14]

They were the sixth Indian delegation to arrive in a three-week period that fall.[15]

The chiefs had to wait for five days until their first meeting with federal officials. President Grant was dealing with a new crisis, only a few weeks in the making. In mid-September, the investment bank Jay Cooke & Co., hollowed out by an unstable financial market and unwise investments in the Northern Pacific Railroad, closed its doors. A panic ensued, and the American economy was in chaos. The New York Stock Exchange had only recently reopened its doors. Grant had meetings every day with eastern businessmen, consulting them about how to keep more firms from failing and to put investment capital into circulation.[16]

While the delegation waited to see the president, they went to Wall's Opera House one night to see a performance of *The Black Crook*, the first modern American musical. If they followed the typical tourist itinerary, they would have walked along newly paved and graveled streets to view the scientific and artistic exhibitions at the Smithsonian Institution and paused to gaze at the Washington Monument, which was 150 feet high but nowhere near completed. The solid block of bluestone gneiss and white marble extracted in Maryland and shipped from Baltimore looked like a massive pedestal missing its equestrian statue.[17] That fall, another delegation had visited Mount Vernon as well. "There is no telling what the effect might be toward inducing these braves to exchange the warpath for agricultural pursuits," a local paper commented, "although it may result badly for the preservation of the cherry trees and 'sich.'"[18]

On November 13, the Northern Cheyenne and Arapaho delegation walked up Seventh Street to the Interior Department building to meet with Secretary Columbus Delano and Edward Smith, the commissioner of Indian Affairs. After the leaders greeted one another, Dull Knife spoke.

"We do not wish to go to Indian Territory," he told Secretary Delano. The Northern Cheyenne wanted to stay on their lands in the North Country and receive their annuities at Fort Fetterman on the North Platte. Commissioner Smith chided them, saying that at the treaty talks at Fort Laramie in 1868, they had ceded their lands in the Powder River valley.

"We never gave up our home," Dull Knife protested. "We did not fully understand the provisions of the Sherman treaty." But Smith was adamant and told them they would have to abide by the treaty and keep their word. "We have come a long way to see the Great Father and to talk with him about these things," the Northern Cheyenne chief retorted. "We did not propose to talk much with the Great Father's subordinate."[19]

The next morning, Little Wolf, Dull Knife, and the delegation waited in the lower hall of the Executive Mansion. They were joined by Southern Cheyenne and Arapaho chiefs, who had arrived in Washington, D.C., just a few days before them. Soon, Commissioner Smith came to fetch the entire group and accompanied them upstairs to a private office, where Secretary Delano introduced the delegation members to President Grant. The president spoke with the Arapaho chiefs first, telling them that they must join their southern kin at their reservation in Indian Territory.

"You agreed to go," Grant told the chiefs, "and there you will be among your friends." The Arapaho chief Little Bear objected, saying that he had thought that his people had thirty-six years from the date of the Laramie Treaty to move southward.

"Before that time the whites will crowd in upon you," Grant replied, "and maybe the Arrapahoes will be gone. If you go south you will be protected by the government; if you remain where you are, you must take care of yourselves." The president then talked up the reservations in Indian Territory, arguing that they would have more game to hunt there, and a genial climate.

When Dull Knife rose to speak for the Northern Cheyenne, he argued once again that he and Little Wolf and the other chiefs had been misled during the treaty talks at Fort Laramie. "When I signed the treaty," Dull Knife protested, "I did not know I was required to go south at all." President Grant blamed the interpreter. He felt sure that his good friend General Sherman, "in making the treaty, would not do them an intentional injury."

The talks were at an impasse. Then a Southern Cheyenne peace chief named Little Robe stood and stepped forward. "I came a good way to see the Great Father," he said to Grant. "I now see him. That is all I have to say." And he sat down.

President Grant laughed. It appeared he had met his match in public speaking.

"That speech was as terse as any of yours," Secretary Delano said to the president.

"I am afraid I shall lose my reputation," Grant replied with a smile.

"You need have no fears on that score," Commissioner Smith chimed in.

The delegation's mood was not so jovial. The chiefs had said what they had come to say, so they rose and left the room. They would return home and consult with their people and find out what they thought about going south to the Arkansas River in southern Colorado, or to Indian Territory (current-day Oklahoma), where the U.S. government had been forcibly removing tribal nations since the 1830s. When they decided what to do, they would send word.[20]

Little Wolf and the others were scheduled to leave Washington, D.C., and go to Philadelphia, but before they left they met with Alexander Gardner. The photographer had been commissioned to take portraits of visiting chiefs. This work was part of a project spearheaded by the Smithsonian Institution, whose directors wanted to create an archive of images of Indigenous peoples before they "vanished" from the earth. Most white Americans believed in the inevitability of their disappearance, which was an integral element of the increasingly entrenched frontier myth. Facing the oncoming wave of white migration, the myth contended, Indigenous peoples would ride into the sunset, never to be seen again.[21]

The chiefs and the photographer had last seen one another outside Fort Laramie five years before. Now Gardner asked Little Wolf to stand while Dull Knife sat next to him in a chair; he placed them in front of a huge drape with a diamond pattern. As Gardner readied his camera, Little Wolf cocked his right hip and held up a blanket wrapped around his waist with both hands. The fringe on his jacket hung down over the sleeves of his shirt. As he and Dull Knife stared off to the left of Gardner's camera, the light picked up the large cross Little Wolf wore around his neck. Its three arms bore Navajo naja pendants, crescents pointed downward toward his moccasins. They resembled horseshoes and were worn to protect both the horse and rider in battle. Little Wolf's naja symbolized fighting prowess and Indigenous resilience in the face of adversity.[22]

Their photo session over, the delegation moved on to Philadelphia, where they stayed at the five-story La Pierre House and attended a concert. In New York City, they were guests at the Grand Central Hotel, one of the largest in the nation and a gathering place for wealthy and glamorous New Yorkers and visitors.[23] By the second week in December 1873, they were back in their homelands, just as the winter began to take hold. They discussed their journey with their families and fellow elders, and the council decided that their position had not changed. They would remain in the North Country and live there until the end of their days.

At the Northern Cheyenne political renewal ceremony in 1874, the council decided they needed to choose leaders who were not only battle-tested and generous but also familiar with the ways of the white men. Dull Knife joined Little Wolf and the other principal "old man chiefs," who were given the responsibility to negotiate with federal Indian agents and make plans for the defense of Northern Cheyenne homelands. Little Wolf was reseated as Sweet Medicine Chief.[24]

These new leaders stepped into their positions at an ominous time. During the summer of 1874, the U.S. government took two actions that changed the course of their relationship with the Great Plains tribal nations. Clearly, Grant had not convinced the Northern Cheyenne to move to a reservation during their visit to Washington, so federal officials abandoned diplomacy. They were not quite ready to declare outright warfare (although generals William Tecumseh Sherman and Phil Sheridan encouraged this option), so they reached what they believed was a compromise. In June, Congress determined that the United States would neither fight the tribal nations of the North Country nor feed them. The Northern Cheyenne and Northern Arapaho would receive no further annuities guaranteed under the Fort Laramie Treaty until they relocated.[25]

A few weeks later, the Department of War approved a thousand-man reconnaissance to explore the Black Hills of western Dakota and eastern Wyoming, led by U.S. Army lieutenant colonel George Armstrong Custer. Ulysses S. Grant's son Fred went along, as a member of Custer's staff. The soldiers were ostensibly searching for a suitable site for a new fort, but Custer brought journalists from New York and Chicago newspapers with him and at least one photographer. There were also a few miners along, "to examine the mineral resources of the region."[26]

In early August, the expedition miners showed Custer the results of their panning just one heap of Black Hills earth: more than forty tiny flakes and nuggets. "Gold has been found at several places," Custer reported to U.S. Army headquarters, "and in paying quantities."[27]

It did not take long for the news to reach states and territories across the nation. For a country in the grip of an economic depression, it was welcome news. Men who had lost their jobs in 1873 rushed to the Black Hills. U.S. Army soldiers tried to enforce the provisions of the Fort Laramie Treaty and keep these new arrivals from settling on Lakota or Northern Cheyenne lands. They failed. By the fall of 1875, there were fifteen thousand American miners in the diggings.[28]

For Little Wolf and the Northern Cheyenne, this was the ultimate desecration. The Black Hills were the center of their world. The prophet Sweet Medicine had gained knowledge of the ceremonial ways of the Northern Cheyenne there, at Nóvávóse (Bear Butte).[29] The Black Hills were also sacred to the Lakota peoples, who placed the hills at the center of their creation history. According to the 1868 Fort Laramie Treaty, the area was part of both the Great Sioux Reservation and the "unceded lands" of the Northern Cheyenne and Northern Arapaho nations.[30]

For the next year, federal Indian agents tried to persuade the Northern Cheyenne and the Lakota to sell the Black Hills to the U.S. government.[31] Both peoples refused, so the government tried to extinguish Northern Cheyenne and Lakota land titles there. This did not work. They were bound by the terms of the 1871 rider protecting previous treaty rights.

In the summer of 1875, Little Wolf and Dull Knife brought their bands to join their Northern Arapaho kin and allies, and the Hunkpapa, Oglala, Minneconjou, and Sans Arc Lakota in a large summer camp in the Powder River country. The Hunkpapa Lakota chief Sitting Bull took part in the encampment's Sun Dance, riding into the ceremonial space on a painted horse.

"The Great Spirit has given our enemies to us," Sitting Bull announced. "We are to destroy them."[32]

By the autumn of 1875, President Grant was nearing the end of his presidency, and he wanted to win the West as his final executive act. Fed up with Indigenous resistance to America's Manifest Destiny and eager to provide economic stability for white Americans, he embraced warfare.

In the first days of November 1875, Grant convened a council of advisers he knew would support his plans for bringing the U.S. West more firmly into the Union by forcibly removing Indigenous peoples to reservations. Included in the meeting was General George Crook, a cousin of Schuyler Colfax's (and therefore Carrie Hollister's) who commanded the Department of the Plains. Crook's soldiers also oversaw the two main roads to the Black Hills, both of which originated at the Union Pacific Railroad tracks and moved through Northern Cheyenne and Lakota lands.[33] Grant told Crook and the other assembled soldiers and politicians that he had a two-part strategy.

First, the U.S. Army would deliver an ultimatum to the Lakota, the Northern Cheyenne, and any other tribal nations that were "roaming" in the Great Plains. They must bring their people to an Indian agency or U.S. military fort and surrender, or the Army would pursue and attack them. Second, Grant would give them a short deadline, one that fell in the dead of winter. The U.S. Army had had success campaigning against

Indigenous peoples as the snow fell and the temperatures plummeted. At that time of year, they tended to stay in their winter encampments, and their food supplies were running low, making them vulnerable. The president anticipated that the Northern Cheyenne and Lakota would have their women and children with them and would not be prepared for battle.[34]

When Little Wolf and the other chiefs received President Grant's order in December 1875, they scoffed at it and did not reply. As Grant anticipated, they stayed in their winter camps, venturing out only for hunts and to cut firewood. The day after the deadline had passed, George Crook received orders to initiate the second part of Grant's plan.

His troops set out from Fort Fetterman, and in early March 1876 they approached what they thought was an Oglala Lakota camp on the frozen banks of the Powder River. They hoped to find the rebellious chief Crazy Horse there and take him prisoner. The horses struggled through ravines and gullies, their hooves slipping on the icy ground. In the dawn quiet, a fifteen-year-old boy herding a small group of horses toward the water saw the soldiers approaching. He immediately raised the alarm.

Families burst out of lodges that were placed alongside nooks and rocks for protection from the wind. As the soldiers rode their horses through the camp, men, women, and children ran toward the bluffs. The men had their guns, bows and arrows, and lances; they paused in flight to shoot at the soldiers' horses, hoping to stop the Americans' rampage through their village. They were outnumbered, however, and the protection of their women and children was primary in their minds. As they left their lodges behind, the U.S. soldiers ransacked them.

They found buffalo robes embroidered with porcupine quills, an elk skin larger than two Army blankets, and war bonnets made of brown and black eagle feathers. The soldiers also discovered baskets and woven bags holding forks, spoons, tin cups, frying pans, and kettles. These were likely procured through a long-standing and far-reaching trade network on the Great Plains, but Crook's officers reported that they were items stolen during attacks on American wagon trains. The soldiers gathered up weapons and ammunition and a herd of seven hundred ponies and then moved from lodge to lodge, putting the shelters and their contents to the torch.[35]

The Americans discovered only later that this was not an Oglala Lakota camp, but a Northern Cheyenne village under the leadership of the peace chief Old Bear. It was also a campsite; the band had been on its way to the Red Cloud Agency to surrender, as Grant had ordered. As the smoke from their burning lodges rose into the frigid air, the Northern Cheyenne men, women, and children began walking through the snow. Four days later, they arrived, half-frozen and starving, at Crazy Horse's camp on the Little Powder River. Oglala men and women came out of their lodges to welcome the refugees and offer them clothing, blankets, and hot stews.

"The Oglalas received us hospitably," the Northern Cheyenne warrior Wooden Leg attested, "as we knew they would."[36] At a council with Crazy Horse, the refugee chiefs told the story of the Army attack on their people and the destruction of the entire camp. "I'm glad you are come," the Oglala chief replied. "We are going to fight the white man again."[37]

The Northern Cheyenne rested, and several days later the combined camp packed up and moved north to the Hunkpapa Lakota chief Sitting Bull's winter village, which sat in the shelter of the Chalk Buttes, a towering white sandstone formation east of the Powder River.[38] Sitting Bull was, like Little Wolf, one of many chiefs of the Lakota people. But he had been gaining prominence among several bands since the 1860s, and many Lakota looked to him for leadership in the fight against American incursions.

At the chiefs' council that convened a few days later, the Northern Cheyenne refugees once again told their story, and Crazy Horse declared his support. Sitting Bull listened with concern. In the past few years, his Hunkpapa Lakota had surveilled and sometimes fought U.S. Army soldiers when they tried to pass through their homelands with Northern Pacific railroad survey teams. But the attack on Old Bear's camp was something different. The Americans had come into Lakota and Northern Cheyenne territory with the express purpose of making war upon them. Sitting Bull sent couriers to his fellow Lakota chiefs as well as Little Wolf, Dull Knife, and the Northern Cheyenne, inviting them to join the Hunkpapa at their summer camp. Once again, tribal nations came together in a widespread alliance to defend their homelands in the American West.[39]

Over the next several months, word spread throughout the North Country about the great summer encampment. Most of the chiefs who had received Sitting Bull's message helped manage their bands' move from winter camps and their springtime hunts. Then they brought them to the lands south of the Yellowstone River. By the end of May 1876, Sitting Bull's camp had grown to more than 3,500 people in a camp almost two miles long. They were on the move constantly, traveling a few miles at a time down Rosebud Creek, seeking fresh green grass for their ponies. "It was the taking down, moving, and setting up again every day of a little city," Wooden Leg remembered. The Northern Cheyenne held a place of honor in the camp, pitching their circle on the southern edge. Little Wolf's Elk Horn Scrapers Society kept watch over them.[40]

Little Wolf himself had not yet joined Sitting Bull's camp. He and his people were out hunting buffalo farther east in the Powder River country. In late June, they were returning to join Sitting Bull on the Rosebud when Little Wolf's scouts reported large numbers of U.S. soldiers riding along the southern bank of the Yellowstone River. Among them were members of 7th Cavalry and Apsáalooke and Arikara scouts under the command of George Armstrong Custer.

Custer had left Fort Abraham Lincoln on the Missouri River the month before, part of a larger column sent out to annihilate the tribal nations of the North Country, once and for all. They were to meet up with another army coming east from Fort Ellis in Montana Territory, and George Crook coming northwest from Fort Fetterman. They would surround Sitting Bull's camp and force his warriors to fight or surrender. On June 22, Custer and the 7th Cavalry had split off from the column to move south along the Rosebud and look for Sitting Bull's camp there and then move westward toward the valley of the Little Bighorn. Little Wolf's band followed at a distance.

They did not engage, for Little Wolf had his family and seven lodges of women and children with him. His had been a hunting party, not a war party. Even a chief without Little Wolf's prodigious experience in war strategy would know that to attack such a large force of armed cavalry would have been madness. Three days later, when Custer and his men encamped in the Wolf Mountains east of the Little Bighorn River, Little Wolf sent scouts to investigate ration boxes that the troops had left behind. They drew the attention of several soldiers of the rear guard, and the Americans shot at them, then rode hard to report to Custer that the Plains warriors had detected them. Custer panicked and ordered his men to split into three groups and advance on Sitting Bull's village on the Little Bighorn, instead of waiting for the other U.S. Army columns to come up.[41]

Little Wolf, who had slowed his surveillance after his men were discovered, arrived at the Little Bighorn battlefield just as Sitting Bull's warriors were decimating Custer's cavalry. Seeing that their allies had the fight well in hand, they waited until the gunfire died down to approach the alliance camp. The Lakotas, sifting through the trophies they had taken off the bodies of Custer and his men, jumped up and surrounded the new arrivals. Why had Little Wolf arrived so late and from the same direction as the soldiers? they wanted to know. Had he been helping the Americans?

"Do these people think I am a crazy man?" Little Wolf retorted. "I have with me . . . families of women and children. They have their tepees, their packhorses, all of their property. Does anybody suppose that is the way to join the soldiers and help them?" Little Wolf was angry that they were questioning his loyalty. "Not any part of me ever was a white man," he declared. "I am all Indian. I am willing to fight any man who says I am not."[42]

The Lakota seemed convinced by this explanation. They grudgingly accepted Little Wolf's gift of the American ration boxes and welcomed his band into the camp.[43] Little Wolf found his kin among the victorious warriors and heard their tales of the battle's many dramas. They also heard about the fight on the Rosebud the week before, where several Northern Cheyenne bands along with Oglala Lakota led by Crazy Horse inflicted enough damage on George Crook's forces that he ordered a retreat. He never made it to the battlefield at Little Bighorn. In the years afterward, U.S. Army personnel debated about the difference Crook's men could have made. If the Northern Cheyenne had not driven Crook back from the Rosebud, perhaps George Armstrong Custer and his men would still be alive.

The next day, when soldiers on the march from Fort Ellis arrived at the site that would become known as "Custer's Last Stand," the alliance camp was gone.⁴⁴ The Lakota bands and the Northern Cheyenne traveled together for another few weeks and then parted ways. Little Wolf took his band southward, toward the Bighorn Mountains and the grasslands east of its slopes, where bison herds still dotted the plains. The men had a good hunting season, and the women prepared the robes, butchered the meat, and sent children out to gather nuts and berries to dry in the sun.

"Most of them had a good summer," one Northern Cheyenne man later remembered. "They did not know it was their last summer of freedom."⁴⁵

CHAPTER 24

On July 6, 1876, the headline in Utah's *Daily Ogden Junction* leapt out from the front page: "TERRIBLE NEWS!" it read. "DEFEAT OF GENERAL CUSTER!" The paper promised to print details of the battle reports that U.S. officers had sent as soon as they reached telegraph lines. Utah's other major papers reported on the Lakota and Northern Cheyenne victory for the next week and then began calling for donations to build monuments to George Armstrong Custer across the western states and territories.[1]

Ovando Hollister was no doubt as shocked as his fellow Utahans when reading this news. He had been advocating for the extermination or removal of Indigenous peoples in the American West for more than ten years, and he still believed that these military campaigns were the key to white settlement and business development in the region. That a large force of allied tribal nations could defeat American troops in the field was inconceivable. It was hard to know what the Department of War would do now.

Ovando and Carrie had been living in Utah for six years. They built a large house in Corinne above a bend in the Bear River surrounded by newly planted trees. It was not Hollister's original land lot. That claim had been canceled because the land had fallen within a section that the Central Pacific Railroad obtained as part of its financing deal with the federal government. The Hollisters liked their new home, however, and they began to build lives for themselves in Corinne.

Hollister helped form a local baseball team, kept tabs on mining discoveries in the Wasatch Range, and made speeches at the yearly "Pioneer Ball," which celebrated the arrival of white non-Mormons in Utah and their role in the westward movement of Americans in the 1850s and '60s. Carrie played the organ during services at the local Presbyterian church. As the federally appointed tax assessor for Utah, Hollister opened an office in Corinne's bank, where business owners reported to him to pay federal taxes on their products. Although taxes were not particularly popular in Utah—or in any other western state and territory—Corinne's civic leaders embraced Ovando and Carrie. "We know of none who could be more welcome to our city," the local paper declared, "than Mr. and Mrs. Hollister."[2]

Therefore, they were sorry to see them go, when the Hollisters decided to move to Salt Lake City in 1873. Corinne had not experienced the growth Hollister had expected in its first few years as a town. Brigham Young and his fellow Mormon business leaders continued to dominate the economy, and Hollister's attempts to raise money for a train line to connect Corinne to towns in Idaho and Montana—and thereby control trade in that corridor—failed. To keep tabs on Utah's Mormon businessmen and make sure they were paying their fair share to the federal government, Hollister felt he had to move to Utah's capital city. He opened an office in the First National Bank and continued his work. Salt Lake's Mormon population was not happy to see him.[3]

"He is an uninteresting man," the editors of the *Deseret News* sniffed, whose only real achievement was that he "married the half-sister of the Vice-President." They identified him as a prominent member of Utah's "Anti-Mormon Ring" and mocked his travels through the territory to confiscate untaxed cigar boxes and beer casks as "voyages of discovery."[4]

Hollister brushed off the scorn. He placed advertisements and editorials in the Mormon papers urging readers to abide by the country's laws. He sang in a local choir and performed Handel's *Messiah* in city theaters and churches. Carrie joined the Salt Lake City Library's board of directors, and the couple regularly attended church services.[5]

As a devoted Republican, Hollister also made sure to attend political meetings and to keep tabs on the party's wins and losses across the nation. In the summer of 1876, he was concerned. The presidential election in November was going to be close, despite the recent entrance of Republican-leaning Colorado into the Union as the nation's thirty-eighth state. President Grant had been on another tour of the U.S. West the year before, trying to drum up support for Republicans. Hollister was both politically and personally invested in Rutherford B. Hayes's victory in the election. A Democratic president would likely remove him from his lucrative position as Utah's tax assessor, and he and Carrie would have to scramble to make a commensurate living.[6]

In Washington, D.C., electoral politics was heating up that summer, but members of Congress broke from campaigning to launch an investigation of the disaster at Little Bighorn. They required reports from officers in the field as well as the secretary of war and his department heads. J. D. Cameron, who had been the head of the War Department for only a few months, admitted in his report to President Grant that mistakes had been made in the battle against the Lakota and the Northern Cheyenne. But the campaign's goals were important, he argued. The U.S. Army must continue to attack Indigenous camps. "It can no longer be delayed," he wrote, "and everything will be done by the Department to ensure success."[7]

General Phil Sheridan sent orders from his headquarters in Chicago to officers stationed across the Great Plains and the West. They were to campaign ceaselessly against the Lakota and Northern Cheyenne that fall and winter until the tribal nations became exhausted. When they finally surrendered at the forts or Indian agencies, officers and officials would disarm them and take their horses. Without means of self-defense or transportation, the Great Plains nations would be fully within the government's power.[8]

In late November 1876, Little Wolf and his people were encamped in the Powder River country south of the Bighorn Mountains, alongside Dull Knife's band. They had brought their winter supplies and planned to spend that season in the mountains, sheltered from howling snowstorms and hidden from the U.S. Army. At a council meeting in the camp, the chiefs argued. Little Wolf and Dull Knife wanted to leave for the Bighorns immediately because scouts had reported seeing signs of U.S. cavalry units in the area. Another chief wanted to stay, however, and feast in honor of the Kit Fox Society. He defied the older men and kept his people encamped. Little Wolf and Dull Knife relented, and the Northern Cheyenne remained where they were.[9]

Early the next morning, 1,500 U.S. cavalry troops led by one of George Crook's officers attacked. Little Wolf, Dull Knife, and their warriors scrambled out of their lodges and grabbed their guns, and someone began beating a drum that the Americans had presented to Dull Knife during their visit to Washington, D.C., three years before.

The battle played out almost exactly like the assault on Old Bear's camp eight months before. The Northern Cheyenne scattered into the bluffs and slopes, the men firing on the soldiers as the women and children took cover as best they could. The warriors exposed themselves to gunfire as they diverted attention from their fleeing families and tried to protect their large pony herd. The nature of the ground meant that part of the battle was fought hand to hand. Several warriors were able to draw a cavalry company into an ambush and kill their commanding officer.

One American soldier shot a warrior and took his gun and gun belt; the latter had a silver plate that read "Little Wolf." When the American rode back to his company, he bragged that he had killed the legendary Northern Cheyenne chief. He was wrong. Little Wolf had gifted the belt—another souvenir from the 1873 trip to Washington—to a fellow warrior as an act of generosity and respect. The two sides fought to a standstill, but the Northern Cheyenne lost more than forty men and women and were, like Old Bear's people, forced to abandon their winter village.

"They killed our men, women, and children, whichever ones might be hit by their bullets," a Northern Cheyenne woman named Iron Teeth remembered. "We who could do so ran away."[10]

Little Wolf, Dull Knife, and their people watched as soldiers burned over two hundred lodges and all their valuables stored inside: the meat the women had preserved for winter, sacks of dried fruit and berries, deerskin clothing along with blankets and buffalo robes.[11]

Some of the soldiers left the battlefield with a grudging respect for the Northern Cheyenne. There were no cowards among them, they wrote in their diaries and battle reports. Throughout the fight, "their courage was unabated." And the Northern Cheyenne battle strategy—gaining the high ground and firing judiciously from behind trees and rocks—was a good one. "Had we foolishly attempted to force them out of their improvised rifle-pits in the crevices and behind the rocks on the hill-sides," one officer wrote, "the loss of life would have been fearful."[12]

Little Wolf directed the evacuation of his band, leading them through the late fall snow toward a creek where he knew Crazy Horse's Oglalas were encamped. When they arrived, Little Wolf's band did not receive the same kind of welcome that Old Bear's people had in March. The Oglalas had been fighting a running battle with U.S. troops that fall, and constant movement and stress had taken their toll. The two groups remained together for a month and then parted ways in the wake of another U.S. Army attack on their camps along the Tongue River in January.[13]

Huddled in their skins and robes and taking meager shelter in makeshift tents, Little Wolf, Dull Knife, and the other chiefs met to decide what to do. Little Wolf wanted to remain in the North Country, near the Powder River. The Northern Cheyenne were born into these lands, he argued, and their sacred places and historical memories were here. Other chiefs argued that the fight was over; they could not win. They should go to the newly constructed Fort Keogh on the Tongue River and surrender. A smaller contingent suggested joining forces with Sitting Bull again, in Lakota country.[14]

By the end of the council, Little Wolf was convinced that his people had few choices. He also received a message from Spotted Tail, Crazy Horse's uncle and an Oglala peace chief. If they surrendered at the Lakota's Red Cloud Agency, the peace chief assured Little Wolf, his band would be fed throughout the winter and have warm places to sleep. They could remain in the region and have access to their homelands.[15]

In February 1877, Little Wolf's band began the three-hundred-mile trek from their winter grounds to the Red Cloud Agency in the Pine Ridge of northwestern Nebraska. The journey took two months, and when the band arrived, the trees that perched atop sandstone towers that gave the place its name were still covered with a dusting of snow. More than 350 Northern Cheyenne men, women, and children gathered outside the agency's ten-foot-high board enclosure, many of them starving and suffering from frostbite. The early spring storms that swept across the northern plains had chilled them to the bone.

Little Wolf asked to meet with the officers of Camp Robinson, whose soldiers provided protection for federal Indian agents and their families and surveillance of encamped Plains nations. He wore black pants and a red shirt, and his hair hung loose down his back. Little Wolf's face was resolute as he informed the soldiers that Dull Knife and his people were several weeks behind, as they had fewer and less hardy horses. They were all there to surrender to the federal government and to discuss a lasting peace.[16]

For the first time in their history, the Northern Cheyenne yielded to the U.S. government.[17]

Little Wolf's band gathered near the agency buildings, warming their chilled limbs by small fires. Medicine men circulated, treating several people for exposure illnesses and frostbite. Although the Northern Cheyenne were clearly exhausted, the Indian agent at the Red Cloud Agency remained cautious. He knew them to be troublesome, especially in the wake of U.S. Army attacks on their people. "They have caused . . . more trouble and anxiety," he wrote to the commissioner of Indian Affairs, "than the Sioux and Arapahoes combined."[18]

After Dull Knife's people and the rest of the bands arrived, there were more than nine hundred Northern Cheyenne encamped at Red Cloud Agency. Soon, a U.S. Army officer named William Clark (no relation to the Corps of Discovery officer) approached Little Wolf and several other chiefs. Through an interpreter, he asked them to join his unit of scouts. There were still several more Lakota bands (including Sitting Bull's Hunkpapa) and other Great Plains nations who had not yet surrendered, and the Army needed the geographic and cultural intelligence that men like Little Wolf offered to continue their campaigns.

Little Wolf and several others agreed. Unlike many of the U.S. Army's officers, Clark seemed at ease with the Northern Cheyenne. Little Wolf liked him, and he and the others nicknamed him "White Hat."[19] Within a few weeks, the chiefs met with General George Crook at his headquarters at Camp Robinson. They offered up their weapons and their ponies and shook hands with the general and his officers. Then they sat on the floor, lit a pipe, and passed it around.

"I am glad you have come in," Crook began, "and I hope you will listen to reason hereafter." He added a few more words of introduction and said offhandedly, "This country is large enough for all of us."[20]

The Northern Cheyenne took these last words to heart and thought Crook meant that they could continue to live in the North Country. A few weeks later, however, he informed Little Wolf that the Northern Cheyenne would be moving to Indian Territory to join their Southern Cheyenne kin on their reservation. The U.S. government would not negotiate on this matter, Crook said. Their punishment for participation in the Battle of Little Bighorn was the loss of their homelands. Several Northern Cheyenne chiefs who surrendered after the battle had signed an agreement to move south, Crook told Little Wolf. And now the rest of the Northern Cheyenne were bound by that agreement.

Little Wolf was outraged. He had agreed to nothing, he insisted. They had surrendered because they thought they would be staying near their homelands. Crook refused to debate the point. They would leave in a few days, he said. And the general would return their ponies to them for the journey.

The Northern Cheyenne chiefs were angry but resigned. They might have their ponies, but they did not have weapons. They could make a run for it and hope that the soldiers could not catch up, but they had to protect their women and children. Little Wolf and the others told themselves that they were going to Indian Territory on a trial basis only. If they did not find everything to their liking, they would leave.

On the morning of May 28, 1877, more than nine hundred Northern Cheyenne left Camp Robinson, their column extending along the prairie for two miles. Little Wolf and Dull Knife, along with several others, rode at the front of the Northern Cheyenne column as they turned south. They carried with them the Medicine Bundle, an item sacred to the Northern Cheyenne. It connected the people to their past and to the Creator who made them. Little Wolf had been tasked with protecting the bundle, and he would not surrender it. If the Northern Cheyenne had this item, they would endure.[21]

For the next seventy days, they followed a route that was at first familiar to them. They skirted the western edge of the Sand Hills, their dunes a constantly changing landscape. They crossed the Union Pacific railroad tracks and then the North Platte, moving through the mixed grass prairie dotted here and there with trees and shrubs. Then they crossed two more railroad lines—the Kansas Pacific and the Atchison, Topeka, and Santa Fe—and the Santa Fe Trail.

Every day of this forced march, the Northern Cheyenne sent scouts in front to look for a camping place and to hunt for antelope and bison. When they passed farms and ranches in Nebraska and Kansas, residents came out to gawk at them. There were many more Americans in the region since the Northern Cheyenne had been down this way. Since 1860, the population of Nebraska had grown from around 28,000 to close to 400,000, and Kansas was closing in on one million residents.[22]

Stopping every few weeks at U.S. Army forts or cattle ranches, the Northern Cheyenne received rations of bacon, beef, sugar, coffee, tea, and tobacco. As they moved toward the Southern Cheyenne reservation and nearby Fort Reno, Little Wolf became uneasy. The land began to buck and break, forming red-hued tablelands. It was midsummer, and the air grew humid as the temperatures soared.[23] Like many of his people, Little Wolf already missed the North Country. The crispness in the air at dawn and dusk, even in the summer. The rushing streams and the lush grasses.

"My people had been raised among the pines and the mountains," he thought. "This is not a good country for us."[24]

On their journey, the Northern Cheyenne passed within one hundred miles of the small town of Lebanon, Kansas. Founded the year before, Lebanon sat between the north fork of the Solomon River to the south and the Republican River to the north. It was also just to the east of the 100th meridian line, which meant that its lands received enough rainfall in any given year to grow crops without irrigation. The lands in Kansas west of that line were already being given over to large herds of cattle. Years later, surveyors would determine that Lebanon was the exact center of the continental United States. It was also the new home of the Watson family.[25]

Thomas and Frances Watson had been living and farming in Ontario, Canada, on a peninsula that jutted out into Lake Huron, for more than fifteen years. They had seven children, and all of them spoke with the

Scottish and Irish accents they had absorbed in conversations with their parents.[26]

It is unclear exactly what had prompted Thomas and Frances to leave Ontario for northwestern Kansas in the spring of 1877, but there was plenty of motivation. Crops had been failing throughout Canada for multiple years and the panic and depression of 1873 had hit businesses in Ontario as hard as those in Chicago and New York. As the Watsons looked around for options, migration to the United States was appealing. The Homestead Act was still providing 160 acres for any citizen—or prospective citizen—who improved upon it. And the recent U.S. Army campaigns against the Lakota and Northern Cheyenne had scattered those tribal nations. The prairie lands of Kansas were therefore available for white settlement. The area around Lebanon was already known as "The Homestead Region."[27]

The U.S. Congress meant the Homestead Act to be both a land act and an immigration policy to promote white settlement, and the Watsons were just the kind of family both Republicans and Democrats wanted to attract. Other migrant communities were not welcome. A few years earlier, Congress had passed the Page Act, restricting the immigration of Chinese "unfree laborers" and women whom officials suspected were transported to the United States for "immoral purposes." It was America's first racially based immigration law.[28]

White Canadians faced no such restrictions. When Thomas and Frances arrived in Lebanon, there were more than 12,500 Canadian-born people living in Kansas, the most of any of the states and territories of the Great Plains.[29] Thomas went to the land office and looked through prior homestead claims that had been abandoned. In April 1877, he printed a notice in a local paper advising the former owner of a quarter section that he intended to file a claim on the land. By the next month, he and Frances and several of their children were starting the arduous, yearlong process of breaking up the prairie sod to prepare it for planting.[30]

The region's grasses had long, thick, compacted roots that helped them reach moisture in the soil. This meant that the Watsons needed a strong team of oxen or mules and a sharp edge on their plow to break it up. Cross-plowing was also required, along with an extended fallow period so that the roots would rot.

"Prairie breaking is no child's play," a historian of Kansas wrote. If done improperly, "forty elephants could not pull it if it remains in the ground and forty more elephants could not hold it in the ground if it wanted to come out."[31]

While most of the family members turned their attention to this process, Thomas and Frances sent their oldest daughter, Ella, to find work in the household of a local family. At sixteen, she was already tall (five foot eight) and strong, but her real talents lay in the kitchen. Her Canadian neighbors attested to her cooking skills, and her dishes were always in demand. There was no work for her in Lebanon, but there was in the town just west of there. As the county seat, Smith Center was full of people when court was in session, and it boasted a hotel, newspaper, a bank, and several middle-class homes. One of the homes belonged to Henry Stone, a merchant and a banker. Ella started working for him and Mrs. Stone as their cook and housekeeper.[32]

Over the next year, Ella brought her wages home to her family and went to social gatherings in Lebanon and Smith Center. At one of these, she met a young farmer named William Pickell. He had light brown hair and blue eyes and a winning way about him. Soon, Ella and Bill were courting. She believed herself in love. Perhaps he did too, and that is why he was on his best behavior around her during their courtship. The couple planned to marry, and Ella seemed to be living the immigrant girl's dream in the American West. She had a good job, a fiancé, and a future in a thriving rural community. It did not take long, unfortunately, for that dream to fall apart.

CHAPTER 25

In the humid lowlands of Indian Territory, Little Wolf and his people were suffering. From the first week, the food rations that the U.S. Army distributed to them were lacking. The cornmeal, coffee, sugar, and a small amount of bacon that Little Wolf, his two wives, and three children received would last for only three days instead of a week.

"They gave us cornmeal ground with the cob," complained another Northern Cheyenne chief named Wild Hog, "much as a man feeds his mule."[1] The cows they received were scrawny and would not feed the family for long after one of Little Wolf's wives butchered it.

The Northern Cheyenne were used to more than twice as much protein in their daily diets. Their federal Indian agent, John D. Miles, had allowed them to go out on a bison hunt the previous winter to augment their rations, but that excursion was a disaster. They did not find any herds, and they nearly froze to death on the frigid, windswept plains. The Northern Cheyenne did not see any deer or antelope either. The entire region had been overhunted by both tribal nations living in Indian Territory and white hunters shooting game for the mass market. During the single year that the Northern Cheyenne had been on the reservation, more than half a million bison carcasses rotted on the plains from Montana to Texas as hunters shipped their tongues and hides back east.[2]

It was no wonder that the Northern Cheyenne began to think of this moment in their history as "The Starving Time."[3]

The winter hunt had convinced Little Wolf that his people could not remain on the reservation in Indian Territory. They were hungry all the time, and more than forty of their band had died since their arrival. These deaths came in forms that were new to them. Malaria and dysentery were rampant on the reservation, and the Northern Cheyenne medicine men did not know how to treat these highly contagious diseases. The reservation's agency had only one physician, and even when he was able to visit Little Wolf's camp, he did not often have enough medicines to treat the sick. Those who survived their bouts of illness were debilitated. "Chills and fever and aching of the bones dragged down most of us," Wooden Leg lamented, "to thin and weak bodies."[4]

Believing that proximity to other bands was spreading illness, Little Wolf moved his people's camp more than ten miles west, up the Canadian River. Here there was more open country, with better water and a reliable wood supply. And the band would not have to clash regularly with the Southern Cheyenne, with whom they had an increasingly tense relationship. The two peoples had not convened for many years, and they had formed alliances with other tribal nations: the Northern Cheyenne with the Lakota and the Southern Cheyenne with the Kiowa, Comanche, and Southern Arapaho. Several Southern Cheyenne chiefs had tried to convince Little Wolf to begin farming, but he had resisted, seeing such a transition as accommodationist. He and several other Northern Cheyenne chiefs ridiculed their southern counterparts by calling them "Agency Chiefs"; they retaliated by calling Little Wolf and the others "Sioux Cheyenne."[5]

In their new camp, Little Wolf and his band were far away from the reservation's agency and the more than two hundred cavalry and infantry posted at its military counterpart, Fort Reno. And they had more privacy, which was good in and of itself. It was also useful for planning a breakout.

Over the summer of 1878, Little Wolf and his fellow chiefs had met with Agent Miles multiple times, asking for more rations, access to guns, and hunting rights.

"[My] people were raised far up in the north," Little Wolf told him in one council. "In that country we were always healthy. There was no sickness and very few of us died. Now, since we have been in this country, we are dying every day." The Northern Cheyenne wanted to return to the North Country, Little Wolf said. "If you have not the power to give us permission to go back there, let some of us go on to Washington, and tell them there how it is." Little Wolf was sure that his people would not last another year in Indian Territory. Illness would take them, or heartbreak.[6]

Miles refused to let them leave, as Little Wolf expected. He also refused to contact the American president, the Republican Rutherford B. Hayes, on their behalf.

Over the next few weeks, Little Wolf, along with fellow chiefs Dull Knife, Wild Hog, and Crow, moved their people once again, to a sharp bend on the northern bank of the Canadian River. Here, a series of sandhills had created a horseshoe, an ideal shape for a defensive stand against approaching soldiers. Warriors dug out a series of rifle pits in the dunes to provide cover for snipers, and women erected the band's lodges in sheltered positions along the bank.[7]

Little Wolf and Dull Knife also sent out their best raiders to capture as many of the Southern Cheyenne and Arapaho horses as they could without drawing too much attention. Some of these horses likely belonged to George Bent, whose family had been attacked at Sand Creek, and who had ultimately moved to the reservation in Indian Territory.[8] The horses' owners did notice, however, and complained to Agent Miles about it. They knew it was the Northern Cheyenne who were stealing their animals and not white settlers who were crossing into the reservation.

"How do you know?" Miles asked them.

"These thieves are particular," the Southern Cheyenne said. "They take only a few good horses from a herd, always picking out the best." White raiders would never do such a thing. "They would just round up the whole bunch and run them off."[9]

Miles sent for Little Wolf, Dull Knife, and Wild Hog and asked them if their young men were stealing horses and planning to abscond. The chiefs feigned ignorance and said that no one had left, or was intending to leave. "It is all a Southern Cheyenne and Arapahoe lie," Little Wolf insisted.[10]

Little Wolf also sent his best traders to Fort Reno to meet with the unsanctioned merchants who always gathered at Army installations.

From them, the Northern Cheyenne bought a range of guns, including Springfield and Sharps carbines, which were excellent weapons for long-range shooting.[11]

The second Monday in September was another ration day, and when the Northern Cheyenne gathered once again at the agency with their baskets, Miles took the opportunity to call Little Wolf and the other chiefs into his office. He had had reports that some Northern Cheyenne were missing, and he wanted the entire tribe to gather for a census. To exert some pressure on them to appear, Miles wanted ten of Little Wolf's men to remain at the agency until everyone came in to be counted. Little Wolf refused. Then he stood up.

"I am going to leave," the Sweet Medicine Chief declared. "I am going north." Before Miles could object, Little Wolf went on. "I do not want to make bloody this ground about this agency. If you are going to send your soldiers after me, I wish you would let me get away from this agency a little way. Then if you want to I will fight you and we will make the ground bloody there."[12]

Miles just stared at them, and the chiefs got up and left. The agent must have believed that Little Wolf was bluffing, because he did not request a unit of cavalry to track the Northern Cheyenne back to their encampment.[13]

At the horseshoe, Little Wolf sent word across the camp that it was time. As the sun sank beneath the horizon, the Northern Cheyenne lit their cookfires as usual. They fed their horses, brought them to the lodges, and began to pack their belongings into saddlebags. Little Wolf had told them to bring only what was necessary. It was imperative that they be able to travel quickly over the 1,500 miles back to their homeland. Some of them found space for treasured items, however.

A man named Little Finger Nail tucked a ledger into his bag; he had been drawing a pictorial record of his people in its pages. Iron Teeth, who had lost her husband in the battle on the Rosebud in 1876, packed clothes, pemmican (dried meat and berries), a revolver, and a hide scraper her husband had given her as a wedding gift. She would not be parted from it. The scraper was a reminder of love and family, and she knew it would be a comfort to her in this chaotic time.[14]

The band did not break down their lodges. Little Wolf planned to leave them standing and the fires crackling so that any soldiers nearby would assume they were still encamped. They also left their travois behind. They would slow down the horses, and dig dark grooves in the prairie soil, creating a track that was easy to follow.[15]

A few hours later, Northern Cheyenne men and women began leaving the camp in small groups. Many of them were members of the Elk Horn Scrapers Society. They quietly sang a war song, making it clear that the Northern Cheyenne would rather fight and die in the running battle with U.S. troops that was sure to follow than stay on the reservation.

The camp emptied out, as 120 women, 92 men, and 141 children moved northwest along the Canadian River in the middle of the night. This was only around one-third of the band who had come south the year before. Little Wolf made sure that they left another one of the Northern Cheyenne's sacred objects, the Buffalo Hat, behind. According to Sweet Medicine's teachings, it must always remain with the largest contingent of the band.[16]

Little Wolf did bring the Medicine Bundle, however. It was his to protect as the Sweet Medicine Chief. As he and Dull Knife rode at the head of the column, with smoke rising from the lodges behind them, one of their fellow chiefs looked at Little Wolf with awe. "He did not seem like a human being," the warrior said, "he seemed like a bear. He seemed without fear."[17]

The Northern Cheyenne traveled for several miles and then came upon a large pony herd in the darkness. Little Wolf had told his raiders to gather the Southern Cheyenne horses here to avoid detection and keep them safe until they needed them. The band members who had been walking in the first hours were now mounted, and they could move much more quickly. Little Wolf organized them into marching order, and by the next night, the group had traveled sixty miles.[18]

They knew the soldiers would be coming for them soon, but they were happy. On the reservation in Indian Territory they had been, as one chief put it later, "homesick and heartsick, and sick in every way."[19] Now they were on the move, traveling toward the high mountains, the clear, fast-running streams, and the scent of the pine trees in winter. They were going home.

The Northern Cheyenne headed northwest and then swung onto an old Indigenous trading and raiding road that white settlers called the Western Cattle Trail. It extended from southern Texas through Indian Territory, then on to Dodge City, Kansas, and western Nebraska. It crossed many creeks and rivers, and there were few bridges—cattle had no need of them. If the soldiers who were following them had wagons with them, they would be slowed at these crossings.[20]

This was a clear advantage for the Northern Cheyenne, as was their knowledge of the country between Indian Territory and their homelands. They had a head start and left almost no trail behind them. They were also seasoned in this kind of military action: a running battle with women and children in tow and many sites in which to lie in wait for pursuers and draw them into ambushes. General Phil Sheridan, who commanded the Military District of Missouri and had a wealth of experience in unconventional warfare, understood this. "It is hard to head off or overtake Indians in an open country, well-known to them," Sheridan noted, especially if the band could procure fresh horses and ride unencumbered by travois.[21]

Two days later, Little Wolf and Dull Knife's bands crossed the Cimarron River and made camp among the broken lands of Turkey Springs, in northwestern Indian Territory. Little Wolf placed his warriors between the camp and the river and the trail. They had seen dust clouds to the south that meant that troops from Fort Reno were in pursuit. The Northern Cheyenne put on their war bonnets and mounted their ponies. Little Wolf sent some of them into a ravine on one side of the trail and told his warriors to wait. "I will go out and meet the troops, and try to talk with them," Little Wolf told them. "Do not any of you shoot until the troops have fired."[22]

When two hundred soldiers of the 4th U.S. Cavalry appeared in front of them, their commander sent an Arapaho scout named Chalk to speak with Little Wolf. The two men acknowledged each other, and then the scout spoke. "The white men want you to go back," Chalk said. "If you will surrender and return, they will give you your rations and will treat you well."

"Tell them that we do not want to fight," Little Wolf responded, "but we will not go back." The Northern Cheyenne would leave Indian

Territory and go to their homelands, where they had been born and raised, and stay there. Little Wolf had no quarrel with the Fort Reno soldiers, but if they tried to stop him, he would fight.[23]

Chalk returned to the soldiers' line and delivered this message. Before the commander could issue any orders, however, an officer on the right side of his line fired at the Northern Cheyenne. In the battle that followed, Little Wolf and his men pushed the soldiers back along the trail. The warriors he had sent fired at them from the side, and they were forced to entrench to protect themselves. Within a few hours, the Americans were in danger of being surrounded with no access to the spring. "The day being very warm and having no water," one soldier wrote, "the outlook was anything but cheery."[24]

That night, Little Wolf's warriors crept close to the Army camp and set the prairie on fire. The soldiers had to fall back seven miles to the Cimarron and camp there. Three soldiers were killed, and many were wounded in the battle; Chalk was one of the casualties.[25] The Americans felt lucky to have escaped what they thought could have been another Little Bighorn.

"None of us wanted to do any more fighting," one soldier admitted. "We were discouraged and as far as I was concerned I did not want to see any more of those Indians."[26]

After resting for a day, the Northern Cheyenne rode on and crossed into Kansas. Little Wolf organized them into small groups. They traveled at night and staggered to avoid detection and to manage water supplies along the route. He and Dull Knife also sent riders out to steal food, cattle, and especially horses. The success of the march depended on a continuous supply of fresh mounts, and the ranches and towns of western Kansas had plenty of those on offer.[27] Over the next week they fought three skirmishes with another regiment of U.S. soldiers and kept moving.[28]

After crossing the Arkansas River, the Northern Cheyenne entered a series of shallow canyons that rose above Punished Woman Creek and wound their way through the otherwise flat lands of the western High Plains. It was the perfect site for an ambush, so Little Wolf called a halt. He and Dull Knife sent the women, old men, and children to a cave on the northern end of the gorge and sent warriors to pound out a more obvious trail leading from a southern valley into the canyon's mouth. They dug rifle pits in front of the cave to protect their families and built sixteen circular breastworks along the canyon top, from which to fire down on the U.S. soldiers. Then they settled in to wait.[29]

Two days later, scouts in the foremost breastworks on the rim spotted an Army command approaching. They were soldiers from Fort Dodge, Kansas, who had marched fifty miles in two days to try to cut off the Northern Cheyenne. They had taken the bait and followed the fake trail into the canyonlands, not realizing that Little Wolf had drawn them into an ambush until it was too late. The Northern Cheyenne were patient. They waited until the soldiers were far enough into the canyon to make a retreat untenable.

"Do not get excited, keep cool, and mind what I say to you," Little Wolf advised his warriors. "Let every shot you fire count for a man."[30]

When the bullets began to ping in the dirt around them, the American soldiers were horrified. "It was a complete surprise," one officer wrote. Clearly, the Northern Cheyenne had "expected to make another Custer business of it."[31]

The battle did not last long. The Americans were able to hold their ground, but their commander was shot (he died the next day). Once again, the U.S. Army had failed to capture Little Wolf, Dull Knife, and their people. Little Wolf was likely pleased at how well his ambush had worked, but one part of the fight did not go his way: the soldiers were able to get between the Northern Cheyenne and most of their pony herd. This was a devastating blow. They lost supplies and personal belongings and transportation for many of their people. That night, when the warriors gathered their families from the cave and moved out through a ravine into the open plains of western Kansas, they were desperate. They needed more horses and more food. Little Wolf and Dull Knife sent their most ruthless foragers out to procure them.[32]

Over the next two weeks, the Northern Cheyenne moved steadily northward, recrossing the Atchison and Topeka and the Kansas Pacific railroad tracks. For hundreds of years, this landscape had been a neutral ground and buffalo-hunting range for northern and southern Plains nations. Now it was dotted with winter wheat farmlands and rangelands cropped down to the dirt by large cattle herds. Along the way to the Platte, their foragers killed more than forty white settlers in western Kansas, many of them European and Canadian immigrants like the Watsons.[33]

When the raiders returned to the group with horses and saddlebags full of supplies, they did not tell Little Wolf how exactly they acquired them.

"They knew I would not like it," the chief said. "I often harangued my young men, telling them not to kill citizens." The raiders disregarded his orders. For them, survival in this moment was paramount, and violent acts of revenge were satisfying.[34]

When news of the Northern Cheyenne raids in Kansas reached U.S. Army posts and larger settlements, Americans were incensed. "Bloodthirsty warriors have made sad work in Northwestern Kansas!" a local paper reported. They killed men and boys, assaulted women, and burned down their houses before leaving to rejoin their people with stolen stock. "Settlement in western Kansas has received a check from which it will not recover for years."[35]

U.S. Army soldiers were deployed from forts across Kansas, and they were joined by "ranch followers": cattlemen who brought no supplies (only their horses and guns) to the pursuit and were bent on revenge for Northern Cheyenne depredations. One gang scoured the country for stragglers and found a wounded old man who had been left behind. They killed him. "The scalp hung in the Pioneer Drug Store in Oberlin, Kansas for many years," one settler noted.[36]

Despite the number of soldiers in the field—almost one thousand of them, in the end—and their ability to use the telegraph and railroad lines for communication and logistics, the U.S. Army was always several steps behind Little Wolf. The Americans consistently underestimated the Northern Cheyenne's speed and determination, and Little Wolf was able to use the mounts that the raiders brought him to replenish their herd.

In early October 1878, the Northern Cheyenne crossed the Platte and the Union Pacific line undetected and unopposed.[37]

Several days later, when they encamped on the southern edge of the Sand Hills in Nebraska, the Northern Cheyenne chiefs met in council.

Bruno Zimm, sculpture of Sacajawea and Jean-Baptiste (Sakakawea), 1904. Photograph reproduced in John C. Luttig, *Journal of a Fur-Trading Expedition on the Upper Missouri, 1812–1813*, ed. Stella M. Drumm (Missouri Historical Society, 1920), frontispiece.

Photograph of Jim Beckwourth, early 1860s. Original in a private collection.

William Gunnison Chamberlain, "Portrait of James P. Beckwourth," 1860s. History Colorado. Accession #89.451.1762.

"James P. Beckwourth in
Citizen's Dress," 1856.
Illustration in James P. Beckwourth and Thomas D. Bonner,
The Life and Adventures of James P. Beckwourth
(Harper and Brothers, 1856), 521.

"Lady Tules," *Harper's Monthly Magazine*,
April 1854.
Palace of the Governors Photo Archives, New Mexico
History Museum, Santa Fe.

"Gambling Saloon in New Mexico," *Harper's Monthly Magazine*, April 1854.
Palace of the Governors Photo Archives, New Mexico History Museum, Santa Fe.

Ovando Hollister, 1860s.
History Colorado. Accession #91.429.263.

C. R. Savage, "O. J. Hollister," 1870s–80s.
History Colorado. Accession #91.429.259.

Little Wolf (detail).
From Alexander Gardner, "Little Wolf and Dull Knife," 1873. "Photographs of North American Indians" Albums, WC054, Manuscripts Division, Department of Special Collections, Princeton University Library.

Alexander Gardner, "Indian Peace Commissioners in Council with the Northern Cheyenne," 1868. William Tecumseh Sherman Collection of Alexander Gardner Photographs, National Museum of the American Indian, Smithsonian Institution.

Ella Watson and her first husband, William Pickell, c. 1879.
Ella Watson and Rustling Figures Photographs, NCA 01.v.2025.03 WyCaC U.S. Western History Center, Casper College Archives and Special Collections.

Ella Watson on horseback, 1880s.
SUB NEG 4104, Bio file—Watson, Ella (Cattle Kate), Wyoming State Archives Photo Collection.

Polly Bemis (in her wedding dress), 1895.
P1975-228.43h, Idaho State Archives.

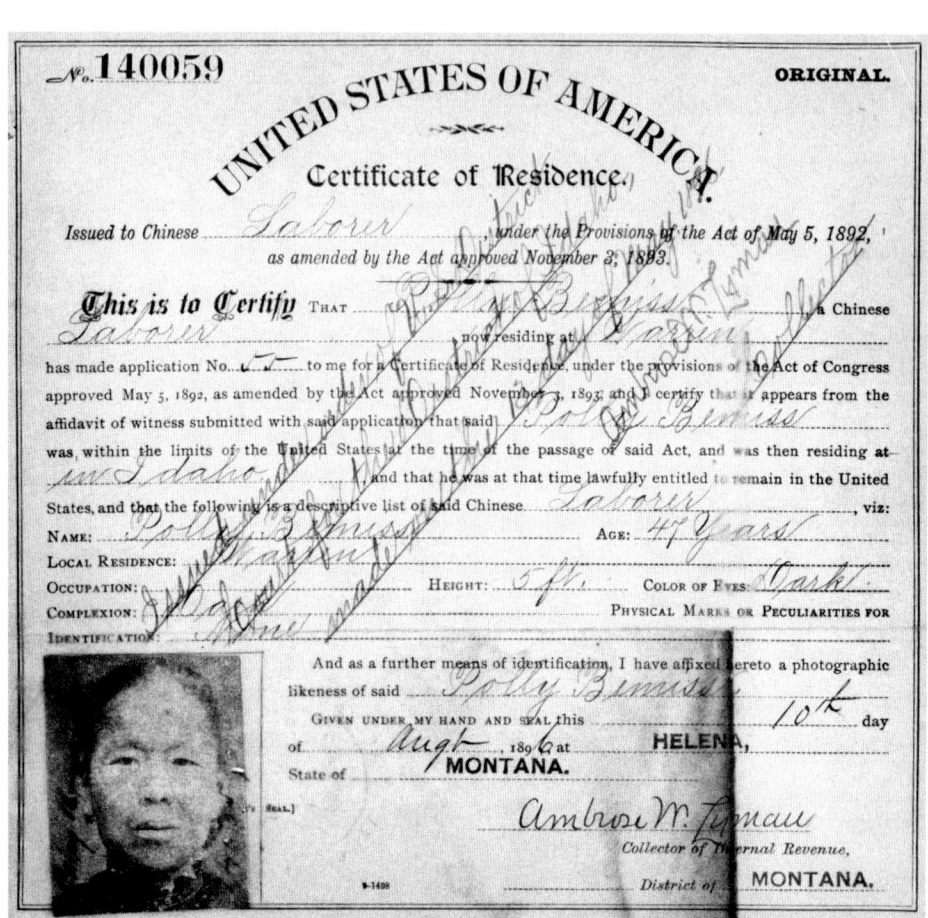

Polly Bemis's Certificate of Residence, 1896. P1975-228.43g, Idaho State Archives.

Polly Bemis in front of her cabin near Warren, Idaho, c. 1920s. P1962-44, Idaho State Archives.

Emanuel Leutze, *Westward the Course of Empire Takes Its Way*, 1862.
Architect of the Capitol Collection.

Frances Flora Bond Palmer for Currier and Ives, *Across the Continent*, 1868.
Black-and-white reproduction of the lithograph courtesy of the Prints and Photographs Division, Library of Congress.

John Gast, *American Progress*, 1872.
Lithograph image courtesy of the Prints and Photographs Division, Library of Congress.

They were all relieved to be once again in their own country, a land they knew well and that could sustain them. Dull Knife wanted to go into the Red Cloud Agency, believing the Indian agents there would protect them. The fighting would be over, and the Northern Cheyenne could move toward their winter camps and live in peace.[38]

Little Wolf disagreed. He wanted to reach the Powder River country, or at least the Black Hills. If they had to fight the U.S. Army again to return to that sacred country, so be it. "You can go that way [toward Red Cloud Agency] if you wish," he told Dull Knife. But "I think it will be better for us all if the party is not divided."[39]

Dull Knife was just as set on his plan as Little Wolf was on his, so the two men parted. As the winter storms started to roll in across the plains, Dull Knife and more than 150 of his people turned northwest into a country of bluffs, tablelands, and hills. Little Wolf and his band headed into the most remote part of the Sand Hills. An area spanning over nineteen thousand square miles with some dunes towering more than four hundred feet above the plains, the Sand Hills were a maze of drifts and alkaline lakes.[40]

"The 'sand hills' form certainly the worst country I have ever seen," one Army officer put it. "They are worse than the worst of Arizona." Pursuing Little Wolf and his band into this landscape without preparation and several weeks' worth of supplies was foolhardy. And of course, the officer admitted, it was "just exactly what the Cheyennes wanted us to do."[41]

Little Wolf and his band spent the winter in the Sand Hills as the cooling temperatures and abundant lakes worked together to create a dense fog through much of the region. They hunted its robust population of deer and antelope and siphoned off cattle from herds turned out to roam in the region as an open range. The false trails they created sent pursuing soldiers off in the wrong direction. In case the soldiers were not fooled, they dug rifle pits in advantageous defensive positions. Occasionally, the Northern Cheyenne and the soldiers caught sight of one another; they fired their weapons, and then the warriors melted back into the fog and disappeared.[42]

In late January 1879, one of their scouts returned to camp with news that Dull Knife's band had surrendered at Camp Robinson (now a fort) and was imprisoned in one of its barracks. The government told them they were going back to Indian Territory, and to avoid that fate, Dull Knife led another breakout. More than sixty Northern Cheyenne men, women, and children were killed in the resulting fight. No one knew if Dull Knife had survived or died in the wind-driven snow of the Nebraska prairie.[43]

This was devastating news, and it likely confirmed for Little Wolf that the U.S. government would send them back to Indian Territory if his band also surrendered. If they could make it back to the Powder River country, however, they could make a stand or elude the troops for long enough to push the government toward negotiation. A few weeks later, Little Wolf's band emerged from the Sand Hills to continue their journey toward the heart of their homelands. The U.S. Army had no idea where they were.

The Northern Cheyenne crossed into Dakota Territory and skirted the Lakota's Pine Ridge Agency. They did not trust Indian agents any more than U.S. Army officers, so they did not want to contact their allies there. Following a trail that moved due north, they rode between the pastel-hued canyons of the White River badlands, with their "boneyards" of plant and animal fossils millions of years old and foothills covered in thick stands of ponderosa pine.[44] Staying in the mixed grass prairie, where their horses would have enough to eat, they soon approached Nóvávóse, the Northern Cheyenne's sacred mountain.

Little Wolf ordered a halt, and the band camped for a few days in foothills. He left his wives and children and urged his horse up Nóvávóse until he found a level spot. Here, he began a four-day fast. He smoked, meditated, and opened the bundle that Sweet Medicine had handed down to the Northern Cheyenne. When he rejoined his band, his head was clear. The people would continue their journey to the North Country, and they would never leave it.[45]

A few weeks later, ice was breaking in Box Elder Creek, a tributary of the Little Missouri, when Little Wolf saw smoke rising a short distance away from the Northern Cheyenne camp. He sent scouts to investigate, and they came back with three prisoners. The men claimed to be Lakota in possession of stolen government stock on their way to join the Hunkpapa chief Sitting Bull in Canada, where he had been seeking refuge for more than a year. Little Wolf was suspicious of their story but was inclined to be generous. He sent two of the men to another lodge and invited one of them, who said his name was Jackson, to stay in his own.

The next morning, Jackson remained, but the other two had sliced open their lodge skin with a knife and escaped. Little Wolf was now even more convinced that the men were U.S. Army scouts, dispatched from one of the nearby forts to find him and his people. Jackson protested his innocence, and Little Wolf kept him close, hopeful that the Lakota would give him some useful intelligence on Army movements in the region or would provide value as a hostage. A few days later, however, Jackson slipped away while the band was hunting for deer. Little Wolf now knew for sure that soldiers were near, probably only a day or two behind them.[46]

He ordered his people to pack up and move to Hole in the Rock, a natural fortress on Box Elder Creek. The men dug into the dirt and piled it up with rocks to make breastworks, while the women arranged the lodges in the best position for protection. A few days later, three Northern Cheyenne men approached the camp. One of them was Little Wolf's brother-in-law. They came to his lodge and told him that they were U.S. Army scouts, and that William Clark—White Hat, from their days at Red Cloud Agency two years before—was a day away with a large contingent of soldiers.

"Lieutenant Clark wants you to know that he has orders to capture or kill you," the emissaries told Little Wolf. "You were an enlisted scout under his command, and so you can have confidence in his message. If you give up ponies and guns, he will not fight you."[47]

Little Wolf considered this and sent the men back to Clark with an offer to meet in council. He had more than one hundred of his people with him but fewer than fifty warriors. If they fought the Americans here, they might win, but the retaliation would be fierce. There was more than one way, Little Wolf knew, to defend his people and their homeland.[48]

The next day, Clark came into the Northern Cheyenne camp unarmed, with an interpreter. The two men greeted each other and then sat down.

"I told my scouts to give you no lies," Clark began, "and I hope they had done so. The guns and ponies must be given up. This is the price of peace, and you must pay it." He would take the guns now and the ponies when they arrived at Fort Keogh, a new Army installation at the confluence of the Tongue River and the Yellowstone. "I am truly and heartily glad we arranged this matter without loss of life on either side," Clark added.[49]

"Since I left you at Red Cloud we have been south, and have suffered a great deal down there," Little Wolf replied. "Our hearts looked and longed for this country where we were born. There are only a few of us left, and we only wanted a little ground, where we could live." He told Clark that he appreciated his offer to talk before fighting. He was the only U.S. Army officer to do so in the seven months since the Northern Cheyenne had left Indian Territory. He and his men would not give up their guns, however.

"My brother, Dull Knife, took one-half of the band and surrendered near Camp Robinson," he reminded Clark. "They gave up their guns, and then the whites killed them all." His band would hand over their weapons and ponies at Fort Keogh, but not before.

The two men reached a compromise. The Northern Cheyenne would keep their weapons, and Clark would issue rations to them and send a doctor to treat their wounds and illnesses. Then the Northern Cheyenne would travel with Clark to his camp, where they would surrender their guns and arrows but keep their horses.[50]

On April 1, 1879, more than one hundred North Cheyenne rode down a tree-lined avenue and into the gates of Fort Keogh. The U.S. Army had built this fort more than two years before, in the wake of the Battle of Little Bighorn; it was named after a 7th Cavalry officer killed in that fight. It had been a base for the campaigns against the Lakota and Northern Cheyenne ever since, and an American flag waved above a large square surrounded by multistory wooden buildings with large windows and porches. The post also had an official photographer, who had his own studio.[51]

The 2nd Cavalry's band played "Hail to the Chief," and the fort's commander, General Nelson Miles, walked out from his headquarters to meet them.[52] The general made it clear to them that they were prisoners of war and that they would need to demonstrate their loyalty to the United States after their actions during the breakout. Congress was trying to decide what to do with them and where their reservation should be. Miles would notify them when decisions had been made. After searching the men for additional weapons (they found none), Miles sent them to join a band of Northern Cheyenne under Two Moons, who had stayed in the North Country and worked as scouts for the U.S. Army after their surrender the year before.[53]

The flight from Indian Territory had taken a toll on Little Wolf and his people. They lost men and women to battle wounds, exposure, and starvation. It was a defining moment in their history, but one that brought both pride and pain. At least now, encamped on the plains near the Tongue River, they were in a country they knew.

"It was a beautiful country, with many high hills covered with pine trees, and plentiful grass and water," one Northern Cheyenne man remembered. "It was one of the last places where there was still some buffalo, and there was much other game as well."[54]

In a letter dictated by Little Wolf, which William Clark included in his report to the Department of War about the campaign, the Sweet Medicine Chief expressed his people's desire to stay in the North Country. "Perhaps if we could see [the Great Father] and plead with him for a little ground . . . he would heed our prayers," Little Wolf wrote. "We are poor, but we are brave, and we can die. We ask for pity, hope and life."[55]

PART VI
SURVIVAL IS A PRESENCE AND AN ABSENCE

CHAPTER 26

Little Wolf and his Northern Cheyenne band had defied the federal government and struck out on their own. They fought bravely in several battles against U.S. troops during their flight from Indian Territory and toward their homeland. To a handful of Americans, these acts may have embodied the spirit of 1776. The vast majority, however, saw the Northern Cheyenne's actions as doomed to failure.

"It was but the latest of a long series of ineffectual struggles by the Cheyennes against the whites," the *Chicago Times* editors wrote, "and against the destiny which was taking from them or rendering worthless their hunting grounds."[1]

By the late 1870s, the frontier myth had fully taken hold in the American imagination, and it had no space for Indigenous resistance in its narrative. The transcontinental railroad had brought photographers and painters to the mountains and deserts, and they produced sublime images of western lands, free for the taking. Commercial prints like Brooklyn-born painter John Gast's *American Progress* (1872) were widely disseminated, urging white Americans to follow the example of the frontiersmen and farmers in the image, who pursue Indigenous warriors and buffalo herds as a railroad and telegraph follow closely behind. Over all of them floats the female figure representing the nation's destiny, with a "star of empire" affixed to her head.[2]

In the decade after the end of the Civil War, hundreds of thousands of Americans traveled on federally funded train lines from the Missouri River and the Pacific Coast and into the western interior, filing claims to buy land under the provisions of the 1862 Homestead Act. The U.S. Army cleared their way, forcing Indigenous peoples onto reservations, far from the main thoroughfares of white migration. Americans believed that the West belonged to white settlers and not to Indigenous peoples. Or Chinese immigrants.

The snow was just beginning to fall in Warren, Idaho, when a handful of white men saw two Chinese miners walking down the town's main street. One of the miners was wearing a pair of boots that the white men believed were stolen from a friend of theirs. They made a citizens' arrest and brought the two Chinese men to the town jail. At a hearing on November 5, 1879, the judge questioned the alleged thieves.

"I bought these boots from another Chinese," the miner protested. He didn't know where the man had gone off to, but perhaps other members of the Chinese community in Warren could track him down. The judge adjourned the session to provide time to find this man and gather more testimony, and the jailer took the prisoners back to the jail. He locked the cell and the front door and left. When the jailer arrived the next morning, he could see that the front door had been broken and thrown open. The Chinese men were gone.[3]

He searched the area and then rode south of town to examine the banks of Slaughter Creek. Near the old Pioneer sawmill, he saw the lifeless bodies of the two men, hanging from a tree.

In the wake of the discovery, Warren's Chinese residents, who made up 80 percent of the population, were incensed. Even if the vigilantes had the right thieves—they did not—the punishment far exceeded the crime. Such acts of violence had been relatively rare in Warren, and this lynching signaled a new era of anti-Chinese aggression in Idaho and the entire West.[4]

White Americans had been growing paranoid and resentful of Chinese migrants since the California gold rush. Their violent attacks on Chinese men and women across the West had increased during and after the panic and depression of 1873.[5] In Washington, D.C., politicians did nothing to prevent or punish these forms of racial violence. Instead, they started passing a series of laws to restrict Chinese immigration.

In 1875, the California Republican Horace Page, who made a career writing and sponsoring anti-Chinese legislation, convinced his fellow congressmen to pass the Page Act, prohibiting involuntary emigration into the United States from China, Japan, and other countries on the Pacific Rim. This was the first piece of legislation in American history that specifically restricted immigration, and it targeted women, on the assumption that all Chinese women had been forced to migrate to the United States as sex workers. After its passage, the number of Chinese women disembarking in San Francisco declined dramatically.[6]

The Chinese inhabitants of Warren, including Polly, had reason to worry after the passage of the Page Act. Few of them had immigration papers or labor contracts to show anyone who might be looking to enforce it. Federal officials were scarce in the remote mountains of Idaho, however, and Chinese men in Warren far outnumbered white men in the 1870s.[7] But it soon became clear that the Page Act had had an impact.

In 1880, a federal census taker in Idaho found that the Chinese population in the mining district around Warren had decreased by almost one-third since 1870. It is possible that the man who had purchased Polly left at this time, or he could have died at some point. In either case, Polly identified herself as a widow to the census taker. There are no records that reveal what her life had been like for the previous eight years; much would have depended on the character of the man who had purchased her and why he had done so.

The census taker found Polly living in the same household as a white entrepreneur named Charles Bemis.[8] Originally from New York, Charlie had come to Idaho with his father in the 1860s. Like so many other men in the West during that period, he was looking to make his fortune. He had been living in Warren for five years before Polly arrived, buying up mining claims, opening a store catering to the town's prospectors, and holding various public offices. Around the time of the lynching of the Chinese miners, he had purchased a collection of businesses on Main Street in a sheriff's sale, including a saloon and a boardinghouse.

Although Polly and Charlie were living together—her occupation was listed as "housekeeper"—it was clear that they were not legally married. An anti-miscegenation law on the books in Idaho, passed in 1864, outlawed marriage between any white person and a person of

Chinese descent. By 1881, residents and visitors to Warren saw something intimate in their relationship, however, and referred to Polly as "Mrs. Bemis."[9]

Charlie's saloon and boardinghouse were centrally located, surrounded by mercantiles, a blacksmith, physicians' offices, a cobbler shop, and a laundry. Polly helped Charlie manage his businesses and ultimately ran the boardinghouse herself. Given the nature of Warren's population, she would have welcomed a mixed clientele.[10]

Polly had established a place for herself in Warren, making it her business to know everything that went on in the town and astonishing her fellow residents with her ability to remember the dates of even the most minor events. She had never been to school, and she could not read. But God had given her a brain, she said later, and "I learn right along."[11]

Polly knew how to cook Chinese food, and there were plentiful ingredients available from the Chinese farmers who harvested vegetables and grains from the terraced gardens they built on the mountains' steep hillsides. When she decided she needed to learn how to make American and European dishes as well, she went to visit the other women in Warren.

There were only five of them in the mining town in the early 1880s: Ah Choy, married to a mule train packer who brought supplies in and out of Warren; Mollie Smead, a Nez Perce woman illegally married to a white man; Carry Smith, the New York–born wife of a farmer and mother of three young children; an Australian named Jenny Church, who ran a boardinghouse with her English husband; and the German immigrant Katherine Clay, who was a mail carrier's second wife and stepmother to four of his children while caring for a baby of her own.[12]

Jenny Church let Polly watch as she cooked for the guests at her boardinghouse, and Mollie Smead, whose husband was a friend of Charlie's, welcomed her into their home as well. In these women's kitchens, Polly learned to make corn bread and scratch biscuits, stews and meat pies. Hearty fare for men who worked in the mines all day. If her boarders ever complained, she appeared in the dining room with a butcher knife and a twinkle in her eye, demanding to know who did not like her meals and her coffee.[13]

Polly regularly left her boardinghouse to walk through town, stopping to talk to and play with children. In later years, she would keep track of every baby born and visit them and their mothers. Given the population and gender disparities in Warren, most of these babies were born to American and European couples.[14] She had lived in the Idaho mountains for more than ten years and was well liked within its white and Chinese communities.

The larger United States, however, was not so welcoming to her and other Chinese immigrants. In 1882, the federal government moved beyond the Page Act and fully embraced racially targeted programs of exclusion. A coalition of Democrats and Republicans representing western states in Congress passed the Chinese Exclusion Act, suspending the immigration of most Chinese laborers into the United States for ten years. Immigrants like Polly Bemis, who had arrived before November 1880, were allowed to remain. If they wanted to leave and return, however, they needed to acquire an identification certificate. And no Chinese person could become a naturalized citizen of the United States.[15]

The Chinese are "aliens to our civilization, aliens in blood, aliens in faith," restriction advocates argued in the congressional debate over the bill. Their presence prevented the "free movement of the wheels of Christian civilization and enlightened progress."[16]

In the same session in 1882 Congress also passed the Edmunds Act, which revoked voting rights for Mormon men who engaged in polygamy.[17] Both pieces of legislation signaled that the federal government intended to Americanize the West, extending federal power into its mountain ranges and cities. It would remain to be seen, however, if they could enforce either law. There were no regulatory or surveillance agencies in place to investigate polygamous families in Utah. And customs officers charged with identifying and turning back Chinese immigrants were few compared to the more than 100,000 Chinese men and women already living in the American West.[18]

In Idaho, some Chinese residents protested the Chinese Exclusion Act. In Lewiston, the river town where Polly Bemis had disembarked and joined the pack train to Warren ten years before, four men who ran laundries in town refused to pay for their city licenses. "They say they will not wash [any]more for the white folks in Lewiston," the local newspaper reported. The men spent a week in jail and were released but continued to refuse service to white residents.[19]

One month later, as the sun set during Lewiston's Fourth of July celebration, Chinese lanterns illuminated Main Street. "The scene was one of the finest we have ever seen in the city," the paper noted. But then a summer thunderstorm descended from the west, bringing with it a bit of rain and a violent wind. Some Chinese lanterns that had been suspended from the trees "were torn into shreds and blown away."[20] To the Chinese residents, this may have seemed an apt metaphor for the times: their labor had helped build towns and cities across the American West, but the nation's patriotic celebrations of itself brought destruction and darkness to their communities.

For Polly, the Chinese Exclusion Act's provisions meant that she could remain in the United States for the time being, but her legal status was precarious. In the years following the passage of the act, a growing sense of uncertainty and fear pervaded Idaho mining towns. Warren's Chinese population declined by half, and power relations began to shift.[21]

That year, Charlie Bemis made a few trips out of town, traveling along the pack trails to Grangeville to file papers or do business deals, but Polly never went with him. She was safer in Warren, where most people knew her, liked her, and understood her relationship with Charlie. Even on the mining town's familiar streets, however, Polly could not be sure that white men and women would protect her from harm.

Although Ella Watson Pickell had nothing to fear from United States immigration authorities, she knew what it meant to be afraid of those closest to you. It was only a few months into their marriage when Bill began to drink almost every day, flying into rages at the slightest provocation and beating her with his horsewhip. For a while, she did not tell anyone about her husband's violent temper and learned to navigate around his moods. Sometimes he would leave the farmhouse for hours on end, and she did not know where he went. It did not occur to her until much later that he was spending that time with other women.[22]

They had been married for two years when Ella appeared at her parents' house, having fled from Bill during one of his violent frenzies. She was covered in bruises and welts and had brought nothing with her.

She had just left, running out of the house and riding all the way back to her family. Bill appeared at the house a few days later, begging her to come back. Ella's mother tried to convince her to go with him, but she was twenty-one years old, and she could support herself with her cooking skills. She was not going back.[23]

Ella worked for a nearby family as a cook but by August 1883, she had decided to get out of Kansas. She did not go far, just over the border to Nebraska. But it probably felt like a world away. Red Cloud was a county seat and a market town, and Ella had been there several times with her family. A summer tornado had damaged many of the town's buildings a few years before, but the residents had rebuilt their homes and businesses, and Red Cloud was flourishing. When Ella arrived, she found work as a cook at one of the town's five hotels.[24]

One of the other arrivals in Red Cloud that year was nine-year-old Willa Cather, who moved to a farm on the outskirts with her family. She remembered arriving at night, struck by the immensity of the landscape of the Great Plains. "There was nothing but land," she later wrote, "not a country at all, but the material out of which countries are made.... I had the feeling that the world was left behind, that we had got over the edge of it."[25]

For Ella, Red Cloud was a place of freedom. She lived there for six months and then, in February 1884, filed for divorce from Bill Pickell, on the grounds of infidelity and extreme cruelty. Divorce was not common in Nebraska—only 7 percent of marriages were dissolved there in the 1880s—but women filed 70 percent of the divorce petitions during that period, many of them citing the same grounds as Ella.[26]

She did not wait for the court to notify Bill or for her case to be heard. Two months later, Ella took the money she had earned at her jobs in Kansas and Nebraska and boarded a Union Pacific train and then a spur line to Denver. One of her younger brothers had moved there, and she stayed with him, but not for long. Ella bought another train ticket, traveling north to Cheyenne and then to the next stop on the western line: Rawlins, Wyoming.[27]

That route took her by dozens of farms and ranchlands in northern Colorado and south-central Wyoming. From the train window, she could see thousands of light brown longhorn cattle walking slowly with their heads down, snuffing at the prairie grasses and then pulling them from the earth with their long tongues. Many of these cows would ultimately end up in a cattle yard in Cheyenne or even in Rawlins. In 1884, Rawlins stood at the intersection of the Union Pacific line and a migrant and cattle trail moving south to north. The town marked the transformation of this part of the West into a landscape of cattle ranching.

Texas cattlemen had been moving longhorns through this area since the early 1860s, overcoming their Confederate sympathies to sell beef in northern markets. Once the Union Pacific line was constructed through southern Wyoming, these drovers moved their bulls and cows to its stations. There, they could sell animals to the railroad to feed its workers or ship them to San Francisco or Chicago. The cattle they could not off-load they turned out to graze on the rolling prairies around towns such as Rawlins. In the 1870s, there was little private land ownership in Wyoming, and cattlemen followed the ethics of the open range: a man could place a herd on any land that was unfenced and let the cows roam through the fall and winter. In the spring, cattlemen hired Anglo, Mexican, and Black cowboys to round up the herd and any calves that had been born and bring them to market.[28]

By the early 1880s, Rawlins was a way station on the way to Wyoming's open range. The town was bustling, and Ella Watson did not have much trouble finding a job as a cook and domestic in one of its better hotels. Rawlins House had forty rooms and a sterling reputation. Its owners were known for providing clean accommodations and excellent food for their clientele.[29]

Ella had been living in Rawlins for a little more than a year when she met a black-haired, blue-eyed widower named Jim Averell. He was four inches shorter than her and ten years older, but he had an easy way about him. The two talked and Ella found out that, like her, he was from a large family who emigrated to the United States from Canada when he was a teenager. Before moving to Wyoming, Jim had served for ten years in the U.S. Army. He had scouted for General George Crook during the 1876–77 campaign that forced Little Wolf and the Northern Cheyenne to surrender.[30]

Jim had been married before and built a cabin on a 160-acre homestead claim for his wife in the Sweetwater River Valley. She had died in childbirth along with their infant son in 1882; he was devastated by the loss and sold the land and the cabin soon afterward. Jim was a man on the rise, however, and he told Ella all about his dream: to farm a nice piece of land and build a road ranch, a small boardinghouse, and a commissary that would welcome travelers and cowboys on the move through Wyoming. He had already claimed a parcel just west of the confluence of Horse Creek and the Sweetwater River, adjacent to a well-traveled military road.[31]

Ella told Jim about her job at Rawlins House and her talents as a housekeeper and a cook. She was a hard worker and good with people. Soon afterward, Jim took her to see his ranch.

They rode through the "sagebrush sea" of central Wyoming, its rolling plains and mesas blue-green with the hardy vegetation. They crossed the Sweetwater River and a few miles later, pulled up alongside two log buildings with easy access to both the road and Horse Creek. Jim had not started farming yet, but he had applied for water rights on the creek. Over the next few months, he planned to dig irrigation ditches to bring that coveted natural resource to his garden and to his ranch buildings.[32]

The Sweetwater Valley, which was Northern Cheyenne and Eastern Shoshone land, was ringed by mountain ranges and sheltered from the worst of Wyoming's strong winds. That white migrants had not yet settled there in large numbers was surprising considering that so many of them passed near the valley on either the Oregon, Mormon, or California Trails. The U.S. Army had cleared the way for white farmers and ranchers in the valley, forcing the Northern Cheyenne to Fort Keogh and the Eastern Shoshone onto a reservation at Wind River.

Ten miles from Jim's ranch along the banks of the Sweetwater, one of Wyoming's most famous landmarks rose above the sagebrush. Independence Rock was a large granite outcropping along the Oregon Trail, a sign that travelers were on the right path. More than five thousand migrants had etched their names and dates of passage on its surface; one traveler called it "the great registry of the desert."[33]

Jim asked Ella if she would like to join him at his road ranch, cooking meals for visitors and running the boardinghouse. He would provide all the supplies, and she could keep whatever money she made from charging hungry travelers fifty cents a plate. Jim would also run the grocery, selling socks, tobacco, and other supplies. At some point, he would build a small saloon next to the boardinghouse and sell whiskey and other libations to thirsty guests.[34] Ella warmed to the idea, and in May 1886, she quit her job at Rawlins House and moved her possessions to the Averell ranch. It was a fateful decision, one that would change her life—and cut it short.

CHAPTER 27

A few months after Ella Watson moved to Jim Averell's road ranch, they applied for a marriage license. Ella told the clerk that her last name was "Andrews," perhaps because she was not sure if she was still married to Bill Pickell; she had not yet heard if her petition for divorce had been granted in Nebraska.[1]

In late August 1886, Ella went back to Rawlins and filed a claim on 160 acres of land adjacent to Jim's. Under the federal Preemption Act and with a claim in hand, Ella could "prove it up," tilling soil and constructing buildings to establish her ownership. She could also defend her claim against any other homesteaders who tried to settle on her land and apply for water rights. Ella and Jim together now controlled access to more than a mile of Horse Creek.[2]

Ella used some of the money she earned in Red Cloud and in Rawlins, along with the profits from the road ranch, to hire a man to build her cabin on Horse Creek. Constructed of fir logs that Jim had cut down and hauled back from the mountains, the cabin was a single room of fourteen by sixteen feet, with one door and one window. The cabin was legally an "improvement," a sign to General Land Office personnel that she had settled on her land. But it was also her home. Although she spent much of her time at the road ranch with Jim, Ella bought a cookstove, a bedstead and bedding, dishes and kitchen utensils, a dining table and six chairs, and a sewing machine for her cabin.[3]

She also built a three-wire fence, strung between cedar posts to enclose sixty of her acres. The fence was the first stage of her long-term plan: she had already started saving money to buy a small cattle herd.[4] At this point, Ella Watson became part of a homesteading wave in Wyoming, during which private ownership of land rose from almost 375,000 to 5.8 million acres. This was still only about 10 percent of Wyoming's land base overall, and ranches were scattered across the plains. But homesteaders and the houses and fences they built were an increasingly common sight in the sagebrush sea.[5]

And although Jim Averell was helping Ella and they had applied for a marriage license, she claimed a separate tract of land and seemed bent on running her ranch mostly by herself. This was a bit more unusual, but it was not unheard of. Women who owned land and cattle, sheep, and horses and built businesses and empires out of these resources, had lived across the West for hundreds of years. Navajo women oversaw the large sheep herds that made their families wealthy and powerful. They sheared these animals, spun their wool, and wove it into blankets that were coveted throughout the American West. Hispano women living in New Spain, whose property rights were respected by the Spanish government, sometimes inherited huge land grants from their husbands or purchased them for themselves. Like Gertrudis Barceló, these Hispanas amassed fortunes by trading in cattle, sheep, and horses.[6]

The frontier myth did not embrace these Indigenous and Hispana ranchers. Instead, nineteenth-century novelists and artists increasingly embraced the cowboy, a western man who seemed to embody all that the West represented: independence, bravery, and adventure. Frederic Remington, one of the most prolific painters and sculptors of American cowboys in the period, first gained fame as an illustrator for *Harper's Weekly* the same year that Ella Watson bought her land. His favorite subjects were western soldiers and cowboys, and he often depicted their battles against Indigenous peoples. In *A Dash for the Timber* (1889), a large (four feet by seven feet) canvas, Remington painted a group of horsemen in a running fight with Indigenous warriors. The cowboys lunge toward the viewer, and some turn to fire over their shoulders at their pursuers. The painting is dynamic and visually powerful, emphasizing the bravery and the brotherhood of the cowboy on the open range.[7]

Western cattlewomen did not inspire such admiring depictions. Dime novelists and newspaper editors did embrace some women with unusual skills and reputations, like the sharpshooter Annie Oakley in Buffalo Bill's Wild West show and master storytellers like the wagon master Calamity Jane. These white women defied gender expectations in thrilling ways, and men could admire their skills because they saw them as performative, instead of a threatening reality.

The lives of women ranchers—or "cattle queens," as some of them came to be called—were not an act. These women were not the "gentle tamers" of the frontier myth, who replicated eastern domesticity and the ideals of "true womanhood" in western cabins and towns. Instead, cattle queens often lived on their own, managing large ranching businesses for their families or themselves. And in the late nineteenth century, their numbers were growing. Western newspapers published features on women like Colorado's Mrs. Bishop Hill Warren, who was reportedly worth more than $10 million in 1887.

"She has made it in cattle with no other business advice," one admiring journalist reported, "than that furnished by her own mother wit."[8]

Teddy Roosevelt, an aspiring New York politician who owned a ranch in western Dakota Territory, knew a few of these cattle queens personally. They are "thoroughly capable of managing their affairs for themselves," he told an audience in 1887, "as if they were the shrewdest of men."[9]

Such competence was intriguing for many American men, but also worrisome. Women across the country were joining clubs to organize and support Progressive causes like temperance and landscape preservation in the 1880s and were agitating more loudly for the right to vote.[10] It was an auspicious time for Ella Watson to establish herself as one of Wyoming's ranch women. She would be the first in Rawlins, and the public response would be unpredictable. Ella decided to wait to purchase her cows until the spring of 1887, when she would have her pick of adults and newborn calves. This turned out to be the best decision she made in her career as a rancher.

In November 1886, snow fell in thick flakes and temperatures plummeted across the Wyoming plains. Winter usually came that early, so Ella and Jim were not concerned. The moisture was a welcome relief;

the summer of 1886 had been scorching, with little rain.[11] The storms continued through December almost without pause, and the snow buried the grass in deep drifts. Cows walked eastward with the storms, bleating and bawling with hunger. And then the blizzard came.

The massive winter storm that descended upon Montana, Wyoming, and Dakota—including the Northern Cheyenne homelands and the Sweetwater Valley—in the first week of January 1887 took almost everyone in the region by surprise.

"It burst upon the country with a fierceness seldom equaled in that land of elemental disturbances," one resident wrote. "The flying snow, which pelts you in the face, stings like so many needles, and nearly drives you mad with pain . . . [the] cattle, becoming confused in the flying crystals, perished in their tracks."[12]

It was the worst winter most western cattlemen had ever seen. Some lost more than half of their herds. Teddy Roosevelt, who liked to ride across his Dakota ranch wearing fringed deerskin, was shocked at the immensity of his loss. "I am bluer than indigo about the cattle," Roosevelt wrote to his sister Anna. "It is even worse than I feared." He estimated he would lose more than half of the $80,000 he had invested in his ranch.[13]

Before that winter, authorities had counted more than 900,000 cattle in Wyoming. The next year, there were only 750,000. Across the region, Westerners referred to this time as the "Great Die-Up."[14]

In southern Montana, the Northern Cheyenne lost more than two hundred cattle that winter when the herd crowded together in the shelter of some cliffs and died. It was a devastating blow because the Northern Cheyenne were already on the edge of starvation.

Since their arrival back in their homelands in 1879, members of Little Wolf's band, along with others (including Dull Knife and the survivors of their breakout), began to gather along the Rosebud River. Their annual fall and winter buffalo hunts had netted fewer and fewer animals as the herds were decimated by American cattle ranchers and tourists bent on killing as many animals as they could.

The U.S. Army officer in command of nearby Fort Keogh, General Nelson Miles, had come to trust Little Wolf and his fellow chief Dull Knife in the years after their arrival back in Montana. Miles understood Northern Cheyenne culture and traditions and was open to talking with them about the future. He knew they wanted to stay in their homelands, but he also knew there were officials in the Department of the Interior and the Department of War who wanted the Northern Cheyenne to return to the Southern Cheyenne reservation in Indian Territory.

The Northern Cheyenne exodus had captured the popular imagination of many Americans, who admired the determination and sacrifices Little Wolf and his band had made in their journey home to the North Country. The Senate created a select committee to investigate both their removal to Indian Territory and their exodus from it, and they interviewed Nelson Miles.

"They behave themselves well" in Montana, he told the committee, because "they are living in a country that is suited to them." Little Wolf and the other chiefs had told him about their horrific year living and dying in Indian Territory and how desperate they were to leave and return home. When they surrendered at Fort Keogh, "something was said about their going back to Indian Territory," Miles added. "They said they would rather die where they were; that we might commence killing them at once."[15]

Miles's testimony reinforced what the committee had already heard from Northern Cheyenne chiefs and from U.S. Army officials who had fought them during their exodus. They wanted to know, however, if it was reasonable to keep the Northern Cheyenne in the region between the Tongue and the Bighorn Rivers.

"Is the country where they are located one that will probably be desired by the whites eventually?" one of the senators asked.

"Well, yes," Miles responded drily. "The same as every other spot of ground that I know of belonging to the Indians in the United States."[16]

That imagined threat soon became real as white ranchers moved into Montana. When they petitioned the U.S. government for the removal of Little Wolf and his people to another part of the territory, Congress launched another investigation and sent an Indian agent to the Rosebud Valley to take testimony.

"We came here to make our permanent home," the chief Two Moons told the agent. The community had grown to seven hundred people, and they had built log houses, tilled land, and grown their cattle herds like the Americans living around them. They were invested in the North Country and would not leave it.[17]

Two Moons had become one of the spokesmen for the Northern Cheyenne by the mid-1880s because Little Wolf had surrendered his leadership role in the wake of a tragedy. Little more than a year after arriving back in Montana, the Sweet Medicine Chief despaired. He had led his people back to their homelands, but still they were prisoners. The Northern Cheyenne nation was fractured and scattered, and their future as a people was uncertain. To ease the pain from all these losses, Little Wolf began to drink whiskey. The post sutler was well supplied with bottles and was happy to trade one for a deerskin or pair of moccasins that one of Little Wolf's wives or his daughter, Pretty Walker, had made.

One day in December 1880, the Sweet Medicine Chief drank an entire bottle of whiskey before leaving the store. In a drunken rage, he had an altercation with a young warrior named Famished Elk and shot him to death. Filled with shame and remorse, Little Wolf smashed his medicine pipe, a sign of his abdication of band leadership, his position as headman of the Elk Horn Scrapers, and as an elder chief on the Council of Forty-Four.

"All of the Cheyennes said, 'How. It is right,'" the warrior Wooden Leg noted. "'Little Wolf shall be not any more a chief among us.' But their hearts were sad, not angry, when they said this."[18]

So it was Two Moons and not Little Wolf who talked with the federal agent, and who ultimately convinced him to recommend that the federal government officially establish a reservation for the Northern Cheyenne in the Rosebud Valley. This would designate official boundaries they hoped would prevent conflict between the Northern Cheyenne and the white ranchers who wanted their lands as open range. In late November 1884, the commissioner of Indian Affairs persuaded President Chester Arthur, who had taken office after James Garfield was assassinated, to act on this recommendation.

From the Executive Mansion, Arthur issued a presidential proclamation marking 765 square miles to be "withheld from sale and settlement, and set apart as a reservation for the use and occupation of the Northern Cheyenne Indians."[19]

For the Northern Cheyenne, this proclamation was double-edged. On the one hand, the U.S. government had officially recognized their right to live in their ancestral homelands. On the other hand, the reservation was small. The cattle herds they were raising to replace the buffalo they had traditionally hunted were also small, so the loss of two hundred animals in the Great Die-Up of 1887 was devastating. This was compounded by the fact that Montana's cattlemen continued to disregard the reservation boundary and sent their own cattle into Northern Cheyenne lands to graze. These animals trampled the gardens and fields that the women had planted to provide vegetables for their families.

Two Moons went to see General Nelson Miles to talk about these incursions. If the Army would not police the reservation's boundaries and arrest Americans who crossed them, then the Northern Cheyenne would have to take matters into their own hands.

"So long as the cattlemen are allowed to range cattle on the reservation," the chief warned the general, "there will be trouble."[20]

Before that terrible winter was over, the Northern Cheyenne received more bad news. In February 1887, the U.S. Congress had approved the Dawes Severalty Act, the latest piece of legislation in the federal government's evolving Indian policy. The law was named for its primary author, Massachusetts representative Henry Dawes, who refused to recognize Indigenous land rights or sovereignty during his long career in Congress. It authorized the president to break up reservation lands, converting them from commonly held territory into private property. Like the Homestead Act, the Dawes Act distributed lots of 160 acres of grazing land or 320 acres of ranchland to each head of a Northern Cheyenne family and smaller parcels to unmarried adults. Any lands remaining—often millions of acres—would revert to "public lands" that the federal government would sell to white settlers.

The Dawes Act and the federal government's intent to implement allotment on their lands confirmed that U.S. Indian policy had shifted, once again, into a new phase. The treaty and removal eras were over. The U.S. Army's large-scale military campaigns had also mostly ceased. Congressmen were now focused on taking as much Indigenous land as they could and destroying the cultures and identities of tribal nations across the American West.

While congressmen tried to argue that this measure was meant to protect tribal nations from further encroachment by white settlers and ranchers, the Northern Cheyenne and other Indigenous peoples immediately understood its real purpose: land dispossession.[21]

Although the snowfall had been as heavy in the mountains of Idaho as it had on the Northern Cheyenne reservation during the winter of 1886–87, the Chinese residents in Warren were used to such extreme weather. They hunkered down and ate preserved meats and other food they had prepared in the fall to get through the winter. When the spring came and the roads opened, Polly and Charlie looked forward to welcoming more miners and travelers to her boardinghouse and his saloon. But in mid-May 1887, disaster struck.

A fire started in the roof of their house (no one seemed to know how) and quickly got out of hand. Polly and Charlie managed to escape, but all their household furniture, food, and most of their clothing went up in smoke.

"The heat was intense enough," the Grangeville newspaper reported, "to fuse silver coins and melt gold watches and chains beyond recognition."[22]

The couple lost these watches and other jewelry that Charlie acquired as collateral for the loans he made to gamblers in the saloon or miners who could not pay their boardinghouse bill in cash. Polly was most distressed, however, to lose a blue dress she had made with silk she ordered from San Francisco and a lining of flour sacks from Grangeville. She did manage to save the buttons: $2.50 and $5 gold pieces that Charlie had cut down to size and she had sewn into the dress.[23]

Polly and Charlie never found out whether the house fire was an accident or an act of arson. And if it was deliberate, whether it was part of the still-strong wave of anti-Chinese violence in mining towns across the West. That spring and summer, white miners killed dozens of Chinese men on the Snake River in Oregon, and assailants burned San Jose,

California's Chinatown to the ground. Newspaper editors across Idaho expressed their disgust and disdain for the state's Chinese residents, mocking their religious rituals and annual festivals.[24]

The Grangeville paper advocated for a wagon road that would open the mineral country to white American migrants exclusively. "Without it," the editors seethed, Idaho County "will remain a Chinese-cursed, low-class county, and we shall continue to suck the hind teat of the territorial sow."[25]

They applauded, therefore, when in May 1888 the U.S. Congress passed a second Chinese Exclusion Act, an amendment to the legislation that they had passed six years before. It was a harsher measure, one that barred all Chinese laborers from entering the United States, even if they had previously resided in the country. This meant that Chinese migrants who had worked in the United States for thirty years could not go back to China to visit family and return; customs officials would no longer honor their "return certificates."[26]

Although President Grover Cleveland was not personally in favor of this new act, he signed it anyway. The first Democrat to win the presidency since before the American Civil War, Cleveland was up for reelection in 1888 and believed that his advocacy of Chinese exclusion would win him much-needed votes in the western states.[27]

For many Chinese residents of Idaho who had chosen to stay after the 1882 act, this new measure was the final straw. It was clear that the United States government and many of its residents would never welcome them, despite all the work they had done to build the infrastructure and stabilize the economy of the West—and the entire country—in the chaotic years after the American Civil War. Many people left and did not return.

Three of them were farmers on the South Fork of the Salmon River named Ah Jake, Ah Kan, and Ah Ming. The three men had worked what had been known as "China Jake Ranch" in an area renowned for its terraced gardens. They grew rhubarb, strawberries, peas, and new potatoes on their irrigated land, and they owned the water rights to the creek that flowed down to the Salmon River. In August 1888, they sold their land, all its improvements, the water rights, farming equipment, and six horses to Charlie Bemis for $500—a reasonable price at the time.[28]

Polly and Charlie did not immediately move out to the ranch. Charlie rebuilt their house in town, and they resumed running their various businesses. Polly replaced all her housedresses and made herself a white apron with lace at the bottom, which she ironed and wore every day. She crocheted curtains for the boardinghouse and trimmed the pillowcases with lace. Her house was immaculate.

"She also washed for the miners," one of her friends, a white miner's wife named Bertha Long reported, "patched their clothes, replacing missing buttons."[29]

For Polly, day-to-day life continued as it had before the passage of the Chinese Exclusion Acts. But the Chinese population in Warren was decreasing once again. There were only three hundred men in the town now (down from four hundred), and Polly was the only Chinese woman. It was a dark time for Chinese immigrants in the American West, and for anyone else, like Little Wolf and Ella Watson, who dreamed of making lives for themselves in a place that white men believed belonged to them.

CHAPTER 28

By the summer of 1888, Ella Watson was prospering on the open range in the company of Jim Averell. She had land, a cabin, and now a small herd of twenty-eight cattle on her Wyoming land claim. The cows weren't much to look at. They were skinny and depleted after the long winter and in need of a copious supply of fresh grass. But they had come cheap, and they were hers. There may have been some mavericks in the bunch, unbranded calves that had been born on the open range and rounded up by rustlers that spring, but she paid that possibility no mind.[1]

Wyoming's cattlemen did not take kindly to rustlers, and there was a territorial law on the books that defined the possession of mavericks as evidence of thievery. Ella believed, however, that she was protected from such accusations. She had a bill of sale, which she kept in the bank in Rawlins, that proved she had purchased unbranded cattle on the open market.[2]

Her cabin was almost two miles from Jim's road ranch, which gave her the comfort of proximity but also a sense of independence. She had enough money to hire a fourteen-year-old local boy named John DeCorey to help her with the harder work on the ranch. And she had befriended and then taken in an eleven-year-old boy named Gene Crowder, whose father often left him alone while out on an alcoholic bender. She felt for the boy, probably because she remembered the traumatic impact of Bill Pickell's drunken rages. And John and Gene were good company and hard workers.

Ella trusted them enough to leave the ranch in their hands in June and July, when Jim drove her to the station in Rawlins. There, she boarded a Union Pacific train to Kansas to visit her parents and her younger siblings. It might have been during this trip that she discovered that her divorce from Bill was finally granted. This was not because her own petition from two years earlier had been successful but because Bill wanted to marry again and had filed his own divorce papers against her in Kansas, on the grounds of desertion. It probably mattered little to Ella how it happened. She was free to marry Jim when they thought an official partnership would be most beneficial for their various businesses.[3]

While Ella was gone, a cattleman named Albert John Bothwell came to see Jim. Born in Iowa, Bothwell had sought his fortune in California and then Colorado before moving north to Wyoming to launch several investment schemes, including a nascent town he named after himself. He owned two ranches in the Sweetwater Valley but claimed tens of thousands more acres as open range. Jim and Ella had filed claims in his favorite hay meadow and cut him off from nearby water supplies on Horse Creek.[4]

Bothwell convinced Jim to sell him irrigation rights on a small section of the waterway. Cattle herds needed to be within a few miles of water, and if they could not drink from the creek directly, Bothwell had to be able to bring water to them. When Ella returned to Wyoming, Bothwell visited her as well. He wanted to invest in her ranch, he said. He would lend her the money to prove it up further, constructing outbuildings and irrigation ditches, and when she was ready, Ella would sell it to him. It was a decent offer, but she refused.[5] The ranch was hers, and no one would take it from her.

Ella was also beginning to agree with Jim, who was a die-hard Democrat and increasingly public about his support of Wyoming homesteaders in opposition to cattlemen. By the 1880s, Republicans were losing some ground in the West, despite supporting the Chinese Exclusion Acts to woo white western voters. This was because they had also turned away from the working class to support the large corporations and other big businesses coming to dominate American life.

These capitalists were running railroads, steel and oil companies, and gold and silver mines, buying out the competition and slashing wages for workers. They were also buying up huge tracts of land in the Midwest and the West, replacing family farmers with large-scale, mechanized agricultural operations. In Wyoming, most open-range ranchers like Al Bothwell who sought to expand their holdings and ranch cattle on a mass scale were Republicans. Homesteaders like Jim and now Ella were Democrats. Wyoming's governor was a Democrat, and he appointed Jim Averell to several positions, including notary public and postmaster.[6]

That fall, Ella Watson's herd had grown to forty-one animals, and she registered her brand with the local authorities. Once she commissioned the iron brand itself and marked her animals, their hides would identify the cows and calves as belonging to her. If any rustlers, or even a big rancher like Al Bothwell, tried to steal or claim them, the brand would prove her ownership.[7]

In February 1889, Jim had had enough of Bothwell's attempts to secure his and Ella's land and decided to publicly decry the grasping land hunger of Wyoming's cattlemen.

"It is wonderful how much land some of the land sharks own in their minds," he wrote to the editors of a newspaper in the town of Casper, "and how firmly they are organized to keep Wyoming from being settled up." While men like Bothwell clearly believed that "a poor man has no say in the affairs of his country," Jim was sure that "he is wrong, as the future landowner in Wyoming will be the people to come." In his view, three or four men should not own the entirety of the Sweetwater River. Homesteading pioneers like him should have access to irrigation water and be able to plant orchards, crops, and raise cattle on small parcels of land. Jim was proud to state such beliefs publicly and so did not hide behind anonymity in his letter.

"Not wishing to disguise myself in the matter," he signed off, "I remain yours truly, James Averell."[8]

After his letter was reprinted in the Rawlins newspaper, Ella and Jim came home from the spring roundup to find skulls and crossbones nailed to their doors.[9] The couple did not take any further action to protect themselves, however. That summer, Gene and John were still living and working with Ella, and they welcomed several guests to the road ranch, including Jim's nephew Ralph and a cowboy named Frank Buchanan.[10]

Shortly after, Ella branded her herd, which included several calves that had been born earlier in the spring. Soon, a cattle detective named George Henderson arrived and checked out her animals, looking for unbranded mavericks and anything else amiss. Henderson, who had been a Pinkerton detective and a strikebreaker in previous years, was working for the Wyoming Stock Growers Association, an organization whose members were the wealthiest cattlemen in the territory.[11]

Henderson went to Al Bothwell and informed him that Ella's calves were newly branded, and the cattleman called a meeting of several of his neighbors and friends. On the morning of July 20, five of them joined him at his ranch, including a former Union Pacific manager named Robert M. Galbraith, a wealthy rancher named John Henry Durbin who financed his cattle concern with money made speculating in mine properties in Deadwood, Dakota Territory, and Thomas DeBeau Soleil (known in the Sweetwater Valley as Tom Sun), a former fur trapper who was one of the first white residents of the region, having built a ranch there in 1872.[12]

"Averell and Watson are rustling and branding our cattle!" Bothwell seethed. It did not take long to convince the other men that the couple were a pair of thieves, and the six men mounted up and rode to Ella's homestead.[13]

That morning, Ella and John had walked down to the confluence of Horse Creek and the Sweetwater River, where a Shoshone band had established a camp. Ella knew the band from previous summers and admired the expertise of their weavers and bead workers. She had purchased a blanket and other items from them before and wanted to see what they had for sale or barter. She and John left Gene behind at the house.[14]

A few hours later, they walked back and Ella reveled in her new pair of moccasins made of soft deerskin, bearing bright red and green triangles. As they neared her cabin, they saw the six ranchers ride up. She was too far away to hear what they were saying to one another, but they were in her corral, looking at her cattle. Then John Durbin began kicking her juniper fence posts and yanking down the barbed wire. If he tore down a large enough section, her cows would escape. Ella and John began to run.

"Stop! Stop!" she yelled, dashing into the corral. The ranchers ceased what they were doing and surrounded her while John came up beside her. "Get into the house," they told the boy. "And don't show your face outside again." He backed away, and Ella turned to them.

"My cattle are not stolen," she said. "I have been pasturing them for almost a year." They scoffed and demanded witnesses. "I bought them and have a bill of sale!" she protested. She could take them to her bank box in Rawlins and show it to them, if they wished.

Suddenly, Gene burst out of the house and leapt onto his horse. He turned its head toward Jim's road ranch, intent on letting him know what was happening to Ella. But one of the ranchers caught his reins and dragged him out of the saddle.

"Get in that buggy," they told Ella, nodding at the vehicle that Tom Sun had driven over. She balked.

"Where are you taking me?" she asked.

"To Rawlins," one of the men said, "to put you on the next train out of the country."

Ella pleaded with them to let her put on some proper clothes. She was wearing a housedress, a bonnet, and her new moccasins.

"Where you are going, you won't need any fancy clothes," Bothwell yelled. He grabbed her arm and forced her into the buggy. While he and four others mounted their horses, Ella sat in the seat behind Tom Sun, stunned. The group headed toward Jim's road ranch.

After about a mile, they saw Jim coming, driving his own wagon. He was on the way to Casper to buy more supplies for his store and for the meals Ella would cook for travelers. When he saw the group coming, he reined in his horses and looked at the cattlemen.

"What do you want?" he asked, confused.

"We have a warrant for your arrest," Bothwell blurted. Jim was immediately skeptical.

"Can I see it?" Jim asked. Bothwell and another rancher swung up their rifles from their saddlebags. "This should be warrant enough," Bothwell said.

Jim saw no way around it, so he got down from his wagon and joined Ella in Tom Sun's buggy. What the couple said to each other for the next few hours went unrecorded. They were unarmed, at the mercy of six men who wanted their land and their water rights and had been thus far unable to secure either.

The horses and the buggy splashed across the Sweetwater River and moved south of Independence Rock toward Sentinel Rocks, a burst of light brown granite formations rising out of the plains and dotted with green pitch pines and juniper trees. Bothwell called out a halt and the cattlemen dismounted. They dragged Jim and Ella out of the buggy, forcing them to walk into a canyon over a pile of jumbled boulders. Soon they found a twenty-foot pine tree, and Bothwell threw one end of his lariat over one of its limbs. He tied the other end into a noose, and another rancher tried to hold Jim still while Bothwell put it over his head.

"We never rustled any cattle!" Jim yelled, resisting. One of the men threw his lariat over a nearby branch and tried to pull the noose over Ella's head, but she was able to dodge it.

Suddenly, bullets began to ping in the dirt and the rocks around them. One of them hit John Durbin in the hip, and he went down. Everyone but Jim and Ella ducked behind boulders and tree trunks. The shooter was Frank Buchanan, the cowboy who had been staying at the road ranch. Gene and John had galloped to Jim's place after the ranchers had left with Jim and Ella, and they told Frank what happened. He had tracked the group to Sentinel Rocks, but he had only twelve bullets. Soon he was out of ammunition and had to retreat.

The ranchers shot at Buchanan as he fled and turned back to their work. They forced Jim and Ella onto a small boulder and finally succeeded in getting the noose around Ella's neck. They shoved Jim off first, then Ella. The drop was not high enough to break their necks instantaneously, so the couple kicked and struggled and tried to free themselves from the nooses. It took more than a few minutes for them to lose enough oxygen to pass out and a few minutes more to stop breathing. The six cattlemen waited a bit longer to make sure Ella Watson and Jim Averell were dead. Then they turned back down the canyon to return to their horses and buggy and disappeared into the Sweetwater Valley.[15]

After he left Sentinel Rocks, Frank Buchanan rode more than sixty miles to the sheriff's office in the town of Casper. He told the sheriff that six ranchers had lynched two homesteaders named Ella Watson and Jim Averell, and he could find their bodies up in the canyon near Sentinel Rocks. The sheriff put together a posse that included a local dentist who could serve as a coroner, and they arrived at Averell's road ranch at 2:00 a.m. on July 22. Buchanan handed around kerosene lanterns and led them to the site of Ella's and Jim's deaths. The sheriff cut down the bodies and the posse tied them to a horse, then brought them back to the road ranch.

They conducted the inquest immediately. The dentist determined suffocation as the cause of death, and Gene and Frank Buchanan told their stories of what happened in Ella's corral and in the canyon. Then Frank, Jim's nephew, Gene, and John placed Ella and Jim into two coffins they had constructed for them in the previous two days. Their friends buried them near the road ranch and marked their graves with two oak wagon wheels, those already famous symbols of the pioneer West.[16]

That day, Al Bothwell sent a telegram to the stock detective George Henderson in Cheyenne. Henderson took it to the editor of the *Cheyenne Daily Leader*, a reliable mouthpiece for the Wyoming Stock Growers Association.

"A man and woman were lynched near historic Independence rock on the Sweetwater river in Carbon County, Sunday night," the newspaper announced the next morning. "Their offense was cattle stealing, and they operated on a large scale, recruiting quite a bunch of young steers from the range of that section." According to the *Daily Leader*, Ella and Jim were "fearless mavericksers," and Ella was a virago, a daredevil, and a holy terror, "the equal of any man on the range." Jim had "murdered two men and would not hesitate to shoot, while the woman was always full of fight."

The paper went on to describe the ranchers as fearless pursuers of justice who surrounded Averell's road ranch and subdued the couple, who resisted and cursed at their captors (especially Ella, whose profanity was particularly shocking) until the end. "It is doubtful if any attempt will be made to punish the lynchers," the *Daily Leader* determined. "They acted in self-protection, feeling that the time to resort to violent measures had arrived."[17]

The *Daily Leader*'s (rather, the ranchers') version of events spread quickly across the nation and the Atlantic Ocean, appearing in New York and London papers in the next few days. Another Cheyenne newspaper that printed its own account the next day confused Ella Watson with a woman named Kate Maxwell, a gambler who socialized with cattle rustlers and ran a dance parlor and brothel in Bessemer, Wyoming. This was probably because the *Daily Leader* had never actually named Ella Watson in their original article but called her only "the woman" or the "female." Ella was almost immediately identified as "Cattle Kate" in the American press, a woman who traded sexual favors for unbranded cattle and who held Jim Averell under her thumb.[18]

Powerful cattlemen had taken Ella Watson's life, and then newspapermen took her reputation. Although subsequent articles tried to correct the record and identify her properly—calling previous articles "dime novels"—and Ella's friends gave interviews testifying to her good nature and generosity, the nickname and the popular image stuck. Even newspapers that expressed outrage at the lynching and framed it as a frontier tragedy believed Ella to be a prostitute.

"There is much that is rough and wild" in the American West, the *Salt Lake Tribune* noted sadly, "but there is generally, withal, a crude chivalry which protects [even] the most abandoned of women."[19]

Although the Carbon County sheriff arrested all six of the cattle ranchers for the murder of Ella Watson and Jim Averell, they were released on $5,000 bail, which they each paid for one another. Only a week after the lynching, Bothwell, Durbin, and Galbraith shipped their first annual trainloads of cattle on the Union Pacific Railroad out of Rawlins. Newspaper editors across the West continued to defend their actions, arguing that the lynching would stand not only as a justifiable act of violence but also as a successful warning to other cattle rustlers to get out of the business, and out of Wyoming as well.[20]

More than a month after her death, Ella's father, Thomas Watson, stepped off the train at the Rawlins depot. He and Ella's mother and siblings had read about her death in the *Omaha Bee*. The family had sent him to gather up or auction off Ella's things and to witness the trial of her murderers. He took a stage and then rode to Ella's ranch house and walked through it, taking in the small and now-deserted space, with its wood furniture, a star quilt Ella had either made or purchased, and her sewing machine.

After the auction, he took Ella's horse and rode to Sentinel Rocks. It must have seemed ironic to Thomas Watson that his daughter had worked so hard to escape a violent husband, only to die at the hands of men who were driven into their own kind of frenzy by her blameless actions. He could see the marks on the trees where the lariats had scraped off the bark and where Ella had kicked off her beautiful new moccasins in her struggle to breathe.

On his way back to the ranch, Watson dropped by Bothwell's house, but the cattleman was not at home. He visited his daughter's grave before heading back to Rawlins. Then he took the train west to the coal mining town of Rock Springs, where he stayed until the grand jury convened in mid-October. There was not much to see in the town, which had its own violent history: four years before, irate white miners had attacked the Rock Springs Chinatown, murdering or wounding more than forty Chinese men before burning eighty homes and businesses to the ground.[21]

The town of Cheyenne was buzzing with people in mid-October 1889 when the grand jury was empaneled for the Averell-Watson case. Al Bothwell and the other five ranchers were present. Their lawyers had been provided by the Wyoming Stock Growers Association. And while the prosecutor had a transcript of the testimony of Frank Buchanan, Gene Crowder, and Averill's nephew Ralph Cole, they did not appear in the courtroom as witnesses. Gene's father had come to collect him, and Frank Buchanan had disappeared. No one knew where John DeCorey was at present. And Ralph Cole had died the previous month, of a mysterious illness.

One of the visitors to Cheyenne during the grand jury deliberations was Owen Wister, a friend of Teddy Roosevelt and future author of Western novels who was traveling through Wyoming for his health. He met the rancher and defendant John Durbin (fully recovered from his gunshot wound to the hip) in the smoking car on a train. "He seemed a good solid citizen," Wister judged, "and I hope he'll get off."[22]

The prosecutor did his best but four days later, the grand jury declined to indict the ranchers.[23] Homesteaders were outraged, and cattlemen were satisfied. The residents of Rawlins likely suspected that the battle between these two Wyoming communities was not over.

Within a few years, the real Ella Watson ultimately became subsumed in the legend of "Cattle Kate." The pioneer myth had room only for women who were obedient wives and mothers or their opposite: rabble-rousing prostitutes. In some ways Watson did fit the "gentle tamer" vision of western women: most of her talents were domestic, and she was warmhearted toward children and strangers. But she was also entrepreneurial and resilient; she persisted in following her dream to become a landowner and a rancher. Ella Watson was, like Sacajawea, María Gertrudis Barceló, and Polly Bemis, a real woman: flawed in some ways but also strong-willed, generous, industrious, and determined. And she was propelled by her desire to live on her own terms in a world that white men—bolstered by the frontier myth and federal policies that reinforced the myth's central beliefs—increasingly defined and controlled.[24]

CHAPTER 29

Two hundred and fifty miles north of Ella Watson's former ranch, two Northern Cheyenne young men rode their horses across their reservation's eastern boundary, heading toward the Tongue River in Montana. It did not take them long to find a cow, browsing in clumps of light brown wheatgrass and wild oats. The animal belonged to one of the ranchers whose lands abutted the reservation, and Northern Cheyenne hunters often targeted this herd when the cows wandered over the boundary line. The older of the two, Vehoneme'ko (Head Chief), was the grandson of a renowned medicine man. It was mid-September 1890, and he had brought fourteen-year-old Heá'ke (Young Mule) with him on this hunting expedition to provide meat for their starving families.[1]

While the Northern Cheyenne had a cattle herd of their own and some fields planted with corn, potatoes, and winter vegetables, these were not enough to feed the more than one thousand people now living on the reservation. Six years after its creation in 1884, Congress still had not appropriated enough money to provide meat, flour, and cornmeal more than twice a month. They expected the Northern Cheyenne to farm and ranch to support themselves, but many families had not yet shifted to an agrarian American culture and so were destitute.[2]

Head Chief and Young Mule dismounted and approached the cow. One of them drew his gun and shot the animal in the head, and they immediately fell to their knees and began to butcher it so they could carry the meat back to their families. Soon they heard a rustling in the brush, and a sixteen-year-old white boy named Hugh Boyle rode up to them, doubtless attracted by the sound of the gunshot. The three young men had words, and Head Chief drew his gun, shooting Boyle in the chest and then the head. Head Chief and Young Mule took the meat they had already cut away from the cow's carcass, stuffed it into their saddlebags, mounted their horses, and rode back the way they came, crossing back into the reservation.[3]

Head Chief went to American Horse, an elder of Little Wolf's generation, and told him what he had done and where Boyle's body could be found. American Horse sent him to consult with his father and several other elders, who were headmen of the Northern Cheyenne warrior societies. Head Chief and Young Mule knew that American Horse would have to report their actions to the federal Indian agent and the commander at the U.S. Army's nearby Camp Merritt and negotiate for their surrender.[4]

The two young men decided they would rather die fighting. Head Chief gathered some supplies from his cabin, and then he and Young Mule rode into the broken, stony hills above the town of Lame Deer. Members of the military societies accompanied them, helping them paint their horses and don their war bonnets. American Horse reported the murder to the agent, and the reservation police—Northern Cheyenne men appointed to keep the peace—fanned out across the reservation.[5]

The next morning, U.S. Army soldiers marched into Lame Deer and joined the reservation police, forming a line at the base of a hill, where they had heard the young men were waiting. Head Chief, the black-and-white golden eagle feathers of his grandfather's war bonnet fluttering in the breeze, turned to Young Mule. They vowed to each other that they would fight to the death, and then they turned their horses down the hill and toward the soldiers.

The sun was high in the sky when "the two renegades were seen coming at full speed in war paint and feathers," a Montana newspaper reported. "They charged along the full length of the line occupied by the troops and Indian police, shooting and yelling like demons."[6]

They approached the soldiers' line and then wheeled away, escaping without damage. They had just started back up the hill when a soldier hit Young Mule's horse and it went down. He disentangled himself and crawled to a rocky outcropping. Head Chief, meanwhile, rode back toward the soldiers, "making directly for the line of troops and police, . . . firing his Winchester as rapidly as possible." He was hit several times but made it through the line before a soldier shot him in the head and he died instantly. Young Mule, singing a death song, came out from the rocks and ran toward the soldiers and was hit in the side.[7]

The troops and the police withdrew, and the Northern Cheyenne military societies came forward to collect the bodies. They buried Head Chief and Young Mule in the traditional manner among the rocks and tied Head Chief's war bonnet above their bodies for all the Northern Cheyenne people, and the white soldiers, to see. This charge was the last time Cheyenne warriors died in a declared battle against U.S. troops, and most Montana newspapers depicted the final charge of Head Chief and Young Mule as a romantic moment of a bygone era.[8]

But this extraordinary event in Lame Deer was not evidence that Indians had nearly "vanished" in the fall of 1890. It was an act of resistance against the cultural annihilation that the federal government was now attempting to enact. The Northern Cheyenne had been fighting American attempts to control them and their homelands since the 1840s. They had won several battles but lost others. They were forced onto a reservation not of their choosing, and after a year, Little Wolf led them back to the North Country in 1879.

When the federal government designated this part of their homelands as a reservation, the Northern Cheyenne gained some protection against trespassers. But then the U.S. Congress and the Grover Cleveland administration threatened to take even more land away from tribal members through allotment and demanded that they send their children to boarding schools. Federal Indian agents cracked down on the performance of the Sun Dance and other ceremonies, arguing that these events undermined the federal program of Christianization that they intended to implement on the reservation. But the Northern Cheyenne regularly took matters into their own hands to defend themselves against interlopers and to continue their rituals and ceremonies.

The Northern Cheyenne had begun hearing about the visions of the Numu (Northern Paiute) prophet Wovoka and the future he promised to all Indigenous peoples about a year before Head Chief and Young Mule killed Hugh Boyle. News had traveled from the Northern Paiute lands in Nevada, through the Shoshone reservations in Idaho and Wyoming. It also came through the Apsáalooke, whose lands bordered the Northern Cheyenne reservation.[9]

The Northern Cheyenne holy man Porcupine went to see Wovoka and confirmed that what they had been hearing about his visions was true. The Great Spirit "told us that all of our dead were to be resurrected," Wovoka told Porcupine, "that they were all to come back to earth, and that as the earth was too small for them and us, he would do away with heaven and make the earth itself large enough to contain us all." To prepare for this moment, Indigenous peoples across the Rocky Mountains and the Great Plains would need to sing and dance in a big circle until they were depleted. Then they would see their dead relatives and plan for their reunion. It was also important that they spread the word.

"We must tell all the people we meet about these things," Wovoka advised.[10]

When Porcupine returned and relayed Wovoka's message about the Ghost Dance, the Northern Cheyenne did as the prophet recommended. They held dances in various locations across their reservation in 1890, evading federal soldiers. They often fasted in preparation for these dances, to bring on the visions more quickly. And they wrote to their Northern and Southern Cheyenne kin in Indian Territory and their Lakota allies at Pine Ridge and Standing Rock in North and South Dakota about this redemptive and transformative act of resistance.[11]

That December, the Northern Cheyenne mourned when they heard about the murder of Sitting Bull at the Standing Rock reservation. The federal agent there had sent reservation police to arrest the Hunkpapa chief for encouraging the Ghost Dance and take him into custody. Instead, the police opened fire on Sitting Bull as he left his cabin to confront them. Two weeks later, 7th Cavalry soldiers (the same regiment Sitting Bull defeated in 1876) massacred hundreds of Minneconjou Lakota men, women, and children as they attempted to flee from their reservation to join their kin at Pine Ridge. The unwarranted attack at Wounded Knee was strongly reminiscent of the 3rd Colorado's massacre of Southern Cheyenne at Sand Creek.

These acts of federal violence did not stop the Ghost Dance. Believers continued to meet and look toward a future of Indigenous interconnection and sovereignty, when the land would be theirs once again.[12]

Energized by the Ghost Dance, Northern Cheyenne leaders decided to hold a reseating ceremony for their political leadership in 1892. The Council of Forty-Four, their central institution of tribal governance made up of chiefs and military society leaders, would meet for the first time in almost twenty years. Several chiefs sent a message to Little Wolf, who was living with his wives and children in the lands between the Muddy River and the Rosebud. Although his standing in the community was still precarious since his murder of Famished Elk, it was important that he attend the ceremony, as he still officially held the position of Sweet Medicine Chief.

At the meeting, the chiefs waited for Little Wolf to appear. When he did not, they sent runners to his cabin to fetch him. Finally, he acquiesced and joined the council elders. He brought the Sweet Medicine bundle with him and did his duty by announcing the successor that the Council of Forty-Four delegates had chosen—a chief named Grasshopper—and handing the bundle to him in a symbolic transfer of power.[13]

As in the 1860s and '70s, the Northern Cheyenne knew they needed strong leadership over the next few years. Congress was considering an expansion of their reservation, and they needed leaders to defend their current boundaries and argue for an extension eastward to the Tongue River. This required diplomacy, and chiefs able to convince federal Indian agents and soldiers that a larger reservation was necessary to their survival.[14]

"I wonder if anyone else," Little Wolf's grandson said, "has ever had to fight as hard to live in Montana as us Cheyennes?"[15]

As the Northern Cheyenne continued to fight for control of their own lands in Montana in the 1890s, federal officials persisted in their attempts to wrest Utah from the Church of Jesus Christ of Latter-day Saints. They continued to prevent the admission of Utah to the Union as a state, demanding that the Saints abandon plural marriage. This was only one of several reasons that Congress—and fifty-four-year-old Ovando

Hollister—objected to Mormonism. They also disliked the power that leaders retained over the people and the economy of Utah. Hollister, for one, believed that this power should belong to everyone who lived in the territory, non-Mormon and Mormon alike.

Although Hollister was often exhausted by this "state of dumb war in which we seem condemned to smoulder" (which had been going on since he and Carrie had moved to Utah in 1869), he saw his work trying to break Mormon power in Utah as part and parcel of his fight for the Union back in 1862. "I could not help taking a hand in the local contest for my country's institutions and honor," he noted, "and once engaged as with a good soldier (or citizen), always engaged."[16]

He had other interests, of course, that took his attention and time. He was still working as a tax collector for the U.S. government, in a huge territory that encompassed Montana, Idaho, and Utah. He traveled often with his brother-in-law Elias Matthews, who was living with him and Carrie and worked as his deputy. When Schuyler Colfax, Carrie's half brother and Ulysses S. Grant's vice president, had died unexpectedly in 1885, Hollister traveled to Indiana for several months to read through his papers. Within a year, he published a well-received and bestselling biography of the former vice president. Hollister had made enough money from this and other projects to build a large three-and-a-half-story house for him, Carrie, and Elias. It was located a few blocks east of the Mormons' Temple Square in Salt Lake City and boasted several porches, Palladian windows, and a turret.[17]

Hollister was now a dominant figure in the non-Mormon social and political community in Salt Lake City. He was a member of the Salt Lake City Chamber of Commerce and helped found and sustain the Salt Lake Academy, a primary school for Gentiles. Given his experiences with the Shakers and the Mormons, he tended to view organized religion with suspicion, but he went with Carrie to services at the First Congregational Church and was an enthusiastic member of its choir. The congregation was constructing a new building across the street from the Hollisters' house, and Ovando helped draw up its architectural plans.[18]

He also continued his involvement in local politics. Presiding over an 1891 meeting of the Liberal Party, formed in Utah to fight Mormon dominance, Hollister had earned thunderous applause from the more than

1,500 attendees for his opening remarks. "It was just twenty-one years ago to-morrow," he said, "since I first made a set speech in Utah for the perpetuation of American ideas and institutions . . . and I have followed it up with voice and pen ever since." Mormon leaders had recently indicated they would give up polygamy, and Hollister thought that the Mormons might move beyond words and toward action sometime soon. "Ideas for which men have suffered so much are not lightly relinquished," he reminded his audience. "The true course for us to pursue is to remain intact until the gradual change which has been going on completes itself."[19]

On a Thursday afternoon in early February 1892, Hollister took a shovel across the street to the First Congregational Church construction site and spent several hours removing fresh snow from the building's foundation and roof. That evening, he sang songs with Carrie and her sister Clara Witter, who was visiting from Denver. He went to sleep but woke up around 2:00 a.m. with a pain in his chest. He could barely breathe. Carrie woke up and fetched Clara, and they called his doctor. Nothing could be done for him, however, and Ovando Hollister died at 5:00 a.m. on February 12.[20]

Word of Hollister's death spread through Salt Lake City. "The sudden death of Colonel OVANDO J. HOLLISTER yesterday morning was a terrible shock to this city," the editors of the *Salt Lake Tribune* lamented, "and filled thousands of hearts with profound grief."[21]

Hollister had been a fixture in Corinne and then Salt Lake City for so long, it seemed impossible to imagine Utah without him. Condolences and memorials poured in from the members of the Chamber of Commerce, the Liberal Party, the Salt Lake Academy, the First Congregational Church, and from friends Hollister had made during all his travels throughout the West. Even the Mormon paper, the *Deseret News*—which had often published articles deriding him and his efforts—printed a memorial that the Chamber of Commerce had written in his honor.[22]

Three days later, mourners crowded into the entryway, dining room, and parlor of the Hollisters' large house. Bouquets covered many of the tables, and the smell of lilies and roses filled the house. Carrie and Clara, with Elias and a few family members who had come from Denver, gathered around his body, which was laid out in the library. It was fitting that in death, as in life, he was surrounded by the written word.

Some of these words were his own. On the shelves were copies of the books and pamphlets he had written, from his Civil War history of the 1st Colorado to his promotional tracts lauding Colorado and Utah to his biography of Schuyler Colfax. He had also collected many issues of the region's early newspapers, including his own Black Hawk *Daily Mining Journal*, and filed them away in the library.[23]

That afternoon, the reverend of the First Congregational Church gave a short memorial sermon. "Never will the city be given quite such another man," the reverend mused, "for the conditions that made him what he was to this city will never again exist here. It takes generations to mold a large, pure, and generous nature. It takes years to fit him for his place in a community, and to set him in that place."[24]

Hollister's friends and allies believed that he was a man for his moment, and for the territory of Utah. He was, in many ways, a prototypical white man at the center of the American frontier myth. Hollister came from nothing and traveled west in search of his fortune. He argued for the extermination of Indigenous peoples to make way for white settlers and believed that it was the fate of the West to be a land of freedom—for white, Protestant men and women. He was also an abolitionist, a women's rights activist, and an ardent Republican who used the power of print to relentlessly promote both Colorado and Utah.

"His death removes from life a pioneer [who was true] to the West," his former newspaper the *Rocky Mountain News* lamented, "whose heart beat in patriotic devotion to the interests of the Rocky Mountain country."[25]

Hollister did not live to see Utah Republicans gain a majority in the territorial council in 1893 or witness the Republican National Committee finally support Utah's bid for statehood. In 1896, Utah achieved what Ovando Hollister had wanted for more than twenty years and became the forty-fifth state of the Union, with a constitution that prohibited plural marriages forever.[26]

Mormons may have been welcomed into the United States as citizens in the early 1890s, but Chinese residents like Polly Bemis continued to face exclusion and possible deportation. In the spring of 1892, Idaho's newspapers began printing accounts of the debates over and ultimate passage of the Geary Act, federal legislation that extended the Chinese Exclusion Act for ten more years. The act went further, however.

"All Chinese laborers now in the United States will be compelled to obtain registration certificates," Boise's *Idaho Statesman* crowed. Any Chinese person found without a certificate after the registration deadline would be deported. And "forging certificates will be punishable by imprisonment for five years."[27]

The certificate also required a photograph so that Internal Revenue collectors tasked with enforcing this new law could ensure that the bearer of the certificate was the person named on the form. The only other American residents required to be photographed in the early 1890s were convicted criminals.[28] The Geary Act's intent was clear: if the federal government could not stop the flow of Chinese migrants into the country, they would control and surveil them—and ultimately deport them, without due process—once they were within national borders.

Over the next year, debates raged about the constitutionality and the moral rightness of the Geary Act. Robert Ingersoll, a politician and orator already famous for his advocacy of free thought in America, debated the act's named author, California politician Thomas Geary. Ingersoll noted that Chinese workers had been invited into the United States in the 1860s to work on one of the West's most important projects, the transcontinental railroad. They had been peaceable and law-abiding residents in the years since. The targeting of the Chinese population was not only unwarranted in Ingersoll's view, but the edge of a slippery slope.

"When the rights of even one human being are held in contempt," he argued, "the rights of all are in danger."[29]

Ingersoll's words had special resonance in the 1890s, a disastrous era for citizenship rights in the United States. In the South, Black women and men who had achieved their freedom during the American Civil War lost most of it again as white Southerners "redeemed" the former states of the Confederacy and passed Black Codes and racial segregation laws that functionally stripped Black Americans of their Fourteenth and Fifteenth Amendment rights. Across the nation and especially in the West, the Northern Cheyenne and other tribal nations had been forced onto reservations that were then reduced in size, and the remaining land sold off to white settlers. Like Chinese men and women, they were not legally citizens of the United States and so had few protections in the face of federal actions against them.

By the 1890s, white Americans had taken control of western lands and their resources. They justified their actions using the ideologies of Manifest Destiny and the American Dream. Most did not care that these national narratives, bolstered by the frontier myth and its exaltation of white pioneer families, led to the political marginalization and social oppression of large populations of Americans.

"The average American," Robert Ingersoll argued, "has but little imagination. People who speak a different language, or worship some other god, or wear clothing unlike his own, are beyond the horizon of his sympathy. He cares but little or nothing for the sufferings or misfortunes of those who are of a different complexion or of another race."[30]

The Chinese Six Companies, a consortium of Chinese businessmen and community leaders based in California, tried to combat this lack of empathy. They filed suit to stop the implementation of the Geary Act, arguing that it violated the constitutional protections of Chinese residents, even though they were not citizens. The Supreme Court majority disagreed, issuing a 6–3 ruling in *Fong Yue Ting v. US* that Congress had the power to both exclude immigrants at the border and expel them from the nation. Deportation, according to the court, was an administrative process, not a cruel and unusual punishment meted out to men and women who had committed no crime.[31]

On the ground, more than 100,000 Chinese men and women still living mostly in the West engaged in acts of strategic noncompliance regarding the Geary Act's requirements. A subsequent law identified a registration deadline of May 4, 1894, but only 10 percent of Chinese residents complied, and those who did waited until the last few weeks before the deadline.[32]

In Warren, Polly Bemis did not seek out a photographer or a registrar to apply for her certificate. Even though the mining town's population had plummeted since 1888 (there were fewer than 150 people living in Warren in 1893), she was still running the boardinghouse and saloon with Charlie.[33] And she had taken on even more of the responsibility for these businesses in the previous few years.

In the fall of 1890, Charlie had run afoul of a gambler named Johnny Cox, who cheated in a game of cards and then demanded the money he had "won." When Charlie ignored his request, Cox pulled out his gun and shot him in the head. The bullet went through his mouth and out his cheek by his ear. His cheekbone shattered into fourteen pieces and injured his eye, and the doctors who attended him could find and extract only one part of the bullet. Everyone was sure that Charlie would die, either of blood poisoning from the bullet shrapnel or some other kind of infection.[34]

He lived, however. Cox was arrested, convicted, and jailed. Over the next few months, Charlie was attended by two doctors, one white and one Chinese, and he had Polly to look after him. By November, Charlie was feeling well enough to help Polly throw a grand ball at the saloon, in honor of John and Bertha Long. Polly's good friend was leaving Warren before the winter's snowfall trapped them there, and they would not be returning in the spring. After Bertha's departure, Polly had few friends left besides Charlie and Mollie Snead, but miners continued to stay in her boardinghouse, and she met a constantly revolving cast of characters in the saloon.

Otherwise, life went on as it did before Charlie's near-death experience. Polly did have to go out hunting with him now, however. He could not see the game given the injury to his eye, but she could. "She used to run up and down and whisk around the hills like a squirrel in a pine-tree," an acquaintance remembered.[35]

There was likely a lot of talk about the Geary Act in Warren but not a lot of action. In the fall of 1893, residents received word that a photographer named John Hanson would be coming from Grangeville. The snows fell before he could make it over the mountain trail, however, so Hanson did not arrive until April 1894. He set up a studio on the side of a log house, spreading hay on the ground and hanging a sheet as a background. A table sat on the left side of the makeshift studio, covered with a striped cloth edged with fringe.

When it came time for Polly to have her picture taken, she walked over and placed her right hand on a book that sat on the tabletop. She was wearing a long skirt and a dark, fitted jacket, long-sleeved with a high collar, and edged with tiny buttons. Lace—likely of her own design—peeked out at her wrists. Her dark hair was parted in the middle and swept back from her face in a neat bun, and she wore a pair of jeweled earrings.[36]

Polly did not have to take such care with her clothes. Hanson would be cropping the photograph to affix only an image of her face to the certificate required by the Geary Act. But she had always taken pride in her appearance, making sure her dresses were neat and clean. She was not going to stop now. As Hanson readied the camera, Polly looked a little to her right. She pressed her lips together with just a hint of a smile. Presenting such an image of elegant, refined femininity to federal authorities, who were so bound and determined to define her as a criminal, was Polly's own act of protest.

After photographing the rest of the town's Chinese inhabitants, Hanson went out on to Main Street and gathered some of the townspeople together. They sat beneath a flagpole as Hanson carried his camera farther up the road. The cluster of wooden buildings, with Polly and Charlie's hotel and saloon at the center of town, dominated the foreground of the photograph as the dark inclines of the mountains rose behind. Charlie and Polly sat together underneath the flagpole, squinting into the sun.[37]

Hanson had arrived only a few days before the May 4 deadline, and Warren's Chinese residents still had not received a visit from an Internal Revenue officer to register them. Then the mining season was upon them, and Polly and Charlie were busy. Charlie bought a mining claim on the Salmon River, seventeen miles from Warren by pack trail. He spent much of the summer hacking out a clearing to build a small cabin close to the riverbank for him and Polly.

On August 13, Polly dressed herself once again in her dark jacket and skirt and joined Charlie in the living room of their house in town. There were two other friends there, and A. D. Smead, Mollie's husband, who was a justice of the peace. As Charlie and Polly promised to honor and obey each other, they legalized what had been a partnership for almost fifteen years. Although Idaho had initially banned marriages between white people and those of Chinese descent in 1864, a recent 1887 law had forbidden miscegenation only between white and Black residents.[38] Soon after their wedding, Polly acquired six tablespoons, all of them engraved "Mrs. C.A. Bemis."[39]

By early April 1896, the federal government finally caught up with Polly Bemis. There had been a complaint filed against her and twenty-two other Chinese people from the mining town, arguing that they had "failed and refused to comply with the provisions" of the Geary Act. Polly and Charlie packed up and traveled to Grangeville. They descended from the mountain trail into a broad valley and approached the gridded town of one thousand people, surrounded by rolling wheat fields.[40]

This was the first time Polly had left Warren since her arrival in 1872, and no one was sure if the white residents there would be hostile to them. They entered the courthouse on Main Street without incident, however. Federal officials must have had a difficult time traveling throughout the rugged mountains and valleys of the American West trying to track down Chinese residents, because the clerk handed Polly what amounted to a fill-in-the-blank document to read through and sign.

"George Miner, a Deputy Internal Revenue Collector for this District in January and February 1894, promised to come to Grangeville, Idaho, and register not only myself but all other Chinamen [*sic*] who were without Certificates," the document read. "I relied on this promise." The document went on to state that Mr. Minor had been delayed by snow and rain, and that the roads were impassable in both directions. "In addition to this: I was poor and without means of travel and had no way of travelling, and I fully relied on Mr. Minor's promise to come and register me, which promise he failed to keep."

A witness, a white man whom Polly and Charlie may or may not have ever met, testified on Polly's behalf. According to him and the document he produced, Polly was a "peaceable law abiding Chinaman [*sic*], inoffensive, and has been continuously engaged in <u>Laundrying</u> for <u>ten</u> years in Idaho County."[41]

The clerk said nothing about the fact that the document misidentified Polly as a man, or that it misrepresented how long she had been living in Idaho. He told her and Charlie that a district court would hear her case. The couple returned to Warren and to their work preparing the hotel and saloon for the summer season. In mid-May, they received word that the district court found in her favor. It was not Polly's fault that she had missed the deadline required by the Geary Act, so her certificate of registration would be issued. On August 10, 1896, Polly Bemis was registered with the federal government through certificate #140059, with her cropped photograph attached to the record.[42]

In the 1890s, white Americans believed that they were protecting the nation by containing the "danger" that people like Polly Bemis, Ella Watson, and Little Wolf represented in the West. Their imaginations were not powerful enough to recognize a Chinese woman, an aspiring cattle queen, and a Northern Cheyenne leader as human beings and as fellow Americans. And if these men and women were not seen as Americans, they could not claim the rights of citizens, and they did not deserve to control the lands of the West.

CHAPTER 30

The 1890s were a tumultuous era in American history. There were now more than sixty million people living across the United States, so many that the Bureau of the Census had determined that there were no longer areas of the continent in the "frontier condition." This was the fact that so alarmed the historian Frederick Jackson Turner that he wrote his manifesto, "The Significance of the Frontier in American History," and presented it at the American Historical Association meeting in Chicago in the summer of 1893.

Even before Turner gave his paper, the idea that there were no longer any frontiers to conquer between the Atlantic and the Pacific had already spurred some Americans to look beyond the nation's borders for a way to demonstrate American greatness. In January 1893, U.S. troops disembarked on the docks in Honolulu, Kingdom of Hawai'i, to overthrow Queen Lili'uokalani. The combined force of sailors and marines invaded the city at the behest of a small group of American businessmen and missionaries who wanted to control the islands' sugar production. Although Hawai'ians actively resisted this coup d'etat, and some American politicians objected to it as an unlawful act of war, five years later, Congress voted to annex Hawai'i as an American territory.[1]

That same year (1898), the United States declared war on Spain, and the ensuing three-month conflict resulted in Spain's relinquishment of Cuba and transfer of sovereignty over the islands of Guam, Puerto Rico, and the Philippines to the United States. On the ground in Cuba, the politician and western historian Theodore Roosevelt (who had so admired Frederick Jackson Turner's frontier thesis) led a motley group of men in a volunteer militia.

"All—Easterners and Westerners, Northerners and Southerners, officers and men, cow-boys and college graduates, wherever they came from, and whatever their social position," Roosevelt wrote proudly, "possessed in common the traits of hardihood and a thirst for adventure. They were to a man born adventurers, in the old sense of the word."[2]

The Rough Riders, in other words, were the new pioneers. They faced hardships in their lives and survived, embraced risk and personal transformations, and were not averse to engaging in acts of violence. In their victorious actions in Cuba, Teddy Roosevelt saw the future of the United States and an answer to Turner's query regarding the closing of the continental frontier.[3]

"As the nation grows to have ever wider and wider interests," he declared in his "Strenuous Life" speech in 1899, "we must build up our power [outside] our own borders."[4]

Of course, the Spanish-American War was only the most recent war of conquest that the federal government had waged outside its borders. The Mexican-American War (1846–48), which brought so many American gamblers into María Gertrudis Barceló's sala, also brought more than half a million square miles of valuable land into the United States. And every nineteenth-century U.S. Army conflict with Indigenous peoples, like Little Wolf's Northern Cheyenne, was an imperial act of aggression.

As Teddy Roosevelt was charging up San Juan Hill in Cuba, the anthropologist George Bird Grinnell visited the Northern Cheyenne reservation with his wife, Elizabeth. He was there to write a history of the tribal nation, through conversations with leaders. Elizabeth was there to take photographs of Northern Cheyenne men and women. Little Wolf agreed to talk with Grinnell and provide material for the books he would publish, *The Fighting Cheyennes* (1915) and the two-volume *The Cheyenne Indians: Their History and Ways of Life* (1923).

Although the Northern Cheyenne had good reason to mistrust white men who came among them professing their allyship in the late nineteenth century, the almost eighty-year-old Little Wolf must have seen his relationship with Grinnell as another way to bolster his people's land claims and to prove to the federal government and its agents that the Northern Cheyenne people persisted. Grinnell soon lobbied President William McKinley on their behalf, arguing that the federal government should buy out the white cattlemen whose lands bordered or overlapped with the reservation. Grinnell was convincing. In 1900, McKinley signed an executive order that almost doubled the size of the reservation. In an era when most Indigenous peoples were losing land to the allotment programs codified in the Dawes Act, the Northern Cheyenne were one of the few tribal nations to expand their borders.[5]

Despite all he had done for his people during his lifetime, Little Wolf spent his final years at the periphery of Northern Cheyenne society. His community had not yet forgiven him for violating the tribal nation's most sacred law when he murdered Famished Elk in 1880. Some Northern Cheyenne blamed Little Wolf's actions for the bad luck and hard times that followed on the reservation. Little Wolf took on this burden, lived with the guilt, and did not complain.

"I loved that young man," Little Wolf told his fellow chief Wooden Leg. "I was crazy when I shot him."[6]

The former Sweet Medicine Chief continued to help his neighbors in need and offered advice when asked. He outlived many of his kin and his fellow warriors and chiefs.[7] It is unclear if he had been sick for some time or if his passing was sudden, but on October 30, 1904, Little Wolf died.

His wives and close friends took his body to a high hill overlooking the grasslands of the Rosebud Valley. The autumn colors were a vivid contrast of golden-brown prairie grasses studded with the dark green spikes of ponderosa pines and junipers. Soon the snows would come to the grasslands and the broken hills, but at that moment, the lands glowed in the midday sun.

Little Wolf's kin collected stones and tucked them around his body, along with his weapons, his pipe and tobacco, and other items he valued. They arranged him so that he could continue to gaze upon Northern Cheyenne lands, for as long as his spirit remained. Once it decided to leave, his spirit would journey along a winding road to a village. There, Little Wolf would join his friends and family who had gone before.

Little Wolf had lived for a long time and had experienced and participated in many eras of Northern Cheyenne history. He had led his people in battle, represented them in diplomatic talks with U.S. officials, and orchestrated the seven-hundred-mile-long journey that brought them back to their homelands. Little Wolf had reason to look upon the Rosebud Valley and all it represented to his people with pride.

When his family left his body on the hillside, it remained there for years. The rock mound that marked his grave site was one of many cairns that Northern Cheyenne men and women had built across the reservation, commemorating important events and village sites. Little Wolf's grave was a historical marker, connecting the former Sweet Medicine Chief to the many roads his people had traveled in his lifetime.[8]

The year that Little Wolf died, a fire destroyed most of the business district in the mining town of Warren, Idaho. Polly Bemis and her husband Charlie lost their hotel, saloon, and boardinghouse. Their twenty-nine-acre ranch on the southern bank of the Salmon River, with its cabin, barn, shed, root cellar, and four acres of planted gardens, became their permanent home for the rest of their lives. They went up into the hills to hunt for elk and deer, and Polly planted cherry, pear, and peach trees, worked in the garden, and fished for salmon, trout, and whitefish in the river. She also kept chickens for eggs and meat and had several dogs, cats, and horses.[9]

The Bemises soon met an Iowan miner named Charlie Shepp, who had made his way to the Salmon River country after the Klondike gold rush in Alaska. He lived north of the river on a small mining claim with a partner named Pete Klinkhammer. In 1910, the two men purchased land directly across the river from Bemis Ranch, and the four of them developed a close friendship. Shepp and Pete were younger than Charlie and Polly, and handy. They fixed tools, harvested potatoes, cut hay, and did other odd jobs around the ranch. In exchange, the Bemises gave them eggs and onions, and Polly baked them pies and fed them chicken dinners.[10]

For the next two decades, Polly and Charlie lived a rural life along the Salmon River, following the rhythms of the seasons. In the late spring, they planted cabbage, carrots, green beans, potatoes, and other vegetables. Polly tended to the garden every morning, digging up worms she would tuck into her apron pocket to use as fish bait later in the afternoon.[11] In June, they did not see Shepp and Pete much because the winter snowmelt turned the Salmon River into a raging torrent. They respected the river and did not try to battle its waves and current until the waters calmed in July.[12]

Every August was busy with visitors. The Bemis Ranch was isolated, but it sat at the center of multiple transportation corridors. Miners and their families riding mules and horses from Warren on their way to the Buffalo Hump Mining District to the north followed a trail to the Bemis Ranch. Charlie would ferry them over the water to Shepp and Pete's place, and they would continue to the mines. Sometimes these visitors bedded down in the Bemises' cabin or outside on the land between it and the riverbank. Polly warned them about rattlesnakes and suggested they lay hemp ropes around their campsite to keep the reptiles out.

Many visitors were strangers, but others were old friends from Warren. Jung Chew, an old friend of Polly's and the owner of Warren's only bathhouse, visited in the early 1920s, as did Ah Kan, the packer who had brought Polly from Lewiston to the mining town back in 1872.[13]

Another set of visitors came from the water, many of them the paying customers of the boat captain Henry Guleke, who had been taking freight and passengers down the Salmon since 1896. The Bemis Ranch sat on a curve in the river where the force of the water had carved out a wide beach full of gravel. It was a pleasant place to stop, and Polly often fed Guleke and his passengers, groups that sometimes included women and children.[14]

Increasingly, August was a time of danger as well. Forest fires became more common, and the air was often full of smoke and ash when Polly woke up to work in the garden. Shepp and Pete worked as volunteer firefighters and helped beat back a major conflagration in 1919 that threatened the Bemis Ranch.[15]

In the fall, Shepp and Pete helped Polly and Charlie harvest their vegetables and took them to Warren or to the Buffalo Hump mines to sell on their behalf. In preparation for winter, Polly made up a list of items she and Charlie needed to get them through the months they would be snowed into the ranch: cans of condensed milk, sugar, flour, and coffee. Shepp and Pete picked up these supplies in Warren or in Grangeville and delivered them to the ranch. Polly cooked festive Thanksgiving and Christmas dinners for all of them, butchering one of her chickens to roast and baking several pies.[16]

The bitter cold and deep snows usually kept them inside during the winter, but when the river froze over, the friends could walk across the ice and visit one another. Shepp obtained a phonograph, and they listened to records, or the men read aloud articles from the *Saturday Evening Post* and other magazines they subscribed to for entertainment. Polly made and mended clothes on her sewing machine and crocheted cuffs and collars for her dresses. She also crafted doilies for decoration, including one that depicted a white swan, a bird she once saw on the river. Charlie also taught her how to fashion melted gold into tiny shovels, picks, and mining pans, which she gave to visitors as gifts.[17]

Shepp bought telephones and strung up a line between the Bemis's ranch and his own, and acquired a radio, so he could listen to shows broadcast from as far away as Los Angeles and Denver.[18] He told Polly and Charlie about the latest news, and how the world "outside" was rapidly changing. By the second decade of the twentieth century, the nation's commercial and imperial desires extended all the way south to the country of Panama, where the United States built a canal to facilitate global shipping; one of President Theodore Roosevelt's pet projects, it opened in 1914, during the Woodrow Wilson administration. That year, a world war began to rage in Europe, and the United States joined the effort three years later, deploying troops to England and France to help defeat Germany.

Despite their frequent visitors, Polly and Charlie were able to avoid falling ill with the influenza strain that sparked a global pandemic in 1918, ultimately killing more than twenty million people worldwide. Charlie did become sick that year with another malady (probably heart failure), however, and was bedridden in their cabin for two years. Polly relied more and more on Shepp and Pete to bring her food and medicines for Charlie.

She may have heard from them about the ratification of the Nineteenth Amendment in 1920, which gave many American women the right to vote. This would not have transformed her life, as Polly was still not considered a citizen of the United States and so could not vote anyway. It was the era of the New Woman, however, a time when white American women went to college, joined Progressive reform movements, rode bicycles, and worked in white-collar jobs. In 1921, a New Woman landed right on Polly Bemis's doorstep.

An American newspaper heiress who had married a European count, Eleanor Gizycka was on a western adventure, riding the strong currents of the Salmon River from Salmon City to Lewiston, Idaho, on one of Harry Guleke's tours. When Guleke steered the watercraft onto the Bemis's rocky beach, Gizycka jumped out and helped push the boat ashore. Polly came to the water's edge to meet them, and the countess took in the sixty-seven-year-old woman, "neat as a pin, wrinkled as a walnut," with her iron-gray hair pulled back into a bun. Polly was "full of dash and charm," she wrote in her travel notes.[19]

Gizycka was surprised to meet Polly Bemis on the banks of the Salmon River. Chinese men and women were not included in the narratives of western history that Gizycka had grown up hearing and reading about. For most Americans, it was impossible to imagine that Polly Bemis or someone like her even existed in the West.[20]

The countess did not meet Charlie. Polly told her that he was too sick for visitors and had been for some time. "You'd better get another husband," she told Polly. The older woman laughed.

"Yes, I think so too," she replied.

The two women chatted while Polly's dog romped around them, and Polly told her visitor about her life before coming to Warren. How she had been taken from her home and sent to Hong Kong, sold for $2,500, and brought by ship and then pack train to the small mining town. Now she fed herself and Charlie by raising chickens, harvesting vegetables, fishing, and hunting.[21]

When Gizycka published her account of the Salmon River trip in the popular magazine *Field and Stream* in 1923, Polly Bemis became famous.[22] By that time, however, Polly was living back in Warren. In August 1922, a fire that started in their stovepipe had burned down the ranch house. Shepp had not been able to cross the river to help until the entire place was engulfed in flames.

"Had a hell of time," he wrote later that day in his diary. "Got the old man out by the skin of my teeth." Polly helped Shepp carry Charlie to his house, and the Bemises stayed with him for two months. They had saved almost nothing from their cabin, but Polly did manage to preserve two documents: her 1894 marriage certificate and her 1896 certificate of residence, which the government had forced her to complete.[23]

Smoke inhalation had made Charlie's condition worse, and he died on October 29, 1922. Polly, Shepp, and Pete buried him on a south-facing hillside above the river, with a view of the water and of Bemis Ranch.[24] Polly wanted to remain in their cabin, but it was uninhabitable, so she moved temporarily to Warren. Fewer than one hundred miners remained in the town or the surrounding hillsides, and most of them were white. Many of the town's Chinese residents had left by that time for other gold diggings, had been forced out of the country by restriction laws, or had died.

While Shepp and Pete rebuilt her house, Polly lived in a cabin on the outskirts of Warren. To make money, she planted another garden and sold the vegetables. She also took in boarders. They were the children of miners and business owners in the region who lived so far away from the school in Warren that they could not go home every day. While they lived with her, the children learned to cook and plant seeds, and they listened to Polly's stories about her life in China and the early days of Idaho mining. Polly also cooked for passersby, serving meals out of the front room at her cabin.[25]

In the summer of 1923, Shepp and Pete picked her up in Warren, and they went together to Grangeville so Polly could see an optometrist and have some eyeglasses made for her. It was the first time she had left Warren, or traveled the pack trail, since she and Charlie had gone there in 1896, to sign documents for her federal registration. After visiting the optometrist and picking out a pair of round glasses with metal frames, Polly toured Grangeville. She rode in an automobile down Main Street, went to the railroad station to see a train, and watched a movie in the small local theater. Polly had known about these technological innovations from Shepp's magazines and radio shows, but this was her first time experiencing them herself.[26] It was all a bit overwhelming. Journalists followed her around, fascinated by Polly's responses to these "modern marvels."

"The little, old, gray-haired woman, . . . sits with a handkerchief held tightly against her face and chuckles, and then bursts into a laughter of tears," a journalist for the *Idaho County News* reported, "as she attempts to describe what she has seen."[27]

Polly stayed with some of her neighbors' friends, wealthy mining entrepreneurs in Grangeville. Once the town residents heard about her arrival, they came in large groups to see her. Polly Bemis told her story again and again, to their delight. To them, it seemed a tale of unimaginable romance: the young girl sold into slavery who ultimately found love with a man in a mining town. There was no talk of Warren's large Chinese majority or the acts of terror perpetrated on them during Idaho's restriction and expulsion eras. Or the stress that Polly must have felt when she was trying to secure her papers to prove her long-term residency in the state.[28]

Instead of being lauded as a bona fide frontier woman, Polly Bemis became a singular curiosity, a woman who suddenly emerged from the isolated, rugged mountains, where she and Charlie had lived—according to the newspaper accounts—"apart from the world." The relative isolation of Warren and the Bemis Ranch had protected her from the worst of the era's anti-Chinese violence in the American West. It also meant that white Westerners literally failed to see her and all that she had accomplished. Her visitors found her pleasing because she presented what seemed to them an impossibility: a Chinese woman who embodied the characteristics of the white pioneer.

One year later, Polly traveled more than 150 miles south from Warren to Boise, this time to see a dentist. She was accompanied by one of the miners who had often stayed in her boardinghouse and his wife. "Mrs. Polly Bemis, Idaho county's modern Rip Van Winkle," a local paper reported, "has made another thrust into the outside world."[29] She rode a streetcar, saw skyscrapers for the first time, and watched several more movies. Polly enjoyed herself, but once again, her senses were overloaded.

"Lots of people, I like it," she told the Boise paper, "but it makes me tired to look so much."[30]

Polly did add one more stop to her itinerary. Along Idaho Street, Boise's Chinatown was still intact, although civic leaders had declared its wooden buildings fire hazards and published an order to tear them down. Chinese restaurants and businesses lined the sidewalk. The neighborhood's residents were almost all from Guangzhou, like Polly, and spoke Cantonese. She wanted to talk with them, especially the women. She had not seen another Chinese woman, she said, for more than twenty years.[31]

When Polly returned from Boise, she lived in Warren for a few more months until October 1924, when Shepp and Pete finished rebuilding her cabin. She moved back in, and a year later, in the fall, a faint roar became louder and louder until an airplane appeared in the sky above Bemis Ranch. It belonged to the U.S. Forest Service, which had a station nearby, and its pilot was scouting the area for forest fires.[32] There were other moments when the outside world intruded on the Salmon River Valley, but for the most part, Polly Bemis lived a quiet but busy life for the next eight years.

She continued to receive a stream of visitors who landed on her Salmon River beach, and Shepp and Pete helped her with ranch work. Then one day in early August of 1933, Shepp rowed over the river and found Polly collapsed outside the cabin. He made sure she was still breathing, then carried her inside.

Pete rowed back over to get Shepp, and they called for an ambulance. They rigged up a sled to take her along the trail to Warren and then to the hospital for the poor in Grangeville.

Her heart was failing, the doctor reported. There was no cure. Polly spent the last three months of her life in the hospital, chatting with her nurse and insisting on visiting all the pregnant women and their newborns. She had always loved babies, and just seeing them cheered her up. Her old friend Bertha Long came to visit her and brought her grandchildren to meet Polly. Her condition worsened, however, and she died in early November 1933.[33]

It had already started snowing in Warren and along the Salmon River, so it was impossible to transport Polly's body home to be buried alongside Charlie. And while Pete had been able to visit her once in the hospital, neither Shepp nor Pete could be at her funeral. Unlike the rest of her life, which was full of daily social interactions and conviviality, Polly Bemis's death was solitary. She was memorialized and buried in the local cemetery—outside town, with only a distant view of the mountains where she lived most of her eighty years—by strangers.[34]

Like Little Wolf, Polly Bemis had lived a long life in the American West. She arrived when there were fewer than sixteen thousand people living in Idaho Territory. By the time she died, the population had topped half a million. There were forty-eight stars on the American flag in 1933, many of them representing western states that had been territories when Polly arrived in San Francisco fifty years before. The country had one transcontinental railroad in 1872, but by the end of her life Polly could have driven in a car from coast to coast or made a quick long-distance telephone call between San Francisco and New York.

In 1872, the United States had been embroiled in an ongoing and long-lasting war to subjugate tribal nations and force men, women, and children onto reservations. In 1924, a federal law determined that Indigenous peoples were citizens of the United States, a status they had been denied since the eighteenth century. Tribal nations continued to struggle with the federal government, however, to determine the extent of their legal and political sovereignty on their own lands.

While the United States had advanced in some ways during Polly Bemis's lifetime, it had not progressed in other ways. The 1924 Immigration Act initiated a national origins quota to restrict European immigration; it excluded immigrants from Asia entirely. A series of laws enacted across the South in the late nineteenth century exploited loopholes in the Thirteenth Amendment to deny Black men the right to vote, and an 1896 Supreme Court decision found that racial segregation was legal, if the accommodations were equal. Women might have gained the vote in 1920, but they were still considered second-class citizens. Striking out on one's own like Gertrudis Barceló and Ella Watson had done became more difficult as the years passed by.

It was a harrowing time in the United States and in the West and the end of an era that had begun with exploration: the promise of movement, of interconnection, and of many possible futures. The dynamism and vitality of a region that was the crossroads of many nationalities and cultures in the early nineteenth century gave way to a bounded, restricted space of inequality in the first decades of the twentieth century. The simultaneous emergence and embrace of the frontier myth as a founding narrative of the United States was a catalyst for these transformations. It marginalized, erased, or revised the actions of people like Little Wolf and Polly Bemis and provided the justification for their removal from the body politic.

EPILOGUE

Because the creators of the frontier myth obscured the real lives of Westerners like Sacajawea, Jim Beckwourth, María Gertrudis Barceló, Ovando Hollister, Little Wolf, Ella Watson, and Polly Bemis during the nineteenth century, it became easier to recast them in American public memory in the years afterward.

One of the people who visited Polly Bemis at her ranch in the 1920s was a cougar hunter, who gave an interview to the *Lewiston Tribune* about her. The hunter invented a story that Charlie Bemis had won Polly in a poker game with a Chinese gambler who purchased her from the Hong Kong traders. This narrative had such romantic appeal that it became part of the popular memory of Polly Bemis for more than fifty years. Along the way, someone gave her the Chinese name "Lalu Nathoy." It is unclear where this additional fiction came from, or why.[1]

In 1981, after finding that the details of Polly's life were too difficult to pin down, Ruthanne Lum McCunn published a biographical novel about her, *Thousand Pieces of Gold*. The novel has sold more than 100,000 copies and its film version was released in 1990 and subsequently shown on PBS. Both fictional versions of her life included the poker bride story as central to their narrative arcs. White Americans bent Polly Bemis's life to fit a narrative that was compelling to them.[2]

"Many strange stories are told of Polly," the *Sacramento Union* reported after her death, "not all of them true, to be sure, for she has become more or less a tradition."[3]

The popular memories of Sacajawea, Gertrudis Barceló, and Ella Watson underwent similar alterations. In 1892, a naturalist named Elliott Coues found the manuscript journals of Lewis and Clark stored on a dusty shelf at the American Philosophical Society. He published an annotated edition of *The History of the Lewis and Clark Expedition* the next year and included details about Sacajawea and her contributions to the expedition in the text. A group of motivated and energetic women involved in Progressive-era social movements took note.[4] These women learned about Sacajawea's botanical collecting and diplomatic efforts and her labor as a translator. They lauded her vote on the location of the Corps of Discovery's winter camp on the Pacific coast in 1805 as the first exercise of the franchise by a woman in America.[5]

In white women's hands, Sacajawea became a mythic figure in her own right in the first decades of the twentieth century.[6] They absorbed her into the frontier myth, and she became a hypervisible symbol of a "vanishing Indian" who enabled Lewis and Clark and the frontier heroes who followed to conquer the West and eradicate its Indigenous peoples.

The first sculpture of Sacajawea appeared at the St. Louis Exposition in 1904, a fair organized to celebrate the one hundredth anniversary of the Louisiana Purchase and the Corps of Discovery. The artist Bruno Zimm sculpted her as a young girl, her long hair parted in the middle and twisted into two braids, wearing an ankle-length fringed dress. Carrying a baby on her back and a walking stick in her right hand, Sacajawea was frozen in mid-stride, looking up and out toward the future. Most artists who produced subsequent images of her represented her in this way.[7]

In the years that followed, Shoshone, Hidatsa, Mandan, and Arikara communities all claimed Sacajawea as an ancestor. In the 1920s, an account circulated in Wyoming, the Dakotas, and Montana that she had not in fact died at Fort Manuel in 1812. Instead, the story went, she left her husband (and presumably Lizette as well) in the 1820s and went to live with the Comanche peoples in northern Mexico and then the Eastern Shoshone at the Wind River Reservation. In this version of Sacajawea's history, she died among family members in Wyoming in

1884. Other narratives track her through the late nineteenth century, raising a family and continuing to live in Upper Missouri Valley Indigenous communities.[8]

As Sacajawea became more famous in the American popular imagination, it became even harder to imagine the realities of her experiences as an Indigenous woman in the early nineteenth century. Other western women, however, disappeared from the historical record even as they shaped regional and national events.[9]

María Gertrudis Barceló was one of the most famous people in the Southwest during the 1830s and '40s. Americans visiting Santa Fe set out to find her, because they had read so much about her in newspaper and magazine accounts of New Mexico Territory. Her gambling empire was part of a continent-wide and international network of currency trading and commerce along the Santa Fe and Chihuahua Trails. And her financial and social alliances with Stephen Kearny's Army of the West helped secure the U.S. military's hold on the northern reaches of Nuevo México in 1846.

A decade after her death, Santa Fe residents dedicated one monument to the Civil War soldiers who defeated both the Confederates and their "savage" enemies (the plaque they placed upon the obelisk's base used this term) and another to Kit Carson, the legendary frontiersman. There were no plaques to mark the location of Barceló's gambling sala or her many properties in town. When Barceló did appear in state or local histories, their authors redefined her as a "courtesan" as well as a card dealer. They mythologized her as the opposite of Sacajawea, a distinctly unmaternal woman who exploited rather than aided western explorers.

Ella Watson received the same treatment in American and western popular memory. After the first news reports of her murder misidentified her as another woman entirely, stories continued to circulate that she built her herd by trading cattle for sex. Even when some historians corrected the record, her real name and actual history as a Canadian immigrant, expert cook, and aspiring rancher were obscured. It was a final indignity, a way for white men to erase all that she had tried to achieve in defiance of their expectations.

The wagon wheels that initially marked Watson's grave site ultimately deteriorated in the harsh Wyoming weather. In 1989, Watson family descendants erected a new gravestone on land owned by a ranching family that continues to erase her actual identity. "Ella Watson," it reads, "Better Known as Cattle Kate."[10]

By the twentieth century, Jim Beckwourth, who like Gertrudis Barceló had been one of the most famous Westerners in America during his lifetime, was little known. Although a town in the Feather Valley and the pass that Beckwourth blazed in 1851 bear his name, the site was not marked as historic until 1937. A monument and plaque at the summit acknowledges Beckwourth and his "discovery" of the pass. But it does not mention his race and dedicates the site both to him and to the white pioneers who traveled over the pass:

> No desert's waste nor redskins bold,
> Could swerve them from this western strand—
> Naught could their courage e'er dismay
> In onward trudging day by day.[11]

While Beckwourth's autobiography in some ways bolstered the frontier myth by emphasizing his heroics in the mountains and Great Plains, Beckwourth's Blackness made him invisible to white historians, novelists, and, later, filmmakers. It did not help that most readers assumed that Beckwourth's autobiography was mostly a work of fiction. One writer thought the book was "as vivid a piece of lying as any of the blood-and-thunder novelists of today ever produced," and another declared that Jim Beckwourth was a "redoubtable prevaricator."[12]

It is unclear how many travelers stop at the historical marker at Beckwourth Pass (it is nestled into a hillside below the road) or wonder for whom the town and pass in northeastern California are named. If Americans remembered him at all, they recall Jim Beckwourth as a "gaudy liar," his achievements unbelievable and therefore unworthy of respect.

While most Americans and Northern Cheyenne acknowledged Little Wolf's actions to protect his people in the nineteenth century, his popular memory also faded, even on his people's reservation. When the federal government forced increasing numbers of Northern Cheyenne children to leave their families and attend boarding schools as part of a program of "civilization" in the late nineteenth and early twentieth century, these

Indigenous children did not learn their own history. Boarding school teachers and Christian missionaries believed that studying chiefs like Little Wolf, who asserted Native sovereignty, fought U.S. forces for years, and successfully negotiated their hold on their homelands, was dangerous. Their goal in the boarding schools was to "Kill the Indian, Save the Man"; acknowledging Little Wolf's history would have directly undermined this goal.[13]

The Sweet Medicine Chief had led his people in multiple battles against Indigenous and American enemies for more than thirty years—and had won many of these fights. He had defended Northern Cheyenne sovereignty in negotiations with Indian agents and the federal government and surrendered only when it became clear that this was necessary for the survival of his people. The seven-hundred-mile exodus that Little Wolf led from Indian Territory to the North Country was a remarkable act of resistance. It is this act that the Northern Cheyenne community has begun to remember and honor today.[14]

One would think that of all the men and women in this book, Ovando Hollister—a white man who traveled from east to west and made a name for himself as a western booster—would have become part of the frontier pantheon. But he too was largely forgotten, outside a small community of scholars interested in the New Mexico battles of the American Civil War.[15] His large house in Salt Lake City changed hands and was then torn down, and the Latter-day Saints—excellent collectors of their own ecclesiastical and community history—have not highlighted his relentless campaign against their dominance in Utah politics and economics in the 1870s and '80s.

Carrie Hollister outlived her husband by fifteen years and ultimately reburied him in the "pioneer" section of Riverside Cemetery in north Denver. The Hollisters lie together in a brick mausoleum tucked into a ridge above the High Line Canal, built to bring water from the Platte and Cherry Creek to white settlers and farmers. To most cemetery visitors, it is hidden from view.[16]

The American West did not appear out of thin air. In the early 1800s, the region began to take shape in the context of momentous social, economic, and political changes across the continent. During that time, the U.S. federal government acquired the lands between the Pacific Coast and the Great Plains through purchase, warfare, and settler colonialism (the replacement of Indigenous peoples with white settlers). The lure of money to be made in the West catalyzed a series of migrations to the region in the early nineteenth century. Before the Civil War, the West was chaotic and unstable, a landscape of transformation. Because of this, men and women from a variety of racial and ethnic communities were able to claim spaces for themselves there.

These women and men journeyed through the West in all directions. Indigenous peoples and other migrants were almost always on the move as they adapted to the region's social and environmental conditions. They built the West into the complex and diverse place that it remains today.

By the end of the nineteenth century, however, the frontier myth had erased, marginalized, or revised their lives. This myth had been taking shape since the Corps of Discovery's expedition. It was the creation of white politicians and boosters, writers, artists, and historians. In their policies and laws and their literary and visual images and books, these powerful Americans centered the frontier myth on the already popular ideologies of Manifest Destiny and the American Dream. They whitened the West, and this transformation resulted in the oppression of Indigenous peoples, women of all races and ethnicities, and migrant communities. In the years since, white Americans have used the frontier myth to justify racist policies of land dispossession, immigration restriction, and civil rights violations. They continue to use it to shore up white supremacy today.

The women and men whose stories are contained in this book—Sacajawea, Jim Beckwourth, María Gertrudis Barceló, Ovando Hollister, Little Wolf, Ella Watson, and Polly Bemis—put the lie to the central tenet of the frontier myth: that the victory of white men over women, people of color, and the natural environment explains American preeminence.

These women and men had singular lives, but their experiences were typical of many others who moved through the region. Their journeys

EPILOGUE

were not linear. They stopped and started again. They moved forward and sideways and backward. They acted in contradictory ways and were impelled by a range of emotions, from fear and anger to love and longing. These kinds of American stories are sometimes difficult to accept and hard to understand. Some are disturbing, and others are joyful.

We can and should recognize ourselves in the messy, complicated lives of the real people who built the West. They reveal a rich regional and national history that belongs to all Americans. If we do not acknowledge this expansive history of the West as a pivotal part of the nation's past, this erasure will continue the work of the frontier myth and usher us into an unjust future.

ACKNOWLEDGMENTS

I have so many people to thank!
   Thank you to:
Heather Schroder, for hearing in my one-sentence pitch an idea that could work as a book and for helping me figure out what that book would be.

Kathy Belden, who always pushes me to be a more incisive thinker and writer. And who has met me for many martinis and Manhattans to talk about everything under the sun.

Madison Than, who answered my panicked emails and shepherded the manuscript through the production process.

The excellent production team at Scribner and Simon & Schuster, particularly production editor Jason Chappell, along with Brigid Black, Annie Craig, Rafael Taveras, and Kyle Kabel. You all make the most beautiful books. And Andy Woodruff, who makes the most glorious maps.

My closest friends with whom I laugh and rage and think through ideas on the regular. Tita Chico, Jen Medearis Costello, and Nancy Serrano-Wu, you are the most supportive, wonderful BFFs.

Lindsay Chervinsky, bestie and fellow historian, who has read parts of this book more times than I can count and hosted me for an amazing writing boot camp in the mountains. Thank you for being a constant source of both wise advice and snarky observations.

The talented writers and historians in all my writing groups, who helped me refine my ideas and made me laugh besides. The members of Classified Writing Group have been especially excellent readers for years now: Lindsay Chervinsky, Rick Bell, Ben Park, and Bob Elder. My friends in Book Squad and Civil War Sisters, you gave me thoughtful feedback on very early, extremely messy chapters—thank you, and I'm sorry you had to go through that.

Gingy Scharff and Kate Carpenter, beta readers extraordinaire. Your comments and suggestions on the manuscript draft were invaluable. I hope you see your influence in these pages.

Shane Doyle, Kate Grandjean, and Joe Beilin Jr., for answering my random and very specific questions that always came out of the blue.

The historians who unearthed sources that illuminated the lives of Little Wolf, Polly Bemis, and Ella Watson, and whose articles and books were essential to me while I was writing *The Westerners*: Leo Killsback, Priscilla Wegers, George Hufsmith, Mary Jean Cook, and Janet Lecompte.

The archivists at the Western History Collection at the Denver Public Library, the Stephen H. Hart Research Center at History Colorado, and the Fray Angélico Chávez History Library at the New Mexico History Museum. In these dark times of decreased funding and fewer hours of operation, you were all shining lights. And Erin Luckett, for providing me with a crucial month of digital access to the Congressional Serial Set.

Sue Juster, who invited me to spend the 2024–25 academic year finishing and revising *The Westerners* as the Rogers Distinguished Fellow in Nineteenth-Century American History at the Huntington Library in San Marino, California. It was a wild ride, and a fun one. Thank you to my long-term fellow cohort, especially Damon Akins, Christine Garnier, Alison Hirsch, Devoney Looser, Tara Lyons, Laura Nelson, Dominique Palanco, Nydia Pineda de Avila, Scotti Parrish, Cori Tucker-Price, Patricia Yu, and Serena Zabin.

The readers of *The Three-Cornered War* and *Saving Yellowstone*, who have embraced my rather unusual approach to writing about the complex histories of the American West. Thank you for choosing to spend your time with my books.

My parents, John and Lynn Fritschel, who showed me very early in my life that histories are written in the landscape.

And finally, Dan. Moving to Southern California for nine months meant that I spent many weeks at a time away from my home base in Boston and from you. It was much harder than I thought it would be. You have always championed this book; thank you for coming along on this and other western adventures with me.

NOTES

Prologue

1. Billington, *Frederick Jackson Turner*, 126; Elliott, "The World's Columbian Exposition."
2. Senturia, "Colorado, Racism, and the 1893 Chicago World's Fair."
3. Dant, *Losing Eden*, 144–45. For a detailed study of Cody and his show, see Warren, *Buffalo Bill's America*.
4. Hamerow, "The Professionalization of Historical Learning," 319–33.
5. Report of the Director, *Annual Report of the Trustees of the Art Institute of Chicago*, 1893, 1–2; Report of the Trustees, June 8, 1893, in *Annual Report of the Trustees of the Art Institute of Chicago*, 1893, 8; *Chicago Tribune* (May 13, 1893): 6; "Today's Program," *Chicago Tribune* (July 12, 1893): 3.
6. *Chicago Tribune* (May 13, 1893): 6; Report of the Director, June 8, 1893, in *Annual Report of the Trustees of the Art Institute of Chicago*, 1893, 6.
7. "Plan of Main Floor, World's Congress Headquarters, Art Institute of Chicago"; *Catalogue of Paintings, Sculpture, and Other Objects*, March 15, 1894, 42, 51–54.
8. Billington, *Frederick Jackson Turner*, 128, 58, 22.
9. Turner, "The Significance of the Frontier," 27.
10. Billington, *Frederick Jackson Turner*, 65–66, 74, 106.
11. Turner, "The Significance of the Frontier," 29–32, 35, 41–42.
12. Turner, "The Significance of the Frontier," 28.
13. Turner, "The Significance of the Frontier," 58.
14. Theodore Roosevelt to Frederick Jackson Turner, February 10, 1894, as quoted in McVeigh, *The American Western*, 25; Grandin, *The End of the Myth*, 2, 3, 7.
15. Billington, *Frederick Jackson Turner*, 119.
16. Turner as quoted in Billington, *Frederick Jackson Turner*, 112.
17. U.S. historians began challenging Turner's manifesto en masse only in the 1980s and '90s, launching what is now known as the "New Western History" movement. The canonical works from this early period are Limerick, *Legacy of Conquest*; White, *The Middle Ground* and *It's Your Misfortune and None of My Own*; Cronon, *Nature's Metropolis* and "The

Trouble with Wilderness," 7–28; Worster, *Rivers of Empire* and *An Unsettled Country*. For a discussion of the philosophy and historiography of this shift in the field, see Limerick, Milner II, and Rankin, eds., *Trails: Toward a New Western History*. Subsequently, scholars have written thousands of articles and books illuminating the Indigenous, Latinx, Asian, and Black histories of the American West and focused many studies on the experiences of women of all races and ethnicities in the region. There are too many excellent works to note here, but you will find citations in the notes for the following chapters, and in the bibliography. Slotkin, *A Great Disorder*, 16.

18 Slotkin, *A Great Disorder*, 2, 4, 12; Dant, *Losing Eden*, 129.
19 Slotkin, *A Great Disorder*, 7, 13.
20 On the connections between national narrative erasure and the removal of marginalized groups from political communities, see Arendt, *The Origins of Totalitarianism*; Grandin, *The End of the Myth*, 12.
21 On the significance of mobility across the American West, see Scharff, *Twenty Thousand Roads*.
22 "The Dry West."
23 Scharff and Brucken, Introduction to *Home Lands*, 1.

Chapter 1

1 Hodge, *Ecology and Ethnogenesis*, 138–39, 144, 165, 174; Jager, *Malinche, Pocahontas, and Sacagawea*, 41.
2 Hodge, *Ecology and Ethnogenesis*, 73; West, *The Contested Plains*, 66–67.
3 Hodge, *Ecology and Ethnogenesis*, 162 167; Lowie, "The Northern Shoshone," 184–85, 188, 191–93, 217.
4 Smith, "Native Borderlands: Colonialism and the Development of Native Power," 180–81; Witgen, *An Infinity of Nations*.
5 Hodge, *Ecology and Ethnogenesis*, 152, 162; Lowie, "The Northern Shoshone," 184.
6 Scharff and Brucken, *Home Lands*, 52; Jager, *Malinche, Pocahontas, and Sacagawea*, 45; Hodge, *Ecology and Ethnogenesis*, 155–56.
7 Hodge, *Ecology and Ethnogenesis*, 164; Lowie, "The Northern Shoshone," 191, 212; Mann, *Sacagawea's People*, 18; Hodge, *Ecology and Ethnogenesis*, 152, 162.
8 Hodge, *Ecology and Ethnogenesis*, 18; Basso, *Wisdom Sits in Places*, 66–70; Momaday, "Values," in Hill, *Words of Power*, 1.
9 Mathews, "Ethnography and Philology of the Hidatsa Indians," 60–62; Fenn, *Encounters at the Heart of the World*, 215; Scharff, *Twenty Thousand Roads*, 15–16; Moulton, *The Lewis and Clark Expedition Day by Day*, 70; Nelson, *Interpreters with Lewis and Clark*, 9; Hodge, *Ecology and Ethnogenesis*, 165.
10 Reséndez, *The Other Slavery*; Brooks, *Captives and Cousins*; Fenn, *Encounters at the Heart of the World*, 156, 215.
11 Meriwether Lewis Journal, July 28, 1805, and Joseph Whitehouse Journal, July 30, 1805, *Journals of the Lewis and Clark Expedition*, University of Nebraska, Lincoln [hereafter UNL]; Fenn, *Encounters at the Heart of the World*, 216. For an account that rejects this narrative of Sacajawea's Northern Shoshone origins, see The Sacagawea Project Board of the Mandan, Hidatsa, & Arikara Nation, *Our Story of Eagle Woman, Sacagawea*.

12 Fenn, *Encounters at the Heart of the World*, 216; Jager, *Malinche, Pocahontas, and Sacagawea*, 41; Mathews, "Ethnography and Philology of the Hidatsa Indians," 54; Slaughter, *Exploring Lewis and Clark*, 102; Nelson, *Interpreters with Lewis and Clark*, 11; Scharff, *Twenty Thousand Roads*, 33.

13 David Thompson Journal, January 1, 2, 9, and 12, 1798, in Raymond and Thompson, "Thompson: the Original Journals," 332–33, 336; Moulton, *The Lewis and Clark Expedition Day by Day*, 70; Stewart, "Mandan and Hidatsa Villages," 296.

14 Metcalf, "Knife River," 36; Hanson, "Adjustment and Adaptation on the Northern Plains," 97; Ronda, *Lewis and Clark among the Indians*, 72, 99.

15 Metcalf, "Knife River," 34 36–38; Thompson Journal, January 1, 1798, 332; Mathews, "Ethnography and Philology of the Hidatsa Indians," 36; Fenn, *Encounters at the Heart of the World*, 24.

16 Ronda, *Lewis and Clark among the Indians*, 50, 67; Fenn, *Encounters at the Heart of the World*, 18, 19, 24; Nelson, *Interpreters with Lewis and Clark*, 14.

17 Metcalf, "Knife River," 34.

18 Fenn, *Encounters at the Heart of the World*, 57, 60–61, 229; Cross, "'Twice-born' from the Waters," 119; Metcalf, "Knife River," 34, 42.

19 Fenn, *Encounters at the Heart of the World*, 264.

20 Fred Last Bull, as quoted in Stands in Timber and Liberty, *Cheyenne Memories*, v; Leiker and Powers, *The Northern Cheyenne Exodus in History and Memory*, 27; West, *The Contested Plains*, 75.

21 Colby, *Sacagawea's Child*, 26–27; Fenn, *Encounters at the Heart of the World*, 238; Nelson, *Interpreters with Lewis and Clark*, 13; Jager, *Malinche, Pocahontas, and Sacagawea*, 82; Dolin, *Fur, Fortune, and Empire*.

22 Fenn, *Encounters at the Heart of the World*, 20, 195, 216–17, 238; Barr, *Peace Came in the Form of a Woman*, 5; Jager, *Malinche, Pocahontas, and Sacagawea*, 46, 82; Richter, *Facing East from Indian Country*, 109; Colby, *Sacagawea's Child*, 41.

23 Scharff, *Twenty Thousand Roads*, 14; Jager, *Malinche, Pocahontas, and Sacagawea*, 82; Hyde, *Born of Lakes and Plains*, xiv; West, *The Contested Plains*, 81.

24 "The Calumet Ceremony in the Mississippi Valley;" Fenn, *Encounters at the Heart of the World*, 37–39, 205.

25 Jager, *Malinche, Pocahontas, and Sacagawea*, 83.

26 Moulton, *The Lewis and Clark Expedition Day by Day*, 75; Jager, *Malinche, Pocahontas, and Sacagawea*, 83; Ronda, *Lewis and Clark among the Indians*, 47.

27 The northern lights are a phenomenon related to solar activity, which scientists have discovered peaks every eleven years or so. Hollabaugh, *The Spirit in the Sky*, 117–20.

28 Momaday, "The Voices of Encounter," 185.

Chapter 2

1 White, "The Louisiana Purchase and the Fictions of Empire," 38; Vidal, "From Incorporation to Exclusion," 62; Kastor, *The Nation's Crucible*, 37; Robinson, "The Louisiana Purchase and the Black Experience," 110; Appel, "The Louisiana Purchase and the Louis & Clark Expedition," 94; Lee, "Accounting for Conquest"; Grandin, *The End of the Myth*, 38–40.

2 Kastor, *The Nation's Crucible*, 36–37; Appel, "The Louisiana Purchase and the Louis & Clark Expedition," 90; Onuf, "Prologue: Jefferson, Louisiana, and American Nationhood," 29.

3   Thomas Jefferson, First Inaugural Address, March 4, 1801; Kovarsky, *The True Geography of Our Country*, 112; Slotkin, *A Great Disorder*, 27.
4   Thomas Jefferson, Secret Message to Congress, January 18, 1803.
5   Appel, "The Louisiana Purchase and the Louis & Clark Expedition," 95–96, 98; Reda, *From Furs to Farms*, 45; Kovarsky, *The True Geography of Our Country*, 120.
6   Reda, *From Furs to Farms*, 47, 49; Appel, "The Louisiana Purchase and the Louis & Clark Expedition," 98.
7   Ronda, *Lewis and Clark among the Indians*, 8–9, 26, 65; Jager, *Malinche, Pocahontas, and Sacagawea*, 79.
8   Fenelon and Defender-Wilson, "Voyage of Domination, 'Purchase' as Conquest, Sakakawea for Savagery," 92; Strang, *Frontiers of Science*.
9   Appel, "The Louisiana Purchase and the Louis & Clark Expedition," 87, 88; Taylor, "Jefferson's Pacific," 16; Kovarsky, *The True Geography of Our Country*, 121; Bellows, *The Explorers*, 19.
10 William Clark Journal, November 4, 1804, UNL. The identity of "one of Charbonneau's wives" has been debated in the years since, with some Indigenous groups believing that it was Otter Woman who was chosen to travel with Lewis and Clark. The fact that Lewis and Clark specifically name Sacajawea in their journals suggests otherwise, but as in so many early American accounts of Indigenous women, their vagueness regarding her identity has created opportunities for many communities to claim her.
11 Clark Journal, November 11, 1804, and John Ordway Journal, November 11, 1804, UNL; Nelson, *Interpreters with Lewis and Clark*, 8; Moulton, *The Lewis and Clark Expedition Day by Day*, 76.
12 Nelson, *Interpreters with Lewis and Clark*, 15; Moulton, *The Lewis and Clark Expedition Day by Day*, 79; Jager, *Malinche, Pocahontas, and Sacagawea*, 147.
13 Capehart, "Crow and Hidatsa Women: The Influence of Economics on Religious Status," 24–25; Fenn, *Encounters at the Heart of the World*, 216; White, "The Louisiana Purchase and the Fictions of Empire," 49; Contini, "Harmonizing the 'West,'" 321.
14 Moulton, *The Lewis and Clark Expedition Day by Day*, 83–89; Nelson, *Interpreters with Lewis and Clark*, 19.
15 Patrick Gass Journal, December 25, 1804, UNL; Nelson, *Interpreters with Lewis and Clark*, 20; Moulton, *The Lewis and Clark Expedition Day by Day*, 89.
16 Clark Journal, January 11 and 20, 1805, UNL; Nelson, *Interpreters with Lewis and Clark*, 21; Moulton, *The Lewis and Clark Expedition Day by Day*, 96, 98.
17 We do not know the specifics of Sacajawea's pregnancy, and every woman's experience is different. I have used the accounts in Knott, *Mother Is a Verb*, to make an informed speculation about her condition at this point. Knott, *Mother Is a Verb*, 63.
18 Wilson, "Notes on the Hidatsa Indians," 272–74; Knott, *Mother Is a Verb*, 68.
19 Earling, "What We See," in *Lewis and Clark Through Indian Eyes*, ed. Josephy, Jr., 36.
20 Clark Journal and Lewis Journal, February 11, 1805, UNL; Nelson, *Interpreters with Lewis and Clark*, 22; Jager, *Malinche, Pocahontas, and Sacagawea*, 83; Moulton, *The Lewis and Clark Expedition Day by Day*, 102; Colby, *Sacagawea's Child*, 19; Wilson, "Notes on the Hidatsa Indians," 275; Knott, *Mother Is a Verb*, 64.
21 Moulton, *The Lewis and Clark Expedition Day by Day*, 107–09, 110–12; Ronda, *Lewis and Clark among the Indians*, 110; Nelson, *Interpreters with Lewis and Clark*, 22.
22 Clark Journal, April 1 and 7, 1805, UNL.

NOTES

23 Moulton, *The Lewis and Clark Expedition Day by Day*, 118; Ronda, *Lewis and Clark among the Indians*, 123; "Fort Mandan Miscellany," UNL; Bellows, *The Explorers*, 26.
24 Nelson, *Interpreters with Lewis and Clark*, 24; Jager, *Malinche, Pocahontas, and Sacagawea*, 85; Fenn, *Encounters at the Heart of the World*, 216; Colby, *Sacagawea's Child*, 49.
25 Lewis Journal, April 7, 1805, as quoted in Moulton, *The Lewis and Clark Expedition Day by Day*, 121.
26 Moulton, *The Lewis and Clark Expedition Day by Day*, 119; Ronda, *Lewis and Clark among the Indians*, xiv.

Chapter 3

1 Meriwether Lewis to Thomas Jefferson, April 7, 1805, as reprinted in the *Alexandria (VA) Gazette* (July 19, 1805): 3.
2 Lewis Journal, June 29, 1805, UNL; Pillow, "Mapping Sex, Race, and Gender in the Corps of Discovery Expedition," 212; Ronda, *Lewis and Clark among the Indians*, 15.
3 "Africans in French America"; Robinson, "The Louisiana Purchase and the Black Experience," 111; Appel, "The Louisiana Purchase and the Lewis & Clark Expedition," 103, 108; Ostler, "Locating Settler Colonialism in Early American History," 444; Le Glaunec, "Slave Migrations and Slave Control," 209, 212; Hammond, "Slavery, Settlement, and Empire," 180, 189; Hammond, "'They Are Very Much Interested in Obtaining an Unlimited Slavery,'" 357.
4 Hammond, "Slavery, Settlement, and Empire," 189; Hammond, "'They Are Very Much Interested in Obtaining an Unlimited Slavery,'" 354–55.
5 Hammond, "Slavery, Settlement, and Empire," 205.
6 Wilson, *Jim Beckwourth*, 12–13; Muddiman, "Agriculture in the Fredericksburg Area," 3–4.
7 Wilson, *Jim Beckwourth*, 14.
8 Burke, *On Slavery's Border*, 26, 27, 32, 49; *Ecoregions of Iowa and Missouri*; "American Land Prices and Policy."
9 Beckwourth and Bonner, *The Life and Adventures of James P. Beckwourth*, 14.
10 Burke, *On Slavery's Border*, 5, 19, 26; Katz, *The Black West*, 39; "Migration and Population Movement."
11 Burke, *On Slavery's Border*, 38.
12 Beckwourth and Bonner, *The Life and Adventures of James P. Beckwourth*, 14; Johnson, *The Broken Heart of America*, 47; Burke, *On Slavery's Border*, 49; Hammond, "Slavery, Settlement, and Empire," 178–79.
13 Thomas Jefferson, Second Inaugural Address, March 4, 1805.
14 Lee, *Masters of the Middle Waters*, 196–97; Saunt, *Unworthy Republic*, 6–7.
15 Jefferson, *Notes on the State of Virginia*; Thomas Jefferson, Second Inaugural Address, March 4, 1805.
16 Black Hawk as quoted in Jung, "Toward the Black Hawk War," 29.
17 Jung, "Toward the Black Hawk War," 30, 46; Beckwourth and Bonner, *The Life and Adventures of James P. Beckwourth*, 18.
18 Jung, "Toward the Black Hawk War," 30–31, 36.
19 Beckwourth and Bonner, *The Life and Adventures of James P. Beckwourth*, 15.
20 Beckwourth and Bonner, *The Life and Adventures of James P. Beckwourth*, 15–16.

21 Beckwourth and Bonner, *The Life and Adventures of James P. Beckwourth*, 16.
22 Beckwourth and Bonner, *The Life and Adventures of James P. Beckwourth*, 16.
23 Beckwourth and Bonner, *The Life and Adventures of James P. Beckwourth*, 17.
24 Beckwourth and Bonner, *The Life and Adventures of James P. Beckwourth*, 14; *Ecoregions of Iowa and Missouri*; Swagerty, "A View from the Bottom Up," 21.
25 Schoenberger, "The Black Man in the American West," 9; Thrapp, *Encyclopedia of Frontier Biography*, 1240; on men like Rose who lived at the nexus of North American slavery, settler colonialism, and Black freedom, see Roberts, *I've Been Here All the While*.
26 Hyde, *Empires, Nations, and Families*, 20, 49–50.
27 Act XII, Laws of Virginia, December 1662. Louisiana's Code Noir (Article 13), also enacted in the seventeenth century, includes similar language.

Chapter 4

1 Kopperman, "'Venerate the Lancet,'" 539.
2 Whitehouse Journal, June 12, 1805, UNL. Clark, Lewis, Whitehouse, and Ordway all wrote about Sacajawea's illness and the captains' treatments between June 10 and June 20, 1805. Clark's bloodletting method is unknown, but he likely used the knife and cup in the field (rather than leeches).
3 Clark Journal, May 8, 1805, Whitehouse Journal, June 19, 1805, and Lewis Journal, June 20, 1805, UNL; Moulton, *The Lewis and Clark Expedition Day by Day*, 142–43, 184–86.
4 The Lewis and Clark journals note many instances in which Sacajawea walked instead of sitting in the white pirogue. Clark, April 9, 18, 30 and May 4, 1805, UNL; Jager, *Malinche, Pocahontas, and Sacagawea*, 116; Moulton, *The Lewis and Clark Expedition Day by Day*, 124, 130, 136; "Montana Plant Life."
5 Jefferson's Instructions to Meriwether Lewis, June 20, 1803.
6 "American Philosophical Society: History."
7 Wulf, "Thomas Jefferson's Quest to Prove America's Natural Superiority"; Taylor, "Jefferson's Pacific," 17, 19, 39; Moulton, *The Lewis and Clark Expedition Day by Day*, 118.
8 Sheehan, "Jefferson's 'Empire for Liberty,'" 360.
9 Strang, *Frontiers of Science*, 5; Miles, *Wild Girls*, 7.
10 Lewis Journal, July 19, 1805, UNL; Moulton, *The Lewis and Clark Expedition Day by Day*, 215.
11 Clark Journal, July 19, 1805, UNL; Moulton, *The Lewis and Clark Expedition Day by Day*, 215.
12 Lewis and Whitehouse Journals, July 21, 1805, UNL; Ronda, *Lewis and Clark among the Indians*, 136.
13 Lewis Journal, July 24, 1805, UNL; Moulton, *The Lewis and Clark Expedition Day by Day*, 219.
14 Moulton, *The Lewis and Clark Expedition Day by Day*, 219–20.
15 Lewis Journal, July 27, 1805, UNL; Moulton, *The Lewis and Clark Expedition Day by Day*, 223.
16 Lewis Journal, July 28, 1805, UNL.
17 Lewis Journal, July 28, 1805, Ordway, Whitehouse Journals, July 27, 1805, Lewis, Clark, Whitehouse Journals, July 30, 1805, UNL.

NOTES

18 Williams, *They Left Great Marks on Me*, 5–7.
19 Lewis Journal, August 15, 1805, UNL; Nelson, *Interpreters with Lewis and Clark*, 38; Moulton, *The Lewis and Clark Expedition Day by Day*, 249–54.
20 Ordway, Whitehouse Journals, August 16, 1805, UNL; Moulton, *The Lewis and Clark Expedition Day by Day*, 254, 257. On the serviceberry and its role in Indigenous cultures across the nation, see Kimmerer, *The Serviceberry*.
21 Whitehouse Journal, August 17, 1805, UNL.
22 Whitehouse Journal, August 17, 1805, UNL.
23 Lewis Journal, August 17, 1805, UNL; Fenn, *Encounters at the Heart of the World*, 216; Scharff, *Twenty Thousand Roads*, 18.
24 Scharff, *Twenty Thousand Roads*, 18, 12–13.
25 It was Lewis who described Cameahwait as having "lank jaws" due to hunger, an indication of a food crisis among the Northern Shoshone in this period: Lewis Journal, August 14, 1805, UNL; Moulton, *The Lewis and Clark Expedition Day by Day*, 252; August 17, 1805, UNL.
26 Jefferson to Harrison, 1803, as quoted in Keller, "Philanthropy Betrayed," 39.
27 Lewis Journal, August 17, 1805, UNL. I have changed the wording slightly from the original, for the purposes of narration.
28 Moulton, *The Lewis and Clark Expedition Day by Day*, 259.
29 Lewis Journal, August 19, 1805, UNL.
30 Clark and Lewis Journals, August 14, 1805, UNL.
31 Hyde, *Born of Lakes and Plains*, xix.
32 Moulton, *The Lewis and Clark Expedition Day by Day*, 279–80, 286; Ronda, *Lewis and Clark among the Indians*, 154.
33 Gass Journal, September 16, 1805, UNL.
34 Lewis and Clark Journals, September 26–October 16, 1805, UNL; Moulton, *The Lewis and Clark Expedition Day by Day*, 308–15.
35 Barr, *Peace Came in the Form of a Woman*, 1, 2, 13.
36 Clark Journal, October 13 and 19, 1805, UNL.
37 Clark Journal, October 16, 1805, UNL; Moulton, *The Lewis and Clark Expedition Day by Day*, 320.
38 Ronda, *Lewis and Clark among the Indians*, 163.
39 Lewis and Clark Journals, October 24–November 5, 1805; Moulton, *The Lewis and Clark Expedition Day by Day*, 328–39; Basch and Basch, "The Ceremony at Ne-Ah-Coxie," in *Lewis and Clark Through Indian Eyes*, ed. Josephy, Jr., 168.
40 Clark Journal, November 20 and 21, 1805 and Ordway, Gass, and Whitehouse Journals, November 21, 1805, UNL; Moulton, *The Lewis and Clark Expedition Day by Day*, 352–54.
41 November 24, 1805, in Moulton, *The Lewis and Clark Expedition Day by Day*, 355–56; Nelson, *Interpreters with Lewis and Clark*, 49; Ronda, *Lewis and Clark among the Indians*, 178.
42 Lewis and Clark Journals, November 24, 1805, UNL; Ronda, *Lewis and Clark among the Indians*, 178; Moulton, *The Lewis and Clark Expedition Day by Day*, 355–56.
43 Lewis Journal and Clark Journal, January 6, 1806, UNL; Ronda, *Lewis and Clark among the Indians*, 177, 186; Moulton, *The Lewis and Clark Expedition Day by Day*, 376; November 18, 1805, Moulton, *The Lewis and Clark Expedition Day by Day*, 350; Nelson, *Interpreters with Lewis and Clark*, 47.

44 Lewis and Clark Journals, January 12, 1806, in Moulton, *The Lewis and Clark Expedition Day by Day*, 383; Ronda, *Lewis and Clark among the Indians*, 189–90, 212; Nelson, *Interpreters with Lewis and Clark*, 54.
45 Lewis and Clark Journals, June 25, 1806, UNL; Moulton, *The Lewis and Clark Expedition Day by Day*, 525–26.
46 Clark Journal, July 14, 1806, UNL. I have changed the wording slightly from the original, for the purposes of narration.
47 Clark Journal, July 14, 1806, UNL; Moulton, *The Lewis and Clark Expedition Day by Day*, 583–84.
48 Clark Journal, July 13, 1806, UNL; Moulton, *The Lewis and Clark Expedition Day by Day*, 582; Nelson, *Interpreters with Lewis and Clark*, 60; Jager, *Malinche, Pocahontas, and Sacagawea*, 117.
49 Clark Journals, July 15–August 14, 1806, UNL; Moulton, *The Lewis and Clark Expedition Day by Day*, 583–610.
50 Fenn, *Encounters at the Heart of the World*, 247.
51 Clark Journal, August 17, 1806, UNL; Moulton, *The Lewis and Clark Expedition Day by Day*, 613.
52 Clark to Charbonneau, August 20, 1806, in Jackson, ed., *Letters*, vol. 1, 315, in Ronda, *Lewis and Clark among the Indians*, Appendix.
53 Conner, "Our People Have Always Been Here," in *Lewis and Clark Through Indian Eyes*, ed. Josephy, Jr., 92.
54 Bellows, *The Explorers*, 38.

Chapter 5

1 Thomas Jefferson to Meriwether Lewis, October 26, 1806, in Jackson, *Letters of Lewis and Clark*, 350–51; Chew, "Jefferson's Indian Hall: Expedition Souvenirs and Specimens"; Foley and Rice, "The Return of the Mandan Chief," 4–5; Fenn, *Encounters at the Heart of the World*, 250.
2 Thomas Jefferson to the Wolf [Sheheke] and the People of the Mandan Nation, December 30, 1806.
3 Thomas Jefferson to the Wolf [Sheheke] and the People of the Mandan Nation, December 30, 1806.
4 Reda, *From Furs to Farms*, 68, 73, 78; Hickey, *The War of 1812*, 20; Lee, *Masters of the Middle Waters*, 210; Fenn, *Encounters at the Heart of the World*, 254, 258, 260; Nelson, *Interpreters with Lewis and Clark*, 68–69; Colby, *Sacagawea's Child*, 71.
5 Luciano, *How the Earth Feels*, 62–64; Keller, "Philanthropy Betrayed," 55; Jung, "Toward the Black Hawk War," 32.
6 Godfrey, "Contact with Northern Plains Indian Villages and Communities."
7 Morris, *The Fate of the Corps*, 107; Fenn, *Encounters at the Heart of the World*, 262.
8 Primm, *Lion of the Valley*, 13–14, 16; Reda, *From Furs to Farms*, 66.
9 Lee, *Masters of the Middle Waters*, 217, 223; Primm, *Lion of the Valley*, 82.
10 Washington Irving (1810), as quoted in Primm, *Lion of the Valley*, 85; Lee, *Masters of the Middle Waters*, 223.
11 Johnson, *The Broken Heart of America*, 38.
12 Johnson, *The Broken Heart of America*, 13–16.

NOTES

13 Buckley, *William Clark*, 68–69, 86.
14 Tucker, "Meriwether Lewis's Mysterious Death."
15 Nelson, *Interpreters with Lewis and Clark*, 69; Reda, *From Furs to Farms*, 73.
16 Colby, *Sacagawea's Child*, 73; Nelson, *Interpreters with Lewis and Clark*, 69; "Introduction," UNL; Johnson, *The Broken Heart of America*, 27; Hyde, *Empires, Nations, and Families*, 30–56.
17 Hyde, *Empires, Nations, and Families*, 1, 30, 45.
18 Colby, *Sacagawea's Child*, 73; Morris, *The Fate of the Corps*, 107; Nelson, *Interpreters with Lewis and Clark*, 69.
19 Morris, *The Fate of the Corps*, 106; Nelson, *Interpreters with Lewis and Clark*, 71; Scharff, *Twenty Thousand Roads*, 22.
20 Lee, *Masters of the Middle Waters*, 158–60; Eustace and Tuete, eds., *Warring for America*, 21; Colby, *Sacagawea's Child*, 67.
21 Morris, *The Fate of the Corps*, 111.
22 Harrison letter (1811), as quoted in Hickey, *The War of 1812*, 23.
23 Jung, "Toward the Black Hawk War," 37; Hickey, *The War of 1812*, 23–24; Keller, "Philanthropy Betrayed," 55.
24 "Strange Happenings during the Earthquake"; Luciano, *How the Earth Feels*, 58, 60; Valencius, *The Lost History of the New Madrid Earthquakes*.
25 Luciano, *How the Earth Feels*, 57–60.
26 Morris, *The Fate of the Corps*, 113; Luttig Diary, August 9 and October 9, 1812.
27 Morris, *The Fate of the Corps*, 114; Reda, *From Furs to Farms*, 74; Luttig Diary, October–November 1812; Nelson, *Interpreters with Lewis and Clark*, 73.
28 Luttig Diary, December 20, 1812. Some Hidatsa, Arikara, and Mandan historians reject this narrative of Sacajawea's death. See The Sacagawea Project Board of the Mandan, Hidatsa, & Arikara Nation, *Our Story of Eagle Woman, Sacagawea*.
29 Morris, *The Fate of the Corps*, 117; Colby, *Sacagawea's Child*, 88, 90; Jager, *Malinche, Pocahontas, and Sacagawea*, 152.
30 *History of the Expedition under the Command of Captains Lewis and Clark*, ed. Allen and Biddle; Thwaites, "The Story of Lewis and Clark's Journals," 37.
31 Clark Journal, June 22, 1805, UNL.
32 Jager, *Malinche, Pocahontas, and Sacagawea*, 253.

Chapter 6

1 Scharff, *Twenty Thousand Roads*, 25; Jager, *Malinche, Pocahontas, and Sacagawea*, 260–63; Slaughter, *Exploring Lewis and Clark*, 92–94, 99, 110; The Sacagawea Project Board of the Mandan, Hidatsa, & Arikara Nation, *Our Story of Eagle Woman, Sacagawea*.
2 Guedea, "The Process of Mexican Independence," 119; James, *Pages from Hopi History*, 71; Gonzales, *Mexicanos*, 3rd ed., 66, 67; Schaefer, "Soldiers and Civilians," 149, 150–51.
3 Sweeney, *Mangas Coloradas*; Hämäläinen, *The Comanche Empire*; DeLay, *War of a Thousand Deserts*; Brooks, *Captives and Cousins*.
4 Bay et al., "Towards a New Interpretation of the Colonial Regime in Sonora, 1681–1821," 396.
5 Cook, *Doña Tules*, 1, 3; "Biographical Sketch," in Nentvig, *Rudo Ensayo*, xx–xxi.
6 Cook, *Doña Tules*, 5–6, 7; Belohlavek, *Patriots, Prostitutes, and Spies*, 88; Toliefson, "The Real Gertrudis Barceló;" González, *Refusing the Favor*, 54.

7 Belohlavek, *Patriots, Prostitutes, and Spies*, 88; Akins et al., "Valencia: A Spanish Colonial and Mexican-Period Site."
8 Sayer, "Traditional Mexican Dress"; Kendall, *Narrative of the Texan Santa-Fe Expedition*, 233–35.
9 Simmons, "Spanish Attempts to Open a New Mexico-Sonora Road," 13.
10 Phillips and Comus, *A Natural History of the Sonoran Desert*, 1st ed.
11 Sweeney, *Mangas Coloradas*, 11, 13.
12 Sweeney, *Mangas Coloradas*, 18, 26, 32, 89.
13 El Paso Historical Society, "El Paso & the Region"; Feit, "A River Used to Run Through It."
14 *El Camino Real de Tierra Adentro*, ed. Palmer, Piper, and Jacobsen, xiii.
15 Simmons, *Albuquerque: A Narrative History*, 96.
16 Gonzales, *Mexicanos*, 3rd ed., 76; Conrad, *The Apache Diaspora*, 51–52.
17 Gonzales, *Mexicanos*, 3rd ed., 54; González, *Refusing the Favor*, 6, 10–11.
18 Guedea, "The Process of Mexican Independence," 128–29.
19 Baur, "The Evolution of a Mexican Foreign Trade Policy, 1821–1828," 225, 232; Reséndez, "National Identity on a Shifting Border," 678–79; Gonzales, *Mexicanos*, 3rd ed., 79–80.
20 Reséndez, "National Identity on a Shifting Border," 678; Cook, *Doña Tules*, 11; González, *Refusing the Favor*, 32; Lecompte, "The Independent Women of Hispanic New Mexico, 1821–1846," 17; Gonzales, *Mexicanos*, 3rd ed., 66, 69, 75, 80; Tyler, "Anglo-American Penetration of the Southwest," 327–28; Weber, *The Mexican Frontier*, 143.
21 Barcelo Church Records, compiled by Chavez, 2016; Pérez, *Colonial Intimacies*.
22 Sherman and Sherman, *Ghost Towns and Mining Camps of New Mexico*, 70–71; "Dolores," in *Lost Treasures and Old Mines*, ed. Lacy and Valley-Fox, 209; Raymond, *Mines and Mining of the Rocky Mountains, the Inland Basin, and the Pacific Slope*, 405; Brevoort, *New Mexico, Her Natural Resources and Attractions*, 80.
23 Truett, *Fugitive Landscapes*, 17; Mountford and Tuffnell, *A Global History of Gold Rushes*, 3.
24 Cook, *Doña Tules*, 25; Lecompte, "La Tules and the Americans," 220–21.
25 Cook, *Doña Tules*, 12–13, 17; Gregg, *Commerce of the Prairies*, vol. 2, pp. 33–34.
26 I have used multiple contemporary accounts, including Matt Field's articles on Gertrudis Barceló and her sala, to create this scene.
27 Sherman and Sherman, *Ghost Towns and Mining Camps of New Mexico*, 70–71; Brevoort, *New Mexico, Her Natural Resources and Attractions*, 80; Weber, *The Mexican Frontier*, 143.
28 González, *Refusing the Favor*, 25, 31–32, 37; Lecompte, "The Independent Women of Hispanic New Mexico, 1821–1846," 17; Gonzales, *Mexicanos*, 3rd ed., 69, 75, 80; Belohlavek, *Patriots, Prostitutes, and Spies*, 69–70; Tyler, "Anglo-American Penetration of the Southwest," 327–28.

Chapter 7

1 Johnson, *The Broken Heart of America*, 34–35, 84.
2 Hyde, *Empires, Nations, and Families*, 239, 254–62, 479–82.
3 Moore, *Sweet Freedom's Plains*, 54, 58, 59, 60, 68, 69–71, 72–73, 74; Johnson, *The Broken Heart of America*, 80, 83, 104.

NOTES

4 Beckwourth and Bonner, *The Life and Adventures of James P. Beckwourth*, 20.
5 U.S. Department of Labor, "Building Trades," 12; "Farmers," in *Historical Statistics of the United States: Colonial Times to 1970*, 163.
6 Beckwourth and Bonner, *The Life and Adventures of James P. Beckwourth*, 20–22.
7 Hyde, *Born of Lakes and Plains*, 1–2, 19.
8 Johnson, *The Broken Heart of America*, 30; Nunis, Jr., "The Fur Men: Key to Westward Expansion," 167; White and Gowans, "Traders to Trappers I," 59; White and Gowans, "Traders to Trappers II," 56–57; Nichols, "The Arikara Indians and the Missouri River Trade," 86; Clayton, "The Growth and Significance of the American Fur Trade," 210–11; Schilz, "Robes, Rum, and Rifles," 4–6.
9 Johnson, *The Broken Heart of America*, 30; Beckwourth and Bonner, *The Life and Adventures of James P. Beckwourth*, 62; White and Gowans, "Traders to Trappers II," 55.
10 Beckwourth and Bonner, *The Life and Adventures of James P. Beckwourth*, 23; Oswald, Introduction, Notes, and Epilogue to *The Life and Adventures of James P. Beckwourth*, 543; White and Gowans, "Traders to Trappers II," 60.
11 "Lewis and Clark: The Maps of Exploration"; Buckley, "Jeffersonian Explorers in the Trans-Mississippi West," 123.
12 Beckwourth and Bonner, *The Life and Adventures of James P. Beckwourth*, 28–31.
13 Beckwourth and Bonner, *The Life and Adventures of James P. Beckwourth*, 32–33, 89–90; Oswald, Introduction, Notes, and Epilogue to *The Life and Adventures of James P. Beckwourth*, 541.
14 Assmann, "How the Mountain Men Trapped Beaver"; Hewit Institute, "Beaver Ecology."
15 Beckwourth and Bonner, *The Life and Adventures of James P. Beckwourth*, 62–69, 73–75.
16 Beckwourth and Bonner, *The Life and Adventures of James P. Beckwourth*, 81–84; Johnson, *The Broken Heart of America*, 41, 53, 65, 67; Saunt, *Unworthy Republic*, xvii.
17 Beckwourth and Bonner, *The Life and Adventures of James P. Beckwourth*, 86.
18 Beckwourth and Bonner, *The Life and Adventures of James P. Beckwourth*, 87–88.
19 Beckwourth and Bonner, *The Life and Adventures of James P. Beckwourth*, 90–92.
20 Beckwourth and Bonner, *The Life and Adventures of James P. Beckwourth*, 93.
21 Hyde, *Born of Lakes and Plains*, 8.
22 Beckwourth and Bonner, *The Life and Adventures of James P. Beckwourth*, 114; Hall, "Before the Medicine Line," 384; Noel and Smith, *Colorado: The Highest State*, 56. On the diplomatic and economic strategy of multiracial marriage in the early American West, see Hyde, *Empires, Nations, and Families*.
23 Beckwourth and Bonner, *The Life and Adventures of James P. Beckwourth*, 126.
24 Beckwourth and Bonner, *The Life and Adventures of James P. Beckwourth*, 139–40.
25 Beckwourth and Bonner, *The Life and Adventures of James P. Beckwourth*, 145.
26 Beckwourth and Bonner, *The Life and Adventures of James P. Beckwourth*, 146, 147.
27 Beckwourth and Bonner, *The Life and Adventures of James P. Beckwourth*, 148–49, 150 [quote].
28 Hoxie, *Parading Through History*, 12, 36.
29 Sore Belly as quoted in Medicine Crow, *From the Heart of Crow Country*, front matter.
30 Linderman, *Pretty-Shield*, 9 [quote]; Medicine Crow, *From the Heart of Crow Country*, 7.
31 Medicine Crow, *From the Heart of Crow Country*, 101; Hoxie, *Parading Through History*, 42; *Pretty-Shield*, 4–5.

32 Medicine Crow, *From the Heart of Crow Country*, 2.
33 Hoxie, *Parading Through History*, 53.
34 Medicine Crow, *From the Heart of Crow Country*, 25; Beckwourth and Bonner, *The Life and Adventures of James P. Beckwourth*, 112 [quote]; Hoxie, *Parading Through History*, 48.
35 Beckwourth and Bonner, *The Life and Adventures of James P. Beckwourth*, 165.
36 Beckwourth and Bonner, *The Life and Adventures of James P. Beckwourth*, 161, 177, 183, 201, 240, 269.
37 Beckwourth and Bonner, *The Life and Adventures of James P. Beckwourth*, 232.
38 Beckwourth and Bonner, *The Life and Adventures of James P. Beckwourth*, 167.
39 Beckwourth and Bonner, *The Life and Adventures of James P. Beckwourth*, 170; "Fort Clark Historic Site."
40 Beckwourth and Bonner, *The Life and Adventures of James P. Beckwourth*, 177–78.
41 Beckwourth and Bonner, *The Life and Adventures of James P. Beckwourth*, 212–13.
42 Fierst, "Rationalizing Removal," 2, 4, 8, 32.
43 "An Act to Provide for the Exchange of Lands with the Indians" [The Indian Removal Act], May 28, 1830; Saunt, *Unworthy Republic*, 82; Ostler, *Surviving Genocide*, 247.
44 Andrew Jackson, First Annual Message to Congress, December 8, 1829; Saunt, *Unworthy Republic*, xvii.
45 Saunt, *Unworthy Republic*, 143, 145, 45 [quote].
46 Beckwourth and Bonner, *The Life and Adventures of James P. Beckwourth*, 213.
47 Beckwourth and Bonner, *The Life and Adventures of James P. Beckwourth*, 216, 298, 301, 336–37.
48 Beckwourth and Bonner, *The Life and Adventures of James P. Beckwourth*, 370–71.
49 Ostler, *Surviving Genocide*, figure 32, "Creek Removal," 259.
50 Beckwourth and Bonner, *The Life and Adventures of James P. Beckwourth*, 376–77; Hoxie, *Parading Through History*, 77, 86; Saunt, *Unworthy Republic*, 108.

Chapter 8

1 Cook, *Doña Tules*, 18, 19; Lecompte, "La Tules and the Americans," 221.
2 Gregg, *Commerce of the Prairies*, 137; Belohlavek, *Patriots, Prostitutes, and Spies*, 69–70.
3 Gregg, *Commerce of the Prairies*, 103.
4 Lecompte, "La Tules and the Americans," 221–22; González, *Refusing the Favor*, 56.
5 Lecompte, "La Tules and the Americans," 222.
6 *Barceló vs. Tenorio*, June 17, 1835, MANM Judicial Proceedings, Box 1, Folder 29, Mary Jean Cook Collection, AC 626, Fray Angélico Chávez History Library, New Mexico History Museum, Santa Fe [hereafter FAC]. I have changed the wording slightly from the original, for the purposes of narration.
7 González, *Refusing the Favor*, 20.
8 Gonzales, *Mexicanos*, 3rd ed., 82.
9 Reno, "Rebellion in New Mexico–1837," 198; Binkley, "New Mexico and the Texan Santa Fé Expedition," 90.
10 Gonzales, *Mexicanos*, 3rd ed., 74; Account of the 1837 revolt, conversation with Aniceto Abeytia, July 19, 1909, Mauro Montoya collection of New Mexican historical documents, 1709–1949, Folder 10B, Box 1, Series II, AC 152, FAC; González, *Refusing the Favor*, 37.

NOTES

11 González, *Refusing the Favor*, 37; Account of the 1837 revolt, conversation with Aniceto Abeytia, July 19, 1909, FAC.
12 Cook, *Doña Tules*, 20; Amado Chaves testimony, in "The Will of Gertrudis Barcelo," typed manuscript, Box 1, Folder 29, Mary Jean Cook Collection, AC 626, FAC; "Consuelo de los Rayos (Rallitos) Gutierres," in "Biographical Sketches," Box 1, Folder 32, Mary Jean Cook Collection, AC 626, FAC.
13 Carl Blumner to his sister, March 18, 1841, Box 1, Folder 1, Hiltrud Von Brandt collection of Carl Blumner letters, 1836–1906, AC 231, FAC.
14 Reno, "Rebellion in New Mexico—1837," 200, 204-5.
15 Gonzales, *Mexicanos*, 3rd ed., 74; Account of the 1837 revolt, FAC; Reno, "Rebellion in New Mexico—1837," 208-209.
16 Lecompte, "La Tules and the Americans," 222–23.
17 "Gambling Saloon in Santa Fe," *Harper's Magazine* (April 1854): 587; Matt Field, "Scenes in Santa Fé: The Monte Bank," *New Orleans Times-Picayune* (August 13, 1840): 2; Cook, *Doña Tules*, 51–52.
18 Kiser, "'A charming name for a species of slavery'"; Reséndez, "North American Peonage." On the complicated networks of godparentage in the Mexican Southwest, see Pérez, *Colonial Intimacies*.
19 Mark L. Gardner, Foreword to Field, *Matt Field on the Santa Fe Trail*, ed. Sunder, v.
20 Matt Field, "Rocky Mountain Sketches: Señora Toulouse," *New Orleans Times-Picayune* (August 18, 1840): 2.
21 Field, "Rocky Mountain Sketches," 2; Kendall, *Narrative of the Texan Santa Fé Expedition*, footnote, 234–35.
22 Barceló Church Records, ed. Chavez; Cook, *Doña Tules*, 30; Lecompte, "La Tules and the Americans," 223.
23 The descriptions of and quotes from the Kirker-La Tules game are from Field, "Scenes in Santa Fé," 2. Field does not identify the player as Kirker, but he describes him as both a trader and a scalp hunter, and Kirker was a known regular at La Tules's sala. Smith, "The Scalp Hunter in the Borderlands," 7.
24 Lecompte, "La Tules and the Americans," 216
25 Gregg, *Commerce of the Prairies* Vol. 2, 33; Lecompte, "La Tules and the Americans," 218.
26 González, *Refusing the Favor*, 50; Gonzales, *Política*, 75.

Chapter 9

1 Beckwourth and Bonner, *The Life and Adventures of James P. Beckwourth*, 379–82 [first quote on 380, second on 381]; Hyde, *Empires, Nations, and Families*, 48–49.
2 Johnson, *The Broken Heart of America*, 67, 73–74.
3 Brown, *Narrative of William W. Brown*, 26–27.
4 Beckwourth and Bonner, *The Life and Adventures of James P. Beckwourth*, 405, 417 [quote].
5 Hyde, *Born of Lakes and Plains*, 155–71; West, *The Contested Plains*, 83.
6 Nunis Jr., "The Sublettes of Kentucky and the Far West," 136; "Fort Vasquez"; Clayton, "The Growth and Significance of the American Fur Trade," 213.
7 *Ecoregions of Colorado*; Sage, *Rocky Mountain Life*, 207.
8 Beckwourth and Bonner, *The Life and Adventures of James P. Beckwourth*, 424.

9. Beckwourth and Bonner, *The Life and Adventures of James P. Beckwourth*, 425.
10. Beckwourth and Bonner, *The Life and Adventures of James P. Beckwourth*, 426.
11. Beckwourth and Bonner, *The Life and Adventures of James P. Beckwourth*, 428.
12. Beckwourth and Bonner, *The Life and Adventures of James P. Beckwourth*, 428 [quote], 429.
13. Leiker and Powers, *The Northern Cheyenne Exodus in History and Memory*, 28; Monnett, *Tell Them We Are Going Home*, 14; Leiker and Powers, *The Northern Cheyenne Exodus in History and Memory*, 23.
14. Beckwourth and Bonner, *The Life and Adventures of James P. Beckwourth*, 462–63. Beckwourth claimed that they believed he was Crow, but it is quite possible that the "affinity of race" that he said explained their trust in him was based on their understanding that he was biracial.
15. Beckwourth and Bonner, *The Life and Adventures of James P. Beckwourth*, 433 [quote], 444.
16. Beckwourth and Bonner, *The Life and Adventures of James P. Beckwourth*, 456.
17. "Taos, New Mexico: Art, Architecture, and History"; Weber, *The Taos Trappers*.
18. Sides, *Blood and Thunder*, 7–22, 42–45; Weber, *The Taos Trappers*.
19. Binkley, "New Mexico and the Texan Santa Fé Expedition," 95; Tyler, "Gringo Views of Governor Manuel Armijo," 31; Kendall, *Narrative of the Texan Santa Fé Expedition*, 200; Gonzales, *Mexicanos*, 3rd ed., 83.
20. Carroll, "Texan Santa Fe Expedition."
21. Beckwourth and Bonner, *The Life and Adventures of James P. Beckwourth*, 464; Ruxton, *Life in the Far West*, 190; Anderson, "J.B. Charbonneau, Son of Sacajawea," 258; Sage, *Rocky Mountain Life*, 206; Bellows, *The Explorers*, 50.
22. Sage, *Rocky Mountain Life*, 206 [quote]; Anderson, "J.B. Charbonneau, Son of Sacajawea," 258; Ruxton, *Life in the Far West*, 190; Oswald, Introduction, Notes, and Epilogue to *The Life and Adventures of James P. Beckwourth*, 586.
23. Hackel, "Land, Labor, and Production: The Colonial Economy of Spanish and Mexican California," 127–28.
24. Gonzales, *Mexicanos*, 3rd ed., 69–70; "History Timeline: Los Angeles County, 1800 to 1847"; Wainwright, "Milestones in California History."
25. Beckwourth and Bonner, *The Life and Adventures of James P. Beckwourth*, 465; Gonzales, *Mexicanos*, 3rd ed., 81.
26. Haas, "War in California, 1846–1848," 333, 334–36, 337; Gonzales, *Mexicanos*, 3rd ed., 86.
27. Beckwourth and Bonner, *The Life and Adventures of James P. Beckwourth*, 473.
28. Beckwourth and Bonner, *The Life and Adventures of James P. Beckwourth*, 473.
29. O'Sullivan, "Annexation," 5.
30. Haas, "War in California, 1846–1848," 339; Wainwright, "Milestones in California History"; Gonzales, *Mexicanos*, 3rd ed., 87.
31. Haas, "War in California, 1846–1848," 339; Wainwright, "Milestones in California History"; Heidenreich, "'I do not like the white man,'" 12–13.
32. Beckwourth and Bonner, *The Life and Adventures of James P. Beckwourth*, 473–74.
33. Gonzales, *Mexicanos*, 3rd ed., 84–86; Gonzales, *Política*, 87.
34. Brown, "U.S. Army Campaigns of the Mexican War," 9.
35. O'Sullivan, "Annexation," 9.

NOTES

36 Beckwourth and Bonner, *The Life and Adventures of James P. Beckwourth*, 474.
37 Beckwourth and Bonner, *The Life and Adventures of James P. Beckwourth*, 475.

Chapter 10

1 Gonzales, *Política*, 90.
2 Gonzales, *Política*, 51–52, 90; Manuel Armijo, Proclamation, August 8, 1846, as quoted in McClure, "Mexican New Mexico, 1837–1846," 108.
3 Gonzales, *Política*, 71–72, 73, 78 [quote], 102; Reséndez, "National Identity on a Shifting Border," 684; Tyler, "Anglo-American Penetration of the Southwest," 336.
4 Tyler, "Gringo Views of Governor Manuel Armijo," 38. I have changed the wording slightly from the original, for the purposes of narration.
5 Gonzales, *Política*, 95.
6 Tyler, "Gringo Views of Governor Manuel Armijo," 38; Hollon, "'A Leap in the Dark,'" 8–10.
7 Emory, *Notes of a Military Reconnaissance*, 25–26; Gonzales, *Política*, 96.
8 Gonzales, *Política*, 101–3; Tyler, "Gringo Views of Governor Manuel Armijo," 40.
9 Hollon, "'A Leap in the Dark,'" 14; Kennerly, *Persimmon Hill*, 185.
10 Beckwourth and Bonner, *The Life and Adventures of James P. Beckwourth*, 476.
11 Journal of Marcellus Ball Edwards, as quoted in Gonzales, *Política*, 105.
12 Emory, *Notes of a Military Reconnaissance*, 32; Gonzales, *Política*, 105.
13 Gonzales, *Política*, 105 [quote]; Emory, *Notes of a Military Reconnaissance*, 32.
14 Emory, *Notes of a Military Reconnaissance*, 32.
15 Emory as quoted in Cook, *Doña Tules*, 40.
16 Document 1113: Stephen W. Kearny, Proclamation, 1846, in Ralph Emerson Twitchell, *The Spanish Archives of New Mexico* (2 vols.; The Torch Press, 1914), AC 229, FAC.
17 Hollon, "'A Leap in the Dark,'" 15; Belohlavek, *Patriots, Prostitutes, and Spies*, 94; Gonzales, *Política*, 118.
18 Beckwourth and Bonner, *The Life and Adventures of James P. Beckwourth*, 476.
19 Report of J.W. Abert, in Emory, *Notes of a Military Reconnaissance*, 448.
20 Kennerly, *Persimmon Hill*, 191; Lecompte, "La Tules and the Americans," 217.
21 Magoffin, *Down the Santa Fé Trail*, 120–21; Cook, *Doña Tules*, 42; Scharff, *Twenty Thousand Roads*, 50–51.
22 Magoffin, *Down the Santa Fé Trail*, 114; González, *Refusing the Favor*, 70.
23 Report of Lt. Col. Phillip St. George Cooke, in Emory, *Notes of a Military Reconnaissance*, 551; *The March of the Mormon Battalion*, 170–72, 187; Emory, *Notes of a Military Reconnaissance*, 45; Tyler, *A Concise History of the Mormon Battalion in the Mexican War, 1846–47*; Belohlavek, *Patriots, Prostitutes, and Spies*, 73, 75, 79; Colby, *Sacagawea's Child*, 135, 145, 159.
24 Gonzales, *Política*, 80; Reséndez, "National Identity on a Shifting Border," 685–87.
25 Lecompte, "La Tules and the Americans," 227; Gonzales, *Política*, 124, 139; Alfred Waud, as quoted in Cook, *Doña Tules*, 46; Report of J. W. Abert, in Emory, *Notes of a Military Reconnaissance*, 511; Gonzales, *Política*, 122.
26 Report of J. W. Abert, in Emory, *Notes of a Military Reconnaissance*, 512.
27 Alexander Brydie Dyer, letter to a friend, February 14, 1847, in Journal of the Mexican-American War, A. B. Dyer Papers, 1846–1848, AC 070-P, FAC; "ARMY OF THE

WEST: Massacre of Governor Bent and Other Americans at Taos!" Government Printing Office, February 15, 1847 [typescript], Mauro Montoya collection of New Mexican historical documents, 1709–1949, Folder 16, Box 1, Series II, AC 152, FAC.
28 Teresina Bent Scheurich notebook, 1847 [typescript], AC 120-P, FAC. I have changed the wording slightly from the original, for the purposes of narration.
29 Teresina Bent Scheurich notebook, FAC; *Kit Carson Home & Museum Guide*, Taos, New Mexico.
30 Teresina Bent Scheurich notebook, FAC.
31 Beckwourth and Bonner, *The Life and Adventures of James P. Beckwourth*, 485.
32 "ARMY OF THE WEST," FAC; Gonzales, *Política*, 126; Alexander Brydie Dyer, letter to a friend, February 14, 1847, in Journal of the Mexican-American War, FAC; Report of J. W. Abert, in Emory, *Notes of a Military Reconnaissance*, 456–60.
33 Henry G. A. Caspers Journal, in Lt. Alexander Brydie Dyer Journal, 1846–48, Box 1, Folder 22, Mary Jean Cook Collection, AC 626, FAC.
34 Alexander Brydie Dyer Diary, February 24, 1847, FAC.
35 Alexander Brydie Dyer Diary, June 27 [quote], September 11 and October 8, 1847, FAC.
36 Belohlavek, *Patriots, Prostitutes, and Spies*, 92; Cook, "Gertrudis Barceló: Woman Entrepreneur of the Chihuahua and Santa Fe Trails, 1830–1850," Box 1, Folder 34, Mary Jean Cook Collection, AC 626, FAC; Henry G. A. Caspers Journal, April 25, 1847, FAC.
37 Belohlavek, *Patriots, Prostitutes, and Spies*, 92; Cook, "Gertrudis Barceló," FAC; "August de Marle," in "Biographical Sketches," Box 1, Folder 32, Mary Jean Cook Collection, AC 626, FAC.
38 Funeral invitation, June 14, 1847, in Manuel Alvarez papers, Business 1847, NMSRCA, in Box 1, Folder 28, Mary Jean Cook Collection, AC 626, FAC. Translated from Spanish into English by Nancy Serrano-Wu.
39 Barcelo Church Records, ed. Chavez; "Maria del Refugio Sisneros," in "Biographical Sketches," FAC.
40 Greenberg, *A Wicked War*, 259.
41 Gonzales, *Mexicanos*, 3rd ed., 88.

Chapter 11

1 West, *Continental Reckoning*, 5–6, 9–10.
2 "Old Spanish National Historic Trail."
3 Beckwourth and Bonner, *The Life and Adventures of James P. Beckwourth*, 502–3; Rohrbaugh, "No Boy's Play," 25–26.
4 James K. Polk, Fourth Annual Message to Congress, December 5, 1848.
5 Polk, Fourth Annual Message.
6 Beckwourth and Bonner, *The Life and Adventures of James P. Beckwourth*, 503.
7 Beckwourth and Bonner, *The Life and Adventures of James P. Beckwourth*, 507; West, *Continental Reckoning*, 22–23.
8 Rohrbaugh, "No Boy's Play," 38; Beckwourth and Bonner, *The Life and Adventures of James P. Beckwourth*, 507.
9 Beckwourth and Bonner, *The Life and Adventures of James P. Beckwourth*, 507.
10 Walton, "Sonora."

NOTES

11 Reyer and Padover, "Placer Mining in California"; Rohe, "Origins & Diffusion of Traditional Placer Mining in the West"; West, *Continental Reckoning*, 382–83.
12 Beckwourth and Bonner, *The Life and Adventures of James P. Beckwourth*, 509; Oswald, Introduction, Notes, and Epilogue to *The Life and Adventures of James P. Beckwourth*, 596.
13 Parsons, *The Life and Adventures of James W. Marshall*, 111–12, 115 [quote].
14 On violence in early Los Angeles, see Faragher, *Eternity Street* and Faragher, *California*, chapter 17; Cleland, *A History of California: The American Period*, 247–48.
15 Cleland, *A History of California: The American Period*, 247–48, 249–50.
16 Beckwourth and Bonner, *The Life and Adventures of James P. Beckwourth*, 506.
17 Katz, *The Black West*, 147.
18 *Pictures of Gold Rush California*, 205–6, 207; *Mountains and Molehills*, 233–35.
19 West, *Continental Reckoning*, 43; Isenberg, "Afterword: Mining, Memory, and History," 399–400.
20 Beckwourth and Bonner, *The Life and Adventures of James P. Beckwourth*, 509.
21 Beckwourth and Bonner, *The Life and Adventures of James P. Beckwourth*, 509; Oswald, Introduction, Notes, and Epilogue to *The Life and Adventures of James P. Beckwourth*, 596; Anderson, "J.B. Charbonneau, Son of Sacajawea," 250–51.
22 Beckwourth and Bonner, *The Life and Adventures of James P. Beckwourth*, 509.
23 Cleland, *A History of California: The American Period*, 251–53.
24 Cleland, *A History of California: The American Period*, 253–54.
25 Smith, *Freedom's Frontier*; Waite, *West of Slavery*.
26 Forbes, "The Early African Heritage of California," 88; Katz, *The Black West*, 124; Smith, "Remaking Slavery in a Free State," 29–30, 34.
27 Katz, *The Black West*, 124.
28 Cleland, *A History of California: The American Period*, 255–56.

Chapter 12

1 West, *The Contested Plains*, 98; González, *Refusing the Favor*, 43; Gonzales, *Política*, 80.
2 Barcelo affidavit [n.d.] and Barceló Affidavit, October 30, 1849, Santa Fe County 1st Judicial District Court Records, Civil cases 1849, NMSRCA, in Box 1, Folder 28, Mary Jean Cook Collection, AC 626, FAC; *Barcelo v Coulter*, Santa Fe County 1st Judicial District Court Records, Civil cases 1848, FAC; "George W. Coulter," Mariposa County Biographies; Reséndez, "National Identity on a Shifting Border," 669–70, 688; Gonzales, *Mexicanos*, 3rd ed., 100, 103.
3 William Raymond testimony, April 24, 1850, *Barcelo v Coulter* trial transcript, Santa Fe County 1st Judicial District Court Records, Civil cases 1848, NMSRCA, in Box 1, Folder 28, Mary Jean Cook Collection, AC 626, FAC.
4 August de Marle testimony, April 24, 1850, *Barcelo v Coulter* trial transcript, FAC.
5 *Barcelo v Coulter* trial transcript, April 24, 1850, FAC.
6 "The Will of Gertrudis Barcelo," typed manuscript, Box 1, Folder 29, Mary Jean Cook Collection, AC 626, FAC; "James Giddings," in "Biographical Sketches," Box 1, Folder 32, Mary Jean Cook Collection, AC 626, FAC.
7 "The Will of Gertrudis Barcelo," FAC; Lecompte, "Barceló and the Americans," 229.
8 "The Will of Gertrudis Barcelo," FAC; "Manuel Alvarez," "Biographical Sketches," Box 1, Folder 32, Mary Jean Cook Collection, AC 626, FAC.

9   The nature of Barceló's empire was unusual but there were other Hispana ricos who played similar roles in New Mexico Territory. See González, *Refusing the Favor* and Montoya, *Translating Property*.
10 Chávez, "Doña Tules, Her Fame and Her Funeral," 232; Statement of Amando Chaves, as quoted in Lecompte, "Barceló and the Americans," 229; Kennerly, *Persimmon Hill*, 192 [quote: "notorious"]; Journal of Henry G. A. Gaspers, as quoted in Cook, "Gertrudis Barceló: Woman Entrepreneur of the Chihuahua and Santa Fe Trails, 1830–1850"; Field, "Rocky Mountain Sketches," 2 [quote: "supreme queen"].
11 Letter from Santa Fe, January 23, 1852, *St. Louis Daily Republican* (March 4, 1862) and *Daily Missouri Republican* (March 27, 1852): 2, Box 1, Folder 29, Mary Jean Cook Collection, AC 626, FAC; Funeral Notice, *New York Daily Tribune* (March 17, 1852): 7; Lecompte, "Barceló and the Americans," 229–30; Belohlavek, *Patriots, Prostitutes, and Spies*, 95; Chávez, "Doña Tules, Her Fame and Her Funeral," 234.
12 Brewerton, *Overland with Kit Carson*, 191; "Farm Laborers–Average Monthly Earnings with Board, by Geographic Regions," 163; Deutsch, *No Separate Refuge*, 14–15, 16.
13 González, *Refusing the Favor*, 77; Gonzales, *Mexicanos*, 3rd ed., 95-96, 103; Belohlavek, *Patriots, Prostitutes, and Spies*, 96; Reséndez, "National Identity on a Shifting Border," 669, 688.
14 Labadie Family Tree, in Twitchell, ed., *The Spanish Archives of New Mexico*, 198; "The Will of Gertrudis Barcelo," FAC; "Rallitos," "Biographical Sketches," Box 1, Folder 32, Mary Jean Cook Collection, AC 626, FAC.
15 *Santa Fe Weekly Gazette* (November 13 and 20, 1852): 2.
16 University of New Mexico, "About *Santa Fe Weekly Gazette*."

Chapter 13

1   "From Santa Fe," *New York Times* (March 16, 1862): 3.
2   Beckwourth and Bonner, *The Life and Adventures of James P. Beckwourth*, 515–16; *Ecosystems of California*.
3   Beckwourth and Bonner, *The Life and Adventures of James P. Beckwourth*, 516.
4   Beckwourth and Bonner, *The Life and Adventures of James P. Beckwourth*, 517–20, 525, 526 [quote], 527; *Chico (Calif.) Weekly Chronicle-Record* (June 13, 1857): 2.
5   Beckwourth and Bonner, *The Life and Adventures of James P. Beckwourth*, v, 172, 175 [quote]; 372.
6   Beckwourth and Bonner, *The Life and Adventures of James P. Beckwourth*, 519–20, 527, 528 [quote].
7   Albright, *Official Explorations for Pacific Railroads*.
8   Douglas, "Speech of Hon. S.A. Douglas, of Illinois, in the United States Senate, March 3, 1854, on Nebraska and Kansas."
9   "The Kansas-Nebraska Act," May 30, 1854; Andrews, "Kansas Crusade," 497; Earle, "'If I Went West,'" 122–23; Karp, "The People's Revolution of 1856," 525.
10 "The Kansas-Nebraska Bill," speech at Chicago, October 30, 1854, in *Frederick Douglass' Paper*, November 24, 1854.
11 West, *Continental Reckoning*, 126–30.
12 Bonner, "Preface," in Beckwourth and Bonner, *The Life and Adventures of James P. Beckwourth*, iii–iv; Davis, Jr., "Research Uses of County Court Records, 1850-1879,"

339, footnote 91, p. 355; Mumey, *James Pierson Beckwourth*, footnote 9, p. 25; "Beckwourth Biography," The Beckwourth Website; Foley, "James Pierson Beckwourth (Beckwith)," Missouri Encyclopedia; "A Temperance Address," *The Pittsfield (MA) Sun* (December 16, 1841): 3; "Five Dollars," *The Pittsfield (MA) Sun* (August 10, 1865): 3.

13 Oswald, Introduction, Notes, and Epilogue to *The Life and Adventures of James P. Beckwourth*, 601. Biographers disagree about whether the autobiography was Bonner's idea, or Beckwourth's.

14 Bonner, "Preface," in Beckwourth and Bonner, *The Life and Adventures of James P. Beckwourth*, iii.

15 Slotkin, *The Great Disorder*, 29, 34.

16 Jones, *Calamity*, 4, 7, 10; Steckmesser, "The Frontier Hero in History and Legend," 168; Smith, *Virgin Land*, 81, 86–88.

17 "Story of James P. Beckwourth," *Harper's New Monthly Magazine*, vol. 13 (September 1856): 455.

18 Deloria, *Playing Indian*.

19 "Agreement with Thomas Bonner and Joseph S. Davis for publication of his life and adventures," Plumas County, California, Bancroft Library, Berkeley, California, as transcribed in Mumey, *James Pierson Beckwourth*, 27–28.

20 Oswald, Introduction, Notes, and Epilogue to *The Life and Adventures of James P. Beckwourth*, 604; Beckwourth, "Agreement with Thomas Bonner and Joseph S. Davis."

21 Bonner, "Preface," in Beckwourth and Bonner, *The Life and Adventures of James P. Beckwourth*, iv.

22 Bonner, "Preface," in Beckwourth and Bonner, *The Life and Adventures of James P. Beckwourth*, iv.

23 Robinson, *Kansas; Its Interior and Exterior Life*, 8, 6.

24 United States Senate, "The Crime Against Kansas: May 19, 1856"; United States Senate, "The Caning of Senator Charles Sumner: May 22, 1856"; Freeman, *The Field of Blood*; Andrews, "Kansas Crusade," 507–8; Miller, "To Make Kansas Free," 6–7.

25 D'Amato, "'The Harper Establishment." In the fall of 1856, bookseller advertisements appeared in newspapers in Louisiana, Iowa, California, Wisconsin, Ohio, Kentucky, Tennessee, South Carolina, Alabama, North Carolina, Pennsylvania, Delaware, New York, Connecticut, and Massachusetts.

26 *Christian Advocate and Journal* blurb, as quoted in "Book Advertisement," *Nashville (TN) Union and American* (November 5, 1856): 2.

27 "Review," *(Washington, D.C.) National Era* (August 21, 1856): 1.

28 "A California Yarn," *Greensboro (NC) Patriot* (December 4, 1857): 4; Mumey, *James Pierson Beckwourth*, 47.

29 "Review," *(Washington, D.C.) National Era* (August 21, 1856): 1.

30 "Story of James P. Beckwourth," *Harper's New Monthly Magazine*, vol. 13 (September 1856): 455.

31 "Story of James P. Beckwourth," 472.

32 "Story of James P. Beckwourth," 458.

33 The illustrations appear in Beckwourth and Bonner, *The Life and Adventures of James P. Beckwourth*, 56, 116, 132, 136, 175, 191, 202, 224, 265, 432, 511, and 521.

34   Another frontier autobiography with "unraced" text is Nat Love's. The images included in that book, unlike in Beckwourth's, represent Love as phenotypically Black. Speirs, "Writing Self (Effacingly)," 302.
35   *The Nevada Journal* (September 26, 1856): 3. My attempts to locate the original issues of the *Mirror of the Times* that published this announcement have been unsuccessful. It is likely that all extant copies were destroyed in the San Francisco earthquake and fire of 1906.
36   George A. Jackson Diary, Folder 10, George Andrew Jackson Collection, 1859–1928, Stephen H. Hart Library and Research Center, History Colorado, Denver, Colorado [hereafter HC].
37   Oswald, Introduction, Notes, and Epilogue to *The Life and Adventures of James P. Beckwourth*, ix.

Chapter 14

1   "The Mines," *Rocky Mountain News* (May 28, 1859): 2; Bancroft, "The Elusive Figure of John H. Gregory," 124; West, *The Contested Plains*, 177.
2   Calvin Perry Clark Diary, June 9, 1859, WHC; David Fletcher Spain Diary, June 8, 1859, Folder 1, and Spain to Ella from "Gregory Diggins," June 12, 1859, Folder 12, David Fletcher Spain Collection (1859), HC.
3   Greeley, *An Overland Journey, from New York to San Francisco, in the Summer of 1859*, 143.
4   Hollister, *The Mines of Colorado*, 76; Blackhawk, *The Rediscovery of America*, 289–90; West, *The Contested Plains*, 145–70.
5   "New Advertisement, Just Arrived for A.P. Vasquez & Co.," *Rocky Mountain News* (December 1, 1859); Mumey, *James Pierson Beckwourth*, 56.
6   Hollister, *The Mines of Colorado*, 89; Wharton, *History of the City of Denver*, 21.
7   John Lewis Dailey Journal, November 25, 1859, WH94, DPL; "Captain James Beckwourth," *Rocky Mountain News* (December 1, 1859): 2.
8   "Captain James Beckwourth," 2.
9   Hollister, *The Mines of Colorado*, 18, 90, 92; Wharton, *History of the City of Denver*, 19, 23, 35.
10 Oswald, Introduction, Notes, and Epilogue to *The Life and Adventures of James P. Beckwourth*, 606; Bill of Sale (Marion to Beckwourth, $100), transcribed in Mumey, *James Pierson Beckwourth*, 57–58; West, *The Contested Plains*, 107–12.
11 Greeley, June 21, 1859, *An Overland Journey*, 157; Blackhawk, *The Rediscovery of America*, 303, 316; West, *The Contested Plains*, 145–46.
12 Wharton, *History of the City of Denver*, 15, 31, 33 [quote], 41, 43; West, *The Contested Plains*, 179.
13 Calvin Perry Clark Diary, 1859–1860, DPL.
14 Calvin Perry Clark Diary, February 1860, DPL; Wharton, *History of the City of Denver*, 47, 49.
15 Wharton, *History of the City of Denver*, 29, 65; Calvin Perry Clark Diary, 1859–1860, DPL.
16 Treaty of Fort Laramie, 1851.
17 "Captain James Beckwourth," *Rocky Mountain News* (December 1, 1859): 2.
18 *Rocky Mountain News* (March 28, 1860): 3; Hafen, "The Last Years of James P. Beckwourth," 135.
19 *Rocky Mountain News* (April 4, 1860): 3.

20 *Rocky Mountain News* (April 4, 1860): 3.
21 Jim Beckwourth, letter to the editor, April 18, 1860, *Rocky Mountain News* (April 18, 1860): 2; Oswald, Introduction, Notes, and Epilogue to *The Life and Adventures of James P. Beckwourth*, 607; Hafen, "The Last Years of James P. Beckwourth," 137; Wharton, *History of the City of Denver*, 71; Hoig, *The Sand Creek Massacre*, 6.
22 Jim Beckwourth, letter to the editor, April 18, 1860, *Rocky Mountain News* (April 18, 1860): 2.
23 Jim Beckwourth, letter to the editor, April 18, 1860, *Rocky Mountain News* (April 18, 1860): 2; Kit Carson testimony, in *Condition of the Indian Tribes: Report of the Joint Special Committee, Appointed Under Joint Resolution of March 3, 1865* [The Doolittle Report], 96–97.
24 "Indian Meeting," *Daily Herald and Rocky Mountain Advertiser* (May 1, 1860): 3; "Indian Meeting," *Rocky Mountain News* (May 2, 1860): 5.
25 "Indian Meeting," *Daily Herald and Rocky Mountain Advertiser* (May 1, 1860): 3; "Indian Meeting," *Rocky Mountain News* (May 2, 1860): 5.
26 "Lo the Poor Indian," *Rocky Mountain News* (April 18, 1860): 2.
27 "A Ride in the Country," *Rocky Mountain News* (September 17, 1860): 2.
28 *Rocky Mountain News* (June 27, 1860): 3; Compiled Marriages from Mesa, Arapahoe, and Boulder Counties, 1859–1900, Colorado, United States; *Western Mountaineer* (July 5, 1860): 6.
29 *Topeka (KS) State Record*, May 5, 1860, Folder 38, MSS 494, Pikes Peak Gold Rush Collection, HC.

Chapter 15

1 Nicoletta, "The Architecture of Control," 354, 360, 367; Graham, "The New Lebanon Shaker Children's Order," 215; "The Shaker Village," *New York Daily Herald* (June 8, 1853): 6.
2 Manget, "The Shaker Connection."
3 Graham, "The New Lebanon Shaker Children's Order," 219.
4 "Financial Ruin at White Haven: The Panic of 1857"; Stampp, *America in 1857: A Nation on the Brink*.
5 Charles May Sears Biography, Sears Family Papers, Manuscripts & Folklife Archives, Western Kentucky University [hereafter WKU]; *The Legislature of 1868, in Transactions of the Kansas Historical Society*, 276; 1880 Federal Census (Eudora County, Kansas); Ponce, "'The Noise of Democracy,'" 89–90; West, *The Contested Plains*, 13, 107.
6 Treaty with the Shawnee, 1831; Roberts, *I've Been Here all the While*; Treaty with the Shawnee, 1854.
7 Charles May Sears, A Concise Journal of Events, 2, WKU; Cordley, *A History of Lawrence, Kansas*, 170–72 [quote].
8 Sears, A Concise Journal of Events, 2, WKU.
9 Hollister, *The Mines of Colorado*, 13, 38, 417, 418.
10 *Rocky Mountain News* (June 6 and June 20, 1860): 2, as quoted in *From Western Deserts to Carolina Swamps*, ed. Wilson, 38–39.
11 Diary of E. H. N. Patterson [letter to the *Spectator*, published August 18, 1859], in Hafen, ed., *Overland Routes*, 187; Greeley, June 9, 1859, *An Overland Journey*, 116.

12 Samuel Mallory, "Overland Route to Pike's Peak," letter to (Danbury, CT) *Jeffersonian* (June 24, 1860), Folder 7, Samuel Mallory Collection, 1860–1869, HC.
13 Hollister, *The Mines of Colorado*, 40; Diary of E.H.N. Patterson [letter to the *Spectator*, published August 18], in Hafen, ed., *Overland Routes*, 187; Greeley, June 9, 1859, *An Overland Journey*, 117.
14 Hollister, *The Mines of Colorado*, 41.
15 Hollister, *The Mines of Colorado*, 41–42.
16 Hollister, *The Mines of Colorado*, 107–8 [quote]; 114, 58 [quote]; Lavender, *The Rockies*, 141–43, 150, 169, 259; West, *The Contested Plains*, 105–6.
17 U.S. Federal Census, 1860, Missouri City, Arapahoe County, Kansas Territory, 13; Hollister, *The Mines of Colorado*, 109; "Missouri City Cemetery, Gilpin County, Colorado"; "Climate and Average Weather Year Round in Central City, Colorado."
18 Sam Curtis to Henry Curtis, November 2, 1858, as reprinted in "Direct from the Gold Mines," *Lawrence (KS) Western Home Journal* (December 9, 1858): 2.
19 Jackson Diary, March 2, 1859, HC; Hogan, *Class and Community in Frontier Colorado*, 121; Noel, "Denver's Curtis Park is a Pioneer Suburb"; Missouri City, Arapahoe County, Kansas Territory, US Federal Census, 1860, 13.
20 "South Carolina Declaration of Secession," 1860.
21 "Declaration of Causes [Texas]," February 2, 1861.
22 Schulten, "The Civil War and the Origins of the Colorado Territory," 22–23.
23 Schulten, "The Civil War and the Origins of the Colorado Territory," 43.
24 "Colorado," *Rocky Mountain News* (March 4, 1861): 2.
25 Hoig, *The Sand Creek Massacre*, 13–14.
26 "Indian Treaty," *Rocky Mountain News* (March 4, 1861): 2; Treaty with the Arapaho and Cheyenne, 1861; Hoig, *The Sand Creek Massacre*, 15.
27 *Rocky Mountain News* (April 18, 1861): 2; "The War Begun," *Rocky Mountain News* (April 19, 1861): 2 [quote].
28 "A Question," *Rocky Mountain News* (March 9, 1861): 2.
29 "A Rebel Flag," *Rocky Mountain News* (April 25, 1861): 3.
30 "Colorado's Role in the Civil War" (1861), 6–7, Folder 28, MSS 118, Civil War Collection, HC; Hollister, *Boldly They Rode*, 3, 5; Chivington, "The Pet Lambs" (1890), Folder 65, Box 2, MSS 141, Colorado Volunteers: Civil War Collection, HC.
31 "U.S. Soldiers Wanted," *Rocky Mountain News* (July 25, 1861): 3; *Daily Colorado Republican and Rocky Mountain Herald* (August 12, 1861): 3. The ad ran for multiple issues in these papers. "Colorado's Role in the Civil War" (1861), 6–7, HC.
32 Hollister, *Boldly They Rode*, 2.
33 Hollister, *Boldly They Rode*, 2; "Cavalry," *Rocky Mountain News* (August 17, 1861): 3.
34 Hollister, *Boldly They Rode*, 80–82; "The Shaker Village," *New York Daily Herald* (June 8, 1853): 6; Stein, The Shaker Experience in America, 66, 205, 208.
35 "To Contractors," advertisement, *Daily Colorado Republican and Rocky Mountain Herald* (August 27, 1861): 3; "Cavalry," *Rocky Mountain News* (August 27, 1861): 3.
36 For work on the Civil War West, see Colton, *The Civil War in the Western Territories*; Josephy, Jr., *The Civil War in the American West*; Adams, "The War in the West"; Frazier, *Blood and Treasure*; Thompson, *Henry Hopkins Sibley* and Thompson, ed., *Civil War in the Southwest*; Hall, *Sibley's New Mexico Campaign*; Waite, *West of Slavery*; Lynch, *Southern California Chivalry*; Masich, *The Civil War in Arizona* and *Civil War in the Southwestern Borderlands, 1861–1867*;

Kiser, *Turmoil on the Rio Grande* and *Illusions of Empire*; Keleher, *Turmoil in New Mexico, 1846–1868*; Brettle, "Confederate Imaginations with the Federals in the Postwar Order," and *Confederate Planning for a Post-Civil War World*; Nelson, "Indian America," "Death in the Distance: The Confederate Campaign for New Mexico, 1861–1862," "Indians Make the Best Guerrillas: Native Americans and the War for the Desert Southwest, 1861–1862," "The Civil War from Apache Pass," and *The Three-Cornered War*.

37 *Daily Colorado Republican and Rocky Mountain Herald* (August 28, 1861): 2; *Rocky Mountain News* (August 29, 1861): 2; Nelson, *The Three-Cornered War*.

38 Ovando Hollister, Muster Record, *Compiled Service Records of Volunteer Union Soldiers Who Served in Organizations from the State of Colorado, 1861–1865*, https://www.fold3.com. I am grateful to Susannah Ural for locating these records for me.

39 Hollister, *Boldly They Rode*, 6, 25; Wallace, "My Experiences in the First Colorado Regiment" (1924), 308–9, Folder 16, MSS 118, Civil War Collection, HC; "Colorado's Role in the Civil War" (1861), 8, HC.

40 Hollister, *Boldly They Rode*, 31–32.

41 Nelson, *The Three-Cornered War*, 5–14.

42 Nelson, *The Three-Cornered War*, 90–96.

43 Hollister, *Boldly They Rode*, 45.

Chapter 16

1 Hollister, *Boldly They Rode*, 59, 61 [quote]; "Colorado's Role in the Civil War" (1861), 11, HC.

2 Hollister, *Boldly They Rode*, 61.

3 Hollister, *Boldly They Rode*, 61.

4 Report of Major John Chivington, March 26, 1862, *OR* I:9, chap. 21, pp. 530–31; *Civil War in the Southwest*, ed. Thompson, 82.

5 Hollister, *Boldly They Rode*, 63–64 [quote on 64]; E. B. Sop, "Engagement with the Enemy in Apache Canyon," Folder 8, MSS 141, Colorado Volunteers: Civil War Collection, HC; Chivington, "The Pet Lambs" (1890), Folder 65, Box 2, MSS 141, Colorado Volunteers: Civil War Collection, HC.

6 Hollister, *Boldly They Rode*, 65; *Santa Fe Weekly Gazette* (April 26, 1862): 1; Nelson, *The Three-Cornered War*, 103–5.

7 Hollister, *Boldly They Rode*, 66, 67.

8 Alberts, *The Battle of Glorieta*, 71.

9 Alberts, *The Battle of Glorieta*, 71–72, 129.

10 Hollister, *Boldly They Rode*, 68.

11 Hollister, *Boldly They Rode*, 71 [quotes]; "A private letter from an officer in the Colorado First, which will be found of special interest to our readers," March 30, 1862, *CR & RMH*, May 1, 1862, Folder 17, MSS 141, Colorado Volunteers: Civil War Collection, HC; *Santa Fe Weekly Gazette* (April 26, 1862): 1; Alberts, *The Battle of Glorieta*, 118; William Davidson, "From Socorro to Glorieta," in Thompson, ed., *Civil War in the Southwest*, 85.

12 Hollister, *Boldly They Rode*, 71.

13 Hollister, *Boldly They Rode*, 71.

14 Report of Major John M. Chivington, March 28, 1862, *OR* I:9, chap. 21, p. 539.

15 Hollister, *Boldly They Rode*, 73.
16 Report of Colonel John P. Slough to Edward Canby, March 30, 1862, *OR* I:9, chap. 21, p. 535.
17 Hollister, *Boldly They Rode*, 102.
18 Hollister, *Boldly They Rode*, 78.
19 Hollister, *Boldly They Rode*, 78–79.
20 Hollister, *Boldly They Rode*, 81.
21 Hollister, *Boldly They Rode*, 97.
22 Nelson, *The Three-Cornered War*, 115–23.
23 Hollister, *Boldly They Rode*, 98.
24 Hollister, *Boldly They Rode*, 116–17.
25 Hollister, *Boldly They Rode*, 118–19; Ickis Diary, April 23, 1862, DPL; Alfred Cobb to a friend, April 29, 1862, Alfred Cobb Correspondence, 1862: Letters from Camp Near Fort Craig (1913), HC.
26 Unidentified letter, Alfred Cobb Correspondence, HC.
27 Hollister, *Boldly They Rode*, 121.
28 Hollister, *Boldly They Rode*, 123.
29 Hollister, *Boldly They Rode*, 128; Chivington, "The Pet Lambs" (1890), HC.
30 Hollister, Service Record, July 1862 and Discharge Papers, January 1863, *Compiled Service Records of Volunteer Union Soldiers Who Served in Organizations from the State of Colorado, 1861–1865*, https://www.fold3.com; Johns Hopkins Medicine, "Inguinal Hernia."
31 Hollister, *Boldly They Rode*, 131–32, 137.
32 Hollister, *Boldly They Rode*, 137.
33 Hollister, *Boldly They Rode*, 141–42.
34 Hollister, Service Record, *Compiled Service Records of Volunteer Union Soldiers Who Served in Organizations from the State of Colorado, 1861–1865*, https://www.fold3.com.
35 Hollister, *Boldly They Rode*, 165.
36 Hollister, Service Record and Discharge Papers, *Compiled Service Records of Volunteer Union Soldiers Who Served in Organizations from the State of Colorado, 1861–1865*, https://www.fold3.com.

Chapter 17

1 Homestead Act, May 20, 1862.
2 John O'Sullivan, "Annexation," 9; Homestead Act, May 20, 1862; Pacific Railway Act, July 1, 1862.
3 Arizona Organic Act, February 24, 1863. The state of West Virginia separated from Virginia and came into the Union in June 1863, but it never held territorial status.
4 *Rocky Mountain News* (March 4, 1862): 3; Oswald, Introduction, Notes, and Epilogue to *The Life and Adventures of James P. Beckwourth*, 614; Hoig, *The Sand Creek Massacre*, 25.
5 Oswald, Introduction, Notes, and Epilogue to *The Life and Adventures of James P. Beckwourth*, 615; *Weekly Commonwealth* (March 5, 1863): 3; "List of Cases," *Rocky Mountain News* (March 13, 1863): 3.
6 *Rocky Mountain News* (March 2, 1863): 4.
7 Bill of Sale, March 4, 1863, as reprinted in Mumey, *James Pierson Beckwourth*, 104; *Weekly Commonwealth* (April 30, 1864): 3.

NOTES

8 "The Great Fire!" *Rocky Mountain News* (April 20, 1863): 2; Wharton, *History of the City of Denver*, 109.
9 "New Book," *Rocky Mountain News* (April 18, 1863): 2.
10 "New Book," *Rocky Mountain News* (April 18, 1863): 2; "NEW BOOK!" advertisement, *Rocky Mountain News* (April 18, 1863): 2.
11 Hollister and Blakely, "Salutory," *Daily Mining Journal* (November 30, 1863): 2; Pioneer Press Advertisement, *Daily Mining Journal* (November 30, 1863): 4.
12 Hollister and Blakely, "Salutory," *Daily Mining Journal* (November 30, 1863): 2.
13 Hoig, *The Sand Creek Massacre*, 35.
14 *OR* Series I, vol. 34, part IV, p. 151, as quoted in Hoig, *The Sand Creek Massacre*, 83.
15 "From Col. Chivington," *Daily Mining Journal* (April 23, 1864): 3.
16 "Death of Bill Payne, The Negro," *Rocky Mountain News* (May 18, 1864): 3.
17 "Death of Bill Payne, The Negro," *Rocky Mountain News* (May 18, 1864): 3; Wharton, *History of the City of Denver*, 29; *Daily Mining Journal* (May 17, 1864): 3; *Daily Commonwealth* (May 18, 1864): 3; *The People, Etc. vs. James P. Beckwourth*, James P. Beckwourth Trial Collection, 1864, HC.
18 Hoig, *The Sand Creek Massacre*, 59.
19 Major T. I. McKinney report, June 15, 1864, *OR* Series I, vol. 34, part IV, pp. 402–4, as quoted in Hoig, *The Sand Creek Massacre*, 78.
20 John Evans, Proclamation, June 27, 1864, *OR* Series I, vol. 41, part I, pp. 963–64, as quoted in Hoig, *The Sand Creek Massacre*, 62–63.
21 John Evans, Proclamation, August 11, 1864, Folder 3, John Milton Chivington Papers, DPL.
22 "Uncle Johnny Evans," *Daily Mining Journal* (August 12, 1864): 1.
23 Hoig, *The Sand Creek Massacre*, 69, 129; Rein, "'Our First Duty,'" 223.

Chapter 18

1 Stands in Timber and Liberty, *Cheyenne Memories*, 42; Moore, "Cheyenne Political History," 336; Leiker and Powers, *The Northern Cheyenne Exodus in History and Memory*, 24–25.
2 Killsback, "The Legacy of Little Wolf," 92; Leiker and Powers, *The Northern Cheyenne Exodus in History and Memory*, 30.
3 Charles Eastman, as quoted in Killsback, "The Legacy of Little Wolf," 89; Monnett, *Tell Them We Are Going Home*, 10.
4 Grinnell, *The Cheyenne Indians*, vol. 2, p. 51.
5 Killsback, "The Legacy of Little Wolf," 88–90; Grinnell, *The Cheyenne Indians*, vol. 2, p. 51.
6 Stands in Timber and Liberty, *Cheyenne Memories*, 58; Killsback, "The Legacy of Little Wolf," 87–88; Moore, "Cheyenne Political History," 338.
7 Stands in Timber and Liberty, *Cheyenne Memories*, 160; Killsback, "The Legacy of Little Wolf," 91; Liberty and Wood, "Cheyenne Primacy," 161; Moore, "Cheyenne Political History," 333–34.
8 Monnett, "'My Heart Now Has Become Changed,'" 48; Monnett, *Tell Them We Are Going Home*, 14.
9 Curtis, *Gambling on Ore*, 43; Rzeczkowski, "The Crow Indians and the Bozeman Trail," 32–33; Northern Cheyenne population number estimated by U.S. Army Colonel Caspar Collins in 1865, as quoted in Spring, *Caspar Collins*, 164–68.

10 Grinnell, *The Cheyenne Indians*, vol. 1, p. 340.
11 Killsback, "The Legacy of Little Wolf," 87–88, 90, 96; Stands in Timber and Liberty, *Cheyenne Memories*, 36; Leiker and Powers, *The Northern Cheyenne Exodus in History and Memory*, 28.
12 Killsback, "The Legacy of Little Wolf," 87–88.
13 Little Wolf quoted in Monnett, *Tell Them We Are Going Home*, 11.
14 Hoig, *The Sand Creek Massacre*, 113; Fowler, "Arapaho and Cheyenne Perspectives," 383–84; George Wakely, "Arrival of Chiefs in Denver, 1864," HC; Kraft, *Ned Wynkoop and the Lonely Road from Sand Creek*, 119–121; Rein, "'Our First Duty,'" 225–26; "Camp Weld Participants, September 28, 1864," HC; Report of the Council, September 28, 1864, in *Condition of the Indian Tribes* (1867), Appendix, 87; Fowler, "Arapaho and Cheyenne Perspectives," 385; Edward Wynkoop Testimony, 1865, *Condition of the Indian Tribes* (1867), Appendix, 77.
15 Orders from General Curtis, 1864, as quoted in Hoig, *The Sand Creek Massacre*, 122.
16 Hoig, *The Sand Creek Massacre*, 124–25, 134–35.
17 Hafen, "The Last Years of James P. Beckwourth," 138; Oswald, Introduction, Notes, and Epilogue to *The Life and Adventures of James P. Beckwourth*, 617; James Beckwourth Testimony, *Report of the Secretary of War* ["The Sand Creek Massacre"], Senate Ex. Doc. 26, February 12, 1867, 68.
18 Annie Ronk to her cousin Redding, November 14, 1864, Charlotte and Anna Ronk Papers, DPL.
19 "The Late Affair of Sand Creek," *Daily Mining Journal* (January 5, 1865): 2; Chivington, "The Pet Lambs" (1890), HC.
20 Chivington, "The Pet Lambs" (1890), HC.
21 Hoig, *The Sand Creek Massacre*, 136; Silas Soule testimony as quoted in Hoig, *The Sand Creek Massacre*, 141. I have changed the wording slightly from the original, for the purposes of narration.
22 Hoig, *The Sand Creek Massacre*, 141.
23 Hoig, *The Sand Creek Massacre*, 144; Samuel F. Tappan to Gen. L. W. Colby [Assistant Attorney General, U.S.], from Washington, D.C., January 18, 1892, Folder 6, John Milton Chivington Papers, DPL.
24 Testimony of Robert Bent, *Condition of the Indian Tribes* (1867), Appendix, 96; Hoig, *The Sand Creek Massacre*, 144. For a history of the Southern Cheyenne Owl Woman, William Bent, and their family, see Hyde, *Born of Lakes and Plains* and *Empires, Nations, and Families*.
25 Hoig, *The Sand Creek Massacre*, 145.
26 Hoig, *The Sand Creek Massacre*, 146.
27 Beckwourth Testimony, *Report of the Secretary of War* ["The Sand Creek Massacre"], 68–69.
28 Beckwourth Testimony, *Report of the Secretary of War* ["The Sand Creek Massacre"], 74.
29 As quoted in Hoig, *The Sand Creek Massacre*, 149.
30 George Bent account, as quoted in Hoig, *The Sand Creek Massacre*, 150.
31 Beckwourth Testimony, *Report of the Secretary of War* ["The Sand Creek Massacre"], 70, 75.
32 Beckwourth Testimony, *Report of the Secretary of War* ["The Sand Creek Massacre"], 70.
33 Beckwourth Testimony, *Report of the Secretary of War* ["The Sand Creek Massacre"], 70; footnote 9, in Hoig, *The Sand Creek Massacre*, 153; Bent to Hyde, March 15, 1905, in Bent and Faller, "Making Medicine against 'White Man's Side of Story,'" 78.

NOTES

34 Bent to Hyde, March 15, 1905, in Bent and Faller, "Making Medicine against 'White Man's Side of Story,'" 77; Hyde, *Born of Lakes and Plains*, 264–70.
35 Beckwourth Testimony, *Report of the Secretary of War* ["The Sand Creek Massacre"], 71, 75; John Smith Testimony, *Condition of the Indian Tribes* (1867), Appendix, 41–42.
36 Hoig, *The Sand Creek Massacre*, 153; Bent to Hyde, March 15, 1905, in Bent and Faller, "Making Medicine against 'White Man's Side of Story,'" 78; Beckwourth Testimony, *Report of the Secretary of War* ["The Sand Creek Massacre"], 71.
37 Chivington quoted in Hoig, *The Sand Creek Massacre*, 155; Beckwourth Testimony, Report of the Secretary of War ["The Sand Creek Massacre"], 72.
38 Curtis to Chivington, September 28, 1864, *OR* Series I, vol. 41, part 3, p. 462; Hoig, *The Sand Creek Massacre*, 112; LeCompte, "Sand Creek," 153.
39 John Chivington, "Additional About the Indian Fight," *Rocky Mountain News* (December 8, 1864): 2; Hoig, *The Sand Creek Massacre*, 154; Kelman, *A Misplaced Massacre*, 9.
40 David Louderback testimony, as in Hoig, *The Sand Creek Massacre*, 156 [I have changed the wording slightly from the original, for the purposes of narration]; Beckwourth Testimony, *Report of the Secretary of War* ["The Sand Creek Massacre"], 71.
41 Beckwourth Testimony, *Report of the Secretary of War* ["The Sand Creek Massacre"], 71 [I have changed the wording slightly from the original, for the purposes of narration]; John Smith Testimony, *Condition of the Indian Tribes* (1867), Appendix, 41–42.
42 Hoig, *The Sand Creek Massacre*, 158–59.
43 Chivington, "The Pet Lambs" (1890), HC.
44 *Rocky Mountain News* (December 22, 1864), as quoted in Hoig, *The Sand Creek Massacre*, 161.
45 *Rocky Mountain News* (January 11, 1865): 3.

Chapter 19

1 Chivington, "The Pet Lambs" (1890), HC; Hoig, *The Sand Creek Massacre*, 163; Robert Rizer, 2nd Colorado Cavalry Journal (1865), 14, Folder 4, Robert Rizer Papers, 1861–1912, DPL.
2 Sandweiss, "Still Picture, Moving Stories," 163.
3 Samuel F. Tappan Diary, January 1, 1865, 3. I am grateful to C.P. Weaver for sharing quotations from this diary with me; Article 37, Lieber Code (1863).
4 Hyde, *Born of Lakes and Plains*, 274–75.
5 Faller, "Making Medicine against 'White Man's Side of Story': George Bent's Letters to George Hyde," 66.
6 On the first Battle of Adobe Walls on November 25, 1864, see Blyth, "Kit Carson and the War for the Southwest."
7 *Report of the Secretary of War* ["The Sand Creek Massacre"], 72–76; Oswald, Introduction, Notes, and Epilogue to *The Life and Adventures of James P. Beckwourth*, 620.
8 Edward Wynkoop as quoted in Hoig, *The Sand Creek Massacre*, 164.
9 *Daily Mining Journal* (February 1, 1865): 2.
10 *Daily Mining Journal* (January 4, 1865): 3.
11 "Editorial Correspondence," *Daily Mining Journal* (February 1, 1865): 2.
12 Samuel F. Tappan Diary, February 8, 1865, 74. I am grateful to C. P. Weaver for sharing quotations from this diary with me; "Court of Inquiry," *Rocky Mountain News* (February 8, 1865): 2.

13. "Court of Inquiry," *Rocky Mountain News* (February 8, 1865): 2; *Daily Mining Journal* (February 14, 1865): 2; *Report of the Secretary of War* ["The Sand Creek Massacre"], 5; Hoig, *The Sand Creek Massacre*, 170.
14. Berwanger, "Reconstruction on the Frontier: The Equal Rights Struggle in Colorado, 1865–1867," 313.
15. Beckwourth Testimony, *Report of the Secretary of War* ["The Sand Creek Massacre"], 68.
16. Beckwourth Testimony, *Report of the Secretary of War* ["The Sand Creek Massacre"], 70.
17. Beckwourth Testimony, *Report of the Secretary of War* ["The Sand Creek Massacre"], 75–76.
18. Berwanger, "Reconstruction on the Frontier: The Equal Rights Struggle in Colorado, 1865–1867," 313.
19. Beckwourth Testimony, *Report of the Secretary of War* ["The Sand Creek Massacre"], 76; Letter from Jim Beckwourth, March 15, 1865, in *Daily Mining Journal* (March 17, 1865): 2 [quote].
20. *Central City Daily Mining Register*, as quoted in *Daily Mining Journal* (March 11, 1865): 3.
21. *Daily Mining Journal* (March 11, 1865): 3.
22. Letter from Jim Beckwourth, March 15, 1865, in *Daily Mining Journal* (March 17, 1865): 2.
23. "The End," *Daily Mining Journal* (April 10, 1865): 2.
24. "Salute," *Rocky Mountain News* (April 11, 1865): 3.
25. "The Homicide Last Night," *Denver City News* (April 24, 1865): 2, clipping in Folder 14, Box 1, Silas Soule Papers, DPL; *Daily Mining Journal* (April 25, 1865): 2 [quote].
26. Hoig, *The Sand Creek Massacre*, 172.
27. Oswald, Introduction, Notes, and Epilogue to *The Life and Adventures of James P. Beckwourth*, 621.
28. "Jim Beckwourth," from Stobie, Autobiography [in manuscript] (1890–91), in Charles S. Stobie Collection, 1865–1928, MSS 609, Series I, Folder 10, HC.
29. *Report of the Secretary of War* ["The Sand Creek Massacre"], 74.

Chapter 20

1. Hollister, *Life of Schuyler Colfax*, 252; McGinty, *Lincoln and California*, 3; *Daily Mining Journal* (May 30, 1865): 2.
2. McGinty, *Lincoln and California*, 3.
3. McGinty, *Lincoln and California*, 3; Hollister, *Life of Schuyler Colfax*, 252; *Daily Mining Journal* (May 30, 1865): 2.
4. Hollister, *Life of Schuyler Colfax*, 255.
5. Hollister, *Life of Schuyler Colfax*, 256.
6. Schuyler Colfax to Carrie Woodhull, July 5, 1865, as transcribed in Hollister, *Life of Schuyler Colfax*, 258.
7. Black Hawk, 1864, from a public history display in Black Hawk, Colorado.
8. *Daily Mining Journal* (May 30, 1865): 2.
9. *Daily Mining Journal* (May 30, 1865): 2.
10. *Daily Mining Journal* (May 30, 1865): 2; Hollister, *Life of Schuyler Colfax*, 251. I have changed the wording slightly from the original, for the purposes of narration.
11. *Daily Mining Journal* (May 30, 1865): 2. I have changed the wording slightly from the original, for the purposes of narration.

NOTES

12 *Daily Mining Journal* (May 30, 1865): 2.
13 *Daily Mining Journal* (May 30, 1865): 2.
14 *Daily Mining Journal* (May 31, 1865): 2; Hollister, *The Mines of Colorado*, 434.
15 *Daily Mining Journal* (May 30, 1865): 2 [quote]; *Daily Mining Journal* (May 31, 1865): 2; *Daily Mining Journal* (June 2, 1865): 2.
16 "Jim Beckwourth," *Rocky Mountain News* (February 5, 1867): 1.
17 Nelson, *Saving Yellowstone*, 55–56; Rzeczkowski, "The Crow Indians and the Bozeman Trail," 32–36.
18 Monnett, Introduction, *Eyewitness to the Fetterman Fight: Indian Views*, ed. Monnett, 5.
19 Haack, "'This Must Have Been a Grand Sight,'" 7, 20, footnote 1.
20 Henry Carrington as quoted in Hoig, *Perilous Pursuit*, 2.
21 Hoig, *Perilous Pursuit*, 2.
22 Hafen, "The Last Years of James P. Beckwourth," 139; Mumey, *James Pierson Beckwourth*, 164.
23 Hafen, "The Last Years of James P. Beckwourth," 139; Mumey, *James Pierson Beckwourth*, 164.
24 Mumey, *James Pierson Beckwourth*, 163–64; Oswald, Introduction, Notes, and Epilogue to *The Life and Adventures of James P. Beckwourth*, 622; "History: Places: Fort C. F. Smith," Bighorn Canyon National Recreation Area; Banfill, "Fort C. F. Smith, Built for Outpost on Bozeman Trail in 1866."
25 George M. Templeton Diary, September 1, 1866, as transcribed in Mumey, *James Pierson Beckwourth*, 168–69.
26 Templeton Diary, September 13, 1866, as transcribed in Mumey, *James Pierson Beckwourth*, 169–71. I have changed the wording slightly from the original, for the purposes of narration.
27 Templeton Diary, 1866, as transcribed in Mumey, *James Pierson Beckwourth*, 171.
28 Templeton Diary, September 29, 1866, as transcribed in Mumey, *James Pierson Beckwourth*, 171. I have changed the wording slightly from the original, for the purposes of narration.
29 Templeton Diary, October 1, 1866, as transcribed in Mumey, *James Pierson Beckwourth*, 171; Oswald, Introduction, Notes, and Epilogue to *The Life and Adventures of James P. Beckwourth*, 624; James Lockwood, *Life and Adventures of a Drummer-Boy*, 156–59, as quoted in Mumey, *James Pierson Beckwourth*, 165.
30 Pope, "Adult Mortality in America Before 1900," Table 9.2, p. 277; Ewbank, "Black Mortality and Health before 1940," Table 1, p. 105.
31 Templeton Diary, October 30, 1866, as transcribed in Mumey, *James Pierson Beckwourth*, 173.
32 Templeton Diary, October 30, 1866, as transcribed in Mumey, *James Pierson Beckwourth*, 173–74.
33 Joseph White Bull account, in *Eyewitness to the Fetterman Fight: Indian Views*, ed. Monnett, 24–26.
34 White Bull account, in *Eyewitness to the Fetterman Fight: Indian Views*, ed. Monnett, 27; Monnett, Introduction to *Eyewitness to the Fetterman Fight* [battle maps 1–2], 6–7.
35 White Bull account, in *Eyewitness to the Fetterman Fight: Indian Views*, ed. Monnett, 29.
36 White Bull account, in *Eyewitness to the Fetterman Fight: Indian Views*, ed. Monnett, 30.
37 White Bull account, in *Eyewitness to the Fetterman Fight: Indian Views*, ed. Monnett, 30–31; Killsback, "The Legacy of Little Wolf," 91.

38 Killsback, "The Legacy of Little Wolf," 93.
39 "Jim Beckwourth," *Rocky Mountain News* (February 5, 1867): 1.
40 *Denver Gazette*, January 22, 1867, as reprinted in the *Gold Hill (Nevada Territory) Daily News* (February 6, 1867): 2; in *Los Angeles Daily News* (February 22, 1867): 1; *Virginia City, Montana Post* (February 16, 1867): 2; *(Helena) Daily Montana Post* (February 12, 1867): 4.
41 "Jim Beckwourth," *Rocky Mountain News* (February 5, 1867): 1.
42 *Rocky Mountain News* (February 20, 1867): 3.
43 "James P. Beckwourth," *American Phrenological Journal* (November 1867): 187.
44 "Jim Beckwourth," from Stobie, Autobiography (1890–91), in Series I, Folder 10, Charles S. Stobie Collection, HC.

Chapter 21

1 The Fourteenth Amendment to the U.S. Constitution, June 13, 1866 (ratified July 9, 1868).
2 Fiege, *The Republic of Nature*, 241, 249–50; Dearinger, *The Filth of Progress*, 113.
3 Fiege, *The Republic of Nature*, 242, 248.
4 "Platte River Valley."
5 Porcupine account of the Plum Creek attack, in Grinnell, *The Fighting Cheyennes* (1915), 257; Stands in Timber and Liberty, *Cheyenne Memories*, 174; "The Massacre on the Pacific Rail Road," *Chicago Tribune* (August 12, 1867): 1; Monnett, *Tell Them We Are Going Home*, 52.
6 "The Massacre on the Pacific Rail Road," *Chicago Tribune* (August 12, 1867): 1.
7 Stands in Timber and Liberty, *Cheyenne Memories*, 174–75; "From Omaha," *Chicago Tribune* (August 17, 1867): 2; Porcupine account of the Plum Creek attack, in Grinnell, *The Fighting Cheyennes* (1915), 255.
8 Stands in Timber and Liberty, *Cheyenne Memories*, 174–75; Porcupine account of the Plum Creek attack, in Grinnell, *The Fighting Cheyennes* (1915), 255; Fiege, *The Republic of Nature*, 256; West, *Continental Reckoning*, 199, 200.
9 Grinnell, *The Fighting Cheyennes* (1915), 256, 258.
10 Stands in Timber and Liberty, *Cheyenne Memories*, 176; Monnett, "'My Heart Now Has Become Changed,'" 48; Leiker and Powers, *The Northern Cheyenne Exodus in History and Memory*, 50–51.
11 *Rocky Mountain News* (August 31, 1867): 4; *{Golden} Colorado {Weekly} Transcript* (September 4, 1867): 1, 2.
12 Hollister, *The Mines of Colorado*, iii, 440; *Rocky Mountain News* (December 1, 1866): 1; *Rocky Mountain News* (January 7, 1867): 3; *Rocky Mountain News* (February 15, 1867): 4. Samuel Bowles published his own book about the West, a series of letters from his 1865 trip, in 1866. Bowles, *Across the Continent*.
13 Hollister, *The Mines of Colorado*, iv.
14 Petrowski, "The Kansas Pacific Railroad in the Southwest," 136, 143; Henry Siebert & Bros., "Map of the Land Grant of the Kansas Pacific Railroad," 1869.
15 "The Mines of Colorado," *Omaha Republican*, reprinted in *Rocky Mountain News* (May 31, 1867): 1; *American Journal of Mining* editorial, reprinted in *Rocky Mountain News* (May 29, 1868): 1; *Rocky Mountain News* (August 31, 1867): 4 [quote].

NOTES

16 Hollister, *The Mines of Colorado*, 448–50.
17 Hollister, *The Silver Mines of Colorado*, 28.
18 Hollister, Preface to *The Silver Mines of Colorado*, np.
19 Hollister to the *New York Times*, July 2, 1867, as reprinted in *Rocky Mountain News* (July 18, 1867): 1.
20 Emanuel Leutze, *Westward the Course of Empire Takes its Way* (1861–62), U.S. Capitol Collection.
21 Hollister to the *New York Times*, July 2, 1867, as reprinted in *Rocky Mountain News* (July 18, 1867): 1.
22 Sandweiss, "Still Picture, Moving Stories," 158–59; Nelson, *Saving Yellowstone*, 49.
23 Doolittle et al., *The Condition of the Indian Tribes*, 1867; Prucha, *American Indian*, 279; West, *The Last Indian War*, 100; Oman, "The Beginning of the End," 36; Jefferson, *Notes on the State of Virginia*, 153.
24 Oman, "The Beginning of the End," 36–38, 48; Prucha, *American Indian Treaties*, 280; Bailey, *The Long Walk*, 231; Sandweiss, "Still Picture, Moving Stories," 163–66.
25 Peace Commission enabling legislation, July 1867, as quoted in Sandweiss, "Still Picture, Moving Stories," 161.
26 Report to the President by the Indian Peace Commission, January 7, 1868, Accompanying Papers A, in *Annual Report of the Commissioner of Indian Affairs, for the Year 1868*, 26.
27 "Union Pacific Railroad, End of Track Dateline, 1865–1869"; Oman, "The Beginning of the End," 38–41; Prucha, *American Indian Treaties*, 281; "Fort Laramie, [Idaho Territory], 1863" [sketch].
28 Report to the President, in *Annual Report of the Commissioner of Indian Affairs, for the Year 1868*, 29.
29 Report to the President, in *Annual Report of the Commissioner of Indian Affairs, for the Year 1868*, 31. I have changed the wording slightly from the original, for the purposes of narration.
30 Demallie, "'Scenes in the Indian Country,'" 44, 46; *Annual Report of the Commissioner of Indian Affairs, for the Year 1868*.
31 William Tecumseh Sherman, Annual Report, 1868, as quoted in Oman, "The Beginning of the End," 48 [quote], 43; Report to the President, in *Annual Report of the Commissioner of Indian Affairs, for the Year 1868*, 30.
32 Union Pacific Railroad, "The Race for Promontory."
33 Treaty with the Northern Cheyenne and Northern Arapaho, May 10; Dusenberry, "The Northern Cheyenne," 24; Killsback, "The Legacy of Little Wolf," 94–95.
34 Alexander Gardner, "Indian Peace Commission in Council with the Northern Cheyenne and Northern Arapaho" [photograph], May 1868, William Tecumseh Sherman Collection of Alexander Gardner Photographs, National Museum of the American Indian, Smithsonian Institution.
35 Alexander Gardner, "Group Cheyenne Chiefs," May 1868 [photograph], Figure 11 in Demallie, "'Scenes in the Indian Country,'" 47, 53.
36 *Rocky Mountain News* (May 13, 1868): 1 [quote]; *Rocky Mountain News* (May 14, 1868): 3.
37 Hollister, "Salutatory," *Rocky Mountain News* (May 4, 1868): 1; William R. Thomas, "To the Readers of the News," *Rocky Mountain News* (May 4, 1868): 4. Notices regarding Hollister's appointment were printed in newspapers across the nation, including the *Atchison (KS) Weekly Champion* (May 23, 1868): 4, the *Leavenworth (KS) Daily Commercial*

(May 9, 1868): 4, and the *Springfield (MA) Republican* (reprinted in the *Rocky Mountain News* (June 13, 1868): 1).
38 Simpson, *Let Us Have Peace*, 244; Waugh, *U.S. Grant*, 104, 113.
39 "Important Arrival," *Rocky Mountain News* (July 21, 1868): 1; Nelson, *Saving Yellowstone*, 8–9; Waugh, *U.S. Grant*, 121.
40 *Rocky Mountain News* (July 22, 1868): 4. I have changed the wording slightly from the original, for the purposes of narration.
41 *Rocky Mountain News* (July 22, 1868): 4.
42 *Rocky Mountain News* (July 24, 1868): 4.
43 Hall and Hafen, "Seventy Years Ago," 162; *Rocky Mountain News* (August 10, 1868): 4; *Rocky Mountain News* (August 8, 1868): 1.
44 *Rocky Mountain News* (August 8, 1868): 4; *Rocky Mountain News* (August 11, 1868): 1.
45 Slotkin, *A Great Disorder*, 38.
46 *Rocky Mountain News* (August 11, 1868): 1; *Colorado Transcript* (August 12, 1868): 2.
47 *Rocky Mountain News* (August 24, 1868): 1; Hall and Hafen, "Seventy Years Ago," 164–65; "The Colfax Party," *Rocky Mountain News* (September 3, 1868): 4; *Rocky Mountain News* (August 11, 1868): 4; *Colorado Transcript*, August 12, 1868): 2; Hollister, *Life of Schuyler Colfax*, 326.
48 Hollister, *Life of Schuyler Colfax*, note 1: "A Tale of Two Wedding Rings," 327.
49 Hollister, *Life of Schuyler Colfax*, note 1: "A Tale of Two Wedding Rings," 327.
50 Demallie, "'Scenes in the Indian Country,'" 48; Prucha, *American Indian Treaties*, 282.
51 Killsback, "The Legacy of Little Wolf," 95.

Chapter 22

1 Frances Flora Palmer, *Across the Continent: Westward the Course of Empire Takes its Way*, Currier and Ives, 1868.
2 Raverty, "Frances Flora Palmer," 8; Fiege, *The Republic of Nature*, 257–58; Beach, "Revisiting America: The Prints of Currier & Ives."
3 Hollister, Letter from Utah No. 8, *Rocky Mountain News* (February 3, 1869): 1.
4 Park, *American Zion*, 127–28, 131.
5 Hollister, Letter from Utah No. 8, *Rocky Mountain News* (February 3, 1869): 1.
6 Park, *American Zion*, 129.
7 Hollister, Letter from Utah No. 8, *Rocky Mountain News* (February 3, 1869): 1.
8 Letter from Promontory, March 25, 1869, in *Deseret News* (April 7, 1869): 5.
9 Hollister, Letter from Utah No. 8, *Rocky Mountain News* (February 3, 1869): 1.
10 Hollister ("Observer"), "Corinne Correspondence," March 31, 1869, *Salt Lake Daily Reporter* (April 3, 1869), as transcribed in Utah Gentiles, http://utahgentiles.com/gentiles/Hollister/Hollister-news1.htm; Hollister, Letter from Utah No. 8, *Rocky Mountain News* (February 3, 1869): 1; Hollister, Letter from Utah No. 11, *Rocky Mountain News* (April 15, 1869): 1; "By Private Letter," *Rocky Mountain News* (April 8, 1869): 1.
11 Hollister ("Observer"), "Corinne Correspondence."
12 Chang, Fisher Fishkin, and Obenzinger, "Introduction," Chang, "Chinese Railroad Workers and the US Transcontinental Railroad in Global Perspective," Hu-DeHart, "Chinese Labor Migrants to the Americas in the Nineteenth Century: An Inquiry into Who They Were and the World They Left Behind," in Chang and Fisher Fishkin, eds.,

The Chinese and the Iron Road, 7, 34, 42, 44; Lew-Williams, *The Chinese Must Go*, 25; Walker, "Gold Mountain Guests," 264; Ngai, *The Chinese Question*, 32; Liestman, "Nineteenth-Century Chinese and the Environment of the Pacific Northwest," 17; Yung, *Unbound Feet*, 17.
13 Ngai, *The Chinese Question*, 21, 36; Lew-Williams, *The Chinese Must Go*, 21.
14 Ngai, *The Chinese Question*, 3, 134.
15 Ngai, *The Chinese Question*, 95, 103.
16 "Arrivals and Departures by Stage: Arrivals, May 26, 1867," (*Helena, MT*) *Weekly Rocky Mountain Gazette* (June 1, 1867): 2; "Arrivals and Departments by Stage: To the West," *Salt Lake Daily Telegraph and Commercial Advertiser* (November 3, 1867): 2; "Arrivals and Departures by Stage: To the North," *Salt Lake Daily Telegraph and Commercial Advertiser* (November 2, 1867): 2. Ping Chong may have been a mining company official working out of Virginia City, Montana: *Daily Montana Post* (October 26 and 30, 1867): 3, 8.
17 Chang, Fisher Fishkin, and Obenzinger, "Introduction," in Chang and Fisher Fishkin, eds., *The Chinese and the Iron Road*, 1, 2, 9, 10.
18 Leland Stanford to Andrew Johnson, October 10, 1865, as quoted in Kraus, "Chinese Laborers and the Construction of the Central Pacific"; Chang, Fisher Fishkin, and Obenzinger, "Introduction," in Chang and Fisher Fishkin, eds., *The Chinese and the Iron Road*, 2.
19 Chang, "Chinese Railroad Workers and the US Transcontinental Railroad in Global Perspective," 33.
20 Chang, Fisher Fishkin, and Obenzinger, "Introduction," in Chang and Fisher Fishkin, eds., *The Chinese and the Iron Road*, 12.
21 Chang, Fisher Fishkin, and Obenzinger, "Introduction," in Chang and Fisher Fishkin, eds., *The Chinese and the Iron Road*, 12–13.
22 Charles Crocker, as quoted in "Key Questions," Chinese Railroad Workers Project, Stanford University.
23 "Key Questions," Chinese Railroad Workers Project; Lee, *The Racial Railroad*, 88–89; Karuka, *Empire's Tracks*, 87.
24 Karuka, *Empire's Tracks*, 92; Chang, Fisher Fishkin, and Obenzinger, "Introduction," in Chang and Fisher Fishkin, eds., *The Chinese and the Iron Road*, 14–15.
25 "Ten Miles in a Day," "Key Questions," Chinese Railroad Workers Project; Chang, Fisher Fishkin, and Obenzinger, "Introduction," in Chang and Fisher Fishkin, eds., *The Chinese and the Iron Road*, 16.
26 Hollister, Letter from Utah No. 7, *Rocky Mountain News* (February 1, 1869): 1.
27 Hollister, Letter from Utah No. 12, *Rocky Mountain News* (April 19, 1869): 1.
28 *Daily Rocky Mountain News* (May 10, 1869): 4.
29 Andrew J. Russell, "East Meets West," May 10, 1869 [photograph], Oakland Museum of California.
30 Andrew J. Russell, "Chinese Laying Last Rail," May 10, 1869 [photograph], Oakland Museum of California; Chang, "Chinese Railroad Workers and the US Transcontinental Railroad in Global Perspective," 30–31; Chang, Fisher Fishkin, and Obenzinger, "Introduction," in *The Chinese and the Iron Road*, 17; Khor, "Archives, Photography, and Historical Memory," 449; West, *Continental Reckoning*, 202–3.
31 Hollister, Letter from Utah No. 7, *Rocky Mountain News* (February 1, 1869): 1; Bowles as quoted in Chang, Fisher Fishkin, and Obenzinger, "Introduction," in *The Chinese and the Iron Road*, 19 and in Dearinger, *The Filth of Progress*, 108.

32 O'Sullivan, "Annexation," 9.
33 Lafayette Wallace Case, *The Hollister Family of America* (Fergus Print Co., 1886), https://www.ancestry.com; US Marriage Records, 1810–1953, https://www.ancestry.com; *Kansas State Recorder* (December 4, 1869): 2; *Fort Wayne (IN) Daily Gazette* (December 4, 1869): 2.
34 "Ovando J. Hollister," *US Register of Civil, Military, and Naval Service*, vol. 1 (1869), 86.
35 Ransmeier, *Sold People*, 2–6, 13, 24, 29, 31; Yung, *Unbound Feet*, 18–19; Wegars, *Polly Bemis*, 7. The documents attesting to Polly Bemis's birthplace are contradictory. A census record lists "Pekin" (Beijing), but in an interview later in her life, Polly herself said that she was from near Hong Kong. Although the interview was mediated by a white interviewer, the statement about Hong Kong came from her. Given this, in addition to the fact that the vast majority of Chinese migrants to the United States came from southeastern China during this period (and not Beijing, which is 1,200 miles north of Hong Kong), I have chosen to privilege Polly's account in my narrative of her sale and journey in the early 1870s. Gizycka, "Diary on the Salmon River: Part II," 278; Washington, Idaho County, Idaho Territory, 1880 Federal Census.
36 Garrett, *Chinese Dress*, chapter 6; Gizycka, "Diary on the Salmon River: Part II," 278; Bertha Long account, in Wegars, *Polly Bemis*, 39.
37 *River Boat* [from the album 50 *Chinese Boats of Various Kinds, Guangzhou, China*, c. 1800], Peabody Essex Museum, Salem, Massachusetts; Lew-Williams, *The Chinese Must Go*, 21.
38 Sinn, *Pacific Crossing*, 227, 237, 262.
39 Sinn, *Pacific Crossing*, 231, 234; Lew-Williams, *The Chinese Must Go*, 21.
40 Sinn, *Pacific Crossing*, 231; Lew-Williams, *The Chinese Must Go*, 22.
41 Carleton Watkins, San Francisco photographs, 1872–1879, University of California.
42 Table I: "Chinese in the United States before the Exclusion Act," Table II: "Chinese Population in the United States, 1852–1900," and Table VI: "Number of Chinese in California by Counties," in *A History of the Chinese in California*, 18–19.
43 Gizycka, "Diary on the Salmon River: Part II," 278; "Polly Bemis Has Big Time On Visit to the State Capital," (Grangeville, Idaho) *Idaho County Free Press* (August 7, 1924): 1; Wegars, *Polly Bemis*, 7; Lew-Williams, *The Chinese Must Go*, 23; Sinn, *Pacific Crossing*, 238, 262; Tracy, "Race, Crime, and Social Policy," 12–13; Chang, Fisher Fishkin, and Obenzinger, "Introduction," 9; Ransmeier, *Sold People*, 2; Yung, *Unbound Feet*, 25.
44 *Ecoregions of Idaho*; Hailey, *History of Idaho*, 30; "A Wagon Road to Warren's," *Idaho Statesman* (November 30, 1872): 2.
45 Wegars, *Polly Bemis*, 12; "Polly Bemis Has Big Time on Visit to the State Capital," 1.
46 "Sketches of Travel in Idaho Number III," (Idaho City) *Idaho Semi-Weekly World* (August 29, 1868): 2; Wegars, *Polly Bemis*, 16.
47 Wegars, *Polly Bemis*, 10–11; "A Wagon Road to Warren's," *Idaho Statesman* (November 30, 1872): 2; Hailey, *History of Idaho*, 32.
48 Wegars, *Polly Bemis*, 11–12; "A Wagon Road to Warren's," 2; "Sketches of Travel in Idaho Number III," 2.
49 "From the North," (Boise, ID) *Statesman* (March 4, 1869): 1; "Chinese Influx," (Idaho City) *Idaho World* (May 13, 1869): 2; Ngai, *The Chinese Question*, 141–42; Wegars, *Polly Bemis*, 17–18, 21; Section F: "Chinese Terraced Gardens," Chinese Sites in the Warren Mining District, National Register of Historic Places Application; Liestman, "Nineteenth-Century Chinese and the Environment of the Pacific Northwest," 19, 22.
50 Boise *Idaho Statesman* (June 25, 1872): 2 and (July 2, 1872): 3.

NOTES 375

51 Boise *Idaho Statesman* (July 2, 1872): 3.
52 "Woman of 70 Sees Railway First Time," (Grangeville) *Idaho County Free Press* (August 16, 1923): 1; Wegars, *Polly Bemis*, 20.
53 Sinn, *Pacific Crossing*, 226, 229, 239, 243, 262; Ransmeier, *Sold People*, 2 ; "Polly Bemis Has Big Time On Visit to the State Capital," 1.

Chapter 23

1 Hoig, *Perilous Pursuit*, 5; Woodward, "Some Experiences with the Cheyennes," 17, 18.
2 Woodward, "Some Experiences with the Cheyennes," 19.
3 Woodward, "Some Experiences with the Cheyennes," 20.
4 Woodward, "Some Experiences with the Cheyennes," 20.
5 Woodward, "Some Experiences with the Cheyennes," 22.
6 Genetin-Pilawa, *Crooked Paths to Allotment*, 87; Stockwell, *Interrupted Odyssey*, 109; Hirsch, "1871: The End of Indian Treaty Making."
7 Casserly, as quoted in Genetin-Pilawa, *Crooked Paths to Allotment*, 87–88.
8 Woodward, "Some Experiences with the Cheyennes," 22.
9 See Nelson, *Saving Yellowstone*, 10, 128–33 and Williams, *I Saw Death Coming*.
10 Ulysses S. Grant, Second Inaugural Address, March 4, 1873.
11 Ulysses S. Grant, Second Inaugural Address, March 4, 1873.
12 "Breaking the Silence: Nineteenth-Century Indian Delegations," Peabody Museum of Archaeology & Ethnology.
13 Col J. E. Smith, "List of names of delegation of Northern Cheyennes & Arapahoes in his charge," Received at Office of Indian Affairs on November 10, 1873, Red Cloud Agency Letters Received File, National Archives and Records Administration roll 717; *Washington, D.C. National Republican* (November 10, 1873): 4; Leiker and Powers, *The Northern Cheyenne Exodus in History and Memory*, 4.
14 Brownell, "The Short-Lived Baltimore & Potomac Railroad Station on the National Mall."
15 "Another Indian Delegation—Cause and Result of Their Visits," *Boston Globe* (November 10, 1873): 1.
16 Nelson, *Saving Yellowstone*, 171–78.
17 *Washington, D.C. Chronicle* (November 11, 1873): 8; Lewis, *Washington: A History*, 186; Khan, *Enlightening the World*, 82–83; Chernow, *Grant*, 696.
18 "Red Men at Mount Vernon," *(Washington, D.C.) National Republican* (November 5, 1873): 4; Mount Vernon Visitor Log, November 1873, George Washington Presidential Library, Mount Vernon, Virginia. Thank you to Lindsay Chervinsky and Rebecca Baird for locating this logbook entry for me.
19 "Indians at the White House," *(Washington, D.C.) Evening Star* (November 14, 1873): 1 [I have changed the wording slightly from the original, for the purposes of narration]; Hoig, *Perilous Pursuit*, 6.
20 My account of this conversation is adapted from multiple sources: "The President's Talk to the Cheyennes," *Chicago Evening Post* (November 14, 1873): 4; "Indians at the White House," *(Washington, D.C.) Evening Star* (November 14, 1873): 1; "The Indian Delegation," *Wheeling (WV) Daily Register* (November 15, 1873): 1, and "Big Talk," *Washington, D.C. Chronicle* (November 15, 1873): 8. Hoig, *Perilous Pursuit*, 6; Wild Hog account, as quoted in Leiker and Powers, *The Northern Cheyenne Exodus in History and Memory*, 6.

21. "The West, 1867–1872," exhibition text, *Dark Fields of the Republic: Alexander Gardner Photographs, 1859–1872*, National Portrait Gallery, 2015–2016.
22. Alexander Gardner, "Little Wolf and Dull Knife," November 1873 [photograph], Bureau of American Ethnology Collection, Amon Carter Museum of American Art, Fort Worth, Texas. It is unclear if the necklace that Little Wolf wears belonged to him and was part of his traditional diplomatic regalia, or if it was one of the props Alexander Gardner used in his studio portraits. Kirkham and Weber, *History of Design*, 448.
23. "Cheyenne and Arrapahoe Indians," *Philadelphia Inquirer* (November 20, 1873): 8; *New York Times* (November 25, 1873): 5; *New England Farmer* (November 29, 1873): 2; Leiker and Powers, *The Northern Cheyenne Exodus in History and Memory*, 8.
24. Killsback, "The Legacy of Little Wolf," 96.
25. Hoig, *Perilous Pursuit*, 8.
26. Dippie, "'Its Equal I Have Never Seen:' Custer Explores the Black Hills in 1874," 2.
27. George Armstrong Custer, Order and Dispatch Book, August 2, 1874, as transcribed in McLaird and Turchen, "Exploring the Black Hills, 1855–1875: Reports of the Government Expeditions," 306.
28. Dusenberry, "The Northern Cheyenne," 25; Monnett, *Tell Them We Are Going Home*, 20; Utley, *Sitting Bull*, 116, 127; Cozzens, "Ulysses S. Grant Launched an Illegal War Against Plains Indians, Then Lied About It."
29. Killsback, "The Legacy of Little Wolf," 96; Leiker and Powers, *The Northern Cheyenne Exodus in History and Memory*, 33.
30. Treaty with the Northern Cheyenne and Northern Arapaho at Fort Laramie, May 10, 1868.
31. "Report of the Secretary of the Commission Appointed to Treat with the Sioux Indians for the Relinquishment of the Black Hills," June 18, 1875, in *Report of the Secretary of the Interior*, 44th Congress, 1st Session, House Ex. Doc. No. 1, 689–90.
32. Liberty and Wood, "Cheyenne Primacy," 169; Utley, *Sitting Bull*, 122–23 [quote]; Killsback, "The Legacy of Little Wolf," 97.
33. Hedren, *Rosebud, June 17, 1876: Prelude to Little Big Horn*, 5–6.
34. Cozzens, "Ulysses S. Grant Launched an Illegal War."
35. *Report of the Secretary of War*, 44th Congress, 2nd Session, House Ex. Doc. 1, 29; Bourke, *On the Border with Crook*, 272–78; Hedren, *Rosebud, June 17, 1876*, 56–57.
36. Hedren, *Rosebud, June 17, 1876*, 57.
37. Hedren, *Rosebud, June 17, 1876*, 57.
38. Hedren, *Rosebud, June 17, 1876*, 62.
39. Hedren, *Rosebud, June 17, 1876*, 63–64.
40. Dusenberry, "The Northern Cheyenne," 25; Monnett, *Tell Them We Are Going Home*, 11; Liberty and Wood, "Cheyenne Primacy," 157 169; Hoig, *Perilous Pursuit*, 9; Utley, *Sitting Bull*, 131–36, 142; Hedren, *Rosebud, June 17, 1876*, 70 and 66 [quote].
41. Killsback, "The Legacy of Little Wolf," 98.
42. Killsback, "The Legacy of Little Wolf," 97.
43. Killsback, "The Legacy of Little Wolf," 98.
44. Stands in Timber and Liberty, *Cheyenne Memories*, 188–89; Agonito and Agonito, "Resurrecting History's Forgotten Women," 8; [Little Hawk] account, in Grinnell, *The Fighting Cheyennes*, 323–24; Spotted Wolf—Yellow Nose Ledger Book, Smithsonian

Institution, National Anthropological Archives, Bureau of American Ethnology; Bourke, *On the Border with Crook*, 317.

45 Stands in Timber and Liberty, *Cheyenne Memories*, 212; Hoig, *Perilous Pursuit*, 9.

Chapter 24

1 "TERRIBLE NEWS!" *Ogden Daily Junction* (July 6, 1876): 1.
2 *Corinne Daily Reporter* (May 26, 1871): 2 and (May 2, 1871): 3; *U.S. Register of Civil, Military, and Naval Service*, Vol. I, 1869, p. 86; *Corrine Daily Reporter* (March 2, 1871): 3, April 29, 1871): 2 [quote], (May 31, 1871): 3, (June 26, 1871): 3, (July 17, 1871); advertisement, *Corinne Daily Reporter* (May 7, 1871); 2; *Salt Lake Tribune* (March 27, 1872): 3 and (March 28, 1872): 3.
3 *Ogden Daily Junction* (November 1, 1873): 5; *Corinne Daily Reporter* (June 19, 1873): 3 and (October 7, 1873): 3; *Utah Mining Journal* (July 31, 1872): 3; Hollister to the editors, February 1, 1873, in "The Mormons on Railways," *Utah Mining Journal* (February 3, 1873): 2.
4 *Deseret News* (November 15, 1871): 6.
5 "Internal Revenues," *Daily Ogden Junction* (April 21, 1874): 3; *Deseret News* (May 20, 1874): 8; *Salt Lake Tribune* (May 23, 1875): 4. Neither Ovando nor Carrie Hollister ever spoke about why they did not have children.
6 *Deseret News* (August 5, 1874): 12; *Utah Mining Gazette* (August 8, 1874): 6; "Died in Salt Lake," *Rocky Mountain News* (February 13, 1892): 1; *Cleveland Plain Dealer* (February 14, 1892): 4.
7 J. D. Cameron to Ulysses S. Grant, July 8, 1876, in "Message from the President of the United States, July 16, 1876," 4.
8 Utley, *Sitting Bull*, 167.
9 Killsback, "The Legacy of Little Wolf," 98.
10 Iron Teeth account, in Monnett, "'My Heart Now Has Become Changed,'" 49.
11 Iron Teeth account, in Monnett, "'My Heart Now Has Become Changed,'" 49; Stands in Timber and Liberty, *Cheyenne Memories*, 217; Dusenberry, "The Northern Cheyenne," 26; Monnett, *Tell Them We Are Going Home*, 11; Killsback, "The Legacy of Little Wolf," 98.
12 Hoig, *Perilous Pursuit*, 10–17 [quote on 15].
13 Monnett, "'My Heart Now Has Become Changed,'" 49–51; Leiker and Powers, *The Northern Cheyenne Exodus in History and Memory*, 35; Agonito and Agonito, "Resurrecting History's Forgotten Women," 9; Stands in Timber and Liberty, *Cheyenne Memories*, 220.
14 Monnett, *Tell Them We Are Going Home*, 13; Stands in Timber and Liberty, *Cheyenne Memories*, 223.
15 *Report, Select Committee on the Removal of the Northern Cheyennes, &c.* Senate Report No. 708 (June 8, 1880), 5.
16 Hoig, *Perilous Pursuit*, 18–19; Bourke, *The Diaries of John Gregory Bourke*, vol. 2, p. 251.
17 Leiker and Powers, *The Northern Cheyenne Exodus in History and Memory*, 35, 36; Monnett, *Tell Them We Are Going Home*, 9–10.
18 James S. Hastings to the Commissioner of Indian Affairs, August 10, 1876, in *Report of the {Secretary of the Interior}*, 44th Congress, 2nd session, House Ex. Doc. 1 part 5, 1877, 437.

19 Hoig, *Perilous Pursuit*, 196.
20 *New York Tribune* (April 23, 1877), as quoted in Hoig, *Perilous Pursuit*, 21.
21 Hoig, *Perilous Pursuit*, 22–23; Monnett, *Tell Them We Are Going Home*, 12.
22 U.S. Census Bureau, "Resident Population of Nebraska, 1860–2000"; U.S. Census Bureau, "Resident Population of Kansas, 1860–2000."
23 *Ecoregions of Kansas and Nebraska*.
24 Killsback, "The Legacy of Little Wolf," 100 [quote]; Monnett, *Tell Them We Are Going Home*, 39–40; Stands in Timber and Liberty, *Cheyenne Memories*, 232; Hoig, *Perilous Pursuit*, 25, 27.
25 *Ecoregions of Kansas and Nebraska*; Hufsmith, *The Wyoming Lynching of Cattle Kate*, 36.
26 Hufsmith, *The Wyoming Lynching of Cattle Kate*, 35; Keppel, Grey North, Ontario, 1871 Census of Canada.
27 "Canadian Farmers Hard Up," (Lawrence, KS) *Spirit of Kansas* (May 24, 1877): 4; Tri-Weekly Mail & Hack Line advertisement, *Osborn County (KS) Farmer* (December 28, 1877): 1.
28 Lew-Williams, *The Chinese Must Go*, 45; Sinn, *Pacific Crossing*, 248; Ngai, *The Chinese Question*, 149.
29 Widdis, "Anglo Canadians," *Encyclopedia of the Great Plains*.
30 "Contest Notice," U.S. Land Office, Kirwin, Kansas, *Smith County (KS) Pioneer* (April 14, 1877): 2; Hufsmith, *The Wyoming Lynching of Cattle Kate*, 36.
31 History of Seward County, as transcribed in Buller and Franz, "Breaking Prairie," January 8, 2017, Buller Time.
32 Hufsmith, *The Wyoming Lynching of Cattle Kate*, 38–39; Smith Center, Kansas, 1880 Federal Census; "Local Items," *Smith County (KS) Pioneer* (September 29, 1877): 1.

Chapter 25

1 Wild Hog as quoted in Hoig, *Perilous Pursuit*, 47.
2 Monnett, *Tell Them We Are Going Home*, 31; Hoig, *Perilous Pursuit*, 37, 39.
3 Leiker and Powers, *The Northern Cheyenne Exodus in History and Memory*, 43.
4 Monnett, "'My Heart Now Has Become Changed,'" 51; Little Wolf to Grinnell, in Monnett, *Tell Them We Are Going Home*, 37; Hoig, *Perilous Pursuit*, 33, 45; Wooden Leg, as quoted in Monnett, *Tell Them We Are Going Home*, 38 [quote].
5 Monnett, *Tell Them We Are Going Home*, 27, 29; Leiker and Powers, *The Northern Cheyenne Exodus in History and Memory*, 39; Hoig, *Perilous Pursuit*, 36.
6 Killsback, "The Legacy of Little Wolf," 100; Monnett, *Tell Them We Are Going Home*, 39–40; Stands in Timber and Liberty, *Cheyenne Memories*, 232; Hoig, *Perilous Pursuit*, 48.
7 Hoig, *Perilous Pursuit*, 49, 51.
8 Hyde, *Born of Lakes and Plains*, 286–87, 299–300.
9 Miles Testimony, *Report, Select Committee on the Removal of the Northern Cheyennes, &c.*, 60; Monnett, *Tell Them We Are Going Home*, 40; Hoig, *Perilous Pursuit*, 48.
10 Miles Testimony, *Report, Select Committee on the Removal of the Northern Cheyennes, &c.*, 60–61.
11 List of weapons confiscated from Little Wolf's band, *Report, Select Committee on the Removal of the Northern Cheyennes, &c.*, Appendix, 249; Hoig, *Perilous Pursuit*, 56.

12 Killsback, "The Legacy of Little Wolf," 100; Hoig, *Perilous Pursuit*, 53; Monnett, *Tell Them We Are Going Home*, 26, 42; Testimony of J. K. Mizner, *Report, Select Committee on the Removal of the Northern Cheyennes, &c.*, 112.
13 Testimony of J. K. Mizner, *Report, Select Committee on the Removal of the Northern Cheyennes, &c.*, 112.
14 Hoig, *Perilous Pursuit*, 54; Monnett, "'My Heart Now Has Become Changed,'" 51.
15 Hoig, *Perilous Pursuit*, 54; John D. Miles to E. A. Hayt [commissioner of Indian Affairs], September 10, 1878, in *Report, Select Committee on the Removal of the Northern Cheyennes, &c.*, Appendix, 239; Monnett, *Tell Them We Are Going Home*, 43; Monnett, "'My Heart Now Has Become Changed,'" 51.
16 Monnett, *Tell Them We Are Going Home*, 42, 51, 52–53; Killsback, "The Legacy of Little Wolf," 100; Monnett, "'My Heart Now Has Become Changed,'" 51; Hoig, *Perilous Pursuit*, 55.
17 Tangle Hair, as quoted in Killsback, "The Legacy of Little Wolf," 100; Hoig, *Perilous Pursuit*, 55.
18 Hoig, *Perilous Pursuit*, 54–55; Monnett, *Tell Them We Are Going Home*, 45.
19 Little Chief Testimony, *Report, Select Committee on the Removal of the Northern Cheyennes, &c.*, 20.
20 Monnett, *Tell Them We Are Going Home*, 45, 49.
21 Phil Sheridan, as quoted in Hoig, *Perilous Pursuit*, 57.
22 Little Wolf, as quoted in Monnett, *Tell Them We Are Going Home*, 53.
23 Chalk and Little Wolf quoted in Monnett, *Tell Them We Are Going Home*, 53–54; Hoig, *Perilous Pursuit*, 68.
24 "The Great Cheyenne Chase," *Ford County Globe* (January 7, 1879), as quoted in Hoig, *Perilous Pursuit*, 70.
25 John D. Miles, Monthly Report, Cheyenne and Arapaho Agency, September 30, 1880, in *Report, Select Committee on the Removal of the Northern Cheyennes, &c.*, Appendix, 240; Monnett, *Tell Them We Are Going Home*, 55; Hoig, *Perilous Pursuit*, 70.
26 Gunther Court-Martial Proceedings, as quoted in Hoig, *Perilous Pursuit*, 82.
27 Monnett, *Tell Them We Are Going Home*, 60; *Report, Select Committee on the Removal of the Northern Cheyennes, &c.*, Appendix, 240.
28 Killsback, "The Legacy of Little Wolf," 101; Hoig, *Perilous Pursuit*, 101; Monnett, *Tell Them We Are Going Home*, 63–66.
29 Leiker and Powers, *The Northern Cheyenne Exodus in History and Memory*, 57; Hoig, *Perilous Pursuit*, 114, 119.
30 Little Wolf, as quoted in Killsback, "The Legacy of Little Wolf," 101; Monnett, "'My Heart Now Has Become Changed,'" 52; Monnett, *Tell Them We Are Going Home*, 71.
31 Lieutenant W. E. Wilder, as quoted in Monnett, *Tell Them We Are Going Home*, 70–71.
32 Monnett, *Tell Them We Are Going Home*, 72–73; Leiker and Powers, *The Northern Cheyenne Exodus in History and Memory*, 59; Hoig, *Perilous Pursuit*, 123, 125.
33 Monnett, *Tell Them We Are Going Home*, 58–60, 75–79; Hoig, *Perilous Pursuit*, 91, 139.
34 Little Wolf, as quoted in Monnett, *Tell Them We Are Going Home*, 92; Leiker and Powers, *The Northern Cheyenne Exodus in History and Memory*, 61; Hoig, *Perilous Pursuit*, 139.
35 "The Bloody Cheyennes," *Parsons (KS) Eclipse* (October 17, 1878): 1.
36 As quoted in Monnett, *Tell Them We Are Going Home*, 89; Hoig, *Perilous Pursuit*, 106.
37 Hoig, *Perilous Pursuit*, 135; Monnett, *Tell Them We Are Going Home*, 105.

38 Dull Knife's words according to Little Wolf, in Hoig, *Perilous Pursuit*, 151; Monnett, *Tell Them We Are Going Home*, 106.
39 Little Wolf, as quoted in Monnett, *Tell Them We Are Going Home*, 110; Testimony of Old Crow, on August 19, 1879, at Fort Reno, Indian Territory, in *Report, Select Committee on the Removal of the Northern Cheyennes, &c.*, 23; Dusenberry, "The Northern Cheyenne," 29.
40 Hoig, *Perilous Pursuit*, 151; Leiker and Powers, *The Northern Cheyenne Exodus in History and Memory*, 68.
41 John Bourke, as quoted in Leiker and Powers, *The Northern Cheyenne Exodus in History and Memory*, 69–70.
42 Hoig, *Perilous Pursuit*, 147, 149, 151–52; Monnett, *Tell Them We Are Going Home*, 108, 110, 162; Leiker and Powers, *The Northern Cheyenne Exodus in History and Memory*, 71.
43 Dusenberry, "The Northern Cheyenne," 29–30; Monnett, "'My Heart Now Has Become Changed,'" 54; *Report, Select Committee on the Removal of the Northern Cheyennes, &c.*, 18.
44 Benton et al., *The White River Badlands: Geology and Paleontology*; Nelson, *Saving Yellowstone*, 3–4.
45 Killsback, "The Legacy of Little Wolf," 102; Monnett, *Tell Them We Are Going Home*, 164.
46 Report of Lt. W. P. Clark, from Fort Keogh, April 2, 1879, in *Report, Select Committee on the Removal of the Northern Cheyennes, &c.*, Appendix, 248; Monnett, *Tell Them We Are Going Home*, 167; Hoig, *Perilous Pursuit*, 197–99.
47 Report of Lt. W. P. Clark, from Fort Keogh, April 2, 1879, *Report, Select Committee on the Removal of the Northern Cheyennes, &c.*, Appendix, 246–48. I have changed the wording slightly from the original, for the purposes of narration.
48 Using multiple strategies to respond to American incursions and defend homelands was common among Indigenous leaders. For an example from Cherokee Nation, see Nagle, *By the Fire We Carry*, 26.
49 Report of Lt. W. P. Clark, from Fort Keogh, April 2, 1879, *Report, Select Committee on the Removal of the Northern Cheyennes, &c.*, Appendix, 248–49; Hoig, *Perilous Pursuit*, 200.
50 Report of Lt. W. P. Clark, from Fort Keogh, April 2, 1879, *Report, Select Committee on the Removal of the Northern Cheyennes, &c.*, Appendix, 249.
51 Laton Alton Huffman was the photographer. L. A. Huffman Photographic Collection, Montana Historical Society.
52 Monnett, *Tell Them We Are Going Home*, 169; *Report, Select Committee on the Removal of the Northern Cheyennes, &c.*, Appendix, 250; Hermann Stieffel, "Fort Keogh, Montana Territory," ca. 1877–81, watercolor on paper, Smithsonian American Art Museum.
53 Monnett, *Tell Them We Are Going Home*, 169; Hoig, *Perilous Pursuit*, 201; *Report, Select Committee on the Removal of the Northern Cheyennes, &c.*, Appendix, 250.
54 Allison, "Beyond the Violence," 94; Monnett, *Tell Them We Are Going Home*, 203.
55 Little Wolf to the U.S. president, as quoted in Hoig, *Perilous Pursuit*, 202.

Chapter 26

1 "The Restless Cheyennes," *Chicago Times*, reprinted in *Kansas City Journal* (October 1, 1878): 3; "Lurking Lo," *Leavenworth (Kansas) Times* (October 1, 1878): 4; "The Indian Question," *Louisville (KY) Courier-Journal* (December 3, 1878): 1; "The Cheyennes," *Omaha Herald* (April 11, 1879): 8; "The Indian Raid," *Lawrence (Kansas) Standard* (October 4, 1878): 4.

NOTES 381

2 Sandweiss, "John Gast, American Progress, 1872," in Picturing United States History.
3 "Hanging," *Lewiston Daily Teller* (November 21, 1879): 2 [quote]; "Chinamen Hanged at Warrens," *Idaho Statesman* (November 27, 1879): 1.
4 "Hanging," *Lewiston Daily Teller* (November 21, 1879): 2; "Chinamen Hanged at Warrens," *Idaho Statesman* (November 27, 1879): 1.
5 "CHINESE INFLUX," *(Idaho City) Idaho World* (May 13, 1869): 2; George, "The Chinese in California," *New York Tribune* (1869), as quoted in Ngai, *The Chinese Question*, 141–42.
6 Lew-Williams, *The Chinese Must Go*, 35, 45; Sinn, *Pacific Crossing*, 248, 251; Ngai, *The Chinese Question*, 139, 149; Paddison, *American Heathens*, 42, 51; Chang, "Chinese Railroad Workers and the US Transcontinental Railroad in Global Perspective," in Chang and Fisher Fishkin, eds., *The Chinese and the Iron Road*, 40.
7 Paddison, *American Heathens*, 3–5, 143; Lew-Williams, *The Chinese Must Go*, 40.
8 Washington Township, Idaho County, Idaho, 1880 Federal Census; Wegars, *Polly Bemis*, 1, 35.
9 Washington Township, Idaho County, Idaho, 1880 Federal Census; Wegars, *Polly Bemis*, 1, 9, 12, 14, 15–16, 28–29, 39.
10 Wegars, *Polly Bemis*, 37.
11 "Woman of 70 Sees Railway First Time," *Idaho County Free Press* (August 16, 1923): 1.
12 Washington Township, Idaho County, Idaho, 1880 Federal Census; "Polly Bemis Has Big Time," 5.
13 "Polly Bemis Has Big Time," 5.
14 "Woman of 70 Sees Railway First Time," 1.
15 Ngai, *The Chinese Question*, 153; Lew-Williams, *The Chinese Must Go*, 5, 10, 87; Sinn, *Pacific Crossing*, 261.
16 As quoted in Paddison, *American Heathens*, 152.
17 "The Edmunds Act," 1882; "Text of the Edmunds Act"; Park, *American Zion*, 149, 152–53.
18 Lew-Williams, *The Chinese Must Go*, 75.
19 *Lewiston (ID) Daily Teller* (June 8, 1882): 3 and (June 15, 1882): 3.
20 *Lewiston (ID) Daily Teller* (July 7, 1882): 3.
21 Lew-Williams, *The Chinese Must Go*, 86–87; 91; 1885 Warren's population statistics cited in Wegars, *Polly Bemis*, 37.
22 Hufsmith, *The Wyoming Lynching of Cattle Kate*, 38–39.
23 Hufsmith, *The Wyoming Lynching of Cattle Kate*, 39.
24 Andreas, *History of the State of Nebraska*.
25 Cather, *My Antonía*, 8; MacGregor, "Explore the World of Willa Cather in Her Nebraska Hometown."
26 Hufsmith, *The Wyoming Lynching of Cattle Kate*, 40; Pfabe, "Divorce in Seward County, Nebraska, 1869–1906," 151–52, 155–56.
27 Hufsmith, *The Wyoming Lynching of Cattle Kate*, 54–55.
28 Allison, "Beyond the Violence," 97; Belgrad, "'Power's Larger Meaning,'" 167; McFerrin and Wills, "High Noon on the Western Range," 71–72; Eaton, "The Wyoming Stock Growers Association's Treatment of Nonmember Cattlemen during the 1880s," 71.
29 Hufsmith, *The Wyoming Lynching of Cattle Kate*, 54–55.
30 Hufsmith, *The Wyoming Lynching of Cattle Kate*, 131, 59, 60–61, 63, 65.

31 Hufsmith, *The Wyoming Lynching of Cattle Kate*, 80–81, 84, 92–94.
32 *Ecoregions of Wyoming*; "The Sagebrush Sesa is Vanishing"; Hufsmith, *The Wyoming Lynching of Cattle Kate*, 101.
33 Lee and Nolan, "Along the Oregon Trail," 26–27; *Millington Journal* (June 23, 1862): 114.
34 John H. Fales and Frank O. Filbey testimonies in Hufsmith, *The Wyoming Lynching of Cattle Kate*, 143, 147.

Chapter 27

1 Hufsmith, *The Wyoming Lynching of Cattle Kate*, 40.
2 Hufsmith, *The Wyoming Lynching of Cattle Kate*, 161, 163, 136.
3 John H. Fales testimony and estate auction records, as quoted in quoted in Hufsmith, *The Wyoming Lynching of Cattle Kate*, 143, 249.
4 Thomas Watson newspaper interview, as quoted in Hufsmith, *The Wyoming Lynching of Cattle Kate*, 252; Hufsmith, *The Wyoming Lynching of Cattle Kate*, 174.
5 Belgrad, "'Power's Larger Meaning,'" 171; McFerrin and Wills, "High Noon on the Western Range," 71; Hufsmith, *The Wyoming Lynching of Cattle Kate*, 156.
6 Palomo Acosta and Winegarten, *Las Tejanas*, 14–19.
7 Lovell, "Dashing for America"; Dant, *Losing Eden*, 143–44.
8 Eliza Putnam Heaton, "The Ranch Woman," *Portland (OR) Morning Oregonian* (May 29, 1887): 3; Jameson, "Women as Workers, Women as Civilizers: True Womanhood in the American West," in *The Women's West*, 146; Armitage, "Through Women's Eyes: A New View of the West," in *The Women's West*, 13.
9 Theodore Roosevelt speech, as quoted in Heaton, "The Ranch Woman," 3; J. M. T. Partello, "Western Heroines," *Cincinnati Enquirer* (April 14, 1888): 11.
10 Jensen, "Butter Making and Economic Development," 813–14; *Neligh (NE) Leader* (September 16, 1887): 4.
11 Clark, "The 1887 Blizzard That Changed the American Frontier Forever."
12 "The Terror of the Plains: A Wild Western Blizzard and its Fearful Destructiveness," *Winnemucca, NV. Silver State* (January 21, 1887): 4.
13 Theodore Roosevelt to Anna Roosevelt, April 16, 1887, Theodore Roosevelt Collection, MS Am 1834 (229), Harvard College Library, Cambridge, Massachusetts.
14 Belgrad, "'Power's Larger Meaning,'" footnote 32, pp. 165 and 171; Sanderson, "'We Were All Trespassers,'" 66; Allison, "Beyond the Violence," 99; Clark, "The 1887 Blizzard That Changed the American Frontier Forever"; Stands in Timber and Liberty, *Cheyenne Memories*, 255.
15 Nelson Miles testimony, in *Report, Select Committee on the Removal of the Northern Cheyennes, &c.*, 13.
16 Nelson Miles testimony, in *Report, Select Committee on the Removal of the Northern Cheyennes, &c.*, 13, 205.
17 Allison, "Beyond the Violence," 99.
18 Wooden Leg quoted in Killsback, "The Legacy of Little Wolf," 103, 105. This crime was uncommon but not unheard of in Northern Cheyenne communities. Little Wolf witnessed another such killing in 1854. Grinnell, *The Cheyenne Indians*, vol. I, pp. 351, 356.
19 Chester A. Arthur, Executive Order—Northern Cheyenne Reserve, November 26, 1884.

20 Two Moons quoted in Allison, "Beyond the Violence," 101.
21 An Act to Provide for the Allotment of Lands in Severalty to Indians on the Various Reservations (The Dawes Act), February 8, 1887; Nagle, *By the Fire We Carry*, 139–40.
22 "Warrens Notes," *(Grangeville) Idaho County Free Press* (September 2, 1887): 1; N.B.W., letter from Warrens, May 18, 1887, *Idaho County Free Press* (June 3, 1887): 4; Wegars, *Polly Bemis*, 33.
23 "Polly Bemis Has Big Time," 5; Wegars, *Polly Bemis*, 32.
24 Lew-Williams, *The Chinese Must Go*, 180; *Idaho County Free Press* (May 20, 1887): 3, (June 24, 1887): 1, (July 1, 1887): 4, and (June 10, 1877): 4; "Warrens Notes," *Idaho County Free Press* (September 2, 1887): 1.
25 "The Wagon Road," *Idaho County Free Press* (December 2, 1877): 4.
26 Lew-Williams, *The Chinese Must Go*, 171, 185–86; Sinn, *Pacific Crossing*, 261.
27 Lew-Williams, *The Chinese Must Go*, 182, 188, 190.
28 Wegars, *Polly Bemis*, 34, 38.
29 Bertha Long account, as quoted in Wegars, *Polly Bemis*, 39.

Chapter 28

1 Hufsmith, *The Wyoming Lynching of Cattle Kate*, 146, 150, 155.
2 McFerrin and Wills, "High Noon on the Western Range," 74; Eaton, "The Wyoming Stock Growers Association's Treatment of Nonmember Cattlemen during the 1880s," 71–72, 76; Hufsmith, *The Wyoming Lynching of Cattle Kate*, 184.
3 Hufsmith, *The Wyoming Lynching of Cattle Kate*, 182, 144–45, 40; Thomas Watson interview, as quoted in Hufsmith, *The Wyoming Lynching of Cattle Kate*, 253.
4 Hufsmith, *The Wyoming Lynching of Cattle Kate*, 101, 115–17, 136.
5 Hufsmith, *The Wyoming Lynching of Cattle Kate*, 144, 163, 181.
6 Hufsmith, *The Wyoming Lynching of Cattle Kate*, 98, 139, 151; McFerrin and Wills, "High Noon on the Western Range," 70–71; Richardson, *How the South Won the Civil War*, 97–99.
7 Hufsmith, *The Wyoming Lynching of Cattle Kate*, 174–75.
8 Jim Averell letter to the *Casper Weekly Mail* (February 7, 1889): 1, as transcribed in Hufsmith, *The Wyoming Lynching of Cattle Kate*, 171.
9 Hufsmith, *The Wyoming Lynching of Cattle Kate*, 174.
10 Hufsmith, *The Wyoming Lynching of Cattle Kate*, 187.
11 Hufsmith, *The Wyoming Lynching of Cattle Kate*, 179, 180.
12 Hufsmith, *The Wyoming Lynching of Cattle Kate*, 180, 110–12, 103-4, 122–23.
13 Hufsmith, *The Wyoming Lynching of Cattle Kate*, 181–82.
14 Hufsmith, *The Wyoming Lynching of Cattle Kate*, 182.
15 The chronology and details of these events were reconstructed from coroner's inquest testimony and other witness statements, as summarized in Hufsmith, *The Wyoming Lynching of Cattle Kate*, 181-204.
16 "The Cattle Queen's Lynching.... —The Actual Facts," *(Washington, D.C.) Evening Star* (July 25, 1889): 1; *Portland (OR) Oregonian* (July 26, 1889): 3; Hufsmith, *The Wyoming Lynching of Cattle Kate*, 205–8.
17 "A Double Lynching!" *Cheyenne Daily Leader* (July 23, 1889): 3; Hufsmith, *The Wyoming Lynching of Cattle Kate*, 214.

18 Hufsmith, *The Wyoming Lynching of Cattle Kate*, 211; *Nashville (TN) Banner* (July 25, 1889): 1; *Chicago Inter-Ocean* (July 24, 1889): 7; *Portland (OR) Oregonian* (July 26, 1889): 3.
19 *St. Joseph (Michigan) Saturday Herald* (July 27, 1889): 1; *(Washington, D.C.) Evening Star* (July 25, 1889): 1; *Salt Lake Tribune* (July 27, 1889), as quoted in Hufsmith, *The Wyoming Lynching of Cattle Kate*, 225.
20 (Akron, Ohio) *Summit County Beacon* (July 24, 1889): 6; "The Range Queen: Her Tragic Death at the Hands of a Wyoming Mob," *(Leadville, CO) Carbonate Chronicle* (July 29, 1889): 7; "Range Thieves Skipping Out," *Rocky Mountain News* (November 17, 1889): 1.
21 Watson to his family [letter printed in Lebanon newspaper], as quoted in Hufsmith, *The Wyoming Lynching of Cattle Kate*, 253; Thomas Watson interview with the *Rock Springs Independent* (1889), as quoted in Hufsmith, *The Wyoming Lynching of Cattle Kate*, 262; Ngai, *The Chinese Question*, 158.
22 Wister as quoted in Hufsmith, *The Wyoming Lynching of Cattle Kate*, 264.
23 "Indictment Doubtful," *Cheyenne Daily Leader* (September 29, 1889): 3; Hufsmith, *The Wyoming Lynching of Cattle Kate*, 266, 278; *Aspen (CO) Daily Chronicle* (October 1, 1889): 1; *Colorado Daily Chieftain* (October 26, 1889): 4; "Lynchers of the Cattle Queen. No Indictments Found, the only Witness Having Disappeared," *Chicago Inter Ocean* (October 22, 1889): 9.
24 Armitage, "Through Women's Eyes: A New View of the West," Graulich, "Violence Against Women: Power Dynamics in Literature of the Western Family," Harris, "Homesteading in Northeastern Colorado, 1873-1920: Sex Roles and Women's Experience," and Jameson, "Women as Workers, Women as Civilizers: True Womanhood in the American West," in *The Women's West*, ed. Armitage and Jameson, 12, 14-15, 113-14, 165, 167, 147.

Chapter 29

1 Killsback, "Crowns of Honor," 16-17; Allison, "Beyond the Violence," 103.
2 "What Shall be Done?" *Helena (MT) Independent-Record* (June 27, 1890): 6; Schrems, "The Northern Cheyennes and the Fight for Cultural Sovereignty," 29; Allison, "Beyond the Violence," 103.
3 Killsback, "Crowns of Honor," 16-17; "He Was Only a Boy," *Helena (MT) Independent-Record* (September 14, 1890): 8.
4 "The Chief Dies," *Great Falls (MT) Daily Leader* (September 17, 1890): 1; "From Miles City," *Anaconda (MT) Standard* (September 17, 1890): 1.
5 Killsback, "Crowns of Honor," 16-17; "From Miles City," 1.
6 "From Miles City," 1.
7 "From Miles City," 1; Killsback, "Crowns of Honor," 17; Allison, "Beyond the Violence," 103.
8 Killsback, "Crowns of Honor," 17; Allison, "Beyond the Violence," 103.
9 Trabert and Hollenback, *Archaeological Narratives of the Northern Great Plains*, 176; Smoak, *Ghost Dances and Identity*, 153, 165; Gage, *We Do Not Want the Gates Closed Between Us*, 147; Warren, *God's Red Son*.
10 Porcupine account, as quoted in Gage, *We Do Not Want the Gates Closed Between Us*, 158.
11 Stands in Timber and Liberty, *Cheyenne Memories*, 257-58; Gage, *We Do Not Want the Gates Closed Between Us*, 147-48, 202; Smoak, *Ghost Dances and Identity*, 165; Dant, *Losing Eden*, 148.

12 Stands in Timber and Liberty, *Cheyenne Memories*, 261–62; Smoak, *Ghost Dances and Identity*, 173; Gage, *We Do Not Want the Gates Closed Between Us*, 238; Gage, *We Do Not Want the Gates Closed Between Us*, 245.
13 Killsback, "The Legacy of Little Wolf," 104; Monnett, *Tell Them We Are Going Home*, 198.
14 Stands in Timber and Liberty, *Cheyenne Memories*, 256; Dusenberry, "The Northern Cheyenne," 39; Allison, "Beyond the Violence," 105.
15 Author interview with Eugene Fisher, grandson of Little Wolf, September 11, 1954, as quoted in Dusenberry, "The Northern Cheyenne," 40.
16 *Salt Lake Tribune* (July 17, 1887): 4.
17 "Col. Hollister's House," illustration in "Chronology of the Year," *Salt Lake Tribune* (January 1, 1891): 31; Salt Lake City, US City Directory, 1893, https://www.ancestry.com; Galli, "Building Zion," 123–24.
18 Salt Lake City Chamber of Commerce Resolution, *Salt Lake Tribune* (February 14, 1892): 6; "In Memoriam," *Salt Lake Tribune* (February 14, 1892): 5; "Death of Colonel Hollister," *Salt Lake Tribune* (February 13, 1892): 4.
19 "Monster Rally. The Liberals Turn Out to Rouse the Town," *Salt Lake Tribune* (August 1, 1891): 5.
20 *Salt Lake City Herald* (February 13, 1892): 2; *Cleveland Plain Dealer* (February 14, 1892): 4.
21 "Death of Colonel Hollister," *Salt Lake Tribune* (February 13, 1892): 4.
22 Salt Lake City Chamber of Commerce Resolution, 6; "In Memoriam," 5; Nicholas Paul to the editors of the *Salt Lake Tribune* (February 15, 1892, printed February 18, 1892): 3; "University Club Banquet," *Salt Lake Tribune* (February 20, 1892): 2; New West Education Commission, *Salt Lake Tribune* (March 4, 1892): 8; "Hollister and Stanley: How and When the Late O.J. Hollister Met the Great Explorer," *Salt Lake Tribune* (May 8, 1892): 6.
23 Carrie Hollister donated Ovando's Colorado newspaper collection to the State Historical and Natural History Society in 1908. *Central City (CO) Gilpin Observer* (March 26, 1908): 6.
24 "Col. Hollister's Funeral," *Salt Lake Tribune* (February 16, 1892): 5.
25 *Rocky Mountain News* (February 13, 1892): 4.
26 Park, *American Zion*, 173, 177.
27 "Exclusion of Chinese," *The (Boise) Idaho Statesman* (May 3, 1892): 1; Wegars, *Polly Bemis*, 52, 55; Ngai, *The Chinese Question*, 161; Lee, "The Chinese Exclusion Example," 54; Johnson, *The Middle Kingdom*, 45.
28 Johnson, *The Middle Kingdom*, 47.
29 Ingersoll, in Ingersoll and Geary, "Should the Chinese Be Excluded?" (1893), 54, 55 [quote].
30 Ingersoll and Geary, "Should the Chinese Be Excluded?" (1893), 52.
31 Johnson, *The Middle Kingdom*, 52, 54; Hernández, *City of Inmates*, 73–74, 76–77, 78.
32 Johnson, *The Middle Kingdom*, 56; Hernández, *City of Inmates*, 73.
33 Wegars, *Polly Bemis*, 51.
34 Wegars, *Polly Bemis*, 41–43.
35 Gizycka, "Diary on the Salmon River Part II," 278.
36 Wegars, *Polly Bemis*, 52; John A. Hanson photograph of Polly Bemis, April 1894, John A. Hanson Photographs, Idaho State Archives.

37 John A. Hanson, "Warrens, Views," 1894, John A. Hanson Photographs, Idaho State Archives.
38 Wegars, *Polly Bemis*, 29, 56; Civil Laws, Title II: Marriage, Chapter 1, Section 2425, *The Revised Statutes of Idaho Territory*, 30.
39 Wegars, *Polly Bemis*, 55.
40 Wegars, *Polly Bemis*, 59–60; Johnson, *The Middle Kingdom*, 65; Hernández, *City of Inmates*, 87.
41 Wegars, *Polly Bemis*, 60–61.
42 Wegars, *Polly Bemis*, 61–62.

Chapter 30

1 On the American conquest and annexation of the Kingdom of Hawai'i, see Coffman, *Nation Within*.
2 Roosevelt, *The Rough Riders*, 19.
3 Roosevelt, *The Rough Riders*, 19–20.
4 Roosevelt, "The Strenuous Life," 6, 10.
5 Allison, "Beyond the Violence," 93, 105–6; Schrems, "The Northern Cheyennes and the Fight for Cultural Sovereignty," 32, 33; Nagle, *By the Fire We Carry*, 98.
6 Wooden Leg account, as quoted in Killsback, 105; Stands in Timber and Liberty, *Cheyenne Memories*, 54–55.
7 Monnett, *Tell Them We Are Going Home*, 198.
8 Wooden Leg account, in Killsback, 105; Stands in Timber and Liberty, *Cheyenne Memories*, 123; Grinnell, *The Cheyenne Indians*, vol. 2, p. 160.
9 Wegars, *Polly Bemis*, 82–83.
10 We know about Polly's everyday activities and ranch products from the detailed diary of Charlie Shepp, who wrote and preserved records of their interactions for almost thirty years. Charlie Shepp diary, as transcribed and synopsized in Wegars, *Polly Bemis*, 74–282.
11 Shepp Diary, in Wegars, *Polly Bemis*, 74, 79.
12 Shepp Diary, in Wegars, *Polly Bemis*, 205.
13 Shepp Diary, in Wegars, *Polly Bemis*, 78–79, 152, 157, 173, 191, 199; Gizycka, "Diary on the Salmon River: Part II," 278. It is possible that this was the same Ah Kan who owned part of Ah Jake ranch and had sold it to Charlie.
14 Shepp Diary, in Wegars, *Polly Bemis*, 95, 152, 161, 173.
15 Shepp Diary, in Wegars, *Polly Bemis*, 146, 179–80, 269.
16 Shepp Diary, in Wegars, *Polly Bemis*, 76, 157, 100.
17 Shepp Diary, in Wegars, *Polly Bemis*, 106, 163.
18 Shepp Diary, in Wegars, *Polly Bemis*, 120, 144, 190–91, 240–41.
19 Gizycka, "Diary on the Salmon River: Part II," 278.
20 "Riggins, Idaho," Salmon River Chamber of Commerce; "Woman of 70 Sees Railway First Time," 1.
21 *Sunday Oregonian* (November 5, 1933): 41.
22 Gizycka, "Diary on the Salmon River: Part II," 278.
23 Shepp Diary, August 16, 1922, in Wegars, *Polly Bemis*, 203; Wegars, *Polly Bemis*, 205.
24 Shepp Diary, in Wegars, *Polly Bemis*, 207; Wegars, photograph of Charlie Bemis grave site, in Wegars, *Polly Bemis*, 209; "Woman of 70 Sees Railway First Time," 1.

25 Wegars, *Polly Bemis*, 209–10, 212–17.
26 "Woman of 70 Sees Railway First Time," 1; Wegars, *Polly Bemis*, 217, 224.
27 "Woman of 70 Sees Railway First Time," 1.
28 "Anson Holmes Has Contract," *Grangeville Globe* (June 23, 1921): 1; "Woman of 70 Sees Railway First Time," 1.
29 "Polly Bemis Has Big Time on Visit to the State Capital," 1.
30 "Polly Bemis of Warren's Diggins Sees City's Sights for First Time," (Boise, ID) *Statesman* (August 4, 1924): 2; reprinted in "Polly Bemis Has Big Time," 1.
31 "Polly Bemis of Warren's Diggins," (Boise, ID) *Statesman* (August 4, 1924): 2; reprinted in "Polly Bemis Has Big Time," 1.
32 Shepp Diary, September 1925, in Wegars, *Polly Bemis*, 244.
33 Shepp Diary in Wegars, *Polly Bemis*, 277; Wegars, *Polly Bemis*, 280, 282.
34 Polly Bemis Death Certificate, Idaho Death Records, 1890–1971, https://www.ancestry.com; *Spokesman-Review* (November 9, 1933): 8; Prairie View Cemetery Inscriptions, Grangeville, Idaho, https://www.ancestry.com; *Sunday Oregonian* (November 5, 1933): 41.

Epilogue

1 "Idaho Chinese Woman Awaits Time to Rejoin Ancestors," *(Boise) Idaho Statesman* (May 8, 1932): 17.
2 McCunn, "Reclaiming Polly Bemis," 76–77.
3 *Sacramento Union* (November 11, 1933): 4; "Colorful Life Comes to End," *Spokesman (Spokane, WA) Review* (November 7, 1933): 10. "Colorful Life" was reprinted in *Idaho Statesman* (November 7, 1933): 2, *Spokesman-Review* (November 7, 1933): 10, *Indianapolis Star* (November 7, 1933): 9, and *Salt Lake Tribune* (November 8, 1933): 15. It was excerpted in *LA Times* (November 7, 1933): 3 and in the *(Washington, D.C.) Evening Star* (November 7, 1933): 26.
4 Coues, *The History of the Lewis and Clark Expedition*, 1893; Jager, *Malinche, Pocahontas, and Sacagawea*, 254.
5 Jager, *Malinche, Pocahontas, and Sacagawea*, 251; Vettel-Becker, "Sacagawea and Son," 34–35.
6 Jager, *Malinche, Pocahontas, and Sacagawea*, 158, 249; Dippie, "The Imagery of Sacagawea," Jackson Hole History.
7 Jager, *Malinche, Pocahontas, and Sacagawea*, 249–50; Scharff, *Twenty Thousand Roads*, 21; Vettel-Becker, "Sacagawea and Son," 29–32; Mussulman, "The Faces of Sacagawea: Interpretations of an Unknown Image"; "1904 St. Louis World's Fair," St. Louis Art Museum.
8 Slaughter, *Exploring Lewis and Clark*, 92–112; The Sacagawea Project Board of the Mandan, Hidatsa, & Arikara Nation, *Our Story of Eagle Woman, Sacagawea*.
9 Scharff, *Twenty Thousand Roads*, 13, 31, 33.
10 Find a Grave entry, Gravestone of Ella Watson and James Averell.
11 "Emigrant Trail" historical marker, Beckwourth Pass, Plumas County, California. The poem is an excerpt from A. W. Wern, "Love Greetings from the Pioneers of Los Angeles," in *From the Last to the First: A Collection of Beautiful Poems* (Glass Book Binding, 1913), 46.
12 Frank Triplett and Hiram M. Chittenden quoted in DeVoto, Introduction to Beckwourth and Bonner, *The Life and Adventures of James P. Beckwourth*, xx, xxii.

13 Killsback, "The Legacy of Little Wolf," 106.
14 Killsback, "The Legacy of Little Wolf," 106.
15 Works that argue that the far-western theater should be included in the overall narrative of the Civil War include Nelson, *The Three-Cornered War* and Kelman, *A Misplaced Massacre*. For an opposing view, see Gallagher, "One War or Two? The United States Versus Confederates and Indians, 1861–1865."
16 "Utah Pioneer Dead," *Bellingham Herald* (December 4, 1917): 3; Riverside Cemetery [later, Fairmount Cemetery] map, DPL; Senturia, "Fairmount Cemetery as an Outdoor Refuge," June 16, 2020.

BIBLIOGRAPHY

MANUSCRIPT COLLECTIONS

Fray Angélico Chávez History Library, New Mexico History Museum. Santa Fe, New Mexico

Mary Jean Cook Collection
Mauro Montoya collection of New Mexican historical documents, 1709–1949
Alexander Brydie Dyer papers, 1846–48
Teresina Bent Scheurich notebook, 1847
Hiltrud Von Brandt collection of Carl Blumner letters, 1836–1906
Translations of selected provincial journals from the Mexican Archives of New Mexico, 1824–46
Ralph Emerson Twitchell, *The Spanish Archives of New Mexico*. 2 Vols. The Torch Press, 1914

Stephen H. Hart Research Center, History Colorado. Denver, Colorado

Scott J. Anthony Collection, 1862–93
John Evans Collection, 1862–1952
Samuel Mallory Collection, 1860–69
Peter G. Scott Collection, 1870–1930
Charles L. and Mary Melissa Hall Papers, 1855–1907
William Henry Jackson Collection, 1875–1942
George Andrew Jackson Collection, 1859–1928
David Fletcher Spain Collection, 1859
John Lewis Dailey Journal
Pikes Peak Gold Rush Collection
Civil War Collection
Colorado Volunteers: Civil War Collection
Charles Porter, *Account of the Confederate attempt to seize Arizona and New Mexico*

Alfred Cobb Correspondence, 1862
James P. Beckwourth Trial Collection, 1864
Charles L. and Mary Melissa Hall Papers, 1855–1907
George Wakely Photographs
Camp Weld Participants photograph
Charles Stobie Collection, 1865–1928

Western History Collection, Denver Public Library, Denver, Colorado

Calvin Perry Clark Diary
Alonzo Ferdinand Ickis Diary
John Milton Chivington Papers
Charlotte and Anna Ronk Papers, 1856–66
Robert Rizer Papers, 1861–1912
Silas Soule Papers
Riverside [Later, Fairmount] Cemetery Map
Rare Books and Pamphlets Collection

PRINT AND DIGITIZED PRIMARY SOURCES AND GOVERNMENT DOCUMENTS

"An Act to Provide for the Exchange of Lands with the Indians" [The Indian Removal Act], May 28, 1830. https://constitutioncenter.org/the-constitution/historic-document-library/detail/indian-removal-act-1830

"Declaration of Causes [Texas]," February 2, 1861. https://www.tsl.texas.gov/ref/abouttx/secession/2feb1861.html

"Fort Laramie, [Idaho Territory], 1863." In Tom Rea, "Peace, War, Land, and a Funeral: The Fort Laramie Treaty of 1868." Wyoming Historical Society, Wyoming Encyclopedia. https://www.wyohistory.org/encyclopedia/peace-war-land-and-funeral-fort-laramie-treaty-1868

"Gravestone of Ella Watson and James Averell," Natrona County, Wyoming. Find a Grave. https://www.findagrave.com/memorial/57378038/ellen_liddy-watson

"Plan of Main Floor, World's Congress Headquarters, Art Institute of Chicago." From "On the Great Stair of the Art Institute," October 3, 2010. Architecture Chicago Plus. http://arcchicago.blogspot.com/2010/10/on-great-stair-of-art-institute-fear.html

"Story of James P. Beckwourth." *Harper's New Monthly Magazine*, vol. 13 (September 1856): 455–72.

"The Code Noir (The Black Code), May 6, 1687." Égalité, Fraternité: Exploring the French Revolution. https://revolution.chnm.org/d/335/

"The Edmunds Act," 1882, in *The Edmunds Act*. Tribune Printing Company, 1884.

"The Kansas-Nebraska Act," May 30, 1854. https://www.senate.gov/artandhistory/history/minute/Kansas_Nebraska_Act.htm

"The Kansas-Nebraska Bill," speech at Chicago, October 30, 1854. *Frederick Douglass' Paper* (November 24, 1854). https://rbscp.lib.rochester.edu/4400

"Utah Gentiles." http://utahgentiles.com/gentiles/Hollister/Hollister-news1.htm

BIBLIOGRAPHY

Act XII, Laws of Virginia, December 1662. In "Legislating Reproduction and Racial Difference." New York Historical Society. https://wams.nyhistory.org/early-encounters/english-colonies/legislating-reproduction-and-racial-difference/

Allibone's Critical Dictionary of English Literature: A Supplement. British and American Authors. 2 volumes. Edited by John Foster Kirk. J. B. Lippincott, 1891.

An Act Erecting Louisiana into Two Territories, March 26, 1804. *Encyclopedia Virginia.* https://encyclopediavirginia.org/primary-documents/an-act-erecting-louisiana-into-two-territories-and-providing-for-the-temporary-government-thereof-march-26-1804/

An Act to Provide for the Allotment of Lands in Severalty to Indians on the Various Reservations" (The Dawes Act), February 8, 1887. https://www.archives.gov/milestone-documents/dawes-act

Andreas, A.T. *History of the State of Nebraska.* Western Historical Company, 1882. https://www.kancoll.org/books/andreas_ne/

Annual Report of the Commissioner of Indian Affairs, for the Year 1868. Government Printing Office, 1868.

Arizona Organic Act, February 24, 1863. https://history.house.gov/Records-and-Research/Listing/lfp_026/

Arthur, Chester A. Executive Order—Northern Cheyenne Reserve, November 26, 1884. https://www.presidency.ucsb.edu/documents/executive-order-northern-cheyenne-reserve-o

Art Institute of Chicago Board of Trustees. *Annual Report of the Trustees of the Art Institute of Chicago.* Art Institute, June 1893. Archives of the Art Institute of Chicago.

Barcelo Church Records. Compiled by Yolanda R. Chavez, 2016. http://files.usgwarchives.net/nm/santafe/church/barcelo.txt

Beckwourth, James and Thomas D. Bonner. *The Life and Adventures of James P. Beckwourth, Mountaineer, Scout, and Pioneer, and Chief of the Crow Nation of Indians.* Harper & Brothers, 1856.

Bemis, Polly. Death Certificate. Idaho Death Records. https://www.ancestry.com.

Bent, George and Lincoln B. Faller. "Making Medicine against 'White Man's Side of Story': George Bent's Letters to George Hyde." *American Indian Quarterly* 24, no. 1 (Winter 2000): 64–90.

Billon, Frederic L. *Annals of St. Louis, In Its Territorial Days, From 1804 to 1821.* Printed for the author, 1888.

Bourke, John G. *On the Border with Crook.* 2nd ed. Charles Scribner's Sons, 1892.

Bourke, John G. *The Diaries of John Gregory Bourke.* Volume 2. Edited and annotated by Charles M. Robinson. University of North Texas Press, 2005.

Bowles, Samuel. *Across the Continent: A Summer's Journey to the Rocky Mountains, the Mormons, and the Pacific States, with Speaker Colfax.* Samuel Bowles & Co., 1865.

Brevoort, Elias. *New Mexico, Her Natural Resources and Attractions.* E. Brevoort, 1874.

Brewerton, George Douglas. "Incidents of Travel in New Mexico." *Harper's New Monthly Magazine* 8, no. 47 (April 1854): 577–96.

Brewerton, George Douglas. *Overland with Kit Carson: A Narrative of the Old Spanish Trail in '48.* 1930; University of Nebraska Press, 1993.

Brown, William Wells. *Narrative of William W. Brown, a Fugitive Slave, Written by Himself.* 2nd ed. The Anti-Slavery Office, 1848.

Cather, Willa. *My Ántonia.* Houghton Mifflin Co., 1918.

Charles May Sears Biography, Sears Family Papers, Manuscripts & Folklife Archives, Western Kentucky University. www.digitalcommons.wku.edu

Civil War in the Southwest: Recollections of the Sibley Brigade. Edited by Jerry Thompson. Texas A&M University Press, 2001.

Compiled Marriages from Mesa, Arapahoe, and Boulder Counties, 1859–1900, Colorado, United States. https://www.ancestry.com

Compiled Service Records of Volunteer Union Soldiers Who Served in Organizations from the State of Colorado, 1861–1865. https://www.fold3.com

Condition of the Indian Tribes: Report of the Joint Special Committee, Appointed Under Joint Resolution of March 3, 1865 [The Doolittle Report]. Government Printing Office, 1867.

Cordley, Richard. *A History of Lawrence, Kansas; from the Earliest Settlement to the Close of the Rebellion.* E. F. Caldwell, 1895.

Cordley, Richard. *Pioneer Days in Kansas.* The Pilgrim Press, 1903.

Coues, Elliott, ed. *The History of the Lewis and Clark Expedition.* 3 volumes. Francis P. Harper, 1893.

Coy, Owen Cochran. *In the Diggings in 'Forty-nine.* California State Historical Association, 1948.

Custer, George Armstrong. Order and Dispatch Book, August 2, 1874. As transcribed in James D. McLaird and Lesta V. Turchen. "Exploring the Black Hills, 1855–1875: Reports of the Government Expeditions." *South Dakota History* (1974): 280–319.

Douglas, Stephen A. "Speech of Hon. S.A. Douglas, of Illinois, in the United States Senate, March 3, 1854, on Nebraska and Kansas." Sentinel Office, 1854.

Emory, W. H. *Notes of a Military Reconnaissance from Fort Leavenworth, in Missouri, to San Diego, in California.* Wendell and Van Benthuysen, 1848. 30th Congress, 1st Session. Ex. Doc. No. 41.

Field, Matt. *Matt Field on the Santa Fe Trail.* Edited by John E. Sunder. University of Oklahoma Press, 1960.

Fourteenth Amendment to the U.S. Constitution, June 13, 1866 (ratified July 9, 1868). National Archives. https://www.archives.gov/milestone-documents/14th-amendment

Gam, Jee. "The Geary Act: From the Standpoint of a Christian Chinese," 1892. In *Chinese American Voices: From the Gold Rush to the Present.* Edited by Judy Yung, Gordon H. Chang, and Him Mark Lai. University of California Press, 2006.

Gender in the Borderlands: A Frontiers Reader. Edited by Antonia Castañeda. University of Nebraska Press, 2007.

Gibson, George Rutledge. *Journal of a Soldier under Kearny and Doniphan, 1846–1847.* Edited by Ralph P. Bieber. Arthur H. Clark, Co., 1935.

Gizycka, Eleanor. "Diary on the Salmon River: Part II." *Field and Stream* (June 1923): 187–88, 276–80.

Grant, Ulysses S. Second Inaugural Address, March 4, 1873. https://www.nps.gov/articles/000/president-ulysses-s-grant-s-second-inaugural-address-march-4-1873.htm

Greeley, Horace. *An Overland Journey, from New York to San Francisco, in the Summer of 1859.* C. M. Saxton, Barker, & Co., 1860.

Gregg, Josiah. *Commerce of the Prairies; or, the Journal of a Santa Fe Trader.* 2 volumes (1844). Edited by Milo Milton Quaife. The Lakeside Press, 1926.

Grinnell, George Bird. *The Cheyenne Indians: Their History and Ways of Life.* 2 volumes. Yale University Press, 1923.

BIBLIOGRAPHY

Grinnell, George Bird. *The Fighting Cheyennes*. Charles Scribner's Sons, 1915.
Hafen, LeRoy, ed. *Overland Routes to the Gold Fields, 1859, from Contemporary Diaries*. Porcupine Press, 1974.
Hailey, John. *The History of Idaho*. Syms-York Company, 1910.
Hall, Mrs. Frank [Sue Matthews]. "Seventy Years Ago—Recollections of a Trip through the Colorado Mountains with the Colfax Party in 1868," as told to LeRoy R. Hafen. *The Colorado Magazine* 25, no. 5 (September 1938): 161–68.
Henry Siebert & Bros. "Map of the Land Grant of the Kansas Pacific Railroad," 1869. Special Collections, Wichita State University Digitized Maps. https://specialcollections.wichita.edu/collections/maps/
History of the Expedition Under the Command of Captains Lewis and Clark. Edited by Paul Allen and Nicholas Biddle. Philadelphia: Bradford and Inskeep, 1814.
Hollister, Ovando J. *Boldly They Rode: A History of the First Colorado Regiment of Volunteers* (1864). Edited by William Macleod Raine. The Golden Press, 1949.
Hollister, Ovando J. *Life of Schuyler Colfax*. Funk & Wagnalls, 1886.
Hollister, Ovando J. *The Mines of Colorado*. Samuel Bowles & Co., 1867.
Hollister, Ovando J. *The Resources and Attractions of Utah*. Tribune Printing and Publishing Co., 1882.
Hollister, Ovando J. *The Silver Mines of Colorado: A Flying Trip*. Collier and Hall, 1867.
Homestead Act, May 20, 1862. https://www.archives.gov/milestone-documents/homestead-act
Houck, Louis. *A History of Missouri, from the Earliest Explorations and Settlements until the Admission of the State into the Union*, vol. 2. R. R. Donnelley & Sons Co., 1908.
Ingersoll, R. G. and T. J. Geary. "Should the Chinese Be Excluded?" *North American Review* 157 no. 440 (July 1893): 52–67.
Jackson, Andrew. First Annual Message to Congress, December 8, 1829. https://www.presidency.ucsb.edu/documents/first-annual-message-3
Jefferson, Thomas to Meriwether Lewis, October 26, 1806. *Letters of the Lewis and Clark Expedition, With Related Documents, 1783–1854*. Edited by Donald Jackson. University of Illinois Press, 1962.
Jefferson, Thomas to the Wolf [Sheheke] and the People of the Mandan Nation, December 30, 1806. National Archives. https://millercenter.org/the-presidency/presidential-speeches/december-30-1806-address-wolf-and-people-mandan-nation
Jefferson, Thomas. First Inaugural Address, March 4, 1801. https://avalon.law.yale.edu/19th_century/jefinau1.asp
Jefferson, Thomas. Instructions to Meriwether Lewis, June 20, 1803. https://www.monticello.org/thomas-jefferson/louisiana-lewis-clark/preparing-for-the-expedition/jefferson-s-instructions-to-lewis/
Jefferson, Thomas. Second Inaugural Address, March 4, 1805. https://avalon.law.yale.edu/19th_century/jefinau2.as
Jefferson, Thomas. Secret Message to Congress, January 18, 1803. https://www.archives.gov/milestone-documents/jeffersons-secret-message-to-congress
Journals of the Lewis and Clark Expedition. University of Nebraska, Lincoln. https://lewisandclarkjournals.unl.edu
Kelly, Lawrence C. *Navajo Roundup: Selected Correspondence of Kit Carson's Expedition Against the Navajo, 1863–1865*. Pruett Publishing Co., 1970.

Kendall, George W. *Narrative of the Texan Santa Fé Expedition.* Sherwood, Gilbert, and Piper, 1846.

Kennerly, William C. *Persimmon Hill: A Narrative of Old St. Louis and the Far West.* University of Oklahoma Press, 1948.

Kit Carson Home & Museum Guide. Taos, New Mexico.

Lieber, Francis. The Leiber Code, 1863. https://avalon.law.yale.edu/19th_century/lieber.asp#sec2

Luttig, John C. Diary, 1812–1813. Transcription, American Mountain Men Association. https://user.xmission.com/~drudy/mtman/html/Luttig/luttig.html

Magoffin, Susan Shelby. *Down the Santa Fe Trail and Into Mexico: The Diary of Susan Shelby Magoffin, 1846–1847.* Edited by Stella M. Drumm. University of Nebraska Press, 1982.

Marryat, Frank. *Mountains and Molehills; Or, Recollections of a Burnt Journal.* Harper & Brothers, 1855.

Mathews, Washington. "Ethnography and Philology of the Hidatsa Indians." *Plains Anthropologist* 14, no. 45 (1877; August 1969): 3–72.

Medicine Crow, Joseph. *From the Heart of the Crow Country: The Crow Indians' Own Stories.* University of Nebraska Press, 2000.

Message from the President of the United States, July 16, 1876, 44th Congress, 1st Session, Senate Ex. Doc. No. 81.

Millington, Ada. "Journal Kept While Crossing the Great Plains [in 1862] . . . Part II." Edited by Charles G. Clarke. *Southern California Quarterly* 59, no. 2 (Summer 1977): 139–84.

Navajo Stories of the Long Walk Period. Edited by Broderick H. Johnston. Diné College Bookstore/Press, 1973.

Nentvig, Juan. *Rudo Ensayo: A Description of Sonora and Arizona.* Edited by Alberto Pradeau and Robert R. Rasmussen. University of Arizona Press, 1980.

O'Sullivan, John. "Annexation." *United States Magazine and Democratic Review* 17 (New York: July/August 1845): 5–10.

Pacific Railway Act, July 1, 1862. https://www.archives.gov/milestone-documents/pacific-railway-act

Parsons, George Frederic. *The Life and Adventures of James W. Marshall, The Discoverer of Gold in California.* James W. Marshall and W. Burke, 1870.

Pokagon, Simon. "The Red Man's Rebuke," 1893. Edward E. Ayer Collection, Newberry Library Special Collections, Chicago.

Polk, James K. Fourth Annual Message to Congress, December 5, 1848. https://millercenter.org/the-presidency/presidential-speeches/december-5-1848-fourth-annual-message-congress

Prairie View Cemetery Inscriptions. Grangeville, Idaho. https://www.ancestry.com

Raymond, Rossiter W. *Mines and Mining of the Rocky Mountains, the Inland Basin, and the Pacific Slope.* J. B. Ford & Co., 1871.

Report of the Secretary of the Interior, 1875. 44th Congress, 1st Session, House Ex. Doc. No. 1.

Report of the Secretary of the Interior, 1877. 44th Congress, 2nd session, House Ex. Doc. 1 part 5.

Report of the Secretary of War ["The Sand Creek Massacre"], February 12, 1867. 39th Congress, 2nd Session. Senate Ex. Doc. 26.

Report of the Select Committee on the Removal of the Northern Cheyennes, &c., June 8, 1880. Senate Report No. 708.

Robinson, Sara T. L. *Kansas; Its Interior and Exterior Life.* Crosby, Nichols, and Co., 1856.

BIBLIOGRAPHY

Roosevelt, Theodore. *The Rough Riders*. Charles Scribner's Sons, 1899.

Roosevelt, Theodore. "The Strenuous Life." In *The Works of Theodore Roosevelt in Fourteen Volumes: The Strenuous Life*. P.F. Collier & Son, 1900.

Ruxton, George F. *Life in the Far West*. Harper & Brothers, 1849.

Ruxton, George F. *Wild Life in the Rocky Mountains: A True Tale of Rough Adventure in the Days of the Mexican War*. Edited by Horace Kephart. Macmillan, 1924.

Sage, Rufus B. *Rocky Mountain Life; or, Startling Scenes and Perilous Adventures in the Far West during an Expedition of Three Years*. Thayer & Eldridge, 1859.

Salt Lake City, Utah U.S. City Directory, 1893. https://www.ancestry.com

Sanford, Mollie Dorsey. *Mollie: The Journal of Mollie Dorsey Sanford in Nebraska and Colorado Territories, 1857–1866*. University of Nebraska Press, 1959.

Senturia, Laura Tuttum. "Fairmount Cemetery as an Outdoor Refuge," June 16, 2020. https://history.denverlibrary.org/news/denver/fairmount-cemetery-outdoor-refuge/

Shaw, Luella. *True History of Some of the Pioneers of Colorado*. W. S. Coburn, John Patterson, and A. K. Shaw, 1909.

Smejkal, Vickie. "Riverside Cemetery—Denver." https://www.riversidecemeterydenver.com

South Carolina Declaration of Secession," 1860. https://constitutioncenter.org/the-constitution/historic-document-library/detail/south-carolina-declaration-of-secession-1860

Standage, Henry. *The March of the Mormon Battalion from Council Bluffs to California* (Taken from the Journal of Henry Standage). Edited by Frank Alfred Golder. The Century Company, 1928.

Stands in Timber, John and Margo Liberty. *Cheyenne Memories*. 2nd ed. Yale University Press, 1967.

The Civil War in the Southwest: Recollections of the Sibley Brigade. Edited by Jerry Thompson. Texas A&M University Press, 2001.

The Edmunds Anti-Polygamy Act, 1882. https://bhroberts.org/records/oO4NVz-SX2vQb/text_of_the_1882_edmunds_act

The Hollister Family of America. Compiled by Lafayette Wallace Case. Fergus Printing Co., 1886.

The Legislature of 1868, in Transactions of the Kansas Historical Society, vol. 10. The Printing Office, 1908.

The Northern Cheyenne Tribe v William Hollowbreast, unanimous decision, March 29, 1976. https://supreme.justia.com/cases/federal/us/425/649/

The Revised Statutes of Idaho Territory. Printed for the Territory, 1887.

The War of the Rebellion: A Compilation of the Official Records of the Union and Confederate Armies. Government Printing Office, 1880–1901.

Thompson, David and Raymond W. Wood. "David Thompson at the Mandan-Hidatsa Villages, 1797–1798: The Original Journals." *Ethnohistory* 24, no. 4 (August 1977): 329–42.

Treaty of Fort Laramie, 1851. https://treaties.okstate.edu/treaties/treaty-of-fort-laramie-with-sioux-etc-1851-0594

Treaty with the Arapaho and Cheyenne, 1861. https://treaties.okstate.edu/treaties/treaty-with-the-arapaho-and-cheyenne-1861-0807

Treaty with the Northern Cheyenne and Northern Arapaho at Fort Laramie, May 10, 1868. https://treaties.okstate.edu/treaties/treaty-with-the-northern-cheyenne-and-northern-arapaho-1868-1012

Treaty with the Shawnee, 1831. https://treaties.okstate.edu/treaties/treaty-with-the-shawnee-1831-0331

Treaty with the Shawnee, 1854. https://treaties.okstate.edu/treaties/treaty-with-the-shawnee-1854-0618

Turner, Frederick Jackson. *The Significance of the Frontier in American History* (July 1893). Unger (Milestones of Thought Edition), 1987.

Tyler, Daniel. *A Concise History of the Mormon Battalion in the Mexican War, 1846–47*. LDS Archive Publishers, 1881.

United States Bureau of the Census. *1910 Census: Indian Population in the United States and Alaska*. Government Printing Office, 1915.

United States Bureau of the Census. *Historical Statistics of the United States: Colonial Times to 1970*. 93rd Congress, 1st Session, House Doc no. 93-78 (Part I).

United States Bureau of Labor Statistics. *Monthly Labor Review* 30, no. 1 (1930).

US Marriage Records, 1810–1953. https://www.ancestry.com

US Register of Civil, Military, and Naval Service, vol. I (1869). https://www.ancestry.com

Wharton, J. E. *History of the City of Denver: From Its Earliest Settlement to the Present Time*. Byers and Daily, Printers, 1866.

When the Texans Came: Missing Records from the Civil War in the Southwest, 1861–1862. Edited by John Wilson. University of New Mexico Press, 2001.

Williams, Mrs. Ellen. *Three Years and a Half in the Army; or, History of the Second Colorados*. Fowler & Wells Company, 1885.

Woodward, George A. "Some Experiences with the Cheyennes" (1878). Reprinted in John E. Parsons, ed. "The Northern Cheyenne at Fort Fetterman: Colonel Woodward Describes Some Experiences of 1871." *Montana: The Magazine of Western History* 9, no. 2 (Spring 1959): 16–27.

DIGITAL SECONDARY SOURCES

"1904 St. Louis World's Fair." St. Louis Art Museum. https://www.slam.org/teachers-students/educator-resources/art-along-the-rivers/art-on-display/1904-st-louis-worlds-fair/

"American Land Prices and Policy." Digital History, 2016. https://www.digitalhistory.uh.edu/disp_textbook.cfm?smtID=11&psid=3836

"American Philosophical Society: History." https://www.amphilsoc.org/about/history

"Beckwourth Biography." The Beckwourth Website. https://beckwourth.org/Biography/

"Breaking the Silence: Nineteenth-Century Indian Delegations." Peabody Museum of Archaeology & Ethnology. https://peabody.harvard.edu/galleries/breaking-silence-nineteenth-century-indian-delegations-0

"Chinese Terraced Gardens" (Section F). Chinese Sites in the Warren Mining District, National Register of Historic Places Application, 1990. https://history.idaho.gov/wp-content/uploads/2018/09/Chinese_Sites_in_the_Warren_Mining_District_64500188.pdf

"Climate and Average Weather Year Round in Central City, Colorado." WeatherSpark. https://weatherspark.com/y/3530/Average-Weather-in-Central-City-Colorado-United-States-Year-Round#google_vignette

"Fort Vasquez." Colorado Encyclopedia. https://coloradoencyclopedia.org/article/fort-vasquez

"George W. Coulter." Mariposa County Biographies, https://www.goldennuggetlibrary.sfgenealogy.org/marcou.htm

BIBLIOGRAPHY

"Golden Currant." Montana Plant Life. http://montana.plant-life.org/cgibin/species03.cgi?Grossulariaceae_Ribesaureum

"History and Culture: Old Spanish National Historic Trail." https://www.nps.gov/olsp/learn/historyculture/index.htm

"History Timeline: Los Angeles County, 1800 to 1847." Los Angeles Almanac. https://www.laalmanac.com/history/hi01b.php

"Lewis and Clark: Maps of Exploration." Exhibition Introduction, Special Collections, Alderman Library. University of Virginia. https://explore.lib.virginia.edu/exhibits/show/lewisclark/westernocean/overview4

"Little Wolf." American Tribes. Edited by Diane and Dietmar Schulte-Moring. https://american-tribes.com/Cheyenne/bio/LittleWolf.htm

"Migration and Population Movement." Encyclopedias, Almanacs, and Maps. Encyclopedia.com. https://www.encyclopedia.com/history/encyclopedias-almanacs-transcripts-and-maps/migration-and-population-movement

"Missouri City Cemetery, Gilpin County, Colorado." Colorado Cemeteries. http://www.colorado-cemeteries.com/Missouri-City-Cemetery-Gilpin-County.html

"Platte River Valley." Rainwater Basin Joint Venture. https://www.rwbjv.org/region/platte-river-valley/

"Riggins, Idaho." Salmon River Chamber of Commerce. https://rigginsidaho.com/history/#

"Strange Happenings During the Earthquake." New Madrid, Missouri City Homepage. http://www.new-madrid.mo.us/132/Strange-Happenings-during-the-Earthquake

"Taos, New Mexico: Art, Architecture, and History." https://www.legendsofamerica.com/nm-taos/

"The Calumet Ceremony in the Mississippi Valley." University of Arkansas, 2007. http://archeology.uark.edu/indiansofarkansas/index.html

"The Sagebrush Sea is Vanishing." The Nature Conservancy, July 30, 2022. https://www.nature.org/en-us/what-we-do/our-priorities/protect-water-and-land/land-and-water-stories/sagebrush-sea/

A History of the Chinese in California. https://himmarklai.org/wordpress/wp-content/uploads/A-History-of-the-Chinese-in-CA-A-Syllabus-Part-I.pdf

Akins, Nancy J. "Valencia: A Spanish Colonial and Mexican-Period Site along NM 47 in Valencia County, New Mexico." *Santa Fe: Archeology Notes* 267 (2001). https://nmarchaeology.org/wp-content/uploads/2024/05/267.pdf

Assmann, Cody. "How the Mountain Men Trapped Beaver." Frontier Life Blog. https://www.frontierlife.net/blog/2019/12/19/how-the-mountain-men-trapped-beaver

Banfill, W. H. "Fort C. F. Smith, Built for Outpost on Bozeman Trail in 1866." https://sites.rootsweb.com/~nalakota/mbbsjttwbb/ft_smith_tt_0933.htm

Beach, Laura. "Revisiting America: The Prints of Currier & Ives." Antiques and the Arts Weekly (October 12, 2021). https://www.antiquesandthearts.com/revisiting-america-the-prints-of-currier-ives/

Beck, David R. M. "Fair Representation? American Indians and the 1893 Chicago World's Columbian Exposition." Forum: Research and Teaching Exhibitions in World History, World History Connected. https://worldhistoryconnected.press.uillinois.edu/13.3/forum_01_beck.html#_ednref4

Brown, John S. "U.S. Army Campaigns of the Mexican War." U.S. Army Center of Military History pamphlet. https://www.officialmilitaryribbons.com/pdf/publications/THE_OCCUPATION_OF_MEXICO_MAY_1846_JULY_1848_mexican_war.pdf

Brownell, Richard. "The Short-Lived Baltimore & Potomac Railroad Station on the National Mall." Boundary Stones, June 2016. https://boundarystones.weta.org/2016/06/29/short-lived-baltimore-potomac-railroad-station-national-mall

Buller, Chris and Malinda Franz. "Breaking Prairie," January 8, 2017. Buller Time. http://bullertime.blogspot.com/2017/01/breaking-prairie.html

Carroll, H. Bailey. "Texan Santa Fe Expedition" (1952; 2020). Handbook of Texas Online. https://www.tshaonline.org/handbook/entries/texan-santa-fe-expedition

Chew, Elizabeth. "Jefferson's Indian Hall: Expedition Souvenirs and Specimens." Discover Lewis & Clark. https://lewis-clark.org/sciences/ethnography/jeffersons-indian-hall/

Chinese Railroad Workers in North America Project. Stanford University. https://web.stanford.edu/group/chineserailroad/cgi-bin/website/

Clark, Laura. "The 1887 Blizzard That Changed the American Frontier Forever." *Smithsonian Magazine* (January 9, 2015). https://www.smithsonianmag.com/smart-news/1887-blizzard-changed-american-frontier-forever-1-180953852/

Cozzens, Peter. "Ulysses S. Grant Launched an Illegal War Against Plains Indians, Then Lied About It." *Smithsonian Magazine* (November 2016). https://www.smithsonianmag.com/history/ulysses-grant-launched-illegal-war-plains-indians-180960787/

D'Amato, Martina. "'The Harper Establishment'; or, How a New York Publishing Giant was Made." Visualizing Nineteenth-Century New York. https://visualizingnyc.org/essays/the-harper-establishment-or-how-a-new-york-publishing-giant-was-made/

Dippie, Brian W. "The Imagery of Sacagawea." Jackson Hole History. https://jacksonholehistory.org/learn/archives-research/the-imagery-of-sacagawea-by-brian-w-dippie/

Ecoregions of North America Maps: California, Colorado, Idaho, Iowa and Missouri, Kansas and Nebraska, and Wyoming. https://www.epa.gov/eco-research/ecoregions-north-america

El Paso Historical Society. "El Paso & the Region." https://www.elpasohistory.com/about/el-paso-the-region/

Elliott, Kimberly Kutz. "The World's Columbian Exposition: Introduction." The 1893 Chicago World's Fair, United States in the 19th Century. Smart History. https://smarthistory.org/worlds-columbian-exposition-intro/

Fees, Paul. "Wild West Shows: Buffalo Bill's Wild West." Buffalo Bill Center for the West. https://centerofthewest.org/learn/western-essays/wild-west-shows/

Feit, Rachel. "A River Used to Run Through It: The Borderlands Cultural Landscape of the Oñate Crossing in El Paso del Norte." National Center for Preservation Technology and Training, February 2020. https://www.nps.gov/articles/000/a-river-used-to-run-through-it-the-borderlands-cultural-landscape-of-the-onate-crossing-in-el-paso-del-norte.htm

Foley, William E. "James Pierson Beckwourth (Beckwith)." Missouri Encyclopedia. https://missouriencyclopedia.org/people/beckwourth-beckwith-james-pierson

Godfrey, Anthony. "Contact with Northern Plains Indian Villages and Communities: An Administrative History of Knife River Indian Villages National Historic Site, North Dakota" (2009). http://npshistory.com/publications/knri/adhi.pdf

Hewit Institute, University of Northern Colorado. "Beaver Ecology." https://www.unco.edu/hewit/doing-history/trappers-traders/trappers/beaver-ecology.aspx

Hirsch, Mark. "1871: The End of Indian Treaty Making." *American Indian Magazine* 15, no. 2 (Summer/ Fall 2014). https://www.americanindianmagazine.org/story/1871-end-indian-treaty-making

BIBLIOGRAPHY

Johns Hopkins Medicine. "Inguinal Hernia." https://www.hopkinsmedicine.org/health/conditions-and-diseases/hernias/inguinal-hernia

Lavender, David. "The Way to the Western Sea: Lewis and Clark Across the Continent." https://lewisandclarkjournals.unl.edu/item/lc.sup.lavender.01.05

Lovell, Margaretta M. "Dashing for America: Frederic Remington, National Myths, and Art Historical Narratives." *Panorama: Journal of the Association of Historians in American Art* 1, no. 2 (Fall 2015). https://journalpanorama.org/article/dashing-for-america-frederic-remington-national-myths-and-art-historical-narratives/

MacGregor, Jeff. "Explore the World of Willa Cather in Her Nebraska Hometown." *Smithsonian Magazine* (July/August 2023). https://www.smithsonianmag.com/travel/in-search-of-willa-cather-nebraska-hometown-180982338/

Manget, Luke. "The Shaker Connection: The Origins of the Botanical Drug Trade in Southern Appalachia." The Southern Highlander. https://www.thesouthernhighlander.org/shakers

Miller, Diane. "To Make Kansas Free: The Underground Railroad in Bleeding Kansas" (May 2008). https://www.nps.gov/npgallery/GetAsset/5c8a5ce2-d40d-4a57-bbef-703aac0b479c

Mussulman, Joseph A. "The Faces of Sacagawea: Interpretations of an Unknown Image." Discover Lewis and Clark. https://lewis-clark.org/people/sacagawea/the-faces-of-sacagawea/

National Park Service. "Financial Ruin at White Haven: The Panic of 1857." https://www.nps.gov/articles/000/financial-ruin-at-white-haven-the-panic-of-1857-comes-to-white-haven.htm

National Park Service. "History: Places: Fort C. F. Smith." Bighorn Canyon National Recreation Area. https://www.nps.gov/bica/learn/historyculture/fort-cf-smith-part-1-the-establishment.htm

National Park Service. "Pecos National Historical Park." https://www.nps.gov/peco/index.htm

Noel, Tom. "Denver's Curtis Park is a Pioneer Suburb." *Denver Post* (April 26, 2016). https://www.denverpost.com/2014/08/15/noel-denvers-curtis-park-is-a-pioneer-suburb/

Oehser, Paul H. and Reed C. Collins. "United States: The Dry West." Encyclopaedia Brittanica. https://www.britannica.com/place/United-States/Strengths-and-weaknesses

Park Ethnography Program, National Park Service. "Africans in French America." https://www.nps.gov/ethnography/aah/aaheritage/frenchama.htm

Sandweiss, Martha A. "John Gast, American Progress, 1872." My Favorite Image, Picturing United States History. https://picturinghistory.gc.cuny.edu/john-gast-american-progress-1872/

Sayer, Chloë. "Traditional Mexican Dress." In *Frida Kahlo: Making Herself Up*. Victoria and Albert Museum. https://www.vam.ac.uk/articles/traditional-mexican-dress

Senturia, Laura Ruttum. "Colorado, Racism, and the 1893 World's Fair" (November 24, 2020). Denver Public Library Special Collections and Archives. https://history.denverlibrary.org/news/western-history/colorado-racism-and-1893-chicago-worlds-fair

Smith, David Michael. "Counting the Dead: Estimating the Loss of Life in the Indigenous Holocaust, 1492–Present." https://www.se.edu/native-american/wp-content/uploads/sites/49/2019/09/A-NAS-2017-Proceedings-Smith.pdf

State Historical Society of North Dakota. "Fort Clark State Historic Site: History." https://www.history.nd.gov/historicsites/clark/clarkhistory.html

Toliefson, Loretta Miles. "The Real Gertrudis Barceló," January 20, 2022. https://lorettamilestollefson.com/2022/01/20/the-real-gertrudis-barcelo/

Tucker, Abigail. "Meriwether Lewis's Mysterious Death." *Smithsonian Magazine* (October 8, 2009). https://www.smithsonianmag.com/history/meriwether-lewis-mysterious-death-144006713/
United States Census. "Resident Population of Kansas, 1860–2000." https://www2.census.gov/library/visualizations/2000/dec/2000-resident-population/kansas.pdf
United States Census. "Resident Population of Nebraska, 1860–2000." https://www2.census.gov/library/visualizations/2000/dec/2000-resident-population/nebraska.pdf
United States Senate. "The Caning of Senator Charles Sumner: May 22, 1856." https://www.senate.gov/artandhistory/history/minute/The_Caning_of_Senator_Charles_Sumner.htm
United States Senate. "The Crime Against Kansas: May 19, 1856." https://www.senate.gov/artandhistory/history/minute/The_Crime_Against_Kansas.htm
University of New Mexico. "About *Santa Fe Weekly Gazette*." Chronicling America, Library of Congress. https://chroniclingamerica.loc.gov/lccn/sn84022168/
Walton, Aaron. "Sonora, California." Western Mining History. https://westernmininghistory.com/towns/california/sonora/
Widdis, Randy William. "Anglo Canadians." Encyclopedia of the Great Plains. http://plainshumanities.unl.edu/encyclopedia/doc/egp.ea.002
Woodard, Colin. "How the Myth of the American Frontier Got Its Start." *Smithsonian Magazine* (January/February 2023). https://www.smithsonianmag.com/history/how-myth-american-frontier-got-start-180981310/
Wulf, Andrea. "Thomas Jefferson's Quest to Prove America's Natural Superiority." *The Atlantic* (March 7, 2016). https://www.theatlantic.com/science/archive/2016/03/jefferson-american-dream/471696/
Yuan, Lynne. "China's Lost Women in the Far West," July 25, 2019. HistoryNet. https://www.historynet.com/chinas-lost-women-in-the-far-west/

PRINTED SECONDARY SOURCES

A Dictionary of North American Authors Deceased before 1950. 10 vols. Compiled by W. Stewart Wallace. Ryerson Press, 1951.
Acosta, Teresa Palomo and Ruthe Winegarten. *Las Tejanas: 300 Years of History*. University of Texas Press, 2003.
Acuña, Rodolfo. *Occupied America: A History of Chicanos*. Pearson Longman, 2007.
Adams, Kevin. "The War in the West." *The Cambridge History of the Civil War*, 554–75. Cambridge University Press, 2019.
Agonito, Rosemary and Joseph Agonito. "Resurrecting History's Forgotten Women: A Case Study from the Cheyenne Indians." *Frontiers: A Journal of Women Studies* 6, no. 3 (Autumn 1981): 8–16.
Alberts, Don E. *The Battle of Glorieta: Union Victory in the West*. Texas A&M University Press, 2000.
Albright, George Leslie. *Official Explorations for Pacific Railroads*. University of California Press, 1921.
Allison III, James R. "Beyond the Violence: Indian Agriculture, White Removal, and the Unlikely Construction of the Northern Cheyenne Reservation, 1876–1900." *Great Plains Quarterly* 32, no. 2 (Spring 2012): 91–111.

Anderson, Irving W. "J.B. Charbonneau, Son of Sacajawea." *Oregon Historical Quarterly* 71, no. 3 (September 1970): 246–64.
Andrews, Jr., Horace. "Kansas Crusade: Eli Thayer and the New England Emigrant Aid Company." *New England Quarterly* 35, no. 4 (December 1962): 497–514.
Appel, Peter A. "The Louisiana Purchase and the Louis & Clark Expedition: A Constitutional Moment?" In *Lewis & Clark: Legacies, Memories, and New Perspectives*, edited by Kris Fresonke and Mark Spence. University of California Press, 2004.
Arendt, Hannah. *The Origins of Totalitarianism*. 1951; Harcourt, 1973.
Arenson, Adam. *The Great Heart of the Republic: St. Louis and the Cultural Civil War*. Harvard University Press, 2011.
Armitage, Susan and Elizabeth Jameson, eds. *The Women's West*. University of Oklahoma Press, 1987.
Aune, Stefan. *Indian Wars Everywhere: Colonial Violence and the Shadow Doctrines of Empire*. University of California Press, 2023.
Bailey, L. R. *The Long Walk: A History of the Navajo Wars, 1846–68*. Westernlore Press, 1964.
Bancroft, Caroline. "The Elusive Figure of John H. Gregory, Discoverer of the First Gold Lode in Colorado." *Colorado Magazine* 20, no. 4 (July 1943): 121–35.
Bank, Rosemarie K. "Representing History: Performing the Columbian Exposition." *Theatre Journal* 54, no. 4 (December 2002): 589–606.
Barr, Juliana. *Peace Came in the Form of a Woman: Indians and Spaniards in the Texas Borderlands*. University of North Carolina Press, 2007.
Basch, Roberta and Richard. "The Ceremony at Ne-Ah-Coxie." In *Lewis and Clark Through Indian Eyes: Nine Indian Writers on the Legacy of the Expedition*, edited by Alvin M. Josephy, Jr. Vintage, 2006.
Basso, Keith H. *Wisdom Sits in Places: Landscape and Language Among the Western Apache*. University of New Mexico Press, 1996.
Baumgartner, Alice. *South to Freedom: Runaway Slaves to Mexico and the Road to the Civil War*. Basic Books, 2020.
Baur, John E. "The Evolution of a Mexican Foreign Trade Policy, 1821–1828." *The Americas* 19, no. 3 (January 1963): 225–61.
Bay, Ignacio Almada, José Marcos Medine Bustos, and María del Valle Borrero Silva. "Towards a New Interpretation of the Colonial Regime in Sonora, 1681–1821." Translated by Jeff Banister. *Journal of the Southwest* 50, no. 4 (Winter 2008): 377–414.
Belgrad, Daniel. "'Power's Larger Meaning': The Johnson County War as Political Violence in an Environmental Context." *Western Historical Quarterly* 33, no. 2 (Summer 2002): 159–77.
Bellows, Amanda. *The Explorers: A New History of America in Ten Expeditions*. William Morrow, 2017.
Belohlavek, John M. *Patriots, Prostitutes, and Spies: Women and the Mexican-American War*. University of Virginia Press, 2017.
Benton, Rachel C., Dennis O. Terry, Jr., and Emmett Evanoff. *The White River Badlands: Geology and Paleontology*. Indiana University Press, 2015.
Berry, Carolyn. "Comenha." *Frontiers: A Journal of Women Studies* 6, no. 3 (Autumn 1981): 17–19.
Berwanger, Eugene H. "Reconstruction on the Frontier: The Equal Rights Struggle in Colorado, 1865–1867." *Pacific Historical Review* 44, no. 3 (August 1975): 313–29.

Billington, Ray Allen. *Frederick Jackson Turner: Historian, Scholar, Teacher.* Oxford University Press, 1973.

Binkley, William Campbell. "New Mexico and the Texan Santa Fé Expedition." *Southwestern Historical Quarterly* 27, no. 2 (October 1923): 85–107.

Blackhawk, Ned. *The Rediscovery of America: Native Peoples and the Unmaking of U.S. History.* Yale University Press, 2023.

Blassingame, John W. "Black Autobiographies as History and Literature." *The Black Scholar* 5, no. 4 (December 1973–January1974): 2–9.

Bloom, John P. "New Mexico Viewed by Anglo-Americans, 1846–1849." *New Mexico Historical Review* 34 (1959): 165–98.

Blythe, Lance. "Kit Carson and the War for the Southwest: Separation and Survival along the Rio Grande, 1862–1868. In *Civil War Wests: Testing the Limits of the United States*, edited by Adam Arenson and Andrew R. Graybill. University of California Press, 2015.

Brettle, Adrian. "Confederate Imaginations with the Federals in the Postwar Order." *Civil War History* 65, no. 1 (March 2019): 43–72.

Brettle, Adrian. *Confederate Planning for a Post–Civil War World.* University of Virginia Press, 2020.

Brooks, James L. *Captives and Cousins: Slavery, Kinship, and Community in the Southwest Borderlands.* University of North Carolina Press, 2002.

Brooks, Joanna. "Sacajawea, Meet *Cogewea*: A Red Progressive Revision of Frontier Romance." In *Lewis and Clark: Legacies, Memories, and New Perspectives*, edited by Kris Fresonke and Mark Spence. University of California Press, 2004.

Buckley, Jay H. "Jeffersonian Explorers in the Trans-Mississippi West: Zebulon Pike in Perspective." In *Zebulon Pike, Thomas Jefferson, and the Opening of the American West*, edited by Matthew L. Harris and Jay H. Buckley. University of Oklahoma Press, 2012.

Buckley, Jay H. *William Clark: Indian Diplomat.* University of Oklahoma Press, 2012.

Burg, David F. *Chicago's White City of 1893.* University Press of Kentucky, 1976.

Burke, Diane Mutti. *On Slavery's Border: Missouri's Small Slaveholding Households, 1815–1865.* University of Georgia Press, 2010.

Campbell, Gregory R. "The Lemhi Shoshoni: Ethnogenesis, Sociological Transformation, and the Construction of a Tribal Nation." *American Indian Quarterly* 25, no. 4 (Autumn 2001): 539–78.

Capehart, Lucy E. "Crow and Hidatsa Women: The Influence of Economics on Religious Status." MA Thesis, University of Montana, 1980.

Chang, Gordon H. and Shelley Fisher Fishkin, eds. *The Chinese and the Iron Road: Building the Transcontinental Railroad.* Stanford University Press, 2019.

Chavez, Fray Angélico. "Doña Tules, Her Fame and Her Funeral." *El Palacio* 57, no. 8 (August 1950): 227–34.

Chernow, Ron. *Grant.* Penguin, 2018.

Clay, T. A. "A Call to Order: Law, Violence, and the Development of Montana's Early Stockmen's Organizations." *Montana: The Magazine of Western History* 58, no. 3 (Autumn 2008): 48–63, 95–96.

Clayton, James L. "The Growth and Significance of the American Fur Trade, 1790–1890." *Minnesota History* 40, no. 4 (Winter 1966): 210–20.

Cleland, Robert Glass. *A History of California: The American Period.* Macmillan, 1922.

BIBLIOGRAPHY

Cleves, Rachel Hope et al. "Interchange: The War of 1812." *Journal of American History* 99, no. 2 (September 2012): 520–55.

Coffman, Tom. *Nation Within: The History of the American Occupation of Hawai'i.* 3rd edition. Duke University Press, 2016.

Colby, Susan M. *Sacagawea's Child: The Life and Times of Jean-Baptiste (Pomp) Charbonneau.* University of Oklahoma Press, 2005.

Colton, Ray C. *The Civil War in the Western Territories: Arizona, Colorado, New Mexico, and Utah.* University of Oklahoma Press, 1959.

Conner, Roberta. "Our People Have Always Been Here." In *Lewis and Clark Through Indian Eyes: Nine Indian Writers on the Legacy of the Expedition,* edited by Alvin M. Josephy, Jr. Vintage, 2006.

Conrad, Paul. *The Apache Diaspora: Four Centuries of Displacement and Survival.* University of Pennsylvania Press, 2021.

Contini, Renaud. "Harmonizing the 'West': Jefferson's Account of Louisiana and American Identity." In *Before the West Was West: Critical Essays on Pre-1800 Literature of the American Frontiers,* edited by Amy T. Hamilton and Tom J. Hillard. University of Nebraska Press, 2014.

Cook, Mary J. Straw. *Doña Tules: Santa Fe's Courtesan and Gambler.* University of New Mexico Press, 2007.

Cordley, Richard. *A History of Lawrence, Kansas, from the First Settlement to the Close of the Rebellion.* E. F. Caldwell, 1895.

Cronon, William. "The Trouble with Wilderness: Or, Getting Back to the Wrong Nature." *Environmental History* 1, no. 1 (January 1996): 7–28.

Cronon, William. *Nature's Metropolis: Chicago and the Great West.* W. W. Norton, 1991.

Cross, Raymond. "'Twice-born' from the Waters: The Two-Hundred-Year Journey of the Mandan, Hidatsa, and Arikara Indians." In *Lewis and Clark: Legacies, Memories, and New Perspectives,* edited by Kris Fresonke and Mark Spence. University of California Press, 2004.

Curtis, Kent. *Gambling on Ore: The Nature of Metal Mining in the United States, 1860–1910.* University Press of Colorado, 2013.

Dant, Sara. *Losing Eden: An Environmental History of the American West.* University of Nebraska Press, 2023.

Davis, Carl M. and Sara Scott. "The Pass Creek Wickiups: Northern Shoshone Hunting Lodges in Southwestern Montana." *Plains Anthropologist* 32, no. 115 (February 1987): 83–92.

Davis, Jr. W. N. "Research Uses of County Court Records, 1850–1879: And Incidental Intimate Glimpses of California Life and Society: Part II." *California Historical Quarterly* 52, no. 4 (Winter 1973): 338–65.

Dearinger, Ryan. *The Filth of Progress: Immigrants, Americans, and the Building of Canals and Railroads in the West.* University of California Press, 2015.

DeLay, Brian. *War of a Thousand Deserts: Indian Raids and the U.S.-Mexican War.* Yale University Press, 2008.

Deloria, Philip J. *Playing Indian.* Yale University Press, 1999.

Demallie, Raymond J. "'Scenes in the Indian Country': A Portfolio of Alexander Gardner's Stereographic Views of the 1868 Fort Laramie Treaty Council." *Montana: The Magazine of Western History* 31, no. 3 (Summer 1981): 42–59.

Dennis, Matthew. *American Relics and the Politics of Public Memory.* University of Massachusetts Press, 2023.

Deutsch, Sarah. *No Separate Refuge: Culture, Class, and Gender on an Anglo-Hispanic Frontier in the American Southwest, 1880–1940.* Oxford University Press, 1987.

DeVoto, Bernard. Introduction to James Beckwourth and Bonner, *The Life and Adventures of James P. Beckwourth.* Alfred A. Knopf, 1931.

Dippie, Brian W. "'Its Equal I Have Never Seen': Custer Explores the Black Hills in 1874." *Columbia: The Magazine of Northwest History* 19, no. 2 (Summer 2005): 1–9.

Dolin, Eric Jay. *Fur, Fortune, and Empire: The Epic History of the Fur Trade in America.* W. W. Norton, 2010.

Drumm, Stella M, ed. *Down the Santa Fe Trail and Into Mexico: The Diary of Susan Shelby Magoffin, 1846–1847.* University of Nebraska Press, 1982.

Dusenberry, Verne. "The Northern Cheyenne: All They Have Asked is to Live in Montana." *Montana Magazine of History* 5, no. 1 (Winter 1955): 23–40.

Eakin, Paul John. *Fictions in Autobiography: Studies in the Art of Self-Invention.* Princeton University Press, 1985.

Earle, Jonathan. "'If I Went West, I Think I Would Go to Kansas': Abraham Lincoln, the Sunflower, State, and the Election of 1860." In *Bleeding Kansas, Bleeding Missouri: The Long Civil War on the Border*, edited by Jonathan Earle and Diane Mutti Burke. University Press of Kansas, 2013.

Earling, Debra Magpie. "What We See." In *Lewis and Clark Through Indian Eyes: Nine Indian Writers on the Legacy of the Expedition*, edited by Alvin M. Josephy, Jr. Vintage, 2006.

Eaton, James Winton. "The Wyoming Stock Growers Association's Treatment of Nonmember Cattlemen during the 1880s." *Agricultural History* 58, no. 1 (January 1984): 70–80.

Etcheson, Nicole. *Bleeding Kansas: Contested Liberty in the Civil War Era.* University Press of Kansas, 2004.

Etulain, Richard W. *Beyond the Missouri: The Story of the American West.* University of New Mexico Press, 2006.

Eustace, Nicole and Fredrika J. Teute, eds. *Warring for America: Cultural Contests in the Era of 1812.* University of North Carolina Press, 2017.

Ewbank, Douglas C. "Black Mortality and Health before 1940." *Milbank Quarterly* 64, no. 1 (1987): 100–128.

Fenelon, James V. and Mary Louise Defender-Wilson. "Voyage of Domination, 'Purchase' as Conquest, Sakakawea for Savagery: Distorted Icons from Misrepresentations of the Lewis and Clark Expedition." *Wicazo Sa Review* 19, no. 1 (Spring 2004): 85–104.

Fenn, Elizabeth A. *Encounters at the Heart of the World: A History of the Mandan People.* Hill and Wang, 2014.

Fiege, Mark. *The Republic of Nature: An Environmental History of the United States.* University of Washington Press, 2012.

Fierst, John T. "Rationalizing Removal: Anti-Indianism in Lewis Cass's *North American Review* Essays." *Michigan Historical Review* 36, no. 2 (2010): 1–35.

Figueredo, D.H. *Revolvers and Pistolas, Vaqueros and Caballeros: Debunking the Old West.* Praeger, 2015.

Foley, William E. and Charles David Rice. "The Return of the Mandan Chief." *Montana: The Magazine of Western History* 29, no. 3 (Summer 1979): 2–15.

Foote, Cheryl J. "Stephen F. Austin and Doña Tules: A Land Agent and Gambler in the Mexican Borderlands." In *Western Lives: A Biographical History of the American West*, edited by Richard W. Etulain. University of New Mexico Press, 2004.

Forbes, Jack D. "The Early African Heritage of California." In *Seeking El Dorado: African Americans in California*, edited by Lawrence B. de Graaf, Kevin Mulroy, and Quintard Taylor. University of Washington Press, 2001.

Foster, Sally. "Maria Gertrudis Barcelo (1800–1852): Entrepreneur." In *Notable Hispanic American Women*, edited by Diane Telgen and Jim Kamp. Gale Research, 1993.

Fowler, Loretta. "Arapaho and Cheyenne Perspectives: From the 1851 Treaty to the Sand Creek Massacre." *American Indian Quarterly* 39, no. 4 (Fall 2015): 364–90.

Frazier, Donald. *Blood and Treasure: Confederate Empire in the Southwest*. Texas A&M Press, 1995.

Freeman, Joanne B. *The Field of Blood: Violence in Congress and the Road to Civil War*. Macmillan, 2018.

Fresonke, Kris and Mark Spence, eds. *Lewis and Clark: Legacies, Memories, and New Perspectives*. University of California Press, 2004.

Frey, Rodney and Robert McCarl. "The Confluence of Rivers: The Indigenous Tribes of Idaho. In *Idaho's Place: A New History of the Gem State*, edited by Adam M. Sowards. University of Washington Press, 2014.

Furtwangler, Albert. "Sacagawea's Son as a Symbol." *Oregon Historical Quarterly* 102, no. 3 (2001): 290–315.

Gage, Justin. *We Do Not Want the Gates Closed Between Us: Native Networks and the Spread of the Ghost Dance*. University of Oklahoma Press, 2020.

Gallagher, Gary W. "One War or Two? The United States Versus Confederates and Indians, 1861–1865. In *The Enduring Civil War: Reflections on the Great American Crisis*, edited by Gary Gallagher. Louisiana State University Press, 2020.

Gallagher, Winifred. *New Women in the Old West: From Settlers to Suffragists, the Untold American Story*. Penguin, 2021.

Garrett, Valery. *Chinese Dress: From the Qing Dynasty to the Present Day*. Tuttle Publishing, 2020.

Galli, Craig D. "Building Zion: The Latter-day Saint Legacy of Urban Planning." *Brigham Young University Studies* 44, no. 1 (2005): 111–36.

Genetin-Pilawa, C. Joseph. *Crooked Paths to Allotment: The Fight Over Federal Indian Policy after the Civil War*. University of North Carolina Press, 2014.

Gitlin, Jay. *The Bourgeois Frontier: French Towns, French Traders, and American Expansion*. Yale University Press, 2010.

Goellnicht, Donald C. "Passing as Autobiography: James Weldon Johnson's The Autobiography of an Ex-Coloured Man." *African-American Review* 30, no. 1 (Spring 1996): 17–33.

Gonzales, Juan. *Harvest of Empire: A History of Latinos in America*. Revised edition. Penguin, 2011.

Gonzales, Manuel G. *Mexicanos: A History of Mexicans in the United States*. 2nd ed. Indiana University Press, 2009.

Gonzales, Phillip B. *Política: Nuevomexicanos and American Political Incorporation, 1821–1910*. University of Nebraska Press, 2016.

González, Deena J. "Gender on the Borderlands: Re-Textualizing the Classics." *Frontiers: A Journal of Women's Studies* 24, no. 2/3 (2004): 15–29.

González, Deena J. "La Tules in Image and Reality." In *Building with Our Hands: New Directions in Chicana Studies*, edited by Adela de la Torre and Beatriz M. Pesquera. University of California Press, 1993.

González, Deena J. and Ellie D. Hernández. "Latina/o Gender and Sexuality. In *Identities and Place: Changing Labels and Intersectional Communities of LGBTZ and Two-Spirit People in the United States*, edited by Katherine Crawford-Lackey and Megan E. Springate. Berghahn Books, 2020.

González, Deena J. *Refusing the Favor: The Spanish-Mexican Women of Santa Fe, 1820–1880*. Oxford University Press, 1999.

Graham, Judith A. "The New Lebanon Shaker Children's Order." *Winterthur Portfolio* 26, no. 4 (Winter 1991): 215–29.

Grandin, Greg. *The End of the Myth: From the Frontier to the Border Wall in the Mind of America*. Henry Holt, 2019.

Greenberg, Amy S. *A Wicked War: Polk, Clay, Lincoln, and the 1846 U.S. Invasion of Mexico*. Penguin Random House, 2013.

Guedea, Virginia. "The Process of Mexican Independence." *The American Historical Review* 105, no. 1 (February 2000): 116–30.

Haack, Steven C. "'This Must Have Been a Grand Sight:' George Bent and the Battle of Platte Bridge." *Great Plains Quarterly* (Winter 2010): 3–20.

Haas, Lisbeth. "War in California, 1846–1848." *California History* 76, no. 2/3 (Summer–Fall 1997): 331–55.

Hackel, Steven W. "Land, Labor, and Production: The Colonial Economy of Spanish and Mexican California. In *Contested Eden: California Before the Gold Rush*, edited by Ramón Gutiérrez and Richard Orsi. University of California Press, 1998.

Hafen, Leroy R. "The Early Fur Trade Posts on the South Platte." *The Mississippi Valley Historical Review* 12, no. 3 (December 1925): 334–41.

Hafen, LeRoy R. "The Last Years of James P. Beckwourth." *Colorado Magazine* 5, no. 4 (August 1928): 134–39.

Hall, Martin Hardwick. *Sibley's New Mexico Campaign*. University of New Mexico Press, 2000.

Hall, Ryan. "Before the Medicine Line." *Pacific Historical Review* 86, no. 3 (August 2017): 381–406.

Hämäläinen, Pekka. *The Comanche Empire*. Yale University Press, 2008.

Hämäläinen, Pekka and Samuel Truett. "On Borderlands." *The Journal of American History* 98 (2011): 338–61.

Hamerow, Theodore S. "The Professionalization of Historical Learning." *Reviews in American History* 14, no. 3 (September 1986): 319–33.

Hammond, John Craig. "'They Are Very Much Interested in Obtaining an Unlimited Slavery': Rethinking the Territorial Expansion of Slavery in the Louisiana Purchase Territories, 1803–1805." *Journal of the Early Republic* 23, no. 3 (Autumn 2003): 353–80.

Hammond, John Craig. "Slavery, Settlement, and Empire: The Expansion and Growth of Slavery in the Interior of the North American Continent, 1770–1820." *Journal of the Early Republic* 32, no. 2 (Summer 2012): 175–206.

Hanson, Jeffery R. "Adjustment and Adaptation on the Northern Plains: The Case of Equestrianism Among the Hidatsa." *Plains Anthropologist* 31, no. 112 (May 1986): 93–107.

Hauptman, Laurence M. "General John E. Wool in Cherokee Country, 1836–1837: A Reinterpretation." *Georgia Historical Quarterly* 85, no. 1 (Spring 2001): 1–26.

Hedren, Paul L. *Rosebud, June 17, 1876: Prelude to Little Big Horn*. University of Oklahoma Press, 2019.

BIBLIOGRAPHY

Heffernan, Michael and Carol Medlicot. "A Feminist Atlas? Sacagawea, the Suffragettes, and the Commemorative Landscape of the American West, 1904–1910." *Gender, Place, and Culture: A Journal of Feminist Geography* 9 (June 2022): 109–31.

Heidenreich, Linda. "'I do not like the white man. He is a liar and a thief': *Testimonios* and the Politics of Resistance." In *California Women and Politics: From the Gold Rush to the Great Depression*, edited by Robert Cherny, Mary Ann Irwin, and Ann Marie Wilson. University of Nebraska Press, 2011.

Hernández, Kelly Lytle. *City of Inmates: Conquest, Rebellion, and the Rise of Human Caging in Los Angeles, 1771–1965*. University of North Carolina Press, 2017.

Hewitt, William L. "'The Cowboyification' of Wyoming Agriculture." *Agricultural History* 76, no. 2 (Spring 2002): 481–94.

Hickey, Donald R. *The War of 1812: A Forgotten Conflict*. University of Illinois Press, 2012.

Hill, Christina Gish. "'General Miles Put Us Here': Northern Cheyenne Military Alliance and Sovereign Territorial Rights." *American Indian Quarterly* 37, no. 4 (Fall 2013): 340–69.

Hill, Norbert S., ed. *Words of Power: Voices from Indian America*. Fulcrum Publishing, 1994.

Hodge, Adam R. *Ecology and Ethnogenesis: An Environmental History of the Wind River Shoshones, 1000–1868*. University of Nebraska Press, 2019.

Hogan, Richard. *Class and Community in Frontier Colorado*. University Press of Kansas, 1990.

Hoig, Stan. *Perilous Pursuit: The U.S. Cavalry and the Northern Cheyennes*. University Press of Colorado, 2002.

Hoig, Stan. *The Sand Creek Massacre*. University of Oklahoma Press, 1961.

Hollabaugh, Mark. *The Spirit in the Sky: Lakota Visions of the Cosmos*. University of Nebraska Press, 2017.

Hollon, Cory S. "'A Leap in the Dark': The Campaign to Conquer New Mexico and California." *Army History* 94 (Winter 2015): 6–26.

Hooper, M. Clay. "'It is Good to Be Shifty': William Wells Brown's Trickster Critique of Black Autobiography." *Modern Language Studies* 38, no. 2 (Winter 2009): 28–45.

Hoxie, Frederick E. *Parading through History: The Making of the Crow Nation in America, 1805–1935*. Cambridge University Press, 1995.

Hufsmith, George W. *The Wyoming Lynching of Cattle Kate, 1889*. High Plains Press, 1993.

Hune, Shirley. "Chinese American Women in U.S. History: Explaining Representations of Exotic Others, Passive Objects, and Active Subjects." In *The Practice of U.S. Women's History*, edited by S. Jay Kleinberg, Eileen Boris, and Vicki L. Ruiz. Rutgers University Press, 2007.

Hyde, Anne F. *Born of Lakes and Plains: Mixed-Descent Peoples and the Making of the American West*. W.W. Norton, 2022.

Hyde, Anne F. *Empires, Nations, and Families: A History of the North American West, 1800–1860*. University of Nebraska Press, 2011.

Irwin, Mary Ann and James F. Brooks, eds. *Women and Gender in the American West*. University of New Mexico Press, 2004.

Isenberg, Andrew C. "Afterword: Mining, Memory, and History." *In Mining North America: An Environmental History since 1522*, edited by John McNeill and George Vrtis. University of California Press, 2017.

Jager, Rebecca K. *Malinche, Pocahontas, and Sacagawea: Indian Women as Cultural Intermediaries and National Symbols*. University of Oklahoma Press, 2015.

James, Harry C. *Pages from Hopi History*. University of Arizona Press, 1974.

Jensen, Joan M. "Butter Making and Economic Development in Mid-Atlantic America from 1750 to 1850." *Signs* 13, no. 4 (Summer 1988): 813–29.

Johnson, Benjamin J. and Andrew R. Graybill, eds. *Bridging National Borders in North America: Transnational and Comparative Histories*. Duke University Press, 2010.

Johnson, Mark T. *The Middle Kingdom under the Big Sky: A History of the Chinese Experience in Montana*. University of Nebraska Press, 2022.

Johnson, Walter. *The Broken Heart of America: St. Louis and the Violent History of the United States*. Basic Books, 2021.

Jones, Karen R. and John Wills. *The American West: Competing Visions*. Edinburgh University Press, 2009.

Jones, Karen R. *Calamity: The Many Lives of Calamity Jane*. Yale University Press, 2020.

Jorgensen, Jeffrey C., Michelle M. McClure, Mindi B. Sheer, and Nancy L. Munn. "Combined Effects of Climate Change and Bank Stabilization on Shallow Water Habitats of Chinook Salmon." *Conservation Biology* 27, no. 6 (December 2013): 1179–89.

Josephy, Jr., Alvin M. *The Civil War in the American West*. Vintage, 1993.

Jung, Patrick J. "Toward the Black Hawk War: The Sauk and Fox Indians and the War of 1812." *Michigan Historical Review* 38 no. 1 (Spring 2012): 27–52.

Karp, Matthew. "The People's Revolution of 1856." *Journal of the Civil War Era* 9, no. 4 (December 2019): 524–45.

Karuka, Manu. *Empire's Tracks: Indigenous Nations, Chinese Workers, and the Transcontinental Railroad*. University of California Press, 2019.

Kastor, Peter J. and Francois Weil, eds. *Empires of the Imagination: Transatlantic Histories of the Louisiana Purchase*. University of Virginia Press, 2009.

Kastor, Peter J. *The Nation's Crucible: The Louisiana Purchase and the Creation of America*. Yale University Press, 2004.

Katz, William Loren. *The Black West: A Documentary and Pictorial History of the African American Role in the Westward Expansion of the United States*. Touchstone, 1996.

Keleher, William. *Turmoil in New Mexico, 1846–1868*. The Rydal Press, 1952.

Keller, Christian B. "Philanthropy Betrayed: Thomas Jefferson, the Louisiana Purchase, and the Origins of Federal Indian Removal Policy." *Proceedings of the American Philosophical Society* 144, no. 1 (March 2000): 39–66.

Kelman, Ari. *A Misplaced Massacre: Struggling Over the Memory of Sand Creek*. Harvard University Press, 2013.

Khan, Yasmin Sabina. *Enlightening the World: The Creation of the Statue of Liberty*. Cornell University Press, 2010.

Khor, Denise. "Archives, Photography, and Historical Memory: Tracking Chinese Railroad Workers in North America." *Southern California Quarterly* 98, no. 4 (2016): 429–56.

Killsback, Leo K. "A Nation of Families: Traditional Indigenous Kinship, the Foundation for Cheyenne Sovereignty." *AlterNative* 15 (2019): 34–43.

Killsback, Leo K. "Crowns of Honor: Sacred Laws of Eagle-Feather War Bonnets and Repatriating the Icon of the Great Plains." *Great Plains Quarterly* 33, no. 1 (Winter 2013): 1–23.

Killsback, Leo K. "The Legacy of Little Wolf: Rewriting and Righting Our Leaders Back into History." *Wicazo Sa Review* 26, no. 1 (Spring 2011): 85–111.

Killsback, Leo K. *A Sacred People: Indigenous Governance, Traditional Leadership, and the Warriors of the Cheyenne Nation*. Texas Tech University Press, 2019.

Killsback, Leo K. *A Sovereign People: Indigenous Nationhood, Traditional Law, and the Covenants of the Cheyenne Nation*. Texas Tech University Press, 2019.

Kimmerer, Robin Wall. *The Serviceberry: Abundance and Reciprocity in the Natural World*. Simon & Schuster, 2024.

Kirkham, Pat and Susan Weber. *History of Design: Decorative Arts and Material Culture*. Yale University Press, 2013.

Kiser, William S. "A 'charming name for a species of slavery': Political Debate on Debt Peonage in the Southwest, 1840s–1860s." *Western Historical Quarterly* 45, no. 2 (Summer 2014): 169–89.

Kiser, William S. *Illusions of Empire: The Civil War and Reconstruction in the U.S.-Mexico Borderlands*. University of Pennsylvania Press, 2021.

Kiser, William S. *Turmoil on the Rio Grande: The Territorial History of the Mesilla Valley, 1846–1865*. Texas A&M Press, 2011.

Knott, Sarah. *Mother Is a Verb: An Unconventional History*. Farrar, Straus and Giroux, 2019.

Kopperman, Paul E. "'Venerate the Lancet': Benjamin Rush's Yellow Fever Therapy in Context." *Bulletin of the History of Medicine* 78, no. 3 (Fall 2004): 539–74.

Kovarsky, Joel. *The True Geography of Our Country: Jefferson's Cartographic Vision*. University of Virginia Press, 2014.

Kraft, Louis. *Ned Wynkoop and the Lonely Road from Sand Creek*. University of Oklahoma Press, 2015.

Kraus, George. "Chinese Laborers and the Construction of the Central Pacific." *Utah Historical Quarterly* 37, no. 1 (Winter 1969): 41–57.

LaChance, Paul. "The Louisiana Purchase in the Demographic Perspective of its Time." In *Empires of the Imagination: Transatlantic Histories of the Louisiana Purchase*, edited by Peter J. Kastor and Francois Weil. University of Virginia Press, 2009.

Lacy, Ann and Anne Valley-Fox, eds. *Lost Treasures and Old Mines: A New Mexico Federal Writers' Project Book*. Sunstone Press, 2011.

Lapp, Rudolph M. "Negro Rights Activities in Gold Rush California." *California Historical Society Quarterly* 45, no. 1 (March 1966): 3–20.

Lavender, David S. *The Rockies*. 1968; University of Nebraska Press, 2003.

Le Glaunec, Jean-Pierre. "Slave Migrations and Slave Control in Spanish and Early American New Orleans." In *Empires of the Imagination: Transatlantic Histories of the Louisiana Purchase*, edited by Peter J. Kastor and Francois Weil. University of Virginia Press, 2009.

Lecompte, Janet. "La Tules and the Americans." *Arizona and the West* 20, no. 3 (Autumn 1978): 215–30.

Lecompte, Janet. "La Tules: The Ultimate New Mexico Woman." In *By Grit and Grace: Eleven Women who Shaped the American West*, edited by Glenda Riley and Richard W. Etulain. Fulcrum, 1997.

Lecompte, Janet. "Sand Creek." In *The American West: The Reader*, edited by Walter Nugent and Martin Ridge. Indiana University Press, 1999.

Lecompte, Janet. "The Independent Women of Hispanic New Mexico, 1821–1846." *Western Historical Quarterly* 22 (January 1981): 17–35.

Lecompte, Janet. "When Santa Fe was a Mexican Town: 1821 to 1846." In *Santa Fe: History of an Ancient City*, edited by David Grant Noble. School of American Research Press, 1989.

Lee, Erika. "The Chinese Exclusion Example: Race, Immigration, and American Gatekeeping, 1825–1924." *Journal of American Ethnic History* 21, no. 3 (Spring 2002): 36–62.

Lee, Jacob F. *Masters of the Middle Waters: Indian Nations and Colonial Ambitions along the Mississippi*. Harvard University Press, 2019.

Lee, Julia H. *The Racial Railroad*. New York University Press, 2022.

Lee, Mary and Sidney Nolan. "Along the Oregon Trail." *Pioneer America* 7, no. 1 (January 1975): 20–35.

Lee, Robert. "Accounting for Conquest: The Price of the Louisiana Purchase of Indian Country." *Journal of American History* 103, no. 4 (March 2017): 921–42.

Leiker, James N. and Ramon Powers. *The Northern Cheyenne Exodus in History and Memory*. University of Oklahoma Press, 2011.

Lew-Williams, Beth. *The Chinese Must Go: Violence, Exclusion, and the Making of the Alien in America*. Harvard University Press, 2018.

Lewis, Tom. *Washington: A History of Our National City*. Basic Books, 2015.

Liberty, Margo and W. Raymond Wood. "Cheyenne Primacy: New Perspectives on a Great Plains Tribe." *Plains Anthropologist* 56, no. 218 (May 2011): 155–74.

Liestman, Daniel. "Nineteenth-Century Chinese and the Environment of the Pacific Northwest." *Pacific Northwest Quarterly* 90, no. 1 (Winter 1998–1999): 17–29.

Limerick, Patricia Nelson, Clyde Milner II, and Charles E. Rankin, eds. *Trails: Toward a New Western History*. University Press of Kansas, 1991.

Limerick, Patricia Nelson. *Legacy of Conquest: The Unbroken Past of the American West*. W. W. Norton & Co, 1987.

Linderman, Frank B. *Pretty Shield: Medicine Woman of the Crows*. Harper Perennial, 2021.

Long, Frances G. and Niles Searls. "Coast to Coast by Railroad: The Journey of Niles Searls—May 1869." *New York History* 50, no. 3 (July 1969): 302–15.

Lowie, Robert H. "The Northern Shoshone." *Anthropological Papers of the American Museum of Natural History* vol. 2, part 2 (January 1909): 169–307.

Luciano, Dana. *How the Earth Feels: Geological Fantasy in the Nineteenth-Century United States*. Duke University Press, 2023.

Lynch, Daniel. *Southern California Chivalry: The Convergence of Southerners and Californios in the Far Southwest, 1846–1866*. PhD Thesis, University of California, Los Angeles, 2015.

Mann, John W.W. *Sacagawea's People: The Lemhi Shoshones and the Salmon River Country*. University of Nebraska Press, 2004.

Masich, Andrew E. *Civil War in the Southwestern Borderlands, 1861–1867*. University of Oklahoma Press, 2017.

Masich, Andrew E. *The Civil War in Arizona: The Story of the California Volunteers, 1861–1865*. University of Oklahoma Press, 2006.

McBride, Spencer W. and Jennifer Hull Dorsey, eds. *New York's Burned-over District: A Documentary History*. Cornell University Press, 2023.

McClure, Charles Robert. "Mexican New Mexico, 1837–1846." MA Thesis, Oklahoma State University, 1972.

McCunn, Ruthann Lum. "Reclaiming Polly Bemis." *Idaho Yesterdays* 46 (Spring–Summer 2005): 22–39.

McFerrin, Randy and Douglas Wills. "High Noon on the Western Range: A Property Rights Analysis of the Johnson County War." *Journal of Economic History* 57, no. 1 (March 2007): 69–92.

McGinty, Brian. *Lincoln and California: The President, the War, and the Golden State*. University of Nebraska Press, 2023.

McVeigh, Stephen. *The American Western*. Edinburgh University Press, 2007.
Meeks, Eric V. *Border Citizens: The Making of Indians, Mexicans, and Anglos in Arizona*. University of Texas Press, 2007.
Metcalf, Fay. "Knife River: Early Village Life on the Plains." *OAH Magazine of History* 9, no. 1 (Fall 1994): 34–47.
Meyer, Balthasar Henry and Caroline E. MacGill, eds. *History of Transportation in the United States before 1860*. Carnegie Institution, 1917.
Miles, Tiya. *Wild Girls: How the Outdoors Shaped the Women Who Challenged a Nation*. W. W. Norton, 2023.
Millett, Nathaniel. "Slavery and the War of 1812." *Tennessee Historical Quarterly* 71, no. 3 (Fall 2012): 184–205.
Momaday, N. Scott. "Values." In *Words of Power: Voices from Indian America*, edited by Norbert Hill. Fulcrum Publishing, 1994.
Momaday, N. Scott. "The Voices of Encounter." In *Lewis and Clark Through Indian Eyes: Nine Indian Writers on the Legacy of the Expedition*, edited by Alvin M. Josephy, Jr. Vintage, 2006.
Monnett, John H. "'My Heart Now Has Become Changed to Softer Feelings': A Northern Cheyenne Woman and Her Family Remember the Long Journey Home." *Montana: The Magazine of Western History* 59, no. 2 (Summer 2009): 45–61, 95–96.
Monnett, John H. Introduction to *Eyewitness to the Fetterman Fight: Indian Views*, edited by John H. Monnett. University of Oklahoma Press, 2017.
Monnett, John H. *Tell Them We Are Going Home: The Odyssey of the Northern Cheyennes*. University of Oklahoma Press, 2001.
Moore, John H. "Cheyenne Political History, 1820–1894." *Ethnohistory* 21, no. 4 (Autumn 1974): 329–59.
Moore, Shirley Ann Wilson. *Sweet Freedom's Plains: African Americans on the Overland Trails, 1841–1869*. University of Oklahoma Press, 2016.
Mora, Anthony P. *Border Dilemmas: Racial and National Uncertainties in New Mexico, 1848–1912*. Duke University Press, 2011.
Moreno Toscano, Alejandra and Carlos Aguirre Anaya. "Migrations to Mexico City in the Nineteenth Century: Research Approaches." *Journal of Interamerican Studies and World Affairs* 17, no. 1 (February 1975): 27–42.
Morris, Larry E. *The Fate of the Corps: What Became of the Lewis and Clark Explorers After the Expedition*. Yale University Press, 2004.
Morsman, Jenry. "Securing America: Jefferson's Fluid Plans for the Western Perimeter." In *Across the Continent: Jefferson, Lewis and Clark, and the Making of America*, edited by Douglas Seelfeldt, Jeffrey L. Hantman, and Peter S. Onuf. University of Virginia Press, 2005.
Moulton, Gary E. *The Lewis and Clark Expedition Day by Day*. Bison Books, 2018.
Mountford, Benjamin and Stephen Tuffnell. *A Global History of Gold Rushes*. University of California Press, 2018.
Muddiman, Jr., Harold J. "Agriculture in the Fredericksburg Area, 1800 to 1840." MA Thesis, University of Richmond, 1969.
Mumey, Nolie. *James Pierson Beckwourth, 1856–1866: An Enigmatic Figure of the West: A History of the Latter Years of His Life*. Old West Publishing Company, 1957.
Myres, Sandra L. *Westering Women and the Frontier Experience, 1800–1915*. University of New Mexico Press, 1982.

Nagle, Rebecca. *By the Fire We Carry: The Generations-Long Fight for Justice on Native Land.* HarperCollins, 2024.

Nankivell, Major John H. *History of the Military Organizations of the State of Colorado.* The W.H. Kistler Stationery Co., 1935.

Neely Jr., Mark E. *The Civil War and the Limits of Destruction.* Harvard University Press, 2007.

Nelson, Megan Kate. "Death in the Distance: The Confederate Campaign for New Mexico, 1861–1862." In *Civil War Wests: Testing the Limits of the United States*, edited by Adam Arenson and Andrew R. Graybill. University of California Press, 2015.

Nelson, Megan Kate. "Indian America." In *Blackwell Companion to the U.S. Civil War* Vol. 1, edited by Aaron Sheehan-Dean. Blackwell, 2014.

Nelson, Megan Kate. "Indians Make the Best Guerrillas: Native Americans and the War for the Desert Southwest, 1861–1862." In *The Civil War Guerrilla: Unfolding the Black Flag in History, Memory, and Myth*, edited by Joseph M. Beilein, Jr. and Matthew C. Hulbert. University Press of Kentucky, 2015.

Nelson, Megan Kate. "The Civil War from Apache Pass." *Journal of the Civil War Era* 6, no. 4 (December 2016): 510–35.

Nelson, Megan Kate. *Saving Yellowstone: Exploration and Preservation in Reconstruction America.* Scribner, 2022.

Nelson, Megan Kate. *The Three-Cornered War: The Union, The Confederacy, and Native Peoples in the Fight for the West.* Scribner, 2020.

Nelson, W. Dale. *Interpreters with Lewis and Clark: The Story of Sacagawea and Toussaint Charbonneau.* University of North Texas Press, 2003.

Ngai, Mae. *The Chinese Question: The Gold Rushes, Chinese Migration, and Global Politics.* W. W. Norton, 2021.

Nichols, Roger L. "The Arikara Indians and the Missouri River Trade: A Quest for Survival." *Great Plains Quarterly* 2, no. 2 (Spring 1982): 77–93.

Nicoletta, Julie. "The Architecture of Control: Shaker Dwelling Houses and the Reform Movement in Early Nineteenth-Century America." *Journal of the Society of Architectural Historians* 62, no. 3 (September 2003): 352–87.

Noel, Thomas J. and Duane A. Smith. *Colorado: The Highest State.* 2nd ed. University Press of Colorado, 2011.

Nunis, Jr., Doyce B. "The Fur Men: Key to Westward Expansion, 1822–1830." *The Historian* 23, no. 2 (February 1961): 167–90.

Nunis, Jr., Doyce B. "The Sublettes of Kentucky and the Far West, 1830–1857." *Register of the Kentucky Historical Society* 58, no. 2 (April 1960): 129–44.

Oman, Kerry R. "The Beginning of the End: The Indian Peace Commission of 1867–1868." *Great Plains Quarterly* (Winter 2002): 35–51.

Onuf, Peter S. "Prologue: Jefferson, Louisiana, and American Nationhood." In *Empires of the Imagination: Transatlantic Histories of the Louisiana Purchase*, edited by Peter J. Kastor and Francois Weil. University of Virginia Press, 2009.

Onuf, Peter S. and Jeffrey L. Hantman, "Introduction: Geopolitics, Science, and Culture Conflicts." In *Across the Continent: Jefferson, Lewis and Clark, and the Making of America*, edited by Douglas Seelfeldt, Jeffrey L. Hantman, and Peter S. Onuf. University of Virginia Press, 2005.

Ostler, Jeffrey. "Locating Settler Colonialism in Early American History." *William and Mary Quarterly* 76, no. 3 (July 2019): 443–50.

Ostler, Jeffrey. *Surviving Genocide: Native Nations and the United States from the American Revolution to Bleeding Kansas.* Yale University Press, 2019.

Oswald, Delmont R. Introduction, Notes, and Epilogue to *The Life and Adventures of James P. Beckwourth.* University of Nebraska Press, 1972.

Paddison, Joshua. *American Heathens: Religion, Race, and Reconstruction in California.* University of California Press, 2012.

Palmer, Gabrielle, June-el Piper, and LouAnn Jacobson, eds. *El Camino Real de Tierra Adentro.* Bureau of Land Management, New Mexico State Office, 1993.

Park, Benjamin E. *American Zion: A New History of Mormonism.* Liveright, 2024.

Pérez, Erika. *Colonial Intimacies: Interethnic Kinship, Sexuality, and Marriage in Southern California, 1769–1885.* University of Oklahoma Press, 2018.

Petrowski, William R. "The Kansas Pacific Railroad in the Southwest." *Arizona and the West* 11, no. 2 (Summer 1969): 129–46.

Pfabe, Jerrald K. "Divorce in Seward County, Nebraska, 1869–1906." *Nebraska History* 97 (2016): 149–64.

Phillips, Jr. David A. "Prehistory of Chihuahua and Sonora." *Journal of World Prehistory* 3, no. 4 (December 1989): 373–401.

Phillips, Steven J. and Patricia Wentworth Comus. *A Natural History of the Sonoran Desert.* University of California Press, 2000.

Pierce, Jason E. *Making the White Man's West: Whiteness and the Creation of the American West.* University Press of Colorado, 2016.

Pillow, Wanda S. "Mapping Sex, Race, and Gender in the Corps of Discovery Expedition." In *Connexions: Histories of Race and Sex in North America*, edited by Jennifer Brier, Jim Downs, and Jennifer L. Morgan. University of Illinois Press, 2016.

Polk, Michael R. "Interpreting Chinese Worker Camps on the Transcontinental Railroad at Promontory Summit, Utah." *Historical Archaeology* 49 no. 1 (2015): 59–70.

Ponce, Pearl T. "'The Noise of Democracy': The Lecompton Constitution in Congress and Kansas." In *Bleeding Kansas, Bleeding Missouri: The Long Civil War on the Border*, edited by Jonathan Earle and Diane Mutti Burke. University Press of Kansas, 2013.

Pope, Clayne L. "Adult Mortality in America Before 1900." In *Strategic Factors in Nineteenth Century American Economic History: A Volume to Honor Robert W. Fogel*, edited by Claudia Goldin and Hugh Rockoff. University of Chicago Press, 1992.

Primm, James Neal. *Lion of the Valley: St. Louis, Missouri, 1864–1980.* 3rd ed. Missouri Historical Society Press, 1998.

Prucha, Frances Paul. *American Indian Treaties: A History of a Political Anomaly.* University of California Press, 1994.

Quaife, Milo Milton, ed. *Pictures of Gold Rush California.* The Lakeside Press, 1949.

Ransmeier, Johanna S. *Sold People: Traffickers and Family Life in North China.* Harvard University Press, 2017.

Ravage, John W. *Black Pioneers: Images of the Black Experience on the North American Frontier.* University of Utah Press, 2008.

Raverty, Dennis. "Frances Flora Palmer: The Pictorial Domestication of the West." *Women's Art Journal*, 38, no. 1 (Spring/Summer 2017): 3–10.

Rabaka, Reiland. "Toward a Critical Theory of the African American West." In *Enduring Legacies: Ethnic Histories and Cultures of Colorado*, edited by Arturo Aldama, Elisa Facio, Daryl Maeda, and Reiland Rabaka. University Press of Colorado, 2011.

Reda, John. *From Furs to Farms: The Transformation of the Mississippi Valley, 1762–1825.* Northern Illinois University Press, 2016.

Rein, Christopher. "'Our First Duty Was to God and Our Next to Our Country': Religion, Violence, and the Sand Creek Massacre." *Great Plains Quarterly* 34, no. 3 (Summer 2014): 217–38.

Reno, Philip. "Rebellion in New Mexico—1837." *New Mexico Historical Review* 40, no. 3 (1965): 197–213.

Reséndez, Andrés. "National Identity on a Shifting Border: Texas and New Mexico in an Age of Transition." *Journal of American History* 86, no. 2 (September 1999): 668–88.

Reséndez, Andrés. "North American Peonage." *Journal of the Civil War Era* 7, no. 4 (December 2017): 597–619.

Reséndez, Andrés. *Caught Between Profits and Rituals: National Contestation in Texas and New Mexico, 1821–1848.* University of Chicago Press, 1997.

Reséndez, Andrés. *Changing National Identities at the Frontier: Texas and New Mexico, 1800–1850.* Cambridge University Press, 2005.

Reséndez, Andrés. *The Other Slavery: The Uncovered Story of Indian Enslavement in America.* Mariner, 2017.

Reyer, Eduard and S. K. Padover. "Placer-Mining in California." *Pacific Historical Review* 4, no. 4 (December 1935): 386–92.

Richardson, Heather Cox. *How the South Won the Civil War.* Oxford University Press, 2020.

Richter, Daniel K. *Facing East from Indian Country: A Native History of Early America.* Harvard University Press, 2001.

Ridge, Martin. "The Life of an Idea: The Significance of Frederick Jackson Turner's Frontier Thesis." *Montana: The Magazine of Western History* 41, no. 1 (Winter 1991): 2–13.

Riley, Glenda. "Frederick Jackson Turner Overlooked the Ladies." *Journal of the Early Republic* 13, no. 2 (Summer 1993): 216–30.

Roberts, Alaina E. *I've Been Here All the While: Black Freedom on Native Land.* University of Pennsylvania Press, 2021.

Robinson, Charles F. "The Louisiana Purchase and the Black Experience." In *A Whole Country in Commotion: The Louisiana Purchase and the American Southwest*, edited by Patrick G. Williams, S. Charles Bolton, and Jeannie M. Whayne. University of Arkansas Press, 2005.

Rohe, Randall. "Origins & Diffusion of Traditional Placer Mining in the West." *Material Culture* 18, no. 3 (Fall 1986): 127–66.

Rohrbough, Malcolm. "No Boy's Play: Migration and Settlement in Early Gold Rush California." *California History* 79, no. 2 (Summer 2000): 25–43.

Ronda, James P. *Lewis and Clark among the Indians.* Bison Books, 2002.

Rosenblatt, Roger. "Black Autobiography: Life as a Death Weapon." In *Autobiography: Essays Theoretical and Critical*, edited by James Olney. Princeton University Press, 1980.

Ruiz, Vicki L. and Virginia Sánchez Korrol, eds. *Latinas in the United States: A Historical Encyclopedia.* 3 vols. Indiana University Press, 2006.

Ruiz, Vicki L. "Nuestra America: Latino History as United States History." *Journal of American History* (December 2006): 655–72.

Rzeczkowski, Frank. "The Crow Indians and the Bozeman Trail." *Montana: The Magazine of Western History* (Winter 1999): 30–47.

Sanderson, Nathan B. "'We Were All Trespassers': George Edward Lemmon, Anglo-American Cattle Ranching, and the Great Sioux Reservation." *Agricultural History* 85, no. 1 (Winter 2011): 50–71.

Sandweiss, Martha A. "Still Picture, Moving Stories: Reconstruction Comes to Indian Country." In *Civil War Wests: Testing the Limits of the United States*, edited by Adam Arenson and Andrew R. Graybill. University of California Press, 2015.

Sandweiss, Martha A. *The Girl in the Middle: A Recovered History of the American West*. Princeton University Press, 2025.

Saunt, Claudio. *Unworthy Republic: The Dispossession of Native Americans and the Road to Indian Territory*. W. W. Norton, 2020.

Schaefer, Timo. "Soldiers and Civilians: The War of Independence in Oaxaca, 1814–1815." *Mexican Studies / Estudios Mexicanos* 29, no. 1 (Winter 2013): 149–74.

Scharff, Virginia and Carolyn Brucken, eds. *Home Lands: How Women Made the West*. Autry National Center of the American West, 2010.

Scharff, Virginia. *Twenty Thousand Roads: Women, Movement, and the West*. University of California Press, 2003.

Schilz, Thomas F. "Robes, Rum, and Rifles: Indian Middlemen in the Northern Plains Fur Trade." *Montana: The Magazine of Western History* 40, no. 1 (Winter 1990): 2–13.

Schoenberger, Dale T. "The Black Man in the American West." *Negro History Bulletin* 32, no. 3 (March 1969): 7–11.

Schrems, Suzanne H. "The Northern Cheyennes and the Fight for Cultural Sovereignty: The Notes of Father Aloysius Van Der Velden, S.J." *Montana: The Magazine of Western History* 45, no. 2 (Spring 1995): 18–33.

Schulten, Susan. "The Civil War and the Origins of the Colorado Territory." *Western Historical Quarterly* 44 (Spring 2013): 21–46.

Seelfeldt, Douglas, Jeffrey L. Hantman, and Peter S. Onuf, eds. *Across the Continent: Jefferson, Lewis and Clark, and the Making of America*. University of Virginia Press, 2005.

Sheehan, Bernard W. "Jefferson's 'Empire for Liberty.'" *Indiana Magazine of History* 100, no. 4 (December 2004): 346–63.

Shelton, Emily Jones. "Lizzie E. Johnson: A Cattle Queen of Texas." *Southwestern Historical Quarterly* 50, no. 3 (January 1947): 349–66.

Shelton, Laura M. *For Tranquility and Order: Family and Community on Mexico's Northern Frontier, 1800–1850*. University of Arizona Press, 2010.

Sherman, James E. and Barbara H. Sherman. *Ghost Towns and Mining Camps of New Mexico*. University of Oklahoma Press, 1975.

Sides, Hampton. *Blood and Thunder: An Epic of the American West*. Vintage, 2007.

Simmons, Marc. "Spanish Attempts to Open a New Mexico–Sonora Road." *Arizona and the West* 17, no. 1 (Spring 1975): 5–20.

Simmons, Marc. *Albuquerque: A Narrative History*. University of New Mexico Press, 1982.

Sinn, Elizabeth. *Pacific Crossing: California Gold, Chinese Migration, and the Making of Hong Kong*. Hong Kong University Press, 2012.

Slaughter, Thomas P. *Exploring Lewis and Clark: Reflections on Men and Wilderness*. Vintage Books, 2003.

Slotkin, Richard. *A Great Disorder: National Myth and the Battle for America*. Belknap Press of Harvard University Press, 2024.

Slotkin, Richard. *Gunfighter Nation: The Myth of the Frontier in Twentieth-Century America*. University of Oklahoma Press, 1992.

Smith, Clinton F. "Native Borderlands: Colonialism and the Development of Native Power." In *Globalizing Borderlands Studies in Europe and North America*, edited by John W. I. Lee and Michael North. University of Nebraska Press, 2016.

Smith, Dale Edwyna. *African American Lives in St. Louis, 1763–1865: Slavery, Freedom, and the West*. McFarland, 2017.

Smith, Duane A. *The Birth of Colorado: A Civil War Perspective*. University of Oklahoma Press, 1989.

Smith, Henry Nash. *Virgin Land: The American West in Myth and Symbol*. Harvard University Press, 1971.

Smith, Ralph A. "The Scalp Hunter in the Borderlands, 1835–1850." *Arizona and the West* 6, no. 1 (Spring 1964): 5–22.

Smith, Stacey L. "Remaking Slavery in a Free State: Masters and Slaves in Gold Rush California." *Pacific Historical Review* 80, no. 1 (February 2011): 28–63.

Smith, Stacey L. *Freedom's Frontier: California and the Struggle over Unfree Labor, Emancipation, and Reconstruction*. University of North Carolina Press, 2013.

Smith, Willard H. "Schuyler Colfax and Reconstruction Policy." *Indiana Magazine of History* 39, no. 4 (December 1943): 323–44.

Smoak, Gregory E. *Ghost Dances and Identity: Prophetic Religion and American Indian Ethnogenesis in the Nineteenth Century*. University of California Press, 2006.

Speirs, Kenneth. "Writing Self (Effacingly): E-Race-D Presences in 'The Life and Adventures of Nat Love." *Western American Literature* 40, no. 3 (Fall 2005): 301–20.

Spring, Agnes Wright. *Caspar Collins: The Life and Exploits of an Indian Fighter of the Sixties*. University of Nebraska Press, 1969.

St. John, Rachel. "Contingent Continent." *Pacific Historical Review* 86, no. 1 (February 2017): 18–49.

Stampp, Kenneth. *America in 1857: A Nation on the Brink*. Oxford University Press, 1992.

Steckmesser, Kent L. "The Frontier Hero in History and Legend." *Wisconsin Magazine of History* 46, no. 3 (Spring 1963): 168–79.

Stein, Stephen J. *The Shaker Experience in America*. Yale University Press, 1992.

Stewart, Frank H. "Mandan and Hidatsa Villages in the Eighteenth and Nineteenth Centuries." *Plains Anthropologist* 19, no. 66 (November 1974): 287–302.

Stockwell, Mary. *Interrupted Odyssey: Ulysses S. Grant and the American Indians*. Southern Illinois University Press, 2018.

Strang, Cameron B. *Frontiers of Science: Imperialism and Natural Knowledge in the Gulf South Borderlands, 1500–1850*. University of North Carolina Press, 2018.

Swagerty, William R. "A View from the Bottom Up: The Work Force of the American Fur Company on the Upper Missouri in the 1830s." *Montana: The Magazine of Western History* 43, no. 1 (Winter 1993): 18–33.

Sweeney, Edwin R. *Mangas Coloradas: Chief of the Chiricahua Apaches*. University of Oklahoma Press, 1998.

Taylor, Alan. "Jefferson's Pacific: The Science of Distant Empire, 1768–1811." In *Across the Continent: Jefferson, Lewis and Clark, and the Making of America*, edited by Douglas Seelfeldt, Jeffrey L. Hantman, and Peter S. Onuf. University of Virginia Press, 2005.

Taylor, Alan. *The Civil War of 1812: American Citizens, British Subjects, Irish Rebels, & Indian Allies*. Vintage, 2010.

BIBLIOGRAPHY

Taylor, Gordon O. "Voices from the Veil: Black American Autobiography." *Georgia Review* 35, no. 2 (Summer 1981): 341–61.
The Sacagawea Project Board of the Mandan, Hidatsa, and Arikara Nation. *Our Story of Eagle Woman, Sacagawea: They Got it Wrong*. The Paragon Agency, 2021.
Thompson, Jerry D. *Henry Hopkins Sibley: Confederate General of the West*. Texas A&M University Press, 1996.
Thrapp, Dan L., ed. *Encyclopedia of Frontier Biography*. University of Nebraska Press, 1988.
Thwaites, Reuben Gold. "The Story of Lewis and Clark's Journals." *Quarterly of the Oregon Historical Society* 6, no. 1 (March 1905): 26–53.
Tiro, Karim M. "The View from Piqua Agency: The War of 1812, the White River Delawares, and the Origins of Indian Removal." *Journal of the Early Republic* 35, no. 1 (Spring 2015): 25–54.
Trabert, Sarah J. and Kacy L. Hollenback. *Archaeological Narratives of the Northern Great Plains*. University Press of Colorado, 2021.
Tracy, Charles A. "Race, Crime, and Social Policy: The Chinese in Oregon, 1871–1885." *Crime and Social Justice* 14 (Winter 1980): 11–25.
Truett, Samuel. *Fugitive Landscapes: The Forgotten History of the U.S.-Mexican Borderlands*. Yale University Press, 2006.
Truett, Samuel, and Elliot Young, eds. *Continental Crossroads: Remapping U.S.-Mexico Borderlands History*. Duke University Press, 2004.
Tyler, Daniel. "Anglo-American Penetration of the Southwest: The View from New Mexico." *Southwestern Historical Quarterly* 75, no. 3 (January 1972): 325–38.
Tyler, Daniel. "Gringo Views of Governor Manuel Armijo." *New Mexico Historical Review* 45, no. 1 (January 1970): 23–46.
Utley, Robert M. *Sitting Bull: The Life and Times of an American Patriot*. Henry Holt, 2008.
Valencius, Conevery Bolton. *The Lost History of the New Madrid Earthquakes*. University of Chicago Press, 2013.
Van Kirk, Sylvia. "The Role of Native Women in the Fur Trade Society of Western Canada, 1670–1830." *Frontiers: A Journal of Women Studies* 7, no. 3 (1984): 9–13.
Van Tassel, David D. "From Learned Society to Professional Organization: The American Historical Association, 1884-1900." *American Historical Review* 89, no. 4 (October 1984): 929–56.
Vettel-Becker, Patricia. "Sacagawea and Son: The Visual Construction of America's Maternal Feminine." *American Studies* 50, no. 1–2 (Spring/Summer 2009): 27–50.
Vidal, Cécile. "From Incorporation to Exclusion: Indians, Europeans, and Americans in the Mississippi Valley from 1699 to 1830." In *Empires of the Imagination: Transatlantic Histories of the Louisiana Purchase*, edited by Peter J. Kastor and Francois Weil. University of Virginia Press, 2009.
Wainwright, Mary-Jo. "Milestones in California History: The 1846 Bear Flag Revolt: Early Cultural Conflict in California." *California History* 75, no. 2 (Summer 1996): 113.
Waite, Kevin. *West of Slavery: The Southern Dream of a Transcontinental Empire*. University of North Carolina Press, 2021.
Walker, Townshend. "Gold Mountain Guests: Chinese Migration to the United States, 1848–1882." *Journal of Economic History* 37, no. 1 (March 1977): 264–67.
Warren, Louis S. *Buffalo Bill's America: William Cody and the Wild West Show*. Alfred A. Knopf, 2005.

Warren, Louis A. *God's Red Son: The Ghost Dance Religion and the Making of Modern America.* Basic Books, 2017.

Washington, Margaret. "African American History and the Frontier Thesis." *Journal of the Early Republic* 13, no. 2 (Summer 1993): 230–41.

Weber, David J. "The Spanish Borderlands of North America: A Historiography." *OAH Magazine of History* 14, no. 4 (2000): 5–11.

Weber, David J. *The Mexican Frontier, 1821–1846: The American Southwest under Mexico.* University of New Mexico Press, 1982.

Weber, David J. *The Taos Trappers: The Fur Trade in the Far Southwest, 1540–1846.* University of Oklahoma Press, 1970.

Wegars, Priscilla. *Polly Bemis: The Life and Times of a Chinese American Pioneer.* Caxton Press, 2020.

Wells, Merle and Arthur A. Hart. *Idaho: Gem of the Mountains.* Idaho State Historical Society and Windsor Publications, 1985.

West, Elliott. *Continental Reckoning: The American West in the Age of Expansion.* University of Nebraska Press, 2023.

West, Elliott. *The Contested Plains: Indians, Goldseekers, and the Rush to Colorado.* University of Kansas Press, 1998.

West, Elliott. *The Last Indian War: The Nez Perce Story.* Oxford University Press, 2009.

White, Linda Harper and Fred R. Gowans. "Traders to Trappers: Andrew Henry and the Rocky Mountain Fur Trade." *Montana: The Magazine of Western History* 43, no. 1 (Winter 1993): 58–65.

White, Richard. "The Louisiana Purchase and the Fictions of Empire." In *Empires of the Imagination: Transatlantic Histories of the Louisiana Purchase,* edited by Peter J. Kastor and Francois Weil. University of Virginia Press, 2009.

White, Richard. *It's Your Misfortune and None of My Own: A New History of the American West.* University of Oklahoma Press, 1991.

White, Richard. *Railroaded: The Transcontinentals and the Making of Modern America.* W. W. Norton & Co., 2011.

White, Richard. *The Middle Ground: Indians, Empires, and Republics in the Great Lakes Region, 1650–1815.* Cambridge University Press, 1991.

Whitford, William C. *Colorado Volunteers in the Civil War.* 1909; Pruett Press, 1963.

Wiegers, Robert P. "A Proposal for Indian Slave Trading in the Mississippi Valley and Its Impact on the Osage." *Plains Anthropologist* 33, no. 120 (May 1988): 187–202.

Williams, Kidada E. *I Saw Death Coming: A History of Terror and Survival in the War against Reconstruction.* Bloomsbury, 2023.

Williams, Kidada E. *They Left Great Marks on Me: African American Testimonies of Racial Violence from Emancipation to World War I.* New York University Press, 2012.

Williamson, G. R. *Forgotten Games of the Old West: Faro & Monte.* Indian Head Publishing, 2021.

Williamson, G. R. *Frontier Gambling: The Games, the Gamblers & the Great Gambling Halls of the Old West.* Indian Head Publishing, 2011.

Wilson, Elinor. *Jim Beckwourth: Black Mountain Man, War Chief of the Crows, Trader, Trapper, Explorer, Frontiersman, Guide, Scout, Interpreter, Adventurer, and Gaudy Liar.* University of Oklahoma Press, 1972.

Wilson, Gilbert L. "Notes on the Hidatsa Indians," edited by Bella Weitzner. *Anthropological Papers of the American Museum of Natural History* 56, part 2. New York, 1979.

Witgen, Michael. *An Infinity of Nations: How the Native New World Shaped Early North America.* University of Pennsylvania Press, 2011.

Woodworth-Ney, Laura and Tara A. Rowe. "Defying Boundaries: Women in Idaho History." In *Idaho's Place: A New History of the Gem State*, edited by Adam M. Sowards. University of Washington Press, 2014.

Worster, Donald. *An Unsettled Country: Changing Landscapes of the American West.* University of New Mexico Press, 1994.

Worster, Donald. *Rivers of Empire: Water, Aridity, and the Growth of the American West.* Oxford University Press, 1985.

Xu, Yixian. "Chinese Women in Idaho during the Anti-Chinese Movement before 1900." MA Thesis, University of Idaho, 1994.

Yung, Judy. *Unbound Feet: A Social History of Chinese Women in San Francisco.* University of California Press, 1995.

INDEX

Academy of Natural Sciences of Philadelphia, 17
Across the Continent (Currier & Ives), 216–17
Adobe Walls, Battle of, 180
Agai-dika, 3–7, 15, 33, 35
Ah Choy, 276
Ah Jake, Ah Kan, and Ah Ming, ranch of, 291
Ah Kan (mule packer), 228, 321
Albuquerque, NM, 52, 53, 55, 94, 146, 154, 155, 158
Alta California, 52, 54, 87–89, 109
American colonies, xv, xvi
American Dream, xviii, 312, 334
American exceptionalism, xvii, 225
American Fur Company, 70, 71
American Historical Association, xiii–xviii, 317
American Horse, 304
American Philosophical Society, 29–30, 330
American Phrenological Journal, 198
American Progress (Gast), 273
American Revolution, 11, 19, 21, 22, 26, 51, 70
American River, 105, 108–10, 219
Anthony, Scott, 172, 180
Antietam, Battle of, 158

Apache, 52, 54, 55, 75, 77, 78, 82, 86, 90, 95, 101, 106, 142, 157, 163–64, 208
Apache Canyon, 151–53, 155, 157, 158, 162, 176
Appalachian Mountains, 4, 70, 140
Apsáalooke (Crow), 5, 8, 38, 62, 63, 84, 168, 169, 193, 194, 208, 211, 243, 306
  Beckwourth and, 66–72, 81, 83, 120, 123, 124, 126, 127, 136, 137, 174, 183, 193–95, 197
Arapaho, 62, 63, 67, 82, 136, 188, 195–97, 206, 236, 239
  in alliance, 191–92, 204
  Northern, 135, 195–97, 198, 210, 211, 235–37
  Peace Commission and, 208
  in Sand Creek Massacre, 188, 191
  Southern, 83, 86, 142, 162–66, 172–77, 178–86, 207, 208, 257, 258
Arikara, 13, 17, 42, 43, 47, 61, 243, 330
Arizona, 145, 157, 161
Arizpe, 53
Arkansas, 20
Arkansas River, 56, 82, 86, 97, 132, 136, 142, 146, 163, 165, 171, 177, 181, 210, 233, 237, 262

INDEX

Armijo, Manuel, 76, 77, 86, 92–95, 99
Army, U.S., 46, 64, 71, 81, 100, 101, 173, 187, 192, 203, 208, 212, 224, 234, 239, 280, 281, 287, 289, 304
   Barceló and, 96–98, 101, 114, 115
   Beckwourth and, 91, 92, 95, 97, 105, 107, 171–77, 178–80, 197
   Black Southerners and, 201
   Bozeman Trail forts of, 192, 193, 195, 196, 209–10, 214, 231–32
   Charbonneau (Jean-Baptiste) and, 110
   in Civil War, 144–47, 151–59, 160–62, 185
   Colorado regiments of, 144–47, 151–59, 161, 162, 166, 171, 172, 175–77, 178, 186, 307, 310
   Indigenous peoples and, 141–42, 157, 163–65, 171–77, 178–86, 191–93, 195–97, 201, 203–4, 207–9, 233, 234, 240–45, 248–51, 253, 254, 256, 261–69, 273, 274, 286, 289, 305, 318
   in Little Bighorn battle, 243–45, 246, 248, 252, 262, 268
   in Mexican-American War, 90–91, 92–97, 100
   rules of warfare for, 179
   Sand Creek Massacre and, 172–77, 178–86, 188, 191, 198, 207, 208, 258, 307
Arthur, Chester, 288–89
Art Institute of Chicago, xiv–xv, 48
Ashley, William, 60–65, 123
Asian immigrants, xix, xxii, 275, 327
   see also Chinese immigrants
Assiniboine, 8
Atlanta, GA, 178
Auraria, 130–34
aurora borealis, 10
Averell, Jim, 280–82, 283–85, 293–95, 297–300
   lynching of, 298–302
Averill, Charles E., 123

Bannock, MT, 169
Bannock people, 5, 63

Barceló, Dolores Herrero, 52
Barceló, María Gertrudis, xx, xxiii, 52–55, 69, 73–80, 86, 93, 97–99, 101, 102, 113–18, 155, 284, 302, 327, 329, 330, 334–35
   Armijo and, 92–95
   civil suits of, 73–74, 113–16
   Coulter and, 113–15
   de Marle and, 101, 114, 115
   estate of, 115, 116
   fame of, 331, 332
   family of, 56, 73, 76, 77, 101, 115–18
   Field and, 77–78
   funeral for, 117–18, 119
   gambling empire of, 56–58, 73, 75–80, 94, 96, 98, 100–101, 113–18, 132, 318, 331
   house of, 73
   husband of, 56, 73, 76, 77
   illness and death of, 115–17, 119
   Kirker and, 78–79
   Mexican-American War and, 92–95, 117
   moneylending by, 113–16
   mythologizing of, 331
   Taos Rebellion and, 75–76
   Thruston and, 73–74, 101
   U.S. Army and, 96–98, 101, 114, 115
Barceló, Juan Ignacio, 52–56
Barceló, María de la Luz, 52, 53, 115
Barceló, Trinidad, 52, 115
Baton Rouge, LA, 12, 21
Baylor, John R., 145, 161
Bear River, 218, 246
Beaverhead River, 32
Beaver Pond, 44
Beckwith, Jennings, 20–27, 60, 62, 64–65, 68, 81, 127
Beckwith, Jonathan, 21
Beckwith, Marmaduke, 21
Beckwith plantation, 21–25, 44, 62, 65, 68
Beckwourth, Elizabeth Lettbetter, 136–37, 162, 164, 185

INDEX

Beckwourth (Beckwith), Jim, xx, xxiii, 60–72, 73, 80, 81–91, 100, 105–12, 113, 119–28, 138, 161–62, 168, 191–95, 197–98, 329, 332, 334–35
- Apsáalooke and, 66–72, 81, 83, 120, 123, 124, 126, 127, 136, 137, 174, 183, 193–95, 197
- autobiography of, 123–28, 332
- as blacksmith's apprentice, 60
- Bonner and, 122–25, 127, 128
- bullet amulet worn by, 120, 194
- Carrington and, 193
- character of, 198
- Charbonneau (Jean-Baptiste) and, 110, 119, 220
- childhood of, 22–27
- daughter of, 162, 185
- in Denver, 130–37, 161–62, 191
- in fur trade, 60–66, 69–71, 82–83, 87, 124–25, 191–93, 197, 198
- at gold camps, 107–8, 198
- Hollister and, 184
- illness and death of, 194–95, 197–98, 201
- "Indian life" of, 65–72, 81, 83, 120, 123, 124, 126, 127, 136, 137, 174, 183, 193, 194
- marriage to Elizabeth, 136–37, 162, 164, 185
- marriage to Luisa, 86, 87, 91
- marriage to Sue, 185, 191, 198
- memory of, 332
- in Mexican-American War, 91, 92, 95, 97, 198
- mountain pass created by, 119–20, 129, 332
- Payne and, 164–65, 184
- portrait of, 198
- relationship with Eliza, 65, 67, 81
- in Sand Creek Massacre, 173–77, 178–84, 198, 208
- Soule's murder and, 185
- Southern Cheyenne and, 83–87, 133–36, 142, 174, 179–80, 186
- spelling of name, 62
- Stobie and, 186, 198
- sunstroke suffered by, 82, 83
- Templeton and, 193–95
- theft charges against, 161–62
- U.S. Army and, 91, 92, 95, 97, 105, 107, 171–77, 178–80, 197

Beckwourth, Julia, 162, 185
Beckwourth Pass, 119–20, 129, 332
Beckwourth Valley, 120–21, 125, 128
Bemis, Charles, 275–76, 278, 290–92, 313–16, 320–25, 329
- Cox's shooting of, 313
- death of, 324, 326
- illness of, 322–24
- marriage to Polly, 314–15, 324
- mining claim of, 314
- ranch acquired by, 291–92
Bemis, Polly, xxi, xxiii, 275–78, 290–92, 302, 311–16, 320–28, 329, 334–35
- Boise trip of, 325–26
- cooking of, 276, 320–22, 324
- death of, 326–27
- fame of, 323–25
- fires and, 290, 320, 323–24
- federal registration of, 314–16, 324, 325
- Gizycka and, 323
- Grangeville trip of, 324–25
- marriage of, 314–15, 324
- myths about, 329–30
- photograph of, 313–14
- ranch of, 291–92, 320–26
- sale to trader and journey to America, xxi, 226–30, 231, 254, 321, 323, 325
Bent, Charles (brother of William), 82, 83, 85, 97, 99–100
Bent, Charles (son of William), 175, 176
Bent, George, 175, 176, 179, 258
Bent, Ignacia, 99, 100
Bent, Robert, 173
Bent, William, 82–85, 97, 173, 175
Benton, Thomas Hart, 59
Bent's Fort, 82, 83, 86, 91, 96, 97, 173
Biddle, Nicholas, 45
Bighorn Mountains, 193, 245, 248–49
Bighorn River, 41, 67, 70, 194, 287

Big Nose, 196, 197
Big Piney Creek, 193
Bitterroot Mountains, 3, 4, 14, 32, 34, 35, 37, 47
Black Americans, xix, xxii, 27, 60, 81, 109
   California laws and, 111–12, 120, 220
   civil rights of, 111–12, 120, 201, 207, 212, 220, 234, 311–12, 327
   enslaved, *see* slavery
   formerly enslaved, 201, 202
   intermarriage and, 26–27, 314
Black Crook, The, 235
Blackfoot, 63, 65–68, 71, 120
Black Hawk (Sauk leader), 24, 71
Black Hawk, CO, 163, 164, 181, 184, 185, 189, 190, 212, 214, 223
Black Hills, 3, 9, 170, 239–40, 265
Black Kettle, 142, 165, 171, 174, 208
bloodletting, 28
Boise, ID, 325–26
Bonaparte, Napoleon, 4, 12
Bonner, Thomas D., 122–25, 127, 128
Boone, A. G., 136, 142
Boone, Daniel, 123, 136
Bosque Redondo, 163
Bothwell, Albert John, 294–301
Bowles, Samuel, 204, 224–25
Box Elder, 179
Box Elder Creek, 266–67
Boyle, Hugh, 304, 306
Bozeman, John, 169
Bozeman Trail, 169, 191–93, 195, 196, 204, 209–10, 214, 231–32
Bridger, Jim, 66, 119, 123, 127, 193, 194
Britain, British people, xv, 4, 8, 9, 12, 17, 26, 33–34, 36, 41, 54, 63, 65, 88, 89
   Embargo Act and, 41
   Hong Kong and, 226–27
   Indigenous peoples and, 26, 27, 46–48
   U.S. relations with, 41, 45
   in War of 1812, 47, 48, 51, 70, 88
Brooks, Preston, 125
Brown, William Wells, 81

Buchanan, Frank, 295, 298–99, 301
Buchanan, James, 134, 142
buffalo, xiv, 5, 8, 9, 14–16, 29, 35, 68, 82–84, 85, 132, 167, 171, 173, 191, 232, 241, 243, 249, 256, 264, 273, 286, 289
Buffalo Hump Mining District, 321
Bull Run, First Battle of, 144, 146
Bumppo, Natty, 123
Butler, Andrew, 125
Byers, William, 129–31, 176, 197, 198

Caddo, 20
Cahokia, 43, 44
Calamity Jane, 285
California, xvi, 88–91, 97, 102, 105, 106, 109–12, 119–23, 131, 137, 145, 156, 157, 187, 191, 225, 281
   constitution of, 110–12, 116
   gold rush in, xxi, 105–10, 113, 118, 123, 128, 133, 198, 218–21, 274
   racially restrictive laws in, 111–12, 120, 198, 220
California, 107
Cameahwait, 33–35, 37
Cameron, J. D., 248
Camp Fortunate, 32
Camp Merritt, 304
Camp Robinson, 251–52, 266, 268
Camp Weld, 146, 159, 161–62
Canada, Canadians, xxi, 8, 9, 41, 43, 48, 65, 68, 233, 253–54, 264, 267
Canadian River, 257, 258, 260
Canby, E. R. S., 146, 151, 154–56
Capitol, U.S., 207
Carrington, Henry, 192–93
Carson, Josefa, 100
Carson, Kit, xviii, 86, 87, 89, 97, 119, 123, 127, 128, 179–80, 331
Carter, Landon, 21
Cass, Lewis, 70–71
Cather, Willa, 279
cattle ranching, 279–80, 287–89, 295, 296, 303, 319
   Northern Cheyenne and, 286, 289, 303
   rustlers and, 293, 296–300

INDEX

water and, 294
Watson and, xxi, 284, 285, 293–302, 303, 331
winter storm and, 286, 289
women and, 284, 285
Census Bureau, 317
Central City, CO, 189, 190, 214
Central City *Register*, 183, 184
Central Pacific Railroad, xxi, 161, 219, 221–24, 229, 246
Chalk, 261–62
Chamberlain, William, 198
Charbonneau, Jean-Baptiste, 18, 29, 31, 32, 34–39, 42, 44, 45, 86–87, 98, 110, 112
   Beckwourth and, 110, 119, 220
   Clark and, 38–39, 44, 45, 48, 86–87
   gold prospecting of, 110
   Sacajawea's pregnancy with and birth of, 10, 15–18
   U.S. Army and, 110
Charbonneau, Lizette, 46–48, 330
Charbonneau, Toussaint, 9–10, 45–47, 51, 66, 330
   Chouteau and, 44–45
   on Lewis and Clark Expedition, 13–18, 31–39, 44, 45
   Sacajawea's marriage to, 9, 34
   in St. Louis, 42–45, 59
Cherry Creek, 130, 132, 162, 333
Chesapeake Bay, 106
Cheyenne, 8, 9, 63, 66–68, 71, 83, 136, 165, 188, 170, 204
Cheyenne, Northern, xxi, 132–33, 135, 142, 162, 167–71, 174, 179, 186, 205, 206, 231, 232, 238, 240–45, 248–53, 256–69, 281, 286–90, 303–7, 318–20, 332–33
   in alliances, 191–92, 195–97, 204, 242–45, 257
   annuities and relocation of, 239
   Black Hills and, 239–40, 265
   Boyle and, 304, 306
   Buffalo Hat of, 260
   Carrington and, 192–93
   cattle of, 286, 289, 303
   Council of 1864 held by, 167–70
   Council of Forty-Four of, 210, 288, 307
   Crook's campaign against, 249–52, 280
   Dawes Act and, 289
   diseases and, 257–58
   Elk Horn Scrapers society of, 167–70, 243, 260, 288
   escape from Indian Territory and return to homeland, 259–69, 273, 286–88, 305, 320, 333
   Fort Fetterman and, 231–32, 236
   Fort Keogh and, 250, 268, 281, 287
   Fort Reno and, 192, 257–59, 261–62
   Ghost Dance and, 306–7
   government schools and, 332–33
   guns purchased by, 257–59, 268
   horses stolen by, 258, 262, 264, 268
   in Hundred Men Killed Fight, 195–97, 214
   Indian agents and, 256–59, 265, 266, 304
   land claims of, 307, 319
   in Little Bighorn battle, 243–45, 246, 248, 252, 262, 268
   Little Wolf as leader of, *see* Little Wolf
   Medicine Bundle of, 252, 260, 266, 307
   Montana and, 169
   North Country homeland of, xxi, 192, 215, 236, 238, 239, 250, 252, 253, 258, 266, 269, 286–88, 305, 333
   Pawnee and, 202–4
   Peace Commission and, 208–11
   photographs of, 318
   railroad and, 202–4
   at Red Cloud Agency, 242, 250–51, 265, 267, 268
   on reservations, 252–53, 256–60, 288–89, 303–5, 307, 312, 318, 319
   rituals and ceremonies of, 238, 305–7
   starvation among, 256, 269, 286, 303–4
   Two Moons as leader of, 288, 289
   in Washington, D.C., delegation, 235–37, 239, 249
   winter storm and, 286, 289, 290

INDEX

Cheyenne, Southern, 132, 163, 164–66, 167–71, 177, 179, 186, 206, 208, 210, 211, 236, 257, 258, 306
   in alliances, 191–92, 204, 257
   Beckwourth and, 83–87, 133–36, 142, 174, 179–80, 186
   on reservation, 252, 253, 287
   in Sand Creek Massacre, 172–77, 178–86, 188, 191, 198, 207, 208, 307
   white allyship and, 318–19
Cheyenne, WY, 204, 213, 301
Cheyenne Daily Leader, 299–300
Cheyenne Indians, The (Grinnell), 318
Chicago, IL, xiii–xvii, 48, 121, 122, 190, 212, 248, 254, 280, 317
Chicago Times, 273
Chicago Tribune, 203
Chihuahua, 55, 93
Chihuahua Trail, 77, 101, 331
China, 219, 220, 225–26, 227, 230, 231
China Jake Ranch, 291
Chinese Exclusion Acts, 277, 278, 291, 292, 294, 311
Chinese immigrants, xxi, 131, 219–21, 225, 229, 274–78, 290–92, 323–26
   Geary Act registration requirements for, 311–16
   immigration restrictions on, 254, 274–75, 277, 278, 291, 292, 294, 311, 312, 324, 327
   intermarriage and, 275–76
   miners, xxi, 220, 227, 229, 274, 275, 278, 290, 292, 324, 325
   photographs of, 313–14
   railroad workers, xxi, 221–25, 227, 229, 311
   violence against, 274, 275, 290–91, 301, 325
Chinese Six Companies, 312
Chinook, 36, 37
Chiricahua Apache, 54
Chivington, John, 151–53, 159, 163–64, 171–74, 176, 177, 178, 181–83, 185
Chouteau, Auguste, 44–45, 59, 66

Christian Advocate and Journal, 126
Church, Jenny, 276
citizenship rights, 59, 97, 102, 112, 311–12, 327
Civil War, xix–xxi, 139, 143–47, 155–58, 160–62, 168, 179, 186, 187, 193, 209, 218, 229, 291, 311, 331, 333, 334
   1st Colorado in, 144–47, 151–59, 161, 162, 176, 310
   end of, 185, 191, 192, 198, 206
   postwar period, 188, 201, 206, 207, 224, 233, 234, 274, 291
   secessions in, 141
   Sherman's march in, 178
Clark, Julia, 44
Clark, Meriwether Lewis, 44, 95
Clark, William, 19, 95, 98
   enslaved man of, 12, 19–20, 43
   as Indian affairs agent, 43–44, 61
   Jefferson and, 43
   Sacajawea and Charbonneau's visit to, 42–45
   Sacajawea's children and, 38–39, 44, 45, 48, 86–87
   see also Lewis and Clark Expedition
Clark, William (White Hat), 251, 267–69
Clark Fork River, 195
Clatsop, 36, 37
Clay, Katherine, 276
Clear Creek, 129, 140, 189, 214
Clear Creek Road, 181
Clearwater River, 35
Cleveland, Grover, 291, 305
Cody, William "Buffalo Bill," xiv, xvii, 285
Cole, Ralph, 301
Colfax, Schuyler, 187–91, 204, 213–14, 225, 240, 308, 310
Collier, David C., 183–84
Colorado, 142, 143, 157, 163–66, 169, 171, 178, 179, 181–82, 189–90, 197, 198, 204–7, 210–13, 229, 237, 248, 310
   gold in, xx, 128, 129–31, 133, 137, 138–41, 143–45, 156, 187, 188–91, 198, 204–6, 212–14, 220

INDEX

silver in, 206, 212, 213
Volunteer Regiments of, 144–47, 151–59, 161, 162, 166, 171, 172, 175–77, 178, 186, 307, 310
Columbia River, 35–37, 228
Comanche, 51, 67, 78, 90, 95, 142, 158, 179–80, 208, 257, 330
Commerce of the Prairies (Gregg), 80
Compromise of 1850, 116
Condition of the Indian Tribes, The, 207
Congress, U.S., 11, 12, 90, 102, 106, 121–22, 125, 131, 136, 142, 160–61, 178, 201, 212, 221, 248, 254, 269, 277, 291, 308
    Indian policies and, 70, 136, 207–12, 215, 233, 239, 289–90, 303, 305, 307
    Peace Commission of, 208–12, 215
    slavery and, 20, 22, 89, 109, 115–16, 121
Consolidated Ditch Company, 141
Constitution, U.S., xvi
    Thirteenth Amendment to, 198, 327
    Fourteenth Amendment to, 201, 311
    Fifteenth Amendment to, 234, 312
    Nineteenth Amendment to, 322–23
Continental Divide, 35, 213
Cook, Sam, 144, 145
Cooke, Jay, & Co., 235
Cooke, Philip St. George, 93, 98
Cooper, James Fenimore, 123
Corinne, UT, 218–20, 223, 225, 246–47, 309
Corps of Discovery Expedition, *see* Lewis and Clark Expedition
Coulter, George, 113–15
cowboys, 87, 280, 281, 284
Cox, Johnny, 313
Crazy Horse, 241, 242, 244, 250
Crazy Woman Fork, 192
Creek, 72
Crocker, Charles, 222, 223
Crook, George, 240, 241, 243, 244, 249–52, 280
Crow (chief), 258
Crow (people), *see* Apsáalooke

Crowder, Gene, 293–99, 301
Cuba, 318
Cumberland Gap, 22
Cumberland River, 23
Currier & Ives, 216–17
Curtis, Samuel R., 176
Curtis, Samuel S., 141, 176
Custer, George Armstrong, 239, 243–45, 246, 263

Daily Mining Journal (Black Hawk), 163, 184, 185, 189, 190, 204, 206, 310
Daily Ogden Junction, 246
Dakota people, 13, 23
Dakota territories, 142, 239, 266, 285, 286, 306, 330
Dash for the Timber, A (Remington), 284
Davis, Jefferson, 145
Davis, Joseph, 124, 125
Dawes, Henry, 289
Dawes Severalty Act, 289, 319
Declaration of Independence, 12, 198
DeCorey, John, 293–99, 301
Delano, Columbus, 236, 237
de Marle, August, 101, 114, 115
Democrats, 88, 109, 115, 142, 160, 207, 212, 248, 254, 277, 291, 294, 295
Denver, CO, 129–37, 140–44, 146, 159, 161–62, 165, 167, 171, 177, 178–81, 183, 185, 188–89, 191, 197, 203–5, 212–14, 224, 279, 333
Denver Gazette, 197
Deseret, 111, 217
Deseret News, 218, 223, 247, 309
Douglas, Stephen, 121–22, 125
Douglass, Frederick, 122
Dull Knife, 232, 233, 235–38, 240, 242, 248–52, 258, 260, 261–63, 265, 266, 268, 287
Durant, Thomas, 223, 224
Durbin, John Henry, 296–98, 300, 301
Dyer, Alexander, 100–101

earthquake, 46
Edmunds Act, 277
El Camino Real de Tierra Adentro, 54–55

El Paso, TX, 95, 96, 145, 146
El Paso del Norte, 54, 55
Embargo Act, 41
Empire, CO, 190
Europe, xv, xvii, 30, 40
  immigration from, 131, 264, 327
Evans, John, 163, 165–66, 171, 180

Famished Elk, 288, 307, 319
farmers, farming, xvi, xvii, xviii, xxii, 4, 23, 25, 30, 42, 43–44, 46, 52, 53, 54, 59, 74, 86, 87, 97, 98, 117, 128, 132, 136, 138, 143, 201, 255, 257, 264, 276, 281, 289, 291, 295, 303, 333
Feather River, 119, 123, 128
Feather Valley, 332
Field, Matt, 77–80
Field and Stream, 323
Fighting Cheyennes, The (Grinnell), 318
Filson, John, 123
Florida, 12, 82, 141
Fong Yue Ting v. US, 312
Fontaine qui Bouille, 172
Fort Abraham Lincoln, 243
Fort Cass, 70–72
Fort C. F. Smith, 193–95, 209
Fort Clarke, 64
Fort Dodge, 263
Fort Ellis, 243, 245
Fort Fetterman, 231–32, 236, 241, 243
Fort Keogh, 250, 268, 281, 287
Fort Laramie, 162, 192, 193, 208–11, 214, 235, 238
  Treaty of, 132, 232–33, 236, 237, 239
Fort Leavenworth, 97, 105, 144
Fort Lyon (formerly Fort Wise), 142, 146, 151, 163, 164, 165, 171, 172, 177, 180
Fort Mandan, 13–17, 44
Fort Manuel, 47, 330
Fort Phil Kearny, 193, 195–96, 209, 214–15
Fort Reno, 192, 257–59, 261–62
Fort Sumter, 143, 161
Fort Union (New Mexico), 146, 151, 153, 154, 158–59
Fort Union (Upper Missouri Valley), 69–70, 72
Fort Vasquez, 83–86, 110, 133
Fox, 24–26, 71
France, French people, 4, 8, 9, 11, 12, 20, 30, 33–36, 41, 54, 68, 89
  Code Noir of, 22, 27
  French Revolution, 51
  intermarriage and, 27
  Louisiana purchased from, *see* Louisiana Purchase
Franklin, Benjamin, 30
Free-Soil Party, 109, 115
Free State Hotel, 125
Frémont, John C., 87, 89–90, 97, 101, 123, 143
frontier
  end of, 317, 318
  trade and, 33
  Turner's thesis on, xiii–xviii, xxi–xxii, 48, 317, 318
  use of term, xv
  see also West
frontier myth, xviii–xxiii, 12, 273, 284, 285, 302, 310, 312, 328, 329, 330, 334, 335
  in art, 207, 216–17, 273, 284
  Cass and, 70
  cowboys in, 284
  Indian disappearance in, xviii, 237–38, 330
  Indian policy and, 186
  Lewis and Clark and, 39
  Manifest Destiny and, xviii, 89, 122, 201, 213, 225, 240, 312, 334
  and rights of Black and Indigenous men, 111–12, 220
  women and, 285, 302
Fugitive Slave Act, 116
fur trade, 8, 9, 27, 41, 44, 45, 47, 68, 72, 82–83, 123
  Beckwourth in, 60–66, 69–71, 82–83, 87, 124–25, 191–93, 197, 198

Galbraith, Robert M., 296, 300
Gallatin Valley, 194

INDEX

gambling, 57, 76
  Barceló's business, 56–58, 73, 75–80, 94, 96, 98, 100–101, 113–18, 132, 318, 331
Gardner, Alexander, 209, 211, 237–38
Garfield, James, 288
Gast, John, 273
Geary, Thomas, 311
Geary Act, 311–16
Ghost Dance, 306–7
Giddings, James, 115, 116
Gilpin, William, 143–46
Gizycka, Eleanor, 323
Glorieta Pass, battle of, 151–54, 157, 162, 172, 176
Glorieta Mesa, 151, 153
gold, 53, 56–58, 73, 132, 137, 145, 160, 168, 169, 187, 191, 221, 294, 324
  in Black Hills, 239–40
  in California, xxi, 105–10, 113, 118, 123, 128, 133, 198, 218–21, 274
  in Colorado Rocky Mountains, xx, 128, 129–31, 133, 137, 138–41, 143–45, 156, 187, 188–91, 198, 204–6, 212–14, 220
Grand Central Hotel, 238
Grangeville, ID, 278, 290, 291, 313, 315, 322, 324–26
Grant, Fred, 239
Grant, Ulysses S., 156, 162, 172–73, 208, 209, 212–13, 225, 234, 235, 240, 248, 308
  Indigenous peoples and, 233–37, 239–42
Grasshopper, 307
Great Basin, 111, 119, 129, 222
Great Falls, 28–30
Great Lakes, 4, 11, 43
Great Plains, xvi, 3, 8, 29, 56, 61, 64, 84, 132, 136, 139, 162, 168, 169, 175, 179, 207, 209, 212, 214, 232, 238–41, 248, 251, 254, 279, 306, 332
Great Salt Lake, 111, 217
Great Sioux Reservation, 239
Greeley, Horace, 129–31, 140, 234
Green River, 62–63, 191, 192

Gregg, Josiah, 80
Gregory Gulch, 129–30, 139–41, 188, 234
Grinnell, Elizabeth, 318
Grinnell, George Bird, 169, 318–19
Guam, 318
Guleke, Henry "Harry," 321, 323
Gulf of Mexico, 11, 43, 106

Hanson, John, 313–14
Harper & Brothers, 126, 127
Harper's Magazine, 284
Harper's Monthly, 124, 126–27
Harper's New Monthly Magazine, 124, 126–27
Harper's Weekly, 284
Harrison, William Henry, 25, 45–46
Hawai'i, 107, 317
Hayes, Rutherford B., 248, 258
Head Chief (Vehoneme'ko), 303–6
Heá'ke (Young Mule), 303–6
Heavy Shield, 65–66
Henderson, George, 296, 299
Herald of Freedom, 125
Hidatsa, 6–10, 11–18, 29, 34, 37–39, 41–43, 45, 47, 51, 67, 330
  Sacajawea's kidnapping and life with, xx, 6–10, 11, 18, 31–34
historians, xiv, xv, xvii–xix, 331, 332, 334
  American Historical Association, xiii–xviii
History of the Expedition under the Command of Captains Lewis and Clark (Allen and Biddle, eds.), 48
History of the First Regiment of Colorado Volunteers (Hollister), 162, 310
Hollister, Carrie Matthews, 213, 214, 225, 240, 246–48, 308–10, 333
Hollister, Ovando, xx–xxi, xxiii, 138–41, 176, 181, 191, 204–7, 217–19, 224, 246–47, 308–9, 329, 333–35
  Beckwourth and, 184
  Bowles and, 204
  in Civil War, xx, 139, 144–47, 151–59, 161
  Colfax and, 190, 213–14, 225, 308, 310
  Colorado gold rush and, xx, 138–41, 187, 188

Hollister, Ovando (*cont.*)
  death and funeral of, 309–10, 333
  First Congregational Church and, 308–10
  Grant and, 212
  hernia of, 157–59
  History of the First Regiment of Colorado Volunteers, 162, 310
  house built by, 308
  Indigenous peoples as viewed by, 164, 166, 181, 206, 207, 246, 310
  marriage of, 214, 225, 247
  memory of, 333
  The Mines of Colorado, 204–6
  Mormons and, 217–19, 247, 308, 309, 333
  as newspaperman and writer, 159, 162–62, 184, 185, 189, 190, 204–6, 211–14, 217–19, 223, 225, 308, 310
  Ping Chong and, 219, 220
  railroads and, 217, 219, 223–25
  as Republican, 247–48
  Shaker upbringing of, xx, 138–39, 144, 217, 308
  tax collector position of, 247, 248, 308
homesteading
  Homestead Act, 160–61, 188, 254, 274, 289
  in Wyoming, 281, 283, 284, 293–95
Hong Kong, xxi, 219–21, 226–28, 323
Horse Creek, 281, 283, 294, 296
Horse Prairie Creek, 32
Hundred Men Killed Fight, 195–97, 214

Idaho, xxi, xxii, 219, 228, 229, 247, 274–78, 290–91, 306, 311, 314, 315, 320, 323, 324, 325, 327
Idaho County News, 325
Idaho Statesman, 311
Illini, 22
Illinois, 22, 121, 217
Immigration Act of 1924, 327
Independence, MO, 56, 59, 74
Independence Rock, 281, 298–99
Indiana, 22, 25, 41, 45, 187, 308
Indian Appropriations Act, 233
Indian Removal Act, 70, 88, 139
Indian reservations, xxi, 70–72, 82, 88, 134, 136, 139, 142, 163, 171, 186, 190, 209, 210, 215, 233, 235–37, 239, 240, 274, 281, 287, 289, 306, 312, 327
  breakup of lands in, 289
  Northern Cheyenne and, 252–53, 256–60, 288–89, 303–5, 307, 312, 318, 319
  Southern Cheyenne and, 252, 253, 287
  Standing Rock, 306
Indian Territory, 70–72, 236–37, 252–53, 256–61, 306
  Northern Cheyenne's escape from and return to homeland, 259–69, 273, 286–88, 305, 320, 333
  see also Indian reservations
Indigenous peoples, xviii, xx–xxii, 4, 7, 18, 24, 72, 75, 81, 100, 102, 109, 132, 157, 186, 190, 197–98, 327, 334
  alliances among, 191–92, 195–97, 204, 242–45, 257, 306
  American schools and, 211, 235, 305, 332–33
  annuities to, 163, 209, 231, 233, 236, 239
  British and, 26, 27, 46–48
  Buffalo Bill's Wild West Show and, xiv
  Bureau of Indian Affairs and agents for, 43–44, 61, 134, 136, 142, 165, 193, 208–9, 211, 240, 248, 251, 256–59, 265, 266, 288, 304, 305
  California laws and, 111–12
  captives taken by, 6
  Chicago World's Fair and, xiii–xiv
  citizenship for, 327
  "disappearance" of, xviii, 237–38, 305, 310, 330
  enslaved, 4, 87, 106
  frontier myth and, xviii, xix
  Grant and, 233–37, 239–42
  Hollister's view of, 164, 166, 181, 206, 207, 246, 310
  in Hundred Men Killed Fight, 195–97, 214

intermarriage and, 9, 27, 66
Jefferson and, 40–41
land taken from, 289–90, 305, 312, 319
Lewis and Clark expedition and, 13–14
literature about, 123–24, 126–27
in Little Bighorn battle, 243–45, 246, 248, 252, 262, 268
northern lights and, 10
photographs of, 211, 237–38, 318
railroads and, 201–4, 208, 210, 235
removal to reservations, *see* Indian reservations
resistance and raids by, 41, 45–46, 64, 135, 142, 157, 158, 162, 163, 165, 167, 179, 186, 188, 191–92, 195–97, 201–5, 208, 235, 262, 264, 273, 305, 333
rituals and ceremonies of, 305–7
in Sand Creek Massacre, 172–77, 178–86, 188, 191, 198, 207, 208, 258, 307
smallpox and, 3, 6
U.S. Army and, 141–42, 157, 163–65, 171–77, 178–86, 191–93, 195–97, 201, 203–4, 207–9, 233, 234, 240–45, 248–51, 253, 254, 256, 261–69, 273, 274, 286, 289, 305, 318
U.S. Congress and, 70, 136, 207–12, 215, 233, 239, 289–90, 303, 305, 307
U.S. treaties with, 25, 132, 142, 190, 208, 210–11, 214, 232–33, 235–37, 239, 240, 289
Washington, D.C., delegation of, 233, 235–37, 239, 249
white settlers and, xvi, xviii, 19, 23–26, 30, 33, 41, 42, 45–46, 52–55, 72, 132–36, 139, 142, 181, 186, 192, 201, 207, 213, 233, 236–38, 246, 264, 274, 287, 288, 290, 310, 312, 334
women and diplomatic relations in, 35, 66
in Wounded Knee Massacre, 306–7
see also specific peoples

influenza pandemic, 322
Ingersoll, Robert, 311, 312
Interior, U.S. Department of, 236, 287
intermarriage, 9, 26–27, 66, 275–76, 314
Iowa, 110–11, 294
Ioway, 43
Iron Bull, 195
Iron Teeth, 249, 259
irrigation rights, 294, 295, 298
Irving, Washington, 43
Isthmus of Panama, 106, 322

Jackson, Andrew, 70
Jackson, George, 128
Jackson (Lakota spy), 267
Japan, 275
Jaramillo, Maria, 97
Jay Cooke & Co., 235
Jefferson, Thomas, 11–12, 15, 17, 19
  Clark and, 43
  Indigenous peoples and, 40–41
  Lewis and Clark Expedition and, 29–31, 33, 39, 40
  Louisiana Purchase and, 12, 24, 41, 131
  Notes on the State of Virginia, 24
  Sheheke and, 40–43
Jefferson Barracks, 64, 81
Jefferson River, 31
Jefferson Territory (later, Colorado), 131, 136, 137
Johns Hopkins University, xiv
Johnson, Andrew, 192–93, 207, 209, 221
Johnston, Albert Sidney, 156
Julesburg, CO, 179, 204
Jung Chew, 321
Junta Popular, 76
Justice Department, U.S., 234

Kansas, xvi, xxi, 121–22, 125, 126, 129, 131, 132, 137, 139, 142, 144, 146, 162, 171, 179, 208, 253–55, 262–64, 294
Kansas City, MO, 204
Kansas-Nebraska Act, 122, 139
Kansas River, 61
Kearny, Phil, 193

INDEX

Kearny, Stephen Watts, 91, 94–101, 151, 193, 331
Kennerly, William Clark, 98
Kentucky, xvi, 11, 19, 22, 43
Kickapoo, 46
Kiowa, 8, 10, 82, 158, 179–80, 208, 257
Kirker, James, 78–79
Kit Fox Society, 249
Klinkhammer, Pete, 320, 326
Knife River, 6–8, 15
Knife River Villages, xx, 7–10, 11, 19, 26, 30, 38, 39, 40–42, 45–48, 51, 54, 58
Ku Klux Klan, 234
Kumeyaay, 110

Labadie, Lorenzo, 118
Lakota, 7, 13, 23, 38, 42, 47, 61, 63, 162, 179, 193–97, 202, 205, 232, 240–45, 248, 250, 251, 266–68, 306
   in alliances, 191–92, 195–97, 245, 257
   Black Hills and, 239–40
   Hunkpapa, 192, 240, 242, 251, 267, 306
   in Little Bighorn battle, 244, 245, 246, 248
   Minneconjou, 196, 240, 306
   Oglala, 196, 209, 240–42, 244, 250
   Peace Commission and, 208–11
   Sans Arc, 240
Lame Deer, MT, 304, 305
Lamy, Jean-Baptiste, 117
Las Vegas, NM, 93
Latter-day Saints, *see* Mormons
Lawrence, KS, 125
Lean Bear, 164
Leaping Fish Woman, 6, 9, 32–34
Lebanon, KS, 253–55
Lee, Light-Horse Harry, 21
Lee, Robert E., 185
Left Hand, 142
Leg in the Water, 180
Lemhi River, 3
Leutze, Emanuel, 207, 216
Lewis, Meriwether, 19, 31, 44
Lewis and Clark Expedition (Corps of Discovery), xx, 10, 12–18, 19–20, 28–39, 40, 59, 62, 123, 334

   botanical specimens and, 29–30, 34, 37, 39
   Charbonneau on, 13–18, 31–39, 44, 45
   at Fort Mandan, 13–17, 44
   Jefferson and, 29–31, 33, 39, 40
   journals of, 39, 44, 45, 48, 61, 330
   Sacajawea in, xx, 10, 14–18, 19, 20, 28–39, 44, 48, 61, 68, 330
   Shoshone and, 13–15, 17, 19, 29, 31–35
Lewiston, ID, 228, 277–78, 321, 323
Lewiston Tribune, 329
Liberal Party, 309
Life and Adventures of James P. Beckwourth, The (Beckwourth), 123–28, 332
Lili'uokalani, Queen, 317
Lincoln, Abraham, 71, 141–43, 158, 160–61, 163, 181, 187–88, 214
   assassination of, 185, 187, 188, 207
   Colfax and, 187–88, 214
Lisa, Manuel, 26, 41, 42, 45, 47
Little Bear, 236
Little Bighorn, Battle of, 243–45, 246, 248, 252, 262, 268
Little Finger Nail, 259
Little Robe, 180
Little Wolf, xxi, xxiii, 168–70, 191, 195–97, 214–15, 238, 240–45, 248–53, 256–69, 287, 292, 304, 307, 316, 318–20, 327, 328, 329, 334–35
   alliances and, 191–92, 195–97
   Black Hills and, 239
   Clark and, 267–69
   death of, 319–20
   drinking of, 288
   escape from Indian Territory and return to homeland, 259–69, 273, 286–88, 305, 320, 333
   Famished Elk murdered by, 288, 307, 319
   at Fort Reno, 192
   Grinnell and, 318–19
   in Hundred Men Killed Fight, 195–97, 214
   leadership role surrendered by, 288
   Little Bighorn battle and, 243–44
   Medicine Bundle of, 252, 260, 266, 307

memory of, 332–33
Peace Commission and, 210–12, 215
photographs of, 211, 238
railroad and, 202, 204
reseating ceremony and, 307
on reservation, 256–57
as Sweet Medicine Chief, 170, 210, 238, 260, 307, 319, 320
Washington, D.C., trip to, 233, 235–37
Woodward and, 231–33
Long, Bertha, 292, 313, 326
Long, John, 313
Long, Stephen, 62
Los Angeles, CA, 87–88, 90, 106, 107, 110, 121
Louisiana, 4, 11, 18, 20–24, 26, 27, 28, 30, 43, 141
Louisiana Purchase, 14, 20, 21, 23, 30, 46, 63, 64, 70, 80, 88, 106, 121–22, 330
Jefferson and, 12, 24, 41, 131
Luiseño, 110
Luttig, John, 47

Madison, James, 70
Magoffin, James, 93–94, 98
Magoffin, Samuel, 98
Magoffin, Susan, 98
Maine, 60
Mandan, 6, 7, 10, 11–13, 16, 17, 38, 39, 40–43, 330
Mangas Coloradas, 54
Manifest Destiny, xviii, 89, 122, 201, 213, 225, 240, 312, 334
Marshall, James, 105, 106, 108–9
Mason-Dixon Line, 60, 121, 122
Matthews, Elias, 308, 310
Maxwell, Kate, 300
McCunn, Ruthanne Lum, 329
McKinley, William, 319
Medicine Lodge Creek, 208
mercury, 110
Merivale, Jose, 231–32
Metaharta, 7–10, 11, 13, 15, 39, 42, 43, 45
Mexican-American War, 90–91, 92–102, 109, 113, 117, 118, 123, 124, 143, 168, 193, 198, 318

Mexican cession lands, 102, 109, 121–22
Treaty of Guadalupe Hidalgo, 102, 105, 109
Mexico, Mexican people, xix, 41, 54–56, 63, 82, 85, 87–90, 100, 118, 137, 145, 330
independence from Spain, 55, 74–75, 77, 89, 90, 116–17
Texas and, 86
women, 74
Mexico City, 51, 52, 55, 67, 75, 76, 86–88, 101
Michigan, 70
Miles, John D., 256–59
Miles, Nelson, 268–69, 287, 289
Miner, George, 315
Mines of Colorado, The (Hollister), 204–6
Mirror of the Times, 128
Mission San Luis Rey, 110
Mississippi, 48, 141, 162, 225
Mississippian peoples, 43
Mississippi River, 4, 11, 12–13, 21, 23, 24, 26, 27, 30, 39, 41–44, 46, 60, 70–72
Missouri, 20, 55–56, 59–60, 63, 77, 81, 93, 121, 125, 126, 137, 146, 261
Missouria, 22, 43
Missouri City, CO, 141, 176
Missouri Compromise (Compromise of 1820), 60, 122
Missouri Plateau, 7
Missouri River, xvii, 4, 6, 7, 10, 13, 14, 19, 20, 21, 26, 27, 28, 30, 31, 38, 41, 42, 44, 45, 47, 61, 64, 68, 97, 107, 160, 181, 188, 225, 243, 266
see also Upper Missouri River Valley
Miwok, 107, 108
Momaday, N. Scott, 10
Monroe, James, 61
Montana, 169, 191, 193, 194, 220, 221, 229, 243, 247, 287, 289, 303–5, 307, 330
winter storm in, 286
Monterey, CA, 105, 107, 110, 111, 116
Monterey Bay, 89–90

Mormons (Latter-day Saints), 98, 110, 111, 116, 138, 169, 217–20, 224, 247, 281, 307–11, 333
  polygamy and, 116, 217–19, 277, 308–10
Mount Lincoln, 214
Mount Vernon, 236
multiracial families, 9, 26–27, 66, 314
Murderer's Bar, 108–12, 119, 220

Natchez Trace, 44
National Era, 126
Native peoples, *see* Indigenous peoples
Navajo, 52, 55, 75, 77, 86, 90, 95, 101, 106, 157, 163–64, 284
Navy, U.S., 145, 156
Nebraska, xvi, xxix, 121–22, 131, 137, 139, 142, 201, 235, 253
Nevada, 142, 221, 222, 306
New England Emigrant Aid Society, 125
New Madrid, 46
New Mexico (Nuevo México), xx, xxii, 2, 53, 55–58, 75–77, 86–88, 91, 105, 106, 109, 113, 115–18, 137, 142, 144–46, 155, 161, 163, 169, 178, 331, 333
  in Civil War, 153, 155–57, 159, 160–62
  in Mexican-American War, 92, 95–97, 99–102, 117, 193
  ricos in, 55, 75, 77
New Orleans, LA, 4, 11, 12, 20, 21, 24, 30, 59, 156
New Orleans Times-Picayune, 79–80
New Spain, *see* Spain, Spanish people
New York (state), 48
New York, NY, 238
New York Daily Herald, 126
New York Stock Exchange, 235
New York Times, 119, 206
New York Tribune, 129, 131, 234
Nez Perce, 35, 63, 228
Nisenan, 108
North American Review, 70
northern lights, 10
Northern Pacific Railroad, 235, 242

North Platte Bridge, 191
Northwest Territories, 20
Notes on the State of Virginia (Jefferson), 24
Nueces River, 89, 90
Nuevo México, *see* New Mexico
Numu, 305–6

Oakley, Annie, 285
Ohio River Valley, xvi, 20, 23
Oklahoma, 82, 237
Old Bark, 84
Old Bear, 242, 249, 250
Olmsted, Frederick Law, xiii
Omaha, NE, 204, 225, 235
Omaha Bee, 301
Omaha Republican, 205
Opium War, 226
Oregon, 63, 88, 105, 106, 108, 290
Oregon Trail, 169, 191, 232, 281
Ortiz Mountains, 56, 57
Osage, 13, 22, 24, 26, 43, 44, 82
O'Sullivan, John, 89, 90, 225
Otoe, 43
Otter Woman, 6, 9, 10, 13–18, 32, 38, 39, 44, 66
Our New West (Bowles), 224–25

Pacific coast, xvii–xx, xxii, 3, 13, 14, 33, 35–37, 39, 48, 61, 89, 90, 102, 106, 122, 145, 156, 187, 188, 225
Pacific Railway Act, 161, 188, 201, 221
Page, Horace, 275
Page Act, 254, 275, 277
Paiute, 106, 305–6
Palmer, Frances Flora "Fanny," 216–17
Panama Canal, 322
Panic of 1857, 139
Panic of 1873, 235, 239, 274
Pawnee, 202–4
Payne, William (blacksmith), 132, 164–65, 184
Payne, Maria, 164
Peace Commission, 208–12, 215
Pennsylvania, 60, 162
Peralta, NM, 155, 162
Pérez, Albino, 75–76

Philadelphia, PA, 237, 238
Philippines, 318
Pickell, William, 255, 278–79, 283, 293, 294, 301
Pike, Zebulon, 62
Pikes Peak, 172
   Colorado gold rush, xx, 128, 129–31, 133, 137, 138–41, 143–45, 156, 187, 188–91, 198, 204–6, 212–14, 220
Pikes Peakers (1st Colorado Volunteers), 144–47, 151–59, 161, 162, 166, 171, 172, 175–77, 310
Pine Leaf, 69
Pine Ridge Agency, 266, 306
Ping Chong, 219, 220
Pioneer Printing Press, 163
Platte Rivers, 62, 83, 85, 86, 128, 129, 132, 136, 163, 171, 173, 179, 181, 202, 208, 214, 231, 232, 236, 253, 264, 333
Platte Road, 162, 167, 179–81, 191–92, 204, 205
Plum Creek raid, 203–4, 235
Polk, James K., 88–90, 101, 102, 105–7
Porcupine, 306
Portage des Sioux, MO, 23–27, 44, 64
Portland, OR, 227–28
Potawatomi, 46
Powder River, 191, 192, 197, 209, 232, 236, 240–43, 248, 250, 265, 266
Preemption Act, 283
Pretty Walker, 288
Price, Sterling, 99, 100
Progressive social movements, 285, 323, 330
Promontory Summit, 218, 222–24
Prophetstown, IN, 41, 45–46
Pueblo, CO, 86, 172
Pueblo peoples, 86
Puerto Rico, 318

Quapaw, 20

railroads, 216, 217, 219, 253, 263, 273, 274, 294, 324

Central Pacific, xxi, 161, 219, 221–24, 229, 246
   Chinese workers on, xxi, 221–25, 227, 229, 311
   Indigenous peoples and, 201–4, 208, 210, 235
   Northern Pacific, 235, 242
   Pacific Railway Act, 161, 188, 201, 221
   Rocky Mountains and, 204–5
   transcontinental, 121, 122, 161, 190, 206, 208, 212, 216, 218, 219, 223–25, 234, 273, 311, 327
   Union Pacific, 161, 188, 201–5, 208, 210, 213, 218, 219, 223–24, 235, 240, 252–53, 264, 279–80, 294, 300
Rawlins, WY, 279–82, 283, 293, 294, 295, 297, 300–302
Rawlins House, 280–82
Real de Dolores, 57–58, 73, 115
Reconstruction, 188, 206, 209, 212
Red Arrow, 6–9, 33
Red Cloud, NE, 279, 283
Red Cloud (chief), 209
Red Cloud Agency, 242, 250–51, 265, 267, 268
Remington, Frederic, 284
Rendón, Doña, 73–74
Republicans, xix, xxi, 142, 143, 160, 161, 163, 187, 188, 207, 209, 212, 214, 234, 247–48, 254, 258, 275, 277, 295, 310
residenters, 8
Revolutionary War, 11, 19, 21, 22, 26, 51, 70
Rio Grande, 4, 52–54, 145, 146, 154–56
Robinson, Sara, 125
Rock Springs, WY, 301
Rocky Mountain Fur Company, 60–66
Rocky Mountain News, 129, 130, 133, 135, 136, 142, 143, 162, 164, 165, 176, 177, 197, 198, 205, 211–14, 217, 219, 223, 310
Rocky Mountains, xvi, xxii, 3, 4, 7, 8, 11, 13, 14, 29–31, 38, 61, 63, 65, 68, 69, 71, 83, 87, 111, 128, 132, 137, 139–40, 142, 144, 156, 169, 187, 190, 205, 213, 306, 310

INDEX

Rocky Mountains (*cont.*)
  Gates of the, 31
  gold rush in, xx, 128, 129–31, 133, 137, 138–41, 143–45, 156, 187, 188–91, 198, 204–6, 212–14, 220
  railroads and, 204–5
Ronk, Anna, 171
Roosevelt, Theodore, xvii, 285, 286, 301, 318, 322
Rose, Edward, 26, 27
Rosebud Valley, 243, 244, 259, 286–89, 307, 319, 320
Rough Riders, 318
Rush, Benjamin, 28
Russell, Andrew, 224
Russian traders, 36

Sacajawea, xx, xxiii, 3–10, 42, 44, 45, 63, 64, 66, 69, 80, 228, 302, 306, 329–31, 334–35
  artistic depictions of, 330
  death of, 47, 51, 330–31
  illnesses of, 16, 28–29, 47
  kidnapping and life with the Hidatsa, xx, 6–10, 11, 18, 31–34
  in Lewis and Clark expedition, xx, 10, 14–18, 19, 20, 28–39, 44, 48, 61, 68, 330
  marriage to Charbonneau, 9, 34
  mythologizing about, 51, 330–31
  pregnancy and birth of daughter, 46, 47
  pregnancy and birth of son, 10, 15–18
  in St. Louis, 42–45, 59
Sacramento Union, 330
St. Charles, MO, 24–27
Saint-Domingue, 4, 51
St. Louis, MO, xx, 12, 13, 17, 19–27, 30, 38, 39, 41–45, 54, 59–62, 64, 65, 68, 69, 71, 72, 81–83
  Exposition in, 330
  racial murders in, 81
  Sacajawea and Charbonneau in, 42–45, 59
St. Vrain, Ceran, 82, 83, 85
Salish (Flathead), 5, 63
Salmon River Valley, 291, 314, 320–21, 323, 326
Salt Lake City, UT, 119, 129, 218, 219, 220, 247, 308, 309, 333
Salt Lake City *Daily Reporter*, 219
Salt Lake Tribune, 300, 309
San Antonio, TX, 145, 146
Sand Creek, 171
  massacre at, 172–77, 178–86, 188, 191, 198, 207, 208, 258, 307
Sand Hills, 252, 264–65
San Diego, CA, 145
Sandoval, Luisa, 86, 87, 91
San Francisco, CA, xxi, 51, 107, 121, 128, 145, 190, 220, 221, 227, 228, 327
San Jacinto, Battle of, 75
San Joaquin River, 107
San Jose, CA, 290–91
Santa Anna, Antonio López de, 75, 88, 90
Santa Fe, NM, xx, 55–58, 59, 61, 73–80, 86, 106, 113, 115, 116, 154–55, 158, 331
  Mexican-American War and, 92–102, 117
  uprising in, 99–100
Santa Fe Pioneers, 86
Santa Fe River, 73
Santa Fe Trail, 56, 58, 59, 73, 77, 80, 81, 82, 83, 93, 94, 101, 143, 146, 151–53, 158, 172, 253, 331
Santa Fe Weekly Gazette, 118
Sauk, 24–26, 71
Scott, Winfield, 101
Seminoles, 82
Sentinel Rocks, 298–99, 301
Service Valley, 32
Seymour, Horatio, 212
Shakers, xx, 138–39, 144, 217, 308
Shawnee, 41, 46, 47, 139
sheep, 284
Sheheke, 40–43
Shepp, Charlie, 320–24, 326
Sheridan, Phil, 212–13, 239, 248, 261
Sherman, William Tecumseh, 178, 208–13, 236, 237, 239
Shiloh, Battle of, 156

INDEX

Shoshone, xx, 3–7, 31, 37, 51, 63, 67, 281, 296, 306, 330
  Agai-dika, 3–7, 15, 33, 35
  Lewis and Clark Expedition and, 13–15, 17, 19, 29, 31–35
  Northern, 3–6, 13, 14
Shoup, George, 171, 172, 175, 177, 178
Sibley, Henry Hopkins, 145, 146
Sierra Madre Mountains, 52
Sierra Nevada Mountains, xxii, 89, 105–8, 111, 119, 145, 156, 187, 220, 222
silver, 187, 206, 212, 213, 221, 294
Sioux, 23, 194, 239
  see Dakota people
  Lakota, *see* Lakota
  Yankton/Yanktonai, 23
Sisneros, Manuel Antonio, 56, 73, 76, 77
Sitting Bull, 179, 192, 211, 240, 242–44, 250, 251, 267, 306
  murder of, 306
Slaughter Creek, 274
slavery, xix, 4, 20, 22, 23, 25, 43, 48, 59, 77, 81, 109, 111, 116, 121, 229
  Beckwourth and, xx, 21–23, 26–27
  biracial families and, 26–27
  Civil War and, 144, 154, 156, 158
  emancipation, 158, 161, 181
  expansion of, 27, 60, 88–89, 115–16, 121–22, 125–26, 141, 142, 144, 160, 161
  formerly enslaved people, 201, 202
  fugitive slaves, 60, 62, 116
  York (Clark's man), 12, 19–20, 43
Slough, John, 152–54
smallpox, 3, 6
Smead, A. D., 314
Smead, Mollie, 276, 313, 314
Smith, Carry, 276
Smith, Edward, 236, 237
Smith, Jack, 175–77, 182
Smith, John, 174–76
Smith Center, KS, 255
Smithsonian Institution, 235, 237
Snake Indians, *see* Shoshone
Snake River, 35, 290
Soleil, Thomas DeBeau (Tom Sun), 296–98

Sonora, xx, 52–54, 56, 107–8
Soule, Silas, 172, 174, 181, 185
South Carolina, 141, 143
Spain, Spanish people, xix, xx, 4, 11, 12, 20, 41, 67, 118
  colonial rebellion, 51–52, 54, 55
  intermarriage and, 27
  Mexican independence from, 74–75, 77, 89, 90, 116–17
Spanish-American War, 317–18
Spanish Trail, 106
Spotted Tail, 250
Springfield, MA, 204
Standing Rock, 306
Stanford, Leland, 221, 224
Stobie, Charles S., 186, 198
Stockton, CA, 107
Stone, Henry, 255
Sublette, Andrew, 82, 83, 85
Sublette, William, 65
Sublette & Vasquez, 82, 85
Sumner, Charles, 125
Sun Dance, 305
Supreme Court, U.S., 312, 327
Sutter, John, 105
Sutter's Mill, 105–8, 219
Sweet Medicine, 9, 170, 202, 239, 260, 266
Sweetwater River Valley, 281, 294–96, 298, 299
Swift Hawk, 196, 197

Taos, NM, 85–86, 91, 97, 99–101
Taos Pueblo, 75, 86
Taos Rebellion, 75–77, 81, 85
Tappan, Samuel F., 152, 172–73, 178–83, 185, 208–11
Taylor, Zachary, 101
Tecumseh, 41, 46
Templeton, George, 193–95
Tennessee, xvi, 11, 43, 162
Tenorio, Josefa, 74
Texas (Tejas), 52, 75, 86, 88–90, 92, 96, 101, 102, 106, 131, 141–42, 145, 179
  in Civil War, 141–42, 152–57, 161

INDEX

Thompson, Jim, 194, 195
Thousand Pieces of Gold (McCunn), 329
Three Forks, 4–6, 13, 14, 18, 31–32, 35, 37
Thruston, Lucius, 73–74, 96, 101
Tillamook, 37
Tillamook Head, 37
Times Publishing Company, 204
Tippecanoe River, 46
tobacco, 20–21
Tohono O'odham, 52
Tongue River, 250, 268, 269, 287, 303, 307
Treaty of Córdoba, 55
Treaty of Fort Laramie, 132, 232–33, 236, 237
Treaty of Fort Wise, 142
Treaty of Guadalupe Hidalgo, 102, 105, 109
Trist, Nicholas, 102
Tubac, 54
Tucson, AZ, 54, 161
Turner, Frederick Jackson, xiii–xviii, xxi–xxii, 48, 317, 318
Turner, Mae, xiii–xiv, xvii
Two Moons, 269, 288, 289

Union Pacific Railroad, 161, 188, 201–5, 208, 210, 213, 218, 219, 223–24, 235, 240, 252–53, 264, 279–80, 294, 300
Upper Missouri River Valley, xx, xxii, 8, 9, 11, 12, 14, 37, 46, 47, 58, 59, 64, 69, 192, 209, 210, 331
U.S. Hotel, 113, 114
Utah, 116, 142, 157, 217–19, 222, 224, 225, 246–48, 307–10, 333
  Mormons in, *see* Mormons
Ute, 82, 86

Valencia, 52, 53, 55, 56, 155
Valverde, 156, 157
Valverde, Battle of, 146
Vasquez, A. P., 130, 134, 136
Vasquez, Pierre "Louis," 83, 85, 130, 131, 133

Vasquez & Co., 130, 134, 136, 140
Vasquez Fort, 83–86, 110, 133
Vehoneme'ko (Head Chief), 303–6
Vigil, Donaciano, 99
Virginia, xx, 20–22, 27, 81, 144, 157, 162
Virginia City, MT, 169
voting rights, 111–12, 198, 220, 234, 277, 285, 322–23, 327

Wabash River, 41
Wanapum, 35
War, U.S. Department of, 64, 160, 166, 178, 193, 209, 210, 239, 246, 248, 269, 287
War of 1812, 47, 48, 51, 70, 88
Warren, ID, 274–78, 290, 292, 312–13, 315–16, 321, 323–26
  fire in, 320
Warren, Mrs. Bishop Hill, 285
Washington, D.C., 39, 40, 100, 105, 111, 116, 136, 143, 225, 235–36, 248, 274
  Indian delegations to, 233, 235–37, 239, 249
  U.S. Capitol, 207
  Washington Monument, 235–36
water rights, 294, 295, 298
Watson, Ella, xxi, xxiii, 255, 278–82, 283–85, 292, 293–302, 316, 327, 329–31, 334–35
  Averell and, 280–82, 283–85, 293–95, 297–300
  as "Cattle Kate," 300, 302, 332
  cattle ranch of, xxi, 284, 285, 293–302, 303, 331
  cooking of, 255, 279–81, 297, 331
  grave of, 331–32
  land and cabin of, 283, 284, 293
  lynching of, 298–302, 331
  marriage to Pickell, 255, 278–79, 283, 293, 294, 301
  in Rawlins, 279–82, 283
  in Red Cloud, 279
Watson, Thomas and Frances, 253–55, 264, 300–301
Weekly Commonwealth (Denver), 162

INDEX

West, xix, 316, 327–28, 333–35
   Buffalo Bill's Wild West Show, xiv, xvii, 285
   Civil War and, xix–xxi
   diverse communities, xix–xxiii
   histories of, xviii–xix
   landscapes of, xxii
   new identities in, 69
   North-South fight for control of, 121, 145
   political appointments and, 105, 134
   popular images of, xvii–xix, 216–17
   U.S. government control of, xix, xxi, 12, 192
   see also frontier; frontier myth
Western Cattle Trail, 261
Western Mountaineer (Golden, CO), 136–37
Westward the Course of Empire Takes Its Way (Leutze), 207, 216
Whigs, 109
White Antelope, 174–75, 182
White Bull, 196
White River, 266
whooping cough, 38
Wild Hog, 256, 258
Wilson, Woodrow, 322
Wilson's Creek, battle of, 146
Wind River, 64, 281
Wind River Mountains, 63, 191
Wind River Reservation, 330
Winnebago, 46
Winning of the West, The (Roosevelt), xvii
Wisconsin Historical Society, xvii
Wister, Owen, 301
Witter, Clara, 309, 310
women, xix, xxii, 116–17, 327, 334
   divorce and, 279
   frontier myth and, 285, 302
   Indigenous, in diplomatic relations, 35, 66
   land and livestock of, 284
   Mexican and Hispano, 74, 284
   New Woman era, 323
   progressive causes and, 285, 323
   ranchers, 284, 285
   voting rights for, 322–23, 327
Wooden Leg, 242, 243, 257, 288, 319
Woodward, George, 231–33
World's Columbian Exposition, xiii–xiv, xvii
World War I, 322
Wounded Knee Massacre, 306–7
Wovoka, 305–6
Wynkoop, Ned, 164, 165, 171, 172, 180
Wyoming, xxi, 191, 231, 239, 279–82, 294, 295, 306, 330–31
   homesteading in, 281, 283, 284, 293–95
   winter storm in, 285–86
Wyoming Basin, 63
Wyoming Stock Growers Association, 296, 299, 301

Yakama, 35
Yankton/Yanktonai, 23
Yaqui, 52
Yellowstone Basin, 65, 194
Yellowstone River, 38, 64, 67–71, 193, 243, 268
York, 12, 19–20, 36, 43
Young, Brigham, 218, 247
Yucatán, 51

Zimm, Bruno, 330